African Language Structures

AFRICAN LANGUAGE STRUCTURES

Wm. E. Welmers

UNIVERSITY OF CALIFORNIA PRESS

Berkeley . Los Angeles . London

University of California Press
Berkeley and Los Angeles, California

University of California Press, Ltd.
London, England

ISBN: 0-520-02210-6
Library of Congress Catalog Card Number: 70-186108

to Bee

Preface

It is the purpose of this work to survey a variety of structural phenomena which appear commonly in African languages, or in languages of one family or group in Africa, but which are not necessarily typical of human language in the broadest sense. No effort is made to isolate linguistic "universals" at a high level of abstraction, nor to investigate the validity of theories of linguistic universals which have been proposed. At the other extreme, it is considered trivial merely to list, for one or another group of languages, certain superficial characteristics of phonology or grammar irrespective of their significance for the total linguistic system, for procedures in linguistic analysis, or for comparison with other languages.

Between the levels of an abstract theory of human language and the trivia of isolated details, however, there are many phenomena which have repeatedly presented problems of analysis to a large number of students of African languages. Inadequately trained investigators have frequently failed to note, or have simply ignored, significant areas of linguistic data. Just as frequently, an unsophisticated analysis has at least partially distorted the picture of a linguistic system. It is hoped that this study of some types of widespread structural phenomena will contribute to more adequate, more thorough, and more consistent analyses of African languages.

A major source of the data on which this work is based is the author's own research and experience, or research with which he has been directly associated, covering a span of thirty years. Much of this research is represented in publications, but some of it is reflected only in rough field notes, and still more of it in hitherto unrecorded memories. Studies contributing to this work have ranged from a few hours to several years per language, with native speakers of perhaps seventy to eighty languages. Substantial experience can be claimed in the case of only about twenty languages, but in many other instances even a very brief exposure has provided significant data for the study of language structures. Languages of the Niger-Congo family account for most of the data, but some Nilo-Saharan and Afro-Asiatic languages are also represented.

The foregoing paragraphs are by no means intended to imply that earlier scholars made no useful contributions to the study of African languages. On the contrary, the utmost respect is due to pioneer analysts such as J. G. Christaller, Diedrich Westermann, Ida C. Ward, R. C. Abraham, and many others. However, it has been the author's privilege to have the opportunity to work independently with most of the languages investigated by these and some other scholars, and to verify or in some cases to modify their conclusions for himself. Thus, for most of the data cited, the same ears have done the hearing, and the same principles of analysis have been applied.

In relatively recent years, particularly within the last decade, there has been an enormous increase in the number of scholars with excellent training in descriptive linguistics working on African languages. For languages with which the author has had little or no direct experience, their publications or personal communications have provided a second important and valuable source of data. At the same time, no apology is offered for relying as much as possible on analyses that could be personally verified. It is not the purpose of this work to survey the vast literature on African languages, which ranges in quality from clearly or apparently excellent to virtually useless. The purpose is rather to present samples of phonologic and grammatical systems in such a way that others can recognize or look for similar or significantly different systems in other languages. Substantial amounts of data are cited from a relatively few languages, some well known and others little known; smaller amounts of data, down to isolated details, are cited from scores of other languages. In some cases, general statements are made for groups of languages such as Bantu or Mande; available literature in many such cases will verify what is here illustrated by data from only a few languages in such groups.

Most of the content of this work has been the subject matter of a graduate-level course taught annually for some fifteen years. Some knowledge of linguistics on the part of the user is naturally assumed; however, the material is presented in such a way that the relative beginner as well as the advanced student can profit from it, in classroom instruction or privately in connection with the study of a particular language. In addition to presenting many of the kinds of structures that the analyst is likely to meet, some suggestions and warnings are included relevant to field procedures. Personal references in connection with work on a number of languages are included only to explain the unavoidable limitations of the data. Otherwise, the sometimes informal and even anecdotal style is intended primarily as a reminder that, in spite of the recognized technicalities of linguistic analysis, we are still dealing with real languages spoken and understood in the work and play, the joys and sorrows, of daily life.

No effort has been made to present all of the material with a single theoretical linguistic outlook. The author's first training was, naturally, in taxonomic linguistics. Developments anticipating many aspects of more recent theories, however, date back to very early work, and are reflected at many points. Some recent work illustrates the application of contemporary theories more explicitly. Fortunately, this variety in approach has never seemed confusing to students.

It would be impossible to acknowledge individually all of my colleagues, students, language informants, and friends who have helped to make this work possible by their advice, their criticism, and especially their encouragement and inspiration. In worldly prestige, they range from distinguished university professors to barefooted children; the relative value of each one's contribution cannot be assessed in terms of any social or educational scale. I hope they will forgive me for not listing their many names. I could not forgive myself, however, if I did not express my unique indebtedness to my wife Beatrice. She has followed me into the most improbable adventures, listened patiently to my efforts to formulate structural statements concerning whatever linguistic data I happened to be working on, become a respectable practical linguist in her own right, successfully accomplished research and teaching tasks for which I had opportunity but no time, learned a substantial amount of at least eight African languages, proven herself an inspired language teacher, been an equal collaborator in major publications, and through it all remained a relaxed and gracious companion and hostess, and my most loyal fan.

In 1853, Sigusmund Wilhelm Koelle closed the Preface of his great *Polyglotta Africana* with the following words, which I would like to make mine on this occasion: "May the following feeble endeavor in behalf of Africa be found useful; and may that land of the natural sun soon be equally distinguished as the land over which the Sun of Righteousness shineth !"

Los Angeles, October, 1971   Wm. E. Welmers

Contents

Chapter 1

The Historical and Classificatory Setting

1.1. Similarities in linguistic structure are in large measure a function of language inter-relatedness. Russian and German have somewhat similar systems of noun genders and cases because they both inherited them from a common Indo-European ancestral language. Tagalog and Malayan have similar systems of verb morphology because the languages have a common origin in proto-Malayo-Polynesian. In the same way, we may expect to find significant structural similarities among African languages primarily within a group or family of related languages, languages with a common origin.

This is not to say that any isolated similarity is proof of language relationship. It is undoubtedly a coincidence that the Mande languages of West Africa and the Mayan languages of Central America have strikingly similar distinctions between alienably and inalienably possessed nouns. The German (but not English) use of the "perfect" to express simple past action is presumably the result of diffusion from French. Conversely, isolated differences in linguistic structure do not disprove relationship. The fact that English has lost virtually every trace of gender and case distinctions in nouns does not make English something other than a Germanic language. Yet in a broader sense a study of common structural characteristics cannot be divorced from considerations of language relationships and language classification. It is relevant, therefore, to survey the present state of scholarship in the field of African language classification.

1.2. The most important, most comprehensive, and most widely accepted genetic classification of the languages of Africa is that proposed by Joseph H. Greenberg (1963).[1] Probably every scholar will agree that earlier attempts at classification were characterized, at least in some respects, by unwarranted assumptions, inadequate evidence, and in some cases sheer guesswork. Greenberg's procedure is a "mass comparison" of language vocabularies, including not only lexical items in major form classes, but also bound morphemes commonly described as having only a grammatical function. If a number of languages show striking similarities in both form and meaning, particularly in items presumed relatively unlikely to be involved in cross-language adoption ("borrowing"), it is concluded that those languages are related. Higher degrees of such similarity reflect closer relationships; lower degrees of similarity reflect more distant relationships. Completely unrelated languages show only a very little random similarity, attributable to coincidence or possibly to adoption of occasional lexical items from one language to another. All of this, of course, has long been recognized by most lin-

---

[1] For a survey of the study of African languages prior to 1945, including classification, see Cole 1971. Some details of Greenberg's classification are further discussed in 1.17-22 below.

1

guists. Greenberg's carefully defined procedure, and the conclusions to which it has led him, have met with widespread approval; but the approval is not universal, and objections to his classification must be considered. Since the major objections are theoretical or have theoretical implications, they can be discussed without detailed reference to specific language groupings.

1.3. To an extent unparalleled in the study of languages anywhere else in the world, African language classification has been beset by persistent hypotheses of language mixture, intermediate or transitional languages, substrata, pervasive external influence far in excess of what is usually recognized as normal, and innovative exuberance unmatched in recorded language history. Perhaps the most dramatic—and preposterous—example of speculation in linguistic history is provided by Sir Harry Johnston (1919, p. 27): "A great jumble of events, and lo!— new languages spring suddenly into existence." Johnston had noted that languages scattered all over West Africa have systems of noun classes, with varying degrees of concord, somewhat resembling the well-known class and concord systems of the Bantu languages. He believed that the most highly developed and regular Bantu languages represented the oldest and most original proto-Bantu type. In some dim period of the past, he speculated, speakers of such a language had contact with West African tribes which at that time spoke languages unrelated to Bantu. By some momentous and amazingly rapid process of fusion, the original West African languages acquired, almost overnight, entire chunks of Bantu morphological structure and a small amount of their most basic vocabulary. Within West Africa itself, Johnston believed that the Moré language (which has a suffix-marked class system) was once unrelated to Fula, but borrowed the entire noun class system—as a morphologic structure and concept!—from Fula. The implication appears to be, theoretically, that a society can, by some concerted and conscious decision, steer its language into substantially new structural shapes. Johnston apparently believed just that, for in another context he says (1919, p. 38), "Zulu-Kaffir will become the second language of South Africa if its exponents are wise enough to eliminate the silly clicks which at present mar its phonology and cause the European to take up instead the ugly and stupid jargon known as 'Kitchen-Kaffir.'"

A theory not very different from Johnston's has more recently been proposed by Malcolm Guthrie as an alternative to Greenberg's hypothesis of a genetic relationship between the Bantu languages and most of the languages of West Africa. Guthrie (1962) attributes the obvious grammatical and lexical similarities between the West African languages in question and Bantu to "the incorporation of Bantu features into languages of a quite distinct origin" in the form of "grammatical contamination" and "loan-words". No explanation is offered for the incredible historical upheavals that must have been involved in such pervasive linguistic restructuring (cf. Welmers 1963b).

Carl Meinhof (1940, p. 164) brought the "Mischsprache" concept more specifically into the picture by his suggestion that "Bantu is a mixed language, so to speak, descended of a Hamitic father and a Negro mother." Perhaps no contemporary scholar would care to defend this specific suggestion (which was based more on cultural than on linguistic considerations), but alleged language mixture is still postulated by some in the case of the so-called Nilo-Hamitic languages, the so-called Semi-Bantu languages, and numerous if not countless individual languages and language groups. E. O. J. Westphal (1957) specifically contends that a given language may be most closely related to one language phonologically, to another morphologically, and to still another lexically. In speaking of "genetic" relationships, he warns against assuming that, for any one language, there is only one "parent" language. M. A. Bryan (1959) has used these theories as the basis for positing extensive language mixtures in Africa, naturally rejecting the basis of Greenberg's genetic classification in the process.

An explicit statement of the theoretical basis for such hypotheses is given by David Dalby (1966). He rejects the traditional concept of genetic relationship and genetic classification, assuming that the term "genetic" has to do with "genes", and that a multiple origin for existing languages, on the analogy of the multiple origin of genes in human heredity, is therefore to be taken for granted. He cites pidgin and creole languages (like Krio of Sierra Leone), and the unusual case of Mbugu in East Africa, as unquestionable instances of mixed languages. Of course, Greenberg and the body of scholars who generally share his theoretical bias never intended the word "genetic" to be associated with "genes" or "genealogy" in the way Dalby assumes; it is associated rather with "genesis" or origin, and "genetic relationships" have to do with linguistic characteristics that are inherited by one generation of speakers from another, as opposed to those which are acquired from other sources. An assessment of the theoretical issues involved may be made on the basis of a relatively elementary outline of the nature of language history.

1.4. Unquestionably the most normal, though by no means the only, variety of language history is the continuous, unbroken transmission of a system of communication from one generation to the next. Parents and children, grandparents and grandchildren, communicate with each other—the "generation gap" has little to do with the basic lexical, phonologic, or grammatical characteristics of the language used. All of the recognized varieties of linguistic change may be, and undoubtedly are, taking place, but the lines of communication are not totally broken.

Assume that a linguistically homogeneous community splits into two groups, through a process such as migration or invasion that creates a geographical separation between them. As long as neither group completely gives up its own language to adopt the language of some other people, there will now be two separate generation-to-generation continua. Linguistic changes will take place within each continuum, but many or all of the changes will be different for the two. After a few generations, members of the two groups, if reunited, will still be able to understand each other, though they will note peculiarities in each other's speech. But after several centuries, enough diverse changes will have accumulated so that members of the two groups will no longer be able to communicate with each other.

They may then be said to speak different languages, each of which is equally a "direct" descendant of the original common language. Some of the changes that have taken place in each are internal—that is, languages change even apart from contact with other languages. Some of the changes, on the other hand, may be, and usually are, the result of external influence; the most conspicuous of such changes is the adoption of foreign words. But no matter how extensive the external influences have been, each resultant language has had a continuous history from its point of origin, the common parent language. Such languages are indeed genetically related, and for several millenia the relationship will remain apparent in parallels discoverable by well-established techniques of comparative linguistics. The similarities of either language to other languages, created by such phenomena as borrowed vocabulary, do not constitute "relationship" or "affiliation;" they merely attest to contact.

1.5. Some internal changes in language are nonsystematic. Such include innovation or invention, the source of such English words as *veep* and *blurb*, or the use of *orbit* as a verb—"to orbit a satellite". Equally non-systematic is analogic change, the source of the modern plural *cows* replacing the original *kine*, or of the neologism *booketeria*. Semantic change, illustrated by modern *prevent*, which once meant "precede," is also nonsystematic. Apart from written records or a great deal of comparative evidence, these types of changes, which apply to individual words or individual grammatical constructions, soon become unrecoverable, and they tend to obscure genetic relationship between languages.

Clearly, changes due to external influence are also nonsystematic. Although the adoption of new vocabulary items is the most obvious and commonest such change, it is not the only one possible. The occurrence of [v] and [z] in word-initial position in English is the result of the adoption of a number of words from French; the appearance of click consonants in some southern Bantu languages, such as Xhosa, is undoubtedly attributable to the adoption of words containing such consonants from the Khoisan languages. Thus the phonologic system of a language may be modified as a result of contact. Similarly, details in the grammatical structure of a language may be affected by external influence. The use of the so-called "perfect" to express past time in German, though not in English, is believed to be the result of diffusion from French.

The only historical change in language that is systematic or regular is phonetic change. In a given language, for example, a [k] sound may change to [č] before a vowel sound like [i]. This change will affect every word in the language that once had the sequence [ki]. In a related language, such a change may not occur. As a result, in every word descended from the common parent language which once had the sequence [ki], the first language will have [či] but the second will have [ki]. The appearance of such regular correspondences demonstrates that the languages are related, and makes it possible to reconstruct something of the phonologic system and the vocabulary of the common parent language.

To cite an African example, consider three languages of Liberia and Sierra Leone—Kpelle, Loma, and Mende. There are a great many words in these three

languages which are similar or even identical. A sizable list can be cited in which
all of the Kpelle words begin with [l], all of the Loma words begin with [d], and
all of the Mende words begin with [nd]; the words are similar in other respects as
well, and are parallel in meaning. The conclusion drawn is that these words have
a common origin, and once began with a consonant which has, regularly, become
[l], [d], and [nd], respectively, in the three languages. The three languages are
genetically related, and the words in question have had a continuous history in
all of them.

1.6. Greenberg has not, to be sure, demonstrated the existence of regular
phonetic correspondences among all the languages in any of the four language
families he posits for Africa, though it has already been implied that such correspondences are the only real proof of genetic relationship. However, failure to
provide what is claimed to be the "only real proof" does not imply the total absence of evidence; in fact, evidence that falls short of clear demonstration of regular phonetic correspondences may nevertheless be overwhelming. What Greenberg has done is, for each family, to cite from a wide variety of representative
languages a number of words which show striking similarity in form and in meaning. That two languages might by accident or by interaction have similar forms
for a few such words is, to be sure, quite conceivable. But that many languages
should have so many similar forms with similar meanings approaches zero statistical probability. The only alternative that has been suggested—and the only
alternative that is even remotely possible—is that some languages adopted the
vocabulary items in question from other languages; just this hypothesis of "loan-
words" has been proposed to explain the lexical similaries between the Bantu
languages and many West African languages. An examination of the evidence,
however, in the light of the nature of vocabulary adoption or "borrowing", makes
this hypothesis incredible. There is ample documentation in the languages of the
world that languages adopt new words primarily for concepts new to the culture
of their speakers. Specialized artifacts and activities, products of a different culture or environment, technical concepts in such areas as religion and law—these
readily move from one society to another, and words for them from one language
to another. But body parts, activities like eating and dying, common environmental items like water and trees, universal concepts like bigness and smallness—
these are not innovations in any culture, and the words for them are seldom given
up in favor of words adopted from another language. Yet it is vocabulary items
of just these types for which Greenberg finds similar forms and similar meaning,
not words for culturally mobile items and concepts. That a few such items in
a few languages might be adopted is possible; but that fifty or more in hundreds
of languages have been adopted is unbelievable. Without a study of regular phonetic correspondences, we may be unable to establish many details of the genetic
interrelationships of the languages in question, and we certainly cannot reconstruct the phonologic system of the parent language with any degree of certainty;
but the nature of the similar forms with similar meanings which Greenberg cites,

and the number of them, is such that the fact of genetic relationship can be considered established.

1.7. The investigation of the genetic relationships of divergent linguistic continua does not in any sense imply a denial of the reality of other important aspects of linguistic history, such as external influence. As has been pointed out, however, language changes due to external influence are non-systematic, and many of them in time become unrecoverable. It is possible to arrive at broad generalizations on the basis of the phonetic and semantic similarities with which Greenberg works; it is not possible to arrive at such generalizations on the basis of a study of proven or hypothetical instances of external influence.

It is difficult if not impossible to assign a linguistically rational interpretation to a statement such as the following (Jacquot and Richardson 1956, p. 22): "Mbo languages show vocabulary affinities with Ewondo, Bulu, N. Mbɛnɛ, and Duala; phonetically their relationship tends toward Bamileke; grammatically they seem to be linked especially to Ewondo, Bulu, and N. Mbɛnɛ." The results of parallel continuous history and the possible results of contact between languages seem hopelessly confused. Greenberg justifiably distinguishes these, and for purposes of language classification confines himself to questions of genetic relationship, which involve only the axis of continuous history. The results of contact, though important and interesting—in so far as they can be recovered—for the study of a language as a totality, have to do with contact only, not with relationships.

Nor does the investigation of genetic relationships on the basis of phonetic and semantic similarity of specific forms imply a denial of the reality of such non-systematic internal changes in languages as innovation, analogic change, or semantic change. It is obvious that such changes take place. In a few cases, Greenberg and others have suggested hypotheses of analogic change that seem reasonable; instances of apparent semantic change are frequently recognizable. But once more, such changes are non-systematic and sporadic. By taking obvious cases into account, we may add to and strengthen our evidence for genetic relationships. But in themselves, they prove nothing more than that such changes actually do take place.

On the other hand, the significance of such types of internal change seems to be ignored by writers who resort to hypotheses of such unexplained phenomena as "intermediate" languages (e.g., Westermann and Bryan 1952, p. 37, for Susu; Westermann 1952, p. 254, for the Benue-Cross languages). The implication of such hypotheses seems to be that independent internal development over a period of centuries or even a millenium or more is of little consequence. Even though we may be unable to reconstruct specific instances of specific types of internal change, it is inevitable and obvious that such changes have occurred.

1.8. It has already been noted that external influence can occasion modifications in the phonologic and grammatical structure of a language. But again, hypotheses of external influence in this area should hardly be the scholar's first resort, and at any time they should be advanced only with the greatest caution.

In all we know of language history, such influences are insignificant when compared with internal change or even with the adoption of foreign vocabulary items. English has borrowed vast numbers of words from French, but the phonology of English has been affected by French in only a few minor details, and the grammar even less, if at all. Similarly, hundreds of demonstrably adopted words can be found in the Kpelle language of Liberia, but only one element in the phonology of Kpelle can possibly be attributed to the influence of neighboring languages and of English, and nothing in the grammar. Swahili has adopted foreign vocabulary items even more extensively, especially from Arabic, but also from English and some other sources. Swahili has experienced external influence to a degree that few languages ever do; in particular, many speakers of Arabic and other languages have used Swahili as a second language and even adopted it as their only language. Such influence has introduced some new consonants, has somewhat modified the rules for syllable structure, and has been responsible for the loss of tonal contrasts. In grammar, however, Swahili is unmistakably a Bantu language. No significant features of Arabic, English, or other foreign grammatical structures have crept into Swahili. There have, to be sure, been some simplifications of rather complex Bantu grammatical patterns, but even these are attested in other Bantu languages where external influence is apparently out of the question.

In the light of these considerations, it indeed seems preposterous to suggest that such complex, abstract, and pervasive grammatical characteristics as the noun class and agreement systems of countless West African languages developed by a process of "grammatical contamination" due to some ancient contact with speakers of Bantu languages. There is simply no known precedent for such a substantive restructuring of grammatical systems. On the other hand, although we may never be able to explain all the details, a hypothesis of common genetic origin would require only the positing of a number of analogic and perhaps some innovative changes which, though admittedly extensive in this case, are commonplace in known language history, and at least as extensive in many well-attested cases.

1.9. Claims that some languages are "mixed languages" fare no better than claims of extensive grammatical restructuring, in the light of known language history and even of common experience. The children of parents who speak different languages natively may learn both of their parents' languages, but they do not develop some new, "mixed" language with structural characteristics and vocabulary derived about equally from each of their parent's languages; at most, their bilingualism may result in a sprinkling of adopted words and traces of other modifications in each language. Nor is there any recorded case of a group of people, even a bilingual community, selecting roughly comparable sets of structural characteristics and amounts of vocabulary from one language, and others from another language, to create anything that can reasonably be called a "mixture." (For pidgin and creole languages, see l. 14-15 below.) To be sure, when a member of the "Pennsylvania Dutch" community says 'he jumped the fence over,' he betrays his German background. But in that community, there is no truly "mixed" language; in fact, there are two languages, German and English, each showing some results of normal external influence from the other.

This is not to say, of course, that in particular the lexical stock of a language may not have a mixed background. In fact, over a period of several millenia—which is undoubtedly the age of the four language families Greenberg posits for Africa—the number of vocabulary items traceable to the original language by direct descent is relatively insignificant. A substantial part of modern English vocabulary has been adopted from French, Latin, and Greek; a substantial though easily exaggerated part of modern Swahili vocabulary has been adopted from Arabic and English. But in structure, and in genetic relationship as reflected in regular phonetic correspondences in inherited vocabulary, English is still Germanic and Swahili is still Bantu.

1.10. Perhaps the most explicit hypothesis of language mixture has to do with Maʔa (Mbugu), a language of Tanzania, which has heen called "a non-Bantu language, which has adopted the Bantu class and concord system" (Tucker and Bryan 1966, p. 270n). It has also been described as having "a large Iraqw [Cushitic] vocabulary and a Bantu grammatical system" (Tucker and Bryan 1966, p. 592). It has been alleged that the Cushitic vocabulary is almost entirely nominal, and that Maʔa verbs are of some other origin (Tucker and Bryan 1957, p. 72). The evidence available in publications is scanty, but unpublished research (Christopher Ehret, personal communication) suggests that the development of Maʔa, though certainly unusual, is within the familiar framework of continuous language history with extensive external influence. Actually, many Maʔa verbs and other words, as well as nouns, are of Cushitic origin. These have parallels not only in Iraqw, but in other southern Cushitic languages, and clearly indicate that the continuous or genetic history of Maʔa is Cushitic. What, then, of the alleged Bantu grammatical system? There are, indeed, a great many Bantu grammatical characteristics in Maʔa. But there are also a number of gaps and inconsistencies in their application, suggesting that they do not belong to the mainstream of the language's history. It appears that the speakers of Maʔa have been bilingual for several generations, their second language being a Bantu language. The Bantu vocabularly in Maʔa is largely among the nouns, which is typical of adopted vocabularly in most languages. The adoption of such vocabulary from a well-known language resulted in Maʔa adopting both singular and plural forms from Bantu, so that a variety if not all of the Bantu noun-class prefixes came into the language. Since it was appropriate in the familiar Bantu second language to use concordial or agreement prefixes with modifiers of such nouns and with verbs, that Bantu usage was transferred along with the nouns for which it was appropriate. Finally, at least to some extent but by no means consistently, the use of noun-class prefixes and concords was extended even to some of the original Cushitic vocabulary of the language. The result is indeed unusual, if not weird, but it is still atrributable to two normal types of language development—continuous internal change and nonsystematic external influence. It should particularly be noted that Maʔa did not adopt Bantu grammatical characteristics in the abstract;

they came into the language as incidentals to the adopted vocabulary. Further, it would appear that such extensive external influence is possible only in a setting of intensive bilingualism throughout the community. Even there, it is by no means inevitable; there are many other bilingual communities in Africa and throughout the world, in which two languages exist side by side with far less influence of either on the other.

In sum, the established principles of comparative and historical linguistics, and all we know about language history and language change, demand that, in the area of divergent linguistic structures, we seek explanations first on the basis of recognized processes of internal change. We should look to external influence, and particularly to anything like language "mixture", only as a last resort. Unfortunately, there has been all too much of fleeing to hypotheses of external influence, alleged secondary affinities, and even mixed languages as a first resort. Maʔa has been triumphantly cited as a case of language mixture, and as evidence that such mixture may be very common in Africa. Even if we were to admit the term "mixed language" for Maʔa—and even there the term as commonly used hardly seems appropriate—it is hardly fair to claim that similar developments may be common. The very fact that Maʔa is so conspicuously unusual suggests that other comparable cases would be readily recognizable and definable. But with the possible exception of one or two other languages for which inadequate evidence is available, no comparable cases have been reported, even where the conditions seem similar. And even Maʔa clearly appears to have had a continuous genetic history which is Cushitic, with remarkably extensive but entirely explicable external influence.

1.11. So far, there have been only passing references to instances in which a group of speakers of a given language adopts a new language which it has not spoken before, and completely loses its own original language. This is outside the realm of unbroken generation-to-generation language history with the usual kinds of language change, and perhaps different rules apply to language change when one language is substituted for another. That such substitutions may take place is obvious—a substantial portion of the population of the United States has experienced language substitution in its own lifetime or within the past few generations. Many people of ethnically Arabic origin speak a Bantu language, Swahili, as their first language. Many people of Malayan origin speak Afrikaans as their first language. Through the largely untraceable history of the indigenous languages of Africa, there have undoubtedly been many cases of language substitution, on the part of sizable groups of people as well as countless individuals. The question may be raised whether such historical events may not vitiate a good many of Greenberg's hypotheses in regard to genetic relationship, and whether something like the "mixed languages" so commonly thought to exist may not actually develop.

1.12. When an individual moves into a new linguistic community and begins to adopt its language in place of his own, he may for years and even decades speak the new language imperfectly, with recognizable characteristics of his first language, especially in pronunciation. But his own children, born in the new community, will probably not learn his first language at all, and in their use of the new language they will conform almost perfectly to the community around them. They actually enter into the unbroken continuum of the language of the community, and for purposes of linguistic history their father's language did not exist. There is no noticeable impact of the first language of one individual on that of the community into which he moves, nor even on the language of his children—or at least grandchildren. Cases of this sort are too commonplace in Africa to make it necessary to cite individual instances.

Africa has certainly known also what has been so common a phenomenon in the United States—that of a sizable group of people moving into a new linguistic environment and adopting the language of that environment. In such cases—as amply attested in the United States—the community may retain its ethnic identity for many generations. It may also retain its original language for a while, though usually not for more than two or three generations. There is a period of bilingualism. Early in that period, the new language may be spoken with recognizable characteristics of the original language—in pronunciation, usage, and some details of vocabulary. Some individuals may also speak their first language, as far as grammatical structure is concerned, with large numbers of words taken from the new language. Later in the period of bilingualism, the second generation may speak the original language only for limited purposes, and with recognizable characteristics of the new language. But by now, they are conforming more and more to the new language around them, so that within another generation or two their speech is virtually or totally indistinguishable from the speech of their neighbors. Only a few details of intonation and word usage are likely to betray the Swedish origin of many a Minnesotan, or the Dutch origin of many a Michigander or Iowan, though such persons may be in only the third generation in this country. The community has by now almost completely joined the mainstream of the unbroken history of the new language, without appreciably disturbing its genetic characteristics.

There are, in fact, some well-attested instances of quite the same phenomenon in Africa. There have been migrations from South Africa to areas farther north, after which the migrating group has adopted the language around them. After a few generations, hardly anything is left, linguistically, to betray their different linguistic origin—perhaps their own name for their people, some proper names, and a few other words. Much like so many communities of foreign origin in the United States, they have retained something of their own identity, but they can by no means be said to speak a mixed or substantially modified language. If caught within a few decades after migration, they may be in a transitional, partly bilingual state, but in time they enter into the new linguistic stream and are lost in that unbroken continuum.

Much the same process takes place when a linguistic community does not move at all, but is overwhelmed by newcomers who speak a new language and whose language the original community adopts. In such cases, bilingualism is far more persistent—English in the United States and Spanish in Mexico have been second languages of countless Indians for a long time, but many of the original Indian languages have survived in addition. Again, however, if the new language eventually predominates, it is not seriously affected by the old. Even to explain the difference between Mexican and Peninsular Spanish, one should look first to the processes of internal change before proposing hypotheses about the influence of Indian languages on Spanish, or on the English of the Southwestern United States.

Again, there are many parallels in Africa. Several tribes in northern Nigeria have adopted Hausa as a second language, and in some cases the first language is gradually dying out—though not as commonly nor as rapidly as some people would like to believe. In Ghana, Efutu was the original language of the coastal town of Winneba, but has almost totally disappeared in favor of Fante. In the northwestern Ivory Coast, a town where Senari was originally spoken has adopted Maninka as its language by local legislation. But in all of these cases, by the time the original language is lost, the new language has been acquired with virtually no modification from the form in which it had been spoken natively in the surrounding community. Minor modifications in phonology and in a few details of usage, and a fair number of adopted words, may later be recognizable, but in nothing like the dimensions posited for supposed mixed languages.

1.13. Suppose, however, that a community which adopts a new language is isolated from its native speakers before the new language is perfectly acquired. Would the result not be the perpetuation of something comparable to the heavily accented broken English of a young immigrant community? The answer would appear to be negative. Not only is it impossible to think of a clear example of such a situation, but the linguistic realities would seem to prevent it. While the second language is still so imperfectly learned, the first language is still retained. If contact with the second language is then lost, the community would—and undoubtedly does—revert to its first language, with hardly a trace of the second language except possibly a number of adopted words.

In short, if a community has reached the point where its first language is used in only a limited way and imperfectly, the second language would have been learned very nearly perfectly, and the community can be considered to have been absorbed into a new linguistic mainstream or continuum. On the other hand, if a community begins to acquire a second language and is interrupted in the process before full mastery has been achieved, it remains in its original linguistic mainstream. In either case, there may be some language change due to the contact of the two languages, but it is not likely to be extensive.

1.14. How, then, would one explain and categorize such a linguistic entity as Krio of Sierra Leone? There is clearly a background of imperfectly learned English in Krio, comparable to what is found in young immigrant communities. There is also a phonology that is in many respects similar to that of any of several West African languages, and a grammatical structure that lacks many English characteristics and in some details resembles West African languages. If there ever was a "mixed" language, Krio would seem to be a noteworthy example. And there are, of course, other languages of a similar type around the world, whose history is quite different from the unbroken history of a language or the virtually total acquisition of a new language described up to this point. In terms of the discussion up to now, Krio is unquestionably aberrant. It is a new language, without any genetic history in the usual sense.

But if such an aberrant language may appear in Africa, with a beclouded or disputable genetic background, may there not be other cases of the same type, unrecorded and buried in the linguistic history of the continent, which would not in any normal way fit into Greenberg's genetic classification? And if so, can we legitimately talk about relationships at all? (See Dalby 1966).

1.15. Before we discard the whole concept of genetic relationship, and with it Greenberg's classification, we should note the highly specialized circumstances under which a language such as Krio may come into being. The origin of Krio is not comparable to the cases of language substitution which have already been discussed. In those, the circumstances were of a homogeneous group, speakers of a single language, adopting a new language in place of their own. During the early stages of the substitution process, they would use the new language only in communicating with native speakers of it; among themselves, they would continue to use their first language. The new language would come into use within the group only after it was well, if not perfectly, learned. The history of Krio is significantly different. As a result of extensive coastal trade, and later in the New World, native speakers of a wide variety of African languages were thrown into each other's social milieu. They were forced, or found it profitable, to communicate not only with native speakers of English, but also with each other. They had no common native language to fall back on. In so far as they communicated with native speakers of English, the usual pressures to conform to English pronunciation and grammar were present. But when they communicated with each other, those pressures were absent. Under such circumstances, habits of imperfect pronunciation and usage were reinforced, and a sort of lowest common denominator of phonology and grammar was arrived at. English lexical items could safely be used in a pronunciation, and in grammatical constructions, which did not seriously violate the patterns of most of the African languages spoken natively by various members of the community. And in time, native speakers of English, in communicating with them, probably found it easier to conform to their newly-developing intertribal code than to impose on them the finer points of English pronunciation and grammar. To the extent that that happened, they no longer had a model of real English to conform to, and the patterns of their pronunciation and grammar became stabilized. Finally, the return of large numbers of the community to African soil further isolated them from an English model.

In such a situation, as long as the native languages of the community are remembered and the newly-developed language is a second language for its speakers, it is known as a "pidgin" language. Within a few generations, however, the children in such a linguistically heterogeneous community may learn only the newly developed language, and it becomes their native language. At that stage it is known as a "creole" language. Sierra Leone Krio is the native language of a sizable population. In the nineteenth century, it was transported by its native speakers to Cameroon, Nigeria, and some other points along the West African coast (though not, as has been alleged, Liberia), where it has become a second language for intertribal communication, and is only in the pidgin stage except perhaps in isolated families.

The unique and significant conditions for the origin of a pidgin and eventually a creole language are, then, a linguistically heterogeneous community, with no predominant native language, and intense pressure to communicate within the community as well as with native speakers of the languages whose vocabulary the community adopts.[2] This has been true not only for Sierra Leone Krio, but also for West African Crioulo (with Portuguese vocabulary), for Liberian "Soldier English" (a pidgin which may not as yet be fully stablized), Haitian and Mauritian and Louisiana Creole, Papiamento and Taki-taki in the Caribbean, Gullah on the islands off the South Carolina coast, Melanesian Pidgin, and all other known pidgins and creoles.

1.16. In this light, the question may once more be asked whether such languages may not have arisen frequently within Africa. It is not enough, in order for such a language to develop, to have migration, some intermarriage, or ordinary language contact and intertribal trade; such factors can account for only the standard forms of external influence in language change, or for ordinary language substitution. Even conquest ordinarily has no greater impact than these. Even slave-raiding must be of such an intensity and such a nature that it results in a substantial heterogeneous community under pressure to communicate within itself as well as with the slave-owners. Such pressure is understandable in such cataclysmic upheavals as the slave communities in the Western Hemisphere, or the trade patterns of European powers within the last few centuries. It does not seem likely that similar pressures would often have developed internally in Africa, even under the great empires of ancient times. The sociology of slavery and the nature of trade within Africa have been, in known times and presumably always, vastly different from the situation in the context of European-African contact; in Africa, the circumstances would have lent themselves far more readily to language substitution rather than to the development of pidgin languages. If unknown pidgin and finally creole languages did develop in the ages of unrecorded history in Africa, there is little reason to believe that they were numerous or large.

---

[2] This view of the necessary and sufficient conditions for the origin of a pidgin and ultimately a creole language, in distinction from a variety of earlier theories, was first explicitly stated in Welmers 1970c. Independently, participants in a conference on pidginization and creolization in 1968 reached the same conclusion; see particularly Whinnom 1971. The view, now widely and probably generally accepted, was foreshadowed in Welmers 1963c, in which the same conditions were described merely as "ideal" rather than necessary and sufficient; the fact that I assumed at that time that the pidgin ancestor of Sierra Leone Krio had its origins in the Western Hemisphere, which is very likely not the case (see Hancock 1971, p. 115), does not vitiate the argument.

We may conceivably find traces of such developments in the future, but it is extremely unlikely that they have been sufficient to distort our picture of language relationships in Africa at all seriously.

There have been, to be sure, other known linguistic developments in the direction of pidginization in Africa. Under the pressures of Belgian administration and missionary education in the Congo, a somewhat pidginized form of KiKongo has developed, known as KiTuba, Trade KiKongo, KiKongo véhiculaire, and by various other names; it has lost the tonal system of indigenous KiKongo, and a few of the subtler grammatical constructions, but is readily understood by native speakers of unaffected dialects of KiKongo. In East Africa, the pressures of centuries of Arabic slave trade followed by a period of European domination have made Swahili a vehicle of intertribal communication. The conditions for the origin of a pidgin have hardly been fully met, because the community is not so much a single heterogeneous community as a cluster of sizable, viable homogeneous communities. Yet the circumstances are somewhat similar, and the result has been the development of somewhat pidginized forms of Swahili such as "Up-Country Swahili", KiSettla, and KiHindi. On the other hand, for all the enormous pressure there appears to be to spread Hausa in West Africa, the circumstances have not been appropriate, or the pressure has been insufficient, to bring about the development of any recognized pidgin or creole language.

A realistic assessment of the situation, therefore, suggests that the possibility of the appearance of new creole languages within Africa throughout its history, sufficient to distort seriously the reconstruction of language relationships, is so remote as to be negligible. In addition, although creole languages may perhaps be called "mixed" languages if one so desires, they are of quite a different type from the kind of mixed languages posited by the fertile imaginations of some writers. And more generally, the tendency evidenced by some to attribute everything possible to language mixture, grammatical and phonological restructuring, or even the adoption of foreign vocabulary, is totally unjustified. The study of externally motivated language change is, of course, justifiable and important. So is, it goes without saying, the study of innovative, analogic, and semantic change which is internally motivated. But such studies can, for the most part, be validated only in the context of the genetic classification of the languages in question. If we begin with a realistic recognition of the nature of continuous language history, everyday communication between old and young, there can be no doubt of the possibility and validity of the genetic classification of languages. And such a classification has important implications for the study of structural characteristics across language boundaries.

1.17. To arrive at a genetic classification of the languages of Africa, Greenberg's procedure of mass comparison of lexical items is certainly valid. Although it does not go so far as a demonstration of regular phonetic correspondences, the similarities cited strongly suggest that such correspondences exist, though we may have inadequate evidence to state them fully. Relying on such approximations may, to be sure, involve the risk of occasional erroneous guesses; but the likelihood that the entire framework of the classification is completely vitiated by reliance on false comparisons is so remote as to be unworthy of consideration.

Granting that Greenberg's procedure is valid, however, the question remains whether he actually applied it with sufficient care and consistency to arrive at a definitive classification. At the grossest extreme, the assignment of individual languages or groups of clearly closely related languages to one of the four language families he posits, there can be little doubt that the assignments are correct, with perhaps a very occasional slip where the available evidence is minimal. For all practical purposes, the validity of Greenberg's four families can be considered established; they are Afro-Asiatic, Nilo-Saharan, Niger-Kordofanian, and Khoisan. Greenberg recognized the possibility of a remote relationship between two or more of these families, but he was not prepared to propose any hypotheses on the basis of available evidence. More recently, E. A. Gregerson (1970) has presented evidence for the ultimate relationship of the Nilo-Saharan and Niger-Kordofanian families; to the super-phylum he posits he gives the name Kongo-Saharan. Gregerson, following Greenberg's procedure and format closely, discusses a number of bound morphemes, and cites comparisons for seventy-five lexical items. Some of the comparisons are highly dubious, but taken as a whole the evidence is reasonably convincing. Within Nilo-Saharan, the most basic subdivision appears to be between Songhai and all the other languages; within Niger-Kordofanian the most basic subdivision is presumably between Kordofanian and Niger-Congo. On impressionistic grounds, Gregerson suggests the possibility that Songhai, the rest of the present Nilo-Saharan, Kordofanian, and Niger-Congo may rather be four "coordinate" branches of Kongo-Saharan. Although some realignment at the deepest levels of relationship may eventually be necessary, the concept of multiple coordinate branches must be handled with extreme care. Language division usually appears to take the form of bifurcation; it must normally be expected that the model for the origin of four branches would be one of the following:

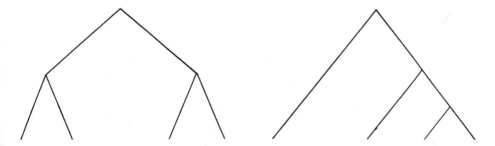

A three-way division from a single node is historically possible, of course; but where there is adequate evidence for reconstructing language history, few such cases have been demonstrated. References to "coordinate branches" should not be taken as actual hypotheses of multiple divisions from single nodes; they are more likely to be, by implication, mere admissions that the order of bifurcations is not clear from the evidence to date. Until unambiguous evidence is available, Greenberg's four-family classification of the languages of Africa remains entirely adequate; the recognition of a probable relationship between Nilo-Saharan and Niger-Kordofanian does not constitute a radical realignment.

1.18. At some points in the subclassification of the four language families of Africa, Greenberg's outline has been questioned with more reason. First of all, in the Afro-Asiatic family, Greenberg recognizes five "coordinate branches": ancient Egyptian (extinct), Semitic, Cushitic, Berber, and Chadic. Once more, it is not to be assumed that the five branches are equally closely or distantly related to each other, but rather that the relative degrees of relationship have not been established. In this case, Greenberg was explicitly reacting against a widely accepted theory that Egyptian, Cushitic, and Berber constituted a unity known as "Hamitic", which was in turn more distantly related to Semitic in a larger "Hami-to-Semitic" family. Greenberg's contention is merely that no such formulation had ever been demonstrated; it was, in fact, merely the result of accidents in the history of comparative scholarship—relationships between Egyptian, Cushitic, and Berber were considered established before many Semitists were prepared to accept the relationship of any of them to Semitic.

Further subclassification within the branches of Afro-Asiatic presents a problem in only two cases. There can, of course, be no subclassification of Egyptian. For the Semitic languages, there is a long tradition of distinguished scholarship, and Greenberg implicitly refers the reader to that; in any case, for Africa, he is concerned only with Arabic and the Semitic languages of Ethiopia. The Berber languages are relatively closely inter-related, and there are no burning issues concerning their subclassification. Greenberg posits five groups of Cushitic languages, and nine groups of Chadic languages. Again the interrelationships among the groups are not established, but there has been no serious disagreement with the groupings themselves.

1.19. In his definition and delimitation of the Nilo-Saharan family, Greenberg (1963) incorporates a number of original hypotheses of relationship and subclassification which could have been based only on careful examination of the evidence and cautious judgment. He includes in Nilo-Saharan seven languages or small groups of languages which he had tentatively listed as separate language families in his earlier classification (1955). In his rejection of the old Nilo-Hamitic hypothesis—the view that certain languages were in some way mixtures of Nilotic and Cushitic elements—he was determined to make as strong a case as possible for the inclusion of the languages in question with the Nilotic languages. For Nilo-Saharan more than for any of the other families, Greenberg's classification worked from the bottom up; even though the evidence for some of the languages is far from extensive, the groupings proposed have a strong claim to validity.

At the same time, the six branches of Nilo-Saharan are listed, as are the branches of other families, without any indication of the relative degrees of interrelationship. Five of the branches are made up of only one to six languages each. The sixth branch, Chari-Nile, is further subdivided into four parts, two of which are still further subclassified into ten and seven groups respectively. It is this latter type of subclassification which, though still capable of refinement, provides a valuable foundation for more detailed and rigid comparative studies.

1.20. In the case of the Niger-Kordofanian family, the situation in regard to subclassification is more complex. In his earlier classification, Greenberg had listed the Kordofanian languages as a separate family. When he concluded that the Kordofanian languages are related to the Niger-Congo languages which he had already defined as a family, it was natural to view Kordofanian and Niger-Congo as unities related to each other as two branches of a larger family. It had already been established (Welmers 1958) that, within Niger-Congo (not including Kordofanian), the Mande languages represent the oldest division from the parent stock; the relationship between the Mande languages and any other Niger-Congo languages is more remote than any other relationship within Niger-Congo apart from Mande. If the dichotomy of Kordofanian and Niger-Congo is valid, then Kordofanian must be more distantly related to all of Niger-Congo, including Mande, than Mande is to the rest of Niger-Congo. It is Greenberg's impression that this is true, but it remains to be proven. It is possible that the relationship between the Kordofanian languages and the non-Mande Niger-Congo languages is closer than the relationship of any of them to Mande. If this should prove to be the case, the divergence of Mande would be the most ancient, and the divergence of Kordofanian from the rest of Niger-Congo would be somewhat later.

Greenberg recognizes five groups of languages as constituting Kordofanian. The major subclassificatory division is between one group (Tumtum) and the other four; the interrelationships among the latter four are not stated in further detail.

For Niger-Congo, Greenberg recognizes six branches: West Atlantic, Mande, Gur, Kwa, Benue-Congo, and Adamawa-Eastern. As mentioned above, the major division among these is between Mande and all of the others. Within Mande, the position of Bobo-Fing (Sya) remains in some doubt. The other Mande languages clearly fall into two groups, each further subdivided into two, and for many of the individual languages the relative degrees of relationship are clear; this is probably the most complete, and perhaps the best established, subclassification of any comparable language group in Africa. Greenberg considers the second major dichotomy to be probably between West Atlantic and the remaining branches. Dalby (1965, 1970), on the other hand, questions the very integrity of the West Atlantic branch, and even suggests that some of the languages assigned to it may be more closely related to languages in other branches of Niger-Congo. If West Atlantic does represent a very old divergence in Niger-Congo, it is to be expected that some inter-relationships within the branch are distant, and the inclusion of some languages may seem dubious. On the other hand, the hypothesis of a closer relationship of some of these languages to Bantu should be easy to demonstrate with a little lexical evidence; demonstration has not been made.

Greenberg considers the Kwa and Benue-Congo branches to be particularly closely related; at least it is clear that the divergences involving the Gur and

Adamawa-Eastern languages are old. Other problems arise, however, in the case of Gur, Kwa, and Benue-Congo. Among some of the languages Greenberg assigns to the Gur branch, inter-relationships appear to be at least as distant as between some of them and some of the Kwa languages. Greenberg's assignment of the Kru group to Kwa is admittedly tentative; Kru may well deserve the status of a separate branch. The assignment of Ijo to Kwa is also considered tentative; Ijo, however, does appear to be about as closely related to Yoruba and to Akan as the latter are to each other. These and several other relationships within Kwa, however, appear to be at least as distant as between some of the easternmost languages assigned to Kwa and languages that clearly belong in Benue-Congo. Within Greenberg's Benue-Congo, the first two subgroups of his Cross-River group (C.1,2) appear to be slightly more closely related to some of the subgroups of Kwa (especially f, g) than to the rest of Benue-Congo.[3]

Definitive reclassification within these branches, however, will be no easy task. There is evidence that, during a relatively brief period in the distant past (perhaps about four millenia ago), there were widespread and complex population movements which resulted in large numbers of language divisions, primarily in groups now found in West Africa. By now, the relative degrees of relationship, and thus the details of classification, are difficult to determine. In some cases, perhaps multiple near-simultaneous division will have to be posited. There is no reason to suppose, however, that anything transpired other than the usual forms of language change. Languages are not life forms that interbreed, transfigure or mutilate each other beyond recognition, or give birth to deformed as well as normal offspring. Languages are what people use in everyday life, and generation speaks to generation in each unbroken continuum.

Whatever other realignments may be found necessary in the complex including Greenberg's Kwa and Benue-Congo, one major conclusion he reached stands out clearly as indisputable, even though there are some who still refuse to accept it. That is the inclusion of the Bantu languages with a number of other languages to the northwest of Bantu in a Benue-Congo branch of the Niger-Congo and ultimately the Niger-Kordofanian family. David W. Crabb has suggested certain features that appear to be innovations within Bantu, and which can therefore be used as diagnostic tests to determine whether a language should be called Bantu or not.[4] Thus, within Benue-Congo, Bantu is specifically delineated. Greenberg does not propose a subclassification of the relatively closely interrelated Bantu languages. The classification of Bantu into geographical zones by Guthrie (1948) is not, and is not intended to be, a full genetic classification. For some of the zones, however, details of the genetic subclassification undoubtedly correspond to his geographical boundaries.

1.21. The Khoisan family is the smallest of the language families of Africa. It includes the so-called Bushman and Hottentot languages of southern Africa plus

---

[3] These suggestions are based on the kind of "statistical pretesting" used by the author in his classification of the Mande languages (Welmers 1958).

[4] Crabb 1965; note especially the Foreword by Joseph H. Greenberg.

Sandawe and Hatsa in Tanzania. Following the view of D. F. Bleek (1927, 1929), Greenberg recognizes that the cultural differences between the Bushmen and the Hottentots do not parallel a linguistic dichotomy. Rather, the South African Khoisan languages fall into three subgroups cutting across cultural boundaries. Sandawe and Hatsa constitute two branches of Khoisan distinct from the South African branch.

Westphal (1971) proposes a classification—perhaps better described as an unclassification—of the Khoisan languages in which he does little more than list numerous groups of the most closely related languages. Since "relationship" to Westphal seems to imply something very close to mutual intelligibility, a more realistic genetic classification is clearly possible. Whether the Bleek-Greenberg classification is valid I am not competent to judge for lack of evidence on hand; it would hardly appear, however, that a drastic revision would be defensible.

1.22. Whatever else may be said in criticism or in defense of Greenberg's classification of the languages of Africa, there is universal agreement on one point: it is time to expand our efforts to work out comparative studies of the most obviously closely-related groups of languages, then to compare group with group, and thus to work from the bottom to the top of the genetic phyla with more detailed evidence and more thorough investigation than could conceivably have been possible for Greenberg. In the process, the assumptions concerning language comparison, language history, and language classification which underline Greenberg's classification can hardly suffer, and there is every hope that hypotheses of language mixture, secondary affiliations, and contamination will be seen for what they are—sheer speculation.

Chapter 2

Vowel Systems

2.1. One of Guthrie's criteria for identifying a language as Bantu is a "symmetrical" vowel system: an odd number of vowels, including one low central vowel and an equal number of front (unrounded) and back (rounded) vowels (see Guthrie 1948, p. 12). Such systems, which are indeed typical though not universal in the Bantu languages, permit variations such as the following:

i	u		i	u		i	u
ɪ	ʊ						
e	o		e	o		e	o
ɛ	ɔ		ɛ	ɔ			
	a			a			a

In citing proto-Bantu forms, a seven-vowel system is used. Because of the nature of the correspondences among Bantu languages, however, most contemporary writers find it convenient to cite the reconstructed system with the following symbols:

į	ų
i	u
e	o
	a

Vowel systems of this sort are also extremely common among the Niger-Congo languages of West Africa. A five-vowel system of this type is found in Jukun and Nupe; seven vowels are found in Yoruba, Bariba, Gã, the Senufo languages, Bambara, Mende, Loma, Kpelle, Mano; and a nine-vowel system appears in at least the Fante dialect of Akan, though the nine vowels of Fante can perhaps be analyzed as five with a prosodic feature. Dan (Gio), which is very closely related to Mano, has a somewhat similar symmetrical system of ten vowels, with a full range of central vowels added; the central vowels have clearly developed rather recently out of allophonic differences, and the contrast between the front and central vowels is still quite restricted:

i	ɨ	u
e	ɨ	o
ɛ	ə	ɔ
	a	

Among the Bantu languages, there are a few with vowel systems of an even number of vowels, probably also symmetrical though perhaps in a different way.

On the basis of a preliminary analysis, KiYanzi seems to have a seven-vowel system including a contrast of unrounded and rounded vowels in the front series:

$$
\begin{array}{ccc}
\text{i} & \text{ü} & \text{u} \\
\text{e} & \text{ö} & \text{o} \\
 & \text{a} &
\end{array}
$$

A number of West African Niger-Congo languages have vowel systems with an even number of vowels, usually paired in such a way that the basic contrast seems to be between unrounded and rounded series. In some of these systems, the phonetic realization of /a/ tends to be rather front, toward [æ]. Tiv and Ewe have systems like that on the left below; the system on the right is that of Igbo, which may perhaps be analyzed as four vowels and a prosodic feature; here, as elsewhere, the symbols chosen are not necessarily those used in works on or in the language:

$$
\begin{array}{cccccc}
\text{i} & & \text{u} & \quad & \text{i} & \text{u} \\
 & & & & \text{ɪ} & \text{ʊ} \\
\text{e} & & \text{o} & & \text{e} & \text{o} \\
\text{a} & & \text{ɔ} & & \text{a} & \text{ɔ}
\end{array}
$$

While symmetry in phonemic systems is common all over the world, it is, of course, not universal. However, one would be hard pressed to find a Niger-Congo vowel system that does not give evidence of at least an underlying symmetry in one of the above ways or perhaps in a slightly different way.

2.2. A peculiarly restricted lack of symmetry is found in Efik. If only a few morphemes in the language are ignored, sounds like [e] and [ɛ] are clearly allophones of one phoneme; [e] occurs only in word-initial position, and [ɛ] occurs only in postconsonantal position. Typical forms are [étó] 'tree', [dέp] 'buy', [ètέ] 'father'. If, on the basis of such forms, [e] and [ɛ] are analyzed as allophones of a phoneme /e/, then Efik has a symmetrical vowel system like that of Tiv or Ewe: unrounded /i, e, a/ and rounded /u, o, ɔ/; the forms cited would be /étó, dép, èté/. In a very few morphemes, however, a sound very much more like the postconsonantal [ɛ] than like the initial [e] occurs in word-initial position; one can hardly be blamed for hearing it as "the same" as postconsonantal [ɛ]. The forms in question include the second and third person singular subject pronouns; depending on the following vowel, the second person has the forms [è-, à-, ɔ̀-, ò-], and the third person has the forms [έ-, á-, ɔ́-, ó-]; the singular forms [έ-] and [έ-] are in minimal contrast with their plural counterparts, which are [è-] and [é-] without variation. Initial [ɛ] occurs also in the third person singular independent pronoun [èɣέ], the demonstrative [έmì] 'this', the noun [έkè] 'possession' (used only with possessors other than singular pronouns, as in [έkὲ ḿmɔ̀] 'theirs'), and a very few other words with a kind of demonstrative meaning—though not, as one might expect, in the singular possessive noun [ésyɛ̌] 'his, hers.'

Considerations of phonetic similarity would seem to favor the identification of the initial [ɛ] of a very few morphemes with the postconsonantal [ɛ]. This solution would, however, leave two phonemes, /e/ and /ɛ/, both with restricted distributions. It would seem preferable to identify the initial [e] of the vast majority of forms with the postconsonantal [ɛ], and interpret the initial [ɛ] of a few morphemes as a separate phoneme /ɛ/; the latter would, of course, have a highly restricted distribution, but the remainder of the vowel system would be more neatly described. Actually, the initial [ɛ] may be a slightly lower vowel than the postconsonantal [ɛ]; particularly in the demonstrative [ɛ́mì], the initial vowel is sometimes heard almost as low as [æ].

The situation is further complicated, however, by the fact that, under special circumstances, a higher vowel like [e] occurs in postconsonantal position where [ɛ] is normal. This is restricted to three verbal construction markers: the completive, which elsewhere has the forms [mɛ́, má, mɔ́, mó]; the contrastive past, which elsewhere has the forms [kɛ́, ká, kɔ́, kó], and the contrastive future, which elsewhere has the form [yɛ́] without variation. If the next vowel after the construction marker is [i] or [ɛ], the forms [mɛ́, kɛ́, yɛ́] appear after the first person singular subject pronoun (a homorganic syllabic nasal with high tone), the second third person singular [è-] and [ɛ́-], and the first person plural [ì-]. If, however, the preceding pronoun is the second or third person plural, [è-] or [é-], the construction markers have the forms [mé, ké, yé]. The foregoing statements are illustrated in the following phonetic transcriptions (no effort is made to reflect the contrastive force of two of the constructions in the English translations):

	[ŋ́kókùt m̀bòró]	'I saw bananas'
	[ókókùt m̀bòró]	'he saw bananas'
	[ékókùt m̀bòró]	'they saw bananas'
	[ń yɛ́kùt m̀bòró]	'I'll see bananas'
	[ŋ́kɛ́dèp m̀bòró]	'I bought bananas'
	[ɛ́kɛ́dèp m̀bòró]	'he bought bananas'
but:	[ékédèp m̀bòró]	'they bought bananas'
	[éyédèp m̀bòró]	'they'll buy bananas'

Again, if the principle of phonetic similarity is determinative, a phoneme /e/ would occur initially in all but a very few forms in the language, and postconsonantally in only three morphemes; conversely, a phoneme /ɛ/ would occur in postconsonantal position in all but three morphemes, and initially in only a handful of forms. Further, the occurrence of [e] in the three verbal construction markers is predictable in terms of the following and preceding vowels (in that order). It has already been suggested that the usual initial [e] and postconsonantal [ɛ] be interpreted as a phoneme /e/, and that only the exceptional initial [ɛ] be interpreted as a second phoneme, /ɛ/. By a similar device, the exceptional postconsonantal [e] could now be interpreted as still another unit in the system, say /e̤/—or, for that matter, also /ɛ/, if /ɛ/ is defined as 'the positionally unexpected allophone of /e/.' This has proven to be a practical and not confusing analysis in teaching Efik to speakers of English; nor are native speakers of Efik confused by it in reading.[1]

The Efik data thus provide an interesting application of the principle of markedness: initial [e] and postconsonantal [ɛ] are unmarked, while initial [ɛ] and postconsonantal [e] are marked. Apart from these special cases of marking, Efik has a typical symmetrical six-vowel system. The above analysis was worked out in 1964-66 (Welmers 1968a).

2.3. Types of allophonic variation within vocalic systems like those outlined above do not differ significantly from variations found in other languages all over the world. Procedures for determining a vocalic inventory, accordingly, are also fairly standard. Brief utterances (three, two, or even one syllable) can usually be elicited early in the analysis to provide minimal or near minimal contrasts displaying the entire vowel system. One negative observation, however, is worth making: tone is rarely if ever a conditioning factor in vowel quality.

Recognizably different allophones of vowels conditioned by preceding consonants are not very common, but they are recorded. In Kpelle, the short unrounded vowels /i, e, ɛ/ are front [i, ɪ, ɛ] in monosyllables only after /y/; after velar consonants they are considerably centralized; after all other consonants they are somewhat centralized. The centralized allophones occur in forms of more than one syllable only in certain special types of combinations (see Welmers 1962).

Allophonic variation in vowels conditioned by following consonants is also uncommon, except in languages which permit syllable-final consonants (i.e., closed syllables). In Efik, which has no phonemic vowel length, vowels in closed syllables are shorter than those in open syllables; in addition, /i/ and /u/ are somewhat lower and slightly centralized in closed syllables. The definition of a "closed syllable" in Efik must await a discussion of the Efik consonant system in the following chapter.

Variations involving progressive derounding of rounded vowels have been recorded in a number of languages. In Kpelle, short /o/ and /ɔ/, when followed by a front vowel, either directly or after an intervening /l, r, n/, have allophones which end unrounded and somewhat fronted; early phonetic transcription of these allophones were [wɪ] and [wə]. There is no contrasting /we/ or /wɛ/, but both pattern congruity and native speaker reaction strongly favor the interpretation of these as /o/ and /ɔ/ respectively. In a number of languages, a similar derounding is recorded, primarily before [r] followed by an unrounded vowel. Sequences first transcribed as [əara] often prove to be best analyzed as /ɔra/ or /ora/.

In some languages, zero allophones of vowels, normally /i/ or /u/, must be recognized. In Senari, word-final /-gì, -lì, -rì, -wì, -mì/, which are sometimes heard as [-gì] etc. in careful speech, are commonly actualized by the consonant articulation alone, syllabic and with low tone. In one dialect of Senari, /u/ in a form

---

[1] The standard orthography of Efik does not distinguish between /e/ and /ɛ/, but some speakers have been taught to read an orthography reflecting the analysis presented here, and make the proper distinctions even when there is nothing in the context to require one or the other reading.

/kpumɔ/ is actualized by the release of the velar closure of the initial /kp/, accompanied by opening of the nasal passage, unvoiced; the lips remain closed until
the release of the /m/. In Fante, /mù/ at the end of a phrase is a syllabic [m] with
low tone, with some rounding of a preceding unrounded vowel.

The citation of further details on allophonic variation could naturally be extensive, but most of it would be trivial. Some widespread phenomena involving
length, nasalization, vowel harmony, and elision are treated in connection with
those topics in the following sections.

2.4. Contrasts between short and long vowels are common among Niger-Congo languages. Phonemically long vocalic segments can, in every known case,
be readily interpreted as double vowels. In innumerable instances, this is demonstrably the best analysis. Long vowels tend to occur with tone glides which do
not occur with short vowels. Such glides may usually be interpreted as sequences
of tones; identical sequences occur with clearly bisyllabic segmental sequences.
Kpelle, for example, has a sequence of mid tone followed by falling tone in bisyllabic forms like /konâ/ 'mortar' or /nɛnî/ 'woman.' A glide from mid to high to
low, accompanying a long vowel, is then best interpreted as the same tone sequence
accompanying a double vowel, as in /tɛɛ̂/ 'black duiker', /sãã̂/ 'tree (sp.)'. But no
comparable tone glide occurs with short (i.e., single) vowels.

This is not to say that tone glides or even phonemic tone sequences occur
only with double vowels in all languages. As will be noted under the discussion
of tone, some languages have glides which can be interpreted as unit tonemes
occurring with short vowels; and some languages have sequences of two or even
three tones, actualized as glides, accompanying short, single vowels. Where long
vowels occur in contrast with short vowels, however, there is frequently evidence
from the tonal system to support an analysis of long vowels as double; and there
is no clear-cut case of such an analysis being impossible or undesirable.

By way of contrast with this typically Niger-Congo pattern, long vowels in
Hausa have a somewhat different status. To be sure, Hodge (1947) analyzes (or
at least writes) them as double vowels, but objections can be raised to this analysis,
and it certainly cannot be defended on the basis of congruence with bisyllabic
sequences. Hausa has five vowels that occur clearly long, or in positions in which
long and short vowels do not contrast; short counterparts of three of these occur
in positions where contrast is possible, but occurrences of short counterparts of
the other two are apparently marginal at best, at least in many dialects. This restriction makes it seem strange to say that there are five vowels plus doubling
or a phoneme of length; the occurrence of two of the vowels by themselves, short
or single, would be questionable. An alternative analysis in terms of five basically
long vowels plus a phoneme of shortening is certainly peculiar, though perhaps
possible. The Hausa system seems rather to be basically one of eight vowels, five
of which are inherently long, and three inherently short. There are also differences in vowel quality between the long and short vowels. The following chart
indicates both the length and quality differences, but treats all eight vowels as
of equal phonemic status; this is strikingly reminiscent of some vowel systems in

some Semitic (also Afro-Asiatic) languages, including ancient Hebrew, Ge'ez, and modern Tigre. The Hausa system then is:

$$
\begin{array}{cc}
\bar{\imath} & \bar{u} \\
\imath & \upsilon \\
\bar{e} & \bar{o} \\
& \textipa{@} \\
& \bar{a}
\end{array}
$$

Even if short [ɛ, ɔ] were to be added to this chart as additional unit phonemes— making a complete set of five pairs—the interpretation of long vowels as double still has no particular merit, as it so commonly does in Niger-Congo languages.

2.5. In Niger-Congo languages which do not have contrastive vowel length (or double vowels), there is frequently allophonic length. In many of the Bantu languages, particularly in southern Africa, the next-to-last vowel of a phrase is very long; length may also appear, though less extremely, with the next-to-last vowel of words within a phrase. In Swahili, some such allophonic length typically accompanies the almost perfectly consistent penultimate word stress.

Length may also be conditioned (as above) in some positions, but phonemic under other (and perhaps restricted) circumstances. Swahili has double vowels which are clearly different from the slightly lengthened stressed short vowels. Some southern Bantu languages have contrasts of short and long vowels in other than penultimate position; such long vowels are rare, but they are phonetically quite similar to the automatically long penultimate vowels. This is a typical problem of phonemic overlapping; but there seems to be no serious objection to analyzing penultimate vowels as automatically long and not indicated as long in any way, while long vowels in other positions are analyzed as phonemically long or double.

Length (or doubling) may condition qualitative as well as quantitative differences in vowels. In Kpelle, as has been noted, the short front unrounded vowels /i, e, ɛ/ have centralized allophones after most consonants in monosyllables and in some types of bisyllabic forms: [ɨ, ɪ, ə]. The double vowels /ii, ee, ɛɛ/, on the other hand, are always front: [iː, eː, ɛː].

In analytic procedure, the problem is again one of simply comparing vocalic segments in maximally similar environments. In due course, if length or doubling exists, one can usually find contrasting pairs like the following in Kpelle:

tí	'that'	tíi	'work, job'
lé	'what?'	wée	'white clay'
tɛ́	'go up'	tɛ́ɛ	'chicken'
ta	'some'	taa	'town'
lɔ́	'enter'	lɔ́ɔ	'market'
ɓó	'leak'	ɓóo	'slippery clay'
pú	'run away'	puu	'ten'

Kpelle also has, phonetically, a long [æ:] without a corresponding short counterpart, as in [kæ:] 'yaws' and [swǽ:] 'weaver bird'. Unlike other long vowels, this does not occur in forms with an additional syllable. This [æ:] by itself is analyzed as /ɛya/; the sequence [wæ:], with derounding, is analyzed as /ɔya/. This analysis, first arrived at with no more evidence than the above, is confirmed by the fact that, in some dialects, these are actually [ɛya] and [ɔya] in slow speech; the analysis also reflects a more widespread native speaker reaction to syllabification, and is reinforced by a pronunciation used in singing. Thus the phonetically transcribed forms above are phonemicized as /kɛya/, /sɔ́ya/.

2.6. The recognition or exclusion of extra short vowels, in apparent consonant clusters separated by a quick release with little evidence of any specific vowel quality, may give far greater difficulty in analysis. In Fante, early analyses interpreted two different verbs as *pra*. It was noted that these verbs differ in the vowel harmony which they determine in prefixes, but the stems were thought to be identical, and one of them therefore irregular. Actually, there is a clearly audible difference in the quality of the release of [p] in the two verbs, and their tonal behavior is also clearly that of bisyllabic stems. The two verbs are /pìrá/ 'hurt' and /pìrá/ 'sweep'; the first vowel in each is voiceless and very short, but there is audible palatal friction with /i/, but not with /ɪ/. Past tense forms like /òpíràà . . ./ 'he hurt' and /ɔ̀píràà . . ./ 'he swept' show a high tone that must be assigned to the vowel that was at first not even recognized as being there; although the vowels are voiceless in these forms as well, they have a tenseness characteristic of high tone, and a high pitch is heard when voicing begins during the /r/. In contemporary othography, the tonal behavior is still ignored; the two stems are written *pira* and *pra* respectively, though their syllabic structure and tonal behavior is identical.

Similar very short vowels occur in first position in Kpelle forms such as /ɣîla/ 'dog', /pêlee/ 'singing and dancing', /kélee/ 'all'. Careful attention to tonal patterns, in particular, will betray the vocalic character of such short segments in most languages where they have been noted. In the case of Kpelle, the qualitative difference between /i/ and /e/ is also audible, though not conspicuous. Dan (Gio) provides another example of an almost identical situation; in this case, early transcriptions showed consonant clusters including *pr, tr, kr, pl, kl*, but not *ll*—almost certainly because only *ll* does not occur in English; the others were reminiscent of English consonant clusters, but the analogy of forms like 'telegraphy' suggested a vowel in the last case. Tone patterns require the presence of a vowel in all of these cases. For Dan, the vowel is identified as identical with the vowel following the /l/ or /r/; a form first transcribed *pla*, for example, is interpreted phonemically as /pala/.

In Gã and Ewe, the orthographies recognize similar consonant clusters, but the tonal evidence suggests that an intervening vowel is present. In Ewe forms like the following, for example, the release of the consonant preceding /l/ or /r/

is slow, voiced, and on the same pitch as that of the following vowel; tone markings are added to orthographic forms here: *flé* 'buy', *dzrá* 'sell', *kplé* 'and', *àgblè*
'farm'. But in the following, the release of the /f/ before /l/ has a high tone, clearly distinct from the preceding and following low tones: *tàf' làtsé* 'excuse me'. By
analogy with such forms, it would appear that there is always a tone-bearing
segment between any consonant and /l/ or /r/, though the tone may be the same
as the following one. And a tone-bearing segment is ordinarily thought of as a
vowel, although other possibilities should also be considered. Although an exhaustive study of Ewe phonotactics has not been made, it would appear that the
tone-bearing segment could be interpreted as /i/, or perhaps as /i/ before unrounded
vowels and /u/ before rounded vowels. If this proves impossible (because of the
occurence of /CilV/ and the like with full vocalic realization), the remaining possibility is to recognize /l/ and /r/ as being themselves tone-bearing. In any case, the Gã
and Ewe data point up the crucial importance of taking tone into consideration
from the beginning of analysis; the recognition of a tone may lead to the recognition of a vowel one might otherwise have ignored.

In some of the Kru languages (or dialects?), the analysis is even less clear
at present. In Tchien, an analyst reports apparent contrasts between CVVlV,
CVlV, and ClV. If there is an intervening vowel between the initial consonant
and the /l/ in the last of these, then apparently three degrees of vowel length must
be recognized. Otherwise, clusters with /l/ or /r/ must be recognized. In general,
such clusters should not be assumed until it is clear that they will not confuse the
tonal analysis; at best, they are rare, and an analysis of any language which recognizes them should be considered suspect unless that analysis is explicitly defended against other alternatives.

Clusters of consonant plus /r/ have also been recognized in the orthography
of Efik, but are best analyzed as having the vowel /i/ between the consonant
and /r/. When a speaker of Efik was first exposed to this analysis, in the word
/tìré/ 'stop', orthographically *tre*, his first reaction was, "But we don't say [tìré]."
Then, having heard himself say it, he thought for a moment and added, "You
know, in some dialects they do say [tìré]." This is hardly conclusive, but it is the
kind of lead that should be followed up. For Efik, considerations of tone are in-
determinative, but there is other convincing evidence for the interpretation suggested. All other CVrV sequences occur with the first vowel readily identifiable;
interpreting the presumed CrV sequences as CirV neatly fills out the pattern.
Further reinforcement comes from negative formations. After verb stems of
the structure CV, a negative suffix consists of /g/ (phonetically usually a uvular
flap) plus a vowel determined by the vowel of the preceding stem. Thus, from a
stem /dí/ 'come', a negative form is /ńdígé/ 'I'm not coming'; from /tá/ 'eat',
/ńtágá/ 'I'm not eating'; from /bɔ̀/ 'receive', /ḿbɔ̀gɔ́/ 'I'm not receiving'. After
clearly bisyllabic verb stems, however, as well as after all consonant-final stems,
the negative suffix is /ké/. Thus, from a stem /ỹéné/ 'have', the corresponding

negative form is /ńỹénéké/ 'I don't have'; from /dómó/ 'try', /ńdómóké/ 'I'm not trying'. From verb stems orthographically represented as CrV monosyllables, negative forms have the suffix /ké/ like negatives from obvious bisyllabic stems; thus, from /tìré/ 'stop', the corresponding negative is /ńtiréké/ 'I'm not stopping'. If the stem were interpreted as */trĕ/ (and a rising tone with a monosyllable is no obstacle in the case of Efik), the expected negative would be */ńtrĕgé/, which does not occur. (A similar argument, in the opposite direction, for interpreting certain Efik sequences as CyV and CwV rather than CiV and CuV, is presented in the following chapter.)

In short, in most cases where adequate evidence is available, apparent Cr and Cl clusters turn out to be illusory; an intervening vowel of some kind is present.

2.7. In a few Niger-Congo languages, types of vowels have been reported which are described as "muffled" or "hollow" (e.g., Kru-Bassa, the Dompago dialect of Kabre). The phonetic character of these sounds has not been clarified by comparing the experience of more than one qualified investigator, nor is it known whether this phenomenon has a special status in the phonemic system. Perhaps some form of tenseness or pharyngeal resonance is involved, as presumably is the case for some vowels in Akan and Igbo; in the latter cases, such distinctions are best treated in connection with vowel harmony, which is discussed later in this chapter.

Among non-Niger-Congo languages, several of the Nilotic languages of the upper Nile valley have a series of vowels commonly called "breathy." Having heard and attempted to imitate such vowels in Anuak (during a period of a few days in 1950), and having heard them on tape recordings of Nuer and Dinka, I consider the impressionistic label to be a good one. Apparently the voicing of these vowels is such that the vocal cords do not entirely close, permitting the air passing through from the lungs to produce an audibly fricative effect.

For Dinka, enough evidence has been available from tape recordings, transcriptions at least partially reliable, and the notes and impressions of a most observant missionary, the Rev. Talmadge Wilson, to arrive at a tentative analysis of the vowel system. If this analysis is correct, it is also remarkable, because the system is quite unlike any other known to me, especially when the morphophonemic alternations operating within it are considered. There appear to be constrasts between (1) very long vowels with extremely clear, "brassy" quality and extreme articulatory positions, (2) breathy vowels of intermediate length and somewhat more neutral (i.e., toward central) tongue positions, and (3) very short, centralized vowels; of the last type, any two vowels with adjacent tongue positions are very hard to distinguish. There are seven contrasting positions for each type. Thus the vowel diagram is like an eight-spoke wheel with the top spoke missing (or, if preferred, like a horseshoe, rather than like the usual vowel "triangle" or trapezoid). The vowel diagram may be depicted as follows; a macron indicates length, a dieresis indicates breathiness, and a breve indicates shortness and centralization:

$$
\begin{array}{ccccccc}
\bar{\imath} & & & & & \bar{u} \\
\ddot{\imath} & & & & \ddot{u} \\
\breve{\imath} & & & \breve{u} \\
\bar{e} \;\; \ddot{e} \;\; \breve{e} & & \breve{o} \;\; \ddot{o} \;\; \bar{o} \\
\breve{\varepsilon} & & \breve{\mathit{o}} \\
\ddot{\varepsilon} \;\; \breve{a} \;\; \ddot{\mathit{o}} \\
\bar{\varepsilon} \;\; \ddot{a} \;\; \bar{\mathit{o}} \\
& \bar{a} &
\end{array}
$$

This analysis is reinforced by a morphophonemic pattern: alternations between noun singulars and plurals appear to involve most commonly a movement clockwise to the next spoke, but in the same position on the spoke; that is, if the singular has /ü/, the plural has /ö/; if the singular has /ö/, the plural has /ɔ/; and so on around until if the singular has /ë/, the plural has /ï/; but if the singular has /ï/ there is no change in the plural (since there is no spoke in the next position clockwise). A less common pattern is precisely the reverse, with the alternation in the plural one spoke counterclockwise from the vowel of the singular; if the singular is on the /u/ spoke, there is no change in the plural. Still other alternations are one step in or out on the same spoke: /ō/ to /ö/, /ă/ to /ä/, and the like. If the above diagram is filled in with lines—three concentric horseshoes and seven spokes—then the morphophonemic alternations permit single moves on any line, never more than one space and never across a gap in a line.

A note on the Dinka vowel system by A.N. Tucker and M. A. Bryan (1966, pp. 402-3) differs from the above analysis in some respects, though they agree in recognizing three types of vowels. They admit, however, being uncertain as to "phonemic boundaries". Eight rather than seven articulatory positions are noted, but quite possibly this represents overdifferentiation. Only four of the very short, centralized vowels are distinguished, but it is even more likely that this represents underdifferentiation. These very short vowels, as well as those of intermediate length, are described as "breathy"; whatever breathiness may be present is certainly not prominent.

It should be noted that, in many contemporary versions of generative phonology, it is impossible to capture the entirely reasonable morphophonemic patterns of Dinka, as described above, in any convenient set of rules. Some phonologists, however, now seem to be prepared to posit distinctive features comparable to moves on a game board.

A number of other Nilo-Saharan languages, including at least Dho-Luo among the Nilotic languages, have vowel systems much more like those typically found among Niger-Congo languages.

2.8. In languages which have long vowels interpreted as double vowels, clusters of unlike vowels are also to be expected. A common problem of analysis in this connection is that of sequences which might be transcribed as [ia, ua, iɔ, ue] etc.; the question often arises as to whether these are to be interpreted as /ia, ua, . . ./ or /iya, uwa, . . ./. The question can often be answered in terms of the overall pattern of vowel occurrences. If double vowels and also sequences of the types /ea, ɛɔ, ou/ occur, then the analysis /ia, ua, . . ./ is likely to be preferable. On the other hand, if there are no double vowels, and at best only restricted vowel clusters such as /ai, ui/, but a pervasive VCV pattern elsewhere, then the analysis /iya, uwa, . . ./ is more likely to be convincing. In a few languages, there may be a contrast between /iV, uV/ and /iyV, uwV/; in such cases, the consonantal quality of /y/ and /w/ is likely to be striking. Another alternative is that sequences may best be analyzed as /yV, wV/; this possibility will be discussed in connection with the occurrence of such sequences after consonants, in the following chapter.

Vowel clusters can present a different type of problem to the analyst who hears primarily in terms of an English system, which is common and understandable among even the best English-speaking linguists at first. The contrast between long, "pure" vowels and diphthongs may not be at all easy to hear at first. In Kpelle, one must learn to contrast /ee, ei, eei, ɛi, ɛɛi/; the additional contrasts of /e, ɛ, ɛɛ/ are relatively easy. But such contrasts need not be permanently confusing. It soon becomes apparent that, in Kpelle, stems with single and double vowels are fairly common, and also that suffixes with the vowel /i/ (actually two different suffixes with different tones) occur after such stems. Thus pairs such as /a, ai; ɔ, ɔi; aa, aai; oo, ooi/ can soon be identified. By analogy with these, .it is not too hard to identify the ones that may give phonetic difficulty; e.g.:

'fé nãa	'it isn't there'	'fêi	'it doesn't exist'
'tée	'cut it'	a 'téeì	'he is cutting it'
tɛ́	'go up'	a tɛi	'he is going up'
tɛ́ɛ	'a chicken'	'tɛ́ɛi	'the chicken'

2.9. Phonemic nasalization is fairly common among the western Niger-Congo languages, though rare among the Bantu languages and the Benue-Congo groups apparently most closely related to Bantu. A frequent pattern is that nasalization occurs with the final vowel of a morpheme; but its scope may include a double vowel or vowel cluster, and often a preceding resonant (e.g., /w, l, r, y/) and the vowel before that. In Kpelle, for example, nasalization is phonemic after stops and fricatives, and after nasals with phonemic tone; in the following examples, nasalization begins at the point marked (or with a preceding nasal), and continues to the end of the form:

sĩi	'spider'	ǹṹui	'the person'
'sŭa	'his nose'	*cf.*	ǹúui	'the fog'
kpɛ́la	'water chevrotain'	m̃ɛ́la	'its horn'
pɔ̃ya	'a design, mark'	*cf.*	m̃éla	'split it'

After stem-initial nasal consonants (which do not have phonemic tone), nasalization is always present. By analogy with corresponding forms in which the nasal has a tone, it seems best to interpret such stems as including the phoneme of nasalization; the rationale of the forms on the right above becomes clearer if the underlying stems are compared: /nũu/ 'person', /lúu/ 'fog', /-mĕla/ 'horn', /6éla/ 'split'.

As the phonology of Kpelle has been described to date, nasalization does not appear after the stem-initial resonants /w, y/. The possibility has been considered, however, of interpreting [ŋʷ, nʸ], which occur only before nasalized vowels, as allophones of /w, y/ before nasalized vowels rather than as unit nasal consonant phonemes /ŋw, ny/. There are distibutional problems at the morphophonemic level which have militated against this interpretation (see Welmers 1962, pp. 73-75). Nasalization does not appear after the implosive-plus-resonant series /6, l, γ/ either. The same distributional problems make it difficult to interpret /m, n, ŋ/ as allophones of /6, l, γ/ before nasalized vowels.

The restrictions on the distribution of nasalization in Kpelle are closely paralleled in Fante, where nasalization occurs only after voiceless stops and fricatives and (noncontrastively) after nasal consonants, but not after voiced stops nor resonants (there are no voiced fricatives).

The scope of nasalization is clearly a syllable in Jukun. This is not obvious after stops and fricatives, which cannot be nasalized; but contrasting oral and nasalized vowels condition markedly different allophones of preceding nasals and resonants. Before an oral vowel, a nasal consonant ends denasalized (i.e., with a homorganic voiced stop). Before a nasalized vowel, a resonant is nasalized to the extent that there is often complete oral stoppage. Thus:

/nè/:	[ndè]	'noise'	/nĕ̃/:	[nɛ̃]	'hoe'
/myā/:	[mbyā]	'make'	/mĕ̃/:	[mɛ̃]	'see'
/wā/:	[wā]	'drink'	/wǎ/:	[ŋwǎ]	'snatch'
/yūrà/:	[yūrà]	'forest'	/yűnù/:	[nyűnù]	'day'

The interpretation of prenasalized stops (or postdenasalized nasals; the commonly used term "nasal compounds" seems meaningless and confusing), [mb, nd, ŋg] and the like, as nasal consonants before oral vowels is completely convincing for Jukun, but it does not seem to be appropriate for any other known African language, though the phonetic sequences are exceedingly common. (The same interpretation is reported, however, for an Indian language along the Paraguay-Argentina border.) The interpretation of phonetic [ŋw, ny] as /w, y/ before nasalized vowels may have a wider application; perhaps even more commonly, [ŋw, ny] may well be interpreted as nasal consonants /w̃, ỹ/, even in languages which do not have phonemically nasalized vowels. The latter is a most attractive interpretation for Efik, and for those dialects of Igbo which do not have phonemic nasalization, and very likely for many more languages.

The restriction of nasalization to a single vowel in a vowel cluster is rare, but it is attested. In Dogon (Habe), forms of the following types have been recorded (from an unusually brilliant, perceptive, and sophisticated male informant aged about thirteen, on a visit to Kankan, Guinea, in 1948; I made no record of the precise consonant-vowel sequences nor of glosses); only the marked vowel is nasalized, so that nasalization may occur with the first, the second, both, or neither of two successive vowels:

$$\text{kĩa} \qquad \text{kĩã}$$
$$\text{kiã} \qquad \text{kia}$$

In languages which do not have phonemic nasalization, there is frequently a degree of noncontrastive nasalization after nasal consonants. This sometimes appears in unexpected places; in Mende, which does not have phonemic nasalization, /h/ and a following vowel are automatically nasalized. In dialects of Igbo which do have nasalization, there are respectable arguments for attributing nasalization to consonants or consonant releases instead of to vowels; again, /h/ is nasalized.

2.10. In many languages, nasalization occurs with only some vowel phonemes in the total inventory. In seven-vowel systems, nasalization is often restricted to five vowels; the following pattern is typical of Kpelle, the Senufo languages, and Bariba, which are by no means closely related to each other:

i		u		ĩ		ũ
e		o				
ɛ		ɔ		ɛ̃		ɔ̃
	a				ã	

(The nasalized /e/ in Kpelle /kpéla/ 'water chevrotain', cited above, is attributed to the scope of nasalization. Nasalization is marked where it begins, to show the extent of the scope; however, the nasalization is properly assigned to the final vowel, from which the scope extends backward.) Where such a pattern of distributionally restricted nasalization is found, it is also likely that the vowels not subject to nasalization (/e, o/ in the above and apparently very commonly) also do not occur, or occur only rarely, after nasal consonants.

In Jukun, as noted in part above, there are only five vowel phonemes, and all occur nasalized as well as oral, but nasalization conditions lower allophones of /e, o/. Thus the phonetic character of the vowels is reminiscent of the distributional restriction of nasalization noted above. The phonetics of the Jukun vowel system are:

[i]		[u]		[ĩ]		[ũ]
[e]		[o]		[ɛ̃]		[ɔ̃]
	[a]				[ã]	

Nasalized syllables are far more frequent in Jukun than in most languages; perhaps forty percent or more of the monosyllabic morphemes of the language are nasalized. In most languages the frequency of nasalization in a morpheme list is more likely to be ten to twenty percent.

In Yoruba, only three contrasts in nasalized vowels occur with any frequency. /ĩ/ and ũ/ are clear; there is also a low nasalized vowel, with allophones farther back than [a] after nonlabial consonants, and somewhat farther forward than [ɔ] after labial consonants. In Yoruba orthography, these are written as though /ã/ and /ɔ̃/ contrasted— the orthographic forms are *an*, *ọn*—but the two could readily be assigned to one phoneme. Whether they are assigned to /ã/ or /ɔ̃/ may well depend on whether a few marginal cases of [ɛ̃] must be analyzed as /ɛ̃/, and on the status that /ɛ̃/ is then given in the system. In the dialects generally considered to conform to "standard" Yoruba, [ɛ̃] occurs only in the demonstrative [ìỹ ɛ̃] (orthographic *iyẹn*) 'that', and occasionally as the result of contractions in rapid speech. The demonstrative is a dialect borrowing, used primarily in formal speech; the contractions can be considered automatic. Excluding or including it would yield one of the following systems of oral and nasalized vowels:

i	u	ī	ū		ĩ	ũ
e	o		OR:			
ε	ɔ				ε̃	ɔ̃
	a		ã			

Since in many Niger-Congo languages consonants either do not occur in final position at all, or do so with considerable restriction, nasalization in exclusively final position may often be analyzed as a final nasal, ordinarily /n/ or /ŋ/. This can be done in the Senufo languages, Bambara, Ewe, and Yoruba with no difficulty. In Kpelle, final /ŋ/ occurs in contrast with nasalization, and does not have the same nasalizing effect over a preceding scope; in such a case, it seems preferable to interpret nasalization as a phoneme of a different type from a final nasal. In Akan, final nasalization contrasts with final /m/ and /n/; there is otherwise no /ŋ/, so that nasalization could be interpreted as that third nasal. Such an interpretation may be acceptable as a linguistic analysis, but it would be awkward if it were incorporated into the orthography; in interior dialects (Asante, Twi, etc.) final /n/ is phonetically [ŋ], but in coastal Fante final /n/ is phonetically [n]. Perhaps it is not out of place to add that my own intuitive reaction, for whatever it is worth, is that nasalization does not "feel" like another final nasal.

A minor detail is well worth noting. In Fante orthography, nasalization is indicated (by a tilde) only in forms which contrast minimally with forms having oral vowels—a wearisomely typical device for avoiding the use of diacritics or anything else that departs from European orthographies. Among the examples given for the application of this principle, a contrast is cited between *nã* 'mother' and *na* 'and' (Methodist Book Depot 1947, p. 11). The two words could never be confused syntactically in any case, but the most ridiculous aspect of the situation is that both words have equally nasalized vowels; nasalization of vowels after nasal consonants is not contrastive. The words do differ, but the difference is in tone. The lengths to which some people will go to avoid marking or mentioning tone are indeed remarkable.

2.11. More or less pervasive systems of vowel harmony are widespread in Niger-Congo languages, and are found in at least some Nilo-Saharan languages. Perhaps the most highly developed systems are found in a few languages such as Igbo and Akan. Igbo has an eight-vowel system, divided neatly into four pairs

by vowel harmony. All vowels belong to one or the other of the following groups;
the orthographic forms of the most commonly used Igbo writing system are included in parentheses, and used in the illustrative material:[2]

i, e, u, o   (i, e, u, o)

ɪ, a, ʊ, ɔ   (ị, a, ụ, ọ)

Some verbal forms to illustrate these in harmonic sequence are:

ó rìrì	'he ate'	ọ́ pị̀rị̀	'he carved'
ó mèrè	'he did'	ọ́ sàrà	'he washed'
ó gbùrù	'he killed'	ọ́ zụ̀rụ̀	'he bought'
ó zòrò	'he did'	ọ́ dọ̀rọ̀	'he pulled'

In the following, the syllable written /nà/ is pronounced [nà] only in very
careful speech, as when correcting the pronunciation of a learner; in normal speech,
the vowel is completely assimilated to the following /è/; the combination is a long
vowel. This assimilation reflects assimilation rules which, while partially overlapping vowel harmony rules, must be separately stated. The underlying /a/ of
/nà/ determines the harmonic group to which the preceding vowel /ọ́/ belongs;
the assimilation rules apply after the vowel harmony rules. What is to be noted
about vowel harmony in the following is the initial or prefix vowel of the last
word, which is a verbal noun:

ọ́ nà èrí	'he is eating'	ọ́ nà àpị́	'he is carving'
ọ́ nà èmé	'he is doing'	ọ́ nà àsá	'he is washing'
ọ́ nà ègbú	'he is killing'	ọ́ nà àzú	'he is buying'
ọ́ nà èzó	'he is hiding'	ọ́ nà àdọ́	'he is pulling'

With few exceptions, Igbo nouns may be analyzed as containing a prefix (a
vowel or syllabic nasal) and a stem; the stem is very commonly monosyllabic,
and its vowel determines the harmonic group to which a prefix vowel belongs.
E.g.,

ìtè	'pot'	ánụ́	'animal, meat'
éwú	'goat'	ụ́kwụ́	'foot'
óbì	'heart'	áfọ̀	'year'
író	'hatred'	ọ́jị̀	'iroko tree'

Noun stems with more than one syllable frequently involve reduplication or
orther derivational processes; in such cases, all vowels in the stem belong to the

---

[2] In the traditions of Bantu linguistics, ị and ụ represent the highest front and back vowels.
In West Africa, it has been customary to use vowel symbols with subscript dots or short vertical strokes for sounds lower than those written without such diacritics.

The form of Igbo cited here and elsewhere in this work has been called "Compromise Igbo";
in all seriousness, it is a type of Igbo very widely used by speakers whose own native dialects
do not have aspirated consonants or nasalized vowels, but who have in large measure adapted
to the phonology of dialects like that of Umuahia (which does have aspirated consonants and
nasalized vowels) in other respects, and to the vocabulary and grammar of the latter. See Welmers and Welmers 1968a, 1968b.

same harmonic group. Occasional violations of vowel harmony are found in nouns which are probably all compounds or adopted words. Verb roots are all mono-syllabic. Composite verb bases are composed of two or more morphemes; in such forms, the application of vowel harmony is highly restricted, and varies to some extent among dialects. The majority of morphemes affected by vowel harmony consist of a vowel alone.

It was a native speaker of Igbo who apparently first thought of interpreting this system as consisting of fewer vowels plus a prosodic feature of vowel harmony (see Ogbalu 1939, pp. v-vii). Actually, he wrote /e/ and /a/ distinctly in any case, but otherwise marked the second harmonic group of vowels with a single word-final *h* to indicate the series to which all vowels in the preceding sequence belong. As noted below, a somewhat similar analysis works rather well for Fante; in Igbo, the frequent mixture of harmonic groups in composite verb bases makes the principle difficult to apply consistently.

In vowel harmony systems of this sort, there may well be some one phonetic feature or articulatory characteristic that distinguishes all the vowels of one har-monic group from those of the other. The presence of pharyngeal constriction or some kind of "tenseness" has been suggested; Peter Ladefoged (1964, pp. 38-40) has demonstrated that, in the second group in Igbo, /i̥, a, u̥, o̥/, the root of the tongue is more retracted, and the pharyngeal opening thus narrowed, by com-parison with the vowels of the first group. Before elaborating on this, a crucially important point must be made. Working only with the symbols used in trans-cription, or relying on the acoustic impression of vowel height and the analogy of the tense-lax distinction of English, it is too easily assumed—and has, indeed, been explicitly stated for Igbo (Swift, Ahaghotu, and Ugorji 1962, p. 50) — that the higher vowels (/i, e, u, o/) are "tense" and the lower vowels (/i̥, a, u̥, o̥/) are "lax." Precisely the opposite is the case; perceptible muscular tension is involved in narrowing the pharyngeal passage. When I was not very used to the sounds of Igbo, I once mistook /u̥/ for /u/ when there were no other harmonizing vowels in the environment which might have made the distinction redundant, and I repeated what I thought I had heard with a very high vowel. The informant said "No," repeated the form with the correct vowel /u̥/, and then added, "You have to tighten up your throat, here," putting her fingers just above her larynx. Instructions to consciously tense and relax the throat are almost indispensable to teaching speakers of English good Igbo pronunciation—and it is the lower vow-els in Igbo that are tense. In the light of all of this, Ladefoged's comments on an interpretation of Igbo vowel harmony in terms of distinctive features deserves underlining.

2.12. In Akan, the vowel harmony system differs somewhat among dialects. In Fante, all vowels within certain definable limits normally belong to one of the following groups:

/ɪ, ɛ, ʊ, ɔ, a/
/i, e, u, o/ and /a/ in last position if /i/ or /u/ precedes.

/e/ or /o/ is rarely the only vowel of a stem, and seems in such cases to have developed historically from /ie/ or /uo/. In a sequence of vowels within a stem, /e/ or /o/ is almost invariably preceded by /i/ or /u/ in the same stem. In the first group, /a/ may occur anywhere in the stem or in a prefix; but in the second group /a/ occurs only in stems, and only after /i/ or /u/ earlier in the stem; in the immediate sequences /ia, ua/, /a/ has a somewhat fronted allophone, toward [æ]. The major application of vowel harmony is alternation in prefix vowels conditioned by the first vowel of a stem. Thus all five vowels in the first series are equally conditioners of prefix vowels, but with a few questionable exceptions only /i/ and /u/ in the second series condition prefix vowels. The system may be conveniently illustrated by some verbal forms with prefixed pronouns and a construction marker:

ɔbésì	'he will say'	òbésì	'he will build'
yèbésì	'we will say'	yèbésì	'we will build'
ɔbéyè	'he will do'	òbéyè	'it will be good'
yèbédà	'we will sleep'	yèbósŭá	'we will study'
ɔbɔ́kɔ	'he will go'	òbópò	'he will bark'
yèbɔ́kŭ	'we will fight'	yèbóhŭ	'we will see'

These data suggest that the vowel system might be analyzed as consisting of five vowels, with a prosodic feature—accompanying /i/ or /u/ in all but a few exceptional cases—to indicate that all the vowels in the sequence belong to the second group rather than the first. The five vowels in the first group can then be rewritten /i, e, u, o, a/; the form written /ɔbésì/ above would then be /òbésì/ and the form written /òbésì/ above would be /òbésì'/, where the apostrophe indicates that all vowels in the form belong to the second rather than the first harmonic group; the same conversion applies to all the other forms, with the apostrophe after the first vowel of the stem if there are two or more vowels. The second group is chosen for marking because the conditioning vowels are more restricted; they are /i'/ and /u'/ except for a half dozen or fewer stems in the language.

As written above, Fante has pervasive morphophonemic alternations—particularly in noun prefixes, subject pronouns, and verbal construction markers—between the pairs /ɪ-i, ɛ-e, a-e, ɔ-o, ʊ-u/. There are secondary alternations in some morphemes of /ɛ-e-ɔ-o/, where assimilation to unrounded or rounded vowels operates in addition to vowel harmony.

As in Igbo, some muscular tension is associated with the vowels of the group /ɪ, ɛ, ʊ, ɔ, a/. Pharnyngeal tension does not appear, impressionistically, to be as strong as in Igbo. But particularly in the case of /ɪ/ and /i/, the tension is visible. In /i/, the lips are at rest; in /ɪ/, the corners of the lips are pulled back and the lips thinned by obvious muscular effort.

In Fante orthography, seven vowels are used: *i, e, ɛ, a, ɔ, o, u*. Both /ɪ/ and /e/ are represented by *e*, and both /ʊ/ and /o/ are represented by *o*. Since /e/ and /o/ hardly ever occur in stems, the orthography is virtually unambiguous; for vowels under the domain of vowel harmony, *e* is read as /ɪ/ or /e/, and o as /ʊ/ or /o/, depending on the first vowel of the stem. However, the orthography fails to reflect the systematic vowel harmony rules of the language. Although phonological analyses—taxonomic phonemic, generative, or whatever—must be carefully distinguished from the establishment of practical orthographies, a maximum parallel is certainly desirable in the absence of compelling external reasons for violating such a parallel. For Fante, an orthography more like that of Igbo might be preferable.

Just to the west of Igbo, centering in the town of Agbor, is a language closely related to Igbo, commonly thought to be a dialect of Igbo, and commonly known as "Western Igbo." It has a nine-vowel system like that of Fante; the additional low front vowel is phonetically [æ]. A very brief investigation[3] has shown that there is vowel harmony, but the rules that involve the low front vowel (and very possibly different rules involving /e/ and /a/) have not been established.

2.13. Dho-Luo, a Nilotic (Nilo-Saharan) language of southwestern Kenya, has a vowel harmony system remarkably like, though in some details differing from, that of Fante. There are nine vowels. As stem vowels which determine the harmonic group of affix vowels, these fall into two groups: /i, e, u, o/ and /ɪ, ɛ, ʊ, ɔ, a/. In the affixes whose vowels are determined, however, /a/ is neutral; it may accompany vowels of the first as well as the second group. Vowel harmony applies within a stem, and also to both prefix and suffix vowels. Harmony within forms not containing obvious prefixes or suffixes is illustrated in the following: glides here interpreted as /u, ʊ/ and /i, ɪ/ before another vowel may be analyzable as /w/ and /y/ respectively, but impressionistically they are syllabic, and they have the vocalic qualities here indicated:

kidi	'stone'	gùɛnɔ̀	'chicken'
riŋò	'meat'	wìnyɔ́	'bird'
ròmbè	'sheep (pl.)'	rɔ́mbɔ̀	'sheep (sg.)'
guòk	'dog'	ŋàtɔ̀	'person'

Harmony in prefix and suffix vowels is illustrated in the following, many of which are incomplete utterances; in each of these examples, only the second of the three vowels is a stem vowel:

nobirò	'he came'	gíwɪtɔ̀	'they're throwing'
gítedò	'they're cooking'	nɔnɛnɔ̀	'he saw'
òbutò	'he is hidden'	nɔculɛ̀	'he returned it'
nalorè	'I shut it'	nalɔkɛ̀	'I exchanged it'
		nɪcamɛ̀	'you ate it'

For Southern Lwo (northern Uganda), which is certainly mutually intelligible with Dho-Luo, Tucker and Bryan (1966, p. 408) report a ten-vowel system, with an additional vowel /ä/ in the first harmonic group. The same type of sys-

---

[3] By Beatrice F. Welmers during a few hours in July, 1966, when an informant happened to be available.

tem is reported by them (1964, p. 194) for Nandi; for at least one dialect of Nandi, however, the additional /ä/ appears to be a dummy phoneme—there seems to be no phonetic difference between [ä] and [ə], but in some forms /ə/ requires the vowels of the first harmonic group in affixes, while in other forms it requires the vowels of the second. This is excellent internal evidence for reconstructing a tenth vowel phoneme for an earlier stage of the language, but at present the relevant data must be accounted for at the morphophonemic level, or perhaps more economically by a prosodic feature marking one of the two groups of vowels, or in the framework of generative phonology.

For Southern Lwo, Tucker and Bryan describe the vowels of the group /i, e, u, o, ä/ as having a "hollow" quality, and those of the group /ɪ, ɛ, ʊ, ɔ, a/ as having a "hard" quality. A phonetic distinction for which such terms might be appropriate, or a distinction comparable to that described for Igbo above, is by no means obvious in Dho-Luo.

For vowel harmony systems of the types described so far, Tucker and Bryan (1966, p. 5) call the two groups of vowels "categories," and the harmonic co-occurrences "category harmony." Category harmony is distinguished from "full harmony," in which the vowel of an affix is identical with the determining vowel of the stem. Following the analogy of musical terminology, the latter could more appropriately be labelled "unison"; the simple term "vowel harmony" has long been used (e.g., for Turkish and other languages as well as West African languages) for systems in which successive vowels are selected from one of two or more groups.

The evidence cited by Tucker and Bryan from a number of languages at least reveals that vowel harmony systems, with some differences in detail or in consistency of application, are by no means uncommon among the Nilotic (including their "Para-Nilotic") languages. As will be seen, less fully developed manifestations of vowel harmony are far more widespread in Niger-Congo than the consistent systems exemplified by Igbo and Fante above.

2.14. In Efik, as has been noted in 2.2 above, the second and third person singular subject pronouns, and two verbal construction markers, have four alternant forms each. In these, the vowel /ɛ/ (with some complications involving markedness) appears before /i/ or /e/ in the following stem; /a/ before /a/; /ɔ/ before /ɔ/; and /o/ before /u/ or /o/. A similar variation applies to the allomorph of the negative suffix after monosyllabic vowel-final verb stems. These, however, are the only clear examples of vowel harmony in Efik. The second and third person plural subject pronouns, /è/ and /é/, are invariable. So are the contrastive plural construction marker /yé/, the first person plural subject pronoun /ì/, the infinitive marker /ndí/, and the other allomorph of the negative suffix, /ké/.

In forms other than verbs, sequences of a vocalic prefix followed by a stem vowel show some restrictions, particularly with the two lowest vowels. Strangely, it seems easiest to define the restrictions in terms of the prefix vowels rather than the stem vowels. Prefix /ɔ/ occurs exclusively before stem /ɔ/. Prefix /a/ occurs almost exclusively before stem /a/, although three of the very few exceptions are in common words: /ànyè/ 'who?' and the independent pronoun forms /àmì/ 'I' and /àfò/ 'you (sg.)'. Prefix /o/ occurs before stem /i, o, u/. The prefixes /i, e, u/ occur freely before all stem vowels.

2.15. LoNkundo (LoMongo) has partial vowel harmony. The vowels /ɛ/ and /ɔ/ may occur together in the same form, and so may /e/ and /o/; but neither /ɛ/ nor /ɔ/ may occur in the same form with /e/ or /o/. The remaining vowels, /i, u, a/, may occur freely with either /ɛ, ɔ/ or /e, o/.

Somewhat similar restrictions on co-occurrences of vowels are found in Yala, Yoruba, and undoubtedly numerous other languages. In some cases, order must be taken into consideration—as in Efik, where */o-e/ is an impermissible sequence, but /e-o/ is common. Systematic or symmetrical restrictions appear to be common, though of course they cannot be expected to be universal.

In many of the Mande languages, two-syllable forms with identical vowels in both syllables are remarkably frequent, but there are enough exceptions to make systematic statements impossible; a mere statistical observation must suffice.

Finally, in some languages, allophonic variations in vowels pattern in such a way as to suggest a form of allophonic vowel harmony. In some of the Southern Bantu languages, and in Swahili and perhaps many other languages, there are five vowels, but /e/ and /o/ have higher allophones, [e, o], before the high vowels /i, u/, and lower allophones, [ɛ, ɔ], before other vowels and in final position. Similar variation is reported (Desmond Cole, private communication), though undoubtedly within a smaller range of articulatory position, in languages that have seven vowel phonemes to begin with. Even in Igbo, which already has a phonemic vowel harmony system, there is some additional allophonic vowel harmony. In particular, /e/ is slightly higher, [e], before the high vowels /i, u/, but slightly lower, [ɛ], before /e, o/ or in final position. For some speakers, /a/ is somewhat more like [æ] before /i̠, u̠/ than before /a, o̠/ or in final position.

2.16. The possibility of some sort of vowel elision exists when two vowels occur in sequence across a morpheme boundary in a phrase. (An elided vowel is, of course, quite different from a zero allophone of a vowel as discussed in 2.3 above. In the case of a zero allophone, a specific vowel phoneme such as /i/ is posited on the basis of nonvocalic phonetic phenomena such as tone, in positions where all other vowels clearly occur. In the case of an elided vowel, any of several vowels attested in other contexts or in slow speech is simply missing, with no evidence in the surface structure of its identity or even its existence.) In a great many languages, vowel sequences across morpheme boundaries are rare, and in a few languages perhaps non-existent. Many Niger-Congo languages have no initial vowels except for a few pronoun forms and other isolated morphemes which consist of only a vowel. In Afro-Asiatic languages, word-initial consonants are generally the rule; in some cases, as Hausa, initial vowels appear in the orthography, but phonetically are always preceded by a glottal stop. In Nilo-Saharan languages, word-initial consonants appear to predominate, and word-final consonants are very common. In Khoisan languages, words in major form classes begin with consonants, more often than not with clicks. Actually, the conditions for possible vowel elision are found by far most commonly in many of the Kwa and some northwestern Benue-Congo languages (all Niger-Congo). In such languages, verbs normally begin with consonants, but most nouns begin with a vowel or a syllabic nasal—which reflects a noun-class prefix in at least an earlier stage of the language. Word-final consonants do not occur at all in some of these languages; in other languages, the number of consonants that may occur in word-final position is restricted. Thus such languages have a great many phrases, consisting for example of verb plus noun object, or noun plus noun, in which vowels occur in sequence across a morpheme boundary. The actualization of such sequences varies considerably from language to language.

2.17. In Akan (the Fante dialect), noun prefixes are /ì ~ ì/, /ɔ̀ ~ ò/, /à ~ è/, and a syllabic nasal homorganic with the following consonant, /m̀ ~ ǹ/. The first two of these four prefixes are exclusively singular in reference. In noninitial position in a clause, they are completely lost. This, however, is more than mere elision after another vowel. The preceding word may end with a consonant (/w, r, m, n/ are permissible final consonants); the noun prefix is still lost. E.g.,

ìpún	'a table'
ɔ̀rútɔ̀ pún	'he's buying a table'
ɔ̀rútɔn pún	'he's selling a table'

The remaining two prefixes, however, are never lost. Nor is there any elision when /à ~ è/ is preceded by the final vowel of a verb or another noun. However, the final vowel of a preceding possessive pronoun (/mí/ 'my', /wú/ 'your (sg.)', /ní/ 'his, her, its'; the plural possessive pronouns end in consonants) is assimilated to the noun prefix /à ~ è/; the result is a long vowel, but with the high tone of the pronoun rather than the low tone of the noun prefix. Thus:

àbɛ́	'palm nuts'
ɔ̀rútɔ̀ àbɛ́	'he's buying palm nuts'
máá'bɛ́	'my palm nuts'

A somewhat similar phenomenon is found in the Wukari dialect of Jukun (known to its speakers as Wàpã̀). In isolated citation or initially in a clause, the vast majority of nouns begins with a prefix /a/ (with mid tone). In noninitial position, this prefix is completely lost; there is no lengthening of the preceding vowel, and no modification of any preceding tone; e.g.,

akwǐ	'chicken'
ku ri hwẽ kwǐ	'he's buying a chicken'
ku ri hwě kwǐ	'he's counting chickens'

A much smaller number of nouns begins with a prefix /à/ (with low tone). In noninitial position, the vocalic quality of this prefix is lost, and there is no lengthening of the preceding vowel; however, the low tone of the prefix is retained after a preceding mid or high tone, combining with it to form a glide (which is in no way a lengthening of the vowel); a preceding low tone is not modified, so that the third of the following examples is completely homophonous with the third of those above:

àkwî	'small-necked gourd'
ku ri hwē'kwî	'he's buying a gourd'
ku ri hwě kwî	'he's counting gourds'

In Efik, on the other hand, prefix vowels (with nouns, adjectives, numerals, and demonstratives) are impervious to elision. They may follow another vowel (although there are also a great many consonant-final stems; /p, t, k, m, n, ŋ/ are permissible final consonants), but there is no elision and nothing approximating full assimilation of either vowel to the other. In cases like the following, both vowels in each sequence are easily identifiable:

sìbé únàm	'cut the meat'	m̀bòró émì	'this banana'
étó ìbà	'two trees'	ébwá órò	'that dog'

Efik does, however, have a few other cases of vowel elision. One is before a sentence-final particle /óó/ which suggests courtesy or personal interest. The verb form /èmésyèré/ 'have you awakened?' is combined with this particle to form a common morning greeting: /èmésyèróó/. A morpheme corresponding roughly to 'at' has the form /ké/ before a word which begins with a syllabic nasal. Before a word beginning with a vowel, however, the vowel of /ké/ is elided; its high tone is retained before a low tone, but only the consonant /k/ remains before a high tone, with no vowel lengthening in either case. E.g.,

ŋkáníká	'bell, clock':	ké ŋkáníká ìbà	'at 2 o'clock'
ùrwà	'market':	kûrwà	'at market'
úfɔk	'house':	kúfɔk	'at home'

2.18. It has been said that Igbo has a considerable amount of vowel elision, particularly of a lower vowel before a higher vowel (see Green and Igwe 1963, p 2). As a general statement, this is a serious oversimplification. For many speakers, there is complete loss of a vowel in one morpheme; the morpheme, with much the same meaning and usage as Efik /ké/, has the forms /ná ~ nà/ before a syllabic nasal, its tone being the same as that of the following nasal. Before a vowel, this is completely reduced to /n/ by many speakers; for others, however, the vowel /a/ is merely assimilated to the following vowel, so that a long vowel results. E.g.,

ŋgbè	'time':	nà ŋgbè áhù̀	'at that time'
m̀bà ànọ́	(place name):	ná m̀bà ànọ́	'at Mbaano'
úlọ̀	'house':	núlọ̀	'at home'
àbá	(place name):	nàbá	'at Aba'

The last two of the above are pronounced by some people (particularly around Aba!) as /núúlọ̀/ and /nààbá/.

In other sequences, the time required to pronounce the first vowel, and its tone, are not affected. The only vowel which is completely assimilated to a fol-

lowing vowel in quality is /a/, and even this complete assimilation is heard primarily in very common expressions or in rapid speech.   In the following examples,
the expressions on the left are written without assimilation; assimilation is indicated in the expressions on the right:

kèdú kà į̀ dì	'how are you?'	:	kèdú kį̀į̀ dì
kà ó mésyá	'goodbye'	:	kòó mésyá
ìrí nà ìsé	'fifteen (ten and five)':		ìrí nììsé
éhí nà éwú	'a cow and a goat'	:	éhí nèéwú
ọ́ nà èrí ń'rí	'he's eating'	:	ọ́ nèèrí ń'rí

In all other sequences, the quality of the first vowel merges very quickly into
the quality of the second.   Thus the second vowel is more prominent, but the first
remains identifiable.   There may be a slight centralization of a front before a back
vowel, or of a back before a front vowel, but all contrasts are maintained.   This
has been strikingly demonstrated by a number of native speakers of Igbo used as
models in teaching Igbo to speakers of English.   Hearing the slight centralization
of /e/ and the rapid transition from /e/ to /o/ in a phrase like /ébé 'ólé/ 'which
place?, where?', students sometimes go to the extreme of saying [ébó'ólé]—and
similarly [ébáà] for /ébé à/ 'this place, here'.   A native speaker of Igbo may hesitate to reject such exaggerations out of hand, but the invariable reaction is a
look of dissatisfaction and a repetition of the phrase in hopes of hearing a more
accurate imitation.   In short, such vowel sequences in Igbo may be difficult to
learn to reproduce accurately, but they are by no means instances of elision, and
not even of full vowel assimilation.

2.19.   Full vowel elision, on the other hand, is typical of some types of phrases
in Edo (Bini).   Nouns regularly begin with vowels, and all words in the language
end with vowels.   In a sequence of verb plus noun object, or in a noun-noun
phrase, the final vowel of the first word is, under many circumstances, totally
elided.[4]   Thus the sequence of /nwɔ́/ 'drink' plus /ènwê/ 'milk' is actualized as
/nwènwê/ 'suckle'.   Final /i/ or /u/ is not normally elided before a vowel different
from itself, though a few exceptions can be found in Melzian's dictionary (Melzian
1937).   Dunn (1968) states that final /o/ with low tone becomes /u/, and final /e/
(apparently with any tone) becomes /i/ before another vowel, and thus do not
elide; there is no evidence of this at all in Melzian, and he regularly indicates
elision of /o/ and /e/—possibly reflecting another dialect.   A final rising tone also
seems to be retained, and accompanies the following vowel; thus the sequence of
/kpě/ 'play' and /ákpátá/ 'a harp' is actualized as /kpǎkpátá/.   Final nasalization
is also retained and accompanies the following vowel.

There may be other details not included in the above statements, but the
fact remains that, in a vast number of Edo utterances containing transitive verbs,
the final vowel of the verb simply does not appear.   After a considerable amount
of elicitation, an investigator may well be tempted to wonder how even a native

---

[4] Such elision was readily noted in my own sporadic work with a speaker of Edo in the early
1950's; the specific data cited here are from Melzian 1937 and Dunn 1968.

speaker of Edo knows what the final vowel of a given verb actually is. The solution is found in an emphatic or topicalized construction, in which the object is transposed to the beginning of the sentence, and the verb appears in sentence-final position. Only in such circumstances do the final vowels of many verbs appear. Speakers of Edo do not restore elided vowels when speaking carefully to beginning learners, but they will readily isolate the verb and pronounce it by itself with its final vowel.

The situation in Urhobo is somewhat similar, except that it is not particularly difficult to elicit careful speech forms without elided vowels. In more normal speech, final vowels other than /i/ and /u/ before a nonidentical vowel elide as far as their quality and duration are concerned. A final low tone is also lost. A final high tone is retained, however, and replaces the tone of the following vowel —a replacement which is recognizable, of course, only if the following vowel would otherwise not have high tone itself. The Urhobo patterns are illustrated by the following, in which the columns are noun, sentence without elision, sentence with elision, and translation of the sentence:

úkó :	ọ̀ dẹ̀ úkó :	ọ̀ dúkó	'he's buying a cup'
àgà :	ọ̀ dẹ̀ àgà :	ọ̀ dàgà	'he's buying a chair'
úkó :	ọ̀ dẹ́ úkó :	ọ̀ dúkó	'he bought a cup'
àgà :	ọ̀ dẹ́ ágà :	ọ̀ dágà	'he bought a chair'[5]

2.20. In all of the cases of vowel elision discussed up to this point, elision is either confined to a few common morphemes, or is largely if not entirely phonologically predictable. In Yoruba, on the other hand, the situation is considerably more complicated. There are patterns of vowel assimilation, in which the quality but not duration of a vowel are affected; and there are also cases of total elision or loss of a vowel. In the latter, phonologic rules may be set up to account for a large majority of the cases, but a number of exceptions remain which can only be said to be lexically determined (see Bamgboṣe 1965).

Assimilation involving subject pronouns in Yoruba is fairly straightforward, and has been adequately described by Bamgboṣe and others; in general, the final vowel of any of several morphemes which may precede a subject pronoun is assimilated to the vowel of the pronoun in quality, though additional statements are necessary for a few cases of full elision. Elision involving the third person singular object pronoun is perhaps best treated in connection with elision in verb-noun sequences. Further comment is appropriate, however, on the striking difference between the actualization of vowel sequences in noun-noun phrases and in verb-object sequences. In noun-noun phrases, initial /i/ in the second noun is assimilated in quality to the preceding vowel, but there is no full elision as is the case in verb-object sequences. There is good reason for such a difference. Nouns in noun-noun phrases are grammatically linked by an "associative" morpheme which, in some phonological environments, appears as a mid tone; the mid tone

[5] For further details, and a discussion of the grammatical function of tone in the Urhobo verbal system, see Welmers 1969.

forms the end of a glide from a preceding high tone, and replaces a preceding low tone.[6] It is marked in the following by a macron between the words:

ogún‑màlúù	'twenty (a score of) cows'
ilé‑Dúkpẹ́	'Dukpẹ's house'
ọ̀na Èkó	'the road to Lagos' (ọ̀nà 'road')
àkpo ẹ̀kpà	'a bag of peanuts' (àkpò 'bag')

In some other phonological environments, however, it would appear that such an associative construction is not overtly marked; sequences such as that of /ilé/ 'house, building' and /ọjà/ 'market, merchandise' are simply of the type /ilé ọjà/ 'store, shop'. The apparent simplicity, however, is grammatically crucial; it is precisely the absence of vowel elision that indicates the presence of the associative morpheme.

Where the associative morpheme is not present, as in a sequence of a verb with a noun object, elision is typical in normal speech. The rules for the resultant tone are simple; statements as to which of the two vowels is elided, apart from tone, are more complex and not without exceptions. In general, the vowels /i/ and /u/ are the most readily elided, though there are some common exceptions: /bí/ 'give birth to' and /ọmọ/ 'child' combine as /bímọ/, and /še/ 'do' and /išẹ/ 'work' combine as /šišẹ/. Other rules with at least some phonological rationality are more complicated, and a residue of lexically determined combinations must always be recognized; a striking example is that the same verb /fọ/ 'wash' combines with /ašọ/ 'clothes' as /fọšọ/ but with /akpẹ/ 'pot' as /fakpẹ/.

2.21. The foregoing discussions of vowel elision and related phenomena have been concerned with a number of languages whose morpheme structure rules are such that vowel sequences at morpheme boundaries are exceedingly common. Even in languages in which this is not the case, it is of course to be expected that at least a few such sequences can be found, and that comparable types of assimilation or elision may well occur. Among the Bantu languages, rather more than the usual amount of elision is found in LoNkundo (LoMongo) (see Hulstaert 1938, pp. 11-13). A number of words begin with vowels, which are noun-class or concord prefixes, and which frequently occur after the final vowel of another word. In the resultant vowel sequences, elision is not permitted only if the second vowel is /ĭ/ (with rising tone). In addition, initial /b/ is normally lost after the final vowel of a preceding word. In the vowel sequences that result from this loss, elision is not permitted if the second vowel is /i/ (with any tone), or a vowel other than /a/ with rising tone. In remaining sequences, final /i/ in the first word becomes /y/, final /u/ becomes /w/ (in both cases with certain other morphophonemic alternations applied from rules which must be stated earlier), and all other vowels (/e, ɛ, a, ɔ, o/) are totally elided. In general, the tones of both the elided vowels and the remaining vowels are retained, but apparently (although Hulstaert's

---

[6] Edward M. Fresco (private communication) reports that he has heard a dialect of Yoruba in which this associative morpheme has a full segmental form /i/. For a fuller discussion of associative constructions, see Welmers 1963a.

description does not make it explicit) there is no additional length left over from the elided vowel.

Similar vowel elision in the presence of vocalic noun class and concord prefixes in Bantu languages is by no means universal, and apparently not even very widespread. Undoubtedly the commonest phenomenon of this type is the appearance of /y/ as an alternant of /i/, and /w/ as an alternant of /u/, in prefixes before vowel-initial stems.

A rather common example of vowel coalescence in many Bantu languages is /e/ resulting from the sequence /a-i/. In Swahili, for example, the stem of the word for 'tooth' is /-ino/. With its appropriate singular prefix /j-/, 'a tooth' is /jino/; but with its appropriate plural prefix /ma-/, 'teeth' is /meno/. Similarly, a set of pronominal forms is preceded by the associative morpheme /a/ to form possessives. The first and second personal plural pronominal forms must be analyzed as /-itu/ and /-inu/, respectively, in the following set:

-angu	'my'	-etu	'our'
-ako	'your (sg.)'	-enu	'your (pl.)'
-ake	'his, her, its'	-ao	'their'

In some languages, a comparable coalescence is /o/ resulting from the sequence /a-u/.

2.22. It is perfectly obvious, of course, that all of the foregoing does not begin to exhaust the details of the analysis of vowel systems in African languages. Experience has amply demonstrated, however, that illustrative descriptions and observations such as these, on the particular topics covered, provide insights that frequently facilitate the solution of problems in languages not previously analyzed, and reveal areas for investigation that might otherwise go unnoticed. In particular, it should be emphasized that apparent irregularities, or even apparent instances of utter confusion, in phonologic systems, are frequently the result of morphophonemic alternations, which may well differ in different morphologic contexts. The rules may be complex, but in many cases they are surprisingly simple. As will be seen in the following chapters, this same principle naturally applies to other aspects of phonology as well.

Chapter 3

Consonant Systems

3.1. A few types of consonant sounds are found in a number of African languages but rarely or never in languages of other parts of the world. These types are doubly articulated stops, implosives, and clicks.

Doubly articulated stops are produced with simultaneous articulation—simultaneous closure if they occur after vowels, and simultaneous release before a following vowel—in two positions, usually bilabial and velar. The voiceless and voiced types are ordinarily transcribed *kp* and *gb*, but the velar component does not in any way precede the bilabial component in pronunciation, and these double stops appear always to function as unit phonemes, not as consonant clusters.

The double closure required to produce these consonants results, obviously, in a space between the two closures. This space can be characterized during the double closure by suction, so that air goes into the mouth when the consonant is released; or it can be characterized by pressure, with a resultant local (not lung air-stream) aspiration; or it may be neutral. In addition, of course, the bilabial and velar articulations may be quite independent as far as the degree of fortisness is concerned. The result is that there are just about as many *kp* sounds as there are languages which have one, and a similar variety of voiced counterparts. In Loma, there is a great deal of suction during the closure, so that the "pop" at release is very clear and conspicuous; in Kpelle, an adjacent language, the suction is noticeably less, and it is much easier to confuse the Kpelle [kp] with an unaspirated [p] and the [gb] with [b]. In Bariba, the velar closure appears to be much more fortis than the bilabial, and there is no discernible suction; at first hearing, the Bariba [kp] can readily be confused with [k] unless one is looking at the speaker's lips. In the Ekpei dialect of Etsako, there is a phonemic contrast between voiceless and voiced doubly articulated stops produced with and without suction—a phenomenon not recorded for any other language. In the following, the stops with suction are transcribed [kp] and [gb], while those with no suction are transcribed [kph] and [gbh]; this is not intended to suggest that the latter pair are aspirated in any way, but merely that there is no inward movement of air at the time of release:[1]

---

[1] These contrasts were first noted by a graduate student, Mr. Baruch Elimelech, in the Spring of 1971. He did not, however, recognize the precise articulatory difference. After I had done so, the presence and absence of oral suction in the two types was confirmed by the marvelous electronic hardware in the phonetics laboratory directed by Professor Peter Ladefoged. In another context, Professor William G. Moulton once characterized a linguist who successfully anticipates the findings of laboratory equipment as a *machina ex Deo*.

ákpá	'cup'	ú'kpháítò	(proper name)
úkpò	'cloth'	ɛ́kphéì	'worm'
úkpêkò	'bread'	àkphémhì	'we thank'
ɛ̀gbéè	'masked dancer'	ɛ̀gbhéè	'house'
àgbàfɛ̀	'rice'	ígbhàsà	'shelf'

In some languages, the bilabial release of [kp] and [gb] is somewhat slower and more relaxed than the velar release, giving the effect of a (non-phonemic) [w] off-glide. Strangely, some investigators seem to hear such an off-glide far more than others do; people with apparently good ears but with little knowledge of phonemic theory have sometimes insisted on writing *kpw* and *gbw* where I, for one, have been unable to detect any slow bilabial release which I might be tempted to transcribe as [w] even in close phonetic transcription. Phonemic clusters of /kpw/ and /gbw/—or, for that matter, of /kp/ and /gb/ with any other phoneme that ever enters into clusters—are exceedingly rare. One example is discussed in a later section.

In Nzema, it is reported (Westermann and Bryan 1952, p. 90) that [kp, gb] occur only before back vowels, while stops with simultaneous bilabial and alveolar closure and release, [tp, db], occur before front vowels. Obviously only two phonemes are involved, which one would presumably choose to interpret as /kp/ and /gb/ respectively.

A few languages also have a doubly articulated nasal, [ŋm]. In Mano, a sound of this sort has been transcribed by some missionaries who did early work on the language; but it is clearly an allophone of /gb/ before nasalized vowels, and at least the informants I have heard begin it orally. A contrast of [ŋm] and [gb] in languages which do not have phonemically nasalized vowels, or such a contrast before nasalized vowels, has been found in some Nigerian languages, but it is not common. Syllabic [ŋm] before /kp/ or /gb/ occurs in a number of languages in which syllabic nasals have allophones homorganic with following consonants. Such an allophone has generally been interpreted as /m/, perhaps because the bilabial closure is visible. I have always interpreted it as /ŋ/ if there is a velar nasal phoneme elsewhere in the language. There is no momentous theoretical issue here. The immediate use of my own analyses has usually been by speakers of English learning African languages; I have felt it more useful to remind the learner of the invisible velar closure. For some unknown reason, in the usual orthography of Efik, *mkp* is written in some words, but *ŋkp* in others. In a few cases, this orthographic distinction may have originated as a device to distinguish words which differ in tone—another devious excuse for avoiding an indication of tone as such. But there is no consistency in using the one spelling for one tone and the other for another; the orthographic distinction seems to be almost totally arbitrary.

There is an interesting geographical distribution of doubly articulated stops in Africa. They occur primarily in languages grouped in a strip from the Atlantic into the Central African Republic, across the West African bulge and somewhat farther east. A number of the coastal languages do not have double stops, and to the north they extend only irregularly beyond the forest into the grassland. Thus northern Bambara does not have either /kp/ or /gb/, but southern Bambara and Maninka have /gb/. Senari (a southern Senufo language) has both, but Suppire (a very closely related language to the north) has neither; Senari /kp/ corresponds to /b/ or /bb/ in Suppire, while Senari /gb/ is of secondary origin.

No language seems to have doubly articulated stops in syllable-final position, although some languages do have final /p, t, k/. In Efik, [kp] appears in syllable-initial position, but [p] does not; [p] appears in syllable-final position, but [kp] does not; in this case, though this is not common among other languages, [kp] and [p] are allophones of one phoneme. Other restrictions, such as the existence of only one double stop, may be part of a more general pattern of phonology in individual languages. For example, Maninka has only /gb/, but it also has /b/ without a voiceless counterpart. Yoruba has both /kp/ and /gb/, but /b/ without a voiceless counterpart (and /kp/ is written *p* in Yoruba orthography); but this seems rather to parallel the absence of a /p/ from the consonant inventory of a number of languages.

3.2. Implosives are voiced stops so produced that the air coming between the vocal cords from the lungs to produce the voicing is more than offset by a simultaneous enlargement of the oral cavity to produce a net suction; thus, when the stop is released, air moves into the oral cavity with a slight "pop." Implosives as envisioned here do not involve complete glottal closure. A similar rarefaction in the oral cavity, with air moving inward at the moment of a stop release, is of course possible with complete glottal closure, but such sounds would more accurately be termed "implosive glottalized stops." Without glottal closure, a bilabial implosive, [ɓ], seems to be the commonest; it is found in a number of Mande languages, and in a variety of other languages throughout Africa, very often in contrast with a nonimplosive [b]. Judging from pronunciations of Swahili by several speakers for whom it is a second language, an implosive [ɓ] may be found in several East African languages, though probably not in contrast with a nonimplosive counterpart. A number of languages also have an alveolar implosive, [ɗ], but other implosives are rare. In Kpelle, implosive [ɓ] contrasts with strongly prevoiced [b] and [gb]. In some dialects of Kpelle, [ɗ] occurs, but is a coallophone with [l], occurring only in word-initial position; [ɓ] occurs almost exclusively in word-initial position in any case, but in its occasional intervocalic occurrences it has the allophone [ʋ] in rapid speech. In the total phonologic system of Kpelle, /ɓ/ and /l/ belong in a set of consonants with /ɣ/, which is a resonant rather than a fricative; the joking suggestion to two informants that we might find a remote dialect in which initial /ɣ/ is a velar implosive was greeted with delighted laughter —the phonetic analogy was immediately obvious to them. Doubly articulated stops, ordinary stops, and implosives all occur in contrast in a number of languages.

In Igbo, there is a clear /kp/, and a contrasting phoneme generally interpreted as /gb/. In the latter, however, the velar closure is never very fortis, and for some speakers the phoneme appears to be phonetically an implosive [ɓ] rather than a doubly-articulated [gb]. The many speakers of Igbo with whom I have checked, however, find a [gb] such as I have used in Yoruba far more acceptable than my Kpelle [ɓ]. I am particularly dubious about an implosive articulation in Igbo after a syllabic homorganic nasal.

3.3. To the beginner, the distinctions between [p], [b], implosive [ɓ], and the doubly-articulated stops [kp] and [gb] are frequently difficult. The distinctions can be instrumentally observed without expensive laboratory facilities, if one can borrow a doctor's stethoscope. In syllables like [ba] and [gba], if the stethoscope is held against the speaker's larynx, the rumble of voicing will be heard throughout, though no appreciable difference between the two syllables will be noticed. In syllables like [pa] and [kpa], the rumble of voicing begins only at the release of the consonant. In a syllable like [ɓa], however, an explosive sound will be heard at the larynx which is somewhat less earth-shaking than, but nearly as impressive as, a sonic boom. If the stethoscope is held against the speaker's cheek opposite the velum, a similar explosion will be heard in [kpa] and [gba].

In learning to produce sounds of these types, [kp] can be approximated by pronouncing the English phrase 'back pocket', artificially prolonging the first vowel, and then rushing precipitously through the rest of the phrase. For that matter, many speakers of English have frequently imitated a hen's cackle as [kpɔ-kpɔ-kpɔ-kpɔ-kpɔ], with simultaneous bilabial and velar articulation at the beginning of each syllable. A [gb] can similarly be approximated by pronouncing the English phrase 'big bag', artificially prolonging the first vowel, and then rushing through the rest. An implosive [ɓ] is a fairly common free variant of American English /b/, especially in exaggerated exclamations like 'Oh, Boy!'. Frequently, beginners need more help with a [b] contrasting with [ɓ]; exaggerated conscious relaxation of the lips and cheeks for [b] will help the learner to become aware of the muscular activity required to produce the suction in the oral cavity for implosive [ɓ].

By closing the glottis, creating a bit of suction in the oral cavity, and opening and shutting the lips repeatedly, one can produce a sound something like that of a cork being removed from a bottle. By closing the velar area and doing the same thing with the oral cavity and lips, one can produce a sound imitative of a liquid being poured out of a full bottle. The resonances of these two types of popping sounds are exactly an octave apart. The lower one, with the glottis closed, is the resonance for [ɓ]; the higher one, with velar closure, is the resonance or [kp] and [gb]. Listening to these popping noises by themselves is sometimes helpful in learning to hear the differences between the consonants in real speech.

3.4. Among non-Niger-Congo languages, Afro-Asiatic languages commonly have a glottal stop and a number of consonants which are either glottalized, pharyngealized, or otherwise similar to each other in some special way. In the Semitic linguistic tradition, such consonants are widely known as "emphatics"; the commonest ones are /ṭ, ḍ, ṣ, ḳ,/; /p/ and /c/ also appear in southern Semitic. Many consonants of comparable types appear also in Berber and Cushitic languages. In Saho, strongly ejective glottalized /t', c', k', s'/ have been recorded. Of these, however, /c'/ was recorded only in one or two words suspected of being *ad hoc* citations (rather than generally used adopted words) from a neighboring Semitic language, and /t'/ and /s'/ occur in words most of which are probably adopted. In addition to /k'/, which appears to belong in the mainstream of Saho phonologic history, there is a retroflex /ḍ/ which may reflect a parallel to the Semitic "emphatic" series.

Glottalized consonants or other types comparable to the above are also typical in the Chadic languages. Hausa has glottalized /'b, 'd, k', s'/, and also a rare /'y/ which is certainly of internal secondary origin. Hausa /'b, 'd/ have sometimes been described as "implosive," but they are articulatorily and acoustically far different from the nonglottalized implosives described above. The voiced articulation is preceded by complete glottal closure, which precludes voicing during its very brief duration. For a layman with no knowledge of phonetic symbols, I would not hesitate to represent the approximate sound of Hausa /hú'dú/ 'four' as *hoot-do*; I would never dream of representing the implosive [ɗ] of some Kpelle dialects by *td*—in a phrase like [ŋá ɗì] 'I went', there is full voicing throughout. The Hausa /k'/ is simultaneously glottalized, with fairly light ejective release most prominent before front vowels; /s'/ (orthographically *ts*) is generally a fricative with a quick glottal closure during part of its articulation; for some speakers it may be a glottalized affricate [ts'], and an affricate [ts] with no appreciable glottalization is accepted from nonnative speakers. Hausa also has a glottal stop, common in initial position (though not written; no word begins with a vowel sound). Intervocalic glottal stop is rare, and confined to words adopted from Arabic.

For Tera, Paul Newman (1970, p. 3) reports a series of voiced "glottalized" consonants in five positions: bilabial, palatalized bilabial, alveolar, palatal, and velar. He also states that these glottalized consonants are implosives. He apparently means that complete glottal closure is involved. In some dialects of Higi, a sound which has been described as a "velar implosive" is reported, but Charles Kraft has produced it for me with clear glottal closure. It would appear that glottalized, not merely implosive, consonants are typical in Chadic. The sounds that do occur form at least a striking typological parallel with other Afro-Asiatic languages; and correspondences for most if not all of them are to be found in specific morphemes.

Most Afro-Asiatic languages in other than the Chadic branch also have a pair of pharyngeal fricatives, voiceless /ḥ/ and voiced /ʕ/, generally in contrast with velar fricatives /x/ and /ɣ/.

3.5. Among Niger-Congo languages, clicks occur only in a few of the Southern Bantu languages, where their origin seems certainly to be through words adopted from the Khoisan languages, in some of which most stems in major form classes have initial clicks; in some cases, however, clicks have been substituted for other consonants in words whose genetic history is clearly Bantu. Otherwise, clicks constitute a striking distinctive characteristic of the Khoisan language family.

Clicks are often transcribed as [c] (dental or alveolar), [q] (palatal or retroflex), and [x] (lateral). A common alternative transcription is [/], [!], and [//] for the same three positions. A bilabial click has also been recorded in a Bushman language, and is transcribed [☉]. Clicks are produced by closure in one of the positions indicated, with simultaneous velar closure and local suction. They may be voiceless, voiced, or nasal (and voiced), and may have unaspirated, aspirated, or glottalized release. These modifications are usually indicated by an additional consonant symbol—no indication for voiceless and unaspirated, but [g-] for voiced, [ŋ-] for nasal, [-h] for aspirated, and [-'] for glottalized. The obligatory velar release is sometimes represented by [-k] for unaspirated and [-kh] for aspirated.

The production of clicks as such is no great problem. To a speaker of English, a bilabial click is a noisy kiss, especially without quadrilabial contact. A dental or alveolar click, usually reduplicated or repeated several times, indicates (or used to a generation or two ago) disapproval or disappointment; it is usually represented by *tsk tsk*. A lateral click, also reduplicated, spurs on a horse, or somewhat outrageously (at least in the 1920's) calls attention to a pretty girl or some other unexpected opportunity. A retroflex or palatal click has no special significance in our paralinguistic communication, but is sometimes heard in imitation of the pop of a champagne bottle cork. By themselves, then, clicks are easy enough. The real trick is to produce a click with a vowel immediately after it, which is not part of our patterns of sound symbolism. Perhaps the easiest starting point is an aspirated click; voiced and nasal clicks are probably next easiest. After the first few successful—if perhaps accidental—attempts, it is surprising how easily most English-speaking learners can imitate almost any of a remarkable variety of them. Occasionally clusters of clicks are found, as in the name of the nearly (?) extinct Bushman dialect //ŋ !ke, with a nasal lateral click followed by a palatal click (with unaspirated velar release indicated in the spelling of the name), all followed by a perfectly prosaic vowel.

It is of interest, but probably of no significance, that the nearest Bantu neighbors of the languages that have click phonemes (e.g., Shona, ShiTswa) have sounds such as lateral fricatives and laterally released affricates with extremely similar local noise effects, though not with the same direction of airstream motion.

Throughout most of Africa, a dental click or other noise produced in the same area, such as the noise of sucking through the teeth or lips, is used as an offensive insult or obscenity; the experimenting field worker must learn to control his unconscious noises, or possibly risk a lawsuit. For another type of sound involved in an insult, an ungui-dental snap, see 15.4. A few phonetic virtuosos are able to produce inspirated trilled clicks, which may be useful under an extremely bizarre set of circumstances. High heels and camera shutters, incidentally, do not produce clicks; they produce clacks. Even the beginner should learn to distinguish between air-stream mechanisms and percussive mechanisms.

3.6. Consonant systems, like vowel systems, tend toward some degree of symmetry; but there is obviously more room for skewing. A number of Niger-Congo languages do, however, show a systematic absence of voiced fricative phonemes. A typical West African consonant system (with no particular language in mind) might well be:

p	t	k	kp
b	d	g	gb
f	s	h	
w	r	y	
m	n	ŋ	

To cite a specific language example, Bariba lacks /ŋ/ in the above chart; has /l/ rather than /r/, but also an /r/ which, except for a few adopted words, would be an allophone of /d/; and has a very rare /z/, phonetically [ž], probably confined to adopted words. Fante has no /kp/ or /gb/, but does have /kw, gw, hw/, and lacks /ŋ/. In these and many other languages, velar /k, g, ŋ/, palatal /y/, and glottal /h/ may well constitute a set of consonants which can together be characterized as postalveolar. There are, to be sure, other languages with voiced fricatives, and other types of consonants are by no means uncommon. Listing all the possibilities would be trivial; but it is striking how commonly one meets systems very much like the above.

Distributionally, resonants and nasals tend to be more free than stops and fricatives in Niger-Congo languages. Many languages do not permit word-final consonants; in those that do, nasals seem to be the most common, though some languages permit final resonants or final stops—usually only voiceless, though perhaps with voiced allophones (or morphophonemic alternants) before a vowel beginning the next word. Resonants and nasals are also more frequent than stops or fricatives in intervocalic position in stems. Consonant clusters are exceedingly rare with the exception of the two special types noted below.

As a sample of a most unusual consonant system among the Nilo-Saharan languages, that of Murle may be cited; it appears to be as follows:[2]

p	θ	t	c	k
b	đ	d	j	g
w	l	r	y	γ
m	ꞃ	n	ñ	ŋ

The articulatory positions are bilabial, interdental, alveolar, palatal, and velar; the types are voiceless stops, voiced stops, resonants, and nasals. There are no phonemic fricatives. /θ/ and /đ/, and also /c/ and /j/, are only very lightly affricated, and even calling their release affricated at all may reflect the bias of a native speaker of English. /l/ is reported to be not visibly interdental, but appears to pattern in this position as opposed to /r/. There are minimal pairs for /ꞃ/ and /n/, though I was unable to hear the difference on a tape recording or in Hostetter's pronunciation when he claimed to be producing different sounds. In exaggerated pronunciation, however, his /ꞃ/ was visibly interdental.

---

[2] Reported to me by the Rev. Paul Hostetter, a missionary with some linguistic training and meticulous work habits, and illustrated by a tape recording of a list of words and phrases.

Dho-Luo has a consonant system almost identical with that of Murle, lacking only /ɣ/ and /ɲ/; fricatives appear in a few words adopted from Swahili or other Bantu languages. Tucker and Bryan (1966, p. 405) give this as "a characteristic basic consonant system" for the Nilotic languages. For the Didinga-Murle group, though they do not specify whether all of this is supposed to be valid for Murle in particular, they cite a similar system (1966, p. 371), but with a few implosives (glottalized or not?) and fricatives added.

In Nilo-Saharan as well as in Niger-Congo, consonant clusters are generally rare. In Afro-Asiatic, though less conspicuously in Chadic than the other branches, consonant clusters and double consonants are common.

3.7. In 1957, the President's address at the annual meeting of the Linguistic Society of America, by W. Freeman Twaddell, was entitled "[č]?"—and was orally introduced as it had been transmitted to the Secretary by telegraph: "Quote, bracket, C, wedge, bracket, question mark, quote." This section might well have the same or a similar title.

The interpretation of consonants with palatal articulation or palatal release —and similarly with bilabial release—might have occasioned even more arguments than it has among beginning analysts except that some have not even noticed a problem where there actually is one. As it is, arguments as to whether to write *Ci* or *Cy* in some African language probably rank next to disputes about the relative merit of various antimalarial drugs for generating heat without light. The fact is that considerations of the phonologic patterns of individual languages can usually provide a simple answer. The results, however, will be disappointing to those who would like to insist on a consistent interlingual orthography, in which the "same" sounds are written in the same way in all languages. Unfortunately, "same" or similar sounds have a perverse tendency to fit into different cubbyholes in different phonologic systems. First, a sampling of the variety of justifiable phonemic interpretations of sounds more or less like the [č, ǰ, š] of English "cheap, jeep, sheep":

In Gourma, there are unit phonemes /c, j, š/, forming a palatal series parallel to a bilabial, alveolar, and velar series of consonants. /c, j/ are stops rather than affricates, quite different from the more slowly released English consonants. No consonant in Gourma clusters with /y/.

In Kpelle, a sort of [š], considerably farther forward than the English /š/, appears in most southwestern dialects, and is an allophone of /s/; it occurs before short vowels, and before double back vowels. In a smaller southwestern area, /s/ is [s] in all positions. In northeastern dialects, /s/ has the allophones [h] and [hʸ] distributed like southwestern [s] and [š].

In Akan, [č, ǰ, š], very much like the English sounds used for comparison, certainly once were, and perhaps still are (depending on the interpretation of certain morphophonemic alternations in adjacent vowels) allophones of /k, g, h/ before /i, ɪ, ɛ/, with certain restrictions in detail. The development of [š] from [h] by a process of palatalization may seem strange and unlikely, but there is nothing unusual about [č, ǰ] as developments from [k, g] by palatalization, and in

Akan /h/ clearly patterns with the velar consonants. In the Fante dialect, the consonant system as a whole shows involvement of the blade of the tongue before high front vowels (see Welmers 1946, pp. 10-12). The morphophonemic alternations referred to above are such that it may seem preferable to consider Akan [č, ǰ, š] as being in contrast with [k, g, h]; in that case, the palatals should be interpreted as /ky, gy, hy/—which is the way they are represented in the standard orthography.

In Jukun and a number of other languages, [č, ǰ, š] (and [ž] if such a sound occurs) are best interpreted as /ty, dy, sy/ (and /zy/). Jukun has obvious clusters of labials and velars with /y/, contrasting with the consonants alone:

pè̌	'roll up'	pyè̌	'front'
bē	'marriage'	byē	'ripen'
fe	'fry'	fye	'pull out'
võ	'hand'	vyõ	'companion'
ma	'arrive' ([mba])	mya	'make' ([mbya])
kànà	'war'	kyànà	'medicine'
ge	'cut'	gye	(in a greeting)
hŭ	'throw away' (Wàpã)	hye	'mushroom' (Wàpã)
ŋa	'try' ([ŋga])	ŋyârà	'hawk' ([ŋgyârà])

(The interpretation of [mb, nd, ŋg] is discussed in another connection below.)

Besides the above, there remain contrasts of [d] with [ǰ] and [s] with [š], as well as [t] with [č] in Wàpã (northern) but not in Dǐyī (southern). Both forms of Jukun have [z], but [ž] was recorded in only one word, and in that word other informants are reported to use [ǰ]. The interpretation of [č, ǰ, š] as /ty, dy, sy/ fills out the /Cy/ pattern almost perfectly. There is also a palatal nasal which one might be tempted to interpret as /ny/, but for other reasons it is better interpreted as /y/ before nasalized vowels. The remaining contrasts of consonants alone with consonants before /y/ are, then:

tò	'bow' (Wàpã)	tyò	'road' (Wàpã)
dì	'body'	dyi	'eat'
se	'until'	syè	'run'

In four different languages, then, something like [š] is interpreted, for perfectly good internal reasons in each case, variously as /š/ contrasting with /s/, as an allophone of /s/, as an allophone of /h/ or perhaps a contrasting /hy/, and as /sy/. It might be added that Mandarin Chinese has two such affricate-fricative series, one more palatal and one more retroflex than English /č, ǰ, š/; they may be interpreted respectively as /cy, zy, sy/ and /cr, zr, sr/ (where /c, z, s/ alone are [ts, dz, s]).

3.8. Apart from phonetically palatal consonants, however, problems often arise in the interpretation of palatal releases of any consonant. Suppose, for example, that a language has a voiced palatal release of a voiced consonant before a vowel—a sequence such as one which might be phonetically transcribed as [bia], perhaps with an indication that the palatal segment is rather short. Should this be promptly interpreted as /bia/ without further ado, or is there a possibility that it might better be interpreted as /bya/? Considerations of superficially apparent syllabicity may sometimes provide an immediate answer: in Fante, the difference between two such types of sequence is apparent in [àbᵞén] 'horn' and [m̀bìá] 'places'; the palatal release in the first case is much faster and more closely associated with the consonant, while in the second case there appear immediately to be two syllables after the consonant—the phonemic interpretation is /àbén/ and /m̀bìá/ respectively, with /b/ having a palatally released allophone before /ɛ/.

In many languages, however, there are no such convenient contrasting forms to make the interpretation so obvious. Considerations of tone, however,—and the languages with which we are concerned are for the most part tonal—will often provide a solution. In such a sequence as [bia], does the palatal segment [i] have contrastive tone in its own right? Or is its pitch conditioned by the tone of the following vowel, or perhaps by the tone of something preceding? That is, are there contrasts such as [bìá] with [bíá] or [bíà]? If there are, than the [i] should be interpreted as a vowel, /i/; it is not likely that a pervasive occurrence of contrastive tone with resonants like /y/ or /w/ will be found. Such tonal contrasts need not, of course, be limited to minimal pairs; a contrast such as [bìá] with [gíɛ́] would normally be adequate to establish the vocalic character of the segment in question.

If this interpretation can be reinforced by the occurrence of a variety of vowel sequences such as /ea, oɔ, ɛə/, the case is definitely strengthened. But even apart from such confirmation, tonal considerations are usually enough; it is not uncommon to find descending (higher to lower tongue position) diphthongs beginning only with /i/ or /u/.

Suppose on the other hand that only sequences of the types [bìà] and [bíá] occur, in which the [i] always has a pitch identical with that of the following vowel. This immediately suggests that the pitch of [i] can be considered conditioned, and raises the possibility of interpreting such forms as /byà/ and /byá/. Then another question can be asked. So far we have been considering only voiced consonants before a palatal release. Are there parallel sequences beginning with voiceless consonants? After voiced consonants like [b], it is to be expected that a palatal segment [i], even if interpreted as [y], will be voiced. But after voiceless consonants, it is quite likely that a voiced palatal segment would be interpreted as /i/, but a voiceless segment as /y/. If sequences such as [pya] occur, in which the phonetic transcription [y] was chosen because the segment was voiceless, and if there is no [pia] with a voiced palatal segment, then the interpretation /bya/ is confirmed by analogy with /pya/. It is conceivable that [pia], with voiced [i], might best be interpreted as /pya/ in some language; but it is hardly likely that [pya], with voiceless [y], would need to be interpreted as /pia/.

3.9. On the basis of just this much analysis, and apart from the evidence given specifically for the Fante dialect above, Akan [bíárá] 'any' can convincingly be interpreted as /bíárá/. The palatal segment has contrastive tone, as shown by the following:

[bíò], /bíò/ 'again'   [èbíèn], /èbíèn/ 'two'

And this interpretation is confirmed by occurrences of voiced, vocalic segments after voiceless consonants:

[fíé], /fíé/ 'home'   [ʃìá], /hìá/ 'meet'

In Jukun, on the other hand, closely similar sequences are best interpreted differently. The palatal segment in [bīē] 'ripen' is not appreciably different from comparable segments in Akan; but in Jukun, unlike Akan, the pitch of such segments is always identical with that of the following vowel. Their pitch, in other words, is conditioned as one would expect the pitch of a voiced consonant to be, not contrastive as one would expect the pitch of a vowel to be. Further, the parallels with voiceless consonants have voiceless palatal release. Thus, for Jukun:

[pỹɛ̃́], /pyɛ̀/ 'front'   [bì̃ɛ̃̀], /byɛ̀/ 'ripen'
[fye], /fye/ 'pull out'   [gie], /gye/ (in a greeting)

For reasons suggested in the preceding chapter and to be reviewed later, Jukun [mb] is interpreted as /m/ before oral vowels. Thus the following forms in Jukun and Akan are remarkably similar phonetically (though differing in melody), but remarkably different in phonemic interpretation; yet each interpretation is justified on internal grounds:

Jukun: [mbia]:   /mya/   'make'
Akan: [m̀bìá]:   /m̀bìá/   'places'

The confirming evidence is not always as complete as in the two languages cited so far. In Tigong,[3] voiced palatal segments occur after both voiced and voiceless consonants; on the basis of that aspect of the data, there is no argument for analyzing such segments as /y/. But their pitch is always conditioned, and the total pattern of the language does not typically include vowel sequences; on these grounds, /CyV/ is the obvious interpretation.

3.10. It would seem likely, and perhaps almost inevitable, that bilabial segments between a consonant and a vowel in a given language would pattern like, and be susceptible to the same kind of interpretation as, the palatal segments discussed above. This is by no means necessarily the case, however. In Akan, there is indeed a /u/ occurring in /CuV/ sequences closely paralleling the occurrences of /i/ in /CiV/. In addition, however, there are three contrasting sequences which are best interpreted as unit phonemes: /kw, gw, hw/. There are no com-

---

[3] Data transcribed by Beatrice F. Welmers in 1949. I have elsewhere referred to the language as "Tigum," which probably reflects a Jukun pronunciation of the name. Mrs. Welmers transcribed the informant's own name of the language, probably on the first day of work, as [mémbé]; this may be a less-than-accurate transcription for what others have written as Mbembe. The latter name is avoided because of possible confusion with another Mbembe to the southwest.

parable */Cy/ unit phonemes or clusters. In Jukun, /y/ occurs, and fairly frequently, after almost every consonant. But /w/ is far more restricted, and may have a different status. In Dìyī, /kw/ and /hw/ occur, and could be interpreted either as comparable clusters with /w/ or—and perhaps better—as unit phonemes; /bw/ occurs in one word, /bwà/ 'thing, event', but this is almost certainly derived from /bu à/, and for some informants the form is /bà/. In Wàpã, there are several occurrences of /kw, hw/, and also of /tsw, dzw/ (Dìyī does not have /ts, dz/ to begin with), which again could be interpreted as unit phonemes; /pw, bw, sw/ are recorded in one word each.

The suggestions for analysis outlined in the preceding sections yield less completely convincing results for Igbo, and the lack of parallelism between palatal and bilabial segments provides no help. In stems, the only sequences with a bilabial segment are /kw, gw, ŋw/, the last of which might well be better interpreted as /w̃/; in /kw/, the /w/ is voiceless. This restriction suggests that these had best be interpreted as unit phonemes. In stem plus suffix, the sequences /ue, ụa, uo, ụọ/ occur after almost any consonant; these are in clear contrast with /kw, gw/ before a vowel, and are obviously vowel sequences.

In the same type of stem plus suffix combination, the sequences /ie, ịa/ occur after almost any consonant, and again are readily interpreted as vowel sequences. Within stems, there are similar sequences—the question as to whether they are identical will be held in abeyance for a moment—after /p, b, f, c, h, r/. After voiceless consonants, the palatal segment is voiced, and phonetically follows the rules for vowel harmony.
Thus:

[í'bị́á] 'come'	[úhíé] 'tree (sp.)'
[áhị́á] 'market'	[órìè] (day name)

The somewhat freer distribution of a palatal than a bilabial segment before vowels in stems, and its voiced quality after voiceless consonants, rules out interpreting these sequences as unit phonemes comparable to /kw, gw/. Judging from the above examples, however, the tone of the palatal segment appears to be conditioned; more importantly, there are no other vowel sequences within stems. This strongly supports the interpretation of these sequences as /Cy/ clusters followed by vowels; the above would be /í'byá, áhyá, úhyé, óryè/.

For two forms, a question may be raised as to whether the tone of the palatal segment is actually conditioned. One of these is the imperative form phonetically transcribed as [bị̀á] 'Come!'. Now, the tone of an imperative is normally low-high—usually with a vowel suffix which does not appear in this form. Although the low-high sequence is here phonetically spread over the sequence [ịa], there is no reason why it could not be assigned phonemically to the vowel [a] alone, and the form analyzed as /byǎ/. Alternatively, the stem which is normally /byá/ could be said to have an allomorph /bị́/ used in the imperative, and the imperative with its normal vowel suffix would be /bị̀á/; that this is not mere hocus-pocus is suggested by the fact that another verb, meaning 'carve', has dialect alternants /í'pyá/

and /í'pí/. In either case, the analysis of certain other sequences as /Cy/ clusters is not overruled.

The other form with a question as to tone was first recorded as [ócìè] and analyzed as /ócyè/ 'old, former'. For some speakers, however, the palatal segment appears to have high tone, which would seem to demand the analysis /ócíè/ (or just possibly /ócíyè/, though this seems less attractive). The word in question is one of a small class of adjectives.[4] Some of the other adjectives have suffixes, though in the other cases the suffix is identical with the stem vowel and has downstep-high tone. It is entirely possible that this form should be analyzed as stem plus suffix, permitting /ócíè/ without yet ruling out the possibility of /Cy/ clusters in stems where the pitch of the /y/ is identical with that of the following vowel.

The question may now be raised as to whether the sequences analyzed as /Cy/ are actually phonetically different from sequences analyzed as /Ci/ and /Cị/ (in stems before a vowel suffix). For analysts who would permit, in the overall phonologic description, different analyses of the same phonetic data in different morphological environments, this question is, of course, not crucial. The reason it was not raised at the beginning of this discussion is that it cannot be easily answered; other evidence was therefore considerd first. Unfortunately, there are no minimal pairs such that a native speaker could be asked whether a stem (/CyV/?) and a stem plus suffix (/CiV/ or /CịV/?) are the same or different. In the usual orthography of Igbo, the two morphologically different types of sequences are written in the same way, with i or ị; informants literate in Igbo presume that they are phonetically the same. An educated and somewhat linguistically sophisticated informant not previously literate in Igbo accepts /Cy/ in stems without objection, but perhaps in recognition of the morphologic rather than any phonetic difference. It is my personal impression—though I would not want to stake my reputation as a phonetician on it—that the palatal segment in stem plus suffix (interpreted as /i/ or /ị/) is very slightly more prominent than the palatal segment in stems (interpreted as /y/), though the latter is voiced after voiceless consonants.[5]

A final and important argument for the interpretation of such a palatal segment as /y/ in stems is based on a detail of tonal behavior. In a noun-noun phrase (and in certain other environments), a final noun whose tones are otherwise high-high has an alternant with downstep before the second syllable. Thus a phrase combining /ánú/ 'meat' with /éhí/ 'cow' is /ánú é'hí/ 'beef'. In the same contexts, a final noun with three syllables and the tones high-high-high has no alternant (except in the marginal Asaba dialect). Thus a phrase combining /úlò/ 'building'

---

[4] The analysis of eight forms and no others as adjectives is justified in Welmers and Welmers 1969.

[5] Our admitted consideration of morphological evidence led us into one misinterpretation. The form we interpreted as /mésyá/ is a verb form from a bisyllabic base. The form in question has a vowel suffix if the base is monosyllabic, or if it is longer and ends in /i/ or /u/. Normally, longer bases with other final vowels do not take a suffix. It developed later, however, that there are a few exceptions, and this is one of them. The base is /mésí/, and the form should be interpreted as /mésíá/.

with /ákwúkwó/ 'leaf, paper, book, education' is /úlò ákwúkwó/ 'school building'.
Forms such as those phonetically transcribed [áhịá] 'market, merchandise' behave in the same contexts like two-syllable rather than three-syllable nouns; the
same /úlò/ combines with this word as [úlò á'hịá] 'store, shop'. This is as close
as one can come at present to making an airtight case for the interpretation /úlò
á'hyá/, and for the recognition of comparable sequences within other stems as
/CyV/.

   3.11. At present, the data from Dho-Luo and apparently mutually intelligible dialects are quite inconclusive. There are both palatal and bilabial segments
between consonants and vowels, which will clearly lend themselves to parallel
interpretations. In Dho-Luo orthography, these are written as *i* and *u*, except
for the sequence *kw* as in *kwal-* 'steal'. In other dialects (including some the names
of which are spelled *Lwo*), they are written as *y* and *w*. In Dho-Luo they are impressionistically syllabic, and are voiced after voiceless consonants; in other dialects, presumably, the impression of syllabicity is not as strong, and they may be
voiceless after voiceless consonants. In the latter case, the interpretation of such
segments as /y/ and /w/ is very likely valid. One would expect that the same interpretation would be applicable in Dho-Luo, but a definite statement to that
effect must await a more detailed analysis of the tonal data. In many forms,
particularly but not exclusively forms cited in isolation, the pitch of the palatal
or bilabial segment differs from that of the following vowel; e.g., with sequences
phonetically mid-low:

   [guòk] 'dog'   [dɪèl] 'goat'

In some contexts, however, the same words have phonetically low tone throughout. It may be that differences such as these can eventually be accounted for
by allotonic statements, or that the nonlevel sequences can be assigned phonemically to the vowel following the palatal or bilabial segment; there is some evidence
for the latter possibility, in that a mid-low glide is sometimes heard also in forms
with obviously only one vowel, though not in forms cited in isolation. The variety
of pitch sequences found in forms of these types is sufficiently restricted as to
suggest that they are probably not sequences of tonemes which must be assigned
to successive vowels. It appears as if either interpretation may be theoretically
possible for Dho-Luo; if so, both on internal grounds and especially in the light
of mutually intelligible dialects, the interpretation of such palatal and bilabial
segments as /y/ and /w/ seems preferable. It is certainly true, as in other languages,
that the acoustic impression of syllabicity is not in itself determinative.

   3.12. In Efik, there are also palatal and bilabial segments between consonants and vowels, which also clearly lend themselves to parallel interpretations.
They are voiced after voiceless consonants, and in the orthography are represented by *i* and *u*. In this case, however, there is evidence of a type different from
any cited for other languages so far which definitely requires that they be interpreted as /y/ and /w/. The tonal evidence is inconclusive. The sequences may
be high throughout, low throughout, low-high, or high-low; but the same tone

sequences occur with single short vowels as well, so that the pitch of the palatal or bilabial segment need not be considered contrastive. E.g.,

[díá]	'eat'	[dá]	'stand up'
[dùòp]	'ten'	[dɔk]	'weave'
[dùɔ́]	'fall'	[kǎ]	'go'
[ìdíà]	'let's eat'	[ìkâ]	'let's go'

There is, however, other evidence that is determinative. In the preceding chapter (2.6), a negative morpheme was cited which has an allomorph /ké/ after a verb stem ending with a consonant, and after any unambiguously bisyllabic stem, but an allomorph consisting of /g/ followed by a vowel determined by the vowel of the stem after unambiguously monosyllabic verbs ending with a vowel. The distribution of these allomorphs was there used to demonstrate that orthographic *Cr V* should be interpreted as /CirV/; verbs with that structure take the allomorph /ké/. Conversely, the distribution of these allomorphs demonstrates that orthographic *Ci V* and *Cu V* should be interpreted as /CyV/ and /CwV/; verbs with these structures take the allomorph which occurs with monosyllabic vowel-final verbs. Thus:

| [ńdíágá]: | /ńdyágá/ | 'I'm not eating' |
| [ńdùɔ́gɔ́]: | /ńdwɔ̌gɔ́/ | 'I'm not falling' |

By analogy, all cases of palatal and bilabial segments before vowels, and they are exceedingly common in Efik, should be interpreted as /y/ and /w/; the four forms transcribed phonetically above are: /dyá, dwòp, dwɔ̌, ìdyâ/.

One of the applications of this analysis is the interpretation of a verb stem [níɔ́ŋ] 'become tall', orthographically *niɔŋ*, as /nyɔ́ŋ/. In contrast with the /ny/ sequence here, there is also a palatal nasal phoneme, represented in the orthography by *ny*, as in *nyɔŋ* 'return home'. The initial palatal nasal in this and other words is interpreted as /ỹ/, paralleling /w̃/ for orthographic *ŋw*; the verb 'return home' is /ỹɔ̀ŋ/. In contrast with both /ny/ and /ỹ/ are forms beginning with a syllabic nasal followed by /ny/, /ỹ/, and also /y/. The sequence of a syllabic /n/ and /y/ has an oral release of the /n/; the sequence of syllabic /n/ and /ỹ/ does not have an oral release. The relevant contrasts, in phonemic transcription and Efik orthography (plus phonetic transcription in one case) are:

/nyɔ́ŋ/	(niɔŋ)	'become tall'
/ỹɔ̀ŋ/	(nyɔŋ)	'return home'
/ńnyɔ̀ŋ/	(nniɔŋ)	'I'm getting tall'
/ńỹɔ̀ŋ/	(nnyɔŋ)	'I'm returning home'
/ńyòm/	(nyom, [ńᵈyòm])	'I want'

3.13. To sum up the preceding sections (beginning with 3.7), a number of languages have /Cy/ clusters. In a few instances, there may be contrasts between the sequences /CyV/ and /CiV/ or even /CiyV/ or both. Where such contrasts appear, they are usually fairly obvious phonetically. But if there are no obvious contrasts, the choice between /CyV/ and /CiV/ (or even /CiyV/) can usually be determined beyond reasonable doubt by considerations of the language's overall syllable structure patterns, parallels between voiced and voiceless beginnings of such sequences, and tone. Parallels between palatal and bilabial segments in such sequences are often found, but in some languages the status of the two is quite different.

In addition to /y/ and /w/ interpreted as such by the above criteria, Kutep also has a post-consonantal velar segment before vowels, here interpreted as /x/. E.g.,

[m̀bàpxú]:	/mbàpxú/	'dog'
[tᵏxí]	: /txí/	'dip'
[fxãp]	: /fxãp/	'roast'
[ǹdgòp]	: /ndxòp/	'weave'
[sxàm]	: /sxàm/	'carve'

In the Eerwee dialect of Bokyi, there are a number of unusual vowel segments, including some centralized vowels with apparently some sort of tense articulation, and a syllabic trill, [r̝]. These are not exceedingly common, and occur after a somewhat restricted number of consonants. After considerable difficulty in imitating some of these to an informant's satisfaction, it occurred to me that they all had something in common phonemically; acceptable imitation soon became easy. The segments in question are interpreted as a consonant release, parallelling /y/ and /w/, followed by vowel phonemes which occur with other allophones where this release is not present. The release may be represented by /x/.[6]

Shona has a phonetically velar release after some consonants; e.g., [vàpxéré] 'children'. This, however, is part of a complex group of postconsonantal segments in complementary distribution. The following types of phonetic clusters occur:

[px]	[txw]	[kw]
[bɣ]	[dɣw]	[gw]
[fx]	[sxw]	
[vɣ]	[zɣw]	
[mŋʷ]	[nŋw]	[ŋw]

[skw] for [sxw] is common as a dialectal or free alternant; [mŋ] without bilabial release is common in slow speech; [w] is voiceless in all cases after voiceless consonants. The general pattern is that what follows the initial consonant adds a velar component if the initial consonant is not velar, and a bilabial component if the initial consonant is not bilabial; both velar and bilabial components are added if the initial consonant is neither. This systematic pattern is reflected in Shona

---

[6] Details of the data are in the possession of the Rev. Paul Bruns, with whom I worked briefly on the field in 1966. I recall a minimal contrast of trills with high and low tone; I believe one is the verb 'eat'.

orthography (which was the product more of common sense than of sophisticated lnguistic analysis or hocus-pocus), which writes the above as *pw*, *tw*, *kw*, *bw*, *dw*, *wg*, *fw*, *sw*, *vw*, *zw*, *mw*, *nw*, *n'w*. Phonetically, of course, [w] has both velar and biliabial articulation. The economy of the Shona allophonic pattern consists in adding only what is missing in the initial consonant. The decision to represent this as *w* in the orthography was undoubtedly made in the light of the fact that these actual allophones of a phoneme /w/ occur most commonly as a morpheme indicating passive, which appears as /w/ in most Bantu languages. The phonemic interpretation of these allophones as /w/ violates, of course, the most rigid form of taxonomic phonemic principles—the "once a phoneme, always a phoneme" concept. For speakers who pronounce /sw/ as [skw], taxonomists may claim that what follows [s] here is the same as initial [kw], and must therefore be interpreted in the same way phonemically. It is hardly a serious violation of taxonomic theory, however, to view something transcribed as [kw] after [s] as being by definition different from [kw] alone. On the other hand, it may be noted that this particular phonetic pattern does not lend itself to a convenient treatment in terms of contemporary theories of distinctive features.

3.14. Another type of postconsonantal segment that is fairly common among Niger-Congo languages is aspiration. Contrasts between unaspirated and aspirated stops occur in a number of Bantu languages and in some West African languages. In Igbo, some dialects have phonemic aspiration while others do not. In some southeastern Bantu languages (e.g., Shona, ShiTswa), nasalized preaspiration occurs also with nasals. Aspiration may usually be interpreted phonemically as /h/, and /h/ usually occurs as a phoneme by itself in the same languages. Interpretations of aspirated consonants as unit phonemes may be preferable in a few instances. In any case, the interpretation of aspiration rarely if ever presents problems comparable to the interpretation of postconsonantal palatal and velar segments. In some Bantu languages, aspiration is part of a morphophonemic pattern which also involves preceding nasals; cases of this phenomenon will be discussed in a later section.

A unique problem involving consonant releases is found in Suppire. /p/ and /b/, but no other consonants, occur in a few forms with strong palatal release before /i/, but with fricative release before /u/ (see Welmers 1950b).[7] These are in contrast with /p/ and /b/ without such releases. E.g.,

[pʸi]	'do'	[pi]	'soften'
[bʸìì]	'drink (pres.)'	[bìì]	'stick'
[m̀pᶠùù]	'hill'	[mpuu]	'spider'
[bᵛũũ]	'hit (pres.)'	[buu]	'kill (pres.)'

Palatally released consonants interpreted as /Cy/ also occur, and /py, by/ do not otherwise occur before /i/. However, the strong release in the first two ex-

---

[7] I believe I recall correctly that the Rev. Ralph Herber, in personal conversation, has reported that [pᶠ] has since been reported also before /o/.

amples above seems quite different from the release interpreted as /y/ in any other environment, and there is certainly no comparable convenient interpretation available for [pˡ] and [bᵛ]. The releases illustrated above are also in complementary distribution with each other, of course, and are phonetically similar in their fortisness. They have been interpreted as a single phoneme; the symbol /'/ was chosen to avoid specifying any articulatory position. The clusters are thus /p'/ and /b'/. In the orthography later established, these are written (perhaps arbitrarily, but also ingeniously) as *pp*, *bb*; the first occurs in the name of the language.

3.15. Palatal and palatally released consonants in Tiv present a problem somewhat different from any discussed up to this point, and no final solution is given here. Such consonants appear as alternants of simple consonants after the vowel /i/ (an environment unparalleled in other examples given above). E.g.,

[átsúl]	'foreheads'	[ìčúl]	'a forehead'
[dzé'ndé]	'a journey'	[íjé'ndé]	'journeys'
[ásémá]	'hearts'	[ìšímá]	'a heart'
[húrúγ]	'a tree (sp.)'	[íhyúrúv]	'trees (sp.)'

This pattern is so prevalent that one is tempted to consider it allophonic. However, the existence of palatal or palatally released consonants in a few instances after vowels other than /i/ indicates that, in the strict traditional sense of the word, the pattern is morphophonemic rather than allophonic; e.g.,

[ášé]	'eyes'	[á'jí]	'eggs'

For those who have no objections to such an interpretation, it would be possible to treat the palatal and palatally released consonants as allophones of other consonants after /i/, but as phonemically distinct in other environments. In any case, the interpretation of [č, ǰ, š] as /tsy, dzy, sy/ appears to be a distinct possibility.

3.16. The only case known to me of doubly articulated stops /kp, gb/ followed by a palatal or bilabial segment (or, for that matter, any comparable type of segment) and then a vowel is in Nupe; and even these have a peculiar status. Following the usual principles of phonemic analysis, Nupe has a five-vowel system, /i, e, a, o, u/. The usual criteria establish the post-consonantal segments in question as /y, w/ rather than vowels. A minimal contrast is found between /kpwà/ 'be cheap' and /kpà/ 'slight, little'. Other /Cy, Cw/ sequences are also attested; it is of the utmost significance that such sequences occur only before /a/. Some examples are:

egyà	'blood'	dá èkpyà	'respect'
kyàkyá	'bicycle'	egbyǎ	'thong'
etswa	'moon, month'	kpwà	'be cheap'
èkwà	'spear'	gbwàrwà	'slippery'

By internal reconstruction, fully confirmed by comparative evidence in the form of cognates with and/or adopted words from Yoruba, all /Cya/ sequences can be shown to come from an original */Cɛ/, and all /Cwa/ sequences from an original */Cɔ/. A seven-vowel system like that of Yoruba, /i, e, ɛ, a, ɔ, o, u/, must be reconstructed for an earlier stage of Nupe. Even synchronically, it would be possible to analyze postconsonantal [ya] as /ɛ/ and [wa] as /ɔ/. Such an analysis would leave Nupe with no /CyV/ or /CwV/ sequences at all, and the record of /kp, gb/ not entering into clusters would remain intact.[8]

3.17. The Southwestern Mande languages (primarily Kpelle, Loma, and Mende) have no sequences of the /Cy/ type. So significant is this restriction, in fact, that in Kpelle, which does have one /Cw/ cluster, /kw/, a /CV/ sequence occurs where /CyV/ would be expected by morphophonemic analogy. The subject pronouns for 'we' and 'they' in their basic forms are /kú/ and /'tí/ respectively. Corresponding independent pronoun forms have an added vowel: /kúa, 'tia/. But the sequence of the subject pronouns and a verbal construction marker /a/ yields /kwa/ for 'we', but /'ta/, not */'tya/, for 'they'; the same rules apply with verbal construction markers /à/ and /aâ/. On the other hand, there is no obstacle to /y/ as a morphophonemic alternant of /i/ in initial position: the subject pronoun for 'you (s.g)' is /í/, and it combines with the construction marker /a/ as /ya/.

A reconstruction of the proto-SWM consonant system, however, reveals a number of correspondences that do not fit into the basic system of simple consonants, but which establish a series of /Cy/ sequences for the parent language— a hypothesis first proposed in the early 1950's by a graduate student who knew nothing of any other African languages. Northwestern Mande (e.g. Bambara) does have /Cy/ clusters.

Adding such evidence to the widespread and varied data discussed in preceding sections reinforces the observation that a major type of cluster in Niger-Congo languages consists of consonants and their releases: palatal, bilabial, velar, aspirated, and other miscellany.

3.18. A second major type of cluster consists of sequences that begin with nasal articulation and end with oral or in some cases also nasal articulation. In one form or another, these are very nearly universal in Niger-Congo, but again their interpretations vary depending on the phonologic patterns of individual languages. The combinations themselves may be restricted in some languages to nasal plus voiced stop; in other languages, nasals may occur before almost all consonants, including themselves. Homorganic sequences—[mp, mb, nd, ŋg] etc. —are perhaps the commonest, but some languages have frequent occurrences of heterorganic sequences, especially beginning with [m]: [md, mk] etc.

Sounds or sequences which may be transcribed [ny] and [ŋw] are ambiguous in their phonetic structure; they may belong to the consonant plus release types discussed above, or to the nasal plus consonant type. Perhaps even more com-

---

[8] The Nupe data and this analysis are treated from the viewpoint of phonological theory by Hyman (1970). Mr. Hyman was a student in a course in Field Methods, in which these clusters were first noted.

monly, however, [ny] and [ŋw] are best interpreted, in languages which have pho-nemically nasalized vowels, as allophones of /y/ and /w/ before nasalized vowels —or, in languages which do not have phonemically nasalized vowels, as unit phonemes /ỹ/ and /w̃/. The first of these is applicable in Jukun and Yoruba, for example, and the second in Efik and Igbo. In a language which has [ny] but not [ŋw], [ny] is frequently a unit phoneme, a palatal nasal in a series such as /m, n, ñ, ŋ/.

Homorganicity is ambiguous in the case of nasal plus [w], since [w] has both bilabial and velar articulation. Thus [mw] in some languages, and [ŋw] in others, may equally represent homorganic clusters. Fante even has [nw]; for Fante, the pattern of nasal plus consonant may be stated as involving homorganicity with the predominant articulation *if any*, or otherwise [n].

Homorganicity may also involve both phonemic and subphonemic differences in the nasals. If a language has /m, n/ as its complete phonemic nasal system, homorganic clusters will include such as /mb, nd/; but there is also likely to be [ŋg], in which [ŋ] can be interpreted as an allophone of /n/ before velars, so that the cluster in question is phonemically /ng/. Of course, if a language has /m, n, ŋ/ as separate phonemes (attested before vowels, for example), then [mb, nd, ŋg] can be interpreted as /mb, nd, ŋg/. For many such languages, the orthographic representation of /ŋg/ is *ng*, and similarly *n* before *k* if such a sequence occurs; this is of course unambiguous. Another common subphonemic homorganicity is with labio-dentals: [ɱf, ɱv], with a labio-dental nasal. In most cases, uncritical analyses have assumed that /f, v/ are to be grouped with the bilabials, and the clusters are accordingly analyzed as /mf, mv/. This is indeed adequate in most cases, though in Fante a case can be made for the interpretation /nf/ by analogy with [nw, nh]; the pattern can be stated as homorganic nasals before stops (in-cluding nasals), but /n/ before fricatives and resonants. In LuGanda, the ho-morganic labio-dental sequences are represented by *nf* and *nv* in the orthography; no reason is known for this atypical representation.

Before doubly articulated stops, nasals also have double articulation, [mŋ]. Such sequences certainly do not have to be interpreted as /mŋkp, mŋgb/ unless /mŋ/ is independently a nasal phoneme, and perhaps not even in such cases. The choice between /mkp, mgb/ and /ŋkp, ŋgb/ (or /nkp, ngb/ if there is no independent phoneme /ŋ/) may be arbitrary. I have personally preferred /ŋkp, ŋgb/ in the cases I have met (cf. 3.1 above), but again no great theoretical issue is at stake.

In any case, of course, if there is a pattern of homorganic nasals before con-sonants, contrasts between nasals that are phonemic before vowels or in final position are neutralized before consonants. The concept of an archiphoneme, say 'N', is applicable; the recognition of this possibility is implicit in many statements that have been made about the morphophonemics of various languages, but it has never been fully incorporated into an analysis, nor reflected in a practical orthography.

3.19. There still remains a variety of possible interpretations of these nasal-plus-consonant sequences from another point of view. Are they to be taken as unit phonemes or as clusters? And if they are clusters, are the nasal components nonsyllabic or syllabic? All possibilities and some combinations of possibilities occur. In some languages, the nasal is always syllabic, and such clusters may occur only in initial position. In other languages, the entire sequence belongs to one syllable with the following vowel. And in at least one case, they are not phonemically sequences of any kind.

In Akan, for example, initial nasals before consonants are syllabic; this is shown by their contrastive tone, as well as by the overall impression of their syllabicity. Such nasals are actually separate morphemes in every case, and some of the morphemes are not always initial. E.g. (from Fante),

m̀pá	'mat'	mím̀báì	'I didn't come'
m̀pʊ̀à	'bananas'	ɔ̀ǹdá	'he doesn't sleep'
ǹtém	'haste'	yɛ̀ǹkɔ́	'we don't go'
ńdɛ́	'today'		
ǹgʊ́	'oil'	wɔ́m̀bá	'they should come'
ǹsú	'water'	ɔ́ńdá	'he should sleep'
ǹwúmá	'skin'	yɛ́ńkɔ́	'let's go'

There are also nonsyllabic final nasals in Akan, which set the pattern for nonsyllabic syllable-final nasals before consonants in medial position, contrasting with the syllabic nasals illustrated above; these are, however, also homorganic with the following consonant. E.g.,

| súnsúm | 'spirit' | àkànfú | 'Akan people' |

At the other extreme, as has been noted in connection with nasalized vowels (2.9), Jukun has phonetic nasal-plus-stop sequences [mb, nd, ŋg] which are interpreted as allophones of the nasal consonants /m, n, ŋ/ before oral vowels. Two important considerations determine this interpretation: (1) the pitch of the nasal is conditioned by (identical with) that of the following vowel, and (2) the sequences occur only before oral vowels, in complementary distribution with the simple nasals [m, n, ŋ] which occur only before nasalized vowels. E.g.,

[m̀bù]:	/mù/	'white'	[mɛ̃́]:	/mɛ̃́/	'see'
[ǹdè]:	/nè/	'noise'	[nɛ̃́]:	/nɛ̃́/	'hoe'
[ŋ̄gā]:	/ŋa/	'try'	[ŋã̀]:	/ŋã̀/	'hate'

With palatal release, the sequences [mby, ŋgy] also occur, and are interpreted as /my, ŋy/ before oral vowels; the latter is one of the rare instances of a sequence /ŋy/ in languages with which I have worked. However, there is no parallel [nɟ], which would be interpreted as /ny/ before oral vowels. The phonemic sequence /ny/ simply does not occur; a palatal nasal which one might at first transcribe as [ny] occurs only before nasalized vowels, as an allophone of /y/. Similarly, [ŋw] is an allophone of /w/ before nasalized vowels. At first, this was recorded only before /ĩ, ẽ, ã/, and the nasal [ŋ] was recorded only before /ã, õ, ũ/; they contrast only before /ã/. However, the apparent [ŋ] before /õ, ũ/ is pronounced with just as much lip-rounding throughout as [ŋw]. It also is therefore interpreted as /w/, leaving the nasal [ŋ] with a highly restricted distribution—only before /ã/. The sequence [ŋg], a co-allophone of /ŋ/, is somewhat less restricted, but is not at all common.

Jukun also has a syllabic nasal which appears before all consonants. In Dìyī it is always /m/ and phonetically [m]; In Wàpã it is homorganic with the following consonant, and may be interpreted as having the morphophonemic alternants /m, n, ŋ/. It is the first person singular subject pronoun. E.g., in Dìyī:

m̀ bi	'I came'		ḿ bi	'I'd better come'
m̀ ya	'I went'		ḿ ya	'I'd better go'

In Igbo, nasals before consonants are always syllabic. Those which occur only before consonants are homorganic and are noun prefixes. (Vowels also occur as noun prefixes.) E.g.,

m̀bè	'tortoise'		ńdí	'people'
m̀pé	'smallness'		ńtì	'ear'
m̀mádù	'man'		ŋ́kwú	'palm'
ḿmà	'knife'		ŋgbá	'wrestling'

There is also a syllabic /m/, again a first person singular pronoun, which also occurs in other positions; and there are a few cases of word-final syllabic /m/. E.g.,

kà m̀ hú 'ya	'let me see it'		dúm̀	'all'
á byàrà m̀	'I came'		òdùm̀	'lion'
á hùrù m̀ m̀mánú	'I saw oil'		gbám̀gbám̀	'sheet metal'

3.20. Syllabic nasals as pronominal morphemes are exceedingly common in Niger-Congo. The pronoun is most frequently a first person singular form, but sometimes third person singular, and in a few cases second person plural.

In Kpelle, homorganic nasals with high tone occur before stops and fricatives as first person singular possessive pronouns before relational (roughly, inalienably possessed) nouns, and as first person singular object pronouns before verbs. The stop or fricative, interpreted phonemically as /p, t, k, kp, f, s/, has a voiced allophone [b, d, g, gb, v, ĵ] in all of the following illustrative forms; the preponderance of following high tones is an irrelevant coincidence:

ḿpòlu	'my back'		ḿpáa	'kill me'
ńtía	'my taboo'		ńtéɛ	'send me'
ŋ́kɔ́ɔ	'my foot'		ŋ́káa	'see me'
ŋ́kpîŋ	'myself'		ŋ́kpέ	'drive me away'
ḿféla	'my wages'		ḿfíli	'cheat me'
ńsũa	'my nose'		ńsóŋ	'catch me'

Kpelle also has syllabic nasals, with contrastive tone, immediately before vowels; these are morphophonemically derived from a nasal with high tone, or from a prefixed low tone, plus a consonant other than a voiceless stop or fricative. In this case, the same first person pronouns as above have high tone; the corresponding third person singular pronouns, which before stops and fricatives are not nasal, have low tone; the latter is a morpheme with the more general meaning of 'previous reference'. /ny, ŋw/ are interpreted as unit phonemes, not clusters. Contrasting forms are:

ḿálo	'heal me'	m̀álo	'heal him'
ńáa	'my name'	ǹáa	'his name'
ŋ́ála	'drag me'	ŋ̀ála	'drag it'
ŋ́wéli	'my friend'	ŋ̀wéli	'his friend'
ńyée	'my hand'	ǹyée	'his hand'

In Swahili, a syllabic /m/ is a third person singular (personal, for nouns of class 1) object pronoun occurring immediately before a verb stem; it is also, as a prefix but usually requiring an accompanying suffix, a second person plural subject pronoun. E.g.,

nilimtafuta	'I looked for him'
(cf.: niliwatafuta	'I looked for them')
mliwatafuteni	'you (pl.) looked for them'

In Efik, a homorganic syllabic nasal with high tone occurs as the first person singular subject pronoun. As in Igbo, syllabic nasals also occur, along with vowels, as noun prefixes; this is true of a number of other languages as well. In some other languages—e.g., Yoruba, Urhobo—only vowels are used as noun prefixes.

A more extensive inventory of languages using syllabic nasals as pronoun forms would hardly be instructive; suffice it to say that such forms are common.

3.21. The nasal component of nasal-plus-consonant sequences is, however, by no means always syllabic. A striking demonstration of this fact is provided by a fluent speaker of Swahili telling how he learned to read and to pronounce Swahili in elementary school. From the early instruction he received in phonics, he recited three sets of syllables in rapid succession; the timing of the third set was precisely the same as the timing of the first two, like the ticking of a watch: /ta, te, ti, to, tu; la, le, li, lo, lu; mba, mbe, mbi, mbo, mbu/.

Swahili has the following such sequences: /mb, nd, nj, ŋg, mv, nz/, all ending with voiced stops or fricatives. Thus Swahili *ndizi* 'banana' and *panga* 'machete' are two-syllable words: [ndi-zi, pa-ŋga], and the name 'Tanganyika' should be syllabified [ta-ŋga-nyi-ka]. Phonetically, such sequences thus have a status comparable to that of /Cy, Cw/ and the like; with a following vowel, they form a single syllable. Such nasal-plus-consonant sequences may be labelled "prenasalized consonants" or "nasal onset consonants". It does not necessarily follow, however, that they are automatically to be interpreted as unit phonemes. Such an interpretation is attractive in view of the fact that they occur within stems in Swahili (as in many other languages). They also occur initially in Swahili, however, and in that position the nasal component is a separate morpheme, a noun or concord prefix, which may make it seem more attractive to interpret the sequences as phonemic clusters. Perhaps the question is not really relevant. What is significant is that these sequences function just like simple consonant phonemes within stems, but include a morpheme boundary in initial position; yet they are phonetically the same. The significance of this distinction in function will become clearer in languages in which the inventories of sequences with these two functions are different.

In Swahili, the noun class and concord prefix in question has a number of morphophonemic alternants: /ny/ before vowels, zero before voiceless stops and fricatives and before nasals, and a homorganic nasal before /b, d, j, g, v, z/, the voiced stops and fricatives. Before stems of more than one syllable, the last of these alternants results in the pre-nasalized consonants under discussion. If the stem is monosyllabic, however, then the nasal is syllabic and stressed. The position of stress is conditioned in Swahili, but is marked in the following examples to point out the syllabicity of nasals before monosyllabic stems. These are all nouns of the same noun class:

mbúzi	'goat'	mvúa	'rain'
ndízi	'banana'	nzíge	'locust'
njúgu	'peanuts'	m̂bwa	'dog'
ngúo	'cloth'	ńgwe	'plot of ground'

In addition to the syllabic /m/ morphemes mentioned in 3.20 above for Swahili, there is another syllabic /m/, which functions as a noun and concord prefix different from the above. Morphologically, this prefix occurs before all consonants. Except before /b/ and /v/, its syllabic character is clearly audible. Apart from the question of syllabicity, the sequences /mb/ and /mv/ may be either the nasal prefix illustrated above plus /b, v/, or this otherwise clearly syllabic /m/ before /b, v/. Some analysts insist that there is a contrast between the two. I have heard the contrast only in artificially slow, careful speech; but it may be normal in some dialects. In the following examples, this syllabic (or problematically syllabic before /b, v/) nasal is written m̂ except when stressed before a monosyllabic stem:

m̂búni	'originator'	m̂píshi	'cook'
m̂dúdu	'insect'	m̂tóto	'child'
m̂géni	'stranger'	m̂kéka	'mat'
m̂ji	'village'	m̂fúko	'bag'
m̂líma	'hill'	m̂shále	'arrow'
m̂méa	'plant'	m̂sóma	'reader'
m̂nyáma	'animal'	m̂tu	'person'

Patterns somewhat similar to that of Swahili are extremely common in Bantu languages. There are frequently complications in morphophonemics that do not involve nasals in the surface phonology, but which result from the presence of a morpheme whose underlying form must be analyzed as a nasal. Even in

some Swahili dialects, a series of aspirated stops is reported in contrast with unaspirated stops: /pʰ, tʰ, čʰ, kʰ/ contrasting with /p, t, č, k/. Morphophonemically,
the aspirated stops are the product of the homorganic nasal prefix described
above, plus the corresponding unaspirated stops as stem initials. The aspirated
stops do not occur independently of this morphological combination. Apparently this contrast is not maintained by many speakers of Swahili today.

3.22. The realization of morphologically underlying nasal-plus-consonant sequences in the surface phonologies of Bantu languages displays a considerable
variety. For any one language, the problem can best be approached from the
morphological viewpoint, by making a study of the phonologic patterns corresponding to a few noun classes and a few pronouns. For some Bantu languages,
this problem is treated rather adequately in the available literature. A particularly interesting example, however, is provided by KiKongo, and this is not fully
described in existing publications, though the principle has been recognized and
a few details sketched out.

The simple consonants of KiKongo, which occur in initial and intervocalic
position, are as follows:

p	t	k
b	d	
f	s	
v	z	
w	l	y
m	n	

In addition, the following prenasalized consonants occur intervocalically in
stems, and thus seem to be part of the basic consonant inventory of the language:

mb	nd	ng
mv	nz	

There is no /g/ to match the prenasalized /ng/, which is phonetically /ŋg/;
although /y/ seems in some respects to pattern with the velar /k/, /ng/ cannot be
interpreted as a cluster of /n/ and /y/, for reasons which will become clear below.
The absence of /g/ paralleling /ng/, along with the fact that this series is restricted
to voiced prenasalized consonants, makes the interpretation of them as a series
of unit phonemes most attractive. The analysis is complicated, however, by the
occurrence of other sequences which include morpheme boundaries.

In initial position, as combinations of two different noun class prefixes (one
of them a prefix identical in two classes, 1 and 3) with the simple consonants
above, there are two kinds of sequences in contrast. In verbal forms, the same
contrasts, not necessarily in initial position, reflect the first and third person
singular object pronouns. There is some morphophonemic coalescence in the sequences involving nouns of class 9 or the first person singular object pronoun.
The following chart lists the phonemically contrasting pairs, in a phonetic transcription, but in a morphophonemic arrangement. What is marked here as as-

piration with voiced stops does not represent a separate segmental aspiration, but merely a general relaxation of the lips and cheeks, with obvious outward air movement at release; the corresponding sounds written without this indication are neutral rather than implosive. The two types of sequences are:

[mpʰ]	[mp]	[ntʰ]	[nt]	[ŋkʰ]	[ŋk]
[mbʰ]	{ [mb] { { [mm]	[ndʰ]	{ [nd] { [nl] { [nn]		
[mᵖf]	[ɱf]	[nᵗs]	[ns]		
[mv]	[ɱv]	[nᵈz]	[nz]		
[ŋᵍw]	[nw]			[ŋᵍy]	[ñy]

Phonetically, it may be noted that the first set of sequences—on the left in each double column—is characterized by aspiration, outward air-stream release, affrication, or stoppage (by [g] in the case of both [w] and [y], and by a bilabial rather than labio-dental nasal in the case of [v]; in the latter, I hear no complete oral stop). The second set of sequences consists of nasals followed by the unmodified simple consonants; [l], which commonly undergoes morphophonemic alternation after a nasal in other languages, remains intact; [w] is preceded by [n], with neither bilabial nor velar closure; and the nasal is labiodental before [f, v] —in every case, the articulation of the consonant after the nasal seems to be "protected."

In the following examples, the prenasalized consonants which occur within stems are written [mb, nd] etc.; this is not intended to imply that there is no conceivable phonetic difference between these and the prenasalized consonants written the same way where morpheme boundaries are present. The status of the stem-internal pre-nasals will be considered again later; the examples here are intended only to illustrate the contrasts listed above in real forms:

[mpʰúku]	'rat'	[mpáaŋgi]	'brother'
[ntʰáaŋgu]	'time'	[nti]	'tree'
[ŋkʰála]	'crab'	[ŋkáaŋgu]	'crowd'
[mbʰu]	'mosquito'	[mbu]	'ocean'
[nᵗsúka]	'end'	[nsúuka]	'morning'
[mᵖfúmu]	'chief'	[ɱváalu]	'horse'
[ndʰooŋga]	'crowd'	[nláambi]	'cook'
[mbʰwéeno]	'vision'	[mmóni]	'one who sees'

(Note: the last of these are from
the same root, with initial /m/.)

[bantʰúŋgila nᵈzo]   [bantúŋgila nᵈzo]
   'they built me a house'   'they built him a house'
[baŋkʰéba]   [baŋkéba]
   'they took care of me'   'they took care of him'
[bamváŋgila kinzu]   [baɱváŋgila kinzu]

'they made a pot for me'   'they made a pot for him'
[bambʰákila kinzu]   [bambákila kinzu]
'they got me a pot'   'they got him a pot'

The question may now be raised whether the stem-internal nasals /mb, nd, ŋg, mv, nz/, irrespective of whether they are interpreted as unit phonemes or clusters, can be assigned to either of the two series illustrated above, and, if so, to which. This is a difficult question to answer merely on the grounds of impressions of phonetic similarity; because of the nature of word structure in KiKongo, including tone, it happens that the stem-internal pre-nasals occur only before the least prominent vowel in the word, while the series illustrated above occur before the most prominent vowel. In terms of outward air movement, stoppage, or affrication, the stem-internal pre-nasals seem neutral—not strikingly more similar to either of the above series. If anything, they appear to be phonetically a little more like the [mbʰ...] series.

Another question, however, is whether the nasal in any or all of the sequences in question is syllabic. In initial position, in the sequences which include a morpheme boundary, the syllabicity of the nasal is questionable. Considerations of tone are not determinative; the nasals do not have contrastive tone. Yet, of course, it does take a little time to pronounce the nasal, and that time might or might not be a syllable. But in examples like the last four pairs above, where the prenasalized consonants occur intervocalically, though not stem-internally, the nasal appears to be more prominent, more likely syllabic, than in the similar pre-nasals within stems. It appears likely that the stem-internal combinations can indeed be interpreted as unit phonemes /mb, nd, ng, mv, nz/ distinct from the other two series, and the latter can be interpreted as clusters. If they are clusters, the question of the syllabicity of the nasals hardly needs to be answered; they are not syllabic in the sense of bearing contrastive tone.

This still leaves important phonetic material in the contrasts of the [mpʰ] series and the [mp] series to be interpreted phonemically. If either or both series were to be interpreted as unit phonemes, there would be an extensive set of prenasalized consonants alongside the simple consonants in the phonemic inventory, and these unit phonemes would include morpheme boundaries. Even if both series are interpreted as clusters, which seems more desirable on other grounds, we would seem to be faced with a second set of phonemes, /pʰ, ts/ etc., which would occur only in clusters after nasals, but in contrast with the simple consonant phonemes listed at the beginning of this discussion.

Another solution seems to be the best of all. That is to interpret both the [mpʰ] and the [mp] series as clusters, but as different types of clusters. That is, the clusters do not contrast as entireties, nor by virtue of having different consonants after the nasal, but rather by virtue of an additional phonemic abstraction. The contrasts are assigned not to the consonants following the nasals, but to something earlier in the cluster. Either there are two different pairs of nasal phonemes involved, or there is one pair of nasals and an added phoneme which differentiates the one set of clusters from the other. The latter seems the better alternative, since there is clearly a closer linkage between the nasal and the following consonant in the [mpʰ] series than in the [mp] series; it was suggested above that the articulation of the consonant in the second series is "protected." The suggested interpretation of the [mpʰ] series is /mp, . . ./, and of the [mp] series is /m'p/.

Phonemically, this interpretation is unusual, but entirely defensible. Morphologically, it is happily reinforced by comparative evidence. Precisely the prefix and pronoun now represented by a nasal alone appear in many other Bantu languages as a nasal before a consonant—often with such allomorphs as the zero or aspiration in Swahili. And precisely the same prefixes and pronoun now represented by /m', n'/ appear in many other Bantu languages as /mu-/.

3.23. LuGanda (see Cole 1967)[9] has nasal-plus-consonant sequences in which the consonant is a stop or fricative. In initial position, the nasal is syllabic and bears tone. In postvocalic position, syllable division precedes the nasal, the nasal is nonsyllabic, and the nasal-plus-consonant sequence functions as a prenasalized consonant. Morphologically, I note only the voiced combinations internally in stems; all combinations occur with a morpheme boundary between the nasal and following consonant.

LuGanda also has a series of double consonants, which occur both intervocalically and initially. All consonants except the resonants occur doubly as well as singly. Double consonants occur within stems, and also as realizations of certain prefixes plus stem-initial consonants. If the stem-initial consonant is /w, l, y/ in other environments, the prefixes in question combine to yield /gg, dd, jj/. Phonetically, intervocalic double consonants are clearly longer than their single counterparts. Initially, the greater duration of voicing in double voiced consonants, and of fricative noise in double fricatives, is audible. Initial double voiceless stops, in contrast with shorter single stops, may seem impossible; the duration of utterance-initial silence hardly seems potentially significant. Actually, if one watches a speaker of LuGanda, the greater duration of an initial double voiceless stop is visible; it is also audible, in the form of a more fortis articulation and more abrupt release than for a single voiceless stop. In both initial and intervocalic position, the first part of a double consonant is defined as syllabic with low tone. The pitch of a voiced consonant can, of course, be heard. The assignment of low tone to a voiceless consonant is justified intervocally by the fact that adjacent tones are realized as they would be if an audible low tone were present. By analogy, low tone is assigned also to initial voiceless segments; their voiced counterparts are always audibly low.

LuGanda displays a wide range of the phonetic combinations that have been under discussion:

[9] Cole 1967 is an admirable model of how to present precisely that information about a language which reveals its structural patterns, with remarkable lucidity and insight.

	C	Cy	Cw
	NC	NCy	NCw
	CC	CCy	CCw

Not all possible combinations are recorded, to be sure. In some cases, primarily where resonants are involved, there are morphophonemic alternations which prevent certain combinations. Apart from these cases, the nonoccurrence of several plausible combinations seems to be simply a statistical limitation, rather than a structurally imposed restriction.

3.24. Reserved for the conclusion of this chapter on consonant systems is a problem of analysis in Efik which I have not seen paralleled in any other language.[10] The phonetic inventory of consonants differs in three different environments, and the problem is how—or even whether—these three inventories can be combined into one inventory of consonant phonemes. In word-initial position, or in syllable-initial position medially if preceded by a nasal or by a vowel allophone which does not occur in closed syllables, the following consonant (sounds) occur:

	t	k	kp
b	d		
f	s		
w		y	
m	n		
w̃		ỹ	

In a few words, [ř] also occurs in syllable-initial position medially, but never in word-initial position; this appears to be a secondary development, since the same words have [d] in some dialects. The following examples illustrate these consonants in medial position; [kp] is put into the labial column here, which is obviously a legitimate alternative:

èkpàt	'bag'	étó	'tree'	ìkó	'calabash'
ébót	'goat'	édèt	'tooth'		
úfɔk	'house'	èsò	'pot'		
ìwá	'cassava'	(áràn	'palm oil')	íyák	'fish'
m̀mɔ́ŋ	'water'	únàm	'meat'		
ìw̃áŋ	'farm'			éỹíŋ	'name'

Secondly, in syllable-final position, the following consonant sounds occur:

	p	t	k
	m	n	ŋ

---

[10] The following analysis is essentially that presented in Welmers 1968a, pp. 101-6; the logical conclusions of the analysis are implicit there, though not explicitly stated in full. The same analysis, with very minor differences in detail, is presented somewhat more fully by Thomas L. Cook (1969).

Examples are:

dép	'buy'	yét	'wash'	kpók	'cut up'
tèm	'cook'	fɔ́n	'be good'	dùŋ	'reside'

From this much data it is clear that [kp] and [p] are in complementary distribution and can be interpreted as a phoneme /p/—itself a most unusual interpretation for a phonetically doubly articulated stop. In addition, [ŋ] and [ỹ] are in complementary distribution, though interpreting them as a single phoneme is not as attractive in terms of pattern congruity. Alternatively, [ŋ] could simply be added to the first chart of consonants, and it would appear that a fairly typical chart of consonant phonemes is the result.

There is a third environment, however, in which a third inventory of consonant sounds occurs. This is after vowel allophones which are elsewhere characteristic of closed syllables, but with a vowel following the consonant as well—that is, intervocalically, but preceded by vowel sounds different from those which occur before syllable-initial consonants as described above. The consonant sounds that occur in this environment are a bilabial flap, an alveolar flap, a uvular flap, and the three nasals which occur also in syllable-final position:

$$ \text{ƀ} \qquad \text{ř} \qquad \text{g̱} $$
$$ \text{m} \qquad \text{n} \qquad \text{ŋ} $$

These are illustrated in the following, in which [ɨ] is characteristic of closed syllables, paralleling [i] in open syllables; the final vowel in these forms is phonetically [ɛ], but that is irrelevant to the analysis at this point:

sɨƀé	'cut down'	tɨřé	'stop'	ńdɨg̱é	'I'm not coming'
nɨmé	'put out'	bɨné	'go to'	nɨŋé	'sweet'

These intervocalic consonants are clearly in complementary distribution with the consonants which occur in syllable-final position. Indeed, in some types of phrases the syllable-final stops may be heard in fairly slow speech, but the flaps in more rapid speech. In the following examples, the closed-syllable vowel sounds, shorter than those in open syllables, are not indicated by a special transcription:

dwòp è bà:	dwòƀè bà	'twelve (ten plus two)'
èfít è nàŋ:	èfířè nàŋ	'nineteen (fifteen plus four)'
úfɔk ìbà:	úfɔg̱ìbà	'two houses'

Of the three inventories of consonant sounds described here, therefore, there is complementary distribution between the first and the second, and between the second and the third. However, there are clearly contrasts between the first and the third within the statements up to this point. Vowel sounds characteristic of closed syllables followed by flaps are in contrast with other vowel sounds followed by syllable-initial stops. In the case of the nasals, the contrasts would apparently have to be assigned to the preceding vowel; the same interpretation is possible, of course, to explain the stop-flap difference. It simply offends the sensibilities, however, to resort to this interpretation with its necessary doubling of the vowel inventory; it would seem that there must be a simpler and more natural solution.

The solution suggested is to posit, in the phonologic system of Efik, a unit that marks syllable division. The flaps described above, as well as intervocalic nasals when preceded by vowels characteristic of closed syllables, may be described as "ambisyllabic" (a term also admirably suited to describe intervocalic consonants before weak-stressed vowels in English, as in *city*, though the structural significance of the phenomenon is not the same). An ambisyllabic consonant functions as the final consonant of one syllable, and simultaneously as the initial consonant of the next syllable. In Efik, then, a vowel may be followed by a syllable-final (including ambisyllabic) consonant, or by phonemic syllable division —which in turn may be followed by a syllable-initial consonant, though also by another vowel, a syllabic nasal, or nothing. Vowels in these two positions have different allophones. The flaps can then be interpreted as /p, t, k/ without preceding syllable division, and the full inventory of Efik consonant phonemes, to which a phoneme of syllable devision must be added, is:

p	t	k
b	d	
f	s	
w	r	y
m	n	ŋ
w̃		ỹ

Since first facing the problems of Efik phonology about 1964, I have been fully aware that a treatment in the framework of generative phonology—which I have had neither sufficient practice, sufficient time, nor sufficient inclination to handle to my own satisfaction, let alone the satisfaction of others—would have certain distinct advantages. I believe and hope that the data outlined above or available from other sources are such that a conversion to a generative treatment would present no insuperable difficulties.

Chapter 4

Tonal Systems

4.1. A missionary candidate and his wife once admitted that, when they learned that the language of their African field was a tone language, they seriously questioned whether the Lord had actually called them to missionary service. Writers of grammars have commonly neglected to describe and write distinctions in tone, on the theory that "tone can be learned only by observation and practice." Leonard Bloomfield aptly commented on this (1942), "Such a statement is nothing less than a downright swindle, for of course observation and practice are the only way anything can be learned." Others dismiss the entire topic of tone with only a brief statement of this sort: "Tone is important, as will be seen from the following examples [two or three examples follow]; however, tone will not be marked in this grammar." One grammar does discuss tone fairly fully, but relegates it to an appendix explicitly added for the benefit of those who are particularly interested and who consider themselves especially gifted. Many more grammars— more than half of over a hundred grammars of African tone languages examined —omit all mention of tone; some go so far as to assert that the language being treated is definitely not a tone language, though a little investigation readily proves that it is. A shocking number of people concerned with African languages still seem to think of tone as a species of esoteric, inscrutable, and utterly unfortunate accretion characteristic of underprivileged languages—a sort of cancerous malignancy afflicting an otherwise normal linguistic organism. Since there is thought to be no cure—or even reliable diagnosis—for this regrettable malady, the usual treatment is to ignore it, in hope that it will go away of itself. With a more optimistic determination, one group of language learners in Africa asked a trained linguist to come and try to "get rid of tone" in the local language.

Now, there is undeniably a danger of oversimplifying the complexities of tonal structure in language; the sophisticate is tempted to be blasé. But at the same time, the presence of tone need not cause us to tremble in our scientific boots, or to bury our heads in the sands of "insufficient data." In principle, the varieties and functions of tonal contrasts in language are of the same order as the varieties and functions of any other contrasts; the problems of tonal analysis are simply typical problems of linguistic analysis.

There have, of course, been some fortunate exceptions to the general disregard of tone. J. G. Christaller (1875), Ida Ward (1933, 1936) and R. C. Abraham (1940b, 1941) in particular made serious efforts to include full descriptions of tonal phenomena in their treatments of several West African languages. In addition, lexical tone is marked in a handful of African language dictionaries. Even in most of these cases, however, tone is treated only at the phonetic level, which is of course to be expected in earlier writings. Pitches are usually indicated by dots or lines representing relative pitches, as [· .] or [⁻ -], without specifying or fully discussing the number and nature of tonal contrasts as structural units in the language. Adequate descriptions of tonal systems are almost entirely confined to recent works reflecting a high degree of sophistication in descriptive linguistics.

4.2. With very few exceptions, the languages of Africa south of the Sahara are tone languages. Within the Afro-Asiatic family, all of the Chadic languages for which there is information are tonal. The Cushitic languages in general are not tonal, although there is at least one demonstrated exception, Moča of south-western Ethiopia (see Leslau, 1958). In Saho, pitch distinctions have been shown to be conditioned by the presence or absence of phonemic stress (see Welmers, 1952b). Somali, one of the largest of the Cushitic languages, has been called a tone language (see Armstrong 1934, Andrzejewski 1964); another investigator (Pia 1963), however, is satisfied that pitch distinctions are, as in Saho, predictable in terms of stress. In the Nilo-Saharan and Khoisan families, tone is present in every language which has been adequately investigated, and there is no evidence that any language in these families is not a tone language. In the Niger-Kordofanian family, the major northern languages of the West Atlantic branch of Niger-Congo—Wolof, Serere, Fula—are not tone languages. Neither is Swahili, at least in its more or less standard forms along the east coast of Africa. Similarly, an inter-tribal or trade language based on KiKongo (KiTuba, Kikongo vehiculaire, and other names) has lost the tonal contrasts typical of KiKongo itself, and some other partially pidginized languages may similarly have become non-tone languages as a recent and secondary development. Otherwise, it had better be assumed that any sub-saharan language is tonal unless the opposite can be demonstrated.

Many of the younger generation of language investigators have been willing to face this fact, but even among them the attitude is all too common that they would prefer first to master the consonants and vowels, most of the grammar, and a great deal of vocabulary, and then they will tackle the supposedly knotty problem of tone. Apart from weightier considerations of the possible functions of tone in a language, there is one intensely practical reason why this procedure is virtually doomed to failure. By the time the investigator decides to settle down and learn something about tone, the people from whom he has been learning the language will already have decided long since that he will never pronounce their language accurately. They will have given up correcting him, and they will utterly fail to comprehend what he is after now. To the native speaker of a tone language, tone is just as basic a part of his speech as consonants and vowels; if no progress is made in that aspect of pronunciation at first, there is no reason to expect that any improvement will be made later.

On the other hand, if speakers of an African language have had some experience with the pitiful efforts that non-Africans have made to learn their language in the past, and with the often unintelligible gibberish that results, then the learner who is prepared to try for accuracy in every detail from the beginning is at a tremendous advantage. He is considered a promising learner, perhaps the first who ever really imitated what he heard; and such a learner will earn patient, thorough help from those with whom he hopes to communicate.

The problems of tone in African languages, therefore, are a most appropriate starting point for the analyst or learner. Nor are they by any means as forbidding as has been widely assumed. Special musical ability has little or nothing to do with ability to hear and reproduce tone in language. Conversely, the claim that one is "tone deaf" is no excuse. Students who literally cannot change the pitch of their voice in singing, and who distinguish different melodies by their rhythm rather than their pitch changes, have mastered tone languages. And advanced students of music, with perfect pitch, who could hear the minutest pitch distinctions in short utterances from their language informants, have been known to completely ignore tone when attempting to speak the language. For reasons not at all clear as yet, some beginners have more difficulty with tone than others. But no one is qualified to predict in advance that he will find tone hopelessly difficult, and many will be surprised at how simple it actually is. Tone has to do with distinctions of pitch in the flow of speech; and every speaker of English notices and produces distinctions in pitch if he can tell the difference between the question "This is living?" and the statement "This is living."

4.3. Why, then, is English not called a tone language, and just what is a tone language? In English, distinctions in pitch apply to phrases separated from each other by slight pauses, or at least marked by a slight prolongation at the end of each phrase. A single phrase may consist of a single word—e.g., "Yes?", "No!" —or of a number of words such as "When I went to see him, . . ." The kind of melody that asks a question in English may be applied to a single syllable, or stretched out over a fairly long sequence of words; but it is basically the same melody, with the same meaning. In English, changing the pitch of one stem, or prefix, or suffix, does not produce a new morpheme in the same class. Such English morphemes consist of consonants, vowels, and in some cases stress in one or another position. Superimposed on entire phrases are intonational melodies, which themselves are morphemes with meanings, but which in themselves contain no consonants or vowels. That is, the morphemes of English include two types: those which have nothing to do with pitch (stems and affixes), and those which consist of nothing but pitch (intonational melodies or contours).

In a tone language, the status of pitch distinctions is quite different. Pike (1948, p. 43) has defined a tone language as "a language having lexically significant, contrastive, but relative pitch on each syllable." This definition really says too much, particularly in associating contrastive pitch with every syllable. Even in Chinese (Mandarin), the language perhaps most widely known as tonal, and in which tone is unquestionably associated with syllables, many syllables must be analyzed as "toneless;" the pitch of such syllables is conditioned by the preceding tone. In some African languages, a single tone may be assigned to a scope of two or more syllables; conversely, sequences of two or more tones may be assigned to a single syllable. Further, tone is not always lexically significant. An affix may have a phonemic tone, but its tone may be conditioned by the tone of the stem with which the affix occurs. There are also tones which function only to distinguish different grammatical constructions; these are not generally called "lexical." And the phrase "relative pitch" is too imprecise. Pitch can be "relative" in several ways—relative to the individual speaker's voice (a soprano or a bass), to the emotional context, to the physical surroundings (e.g., murmuring in privacy as opposed to shouting in a noisy market), or to neighboring pitches. It is, of course, the pitch of a given segment relative to the pitch of neighboring segments that is linguistically significant, but more than mere pitch relationship is usually involved. Given the same physical surroundings, the same conditions of speech, and the same purpose, repeated recordings have shown that a given speaker will hit almost precisely the same pitch for a given tone at intervals of hours and even days; on the other hand, to be sure, if a tired informant is given an opportunity to rest, his entire pitch range is likely to go up, and his pitch intervals to increase. That more than mere relative pitch is involved, however, is clear from the fact that, more often than not, an isolated monosyllabic utterance can be identified as low or other than low; in most languages, low tone, especially in isolation or in final position, is characterized by relaxation, often a progressive relaxation accompanied by a slight downward glide of pitch.

A definition of a tone language proposed as more adequate is this: "A tone language is a language in which both pitch phonemes and segmental phonemes enter into the composition of at least some morphemes" (Welmers 1959). Like Pike's definition, this excludes intonational languages like English. Such languages have many morphemes composed of segmental phonemes (and perhaps stress) without pitch phonemes, and some intonational morphemes composed of pitch phonemes without segmental phonemes; but they have no morphemes that include both types of phonemes. A tone language may conceivably have some morphemes that contain no pitch phonemes, and certainly many tone languages have some morphemes composed exclusively of pitch phonemes. But the distinctive characteristic of a tone language is that some of its morphemes—usually nearly all of them—contain both segmental phonemes and pitch phonemes. There seems to be no known language in which pitch is significant only for units larger than a morpheme (such as words), but smaller than a phrase.

4.4. The kinds of pitch phenomena that enter into phonemic contrasts in tone languages are varied; and the recurrence of similar contrasts in restricted areas, such as Southeast Asia or West Africa, suggests that a typological classification of tone languages may be useful. Pike classified the tone languages with which he was acquainted in 1948 as having either "register systems" (definable in terms of levels of pitch) or "contour systems" (definable in terms of direction of pitch change), and added that some languages are basically of one type with an overlay of the other type. Actually, such "combinatory types" appear to be far more common than unadulterated "register" or "contour" types; a striking example is Cantonese, with four level tones and four glides. Pike was unquestionably correct in recognizing an important difference between the tonal systems of a great many Asian languages and those of many Amerindian and African languages; his definitions, however, can profitably be refined. The term "contour" may be retained, but I would define a contour tone language more specifically as one in which at least one unit toneme must be described in terms of two distinct components: the direction of pitch change, and also the position of the entire glide within the pitch range of the environment. For example, Vietnamese has unit tonemes that must be described as "high rising" and "low rising"; Cantonese has "high rising", "low rising", "high falling", and "low falling" (in addition to the four level tones); Mandarin has "high rising" and "complete falling". As described to me, Thai, on the other hand, is not a contour language; it has one "rising" and one "falling" tone, along with three level tones, but the position of the glides within the environmental pitch range is apparently not significant. Within a few minutes after I first learned that, I happened to hear Thai spoken, just loudly enough for me to be able to hear the tones, but not loudly enough so that I could distinguish consonants and vowels to any extent; to my gratification, it sounded far more like an African language than like Chinese or Vietnamese. By the same definition, no known language of Africa is a contour language, though unitary rising and falling tonemes may sometimes be found, without contrastive positions in the pitch range.

Many languages of West and Central Africa, as well as the few American tone languages of which I have any knowledge, can be rather simply described as having two, three, or four level tones, and perhaps also a unit rising tone and/or a unit falling tone. In many such languages, each level tone is restricted to a relatively narrow range of absolute pitch (absolute for a given speaker under given environmental conditions) within a phrase, and these tonemic ranges are discrete —never overlapping, and separated by pitch ranges which are not used—throughout the phrase, though they may all tilt downward at the very end of the phrase in a brief final contour. Thus, in a three-level system, high tone near the end of the phrase has virtually the same absolute pitch as a high tone at the beginning of the phrase, and is higher than any mid tone in the phrase. Usually there are few restrictions in tone sequences. These phenomena may be illustrated by the following sentence in Jukun (Dìyī):

> áku pèrè ní zè budyi à syi ní bi kéré.
> [‾ – _ _ ‾ _ – – _ – ‾ – ‾]
> 'That person brought this food here.'

Every possible sequence of two successive tones occurs in this sentence. The three levels are discrete throughout the sentence, and so precisely limited that playing them on three notes on a piano (a major triad does very well) does not appreciably distort the pitches of normal speech.

Such a tonal system may be called "discrete level." Details concerning the analysis and characteristics of some discrete level languages will be outlined after defining another type of tonal system.

4.5. Quite a different type of pitch relationship within a phrase is found in a number of Bantu languages and in some West African languages—among them Tiv, Efik, Igbo, Gã, and Akan. In these languages, sentences can readily be found with seven, eight, or even more perceptibly different levels of pitch. Recurrent low pitches in a phrase can be rather easily identified, and can safely be interpreted as representing a toneme "low". But to identify each of eight or more non-low pitches as a separate toneme would require positing a highly unlikely number of tonemes. In addition, the morphophonemic statements required by such an analysis would be incredibly complex; just as an example, a given monosyllabic morpheme with a non-low pitch might occur with as many as eight or more different tonemes in different sentences. The restrictions in pitch sequences, however, suggest a different analysis. After a low tone at any point in a phrase, there are only two possibilities: the next syllable may have the same pitch and thus also have low tone, or it may have a nonlow pitch; if there was a nonlow pitch earlier in the phrase, this one will be a little lower. (An exception in ShiTswa, important to the history of the analysis of languages of this type, will be discussed later.) After a nonlow pitch at any point in a phrase, there are three possibilities: the next syllable may be low, or it may have the same nonlow pitch, or it may have a slightly lower nonlow pitch. What is significant is not the absolute pitch (for a given speaker under given conditions) of a syllable in a phrase, as in a discrete-level language, but the pitches of nonlow syllables relative to preceding nonlow syllables.

It follows from the above statements that, in a phrase in such a language, the first nonlow pitch is the highest. After that, there may be successively lower nonlow pitches, but never a return from a lower pitch to the same level as a preceding nonlow. The sequence of nonlow pitches in a phrase may be likened to a series of terraces or a set of steps, with low tones intervening here and there—like gaps between the steps where the floor is visible if one looks down. In the following illustrative sentence from Igbo, the successively lower non-low pitches are represented under the line by the letters a, b, ..., and low tone by z:[1]

> ŋwa nne m na onye ŋkuzi ya byara ụlọ anyị.
> a a b b z c c c c c d z z e f g g
> 'My brother and his teacher came to our house. '

Such a tonal system may be called "terraced level". In such a system, there are two contrasts after low: low and nonlow, with the actual pitch of the nonlow determined by the preceding nonlow if there is one. There are three contrasts after any nonlow: the same pitch, a slightly lower pitch, and low. Arbitrarily, the first nonlow could be identified with either a same or a lower pitch after nonlow.

---

[1] This notational device was apparently first used by Paul Schachter (1961). Its use is not meant to imply an acceptance of Pike's convention of numbering tone levels (in discrete level systems) from top to bottom; numbering from bottom to top, by analogy with the stories of a building or the letters of a musical scale, seems more acceptable.

It follows that the two identical pitches marked *b* in the above have a different phonemic status, as do the two marked *g*. Conversely, the first *b* and the first *g* have the same phonemic status, along with the *d* and *f*. Similarly, the second *a*, the second *b*, every *c* after the first, and the second *g* all have the same phonemic status. The status of nonlows initially and after low will be considered later; for the moment, it is enough to note that attributing a different phonemic status to phonetically identical pitches (and perhaps also attributing the same phonemic status to different pitches) may appear to be a gross departure from the traditional concept of the phoneme. Yet it is necessary with this kind of data to attribute contrasts—phonemic status—to pitch relationships rather than to pitches as such.

4.6. The recognition of phonemic contrasts of this type is relatively recent. In many cases, analysts seem to have considered tone—if at all—only at the lexical level, in individual words cited in isolation. In the very early stages of analyzing a language of this type, one's attention is likely to be focused on very short utterances—sequences of two or three syllables. It may well be noticed that three pitches occur in such forms, and perhaps a restriction in their distribution will not be thought strange so early in the work. Two-syllable forms would show five possible sequences:

$$\lceil\;\;\rceil \quad \lceil\;\;\rfloor \quad \lfloor\;\;\rceil \quad \lfloor\;\;\rfloor \quad \lceil\;-\rceil$$

In Efik, for example, just these and only these sequences are found in typical bisyllabic nouns:

iyak	$\lceil\;\;\rceil$	'fish'		iwa	$\lceil\;\;\rceil$	'cassava'
ufɔk	$\lceil\;\;\rfloor$	'house'		eso	$\lfloor\;\;\rfloor$	'pot'
		ɔbɔŋ	$\lceil\;-\rceil$	'chief'		

With no more evidence than this, one might very possibly conclude that these sequences can be labelled, respectively, high-high, high-low, low-high, low-low, and high-mid. Sequences of three syllables would very likely strengthen this impression at first; one might note only the restricted distribution of the apparent mid tone. A descending sequence of three tones, with even the last one not being low, should certainly be disturbing, but it might well not occur in a substantial body of lexical data.

If tone is considered only at the lexical level—as has frequently been the case, apparently on the assumption that lexical contrasts will exhaust the tonal system —the validity of the labels "high", "mid", and "low" may never come into question. Some who have considered contrasts in longer utterances have attributed all of the descending pattern of nonlow tones to a descending intonational contour, without recognizing that the point at which the pitch level is lowered is by no means predictable in every case. Such an analysis would account for most of the data in some languages, such as Tiv, in which three successive nonlow levels are rare. But occasional occurrences of such sequences invalidate this analysis. For Tiv, R. C. Abraham (1940b) noted such occurrences, but treated them as exceptions in which the first tone is high, the second mid, and the third also mid but specially noted as being lower than the preceding mid. For Igbo, he (1967) attempted a more rigidly phonetic treatment and recognized seven tone levels, though such a treatment would require even more. My own early failure to recognize the crucial contrasts in Fante (Welmers 1946) is attributable to my reliance on overly slow, careful speech;[2] I distinctly recall eliciting phrases which in normal speech would have the pitch sequence *a-b-c*, but they were pronounced as if the two words were being cited separately, so that the effect was *a-c*, *b*, which I interpreted as high-mid-high.

4.7. Those who have clearly recognized three contrasts in these languages as described in 4.5 above have treated them tonemically in three different ways. Perhaps from a reluctance to depart from the labels first assigned in very short utterances, or from the labels traditionally used in describing other (discrete level) languages, some have persisted in labelling the three contrasting phenomena "high", "mid", and "low." This is done by (among others) M. M. Green (1963) and Lloyd Swift (1962) for Igbo, Jack Berry (1969) for Gã, and Bertha Siertsema (1963) in discussing my own treatment of terraced-level languages. This requires a redefinition of "high" and "mid" in terms of pitch relationships rather than pitch levels, which seems unnecessarily tortuous. Green provides the most explicit and lucid such redefinition. In handling the data in this framework, an initial nonlow is interpreted as "high". A nonlow after low is also interpreted as "high," with a statement that it is automatically lower than the last preceding nonlow if there was one. A nonlow which is the same as an immediately preceding nonlow is also called "high." Only a nonlow lower than an immediately preceding nonlow is called "mid." The Igbo sentence cited above is then written, with "high" unmarked, as follows:

ŋwa nnẹ́ m nà onye ŋkuzi yá byàrà ụlọ̀ ányị.
a a b b   z c   c c c c   d   z z e f   g   g

This treatment is unambiguous, to be sure. My only objection to it is the use of the terms "high" and "mid" to describe the pitch relationships involved. Although Green is perfectly clear in describing the sequences high-high and mid-high as level, but high-mid and mid-mid as descending, this labelling jars the semantic sensibilities of an old discrete level hand. I prefer to reserve the terms "high" and "mid" for the recurrent levels of discrete level languages—in which any mid is lower than any high, any high is higher than any mid, and two mids are the same—rather than subject the terms to quite different definitions for different types of languages.

4.8. A second way of handling such data is that suggested by myself (Welmers 1959) in what appears to be the earliest treatment recognizing that there are a

---

[2] J. M. Stewart (1965) notes and corrects my crucial error, but seems not to have realized that it excluded from my mind the very pitch sequences that make this type of tonal system what it is. Given my inexperience and the principles of linguistics when I worked on Fante (1942-43), if I had heard correctly I might have given up in despair, or just possibly an amazing discovery, for its day, would have been made.

number of languages of this type. This interpretation was first arrived at while working with taperecorded material in ShiTswa in 1953. I also recognized the three contrasts as three tonemes, but gave them different labels and treated the nonlow pitches in a different way. My original labels for the three tonemes were "same," "drop," and "low." An initial nonlow would arbitrarily be identified with either "same" or "drop;" the terms themselves are both relational, and imply a preceding nonlow point of reference. A convenient relabeling avoids this arbitrary choice. In terminology developed later, by analogy with a staircase, the first nonlow and every subsequent "drop" is labeled "step," and the three contrasting units are then "same," "step," and "low." "Step" then refers to the highest level in a series of terraces, and to any lower nonlow level thereafter. That is, initial nonlow, nonlow after low, and nonlow lower than an immediately preceding nonlow are all "step". "Same" is applied, of course, only to those pitches which are the same as a preceding nonlow. In the following transcription of the same Igbo sentence, "same" is unmarked; any low after the first in a series is also unmarked; "step" is indicated by an acute accent:

ŋwá nné m nà ónye ŋkuzi yá byàra úló ányị.
a a b b   z c   c c c c   d   z z e f g g

This transcription lends itself to the convenient characterization that, after the first syllable, every mark indicates a change, and every change is marked. This interpretation of the contrasts involved has proven highly practical in teaching Igbo (see Welmers and Welmers 1968b). It has been criticized on the ground that it makes the morphotonemics of Igbo unnecessarily complicated. The fact is, however, that the morphotonemics of Igbo are complicated to begin with, and no other interpretation or transcription would make them appear significantly simpler.

4.9. A third interpretation of such data was first foreshadowed by a nameless author (very likely Ida C. Ward) in a very brief note on Igbo in 1949 (see International Phonetics Association 1949, p. 45), apparently the earliest valid analysis of a tonal system of this type. The "essential tones" are described as high, low, and "a lowered high tone shown by ᵛ preceding the syllable." Although the terminology suggests three tonemes, the transcription suggests that the lowering itself has a phonemic status; some syllables have lowering plus a high tone. This was apparently first incorporated into an explicit phonemic analysis by F. D. D. Winston (1960). Winston recognizes "a unit of 'downstep', which may be symbolized by a superior exclamation mark, contrasting with its absence." "Downstep" accounts for any nonlow tone (which may now safely be called "high") being slightly lower than an immediately preceding nonlow. The lowering of nonlow tones after low is considered automatic. Thus the same Igbo sentence would be transcribed, with high tone unmarked and a vertical stroke indicating downstep:

ŋwa nⁱne m nà onye ŋkuzi 'ya byàrà ụ'lọ 'anyị.
a a   b b   z c   c c c c   d   z z e f g g

This transcription is instantly convertible to or from the transcription used by those who speak of high, mid, and low tones; the mark which they use for "mid" is simply redefined as "downstep followed by high." There is a significant difference, however, in the nature of the linguistic description. In both the re-defined "high-mid-low" interpretation and in my "same-step-low" interpretation, three tonemes are envisioned with coordinate status. In Winston's interpretation, there are two tonemes, high and low, and a phoneme "downstep" which is not a toneme; it is rather something that conditions the actual pitch of the following high toneme.

From the viewpoint of linguistic theory, Winston's interpretation may cer-tainly be judged the most elegant. It attributes the actual pitches within a phrase to tonemes, but the significant relationships between non-low pitches to the pre-sence or absence of a phoneme belonging to a different class. Winston's inter-pretation has since been applied by other scholars to other terraced level langu-ages. (e.g., Meeussen 1964, p. 3). It underlies my more recent treatment of Efik (Welmers 1968), though for practical pedagogical purposes (not just to be per-verse) I abbreviate the awkward phrase "downstep plus high" to my familiar "step," and transcribe it with an acute accent in other than word-initial position. In general, a transcription recognizing downstep as an independent phoneme will be used in the remainder of this work in citing forms from terraced level languages. At the same time, of course, there is no reason why one should not use the "same-step-low" framework in such practical situations as the language classroom if one chooses.

4.10. J. M. Stewart (1965) has suggested that too much of an issue has been made of distinguishing discrete level and terraced level languages as different types.[3] He maintains that the latter are simply straightforward examples of Pike's "register" languages with the addition of a phonemic downstep. But that is pre-cisely what is so momentous. It was over a decade after the appearance of Pike's *Tone Languages*—a masterful work for its day and still indispensable to the beginning analyst of a tone language—before scholars began to be aware that there are languages in which pitch levels are not (to oversimplify the matter just a bit) like a two- to five-note scale on which one can play a wide variety of melodies, but in which there may be many more than five levels in a phrase, with rigid restrictions in the sequences of levels, yet all analyzable in terms of three phonolo-gically distinctive units.

As noted above, the "same-step-low" interpretation of a terraced level lan-guage identifies a lowered nonlow after low with a lowered nonlow after nonlow. That is, the sequence *a-z-b*, using the transcriptional device introduced above, is called "step-low-step", and *a-b* is "step-step". Stewart lays considerable em-phasis on the automatic nature of lowering after low. To be sure, in Twi—and in Gã, Igbo, Efik, Tiv, and many other languages—two contrasting nonlow levels

[3] My comments in Stewart 1965 are not worded as graciously or as concisely as I would have desired; a delay in the mails, not the fault of anyone concerned, compelled me to write and send them within a few hours after receiving Stewart's manuscript.

do not occur after low. But it should be noted that the first conscious analysis of a terraced level system was made for ShiTswa, and in that language—using only a rather limited amount of tape-recorded material, to be sure—a clear contrast was recorded, after low, between a nonlow at the same level as the preceding nonlow and a nonlow at a slightly lower level. It was later discovered that the same overall analysis could be applied to many other languages, even though this particular contrast did not occur. More recently than any of the discussions of this subject in print, a more sophisticated treatment of the ShiTswa data has suggested itself, which will be outlined in another connection below. It remains true that, in general, the typological distinction between discrete level and terraced level tonal systems makes it possible to characterize in a few words a very large number of the tone languages of Africa. Details relevant to individual languages must, of course, be separately described; several are discussed in the remainder of this chapter.

The status of downstep in terraced level languages has also received a good deal of attention from another point of view. It has been noted for some individual languages, and I have heard it suggested as a possibility for all terraced level languages, that downstep may be historically, or morphophonemically, the result of a low tone between two high tones which has been lost or assimilated. Since the lowering of a high tone after downstep is just like the lowering of a high tone after low, it is attractive to associate the two in some way. In some languages this is unquestionably valid. In at least the Bandi dialect of Mende (the only dialect I have heard at all extensively), a sequence like [H 'H H] (a-b-b) occurs only in rapid speech as an alternate of [H L H] (a-z-b); the latter is also commonly heard. The assimilation in rapid speech takes place only with a single syllable which is otherwise low, never more than one syllable. In its present form in Bandi, I would simply interpret this as /H L H/ and describe the optional assimilation. A terraced level system may well be in the process of developing.

Associating downstep with low tone also readily accounts for by far the most part of the data in Akan (including Fante, Twi, Asante; see Schachter and Fromkin 1968), though it does seem arbitrary to posit an untraceable low tone between the two syllables of a rather small number of nouns in which downstep precedes the second syllable. In phrases like /hɛn 'dán/ 'their house', the downstep reflects the low tone of an elided syllable; by itself, 'house' is /ìdán/. In phrases like /hɛn á'dán/ 'their houses', the downstep reflects a low tone which has been assimilated to the level of the preceding high; by itself, 'houses' is /àdán/.

In other languages—Igbo, for example—there seems to be no motivation for such a reconstruction, historically or at some subsurface level of the phonology. In fact, there is good evidence that a downstep in some environments may have developed from a high tone, rather than a low tone, that is no longer present. Consider, for example, the following:

| úlò | 'house'; | àtó | 'three': | úlò àtó | 'three houses' |
| úlò | 'house'; | ànyí | (1 pl.): | ú'ló 'ányí | 'our house' |

The tones of the second phrase can be accounted for, because of their contrast with the tones of the first, only by recognizing a different grammatical relationship between noun and numeral on the one hand, and noun and possessor (actually noun and noun) on the other. In the latter, an additional morpheme between the nouns must be posited, which presumably was once a syllable with a tone. The most reasonable hypothesis is that that tone was high. Then */H L H L H/ (a-z-b-z-c) underwent two assimilations yielding a second stage */H 'H H 'H H/ (a-b-b-c-c); each low syllable was assimilated to the level of the following high. Finally, the middle syllable was lost, leaving the present tones /H 'H 'H H/ (a-b-c-c).

Thus, historically or morphophonemically, downstep may have different ultimate explanations in different languages, or even in different environments in the same language. The fact remains that, at the level of surface phonology, there are a lot of strikingly similar terraced level languages in Africa.

4.11. Those who have had considerable experience in this field may understandably be impatient or critical that certain types of data have been ignored up to this point. There is admittedly much more to be said, and a great deal of it will be said, but before going farther it seems appropriate to mention some problems that relative beginners are likely to have. As the nature of a terraced-level language becomes clear, students have frequently asked whether, in such a language, all low tones are on the same level, or is there a downward slope with successive low tones? Before a pause in speech, a final low or series of lows may show something of a downward tendency in pitch, reflecting a phrase-final relaxation. But earlier in a phrase, in most languages with which I have had experience, the low tones are remarkably close to the same absolute level; there is certainly no striking drop in pitch. Nor is it difficult to distinguish a low tone from a lowered high tone.

Another question frequently asked concerns the actual pitch intervals between successively lower manifestations of high tone. If a single sequence can include anywhere from two to eight or more distinct levels of pitch, doesn't a speaker have to plan ahead to determine either the absolute pitch level at which he should begin, or the size of the intervals he should use, or both, to accomodate just the number of levels he will need? The answer is simple: of course he does. It may not be a commonly stated fact, but it should be obvious that a native speaker of any language is (perhaps not entirely consciously) aware of what he is going to say, and does plan ahead.

A vivid and amusing illustration of this is provided by a circumstance in which the normal conditions of extemporaneous speech were not present. Included in the tape recording of ShiTswa with which I have worked is a section in which the speaker is reading a folk story from a book. Just before he turns a page (the rustle of paper is clearly audible), he has read a sizable portion of a sentence, including several levels of pitch. The structure of the sentence is such that he apparently expected it to end within a few words over the page. It develops, however, that the writer added more than was expected, without a convenient place for a phrase break. Without a pause or hesitation, the reader lowered the overall level of his low tones, and continued the series of successively lower high tones—but to the point where he was clearly pushing the pitch of his voice to a considerably lower level than was comfortable for him.

4.12. It has sometimes been reported to me orally that a phenomenon appears in one or another language which functions as the converse of "downstep," and which may therefore be termed "upstep." For the most part, such reports have turned out to reflect nothing more than a grave misunderstanding of what constitutes a statement of tonemic structure, and a serious confusion between tonemic structure and morphotonemic alternations. The evidence presented to me has been precisely analagous to an Igbo phrase cited above, in which the word for 'house' ends with a higher pitch (downstep plus high) than in isolation (where the final tone is low):

ụ́lọ́   'house';   ànyị́   (1 pl.):   ụ́'lọ́ 'ányị́   'our house'

The analysts in question would suggest that the higher pitch (and tone) of the syllable /lọ/ in the phrase than in the word by itself (and similarly of the syllable /a/) represents an "upstep." But two different utterances are involved, and this is simply an instance of morphotonemic alternation. "Downstep" is defined as a phoneme conditioning a lowering of the pitch of high tone; it applies to a sequence of syllables in one utterance. Similarly, "upstep" should be posited only if there is a sequence of a nonlow pitch followed by a slightly higher nonlow pitch in the same phrase—and in a language which cannot be described as having a discrete level system, in which such a sequence would be something like mid-high. "Downstep" and "upstep" should not be used to describe the relationship of the pitches of a given form in two different utterances.

The term "upstep" has also been suggested for a somewhat different phenomenon (Stewart 1965, p. 3). The succession of descending nonlow levels characteristic of a terraced level system can hardly, of course, go on indefinitely. It is specifically restricted to sentences, clauses, or phrases the terminal points of which may be identified as the loci of terminal phonemes; the use of a period or comma in transcription may be an ingenuous, but is also an ingenious, reflection of such an analysis. After such a terminal, a new succession of descending levels begins; its onset is usually distinctly higher than the last nonlow before the terminal. Such a phenomenon need not be called "upstep"; it is simply the beginning of a new tonal sequence after a phonemic terminal.

Actually, as will be seen, "upstep" is attested in a few languages, though it is certainly an unusual phenomenon. But the terms "downstep" and "upstep" should be reserved for contrastive changes in nonlow pitch levels within a single phrase.

4.13. Once "downstep" in a terraced level system is recognized as a phoneme with a status different from that of the high and low tonemes, there is reason to wonder whether it may be found operating on a tonemic system which has more than two contrasts. Three contrasts apart from the possibility of downstep can be demonstrated if a language has contrasting sequences such as [_ _], [_ -], and [_ ¯]; the sequences would be analyzed as low-low, low-mid, and low-high. In addition to these contrasts, is it not possible that, in longer and more complex sequences, a phonemic lowering could occur with high or mid or both? In such a system, the pitch of downstep plus high would be higher than the pitch of imd, but it would still be possible to have a sequence mid-high.

Considering such a system as an abstract possibility, the complexities may seem forbidding. Theoretically, however, there is no reason why such a system could not appear in some language—a possibility which I had noted, in an unpublished manuscript, three days before I received information that a language with just such a system had been discovered. Pike (1966, pp. 137-39) notes a system apparently of this type in Bette, but finds that the downstep is non-phonemic, appearing automatically after a stressed high tone. He suggests that this might easily develop into a system with three tonemes and a phonemic downstep. A few months after this report of Pike's appeared, Robert G. Armstrong (1968) reported a confirmed case of downstep in a three-toneme system in the Ikom dialect of Yala.

Three dialect areas are distinguished for Yala: Ogoja, Obubra, and Ikom. On the basis of his own comparisons, Armstrong states that the dialects of Ogoja and Obubra have straightforward discrete level systems; for Ogoja, this is amply confirmed by the analysis of Eugene Bunkowske (not yet published), which I in turn have checked with his informants. But in Ikom, there is an automatic lowering of high tone after mid or low, and of mid after low; and in addition, there is a phonetically distinct and contrastive lowering of high after high, and also of mid after mid. That is, phonemic downstep occurs with both high and mid. A phonetic sequence high-low is analyzed as high-downstep-low; without downstep, the phonetic realization of low after high is a falling glide. Morphophonemically, the presence of downstep appears to be the result of the deletion of a syllable with low or mid tone. Armstrong's description of this system is so explicit and fully documented as to be completely convincing. In addition, it further strengthens the case for considering downstep to be a phoneme operating on a tonemic inventory, rather than for attempting to incorporate all pitch phenomena within a tonemic inventory.

4.14. A phonemic upstep appears to be the only reasonable interpretation of the raising of a high tone in Yombe, as reported by A. E. Meeussen (Meeussen and Ndembe, 1964). Such an upstep appears in only a few constructions, and it is conceivable on the basis of the limited evidence cited that it should be attributed to an intonational pattern having a status different from that of downstep, which occurs more commonly in the language. The latter alternative, however, seems quite unlikely in the light of some details of the available data, and in the light of Meeussen's entirely sophisticated reaction to the data. After an upstep, following highs continue on the same level until a low or downstep; the upstep simply shifts the entire sequence of terraces back up one level.

There are also instances of a rise in pitch within a phrase which are non-phonemic. In Xhosa, in a sequence of high tones followed by low, there is a general ascending pattern of pitch, and the last high in particular is noticeably higher than those preceding. This is, however, clearly conditioned rather than contrastive.

A somewhat similar phenomenon is heard in some dialects of Ewe. Ewe is one of a small number of known languages in which some mutually intelligible dialects have a discrete level tonal system, but other dialects have a downstep. In the terraced level dialects, for at least some speakers, the last high tone before a downstep and another high is considerably raised. It is easily demonstrable, however, that it is the downstep that is phonemic, and that the raising of a high tone before it is conditioned.

A similar analysis may well be applicable to the data described by Pike (1966, pp. 133-35) for Degema and Engenni, closely related languages (or dialects?) of the Edo (Bini) group in Nigeria. In one of its occurrences in both languages, what Pike calls "extra high tone" is characteristic of a negative verbal prefix. In another occurrence in Engenni only, the same "extra high tone" appears with a syllable preceding a deleted pronoun the normal tone of which is high. That this is not a case of "upstep" is verified by the fact that following high tones do not continue on the same level—in fact, Pike explicitly points out that following high tones are lower than they would normally be. The interpretation posited for Ewe is apparently applicable here as well—there is actually a phonemic downstep, which is automatically preceded by a raised high tone.

In the history of the recognition and analysis of terraced level tonal systems, it was accidental but peculiar that the first language for which such a system was clearly stated, ShiTswa, does not have a completely automatic lowering of high tones after low. My interpretation of certain pitch phenomena as "same" and "step" included a recognition that there is such a contrast after low tone as well as after nonlow, a contrast not to my knowledge attested for any other terraced-level language. The sequence of successively lower non-low tones with intervening low tones, typical and invariable in other terraced level languages, is common enough, to be sure; for example:

> vámùwóná mùfánà.   'They see the child.'
> a z b b   z c z

In the following phrase, however, the syllable /wa/, unmarked, has the same pitch as the nonlow before the preceding low:

> mùfánà wa'hósí   'the chief's child'

This is not, as Stewart (1965, pp. 9-10) considered possible, an attempt on my part at a morphophonemic representation, calling the syllable /wa/ "same" because it would be on the same pitch level as an immediately preceding nonlow. Nor is it a case of a new phrase beginning with /wa/, such that beginning again at the highest level of pitch is permissible. Contrary to Stewart's first assumption, I would indeed distinguish two contrasting nonlow levels after low—one the same as the last preceding nonlow, and one a little lower. Although based exclusively on tape-recorded materials, the data is sufficient, and the pronunciation so clear, that such a conclusion seems inescapable. A reinterpretation of this phenomenon seems possible, however, and highly desirable.

It has occurred to me recently that, to the best of my knowledge, the "same" level after a low tone occurs with only one morpheme in the language—the associative porpheme /á/, which occurs in a number of syllables preceded by a consonant representing a concordial prefix. (If there are other occurrences, they are probably few, and very possibly of a similar morphological type.) The associative morpheme has a high frequency of occurrence, perhaps especially in the type of data selcted for recording, but it is still only one morpheme. Apart from it, ShiTswa seems to display the usual automatic lowering of high after low. It is this associative morpheme, then, which is unusual if not unique. This suggests that the lowering of high after low could be considered normal and nonphonemic, as in other terraced level languages, while the nonlowering of the tone of the associative morpheme could be considered the unusual case and selected for phonemic marking. (For a theoretically similar solution to a problem in the Efik vowel system, see 2.2.) Since the pitch in question is higher than the normal, expected, noncontrastive lowered high, it can be interpreted as a high tone preceded by a phonemic upstep. (This appears only after low; after high, the same morpheme has a normal high tone.) In the following example, all high and low tones are marked, downstep is marked /ᵛ/, and the posited upstep is marked /ᴧ/:

> vámùwóná mùfánà ᴧwáᵛhósí.   'They see the chief's child.'
> a z b b   z c z   c d d

This is not like the phenomenon described above for Ewe, Degema, and Engenni—a raised high before a downstep. The same morpheme shows the same pitch relationship if a low tone follows, contrasting with the usual lowered high. E.g.,

> mùfánà ᴧwá mùbìkì   'the cook's child'
> z a z   a z zz

Pending a more thorough analysis of the ShiTswa tonal system, with informants available in person, the contrasts as described here seem inescapable. Positing a phonemic upstep for one unique (or perhaps only near-unique) case appears at present to be the best solution. Apart from this, ShiTswa displays very much the same kind of tonal system as other terraced level languages. The three tonemes of the Yala of Ikom, and the presence of a phonemic upstep in Yombe and ShiTswa if the above analyses are correct (and they certainly are not unreasonable), are relatively minor additions to the very widespread underlying theme of terraced level languages: two tonemes and a phonemic downstep.

4.15. A number of analysts have recognized, in terraced level languages, the different status of a phonemic lowering of high tone by downstep and the non-phonemic lowering of high tone after low, and have used the term "downdrift" to describe the latter. Downstep does not seem to occur in a language unless downdrift also occurs—a fact which may have led some to the undoubtedly premature conclusion that downstep always reflects the deletion or assimilation of a syllable with low tone, so that downstep is the phonemic product of a once non-phonemic downdrift. It is true, on the other hand, that some languages with two tonemes have downdrift—the nonphonemic lowering of high after low—without having downstep. This is true, for example, of Bandi, which also has an allophonic assimilation yielding a nonphonemic downstep in rapid speech. The dialect of KiKongo spoken in Ngombe has two tones and such a descending contour with high tones, although the dialect recorded by Laman (1936) seems to be a classic example of a terraced level language, with an apparently phonemic downstep. Judging from a variety of descriptions I am not prepared to accept as complete, it would appear that downdrift is typical of a number of Bantu languages; in some cases, the writers may have included downstep without recognizing its phonemic status. It would appear, therefore, that many two-tone systems should, on the basis of the general patterning of pitch levels, be classed with terraced level languages. The term "terraced level", then, would not be restricted to those systems which include a phonemic, contrastive lowering of nonlow tone (downstep), but would be extended to include all systems characterized by successively lower non-low levels, or downdrift.

Although downdrift seems to be typical of many languages with two tonemes, it is certainly not safe to assume that it is universal. The literature is of little help here; an analyst with experience in only one language might point out the presence of a descending contour throughout a phrase, but he would hardly be likely to point out its absence. My own experience with two-tone systems is restricted to a very few languages, most of them heard before this was recognized as a possible problem. In the case of Loma, however, I do not recall any temptation to transcribe a higher-lower-higher sequence as tentatively "high-low-mid", which I probably would have done if there were an appreciable lowering of high after low. Throughout an utterance, Loma (which is adjacent to and fairly closely related to Bandi) seems to show little if any such lowering, except perhaps in phrasefinal position. In Upper Volta, I once overheard an animated conversation in a language unknown to me, which was characterized by clearly marked, almost staccato, syllabification; I observed to another American present that it sounded as if the tones of a single speaker could be played accurately on two notes, with the interval of a minor fifth. In the interests of more accurate descriptions, it seems useful to distinguish allophonic terracing, in the form of downdrift, from recurrent discrete levels even for two-tone systems. Even where overall terracing is not present, however, a perceptible lowering in final position appears to be exceedingly common in discrete level systems.

4.16. Hausa illustrates a clearly marked type of terracing with two phonemic tones.[4] Both high and low tones are involved. In declarative utterances, five levels of pitch may be recognized. An initial low tone is normally at the next-to-lowest level; a final low tone is always at the lowest level. Uninterrupted sequences of either high or low are level. Apart from initial and final low, alternating high and low tones begin at the highest level, go down two levels and up one, down two and up one, so that a maximally long sequence has its last high tone on the next-to-lowest level. Potentially longer sequences must be broken up into two or more; in each new sequence, the first high returns to the highest of the five levels. Such breaks normally occur at certain types of syntactic boundaries. Thus the two tones of Hausa might be diagrammed on two downward-slanting lines; a low tone is always lower than both the preceding and the following high tone, but the fourth high tone level is lower than the first noninitial low tone level, and the same as the second, in a series of alternating tones. Using the letters *a* through *e* to represent the five possible pitches, from highest to lowest, a maximum sequence is illustrated in the following Hausa sentence:

> íyà tá dáfà dànkáli dà námà.
> a c b bd d ce e   d e
> 'Mother cooked sweet potatoes and meat.'

An interrogative intonation, superimposed on such a sequence, is characterized by two discrete levels for high and low, plus an additional raising of the last high tone.

Hausa is one of the few languages I have heard in which a high tone relatively late in a sentence may be on a lower absolute pitch than a low tone earlier in the sentence. Few languages, it would seem, have low tones in such clearly audible descending relationships, though in other languages low tones are not necessarily on the same absolute pitch; commonly, however, low tone gives the effect of a drone bass accompanying whatever is happening up on the steps. Pike (1966, pp. 139-41) cites other cases of assimilative intersection of the absolute pitch levels of different tonemes. Whether they can be described as reflecting a form of downdrift is not entirely clear. In any case, of course, the details must be described independently for each language.

4.17. Prior to 1959, I had worked on Shona for no more than a few hours one afternoon. That was enough time to notice a phonetic downstep between successive high tones, which I presumed to be phonemic; I accordingly cited Shona as an example of a terraced level language without further comment. It has since come to my attention that this apparent downstep is conditioned by the identity of the consonant or consonant cluster beginning the syllable.[5] Actually, both high and low tone are affected by such consonants: a high tone is realized as a rising glide beginning at a pitch lower than the preceding high, and a low tone is

---

[4] This system was first described by Hodge and Hause (1944).

[5] The principles of this system are described, though not in comprehensive detail, by Stevick (1960, p. 32).

simply lower than it would otherwise be. The consonants and clusters that condition this lowering have been termed "depressor onsets"; a complete list is provided by Derek Fivaz (1969). The depressor onsets do not seem to constitute a very neatly definable class of phonemes and clusters; they include some but not all of the voiced stops and fricatives of the phonemic inventory, most but not all of the voiced nasal-onset combinations, and apparently all clusters of voiced consonants with /w, y, h/ (/h/ is voiced in Shona). Shona also has the phenomenon described above as downdrift, a nonphonemic lowering of high tone after low. It is thus a terraced level language in the broader sense, with a nonphonemic conditioning of tones that makes it sound much like a language with phonemic downstep.

A very similar conditioning of both high and low tones by depressor onsets is found in Xhosa (see Lanham 1963), Zulu, and possibly other South African Bantu languages. In Xhosa, there is also a downstep reflecting the deletion of a vowel with low tone. The one native speaker of Xhosa with whom I have worked readily restored the elided vowel in slow speech; whether this is typical, and whether the low tone can be recognized as phonemically present (as in Bandi) is uncertain to me at present.

4.18. The three-tone discrete level system of Jukun (Dìyī) was very briefly described in 4.4 above, in order to provide a point of departure for the discussion of the quite different systems characterized as terraced level. The extent of the ensuing discussion must not be interpreted as implying that discrete level systems are at all uncommon. Countless Niger-Kordofanian languages clearly have discrete level systems with two to four tones. At least some Chadic and Nilo-Saharan languages also have, and a Bushman (Khoisan) language with such a system has been described to my satisfaction in private conversation by Desmond T. Cole. The actual tonemic contrasts are usually rather easy to identify, though there may be complications at the level of morphotonemic alternations.

A convenient procedure for beginning tonal analysis is to elicit the equivalents of several English nouns, particularly nouns referring to countable items, such that one can soon afterwards elicit phrases in which the same nouns are used with the equivalents of numerals, demonstratives, possessives, and as objects of verbs such as 'want, see, buy' and so on. In some languages, a simple comparison of the nouns with each other is sufficient to reveal the contrasting tones. Such is the case in Jukun (Wàpã) (see Welmers 1968a). Of the first twenty or so nouns recorded, a very few would have the segmental structure CVCV. Setting these aside for the moment, the remaining nouns are all similar in segmental structure, and lend themselves to direct comparison for tone. Within fifteen minutes or less, one might well have recorded fifteen nouns like those listed below, and be fairly certain that tone has been accurately recorded. Many informants volunteer additional nouns showing minimal contrasts in tone. To assure random order, the following nouns are listed in the alphabetic order of their English equivalents; mid tone is unmarked:

awi	'animal'	àkwǐ	'gourd'	abyù	'oil'
akwǐ	'chicken'	avī	'horse'	apà	'person'
akù	'chief'	atã	'house'	àdǔ	'sheep'
abá	'dog'	akwí	'knife'	atswí	'thorn'
abyí	'goat'	akwī	'millstone'	así	'yam'

These nouns may now be regrouped according to tone for better-controlled comparison. Having the informant repeat all the nouns in each group, or pronouncing them for his approval or disapproval, reveals that all the nouns in each group are indeed indentical in tone. Comparing the first noun in each group reveals that there are indeed four contrasting tone sequences, and three levels:

akwǐ	'chicken'	akwí	'knife'
akù	'chief'	abá	'dog'
abyù	'oil'	abyí	'goat'
apà	'person'	atswí	'thorn'
		así	'yam'
akwī	'millstone'		
awi	'animal'	àkwǐ	'gourd'
avī	'horse'	àdǔ	'sheep'
atã	'house'		

4.19. Checking the above contrasts in short phrases soon provides data which present a significant problem in the scope of tone—the assignment of tonemes to segmental units. The numerals through ten, in the form used in counting, are:

ázū	'one'	átyǐdyē	'six'
ápyǐnǎ	'two'	átsǔpyǐ	'seven'
átsara	'three'	átsùtsa	'eight'
áyěnã	'four'	átsǔyō	'nine'
átswãnã	'five'	ádzwe	'ten'

Numerals are used after nouns. If the final tone of the noun is high, the initial vowel of the numeral is elided, and there is no perceptible lengthening of the final vowel of the noun. One would have no hesitation in transcribing combinations like:

abá tsara 'three dogs'   abiyí tsara 'three goats'

If the final tone of the noun is mid or low, however, the tone of the initial vowel of the numeral remains; there is a quick glide from the final mid or low tone of the noun to high, but again there is no perceptible lengthening of the final vowel of the noun. Phonetically, the sequences mid-high and low-high accompany the final short vowel of the noun, as suggested by the following transcriptions:

awi'tsara 'three animals'   akwǐ'tsara 'three chickens'

Following Pike's definition of a tone language, which suggests a rule of one tone per syllable and one syllable per tone, a number of linguists have assumed that an additional vowel must be posited to accommodate the extra tone in phrases such as the above; they would analyze these as /awií tsara/ and /akwií tsara/. Particularly in light of the phrases with nouns having final high tone, there is absolutely no phonetic justification for such an analysis. For phrases of this particular type, it may be theoretically possible to posit such an "empty" vowel, which has no duration; but further analysis (undoubtedly much later than the first hour, to be sure) reveals contrasts which make such an interpretation hopelessly awkward.

Thirteen of the fifteen nouns cited in the preceding section begin with /a/, with mid tone. If anything precedes a noun in an utterance, this vowel is completely lost; the following sentences illustrate this, and also constitute the first six of a remarkably large set of utterances minimally different in tone:

ku hwẽ kwí	'he bought a knife'
ku hwẽ kwī	'he bought a millstone'
ku hwẽ kwì	'he bought a chicken'
ku hwẽ̌ kwí	'he counted the knives'
ku hwẽ̌ kwī	'he counted the millstones'
ku hwẽ̌ kwì	'he counted the chickens'

The remaining two nouns begin with /à/, with low tone. In similar environments, this vowel is completely lost after low tone, but its tone is retained after mid or high, with no lengthening of the preceding vowel. This adds one more to the six contrasts above; the second of the following sentences is completely homophonous with the last of the above:

ku hwẽꞌ kwì	'he bought a gourd'
ku hwẽ̌ kwì	'he counted the gourds'

There is a morpheme indicating identification, used before nouns, which in utterance-initial position has the form /á/, with high tone. E.g.,

á kwì	'it's a chicken'	áꞌ kwì	'it's a gourd'

Before an object noun, and after mid or low tone, the vowel quality and duration are lost, but the high tone is retained as part of a glide. This results in sequences of two and even three tones without any lengthening of the final vowel of the verb, adding eight more contrasts to the seven above:

ku hwẽ′ kwí	'it's a knife he bought'
ku hwẽ′ kwī	'it's a millstone he bought'
ku hwẽ′ kwì	'it's a chicken he bought'
ku hwẽ′ꞌ kwì	'it's a gourd he bought'
ku hwẽ̌′ kwí	'it's knives he counted'
ku hwẽ̌′ kwī	'it's millstones he counted'
ku hwẽ̌′ kwì	'it's chickens he counted'
ku hwẽ̌′ꞌ kwì	'it's gourds he counted'

A test has been made, having an informant say about five of these sentences, randomly including examples with one, two, and three tones accompanying the vowel of the verb, one after another. All the sentences were identical in timing. With a pause equivalent to the length of one syllable after each sentence, the list sounded like counting cadence. The conclusion is simply that, in some languages, the scope of tone need not be an entire syllable; sequences of two or more tones may accompany a single syllable.

Incidentally, fifteen more minimally contrasting sentences can be added to the above. If the initial syllable is /kú/, with high tone instead of mid, the sentences mean 'he should buy a knife' rather than 'he bought a knife', etc... Further, all thirty contrasting sentences can be transformed into questions by lengthening the final vowel, with a slight downward glide after high or mid tone. In spite of such an unusual variety of tonal contrasts, I have found Wàpã, of all the languages I have worked with, to be one of the easiest to learn.

4.20. In Dìyī, sequences of two tones with a single short vowel appear under quite different circumstances. There are the same sequences in noun-numeral phrases, but nouns have no initial vowel, and the identification construction found in Wàpã was not recorded. In Wàpã, nouns typically consist of an initial vowel plus a single syllable. In Dìyī, many nouns consist of two syllables, the first of which is clearly cognate with the single syllable in Wàpã. In most such nouns, the final syllable is /rà/ after an oral vowel, and /nà/ after a nasalized vowel. E.g.,

súrà	'yam'	kũnǎ	'knife'
dàrà	'farm'	kũnà	'millstone'
bàrà	'bag'	kǔnǎ	'chicken'

The final syllable in such nouns—and only nouns have such a structure—can readily be analyzed as a suffix, even though it has no grammatical function. Several other nouns consist of one syllable, with a tone falling from high or mid to low, or with low tone alone. The high-low and mid-low glides are interpreted as sequences of tone accompanying a single vowel. E.g.,

bé	'dog'	za	'guinea corn'	bè	'money'
dyî	'dirt'	dyì	'year'	nê	'hoe'

No words other than nouns have high-low or mid-low sequences, and with the exception of a very few kinship terms no one-syllable nouns have high or mid tone without a following low. The low tone can thus be interpreted as a second noun suffix. By analogy, it may be assumed that almost all monosyllabic nouns with low tone (excepting possibly a few kinship terms) are derived from nouns with the same suffix. The two above would be */bè/ and */nê/. The suffix, however, has no vocalic content of its own; it is only a tone following the preceding tone and accompanying the same vowel. The noun /nê/ 'hoe' is homophonous with a verb /nê/ 'boil', which cannot have a suffix in its underlying structure.

Ewe has similar tone sequences with single vowels, involving a noun suffix which consists of high tone. Among terraced level languages, Efik has a falling glide and a rising glide with single vowels, which can with no seeming difficulty be interpreted either as unit tonemes or as high-low and low-high sequences; arguments for the latter are perhaps slightly better.

4.21. In Mano, very much as in Wàpã, the earliest steps in analysis—the elicitation of a number of nouns in isolation and then with a few numerals—again quickly revealed three contrasting levels of pitch. Monosyllabic nouns with each of the three tones were found within the first few minutes of elicitation; hearing them repeated in various orders was like hearing someone play around with the three notes of a major triad; an example of each is:

> gɔ́   'leopard'   fo   'toad'   6ò   'goat'

Disyllabic nouns—with double vowels, vowel sequences, or a second syllable beginning with a consonant, were found to illustrate every possible sequence, though some sequences are much more common than others. E.g.,

yílí	'tree'	kpaá	'rat trap'	6ɔ́ɔ́	'bag'
fɔ́lɔ	'hoe'	mɛnɛ	'moon'	mènɛ	'snake'
gbíyè	'machete'	gbilì	'hamper'	mènè	'tsetse fly'

Comparisons of these tones with the initial tone of a following numeral provided ready confirmation of the preliminary identifications. Convenient numerals are the first five:

Initial high:	sɔ́ɔ́li	'five'
Initial mid:	doó	'one'
Initial low:	pèèlɛ	'two', yììsɛ 'three', yààka 'four'

Various combinations make the sameness of the final tone of a noun and the initial tone of a numeral conspicuous, or provide clearly distinct examples of every possible interval. In short, everything seemed amazingly simple; apart from a few cases of a falling glide which were simply set aside for the moment, and later proved to be best interpreted as a unit toneme, the tonemic inventory of Mano seemed to be comprehensively illustrated.

When the analysis progressed from phrases of the noun-numeral type to short verbal sentences, however, everything seemed to fall apart; in simple subject-object-verb sequences, the final verb did not fit into the tonal framework already established. There appeared to be no final high tone at all; and after some initial confusion about final low tone, a contrast was recognized between a low level pitch and a low falling glide. Ultimately, it became clear that two intonational patterns were involved. Citations in isolation regularly—and unusually as languages go—show the same characteristics as complete utterances which are questions: three truly discrete, invariable pitch levels. In declarative utterances, however, the last tone, or the last sequence of identical tones after a phonemic juncture, is lower than the same tone at any earlier point in the sentence. Final high is at about the level of an earlier mid; final mid is at about the level of an earlier low, level and steady in intensity; final low begins at the level of an earlier low, but falls slightly lower and dies out in intensity. The discrete levels of the earlier part of the sentence tip down, as it were, at the very end. This is quite a different phenomenon, however, from a pattern of descent distributed more or less evenly over an entire utterance. It is simply a phenomenon which must be specially described for Mano and some other languages, superimposed on an otherwise simple discrete level system.

Before full treatments of tone languages were common, some linguists believed that it was impossible for intonational contrasts to be superimposed on a tonal system. The evidence from Mano and Hausa (4.16 above) amply contradicts that assumption. Intonational contrasts, however, usually seem to be restricted to intonations for statements, yes-no questions, and nonfinal clauses. On the other hand, many tone languages do not have intonational contrasts; and it is by no means true that questions in all languages, even those with intonation, involve "raising the voice" at some point in a question. Perhaps the commonest fault among beginning learners of tone languages is to attempt to imitate what was said, but largely ignoring the tones and superimposing on the utterance an Enlish question intonation, as if to ask, "Am I saying it right?"

4.22. Both a problem in the scope of tone, and intonation superimposed on tone, are found in Kpelle (see Welmers 1962, pp. 82-92). Three contrasting levels are readily established, and a falling glide (high to low) also occurs with monosyllables:

ká ˈkὲ	'you (pl.) did it'
ka ˈkὲ	'you (pl.) do it (customarily)'
kà ˈkὲ	'when you (pl.) do it'
kpɔ̀ŋ	'door'

In morphemes of more than one syllable (disyllabic morphemes are predominant, with double vowels, vowel sequences, or a second syllable beginning with a consonant), five pitch sequences are found. For reasons which will be stated after illustrations are given, each of these sequences is interpreted as the realization of a single toneme, whose scope is the entire form. Obviously, the diacritics used to indicate these tonemes are here used rather differently than in transcriptions of other languages. The five sequences are:

High throughout:
      tɛ́ɛ   'chicken'   kɔ́li   'leopard'

Mid throughout:
      taa   'town'   kɔli   'iron'

First syllable high, low thereafter:
      tɔ̂a   'pygmy antelope'   kâli   'hoe'

First syllable mid, high-low thereafter:
      tɛɛ̂   'black duiker'   konâ   'mortar'

Low throughout:
      kpɔ̀o   'padlock'   tòloŋ   'dove'

A phoneme of open transition must be recognized. There is a contrast between /kâli/ 'hoe' and /ká lì/ 'you (pl.) went'; the pitch sequences are identical, but in the latter the second syllable is slightly more prominent. When forms such as those cited above are used in longer utterances, each toneme is assigned to a segment between two open transitions. The tones of monosyllables between open transitions are identified with the first three and the last of the five sequences described above.

When mid is followed by mid or by preconsonantal low after open transition, its allotone is a slight rise spread over the entire scope of mid. (This statement requires slight modification for dialects other than the one used here, but the implications of the allotonics are the same.) Such a rise accompanies the first word in each of the following:

ka kpɔŋ mâ.	'Help me (pl.).'	taa puu	'ten towns'
a 'kè.	'He does it.'	kula 'sù.	'Get out of it.'

Now, when this rising allotone of mid is spread over two or more syllables, as in the forms on the right, it is realized as a slightly higher pitch with the last vowel than with the first. If tones were assigned to individual syllables, there would seem to be no alternative to identifying this higher pitch as a high tone. By analogy, the short rising pitch of a monosyllable in the same environment should then also be analyzed as a sequence of mid-high. Recognizing segments between open transitions as possible scopes for single tonemes obviates this difficulty and simplifies the analysis.

In utterance-final position, high and mid, as well as the beginning of high-low, have slightly lowered allotones after low; the low may be preconsonantal, or may belong to the preceding word. Again, this phenomenon applies throughout the scope assigned to high or mid, which may be more than a single syllable. In the examples below, the lower allotones of high and mid are heard in the phrases on the right:

píli.	'Jump.'	'píli.	'Throw it.'
kula.	'Get out.'	'kula.	'Get it out.'
téɛ lɔ́ɔlu	'five chickens'	konâ lɔ́ɔlu	'five mortars'
taa puu	'ten towns'	tòloŋ puu	'five doves'

Question intonation is superimposed on the last toneme other than low in a sentence, unless all tonemes in the sentence are low. High tone, including the beginning of high-low, is extremely high and tense, often falsetto. Mid tone is a sharp rise to a similar level. (English speaking learners of Kpelle usually use a raised level far too low; in terms of English intonations, Kpelle questions sound astonished or rude.) Any low after this realization of question intonation is just as low as in statement intonation. A question which contains only low tones is pronounced on a very level pitch, with sustained intensity; in a statement with only low tones, there is a slight fall in pitch, and diminished intensity toward the end. Questions provide more examples of the unity of a segment between two open transitions; in the following, question intonation is realized with the single tonemes of such segments (underlined), spread over more than one syllable:

è pà à tɛ́ɛ lɔ́ɔlu ?	'Did he bring five chickens ?'
'káa 'pérɛi mǔ ?	'Is he in the house ?'
'káa nãa ?	'Is he there ?'
í lee è pà ?	'Did your mother come ?'

A disyllabic or longer segment between two open transitions may thus be the domain of a single toneme. Such segments may, however, contain more than one toneme. Initial preconsonantal low tone, or initial high tone with a nasal, may precede any toneme in the rest of the segment; e.g.,

'tóli.	'Call him.'	ńtóli.	'Call me.'

High-low and low may be followed by mid with the final phoneme of the segment (always /i/ or /ŋ/). In this case, the drop in high-low goes down only to mid, and continues at mid through the final phoneme, to which the mid toneme is actually assigned. Final mid is indicated by /⁻/ in the following:

'pâraī	'the swamp'	'tɔnəī	'the chisel'
'tɔ́ŋ̄	'the law'	'tòloŋ̄	'the dove'

High with a scope of more than one syllable may be followed by low with a final vowel (always /i/):

a pílìì	'he is jumping'	a lɛ́ɛì	'he is lying'

And finally, verb phrases like the above may be followed by /ī/; the second of the following examples illustrates the maximum sequence of tonemes between two open transitions, and one of them still has a scope of more than one syllable:

'surɔ́ŋ a pílìī	'the boy who is jumping'
'kənii a 'pílìī	'the stone which he is throwing'

A toneme always begins after the first consonant following open transition. Its scope is up to the next toneme or the next open transition, whichever is first.

4.23. The characteristics of some discrete level systems with three contrasting levels have been described. Systems with four contrasting levels are probably less common, but are clearly established for several languages. Bariba is one of these (see Welmers 1952a), though the Kandi dialect has only three level tonemes, with an allotonic fourth level; four contrasting levels are established for the Nikki and Parakou dialects by a variety of minimal and subminimal pairs. The four levels have been labeled, starting from the lowest, low, mid, high, and top. There is also a rise (from mid to top, or perhaps slightly lower in rapid speech) and a fall (from mid to low after mid, otherwise high to low). The rise and fall accompany short vowels, including one of a sequence of identical vowels. They are perhaps best treated as a unit rising toneme and a unit falling toneme, though the rise is always, and the fall sometimes, morphologically complex; only the fall occurs as part of a stem. In forms with double vowels alone, a variety of sequences illustrates the contrasts; in the following, the unmarked tone is high, and top is marked /'/:

boo	'goat'	yaa	'meat'
bòo	'water pot'	yaá	'there's meat'
bòō	'ulcer'	waā	'snake'
ya wǎǎ	'is there some?'	waǎ	'there's a snake'
ya wâǎ	'is it good?'	dǎǎ	'tree'

All four level tonemes occur in a descending sequence in the sentence /nέ na nā kɔ̀/ 'I am the one who came'.

Preconsonantal nasals are always syllabic and carry a tone. Syllabic /m/ with a tone occurs postvocalically in final position, with the morphophonemic alternant /n/ in utterance-medial position before consonants other than /p, b, m/. There are no nonsyllabic final consonants; in the following examples, an unmarked preconsonantal or final nasal has high tone:

ko n dī	'I'm going to eat'	nέm̀ boo	'my goat'
tìm̄	'medicine'	nέǹ duma	'my horse'
nim	'water'	sέm̀bù	'comb'
na nin takā	'I drew water'	tendu	'bow'

There is no allophonic lowering of tones in final position. Morphophonemically, however, a series of one or more high tones (attested in utterance-medial position) has the alternant mid in final position after low.

4.24. What may have been a *tour de force* in tonal analysis took place on a roadside perhaps fifty miles southeast of Bamenda, Cameroon, about mid-January, 1950. The language is unidentified. We had stopped for lunch out of sight of any habitation, and were standing around the tailgate-cum-lunch-table of our pickup truck, when a woman and a child of perhaps eight came past on foot. With understandable curiosity at this display of foreign culture, the child kept turning to look at us, and fell perhaps fifty feet behind his mother. His mother turned and said something which consisted of four syllables. The first syllable had the lowest pitch; the second was higher; the third was higher than the first but lower than the second; the fourth was the highest of all—in Bariba, the sequence would be low-high-mid-top. I immediately said to my wife, "Behold a language with four tones!" I had reasoned that the circumstance and the child's lack of verbal response made it highly unlikely that the utterance was a question; had it been, the possibility of a rising intonation would have to be considered. More likely the utterance was an imperative; possibly it was a statement. Intonational or allophonic conditioning to account for a pitch sequence of this type seems highly unlikely. It just shows—in all likelihood—how simple tonemic analysis can sometimes be.

Just a few weeks earlier, under more serious and scientific circumstances, Ndoro had proven to have a discrete level system with four tones. First several

nouns were elicited in isolation, with somewhat inconclusive results; three tone
levels were obvious, but four were possible. Then the informant was asked to
count from one through five. Four seconds and five short words later, it was
obvious that four tones had to be recognized; the next-to-last level was reminiscent
of a beginner on the trumpet accidentally playing a note two steps higher than
expected:

[yɛɛrì] — [hààlā] — [tāārā] — [nyǣǣ] — [sóónɪ]

[⁻_] 　 [_-] 　 [— -] 　 [—-] 　 [　 ⁻]

Hearing the series said twice in succession confirmed that the pitch at the end of
'five' was precisely the same as that at the beginning of 'one'. Further comparisons of the tones of nouns with those of numerals, and of tones in a variety of
utterances, readily confirmed this analysis. Unfortunately, the few hours available with a speaker of Ndoro did not permit a full analysis of the segmental
phonemes, but confirmed tonal contrasts are illustrated in the following, the transcription of which is otherwise tentative; again the next-to-highest tone is unmarked:

símá	'adze'	mōŋɪ	'farm'
čarɪ	'axe'	ʔwɛ̄rá	'pot'
čēlā	'stone'	šìɛ̀	'dog'
šòrà	'chicken'	kumù	'chief'
bìæ	'baboon'	tanā	'house'

A procedure for testing is illustrated by the following series of phrases and
what each confirms:

sím sóónɪ	'five adzes'	(top same as top)
čar sóónɪ	'five axes'	(high lower than top)
čar tāārā	'three axes'	(high higher than mid)
čēl tāārā	'three stones'	(mid same as mid)
šòr tāārā	'three chickens'	(low lower than mid)

The four contrasting levels are equally clear in final position after the sequence mid-high:

mə̄ ʔi símá	'I have an adze'
mə̄ ʔi čarɪ	'I have an axe'
mə̄ ʔi čēlā	'I have a stone'
mə̄ ʔi čòrà	'I have a chicken'

Twenty-six verbs were recorded in monosyllabic forms which appear to be
allomorphs of stems, in some cases without a stem-final consonant which appears
before a vowel suffix. Of the twenty-six monosyllables, ten were recorded with
low tone, three with mid, thirteen with high, and none with top. A restriction
of this type is attested in several languages in more than one branch of the Niger-

Congo sub-family. Jukun (both Wàpã and Dìyī) has three level tones, but verb stems have only low or mid tone. Another case is noted below.

4.25. Another four-tone system is found in Tigong.[6] In this case, the four levels quickly became conspicuous when singular and plural forms of nouns were compared. Most plurals have a prefix /e-/, with the next-to-highest tone, providing a convenient frame for recognizing the following tone as higher, same, or lower; other tests were found for distinguishing the (lower) mid from low, though the contrast was not hard to hear in any case. In addition, many noun stems have a tone one step higher in the plural than in the singular, while others have a tone one step lower in the plural than in the singular; some stems show no tonal alternation, and there is frequently a vowel alternation as well. A comparison of singular and plural forms spoken in immediate succession thus provides a wide variety of sub-minimal pairs illustrating the four contrasting levels. Plural forms and singular-plural pairs illustrating the tones are as follows; again, the analysis of the segmental phonemes is tentative in some details:

efíkpí	'axes'	venyī, evényi	'elephant(s)'
esye	'holes'	bwā, ebwa	'chimpanzee(s)'
enwā	'men'	kwê̌, ekwē̄	'mountain(s)'
ekì	'canoes'	yu, eyī	'millstone(s)'
kpī, ekpī	'tree(s)'	jõ, ejê̌	'house(s)'

The fact that the vowels of plurals are recorded in some cases as the same as the vowels of the singulars in tone, in some cases higher, and in some cases lower, may lead to the suspicion that the recording was not entirely accurate, rather than that the language actually has such complications. Apart from an assurance that the investigator's hearing, transcription, and reproduction of tone are unusually reliable, it is fortunate that almost every singular-plural pair (over fifty) was recorded independently on two different occasions, probably for the most part on different days; the independent transcriptions are identical in every case but one. In addition, I had the opportunity to check a number of the crucial pairs myself.

4.26. In Kutep, four-syllable sentences with a tone sequence like that heard in the unidentified Cameroon language have been recorded (see Welmers 1956). For example:

 m̀ nuŋ kūsók.   'I saw a house.

Four contrasting levels are amply attested from other data as well. The distribution of tones with stems, however, is peculiar. Most nouns consist of a prefix and a monosyllabic stem. For most nouns, the prefix has low tone in initial position or after low, but mid after other tones. A few nouns have a prefix with high tone. Noun stems have low, mid, or top tone—never high. An example of each possibility, with a sentence showing how the tones were tested, is:

[6] Data gathered in December, 1949, by Beatrice F. Welmers.

ùswàm	'baboon':	ū nuŋ ūswàm	'he saw a baboon'
ìyāk	'buffalo':	ū nuŋ īyāk	'he saw a buffalo'
ìwák	'fish':	ū nuŋ īwák	'he saw a fish'

Verb stems, on the other hand, have low, mid, or high tone, but not top. An example of each is:

ū ku yě ùyín	'he is crossing the river'
ū ku rū	'he is going'
ū ku ba	'he is coming'

Taking either verbs or nouns by themselves, therefore, one would soon judge that Kutep has three tone levels. But the levels in nouns and in verbs are not the same; when tones are compared even in short utterances containing both verbs and nouns, four tones must be recognized.

Some years after working out this analysis of Kutep, I began to question its validity in the light of newer discoveries about the variety of tonal systems in African languages. In the early 1960's, however, I had the opportunity to check on the analysis with a missionary who had learned something about linguistics and an informant who was himself remarkably sophisticated. They had no doubt, and left me with none, that the analysis and the statements on the tones of noun and verb stems are competely valid.

4.27. The tonal system of Yoruba warrants special attention. In most dialects, there is a phenomenon which might be interpreted as a phonemic downstep, but which is more conveniently treated as a fusion of low and mid (in a three-level system). In addition, a rising glide is interpreted as an allotone of high if low precedes, but as a sequence or fusion of low and high in other environments.

In the simplest two-syllable utterances, nine tonal sequences are readily found. Seven of these are sequences of level pitches showing clear contrasts of high, mid, and low. Two of the nine possible sequences of levels do not occur: *low-high and *high-low. There is, however, a sequence of low and a rising glide, and a sequence of high and a falling glide. These sequences may be interpreted tonemically as low-high and high-low respectively. Thus a rising glide is the allotone of high after low, and a falling glide is the allotone of low after high. The facts up to this point are summarized in the chart below. Mid tone is unmarked. Word division does not represent anything phonemic. Glosses are given in a separate and parallel chart in order to preserve the graphic value of the Yoruba forms and representations of their tones.

	H—	M—	L—
—H:	ó wá [⁻ ⁻]	ajá [– ⁻]	ìwé [_ /]
—M:	ó lọ [⁻ –]	ẹja [– –]	àga [_ –]
—L:	ó wà [⁻ \]	iyọ̀ [– _]	ìlù [_ _]
	'he came'	'dog'	'book'
	'he went'	'fish'	'chair'
	'he is (there)'	'salt'	'drum'

This much analysis is adequate to account for all of the tonal contrasts of Yoruba at the lexical level. It is also all that was reported about Yoruba tone until relatively recently; as with other languages, a common practice has been to overlook tone totally in contexts larger than single words—if, indeed, it is noted even there. Yoruba is one of the rare African languages for which tone marking has been learned by a substantial number of native speakers, but again only lexical tone, as summarized above, is taught and learned.

One detail was omitted from the description above, which is related to the analysis of tone in longer sequences. Mid tone after low is slightly lower than in other environments. This seems natural enough, and at the lexical level is hardly worth mentioning. In longer sequences, such a lower allotone of mid is most noticeable in final position. For example, in the following two sentences the second tone—mid in both, but after high in the first and after low in the second—is commonly pronounced, and is always acceptable, at the same pitch; but the final mid tone is always lower than the mid of the second syllable:

ó ra àga   'he bought a chair'
kò ra àga   'he didn't buy a chair'

Thus the allotonic lowering of mid after low is not entirely parallel to "automatic downstep" or "downdrift" in terraced level languages. It is not confined to final position, as might be suggested by the above illustrations, but neither is it obligatory in every occurrence of the sequence low-mid. Toward the beginning of fairly long utterances, the lowering of mid after low is optional, or at least very slight. At the same time, the potential for such a lowering proves to be most important for the analysis of another phenomenon in the Yoruba tonal system.

The numeral 'one', in a form used nominally, is /ɔ̀kan/. When used attributively after a noun, the initial vowel of this form does not appear. However, the tone of the final syllable is the lower mid level which is elsewhere conditioned by the presence of a preceding low. If the preceding noun ends with low, the lower mid level of /kan/ can be explained as the usual conditioned lowering. But if the preceding noun ends with mid or high, the tone of the numeral contrasts with what has already been established as mid. In all three of the following examples, the final tone is slightly lower than the initial tone; in the first example, this is interpreted as conditioned by the preceding low, but in the second and third it is contrastive, and here indicated by a macron:

ẹtù kan   'one guinea fowl'
ẹja kān   'one fish'
ajá kān   'one dog'

After mid or high, the tone of the numeral can be interpreted as a fusion of low and mid; that is, both the low and mid tonemes are present, simultaneously. Morphophonemically, this is obviously attractive: the low tone which in other contexts precedes the numeral stem is transferred to the stem itself; its presence is apparent in its conditioning effect, though its own pitch combines with the usual pitch of mid to result in a compromise between them. Phonemically, this interpretation is strengthened by two further considerations.

First, there is a close parallel involving the sequence low-high. The demonstrative 'this' has a nominal form /èyí/, in which the second tone has the normal rising allotone of high after low. When used attributively after a noun, the initial vowel of this form does not appear. The tone of the final syllable remains a rise, starting at the level of low. If the preceding noun ends with low, this rise can be explained as the usual allotone of high. But if the preceding noun ends with mid or high, the rise is contrastive. In all three of the following examples, the tone of the last syllable is rising; in the first, this is interpreted as conditioned by the preceding low, but in the second and third it is contrastive, and here indicated by a wedge:

ẹtù yí	'this guinea fowl'
ẹja yǐ	'this fish'
ajá yǐ	'this dog'

After mid or high, the tone of the demonstrative is interpreted as a sequence or fusion of low and high; that is, both the low and high tonemes are present.

Second, a comparison of other dialects reinforces this interpretation. Other numerals provide a convenient illustration. One form of 'three' used in counting is /ẹ̀ta/; the corresponding form of 'ten' is /ẹ̀wá/. Attributive forms of these numerals add a prefix which may be symbolized as /m'-/. The resultant forms in the dialects considered up to now are /mẹ́tā/ and /mẹ́wǎ/. In some other dialects, however, the low tone attested in the counting form is not transferred to the numeral stem, but is simply retained; the resultant forms are /mẹ́ẹ̀ta/ and /mẹ́ẹ̀wá/. A similar situation is found in the negative imperative of verbs. For the verbs /lọ/ 'go' and /wá/ 'come', the negative imperatives in the dialect under consideration are /má lọ/ and /má wǎ/; but in other dialects the forms are /máà lọ/ and /máà wá/.

This is, of course, a classic problem of neutralization and phonemic intersection. Two levels between high and low contrast after high or mid, but not after low; high and rise contrast after high or mid, but not after low. The above interpretation is presented as a legitimate and defensible one, but not necessarily as the only possible one. An alternative description would state that high and mid simply do not occur after low, but that rise and lower mid (treated as unit tonemes rather than sequences or fusions in this interpretation) do. Apart from one's theoretical preference or bias, it is clear that this interpretation would also simplify the description of the limited number of examples cited above. It would, however, introduce an incomparably greater complexity throughout the morphotonemics of the rest of the language. At the purely pragmatic level, it may be added that both interpretations have been tested; both native speakers and English-speaking learners find the interpretation outlined in the preceding paragraphs far easier to work with.

The lower level of mid after low in Yoruba resembles the downstep of a terraced level language in that—at least in relatively short utterances—it becomes
the point of reference for following tones. Yoruba is not characterized as a terraced level language, however, because it can be described in terms of three non-
overlapping levels and certain clusters of these; the basically relational terminology required for a terraced level system is inappropriate.

In isolation and in final position, low tones in Yoruba are short falling glides,
giving the impression that the pitch is "pushed" to low. Low tone is also very
commonly associated with a creaky voice quality—so much so that native speakers
of Yoruba have sometimes interpreted a habitually creaky voice in an American
learner as signalling low tone even when the pitch relationships represented an
adequate imitation of mid and high.

4.28. As has been noted above (4.14), some dialects of Ewe have a phonemic
downstep, while others do not. Apart from this downstep, three pitch levels are
clearly distinguishable, phonetically, in both types of dialects. The distribution
of the mid and low levels, however, is such that the reality of a phonemic contrast
between mid and low may be questioned. In noun stems, mid and low are clearly
in complementary distribution in terms of stem-initial consonants. In verb stems
and at least the vast majority of other morphemes, mid and low are in complementary distribution in terms of adjacent tones. The difference between the
conditioning factors for noun stems and other morphemes suggests that it should
be possible to find some syllable sequences, with different morphemic composition, in which mid and low contrast. In fact, however, the conditions interlock
in such a way that contrasts are rare, and perhaps never minimal.

Three classes of consonants may be distinguished in Ewe, differing in the
way in which they condition tone in noun stems and a noun prefix:

A.	Voiced stops and fricatives:					
	b	d	d	dz	g	gb
	ʋ	v		z	h	
B.	Voiceless stops and fricatives:					
		t		ts	k	kp
	ʃ	f		s	x	
C.	Resonants and nasals:					
	w	l	y	ɣ		
	m	n	ny	ŋ		

The three recognizable pitch levels will tentatively be called tones. In utterance final position or before low tone, only high and low tone occur. Before
mid or high tone, however, all three levels occur; the tones of noun stems are
identified in this environment. All noun stems that have low tone begin with consonants of class A, and conversely all noun stems that begin with consonants of
class A have low tone. Noun stems with mid or high tone begin with consonants
of class B or C; at this point, class B and C are not yet distinguished by their tonal

conditioning. Examples of monosyllabic nouns, as they appear before mid or high tone, are:

dà	'snake'	ka	'rope'	kpé	'stone'
dzè	'salt'	nyi	'cow'	yí	'machete'
gà	'money'	tsi	'water'	só	'horse'

Many nouns have a vowel prefix; apart from tone, the vowel is always /a/. Before stems with low tone, the tone of the prefix is always low. Before stems with mid or high tone, the tone of the prefix is, in one dialect with which I have done some work, always mid; in another dialect, however, it is low before consonants of class B, and mid before consonants of class C. Examples from the latter dialect are:

àgà	'cliff'	àfi	'mouse'	àfí	'ashes'
àgbà	'load'	àsi	'market'	àtí	'tree'
àhà	'palm wine'	awu	'dress'	anyí	'mud'

In verb stems, high contrasts with non-high irrespective of stem-initial consonants. In final position and before low tone, only high and low occur; examples are:

dí	'want'	ɗà	'cook'
dzrá	'sell'	dzè	'split'
tó	'pound'	tɔ̀	'fry'
yɔ́	'call'	yì	'go'

Before mid or high tone, nonhigh tone with verb stems is low or mid following the same rule as for the noun prefix described above, and mid before a noun prefix with mid. Before the verb, a subject pronoun with non-high tone has the same tone as the verb stem. Thus, in a typical subject-verb-object sequence (and also in more complex sequences by further applications of the same rules), there is a chain of conditions for the choice of mid or low at any point, as long as the distinction between noun stems and other morphemes is recognized.

The same rules require, however, that there must be a contrast between low-high and mid-high, with consonants in each position belonging to the same class, in combinations like the following:

| àgà lá | 'the cliff' |
| eɗe yí | 'you picked up a machete' |

Presumably the above might be complete utterances under unusual circumstances, and minimal pairs might possibly be found, but in ordinary speech such contrasts are in the nature of the case extremely rare in compared utterances.

Other morphological conditioning of tonal alternations provides some other contrasts between low and mid. For all verb stems, the imperative is low no matter what follows; a monosyllabic noun beginning with a consonant of class B or C may have mid tone before mid or high. Thus the following contrast:

tsɔ̀ yí	'pick up a machete'
tsi lá	'the water'

In a dialect which does not have downstep, mid tone is recorded in final position, and before low, in two demonstrative stems. With what appears to be a prefix which does not appear when these are used attributively after a noun, they are /ésia/ 'this' and /éma/ 'that'. In a dialect which does have downstep, the stem of the first of these can be interpreted as beginning with a downstep and having high tone; this level is identical with a preceding mid. In the same dialect, the second of these demonstratives is simply high-high.

In the dialect with downstep, a minimal contrast is recorded between the following:

metɔ akɔdú	'I fried bananas'
mètɔ akɔdú	'you didn't fry bananas'

In the dialect without downstep, however, the second of these is recorded with a rise from low to high accompanying the first syllable; this may be interpreted as /m̀étɔ akɔdú/.

Not all of the details of the Ewe tonal system have been exhausted by the foregoing description—and, indeed, my own experience with the language has been too limited to make complete statements. It is clear, however, that any taxonomic or neotaxonomic treatment must recognize three tonemes. On the other hand, almost all choices between mid and low are determined if grammatical as well as phonological conditions are taken into account. It would appear that a generative treatment of the Ewe tonal system—or rather, systems—would more elegantly reflect the structure of the language.[7]

4.29. Some other languages clearly show dialect differences in their tonal systems. Although the evidence is not entirely clear, Edo (Bini) may be one of them. Ernest F. Dunn (1968) has described the tonal system as having two tones and a lowering of high tone after low (downdrift); his description suggests that he has listened carefully for other alternatives, and it may be valid for the dialect with which he worked. I had previously worked on Edo on two different occasions, with two different informants; unfortunately, I had little more than a few hours with each, and was unable to work out a satisfactory description of the tonal system, but I was reasonably certain that there was more to the system than two tones and downdrift. More recently, with a third informant, I have been able to reach more definite conclusions. I report that Edo, at least as I have heard it, has a terraced-level tonal system, but with a most unusual feature. Throughout most of an utterance, the usual high and low tones, as well as occasional rising and falling tones, and a clear phonemic downstep can be identified. With a clause-final (prepausal) syllable after high, however, there are two contrasting down-stepped levels, as well as high without downstep and low. The more common of

---

[7] An excellent treatment of at least most of the data for one dialect, too recent to be fully discussed here, is found in Stahlke (1971).

these, the derivation of which is usually easy to explain, is unusually low, and may
well be mistaken for a low tone at first; it is, however, noticeably more tense than
low, and level in pitch rather than having the slight down-glide and progressive
relaxation of a final low tone. This large-interval downstep is marked /'/ in the
following:

ὲwé   'goat' :   ì dέ'wé   'I bought a goat'

The small-interval downstep, which is much more like the downstep of most
other terraced-level systems, is recorded primarily in a limited number of grammatical constructions, but the conditions for its appearance have not been fully
defined. It is marked /ᵛ/ in the following:

ʋɔ́ré   'when he came' :   ɔ́ ná ᵛré   'if he comes'

The two downsteps are in clear contrast in the following:

ὲmíɔ́'wó   'money'   ìɣúᵛhṹ   'taxes'

In other than clause-final position, a downstep is very much like in other
languages. One detail not attested in other languages is the occurrence of a glide
from high to downstep-high accompanying a single short vowel. In the following,
the first downstep is a very small interval, the second much larger:

ɔ́ ná''ré 'ʋá   'he was already there'

A single low tone, initially or between two high tones, is usually higher than
a clause-final large-interval downstep-high. A sequence of two or more low tones,
however, is lower than anything else in the clause. In any case, a low tone can
always be identified as low by the fact that a higher pitch occurs later in the same
clause, or, in final position, by the slight downward glide and dying out of the
voice.

A remarkable parallel to the two contrasting downsteps with clause-final syllables in Edo is found in another language in the same group, Urhobo (Welmers
1969a). Throughout most of an utterance, tones can readily be identified as high,
low, rising, and falling. There is no appreciable downdrift, and the system would
seem to be a fairly simple discrete-level system with two tones and probably two
clusters of tones. In clause-final position, however, and only after high, there are
three contrasting levels: high, low, and an intermediate level which can validly
be called mid in this system. In disyllabic nouns in isolation, the sequence high-
mid is considerably more common than high-high or high-low, though low-high
is about as common, and low-low even more so. These five sequences, which are
usually characteristic of terraced-level systems rather than of the system found
in the rest of Urhobo utterances, are illustrated by the following:

úkó   'cup'   òzé   'basin'
ébò   'bag'   àgà   'chair'
         íwē   'thorn'

If a noun with high-mid in isolation is used in other than clause-final position is, it has the tones high-low in all recorded cases.

It would obviously be interesting to study the tonal systems of other Urhobo dialects, and other languages in the Edo group.

4.30. The occurrence of both intonation and tone in a single language has already been noted. The question should also be raised as to whether a tone language may also have phonemic stress. As far as Africa is concerned, no language has been reliably reported to have both tone and stress in the phonemic system. Syllable prominence or phonetic stress may be conditioned by tone. In Kpelle, the tonemes high throughout, first syllable high and low thereafter, and low throughout have initial stress. First syllable mid and high-low thereafter is stressed at the high point. In mid throughout, no syllable is appreciably more prominent than any other.

In Jukun, in some similar short sentences with only mid tones, I recorded different apparent stress sequences within a few minutes from the same speaker; e.g., [ku ri ˌsa buˌso] and [ˌku ri sa ˌbuso], both glossed as 'he is working', I reproduced each and asked if there was any difference in meaning. The informant assured me that there was no difference (to him) even in sound.

4.31. Since so little has been reported even on lexical tone in most African languages, it is natural that hardly anything has been said about tone in comparative linguistic studies. Tones are phonemes just as consonants and vowels are, and where data is available it is possible to establish regular correspondences in tone as well as in other phonemes. In three Southwestern Mande languages, for example, two readily attested correspondences are:

	Kpelle	*Loma*	*Mende*
*high-high:	high . . .	high-high	high-high
*low-high:	mid . . .	high-high	low-high

A few representative examples (out of scores recorded for each correspondence) are:

	Kpelle	Loma	Mende
'house':	pérɛ	pélé	pélé
'medicine':	sále	sálé	hálé
'cook':	ɣíli	gílí	ŋgílí
'path':	pere	pélé	pèlé
'town':	taa	táá	tàá
'tie':	ɣiri	gílí	ŋgìlí

Unfortunately, in comparative as well as descriptive studies, tone has sometimes been treated as if it has some special status in its own right. In an article that has even been cited as a promising beginning in the use of tone in comparative studies, M. M. Green (1949) makes a completely typological comparison of tone in Yoruba, Igbo, and Efik. Her conclusion (which happens to be correct, but for totally different reasons) is that Igbo and Efik are more closely related to each other than either is to Yoruba. To establish such a classification, she suggests that "we need to know (a) the number of essential tone levels in any one language; (b) whether semantic or lexical tone exists; (c) whether what might be called dynamic or relational tone exists, and if so whether or not this tone system is grammatical." In more familiar terminology, "dynamic or relational tone" refers to morphotonemic alternations and/or morphemes whose only phonological realization is tonal; such phenomena are "grammatical" if tonally realized morphemes are included.

It requires little reflection to realize that none of these criteria is relevant in a comparative study. The number of "essential tone levels" (tonemes) may differ in mutually intelligible dialects of the same language (e.g., Bariba), or may be the same in completely unrelated languages (e.g., Loma and Hausa). Are we to set up three language "families" in Africa depending on whether a language has two, three, or four tonemes? There is, of course, no more reason for basing classificatory hypotheses on the number of tonemes in the languages being studied than on the number of consonant or vowel phonemes they have. Nor does the presence or absence of a phonemic downstep tell us anything conclusive about language relationships. One dialect of Yala has a downstep, while other mutually intelligible dialects do not; the same is true for Ewe and Dyimini. But in either type of dialect these three languages are by no means closely related.

The existence of lexical tone as a classificatory criterion is even more easily dismissed; it is highly dubious that there is any tone language in Africa which does not have lexical tone—tone as a constituent part of morphemes which also contain consonants and vowels, especially in major form classes.

Morphotonemic alternations, whether phonologically or morphologically conditioned, are also very nearly universal in African tone languages; I cannot cite any for Jukun, but they are commonplace in most languages. Further, the complexity of morphotonemic alternations may vary widely in closely related languages; Suppire has an unusually complex set in object-verb sequences, while Senari, barely beyond the bounds of mutual intelligibility, has nothing of the same type. Again, of course, there is no more significance for comparative purposes in the mere existence of morphotonemic alternations than there is in consonantal or vocalic alternations. The occurrence of the same alternation under the same conditions in two languages may, of course, be important, since it may reflect a shared development.

The presence of morphemes whose only realization is tonal—whether by prefixation, suffixation, or replacement of a lexical tone—is also attested in virtually every African tone language. In some languages (e.g., Jukun and Yoruba) there are relatively few such morphemes; in others (e.g., Efik) there are many more. In Kpelle, tonal morphemes are an important part of the grammatical system; in Loma, quite closely related, the same grammatical distinctions are made by suffixes which are not exclusively tonal. The presence or absence of tonal morphemes is no more significant for comparative studies than the presence or absence of ordinary prefixes or suffixes.

Green is critical of "the tendency, in much language classification, to stress questions of vocabulary rather than of grammar." Yet no comparativist has ignored affixes, which have a "grammatical" function, and concentrated exclusively on stems, which are "lexical," given available data. The insistence has simply been on comparing specific morphemes in terms of both form and meaning. Where Green's argument is strongest, she does precisely that. Igbo and Efik have somewhat similar tonal manifestations of an "associative" morpheme. Actually, as Green does not note, an associative morpheme in Yoruba is also realized tonally, but admittedly in a somewhat different way. This may well be valid evidence for a closer relationship between Igbo and Efik than between either of them and Yoruba, but Green does not recognize the evidence for what it is; she rather treats it as typological data, which is of little use in comparative linguistics.

It has been the purpose of this chapter to outline the types of tonal systems and tonal phenomena that are found in African languages, irrespective of language relationships, largely on the phonological level. It has been convenient and perhaps necessary to mention instances of restricted tonal distribution, morphotonemic alternations, and morphemes actualized only as tone, but this has been only incidental to the description of tonemic systems as such. A more detailed discussion of these topics is presented in the following chapter. The crucial assumption underlying all that has been and will be said is that tonal systems, like consonant and vowel systems, are simply part of phonological systems. This is as true for comparative studies as it is for descriptive studies. Tonemes enter into regular correspondences, as illustrated for Southwestern Mande above, just as other phonemes do. Comparative linguistics and language classification will be served by investigating such correspondences in specific morphemes in related languages.

Chapter 5

Functions of Tone

5.1. It is inherent in every proposed definition of a tone language that at least one of the functions of tone is to participate in distinguishing different lexical items in a language from each other. Commonly, there are some pairs or sets of words in which tone is minimally contrastive—that is, the consonants and vowels in such words are identical, and the words differ from each other only in tone. In Jukun, for example, minimal pairs are abundant, and sets of three or even four words showing minimal contrasts in tone are recorded; e.g., in Wàpã:

akwí	'knife'	akwì	'chicken'
akwī	'millstone'	àkwì	'gourd'

In Igala, a six-way minimal contrast is reported (by Raymond O. Silverstein, private communication):

áwó	'guinea fowl'	àwó	'a slap'
áwo	'an increase'	àwo	'a comb'
áwò	'hole (in a tree)'	àwò	'star'

In nontechnical references to tone language, one is frequently told that there are some words which can be pronounced with two or three different tones or tone sequences to give them different meanings. In the written forms of most African languages, tone is not indicated, and it is assumed that a "word" is a sequence of consonants and vowels. Thus sets of forms like the above are considered to be one "word" each; in speech, those mysterious things called tones are superimposed on one such word, and it comes out with four or six different meanings. Even in some dictionaries in which tone is marked, sets like the above are listed as numbered subentries under a single main entry, which consists of consonants and vowels only (e.g., Bargery 1934, Abraham 1940a). All of this misses the elementary principle that words in a language are not letters on a page, and that tones are phonemes just as consonants and vowels are. Lexical items that differ only in tone are just as much different words as items that differ in any other way.

5.2. Although minimal contrasts in tone can usually be found in a tone language, and are a convenient and convincing way to illustrate tonemic contrasts, they are not essential to identifying a language as tonal. Nor should it be assumed, if minimal contrasts are not found in a given language, that that language is not tonal. If words with the same number of syllables can be divided into two or more sets, such that each set, in a given environment (citation in isolation included), is characterized by a particular pitch or sequence of pitches different from

116

that of the other sets, and if there are no reasonably definable conditioning factors that can be said to determine the differences in pitch, then there are tonemic contrasts. Data like the following from Igbo are sufficient to establish tonemic contrasts even though no minimal pairs are included:

ọ̀kà	'corn'	éwú	'goat'	àkwá	'egg'
úlọ̀	'house'	ákpụ́	'cassava'	ìkó	'cup'
ézì	'pig'	ócé	'chair'	ọ̀sá	'squirrel'
		ìtè	'pot'	é'gó	'money'
		àkpà	'bag'	ọ́'jí	'kola nut'
		ùdọ̀	'rope'	á'gụ́	'leopard'

There are no systematic restrictions on the co-occurrence of any pitch sequence with particular vowels or particular types of consonants. Tone must be recognized as an essential ingredient of each word. Apart from minimal pairs, changing the tones that accompany a given segmental sequence does not produce a different recognizable word; it simply produces no word at all. In terms of the definition of a tone language proposed in the preceding chapter, tones as well as consonants and vowels enter into the composition of these forms.

Perhaps there is no tone language which is completely devoid of minimal contrasts in tone at the lexical level. There are, however, many languages in which such minimal contrasts are far from numerous. Minimal pairs are uncommon in many Bantu languages, in Akan, and in Hausa. In Baule, hundreds of words were transcribed before the first minimal contrast in tone was found, although tonemic contrasts had been established long before. In some other languages—Yoruba and Jukun are good examples—minimal contrasts in tone are exceedingly common. As will be seen, however, tone contrasts may be other than "lexical" in the narrow sense, and minimal contrasts between utterances may be common and crucial even though such contrasts between lexemes in identical environments may be rare.

Beginners in tone languages frequently ask whether a systematic correlation between tone and semantic categories is ever found. That is, in a given language, do nouns that share a common semantic feature, such as perhaps terms for animals or large objects, tend to have the same tones? The answer is simply no. A few minimally contrastive pairs in Jukun show some semantic similarity, as /tè/ 'push' and /te/ 'press', but a comparison of all such pairs shows no common semantic distinction (such as 'more intensive action' for low tone) that correlates with the tonal distinction. There are so many minimal pairs in Jukun that a few such coincidences can be expected. There is no reason to expect a correlation of this type; we do not look for semantic correlates with particular initial consonants and the like. Once more, tones are phonemes like consonants and vowels. (A special case of partial sound-meaning correlation involves what has been called "phonaesthemes," e.g. the frequency of initial /sn/ in English words alluding in some way to the nose: snout, snort, sniff, snob (with upturned nose), etc. There may very well be a comparable correlation of tone and meaning at this level in some languages, particularly in words known as "ideophones". See 15.4.)

It has been an exceedingly common practice in writing African languages to leave tone unmarked unless a minimal contrast is involved so that the reader would have to guess which of two possible alternatives is intended. This may be acceptable when writing only for readers who are native speakers of the language; it is generally comparable to leaving stress unmarked in written English. This procedure, however, assumes that the writer is aware of every possible minimal contrast in the language, and even then the writing system is full of special rules; in practice, this has rarely if ever been done with any consistency. For the analyst and language learner, of course, full and consistent marking of all tones is essential —and virtually every written African language sooner or later receives the attention of analysts and learners. It has proven far too easy to underestimate the importance of indicating tone. In recording a Bassa (of Liberia) reading of a portion of the Bible for broadcast purposes, it was noted that, no matter who the reader was, he could record only one sentence at a time; for each sentence, he had to experiment with various combinations of tone before settling on a combination that seemed the most reasonable. (In languages with very little written material available, apparent reading out loud may be deceptive; many people are known to have memorized everything that has been printed.)

5.3. In a given language, the function of tone in making lexical distinctions may differ for different classes of morphemes. In Kpelle, for example, there are numerous minimal contrasts in tone among nouns, and between nouns and verb stems; but no two verb stems differ from each other only in tone, except that in dialects which have /l/ but no /r/ the verbs /ɣíli/ 'cook' and /ɣíri/ 'tie' contrast in tone only. As has already been noted, the distribution of tones in nouns and verbs differs in several languages. In Baule, there are tonal contrasts (rarely minimal) between nouns, but, as reported to me, all verbs with the same syllable structure have the same tone or tones.

In Akan, rather closely related to Baule, a somewhat similar situation obtains. In Fante, a distinction between low and high in monosyllabic verbs appears only in some verbal constructions; e.g., /yɛ̀/ in /ɔ̀béyɛ̀ .../ 'it's going to be ...', but /bá/ in /ɔ̀bébá/ 'he's going to come'. In other constructions, all monosyllabic verbs have either high or low tone. Disyllabic verb stems are of two types; their tones are conditioned by the syllable structure. If the first vowel of the stem is a high vowel (/i, ɪ, u, ʊ/), and if the second vowel follows immediately or after a resonant or nasal, the tones of the stem are low-high. If either of these conditions is not met, the tones of the stem are high-low. E.g.,

bʊ̀á	'help'	kásà	'speak'
pìrá	'hurt'	bísà	'ask'
kyìréw	'write'	nántìw	'walk'
fʊ̀ná	'tire'	páà	'split'

In some constructions, each of these types of stems has other tones, but tone is not lexically significant for disyllabic verb stems.

In ChiNyanja also, all verb forms with the same number of syllables have the same tones in any given construction (see Harding 1966), but there is evidence of considerable dialect variation in the rules for verb tones.[1] Urhobo also has no lexical tone in verbs, and this may be true of many more Niger-Congo languages.

In sum, tone has a lexical function in every known tone language, but the details of this function vary considerably from language to language.

5.4. Like consonants and vowels, tones also participate in morphophonemic alternations, which in the case of tone may be called morphotonemic. Beginning learners are sometimes discouraged when they discover that a given word does not always have the same tones, and indeed the morphotonemic rules in some languages are rather complex. But they are none the less rules. The restricted variations that result from morphotonemic alternations do not provide an excuse for using just any tone; it does not follow from the fact that variation exists that the wrong variant in a given environment is unimportant for comprehension.

Morphotonemic alternation may be phonologically conditioned in fairly simple ways. In Bariba, there are five such alternations; the first three are instances of dissimilation, while the last two are instances of assimilation (for the system of tone marking, see 4.23):

(1) High has the alternant top before low:

na tasu dūūrā	'I planted yams'
na tasú dùùrè	'I plant yams'

(2) In the sequence low-mid (attested in phrase-final position), mid has the alternant low before any tone other than low:

kpèrū	'a stone'
na kpèrù sūā	'I picked up a stone'

(3) In the same sequence low-mid, mid has the alternant high before low:

gònā	'a guinea fowl'
gòna yèní	'that guinea fowl'

(4) In the sequence high-mid, high has the alternant top after top:

naā	'a cow'
nén náā	'my cow'

(5) A sequence of one or more high tones has the alternant mid after low in phrase final position:

na bòra buā	'I broke a stick'
bòrā	'a stick'

In alternations of this sort, it is not always immediately apparent which alternant is to be considered the underlying or basic form, and which the product of morphotonemic alternation. In the first four of the above alternations, the form considered basic is the form which occurs in isolated citation; this is by far the commonest situation, but it is by no means invariable. In the last of the above, the form considered basic occurs only if something else follows. This analysis is made on the principle of maximum variation. In isolation or in phrase-final posi-

---

[1] Informants used by Beatrice F. Welmers, 1969-70, differ considerably in their tones.

tion, /kpèrū/ (2), gònā (3), and /bɔ̀rā/ (5) have the same tones. They also have the same tones before low (3 and 5). Before a tone other than low, however, there is a contrast; the forms are, respectively, /kpèrù/, /gònà/, but /bɔ̀ra/. Thus, for either the first two or the third, or perhaps for both, the form which occurs before a tone other than low must be considered basic. However, the low-low of the first two in this position cannot be taken as basic for another reason. In phrase-final position or in isolation, these forms have low-mid, but there are other forms which, in contrast, have low-low; /kpèrū/ and /gònā/ contrast with forms like /yàrì/ 'throw away (habitual)'. This establishes low-mid as the basic tones of these two nouns. (Low-low is recorded in only one noun in isolation; this may be an error in transcription. There are, however, some three-syllable nouns with low-low-low in isolation, contrasting with low-low-mid.)

To word this argument differently, if it is assumed that the isolation forms /kpèrū, gònā, bɔ̀rā/ are all basic, then the difference in tone between the first two and the third before a tone other than low can be explained only on the basis of lexical rather than phonological conditioning. But if the low-low of the first two in this position is considered basic, then the contrasting tone of some verb forms in final position must involve lexical or at least morphological conditioning (e.g., low-mid if the form is a noun). By taking the isolation forms of the first two nouns, but the nonfinal form of the third, as basic, all of these morphotonemic alternations can be stated in terms of phonological conditioning. If there are alternative possibilities, phonological conditioning is the first choice.

5.5. Another instance of phonologically conditioned alternation is found in Kpelle, in which low (throughout) has the alternant high-low (first syllable high, low thereafter) after mid. (For the system of tone marking, see 4.23.) E.g.,

pérɛ tɔ̀nɔ	'one house'	konâ tɔ̀nɔ	'one mortar'
kâli tɔ̀nɔ	'one hoe'	tòloŋ tɔ̀nɔ	'one dove'
but: koni tɔ̂nɔ	'one stone'		

To establish this as a phonologically conditioned alternation, of course, it must be verified that all forms which have low tone after tones other than mid have high-low after mid, irrespective of the morpheme in which the mid appears. Examples are indefinitely numerous—the second noun in a noun-noun compound, any verb stem in some constructions, and a number of other stems whose tone is low, after any morpheme with mid. An example of each type is:

tɛ́ɛ-pèrɛ	'chicken house'	ɓoli-p êrɛ	'goat house'
è tɛ́ɛ kàa	'he saw a chicken'	è koni kâa	'he saw a stone'
ǹɔ́ɔi sù	'in the market'	ǹɔɔi sù	'in the forest'

Conversely, however, it must not be true that all forms which have high-low after mid have low elsewhere. If that were true, low and high-low would be in complete complementary distribution rather than in phonemic contrast. After tones other than mid, low and high-low do contrast; e.g.,

| kú pèlaŋ | 'we got down' | kú pêlaŋ | 'let's get down' |

The neutralization of this contrast after mid is strikingly illustrated if an object ending with mid tone is inserted before the verb in each of the above sentences. The equivalents of 'we got the stone down' and 'let's get the stone down' are homophonous: /kú 'kɔnii pêlaŋ/.

It is interesting to compare the morphotonemic alternation of low-throughout to high-low after mid with the allotonic variations characteristic of the sequence mid-mid. Consider a phrase such as /taa puu/ 'ten towns', in which each word has mid tone throughout, and the words are separated by a phonemic open transition. In all dialects, such a phrase begins and ends on the same phonetic pitch. In the dialect primarily under consideration, the mid tone of the first word ends slightly higher, but the mid tone of the second word is level. In some other dialects, the mid tone of the first word is level, but the mid tone of the second word starts slightly higher and quickly falls to the preceding level. In still other dialects, the mid tone of the first word ends slightly higher, and the mid tone of the second word begins at that level and quickly falls to the preceding level. In all three cases, the sequence mid-mid involves an upward pressure: at the end of the first mid, at the beginning of the second, or both. The morphotonemic alternation of low to high-low reflects the same upward pressure of mid. In one small area, this alternation is restricted to the point where question intonation raises a high tone; elsewhere, low-low occurs after mid, but the preceding mid ends higher than it begins.

An amusing demonstration of the significance of tone, and a striking contradiction of the widespread assumption that native speakers can readily guess what the foreign learner intended to say "from context," is provided by a bargaining exchange overheard many years ago, in which this morphotonemic alternation plays a major role. A man approached an American woman sitting on the porch of her home, with a few eggs in a small basket. The American woman asked, in accurate Kpelle, how much they were. He replied, /kâpa feerɛ, kâpa feerɛ/ 'two cents each' (/kâpa/ 'a penny'). Following the proper traditions of bargaining, the American woman attempted to offer one cent each; she should have said /kâpa tɔnɔ/. But she superimposed on this phrase an English intonation with contrastive stress accompanying the numeral, which could only be interpreted as mid tone with the first word and high-low—the appropriate alternant of low after mid— with the second: */kapa tɔ̂nɔ/. In spite of the almost unmistakable context, the man looked completely mystified, and looked around to see if she had seen something he wasn't aware of. He was plainly wondering, "What in the world is a /kapa/?" There is no such word. I don't recall what happened to the eggs.

5.6. Morphological or lexical conditioning may also be involved in morphotonemic alternations. An alternation in Senari noun stems is of this type. Final low tone in a noun stem has the alternant mid before certain suffixes, including the singular and plural definite suffixes. These suffixes always have low tone. The alternation is not phonologically conditioned, however, since the singular indefinite suffix also has low tone after most stems ending with low. Thus:

tè-gè	'a hoe'	te-gì	'the hoe'
sèʔὲ-lὲ	'a basket'	sèʔɛ-lì	'the basket'
gbὲ-mὲ	'light'	gbɛ-mì	'the light'

That the alternation is from low to mid and not the reverse is obvious from the fact that there are also stems with final mid tone (after which the indefinite suffix also has mid in all but a few words); e.g.,

kpa-ʔa   'a house'   kpa-gì   'the house'

The contrast of low and mid in stem-final position is also attested in an identical environment:

tè-kpɔʔɔ   'a large hoe'   kpa-kpɔʔɔ   'a large house'

The above alternation is an instance of a small number of morphemes in a restricted class (suffixes in this case) conditioning a morphotonemic alternation in a large number of stems. The converse is also found: a large number of stems conditioning a morphotonemic alternation in a small number of morphemes in a restricted class. In general, the indefinite suffixes of Senari have low tone after low and mid after mid. There are a few exceptions, however, which can only be described as lexically conditioned. After high tone, the indefinite suffixes have high after a few stems, and mid or low after about equal numbers of the rest, again only by lexical conditioning. Thus:

zà-ʔá	'rain'	sépí-lé	'a bee'
kpana-ʔà	'an axe'	ŋɔ́rɔ́-lɔ	'a star'
sísyɔ̃-ɔ̃	'a fly'	súgé-lè	'millet'

5.7. In Loma, there is a pervasive pattern of lexically conditioned morphotonemic alternation (see Sadler 1951). All stems are divided into two morphotonemic classes, which may be referred to as A and B. In a sequence of stems both of which belong to class A, high tones in the second have the alternant low. If either stem belongs to class B, there is no alternation. The following illustrate the presence and absence of this alternation; there is also some consonant alternation involved, but it is irrelevant to the tonal alternation:

A-A:	gúlú	'stick',	tévé	'cut it':
	gúlú lèvè	'cut a stick'		
A-B:	gúlú	'stick',	pílí	'throw it':
	gúlú vílí	'throw a stick'		
B-A:	gálú	'rope',	tévé	'cut it'
	gálú lévé	'cut a rope'		
B-B:	gálú	'rope',	pílí	'throw it':
	gálú vílí	'throw a rope'		

Suffixes apparently fall into the same two classes. A number of suffixes have low tone after a stem of class A, but high after a stem of class B; such suffixes would belong to class A. At least one suffix takes the tone of the preceding vowel, including high after a stem of class B; this suffix would belong to class B.

This suffix creates a slight complication in sequences of three morphemes. In the alternation illustrated above, both syllables of a stem of class A have the alternant low after a stem of class A. In the following, a stem of class A, /pɛ́lɛ́/ 'house', occurs after a pronoun of class A but before this suffix of class B; in this case, only the first syllable of the stem has the alternant low: /nà pɛ̀lɛ́í/ 'my house'.

For comparative purposes it is significant that, on the basis of a preliminary check, the morphotonemic classes of Loma stems appear to correspond to stems with different tones in Kpelle and Mende. High-high in class A corresponds to high throughout in Kpelle and high-high in Mende; high-high in class B corresponds to mid throughout in Kpelle and low-high in Mende. One exception, included in the above illustrations, is of special interest: Loma /pílí/, in class B, has cognates with high throughout in Kpelle and high-high in Mende, like a class A stem; however, in Mende this particular stem is in a special morphotonemic class.

5.8. A particularly complex set of lexically conditioned morphotonemic alternations is found in Suppire (see Welmers 1950b). Nouns with any final tone (there are three levels) fall into two morphotonemic classes, one far larger than the other. Alternations are conditioned by both the actual final tone of the noun and by its morphotonemic class. Further, different alternations appear with the word after a noun in some cases, depending on whether that word is an identifier, the stem of a verb, or the present base of a verb (and perhaps other unrecorded possibilities). Pronouns fall into three morphotonemic classes. An object pronoun in the third class conditions still different alternations in a following verb. Object and possessive pronouns in themselves have identical forms, but they condition different alternations in a following verb and in a following noun. The construction of possessive plus noun may involve an associative morpheme; unfortunately, noun-noun phrases were not recorded, since much of the four weeks spent on the language was devoted to sorting out the alternations so far mentioned, but an associative construction can be expected in such phrases, very possibly with still different morphotonemic alternations. Some of the recorded alternations are outlined below; nouns in the smaller morphotonemic class are indicated by an asterisk; pronouns in the third morphotonemic class can be identified without indication because they are the complete set of third person pronouns (including concords for a number of noun classes).

Identifiers (one for each noun class) have mid tone; after nouns* (i.e., nouns of the smaller class), their tone is the same as the preceding. Obviously, this provides no basis for distinguishing mid and mid*. An example with each final tone and each morphotonemic class is:

bílí wi	'it's a slave'
búrú* wí	'it's bread'
baga ki	'it's a house'
yaga* ki	'it's a thing'
fàŋà wi	'it's cloth'
dùbà* wì	'it's a mirror'

The two classes of mid are distinguished by different alternants of the nouns themselves (in a definite form) after a possessive pronoun:

mi bagé	'my house'
mi yáge*	'my thing'

Three contrasting tones are recorded in verb stems only after pronouns of the third morphotonemic class; e.g.,

mi á ku nyà	'I saw it'
mi á ku bbũã	'I hit it'
mi á ku wíí	'I looked at it'

After other pronouns and after any noun object, stems here established as having mid and high tone have identical morphotonemic alternants. (In a nearby dialect, mid and high are not distinguished even in the above; there are only two verb stem tones.)

The present bases of verbs after the same pronouns of the third morphotonemic class have a different set of alternants; for the same three verbs:

mi ná ku nyàà	'I see it'
mi ná ku bbũũ	'I am hitting it'
mi ná ku wìì	'I am looking at it'

The alternations in noun-verb sequences are so random that a chart of all the possible combinations is more useful than a list of statements. A verb stem with low tone has alternants with each tone level. So does a verb stem with mid or high tone. But after any particular noun, low tone stems are always distinct from mid or high tone stems; mid and high tone stems are identical. The following chart shows the alternations for verb stems. Admittedly some of the sentences, the translations of which can be completed by consulting the glosses of the nouns as given above, are semantically rather unrealistic, but this seems the best way to present the data; for the three columns, the meanings are 'I saw . . .', 'I hit . . .,' and 'I looked at . . .'; on the left is the final morphotoneme of the noun object:

	nyà	*bb ã*	*wíí*
H	mi á bílí nyá	mi á bílí bbǔǎ	mi á bílí wìì
H*	mi á búrú nyá	mi á búrú bbũã	mi á búrú wii
M	mi á baga nya	mi á baga bbǔǎ	mi á baga wíí
M*	mi á yagá nyá	mi á yaga bbǔǎ	mi á yaga wíí
L	mi á fàŋà nya	mi á fàŋà bbǔǎ	mi á fàŋà wìì
L*	mi á dùbà nyà	mi á dùbà bbǔǎ	mi á dùbà wíí

For verb stems with mid or high tone, the present bases have morphotonemic alternants after nouns identical with those of the stems as given above. Substitute /ná/ for /á/, and in the second column the segmentals /bbũũ/ for /bbũã/, leave all tones the same, and each of the sentences in the second and third column will

be present in meaning. For verb stems with low tone, however, the present base
has a different set of morphotonemic alternants, as given in the following:

H	mi ná bílí nyàà
H*	mi ná búrú nyàà
M	mi ná baga nyáà
M*	mi ná yaga nyáà
L	mi ná fàŋà nyàà
L*	mi ná dùbà nyáà

In a sequence of possessive pronoun plus noun, the three morphotonemic
classes of pronouns condition different alternants, in combination with different
initial tones in the noun form. Using the definite forms of the same nouns, the
combinations for 'my . . .', 'your . . .', and 'his . . .' are:

mì bíliŋi	mu bíliŋi	u bíliŋi
mì búrúŋi	mu búrúŋi	u búrúŋi
mi bagé	mu bagé	u bagé
mi yáge	mu yáge	u yáge
mí fàŋi	mu faŋí	ú fàŋi
mí dùbàŋi	mu dubáŋi	ú dùbàŋi

There are other details involving nouns and verbs with sequences of different
tones, but the above is a sufficient outline of the basic types of morphotonemic
alternations recorded for Suppire. At the time these data were gathered and analyzed, the whole picture seemed so complex and unsystematic that the prospect
of learning to speak the language fluently appeared extremely difficult. It was
most rewarding, some six months later, to receive a letter from the first American
to learn Suppire, who had followed me through the initial work, saying approximately, "At first it seemed hopelessly complicated, but now it's getting so that,
when I make a mistake in tone, it just *sounds* wrong!" The analytic procedure,
of course, was to elicit a far larger number of nouns and verbs than those cited
above, in a variety of fairly simple environments; then the various tone sequences
were grouped together, until eventually sets of nouns and verbs were identified
which displayed the same tonal behavior. Finally, when diagnostic environments
were found for each tone and each morphotonemic class, additional vocabulary
could be quickly tested. It was an unusual four weeks of elicitation, analysis,
and writing, during which we also enjoyed West Africa's finest supply of fresh
vegetables, and government-inspected filet mignon at 8 cents per pound.

5.9. In Kpelle, there is one morphotonemic alternation which must be stated
in terms of a combination of phonological, morphological, and lexical conditioning.
The alternation occurs only after mid or high tone, only in some verbal constructions, and only in some verbs whose stem tone is mid.

Verbs with mid stem tone fall into two morphotonemic classes, one about
twice as large as the other. Under the appropriate conditions, verbs in the larger
class have alternants with high tone. Verbal constructions in which the stem tone

of verbs is used, and in which there is no suffix, include the imperative, hortative, completive, experiential, and past negative. The alternation in question takes place in all of these except the past negative, after mid or high tone. The alternation is illustrated for the stem /kula/ 'exit, remove' in the following:

kú kúla	'let's get out'
aâ 'kɔnii kúla	'he has gotten the stone out'

But the alternation is not found after low tone, in the past negative, or with a stem from the other morphotonemic class:

kú 'kula	'let's get it out'
kú fé kula ní	'we didn't go out'
kú 'kpáwɔi kpɛtɛ	'let's fix the bridge'

5.10. In Kikuyu, for which I must rely on reports from other responsible linguists, there are morphotonemic alternations which in some cases are not realized until two or more syllables after the conditioning syllable or word. Such a delayed reaction is hardly common, but is obviously another of the varied types of alternation under a variety of conditions. In Sapiny, a verb form may include a large number of morphemes in sequence. The morphotonemic alternations conditioned by various combinations of morphemes in various positions in the forms are so ebulliently complex that full statements have not as yet been made, and will probably not reduce to anything like a concise set; a suggestion has been made that the problem be computer filed for multiple sorting. But whether the morphotonemic alternations of a language can be covered by a few simple rules or require the separate memorization of scores of different combinations, the fact remains that five-year-old native speakers of such languages have the morphotonemic systems pretty well mastered. A patient analyst can also discover and describe such systems in due time.

5.11. Lexical tone and morphotonemic alternations conditioned in the ways outlined above do not, however, exhaust the description of tone. In most African tone languages—possibly all—there are also morphemes whose only realization is tonal, or morphemes which have allomorphs whose only realization is tonal. Such morphemes may be affixes, particles, or pronouns. There are also affixes which include segmental phonemes, but which in addition have a tonal realization accompanying the stem with which the affix is used; this might be covered under morphotonemic alternations, but it seems more convenient to treat it a little differently. And finally, there are affixes which consist of a tone which occurs with the consonants and vowels of a stem, instead of the lexical stem tone.

In connection with the discussion of assigning sequences of tones to single short vowels (4.19, 20), a noun suffix consisting of low tone only has been identified in Jukun (Dìyī). It has also been shown that there is a noun prefix /à/ in Jukun (Wàpā) which has an allomorph consisting of low tone only after mid or high (and a zero allomorph after low). A particle /á/ has also been described which has an allomorph consisting of high tone alone. A noun suffix consisting of high tone alone appears in Ewe. Not many such suffixes and particles, realized as an audible tone without an added vowel, have been recorded, but in all likelihood they may be found in some other languages as well.

In Yoruba, the third person singular object pronoun, in fairly deliberate or formal speech, is realized as a slight prolongation of the vowel of the verb stem, with mid tone after high but high tone after mid or low. In rapid colloquial speech, the sequence high-mid is realized as mid tone accompanying the high-tone stem, and the sequence mid-high is realized as high tone accompanying the mid-tone stem, without prolongation. Anticipating further analysis, the longer forms in the following illustrations are treated as if the pronoun consists of tone alone:

> mo rí⁻ : mo ri   'I saw him (her, it)'
> mo jẹ' : mo jẹ́   'I ate it'
> mo rà'   'I bought it'

The longer forms have commonly been treated as if the pronoun is a full vowel with the appropriate tone; the vowel of the pronoun is then identical with the vowel of the preceding verb stem. There are, however, good reasons for questioning this analysis. A second person singular object pronoun is segmentally /ọ/ in some dialects and /ẹ/ in others; it follows the same tone rules as the third person object pronoun in the longer forms above. Taking a verb /wẹ̀/ 'bathe' and the second person object form /ẹ/, the verb with the third and with the second person object should be homophonous if the third person form is a full vowel. They are not, however. The contrast is clearest if a high tone precedes the verb stem, as in:

> ó wẹ̀'   'she bathed him'
> ó wẹ̀ ẹ́   'she bathed you'

Ordinarily, low tone has a falling allotone after high. This is audible in the second of the above examples; the tone of the uninterrupted sequence of verb stem vowel and object pronoun is a quick fall followed by a rise. In the first of the above, however, the sequence of verb stem vowel and object pronoun begins at the low level, and is simply a rise. This may be stated in a rule that the falling allotone of low after high does not appear if the syllable with low tone is immediately followed by another tone, without a vowel. A parallel situation is found in which the usual rising allotone of high after low does not appear if the syllable with high tone is immediately followed by another tone, without a vowel. In the following, the sequence of verb stem vowel and object pronoun begins at the high level and falls to mid; the usual rise after low is not present:

> kò rí⁻   'he didn't see it'

The conclusion is that, in deliberate speech, the third person singular object pronoun consists of a tone alone, without a vowel, even though the vowel of the preceding verb stem is slightly prolonged.

The third person subject pronoun in Yoruba also has an allomorph which consists of tone only. If there is no noun subject, the pronoun form is /ó/. After a noun or noun phrase subject which ends with mid or low tone, and when not followed by the morpheme /ń/ indicating present continuous action, the pronoun is realized as high tone appended to the final tone of the subject; e.g.,

Ayọ̀′ rí⁻   'Ayọ saw it'

If the noun or noun phrase subject ends with high tone, that high tone may be interpreted as simultaneously representing the high tone of the pronoun. The same interpretation may be applied to the high tone of the present morpheme /ń/. There is no tonal realization of the pronoun in negative constructions either, but that simply parallels the fact that, if there is no noun subject, the third person singular pronoun has a zero allomorph in negative constructions.

If the noun subject in sentences like the above ends with the sequence high-low, low tone does not have its usual falling allotone, following the same rule as stated above in connection with the third person singular object pronoun.

The usual failure to be concerned with anything but lexical tone is reflected in written Yoruba. The third person object pronoun is indicated by a tilde over the vowel of the verb stem, suggesting the prolongation but not specifying the tone. Other tonally realized morphemes are not indicated in any way.

5.12. A similar tonal realization of a morpheme is found in the associative morpheme in Yoruba, which has been discussed in 2.20 in connection with vowel elision. One of its allomorphs, the choice of which is phonologically predictable, is a mid tone between two nouns. A second allomorph is realized as a morpho-tonemic alternation, and a third as a morphophonemically significant absence of vowel elision.

One of the uses of the associative construction—probably by far the commonest, but by no means the only one—is to express possession. In sequences of noun plus possessive pronoun in Yoruba, there is also a tone which does not accompany a separate vowel. This may well be another manifestation of the associative morpheme, although the tone is low for the first and second person singular pronouns, a characteristic which seems to belong to the pronoun itself. Further, in the second person plural pronoun, the preceding mid tone is found even where the associative construction cannot be present. The possessive pronouns of Yoruba are illustrated in the following:

ilé'mi	'my house'	ilé⁻wa	'our house'
ilé'rẹ	'your (sg.) house'	ilé⁻yín	'your (pl.) house'
ilé⁻rẹ̀	'his house'	ilé⁻wọn	'their house'

In the second person plural, the mid tone is found even in the object pronoun form:

mo rí⁻yín   'I saw you (pl.)'

5.13. Prefixes consisting of tone alone have not, to my knowledge, been recorded in any language except Kpelle, but they are clearly present there. A portion of the relevant data has been discussed in 3.20 in connection with syllabic nasals.

The first person singular possessive pronoun with relational nouns, and object pronoun with verbs, is a nasal with high tone, not merely a tone. This is obvious before stems with initial voiceless stops and fricatives. With stems having other initial consonants, it is less obvious but equally true. By analogy with forms like /m̀pôlu/ 'my back' (in which /p/ has a voiced allophone [b]), the interpretation of a form like /ńáa/ 'my name' is that the initial /ń/ is simultaneously the nasal-plus-high-tone pronoun and a morphophonemic alternant of the initial consonant of the stem—which happens to be /l/, as attested in /í láa/ 'your (sg.) name'. If the stem has an initial nasal, as in /í nâŋ/ 'your father', the initial /ń/ of /ńâŋ/ 'my father' is interpreted as being simultaneously the pronoun and the initial consonant of the stem without alternation.

The corresponding third person singular pronoun, however, is interpreted as consisting of low tone alone. In /ǹáa/ 'his name', only the low tone of the initial /ǹ/ is considered a manifestation of the pronoun; the nasal is a morphophonemic alternant of /l/ in the presence of this low tone. In /ǹâŋ/ 'my father', only the low tone is the pronoun; the nasal is the stem-initial consonant without alternation. The morphophonemic alternants of stem-initial non-nasal consonants are as follows, with relevant illustrations for each:

ɓ : m	'tí ɓálo	'heal them'	m̀álo	'heal him'
l : n	'tí láa	'their name'	ǹáa	'his name'
ɣ : ŋ	'tí ɣála	'drag them'	ŋ̀ála	'drag it'
w : ŋw	'tí wéli	'their friend'	ŋ̀wéli	'his friend'
y : ny	'tí yée	'their hands'	ǹyée	'his hand'

The fact that the stem-initial consonants in question have morphophonemic alternants which happen to be nasal has nothing to do with the underlying phonemic composition of the pronoun. In a small extreme western dialect area, the third person pronoun plus /ɓ/ is realized as low tone accompanying /ɓ/, without nasality; similarly, the pronoun plus /ɣ/ is realized as low tone accompanying /ɣ/; /l/, however, has a nasal alternant, and if memory serves me correctly /w/ and /y/ do also. In other dialects, one can only say that the phonotactics do not permit low tone to accompany these consonants, but it may accompany their nasal counterparts.

The analysis of the third person pronoun as low tone alone, but the first person pronoun as nasal plus high tone, when the forms cited thus far differ only in tone, is justified by analogy with the pronoun forms accompanying stems whose initial consonants are voiceless stops and fricatives. The analogy has already been cited for the first person pronoun. For the third person, the realizations are interpreted as "prefixed low tone". For each stem-initial voiceless stop and fricative, the form with the third person pronoun begins instead with a voiced consonant, an allophone of the voiceless counterpart, and this voiced consonant begins on a low pitch; it is this low pitch, interpreted as low tone, which signals the presence of the pronoun. (Intervocalically in stems, there are occasional contrasts of /p/ and /b/, /t/ and /d/, etc., but the intervocalic voiced consonants do not begin with low pitch. Initially, [b, d, g, gb, v, ɉ] do not occur without low pitch, and may thus be interpreted as allophones of /p, t, k, kp, f, s/ conditioned by the presence of low tone.) In the phonetic transcription of the following forms, the low tone must be read as accompanying the first part of the strongly voiced consonant:

'pôlu	['bôlu]	'his back'	'kpîŋ	['gbîŋ]	'himself'
'tía	['día]	'his taboo'	'féla	['véla]	'his wages'
'kɔ́ɔ	['gɔ́ɔ]	'his foot'	'soŋ	['ɉoŋ]	'catch him'

This is, of course, the Kpelle form of the "initial consonant alternation" in Southwestern Mande which has attracted the attention of many writers (Welmers 1971b, pp. 132-36). I cannot see that it has any conceivable connection with an original nasal, as Manessy (1964) assumes, followed by Bird (1971). As noted above, a nasal appears before (voiced allophones of) voiceless stops and fricatives in the first person pronoun. In environments identical except for tone, no nasal appears in the third person pronoun. It seems extremely unlikely that the difference in tone would be sufficient to account for the retention of a nasal in one case and its loss in another, and there is no other available or suggested explanation for what would be a clear violation of regular phonetic change. In Loma and Mende, there is a real consonant alternation, which cannot be reinterpreted in a comparable way in the languages as they now are. Morphologically, comparing the basic consonants with their alternants, the Loma and Mende alternations function in a way almost precisely the reverse of the situation in Kpelle. Apart from a few irrelevant grammatical differences among the languages, prefixed low tone in Kpelle corresponds to the absence of consonant alternation in Loma and Mende, and the basic consonants in Kpelle correspond to the morphophonemic alternants in Loma and Mende. In Loma, /l/ is the alternant of both /t/ and /d/, and in Mende /l/ is the alternant of both /t/ and /nd/, which demonstrates that /t/ and /d/ or /nd/ are indeed the underlying consonants; the reverse grammatical situation in Kpelle and these languages is shown in the following:

Kpelle:	tɛ́	'go up, climb',	'tɛ́	'lift it'
Loma, Mende:	tɛ́	'lift it',	lɛ́	'go up, climb'

In Kpelle, prefixed low tone in the forms in question can readily be interpreted as a morpheme. In Loma and Mende, stem forms such as /tɛ́/ 'lift it' can—more clearly in Loma—be interpreted as including an additional morpheme in the underlying structure. In other branches of Mande, the corresponding morpheme appears as /à/, so that */à/ appears to be the logical reconstruction of Kpelle prefixed low tone, and of the absence of consonant alternation in Loma and Mende. (Other Southwestern Mande third person pronoun forms contain nasals, to be sure; e.g. Kpelle /ŋɔ̀/, possessive for free but not relational nouns, and Mende /ŋgì/, possessive for all nouns. These forms, however, are grammatically different from, and irrelevant to, the problem of prefixed low tone in Kpelle corresponding to the absence of consonant alternation in Loma and Mende.) Without going into all of the minute details (which can, to be sure, be accounted for), my hypothesis is that the presence of this original */à/—or perhaps more accurately developments in its phonological realization which ultimately led to its loss as a separate segmental entity—resulted, in all three Southwestern Mande languages, in a strengthening (fortition, *Verschärfung*) of the following consonant. In Kpelle, this took the form of strong voicing, with the low tone of the */à/ remaining; that strengthening is involved in this voicing (rather than the lenition usually associated with voicing) is attested also by the affricate [ǰ] as a counterpart of [s] (the former is palatal in all environments, the latter in some). In Loma and Mende, strenthening may have taken the form of a more fortis articulation of all stem-initial consonants, as suggested by the fact that the Loma /kp/ is produced with considerably more oral suction than the Kpelle /kp/, and by the fact that Mende has initial /nj/, and Loma initial /z/, corresponding to Kpelle /y/; in any case, voiceless consonants remained voiceless after */à/, and reconstructed initial voiced stops are reflected as stops in Loma and prenasalized stops in Mende. Where */à/ was not present, stem-initial consonants underwent lenition. These consonants, the present morphophonemic alternants, are not strongly voiced, and for the most part are resonants rather than voiced stops or fricatives; e.g., as noted above, the alternant of both /t/ and /d/ in Loma, and of both /t/ and /nd/ in Mende, is /l/. After these processes of fortition after */à/ and lenition elsewhere had introduced a distinction between two sets of consonants, */à/ lost both its vowel and its tone; it is now realized only by the presence of the stem-initial consonant rather than the weakened alternant.

The morpheme in question, realized as prefixed low tone in Kpelle, is far more than a third person pronoun. It has a more general meaning of "previous reference". It can be used with a free noun stem as in Kpelle /'pérɛ/ 'a house for it' (heard in a conversation about a goat for whom we wanted a shelter built). It is always used, along with a suffix, in the "specific" form of a free noun: /'pérɛi/ 'the house'; in Loma and Mende, there is no consonant alternation in free nouns in citation or in phrase initial position, paralleling the frequent occurrence of the specific form in Kpelle for purposes of citation. It is used with numerals in forms like /'feerɛ/ 'two of them'. In counting a number of items, it is used with the numerals two through nine, but not with ten unless there are exactly ten items. Above ten, counting starts over with one, and again prefixed low tone is not used with ten. The form is /puu/ 'a ten', but then the person counting pauses and adds, /'puu feerɛ/ 'twenty (two tens) of them'. The comparable procedure is followed for every multiple of ten. Prefixed low tone is also used to express the topic of a predicative adjective: /'kétɛi/ 'it is big'.

Not every instance of word-initial low tone is, however, a manifestation of this morpheme. Some free nouns have initial low tone as part of their stems; e.g., /'kêli/ 'Diana monkey', /'pɔ̂ki/ 'bucket'. Many such nouns are clearly adaptations from neighboring languages or from English, and it is only reasonable to assume that all of them are (see Welmers 1961). With such stems, the morpheme described as prefixed low tone has a zero allomorph, or it could be said that the initial low tone is simultaneously part of the stem and prefixed low tone: /'kêliĩ/ 'the Diana monkey'.

5.14. Another type of tonally realized morpheme is "replacives" (See Gleason 1961, p. 74). That is, the inherent or stem tone of a morpheme does not appear; in its place is another tone which has morphemic status in its own right. A simple example may be cited from Jukun. In most verbal constructions, the first and second person singular subject pronouns have low tone; all other subject pronouns have mid tone. In the hortative construction, however, all subject pronouns have the same consonants and vowels as in other constructions, but have high tone. Because of their appearance in most verbal constructions, and more especially on the basis of the principle of maximum differentiation, the pronouns in the phrases on the left below are taken to be the basic or stem forms of the pronouns. The first syllable in each phrase on the right is taken to be the pronoun plus a morpheme defined as "high replacing stem tone" and having the meaning "hortative." The past construction is simply pronoun plus verb stem, with no additional morpheme having "past" significance. Thus:

m̀ ya	'I went'	ḿ ya?	'Should I go?'
ù ya	'you (sg.) went'	ú ya	'Go (sg.).'
ku ya	'he went'	kú ya	'have him go'
i ya	'we went'	í ya	'let's go'
ni ya	'you (pl.) went'	ní ya	'Go (pl.).'
be ya	'they went'	bé ya	'they should go'

For those who dislike the concept of "replacives", perhaps because it smacks too much of "process" description, there is another technique available to account for such data. Each pronoun could be described as having two allomorphs: one with low or mid tone as the case may be, and another with no tone. The allomorph with no tone occurs in the environment of an accompanying morpheme which consists of tone only. The result is obviously the same. With the latter analysis, however, it would be necessary in a rigidly formal lexicon to list two allomorphs for a number of morphemes—only six in Jukun, but virtually every morpheme in the lexicon in some other languages. The importance of this cavil may be minimal, but I personally find it more elegant to incorporate more in the definition of a replacive, which occurs with (or operates on) whole classes of morphemes.

A replacive may be said to be present even when it has replaced a tone identical with itself. In Kpelle, five of the six subject pronouns have high tone in what is analyzed as their stem forms; the other has low. The subject pronouns are:

1s	ŋá	1pl	kú
2s	í	2pl	ká
3s	è	3pl	'tí

These subject pronouns are used without modification only in the past construction. In the hortative, as in Jukun, they have high tone replacing stem tone. This produces a different tone only in the third person singular, but the difference between the past and the hortative is marked also by a difference in tone in the verb stem. E.g.,

| è pìli | 'he jumped' | é píli | 'he should jump' |
| kú pìli | 'we jumped' | kú píli | 'let's jump' |

To say that high tone replaces stem tone in subject pronouns makes for a neat grammatical statement, even though in five cases high simply replaces high. An analogy in the physical world is a fence made of vertical boards, in which all the boards are green except one that is white. If the entire fence is covered with a coat of green paint, only the white board changes color—but the entire fence has nevertheless been painted.

5.15. As suggested by the last examples above, Kpelle also has a replacive with verb stems. As shown in 4.22, five tones, with a scope from one open transition to the next, occur with stems; they are high, mid, high-low, mid-fall, and low. Of these tones, low occurs almost exclusively with free noun stems, all of which are undoubtedly adaptations from other languages (see Welmers 1961). The other occurrences of low as a stem tone are with one pronoun and with some ideophones, which are atypical in any case. Low does not occur as a stem tone with verbs. Further, as noted in 5.3 above, no two verb stems contrast minimally in tone. The four possibilities are illustrated in the following:

| píli | 'jump, throw' | pêlaŋ | 'get down' |
| kula | 'exit, remove' | tuâŋ | 'move over' |

A morpheme defined as "low replacing stem tone" appears, however, in a number of verbal constructions with all verb stems. The constructions in question are also differentiated by different morphemes appended to the subject pronouns. Since the constructions using the low tone replacive share no common semantic feature, one might prefer to say that there are several homophonous morphemes involved; nothing is gained by such an interpretation, however, since there are other morphemes present to which the semantic differences can be attributed. In the following, the stem tone of verbs appears in the completive construction, while low replacing stem tone appears in the past:

aâ píli	'he has jumped'	è pìli	'he jumped'
aâ kula	'he has gone out'	è kùla	'he went out'
aâ pêlaŋ	'he has gotten down'	è pèlaŋ	'he got down'
aâ tuâŋ	'he has moved over'	è tùaŋ	'he moved over'

Other constructions in which low replacing stem tone appears are the following, which also include examples of high-low as a morphotonemic alternant of low after mid (5.5 above):

Conditional:	à pìli	'when/if he jumps'
Customary:	a kùla	'he goes out'
Cust. Neg.:	'fa kùla	'he doesn't go out'
Desiderative:	èi pèlaŋ	'if only he'd get down'
Desid. Neg.:	'fêi pèlaŋ	'if only he wouldn't get down'
Hortative Neg.:	'fé tùaŋ	'he shouldn't move over'

In each of these constructions, of course, an alternative analysis is possible; it could be said that each construction contains a morpheme composed of whatever (including zero) is appended to the pronoun or negative marker plus the replacement of verb stem tone by low. Such posited morphemes would, however, be discontinuous in all sentences containing a verbal object, since the object (which may be a phrase of considerable length) comes between the pronoun with its affix and the verb.

In phrases or compounds consisting of two or more nouns, an identical (but presumably not the same) morpheme of low replacing stem tone appears with each noun stem after the first. The following examples show a variety of combinations in terms of the independent stem tones of the nouns; again low has the morphotonemic alternant high-low after mid:[2]

tóu	'palm nut',	wúlɔ	'oil'	:	tóu-wùlɔ	'palm oil'
kɔlɔ	'book, paper',	láa	'leaf'	:	kɔlɔ-lâa	'page'
kéleŋ	'vehicle',	pere	'path'	:	kéleŋ-père	'road'
kali	'snake',	pala	'sore'	:	kali-pâla	'snake-bite'
ɣâla	'God',	taa	'town'	:	ɣâla-tàa	'heaven'
kpɔŋô	'young bush',	kwala	'monkey'	:	kpɔŋô-kwàla	'monkey (sp.)'
taa	'town',	kâloŋ	'chief'	:	taa-kâloŋ	'town chief'
pala	'sore',	kpɔlɔ̂ŋ	'scar'	:	pala-kpɔ́lɔŋ	'scar of a sore'
-kpó	'excrement',	pérɛ	'house'	:	kpó-pèrɛ	'outhouse'
ɓála	'sheep',	-kɔlɔ	'skin'	:	ɓála-kɔlɔ	'sheep skin'
pala	'sore',	kɔlɔ-fêla 'sickness'	:	(/fela/ is not attested independently; its stem tone is unknown): pala-kɔ́lɔ-fêla 'sickness caused or characterized by sores'

A personal relational noun may be combined with the noun /nṹu/ 'person', with low replacing stem tone (certainly a different though homophonous morpheme in this case) accompanying the first as well as the second component, to produce a noun with the meaning of the relational noun, but for which no possessor need be expressed; e.g.,

| -nâŋ | 'father', | nṹu | 'person' | : | nàŋ-nùu | 'a father' |

In Akan, there are somewhat similar noun-noun phrases or compounds, with a replacive accompanying the first rather than the second component. Throughout the first noun, low tones replace the tones of the noun in its independent form. E.g., from Fante:

| ǹkàtí | 'peanuts', | ǹkwán | 'soup' | : | ǹkàtì-ǹkwán | 'peanut soup' |
| dén'kyɛ́m | 'crocodile', | ɔ̀bú | 'stone' | : | dènkyɛ̀m-bú | 'diamond' |

5.16. When different tones accompany the consonants and vowels of a number of morphemes in a language under different circumstances, it is not always immediately apparent whether it is morphotonemic alternation under definable

---

[2] For further details and additional examples, see Welmers 1969b.

conditions, or the presence of a tonally realized morpheme, that is responsible for the variation. In some cases, both may be present. Igbo provides some interesting complications in the identification and interlocking functions of morphotonemic alternations and tonally realized morphemes; a few details restricted to relatively uncommon constructions or to individual words with a unique structure are omitted in this treatment, but all of the relevant principles of analysis and interpretation are amply illustrated.[3] It is recognized that there are dialect differences in some details, but the statements made here represent patterns that are known to be widespread. For other dialects, an occasional statement would have to be omitted, added, or modified, or the order in which some statements are made would have to be changed. A few conspicuous dialect differences are noted.

This section is confined to a few details of tonal identification and behavior which can then be assumed in the remainder of the discussion. First, there is a set of independent pronoun forms which in most respects function as nouns. Three of these are monosyllabic, and in their underlying structure are interpreted as having initial downstep followed by high tone. The initial downstep is, in all probability, historically derived from a vowel with low tone. The six forms are:

m̀mụ́	'I'	ànyị́	'we'
'gị́	'you (sg.)'	únù	'you (pl.)'
'yá	'he, she, it'	'há	'they'

Downstep with the monosyllabic forms is shown in the following:

ọ́ bụ́rụ́ 'yá byàrà 'if it is he (who) came'

These forms are also used as possessives. Downstep with the monosyllabic forms is again attested; after low tone, of course, downstep is automatically deleted. E.g.,

éwú 'yá	'his goat'	ụ́lọ̀ yá	'his house'

As verbal objects, the same forms are used except for the first person singular, which is a syllabic /m/. This and the other three monosyllabic forms have downstep-high after high, but in the particular dialect under consideration have the alternant tone low after low. E.g.,

ọ́ kpọ́ọ́ 'ḿ	'if he calls me'	ọ́ kpọ̀rọ̀ m̀	'he called me'

As verbal subjects, the plural forms listed above are again used. There are, however, special singular subject pronouns. The second person form is /ị́/ or /í/ (the choice depending on vowel harmony). The third person form is /ọ́/ or /ó/. In some constructions, the first person form is /ḿ/. In other constructions, the first person form consists of /á/ or /é/ before the verb plus a syllabic /m/ after the verb; the tone of the latter is downstep-high after high, but low after low. E.g.,

[3] The substance of 5.16-19 is separately published as Welmers 1970b.

í méé 'yá	'if you do it'
ọ̀ bụ̀ ìtè	'it's a pot'
ḿ méé 'yá	'if I do it'
é 'méélá 'ḿ yá	'I have done it'
á hụ̀rụ̀ m̀ yà	'I saw him'

Perhaps to be identified with the vowel component of the first person form above is an impersonal subject pronoun, /á/ or /é/.

In negative constructions, with subjects other than the above singular pronouns, the verb form has a vowel prefix. Before this prefix, the plural subject pronouns listed above function as nouns and undergo no alternation. With singular subject pronouns, however, the verb form has no prefix, but the pronouns have low tone replacing their inherent high tone. This is interpreted as a morpheme with the meaning 'unreal'. E.g.,

| únù á'byághị | 'you didn't come' |
| ọ̀ byá'ghị | 'he didn't come' |

In affirmative verbal constructions, the same replacive is used with both singular and plural subject pronouns. Such combinations are usually translated as, and have generally been described as, questions. After a noun subject, the third person form /ọ̀/ or /ò/ is required. E.g.,

ọ̀ gàrà áhyá	'did he go to market?'
ùnù èméélá 'yá	'have you (pl.) done it?'
ńnà gị́ ọ̀ byàrà	'did your father come?'

The meaning 'unreal' is here more specifically 'hypothetical'. The identification of the replacive here with that in negatives is possible because there are no negative questions in Igbo, but there are common circumlocutions such as the equivalent of 'I think he didn't go', which expects a response. By analogy, the above are interpreted as having the more basic meaning 'I suppose he went to market' etc. As in English, such hypothetical statements expect a response. (In English, speakers of Igbo sometimes say, e.g., 'I think you are going to go to Aba tomorrow', where a native speaker of English would invariably use a question.)

A few monosyllabic morphemes are interpreted as being inherently toneless. These include four suffixes which repeat the tone of the preceding syllable, high or low: the negative imperative suffix /-la/, the negative suffix /-ghị/, the applicative verbal extension which consists of /-r/ plus a repetition of the preceding vowel, and the additive verbal extension /-kwa/. These all follow the pattern illustrated in the following:

é'mélá yá   'don't do it'   ázàlà yà   'don't sweep it'

A few other suffixes found in verb forms could also be considered toneless, but they appear only after high or only after low tone, so that their high or low tone can equally well be considered an inherent part of the suffixes themselves.

The remaining toneless morpheme is a sort of preposition, the underlying form of which is /na/. Before a consonant (which is extremely rare) this morpheme has low tone. Before a syllabic nasal, it takes the tone of the following syllable. Before a vowel, its vowel and tone are elided, as indicated by an apostrophe in the transcription used here. E.g.,

ná ŋ́gbèdè	'in the evening'	n'úlò̩	'at home'
nà m̀bú̩	'in the beginning'	n'ò̩bò̩dò̩	'in town'

Significantly, the presence of this morpheme, even when it consists of a consonant only, inhibits in what follows the operation of any morphotonemic alternation conditioned by what precedes.

One morphotonemic alternation must be included here, prior to the three alternations described in the following section, which have a different type of conditioning. Before any modifier except a monosyllabic form with the inherent tone downstep-high, in nouns which independently have the tones high-downstep-high, the downstep is deleted. The exception, though included in the illustrations below, is covered by the first alternation stated in the following section; in many dialects, as shown by the parenthesized alternant below, this exception does not apply. That the crucial environment here is a modifier is shown by the fact that this alternation does not take place before a verb. E.g., from /é'gó/ 'money, shilling':

á cò̩rò̩ m̀ é'gó	'I want money'
é'gó dì m̀'má	'money is fine'
égó únù	'your (pl.) money'
égó 'átó̩	'three shillings'
é'gó yá (égó 'yá)	'his money'

5.17. It seems most convenient next to describe three morphotonemic alternations which are largely conditioned by the preceding tonal environment. The derivations of the conditioning environments are assumed here, but will be explicitly stated in the following section, after which a number of apparent or real exceptions will be accounted for. The alternations described in this section will be referred to as A1, A2, and A3.

A1: After one or more high tones preceded by a downstep, in forms with an initial vowel or nasal whose first two tones are low-high, initial low tone has the alternant high. In this environment, therefore, forms whose first two tones are independently low-high have the same tones as forms whose first two tones are independently high-high. Both are illustrated in the following:

Àbá	'Aba (town)':	ò̩ gá'ghí Ábá	'he didn't go to Aba'
m̀mánú̩	'oil':	ó̩ cò̩rò̩ í̩'zú̩tá m̀mánú̩	'he wants to buy oil'
ánú̩	'meat':	ó̩ cò̩rò̩ í̩'zú̩tá ánú̩	'he wants to buy meat'

A form of this alternation applies in monosyllabic forms with the inherent tone downstep-high; the alternation takes the form of deleting the downstep (compare the end of the preceding section). E.g.,

zùtá 'jí	'buy yams' :	ò zú'tághị́ jí	'he didn't buy yams'
mèé 'yá	'do it'	ọ́ cọ̀rọ̀ í'mé yá	'he wants to do it'
ánụ̣ 'gị́	'your meat' :	é'gó gị́	'your money'

A2: After high tone when no downstep precedes, also in forms whose first two tones are independently low-high, initial low tone has the alternant downstep-step-high. A modification of this alternation appears only in forms with more than two syllables and an initial nasal; in such forms, initial low tone has the alternant high and downstep precedes the second syllable—that is, an initial nasal delays the downstep for one syllable. The fourth example in the following illustrates this modification:

àkwá	'egg'	:	wètá 'ákwá	'bring eggs'
ị̀gbá	'wrestling'	:	há nà àgbá 'ị́gbá	'they're wrestling'
ụ̀fọ́dụ́	'some'	:	wètá 'ụ́fọ́dụ́	'bring some'
m̀mánụ̣	'oil'	:	wètá ḿ'mánụ̣	'bring oil'
Àbá	'Aba (town)':	ónyé 'Ábá	'a person from Aba'
àtọ́	'three'	:	àkwá 'átọ́	'three eggs'
únù èméélá 'yá	:		ànyị́ 'éméélá 'yá
'you (pl.) have done it'		'we have done it'

In the last of these, the downstep of /'yá/ cannot be deleted by the A1 rule, since the downstep of the preceding word is derived by A2 after A1 has ceased to apply.

A3: With the syntactic restrictions stated below, also after high tone when no downstep precedes, in nouns with two syllables only and the tones high-high, the second high tone has the alternant downstep-high. This alternation applies to a noun used by itself (i.e., without a modifier after it) immediately after a verb, and to the second noun in a noun-noun phrase. It does not apply, although A2 does, in the second of two nouns after a verb if the nouns do not belong to the same phrase; the conditioning for A2 is phonologic, while the conditioning for A3 is in part syntactic. Examples of this alternation and its restriction to two-syllable nouns are:

ánụ̣	'meat'	:	wètá á'nụ̣	'bring meat'
éwú	'goat'	:	ánụ̣ é'wú	'goat meat'
ósísí	'plant'	:	ị̀kpụ́rụ́ ósísí	'fruit, nut, seed'

This alternation applies only in nouns; in the following, /ọ́cá/ 'light-colored' is an adjective, which indicates the category or class to which a preceding noun belongs (see Welmers and Welmers 1969):

ónyé ọ́cá   'a Caucasian'

Nor does A3 apply if a noun is followed by a modifier, as /éwú/ in the first two of the following; by contrast, in the third, /éwú/ is the second noun in a noun-noun phrase, and the demonstrative modifies the entire phrase, not /éwú/ alone:

kpʊ̀tá éwú ꞌátọ̀   'bring three goats'
ísí éwú áhʊ̀   'the head of that goat'
ísí éꞌwú áhʊ̀   'that goat head'

Finally, A3 does not apply in the second of two nouns, not in the same phrase, after a verb. As shown in the third and the last of the following, however, A2 does apply in this environment:

écí   'yesterday, tomorrow': kpʊ̀tá éꞌwú écí 'bring a goat tomorrow' (cf.: gàá éꞌcí 'go tomorrow')

ánʊ́   'meat'   : ó sììrì ànyị́ ánʊ́   'she cooked meat for us'
àkwá   'eggs'   : ó sììrì ànyị́ ꞌákwá   'she cooked eggs for us'
író   'hatred'   : há hʊ̀rʊ̀ ànyị́ író   'they hate us'
                                                  (lit. 'they see us hatred')
àhʊ́   'body'   : há mèrʊ̀rʊ̀ ànyị́ ꞌáhʊ́   'they hurt us'
                                                  (lit. 'they spoiled us body')

An instance was cited earlier in which A1 cannot apply if the phonologic environment which otherwise conditions it is derived by the application of A2. In the environment just discussed, however—in the second of two nouns, not in the same phrase, after a verb—A1 applies after itself, after A2, or after A3. The rationale of this appears to be that the verb and the first noun are treated as a unit; any downstep followed by high tones in the total unit, whether it is in the verb before the first noun, or in the first noun as a result of A2 or A3, conditions A1 in the second noun. This is confirmed by the first of the following examples, in which A1 also applies after a high tone which is not the result of any alternation; the conditioning factor is the downstep in the preceding verb:

éwú   'goat', àhʊ́ 'body',   no alternation and A1:
  há éꞌmérʊ́ghị̀ éwú áhʊ́   'they didn't hurt a goat'
ànyị́   (1pl), àhʊ́ 'body',   A1 and A1:
  há éꞌmérʊ́ghị̀ ànyị́ áhʊ́   'they didn't hurt us'
ànyị́   (1pl), àhʊ́ 'body'   A2 and A1:
  há nà èmérʊ́ ꞌányị́ áhʊ́   'they're hurting us'
éwú   'goat', àhʊ́ 'body',   A3 and A1:
  hạ́ nà èmérʊ́ éꞌwú áhʊ́   'they're hurting a goat'

In other environments than the above, A2 applies after itself and after A3. This recursive application of A2 is illustrated by the following, in which the alternation with the second word must precede the alternation with the third:

àtọ́   'three', ànyị́ (1pl),   A2 and A2:
  éwú ꞌátọ̀ ꞌányị́   'our three goats'
éwú   'goat', ànyị́ (1pl),   A3 and A2:
  ánʊ́ éꞌwú ꞌányị́   'our goat meat'

The following example shows the same surface realization of tonal alternations, but is derived differently; the alternation with the third word precedes, and is then unaffected by, the alternation with the second:

ìkó   'cup',   ànyị̀ (1pl):
wètá 'íkó 'ányị̀   'bring our cups'

In the following, A2 appears four times; the order of the four applications is 3-4-2-1:

ànyị̀ 'éwétálá 'íkó 'átọ́ 'ányị̀
'we have brought our three cups'

A contrast between the sequence of A3-A1 and A3-A2 is shown in the following. A3 appears in /m̀mányá ŋ́'kwú/ 'nut palm wine'; /m̀bú/ is a noun meaning 'the first time', here '(n)ever':

ànyị̀ á'ŋụ́bèghị̀ m̀mányá ŋ́'kwú m̀bú
'we've never drunk nut palm wine'
ànyị̀ á'ŋụ́bèghị̀ m̀mányá ŋ́'kwú 'ányị̀
'we haven't drunk our nut palm wine'

For some speakers, peculiarly, in a monosyllabic modifier after a noun (but not in a verbal object), A1 reapplies after A2; further, A3 applies in a noun before a monosyllabic modifier, and then A1 reapplies. (As one might guess from this and other statements, these pronoun forms are perhaps the prime nuisance in Igbo when working with a number of speakers.) E.g.,

ìkó 'yá   'his cup' : wètá 'íkó yá   'bring his cup'
 (cf.: ànyị̀ 'éwétálá 'yá   'we have brought it')
ánụ́ 'yá   'his meat' : wètá á'nụ́ yá   'bring his meat'

5.18. The conditioning environments for the alternations stated in the preceding section may appear in nouns, numerals, verbs, and very occasionally other words. For all forms other than verbs, these are lexical tones or tones derived by the alternations themselves. For verbs, it is necessary, before applying the above alternations, to derive the tones of bases and constructions. Such derivations, in so far as they present no problems in the application of the alternations stated, are outlined in this section.

It is first necessary to make statements deriving the tones of verb bases.[4] Verb stems are monosyllabic, and may have high or low tone; a single verb stem may consitute a verb base. In a base of more than one syllable, the first syllable must be a verb stem; one or occasionally two stems may follow, and morphemes of a different class, base formatives, may also be included. The inherent tones of base formatives are identified by comparing their tonal behavior with that of stems which may be used independently. Bases of two and three syllables are common, and some longer bases are recorded. The tones of a verb base are determined by the independent (lexical) tones of the first two syllables. If the tones of the first two syllables are both independently high, the base has high tone throughout. If their tones are independently low and high, in that order, the

---

[4] This supplements Welmers 1970a, in which the derivation of tones is not discussed.

first syllable of the base has low tone, and all following syllables have high. If their tones are independently high and low, or low and low, the base has high tone with the first syllable, low with the second, and high with all syllables following. Examples of these derivations are:

mé	'do, make',	cí	'be stopped up':	mécí	'close'

mécí (from above), sị́ (indicating action done to completion or to a stopping place): mécísị́ 'tie up, fasten up completely'

kwà	'push',	cí	'be stopped up':	kwàcí	'push shut'
gá	'go',	fè	'cross, pass over' :	gáfè	'go across'
wè	'take, pick up',	pù	'exit' :	wépù	'remove'

wépù (from above), tá (indicating action toward or for the speaker or subject): wépùtá 'bring out'

Statements may now be made deriving certain verbal constructions. There is no construction in which the verb base is used by itself; some other morpheme is always present, though in some cases with a zero allomorph. The following numbered statements also establish a number of tonally realized morphemes in verbal constructions.

(1) A morpheme consisting of low replacing stem tone occurs with a limited number of verb stems, marking a "stative" construction. Two stems which may be used for illustrative purposes are /dị́/ 'be described as; be located at (of inanimates, sometimes non-human animates)' and /nò/ 'sit, be located at (of humans, usually non-human animates)'. E.g.,

ọ́ dì n'ébé à	'it is here'
ọ́ nò n'ébé à	'he/she is here'

(2) A "factative" construction includes a replacive which can be identified with that of the stative. For all bases except those which begin with high-low (see above), low replaces stem tone throughout the base; for bases with initial high-low, the replacive has the alternant downstep-high with the first syllable and low with all following syllables; the downstep is, of course, overt only after a high tone. In addition to the tonal replacive, the factative has a suffix consisting of /r/ plus a repetition of the preceding vowel, also with low tone. E.g., from some of the bases cited above:

ọ́ gàrà áhyá	'he went to market'
ó wèrè ósísí	'he took a stick'
ó mècìrì úzọ̀	'he shut the door'
ọ́ kwàcìrì úzọ̀	'he pushed the door shut'
ó 'wépùtàrà ḿmà	'he brought out a knife'

(3) An infinitive is formed by a prefix, with a morphotonemic alternation in one type of base. The prefix includes a downstep, which is of course deleted before low tone; it is /í'-/ or /i'-/. After a low tone in the base, all following tones have the alternant low. Examples of infinitive derivation are:

rí : í'rí   zà : ịzà   mécí : í'mécí
    kwàcí : ịkwàcì   wépụ̀tá : í'wépụ̀tà

(4) A negative imperative has a prefix /á'-/ or /é'-/, the same morphotonemic alternation in the base, and a toneless suffix /-la/. For the bases used above, negative imperatives are as follows; A1 applies in the object in the first and third:

é'rílá yá	'don't eat it'
ázàlà yà	'don't sweep it'
é'mécílá yá	'don't close it'
ákwàcìlà yà	'don't push it shut'
é'wépụ̀tàlà yà	'don't bring it out'

(5) Next to be considered is a relative construction in which the antecedent noun is the subject of the relative (as in 'the man who came', not 'the man I saw'). Many speakers of Igbo form affirmative relatives only from the stative and factative constructions, and these are the only types considered here. Two tonal replacives must be recognized in such relatives. First, downstep-high replaces a final low tone in the antecedent. Second, in statives and in those factatives which have only low tones, there is an initial downstep, and high tone replaces low throughout the form; in factatives which begin with downstep-high-low (all of which have at least three syllables), there is no alternation in the first two syllables, but high replaces low in all following syllables. (Such high tones appear also in the base, but here they are the product of two successive replacives: low replaces high in the base to form the factative, and then high replaces low in the factative to form the relative.) Examples of relative derivation are:

ŋwátàkịrị byàrà.	ŋwátàkịrị 'byárá
'A child came.'	'the child who came'
ŋwáànyị mècìrì ụ́zọ̀.	ŋwáànyị 'mécírí ụ́zọ̀
'A woman shut the door.'	'the woman who shut the door'
únù wépụ̀tàrà yà.	ú'nú 'wépụ̀tárá 'yá
'You (pl.) brought ito ut.'	'you who brought it out'

Relatives are strikingly similar to, and in all probability historically related to, an associative construction which is discussed later. Because of the ways in which tonal alternations are conditioned, however, it is necessary to separate them.

(6) In a number of constructions, there is a suffix which, after most monosyllabic bases, longer bases ending with /i/ or /u/, and a few other bases which must be individually listed, is a vowel with high tone; the identity of the vowel need not concern us here. After some monosyllabic bases, there is an allomorph consisting of /r/ plus a repetition of the preceding vowel, also with high tone. After some monosyllabic bases, and after most longer bases ending with vowels other than /i/ or /u/, there is a zero allomorph of this suffix. Before this suffix, including its zero allomorph, bases have their inherent tones as described above in all constructions but one. E.g.,

ọ́ byàrà ríé 'yá	'he came and ate it'
ọ́ byàrà zàá 'yá	'she came and swept it'
ó mécíé 'yá, ọ́ dì m̀'má	'if he closes it, fine'
kà ọ́ kwàcíé 'yá	'he should push it shut'
kà ànyị́ wépùtá 'yá	'let's bring it out'

(7) The imperative uses this suffix, but also includes a morpheme of tonal replacement. Except in bases which begin with high-low, low replaces stem tone with the first (or only) syllable of the base. For bases beginning with high-low, it is entirely reasonable to suppose that the replacive inherently has the alternant downstep before the base; this is not recoverable, however, since nothing can precede an imperative in the same clause. E.g.,

rí	:	rìé 'yá	'eat it'
zà	:	zàá 'yá	'sweep it'
mécí	:	mècíé 'yá	'close it'
kwàcí	:	kwàcíé 'yá	'push it shut'
wépùtá:		wépùtá 'yá	'bring it out'

A special morphotonemic alternation involving an imperative from a base with two syllables and the tones high-low will be noted in the following section.

What the foregoing statements have done is to establish particular instances, other than lexical, of the conditioning environments for the alternations stated in the preceding section. Low tone in some verbal constructions has been shown to be a morpheme of tonal replacement (1, 2, 7 above); this is irrelevant to the morphotonemic alternations, but, in (1) and (2), prerequisite to the derivation of relatives. With the appropriate types of bases, downstep followed by all high tones in infinitives, negative imperatives, and relatives conditions A1 (3, 4, 5 above). The final high tone of a suffix in a number of verbal constructions conditions A2 and A3 (6, 7 above).

5.19. The statements concerning morphotonemic alternations in 5.17 above were intentionally somewhat oversimplified in the interests of clarity. Special exceptions to them remain to be stated, and a few statements of more restricted alternations must be added.

(1) Apart from the negative imperative described above, there is only one negative construction in Igbo. Downstep is a characteristic of this negative construction, but with a unique morphotonemic alternation. After subjects other than singular pronouns, there is a prefix /á'-/ or /é'-/—with automatic deletion of downstep before low, of course. After low tone in the base, all following tones have the alternant low. There is also a suffix, /-ghị/, which is toneless. Examples of this negative construction are:

ànyị́ é'ríghị́ ńrí	'we didn't eat (food)'
há ázàghì ụ́lọ̀	'they didn't sweep the house'
Okóyè é'mécíghị́ ụ́zọ̀	'Okoye didn't shut the door'
há ákwàcìghì ụ́zọ̀	'they didn't push the door shut'
únù é'wépùtàghì yà	'you (pl.) didn't bring it out'

After a singular pronoun subject, which has low tone in the negative, the prefix
has an allomorph with no vowel, but with its high tone and downstep replacing
the first tone of the verb base; if that tone was low, all following syllables in the
form have low tone—in the second and fourth of the following examples, the
second syllable of the verb form had already acquired its low tone by the rule
above, before the preceding low was replaced by high according to this rule. Counterparts of the above with singular subject pronouns are:

ò rí'ghį́ ńrí	'he didn't eat'
ọ̀ zághì úlọ̀	'she didn't sweep the house'
è mé'cíghį́ ḿ úzọ̀	'I didn't shut the door'
à kwácìghì ḿ úzọ̀	'I didn't push the door shut'
ì wépụ̀tàghì yà	'you didn't bring it out'

Downstep followed by one or more high tones in the negative conditions A1,
as expected, except in one type of form. Before stating the exception, it is necessary to describe a "verbal noun." A verbal noun, which in most respects functions
like other nouns, has a prefix which is segmentally /a-/ or /e-/, with low tone before high in the first syllable of the base, and high tone before low. The verbal
noun is used after the stative of a verb /ná/ (which is not independently used,
but to which a meaning may be assigned something like 'be at, be with') to form
an "incompletive," and after the stative of /gá/ 'go' to form a "future." E.g.,

ọ́ nà èrí ń'rí	'he is eating'
ọ́ gà ázà úlọ̀	'she's going to sweep the house'
á gà ḿ èmécí úzọ̀	'I'm going to shut the door'
á gà ḿ ákwàcí 'yá	'I'm going to push it shut'
á nà ḿ èwépụ̀tá 'yá	'I'm bringing it out'

In the negative of the incompletive and future, the formation described a-
bove applies to /ná/ and /gá/. This yields forms which have a downstep followed
by one or two high tones. According to A1, it would be expected that low tone in
the prefix of a following verbal noun would have the alternant high. An exception must be incorporated into the statement for A1: the alternation does not
apply in a verbal noun after a negative. E.g.,

há á'gághį̀ èrí ń'rí	'they're not going to eat'
ọ̀ ná'ghį̀ èwépụ̀tá 'yá	'he's not bringing it out'

(2) A similar exception must be incorporated into the statement of A2. A
verbal noun may occur after a "consecutive" construction with /ná/, in which
/ná/ has the zero allomorph of the previously described suffix with high tone. According to A2, it would be expected that low tone in the verbal noun prefix would
have the alternant downstep-high; in this environment, however, the alternation
does not apply. E.g., in the next-to-last word of the following:

há nà èrí ń'rí, ná àŋú ḿ'mányá
'they're eating (food) and drinking (booze)'

In spite of the above, it cannot be said that the verbal noun prefix before a high tone is an invariable low tone; A1 applies regularly after a relative:

ónyé 'ná érí ń'rí   'the person who is eating'

(3) In a "completive" construction, after a subject other than a singular pronoun, there is also a prefix /à-/ or /è-/. After high tone, the tone of this prefix has the alternant downstep-high before high according to A2. After a singular pronoun subject, the vowel of the prefix does not appear; the allomorph of the prefix is downstep alone. With appropriate verbal bases, these statements yield forms which have a downstep followed by all high tones, which is otherwise the conditioning environment for A1. However, this allomorphic downstep is itself the product of A2, with a statement added here deleting the vowel after singular pronouns, so that A1 can no longer apply. After such completive forms, A2 and A3 apply. E.g., with objects /àkwá/ 'egg' and /ńrí/ 'food':

únù èríélá ń'rí   'you (pl.) have eaten'
ànyí 'éríélá 'ákwá   'we have eaten eggs'
ó 'ríélá ń'rí   'he has eaten'

(4) A morpheme with the meaning "associative" is recognized as present in phrases such as /ú'ló 'ányí/ 'our house', which is /úlò/ 'house' associated with /ànyí/ 'us' (cf. 4.10). The tones of this and certain other types of phrases are not accounted for by the morphotonemic alternations stated so far. Nor can they be directly accounted for by other alternations, because the same independent tones do not have alternants in a sequence of noun plus numeral, as /úlò àtó/ 'three houses'. It might, of course, be suggested that morphologic conditioning is present; the alternation takes place if the second word in the phrase is a noun, but not if it is a numeral. A numeral, however, may also participate in the associative construction. There is a minimal and morphemic contrast between /úlò àtó/ 'three houses' and /ú'ló 'átó/ 'the third house'. The alternations in question can be accounted for if the associative morpheme is interpreted as having the underlying form of a high tone between two nouns, or between a noun and another word used nominally. (Historically, the high tone undoubtedly originally accompanied a vowel.)

One morphotonemic alternation conditioned by this underlying high tone is here derived after A1 but before A2 and A3; an alternative possibility is to derive it after A3, but the required statements would be more complicated and less reasonable. If the associative morpheme is followed by a low tone (before the application of A2 if a high tone follows that), final low tone in the preceding noun has the alternant downstep-high; i.e., it is assimilated to the level of the associative high tone. This, with deletion of downstep after low, accounts for the tone of the final syllable of the first word in each of the following; the last two of these include the later application of A2, and all of them show the still later deletion of the associative high tone:

áhà	'name' :	á'há òbòdò áhụ̀	'the name of that town'
òbòbò	'town',	à 'this' :	òbòdó à	'this town'
ụ́lọ̀	'house',	ànyị́ (1pl) :	ụ́'lọ́ 'ányị́	'our house'
ìtè	'pot',	ànyị́ (1pl) :	ìté 'ányị́	'our pot'

The underlying high tone of the associative morpheme is deleted only after the application of A3. It is only this that can account for A3 applying after low tone in the surface manifestation in phrases like the following:

ụ́lọ̀   'house, building',   áhyá 'market, merchandise':
ụ́lọ̀ á'hyá 'store, shop'

It now becomes apparent that, in many of the examples previously cited for A2 and A3, though by no means all of them, the alternation is actually conditioned, in the deeper structure, by the high tone of the associative morpheme rather than by the final high tone of the preceding word. These include cases like the following:

é'gó	'money',	ànyị́	(1pl) :	égó 'ányị́	'our money'
ìkó	'cup',	m̀mánụ́	'oil' :	ìkó m̀'mánụ́	'a cup of oil'
ánụ́	'meat',	éwú	'goat' :	ánụ́ é'wú	'goat meat'

Implicit in the foregoing is an interesting ambiguity. As noted above, in /ụ́lọ̀ àtọ́/ 'three houses' the associative morpheme is not present, but in /ụ́'lọ́ 'átọ́/ 'the third house' it is present and conditions two morphotonemic alternations. In a phrase such as /éwú 'átọ́/, however, there are two possibilities: the application of A2 in the second word could be conditioned directly by the final high tone of the preceding noun, in which case the phrase would mean 'three goats'; or it could be conditioned by the underlying and later deleted high tone of the associative morpheme, in which case the phrase would mean 'the third goat'. This ambiguity is normally avoided by using, for the ordinal, the noun /ŋ̀kè/ 'thing, the one' in association with the numeral, yielding /ŋ̀ké 'átọ́/ 'the third'. The noun is then used in association with this phrase, yielding /éwú 'ŋ́ké 'átọ/. In the relatively careful speech characteristic of linguistic analysis and language teaching, /éwú ŋ̀ké 'átọ́/ is often heard, without the normal manifestation of the associative morpheme after the first word. This is presumably appositional: 'a goat, the third one'. The technically ambiguous /éwú 'átọ́/ is assumed to refer to 'three goats'.

By analogy with the use of /ŋ̀kè/ to avoid ambiguity in ordinal phrases after a high tone, it is commonly used also after a noun with inherent final low tone, where there would be no ambiguity in any case. Thus 'the third house' is often, if not usually, expressed as /ụ́'lọ́ 'ŋ́ké 'átọ́/. On the other hand, in some combinations where the ordinal is the only reasonable semantic possibility, /ŋ̀kè/ is not used; e.g., /n'élékéré 'átọ́/ 'at the third bell, at three o'clock'. All numerals ('two' through 'ten' and derived phrases) are included in these statements; they all begin with low-high. (The words for 'one', 'twenty', and 'four hundred' are grammatically nouns, not numerals.)

The foregoing discussion of the associative construction is, of course, in the context of a treatment of tonology. It may not be out of place, however, to add that it is presented with a full consciousness of the striking grammatical parallelism with associatives in Bantu and other languages (see Welmers 1963a). There are also some differences in grammatical detail, as will be seen in connection with possessive pronouns.

(5) After nouns other than verbal nouns, the combination of a noun with a monosyllabic modifier (a pronoun) does not include the associative morpheme. This is attested by the fact final low tone in such a noun does not have the alternant downstep-high as required before the associative. E.g.,

         ụ́lọ̀ yá   'his house'   ìtè gị́   'your pot'

For some speakers, the same is true regularly after verbal nouns; thus, from a verb stem /bè/ 'cut':

         ọ́ nà ébè yá   'he's cutting it'

For many other speakers, however, the combination of verbal noun with pronoun must be interpreted as including the associative morpheme; thus, probably more commonly:

         ọ́ nà é'bé 'yá   'he's cutting it'

A verbal noun with a following noun ("object"), however, always uses the associative construction:

         ọ́ nà é'bé ùdọ̀   'he's cutting a rope'
         ọ́ nà á'zá 'ézí   'she's sweeping the compound'

The grammar of these may be reflected by 'he is-at rope-cutting' and 'she is-at compound-sweeping'.

(6) In the sequence of an imperative from a two-syllable base with the tones high-low and a noun or pronoun object with initial low (or downstep), a complex of alternations identical with those conditioned by the associative morpheme, attributable to an original verbal suffix, a vowel with high tone, is found. E.g.,

         há'pụ́ 'ányị́   'leave us alone'
         há'pụ́ 'yá   'leave him alone'
         (cf.: hápụ̀ éwú à   'leave this goat alone')

(7) Two special alternations apply in the subject of a verb if something precedes it in the same clause. The first of these is A1 after high tone in this additional environment: initial low followed by high in the subject has the alternant high. The second is identical with the alternation before the associative morpheme, though the presence of that morpheme is out of the question: before low tone, final low in the subject has the alternant downstep-high. Both of these alternations are attested in relative clauses (of the type 'the man I saw', not 'the man who came', in which the antecedent is the subject). Only the second is at-

tested anywhere else. The reason for this is that anything other than the antecedent of a relative, before the subject of a verb in the same clause, must be followed by the morpheme /kà/, which does not have the conditioning high tone. In the relative clauses among the following examples, the antecedents are nouns meaning, respectively, 'thing, matter' and 'place'; the alternation illustrated in each is shown by a numeral:

(1)	:	ànyí	:	íhé ányí mèrè	'what we did'
(2)	:	únù	:	íhé ú'nú mèrè	'what you (pl.) did'
(1, 2)	:	Òkóyè	:	íhé Ókó'yé mèrè	'what Okoye did'
(1, 2)	:	ìkó únù	:	ébé íkó ú'nú dì	'where your cups are'
(2)	:	únù	:	ébé 'ólé kà ú'nú nò	'where are you?'
(2)	:	únù	:	ó bù yá kà ú'nú hùrù	'it's he that you saw'

It has been assumed that the third person plural pronoun form, which among other things may be used as a verbal subject, has an initial downstep: /'há/. For the singular subject pronouns, there is no evidence that there is or is not inherently an initial downstep. If there is, they are also included in a minor extension of the first of these alternations: after high, initial downstep in the subject is deleted. E.g.,

ébé há nò	'where they are'
íhé ó nà èmé	'what he is doing'

(8) Two expressions in adverbial usage are exempted from A1 and A2; their initial low tone does not undergo alternation. These are /òzó/ 'again, any more', and /ùgbú à/ 'now'. The latter of these is apparently a noun meaning 'time' and the demonstrative 'this', but the noun is not attested in any other combination. Instances of these in the conditioning environments for A1 and A2 are:

ó còrò í'byá òzó	'he wants to come again'
kà ó byá òzó	'he should come again'
mèé 'yá ùgbú à	'do it right now'

The first of these also appears without alternation in what otherwise seems to be an associative construction after the words /ízù/ 'week', /óŋwá/ 'month', and /áfò/ 'year', with the meaning 'next'. The three expressions are:

í'zú òzó   óŋwá òzó   á'fó òzó

It cannot be said, however, that initial low tone is simply invariable in these expressions. A completely regular associative construction using /òzó/ is also found, similar to the ordinal expressions previously noted. E.g.,

ú'ló 'ŋké 'ózó   'the other house'

Nor does it seem feasible to assign the instances of nonalternation in these expressions to adverbial use in general. There are some constructions in which a noun /m̀bú/ 'the beginning, the first time' appears in comparable adverbial usage, but with regular alternations; note the contrast in the following:

ọ́ gàrà Àbá ọ̀zọ́   'he went to Aba again'
ọ́ gàrà Àbá 'm̀bụ́   'he went to Aba first'

A rigidly formal presentation of all that has been said about Igbo tone would inevitably be more difficult to follow, or more lengthy, but it is of course possible. It would follow this order:

(1) Identify lexical tones, including the high tone of the associative morpheme.
(2) Derive the tones of verb bases.
(3) Derive the tones of verbal constructions, including the tones of subject pronouns.
(4) Make statements concerning monosyllabic nouns, including the pronominal types.
(5) State the alternation illustrated by /égó . . ./ from /é'gó/.
(6) State A1, A2, A3 with the exceptions noted.
(7) State the alternations in (7) and (8) above.

5.20. In Efik, there are two kinds of tonal alternations in nouns in different environments. Historically, these alternations are very probably reflexes of an associative morpheme between two nouns. They are also found, however, in a type of phrase in which an associative morpheme is hardly expected; the conditioning environments in the two types of phrase are partially different. Personal names and five kinship terms (meaning 'father', 'mother', 'husband', 'namesake', and 'friend', but not the word for 'son, daughter' and some others) are exempt from these alternations. Also exempt are the very few nouns which begin with a consonant.

There is a class of words in Efik which may legitimately be called adjectives. In some languages, many words that have often uncritically been called adjectives (usually, apparently, for no better reason than that they parallel English adjectives in meaning) can be shown to be nouns. The words classed as adjectives in Efik, however, differ morphologically and syntactically from words which are obviously nouns. In nouns, except for a few indicating persons, there is no singular-plural distinction; but adjectives have singular and plural froms distinguished by different prefixes. Adjectives are used attributively before nouns—by no means the typical order in Niger-Congo languages; adjective-noun phrases, therefore, have the structure modifier-head. In noun-noun phrases, however, the first noun is the head and the second (in an associative relationship) is the modifier. The demonstratives /émì/ 'this', /órò/ 'that (near you)', and /ókò/ 'that (away from us)', used attributively after nouns, are themselves a sub-class of nouns.

For purposes of stating tonal alternations, Efik nouns fall into two tonal groups: (1) those whose first tone is low or high-downstep and whose second tone is high, and (2) those whose first two tones are any other sequence. These are illustrated in the two columns below. Since only the first two tones are relevant, the tones of the first and second noun in each column need not be distinguished; / ∧ / indicates a high-low sequence with a single vowel. They are listed separately merely to illustrate all possible tone sequences in two syllable nouns. The sequences in the two tonal groups are shown in the following:

	(1)		(2)
ìkpáŋ	'spoon'	ébót	'goat'
àw̄â	'cat'	íkwâ	'knife'
íˈnwén	'bird'	úfɔk	'house'
		ùsàn	'dish'

Under alternation, all nouns in the same group have the same tones in the same environment; for each group, there are two alternant sequences. For (1), in the first alternant, the first two tones are high-downstep-high and all remaining tones are unchanged (this has a zero effect for the third sequence illustrated above); in the second alternant, the first two tones are low-high and all remaining tones are unchanged (this has a zero effect for the first two sequences). For (2), in the first alternant, the initial tone is high and all remaining tones are low (with a zero effect for the third sequence illustrated above); in the second alternant, all tones are low (with a zero effect for the fourth sequence). Before stating the conditioning environments, these alternations are illustrated after two adjectives, the first alternant for each group on the left and the second on the right:

			'a big . . .'	'a little . . .'
ìkpáŋ	'spoon'	:	àkámbá íˈkpáŋ	èkpírì ìkpáŋ
àw̄â	'cat'	:	àkámbá áˈw̄â	èkpírì àw̄â
íˈnwén	'bird'	:	àkámbá íˈnwén	èkpírì ìnwén
------	---------	---	----------------	----------------
ébót	'goat'	:	àkámbá ébòt	èkpírì èbòt
ìkwâ	'knife'	:	àkámbá íkwà	èkpírì ìkwà
úfɔk	'house'	:	àkámbá úfɔk	èkpírì ùfɔk
ùsàn	'dish'	:	àkámbá úsàn	èkpírì ùsàn

The conditioning environments for the first alternants are: after an adjective ending with high tone (as above), or after a noun ending with either high or low (but not high-low accompanying the final syllable). The conditioning environments for the second alternants are: after an adjective ending with low tone (as above, and including high-low with the final syllable), after a noun having high-low with the final syllable, or (a strikingly restricted instance) after a noun whose inherent tones are all high after it has undergone either alternation. The alternations after adjectives have already been illustrated; the conditioning environments after nouns are illustrated in the following, using /ówó/ 'person' and, for the last condition, /órò/ 'that (near you)':

ébót ówò òrò	'that person's goat'
úfɔk ówò òrò	'that person's house'
íkwâ òwò òrò	'that person's knife'

If adjectives alone are considered in the conditioning environment, these alternations can be simply stated as phonologically conditioned: the first alternants appear after high, the second after low. If only nouns of the tonal types represented by /ébót/, /úfɔ̀k/, and /ùsàn/ are considered, the same phonologic conditioning can be derived by positing, in the deep structure, an associative morpheme with high tone which is the actual conditioning environment before its deletion; the first alternants follow. Especially in light of the Igbo data discussed in the preceding section, this is an extremely attractive hypothesis. Two instances of the second alternants after nouns, however, remain to be accounted for; in each case, the associative morpheme must be assumed to be present in the deep structure, and a rationale must be sought for its deletion prior to the application of the tonal alternations and its subsequent deletion elsewhere. In the first of these cases, the associative morpheme appears after high-low accompanying a final vowel; the associative morpheme is assumed to be a vowel with high tone in its most underlying form. The first rule to be stated is that the vowel (but not the tone) of the associative morpheme is lost in all its appearances, leaving a variety of tone sequences accompanying single vowels. If the preceding vowel has the sequence high-low, this rule yields a sequence of three tones with a single vowel: high-low-high. The second rule posits the nonpermissibility of such sequences of three tones, and deletes the last, which is the high tone of the associative morpheme. In the second case in question, at least three words must be in sequence, with two occurrences of the associative morpheme. If a noninitial and nonfinal word in such a phrase has only high tones, the first rule above yields both a preceding and a following high tone. The third rule posits the nonpermissibility of such a complexity, and deletes the high tone after the word in question. The stage is now set for the application of the alternations stated above. In any noun phrase, the first alternants appear after high and the second after low; in the two cases where the associative high tone has already been deleted, low rather than high is now the conditioning environment. Finally, the associative high tone is deleted in all remaining environments, and the present surface structure is left. Noun-noun and adjective-noun phrases must still be recognized as grammatically distinct.

5.21. It is not at all uncommon to find morphotonemic alternations or morphemes of tonal replacement which have a zero effect, where the alternant or replacive is identical with the inherent tone or tones to which it applies. This results in formal neutralization, but rarely in ambiguity; there usually seems to be enough redundancy lurking around to make the choice between derivations clear. A case of ambiguity involving ordinal phrases in Igbo, and its resolution, has already been noted. In the Efik verbal system, there is an interesting, though still restricted, instance of neutralization with unresolved ambiguity.

As a point of departure, consider the tones accompanying the segmental sequence /dep/ in the following; both forms are derived from /dép/ 'buy':

ŋkédèp m̀bòró	'I bought bananas'
m̀bòró ké ŋké'dép	'it's bananas I bought'

It would appear from the translations that the second of these is contrastive, distinguishing 'bananas' from all other possible purchases, while the first is not. This is not entirely true, in that the first is an appropriate answer to the question 'What did you buy?' (and says 'bananas, not something else'), but not to the question 'What did you do?', to which the answer might require a different verb. In answer to 'What did you do?', there is a truly neutral past construction which is quite different:

ḿ'má ń'dép m̀bòró   'I bought bananas'

The distinction is rather that the first example, with a morpheme of tonal replacement (low replaces stem tone), indicates contrast or emphasis accompanying something which follows the verb, which may be an object or an adverbial complement; the second example, with the verb's stem tone, indicates contrast or emphasis with something preceding the verb and its subject pronoun prefix, which may be a transposed object or adverbial complement followed by /ké/ (as above) or, if nothing is transposed, an expressed noun subject.[5] The latter includes independent pronoun forms; in the English translations of the following, the contrasted subject is italicized to suggest the appropriateness of contrastive stress:

Ákpán éké'dép m̀bòró   *'Akpan* bought bananas'
àmì ŋ̀ké'dép m̀bòró   *'I* bought bananas'

The same distinction is made in the same way, tonally, in the present, without the past marker /-ké'-/; the corresponding verb forms, in the first person singular, are /ńdèp/ and /ńdép/. In the future, a "neutral" form, /ńyé'dép/, is distinguished from a "contrastive", /ńdîdêp/, but the latter does not indicate whether the contrasted item follows or precedes the verb.

Apart from other clues which may be present, therefore, tone alone may be sufficient to distinguish following contrast (with replacive low) from preceding contrast (stem tone) in the past and present. There are, however, verbs whose stem tone is low to begin with; with such, the replacive low tone has a zero effect, and the contrast is neutralized in the verb form (as it is in the future as noted above). Sentences paralleling the first two examples above with /ỹàm/ 'sell' are:

ŋ̀káỹàm m̀bòró   'I sold bananas'
m̀bòró ké ŋ̀káỹàm   'it's bananas I sold'

Without a tonal distinction in the verbs in these sentences, it is still possible to determine what is contrastive. In the first, nothing precedes the verb with its subject pronoun prefix, so only what follows can be contrastive. In the second,

---

[5] Ida C. Ward (1933, pp. 63-65), though primarily concerned with phonology, demonstrates her usual insight by suggesting that these contrasts "may indicate some kind of emphasis". M. M. Green (1949) recognizes the indication of emphasis or contrast more clearly, but only as applied to object and subject, which is by no means the entire story.

the transposed object followed by /ké/ is by definition contrastive. Ambiguity arises, however, if there is an expressed noun subject and nothing transposed; but even here an independent pronoun may be assumed to be contrastive, because it would otherwise not be required. E.g.,

Ákpán ákáyàm m̀bòró   'Akpan sold *bananas*'
                      or: '*Akpan* sold bananas'
àmì ŋ́káȳàm m̀bòró   '*I* sold bananas'

In written Efik, independent pronoun forms are very commonly used where they are not required or are even inappropriate in the spoken language. A major reason for this is that four different subject pronoun prefixes in some vowel harmony contexts, and two pairs in other contexts, are written identically; /e/ and /ɛ/ are not distinguished, and tone is not written, with the result that second and third person pronouns are never distinguished, and in some cases the singular and plural forms are identical. The independent pronoun forms are added to resolve the ambiguity. Because of the emphasis on the written language in schools, and because non-African learners are likely to miss those very contrasts, this usage sometimes spills over into the spoken language. This introduces a new ambiguity, between contrastive after and contrastive before the verb, into sentences like the last above !

5.22. In the preceding few sections, downstep has been assigned, without comment, to the beginning of some morphemes and to the end of others. Most of the morphemes in question have been prefixes. In some languages, downstep, wherever it appears, is the final phoneme of a morpheme, and stems also may have a final downstep. Downstep has no phonetic realization, of course, when such a form is cited in isolation. But, in such languages, some morphemes are typically followed by either downstep-high or low, while other morphemes are typically followed by (the same) high or low. This, with some complications in detail, is the situation in Ukele.[6] In some other languages, downstep may normally be the initial phoneme of some morphemes,

In Tiv, there are three possibilities.[7] First, downstep is the final phoneme of some morphemes with high tone, but not of others. In the second of the following examples, downstep is written, as usual, before the syllable after it; but it must be interpreted as belonging to the preceding morpheme:

má méɣ   'drink the poison'   ká 'méɣ   'it is poison'

In other cases, downstep is the initial phoneme of a morpheme. In the following, the initial vowel of each word is a prefix, and it is the same prefix; the contrast between high and downstpe-high must therefore be attributed to the following stems:

íkọ́n   'trees'   í'jí   'egg; flies'

---

[6] As convincingly reported by John Fajen, presently engaged in research on Ukele.

[7] The Tiv data are taken from R. C. Abraham (1940b), but retranscribed. See also Arnott 1964, McCawley 1970.

In still other cases, downstep must be interpreted as having morphemic status by itself. In some verbal constructions, downstep appears before all verb stems which do not have or begin with low tone. In other constructions, this is not true. Downstep is thus the morpheme which marks the past construction; it appears in some other constructions also. The vowel difference in the following is irrelevant:

> á vé   'he has come'   á 'vá   'he came'

In the first of these constructions, however, downstep appears after the first or second person singular subject pronoun; in this case, downstep must be assigned to the pronoun. (The cognate pronouns in Jukun are the only ones which have low tone.) E.g.,

> ḿ 'vé   'I have come'   ú 'vé   'you have come'

5.23. In the languages cited so far for illustrative purposes, it has generally been possible, and usually not difficult, to distinguish lexical tones, morphotonemic alternations, and tonally realized morphemes, and to state their interacting manifestations. In the Bariba verbal system, the interaction of all of these plus final vowels creates such an unusually complex set of verbal forms that one is tempted to wonder if it is profitable, or even possible, to make morpheme cuts in every form. At best, there is some unusual variation among allomorphs; at worst, a number of portmanteau forms might be posited.

In working on Bariba for one month in 1949, and for the most part communicating with informants through a missionary's Yoruba, it was most fortunate that one of the first verbs chosen to elicit a variety of verbal constructions was the verb meaning 'plant'. Out of 145 verbs checked, there are only three that show the maximum variation of seven different forms; this is one of them. Without the data provided by such a verb, it would have been impossible to arrive at a complete outline of the system; for 85 of the remaining verbs, three of the corresponding forms are identical, and for the other 57 two to five forms are identical, but not always the same combinations. Various verbal constructions are distinguished by an assortment of particles in addition to the different verbal forms. Thus the variation in the verbal forms themselves is redundant. The selection of the correct form is nevertheless obligatory, as was amusingly demonstrated by an argument between two informants who disagreed on a form that would probably not be used often. The argument was settled when one informant cited two other forms of the same verb, exactly as a Latin teacher might cite the principal parts of a verb to show an erring student where he went wrong! Because of the limitations of time and the problems created by indirect elicitation (particularly when I was totally unfamiliar with the Yoruba verbal system), the labels here given to the relevant constructions may not be ideal in every case, but they will at least serve to show that different constructions are indeed involved.[8] For

---

[8] The labels used here for four of these constructions differ from those in Welmers 1952a. Cf. 13.4.

three sample verbs, meaning respectively 'plant', 'sell', and 'count', the forms
used in the relevant constructions are as follows:

Hortative	dūūrē	dɔ̄ɔ̄rā	garì
Past	dūūrā	dɔ̄ɔ̄rā	garà
Incompletive	duurù	dɔɔrà	garì
Customary	dùùrè	dɔ̄ɔ̄rē	garì
Experiential	dūūrū	dɔ̄ɔ̄rā	garì
Imperative	dūūrūō	dɔɔrō	garìō
Past negative	dūūrè	dɔ̄ɔ̄rè	garà

The linguist always hopes to find a relatively simple set of rules, but none
are obvious in Bariba. The past does not always end in the vowel /a/; with the
third column above, compare the first two forms from a verb 'tether': /sɔ̄rī, sɔ̄rī/.
The incompletive does not always have the tones high-low; the first three forms
from a verb 'tie up' are /bɔ̄kē, bɔ̄kūā, bɔ́kù/. The final vowel of the imperative is
always /o/, but it does not always have mid tone; the imperative of a verb 'break'
is /buó/, and there are eighteen more verbs like it. In 141 verbs, the hortative
and past have the same tones; but in four they have different tones (though at
least the four agree with each other). Nothing, in fact, seems to be susceptible
to simple and reasonable statement.

Well into the month of work, as might be expected, even a tabulation like
that above (which does incorporate a rationale not yet revealed) had not been
arrived at. The data consisted of a table full of piles of 3 × 5 slips, which had
been attacked from more angles than a ball of string whose principal investigator
is a kitten. By way of comment on practical aspects of field work, it is by no means
irrelevant to relate that, at about 10 P.M. after a twelve-hour work day, it was
suggested that the following day's rat-race be scratched, and a group of us go hunting. A choice of big game was guaranteed within a reasonable radius—from *an-
tilope cheval* to *phacochere* to lion to hippopotamus. After eight hours of traipsing
through park savannah the next day, game sighted: two ground squirrels and three
guinea fowl (one of which was drilled through the neck by a blind shot from a
22, fired into the tall grass where they had disappeared, in an effort merely to
flush them into flight; the other two took off at different angles, and your red-
faced reporter succeeded in spraying a 12-gauge shell of birdshot squarely between
them).

Let this be a lesson to inexperienced field workers who may not appreciate
the invaluable contributions available to linguistic research from a day of hunting
(or possibly other relaxation). While looking over the slips that evening, and
chewing a meditative pencil, light suddenly dawned. Of all the sets of forms, the
hortative shows the least evidence of being derived. The past frequently ends
with the vowel /a/. In some verbs, the incompletive and experiential end with
the vowel /u/; most of the corresponding hortatives end with /e/, but a few with
/i/. The customary frequently ends with low tone. The imperative always ends
with the vowel /o/. And the past negative frequently ends with the vowel /e/.

Thus the hortative must be taken as the basic form from which all other forms are derived. Further, in deriving the other sets, it quickly became obvious that, irrespective of the identification of morphemes, it would be simplest to start by making separate statements for final vowels and for tones (the latter in most cases only the tones of the final vowels, but in some cases the tones of the entire form). A complete, if not simple or very satisfying, set of statements was then worked out with relatively little difficulty.

Verbs are first devided into five major classes depending on the formation of the past. For four of these classes, only the final vowel and/or a suffix is involved; for the fifth, all verbs in which are monosyllabic, mid tone replaces falling tone to form the past. For verbs with final mid tone in the hortative, there is a lexically conditioned morphotonemic alternation in the incompletive, creating two subclasses in four of the five classes. Apart from this, the tones of all forms can be stated as derivations from the tones of the hortative, except that in one class the final vowel of the hortative is an additional conditioning factor. In another class, there are two instances of lexical conditioning in the derivation of final vowels. The possible permutations of these various factors yield twenty-five theoretically possible paradigms for the seven forms. Twenty-three of these are attested by a number of verbs ranging from one to twenty-nine.

The details of this complex of paradigms need not be presented here; the chart above would merely have twenty-five columns instead of three, two of them blank. And the derivational statements by themselves would be uninteresting lists. What is of interest, however, is the theoretical problem of the interdependence of the final vowel and tone. In one set of forms, a morphotonemic alternation has been recognized. In the remainder of the data, however, are the final vowel and the tone (of the final vowel or of the entire form) separate morphemes, or are they components of single morphemes? The latter appears to be the preferable interpretation; classes and subclasses condition different segmental allomorphs in every construction, but in addition to what has already been eliminated there are only two constructions for which morphotonemic statements turn out to be required. The morphotonemic alternants of final vowels and in some cases entire forms can be considered conditioned by morphemes defined as to segmental shape.

A final question concerns the composition of the consecutive form itself. Is this to be considered a stem, or is it also composed of a stem plus another morpheme—presumably the final vowel, at least in forms of two or more syllables? In disyllabic and longer forms, the final vowel is /a/ in over half of the verbs recorded. It is /i/, /e/ (with the regular alternant /ɛ/ after nasals), or /u/ in all other forms. Except immediately after a nasalized vowel, the final vowel is recorded as nasalized in only one verb; this may have been an error. These restrictions suggest that the final vowel is a suffix. In about two-thirds of the verbs recorded, its tone is mid; instances of high and low (top does not occur) may be considered lexically conditioned by the stem. The suffix may be interpreted as having a zero allomorph in monosyllabic hortatives; all seven vowels except /ɔ/

are found, and nasalization (including /ɔ̃/, but /o/ does not occur nasalized) is common.

Complex as the Bariba verbal system is, therefore, its seemingly exuberant tonal variations all boil down to lexical tone and a surprisingly few morphotonemic alternations.

5.24. As noted in 5.3 above, ChiNyanja has no lexical tone in verbs. In any given construction, all verb forms with the same number of syllables have the same tone sequence. Different constructions differ from each other in tone, however. Five different tone sequences are recorded by Deborah Harding (1966, pp. 114-22). For each, statements are made for forms using verb bases from one to five syllables. The conditioning factor for each sequence is the prefix which marks the particular construction.

On the basis of considerably less data, Beatrice Welmers has recorded four tone sequences in ChiNyanja verbs. A fifth may possibly occur in constructions not recorded. Enough data is available, however, to show remarkable differences between the verb tones as recorded by two different people. The informants for each speak a dialect known as ChiNgoni, spoken by the ANgoni people, who came to Zambia from South Africa some generations ago and have adopted ChiNyanja as their only language. There are, however, two nonadjacent ANgoni communities, and it may be that two rather different dialects are being reported. An example of the difference is a verb form meaning 'he can sell', recorded by the two investigators respectively as /àngàgùlítsé/ and /àngágùlìtsè/. There is also evidence that the conditions for the occurrence of a given tone sequence are considerably more complex in the data recorded by Miss Harding. In spite of the drastic differences between them, however, each system can be treated in the same way.

The four tone sequences recorded by Beatrice Welmers are illustrated in the following:

ànàwérèngà	'he read' (recent past)
ámàwèréngà	'he reads'
ànkáwèrèngà	'he read' (remote past)
ádzáwèrèngà	'he will read'

The conditioning factor is the prefix, respectively /nà/, /mà/, /nká/, and /dzá/ in these forms. Each of these conditions the tone of the preceding pronoun and the following verb base. The pronoun tones are obvious in the above. After the prefix, the first prefix conditions high tone with the next syllable, and low with all remaining syllables. The second prefix conditions high tone with the next-to-last syllable of the form (that it is the next-to-last syllable and not the second syllable after the prefix is shown by forms with one or two more syllables), and low with all other syllables. The third and fourth prefixes condition low tone throughout the remainder of the form.

In such a situation, tone is not separately significant for each syllable; the tones of the entire form are conditioned by the presence of one prefix syllable.

It is suggested that this be labelled "focus tone"—the prefix is the focal point from which the tones of all other syllables are determined.

In Shona, and apparently commonly in Southern Bantu languages, verbs fall into two classes tonally. E.g., Shona has contrasts such as /kùfùrà/ 'to graze' and /kùfúrá/ 'to blow'. For each tonal class, there is a paradigm of tone sequences in different verbal constructions, similar to the system(s) found in ChiNyanja. This may be viewed as a combination of lexical and focus tone. Derek Fivaz (1969, pp. 20-21) treats the two tonal paradigms as sets of morphemes of tone replacement, and views verb stems themselves as toneless. The assignment of one or the other sets of morphemes to a given stem is nevertheless by lexical conditioning. It is true, however, that tone is not separately significant for each syllable in any verb form, while it is in words other than verbs.

5.25. Finally, tone functions at the syntactic level in some languages. Kay Williamson (1965) describes "tone groups" and "tone phrases" in Ijo; the tones of one or more words in a sequence may be determined by their grammatical relationship to a key or focal word. A somewhat similar phenomenon is reported in Ukele (John Fajen, personal communication), in which a negative verb conditions a special set of morphotonemic alternations throughout all of what follows in the sentence. In KiKongo, topicalization and relativization are marked solely by the tones of the verb forms in those constructions, though the rules may result in a zero effect in some cases; a similar phenomenon was described for Igbo in 5.18 above. It is quite possible that the occurrence of different tones with verbs used in at least some subordinate clauses is widespread.

In Akan, verb forms in three types of subordinate constructions have different tones than in other environments. The clauses are those introduced by a conjunction of which the Fante form is /déè/ 'that, in order that', by the relative marker /áà/, and by the contrastive morpheme /nà/, which appears regularly after question words but also after other forms. In Fante (the rules are slightly different for Twi and Asante; see Schachter and Fromkin 1968), all low tones up to the first high in a verb form are replaced by high in such clauses, and a final low tone after high is replaced by downstep-high if nothing else follows in the clause. E.g.,

ɔbébá	'he will come':	mígwìn déè ɔbébá
		'I think he will come'
ɔríbà	'he's coming':	mígwìn déè ɔrí'bá
		'I think he's coming'
ɔbáà há	'he came here':	mígwìn déè ɔbáà há
		'I think he came here'
ɔrùfùná	'he's tiring':	pɔnkɔ́ áà ɔrúfúná
		'a horse that's tiring'
ɔrìkásà	'he's speaking':	wáná nà ɔríká'sá
		'who's speaking?'

Chapter 6

Noun Class and Concord Systems: An Introduction

6.1. In all branches of the Niger-Kordofanian language family with the exception of Mande, it typical that a noun in its simplest form can be analyzed as consisting of a stem and an affix. In some languages—e.g., Yoruba, Igbo, Efik—the affix has at best a minimal grammatical function such as deriving a few nouns from verbs, and there are only slight traces of semantic correlation, which one might hardly recognize except through comparative studies. At the other extreme, there are many languages and groups of languages in which affixes with noun stems constitute a major criterion for dividing nouns into a number of noun classes which differ from each other in a variety of grammatical constructions. The nature and functions of these noun classes, and to some extent their form, show a number of striking similarities even when languages belonging to rather distantly related groups are compared.

It is the Bantu languages which are the most commonly associated with noun class systems. In this very large group, there is a substantial amount of homogeneity in the noun class systems and in their grammatical functions. Many Bantu languages have a large number of noun classes, and their grammatical functions are maximal. The significance of a small group of languages in West Africa, with a relatively few noun classes whose grammatical functions are fairly restricted, may seem to pale by comparison. Bantu, however, is by no means unique; it is merely somewhat overpowering at first glance. Noun classification, with its grammatical implications, is just as basic to the structure of many non-Bantu languages as it is to Bantu structure.

Bantu and other Niger-Kordofanian noun class sytems have sometimes been compared to the gender systems of Indo-European and some other languages. There is, indeed, some typological similarity, in that different sets of nouns are distinguished by affixes, and grammatical agreement is found between nouns and their modifiers and other morphemes referring to them. In gender languages, however, there are typically only two or three sets of nouns, and there is a partial correlation between them and sex distinction. In Niger-Kordofanian noun class languages, there are ordinarily many more thon three classes, sex distinctions are irrelevant, and there are a number of other partial semantic correlations. Another difference is of considerable interest. In Indo-European gender systems, gender and number are at least to some extent separately identifiable (as in Greek singular-plural pairs, masculine *-os, -oi*, feminine *-a, -ai*); in Niger-Kordofanian noun class systems, on the other hand, each singular and each plural affix is autonomous and mono-morphemic.

As suggested in the title, this chapter is intended primarily for students who have had little or no prior experience with noun class and concord systems. Scholars with vast experience in Bantu languages will find little if anything by way of new contributions, and may see evidence of oversimplification in some details. A full treatment of all of the details and problems in Bantu, on the basis of readily available evidence, could of course fill more than one volume. The purpose of this chapter is by no means to exhaust a topic, but simply to acquaint the relative beginner with what might be called the *mystique* of noun class and concord systems, and to prepare him for deeper and more varied investigations. With this purpose in mind, Bantu has been chosen as a starting point, and the illustrative material is taken largely from Swahili.

6.2. In any Bantu language, a very large number of noun forms can readily be analyzed as consisting of a prefix and a stem. It may be possible to recognize from ten to twenty different prefixes in a given language. Many noun stems will be found commonly with two of these prefixes; such a pair is ordinarily singular and plural. Some stems may occur with only one prefix; these are usually mass nouns, abstracts, and other types for which enumeration is irrelevant. In addition, some stems may be found, at least fairly frequently, with more than two prefixes; this variety is likely to reflect semantic differences in addition to number.

There is no reason why the first examples should not be amusing as well as instructive. In Swahili, the English instruction on a road sign has been adopted to refer to a traffic circle or roundabout; the Swahili form is /kipilefti/. By analogy with a great many nouns in which /ki-/ is a singular prefix and which have plural forms with a prefix /vi-/, the first syllable of this noun is re-analyzed as a prefix, and more than one traffic circle is, of course, /vipilefti/. Similarly, the (British) English word *mudguard* has been adopted in the form /madigadi/; the syllable /ma-/, however, is a plural prefix, so that the form is taken to mean 'fenders'; the corresponding Swahili singular prefix has a zero allomorph with polysyllabic consonant-initial stems, so that 'a fender' is /digadi/. Now, this pair of forms has further been adopted in a language known as KeRezi, for which a vocabulary and some grammatical information exist through the good offices of Desmond T. Cole, with a little help from his friends. In KeRezi, however, the stem is also used with a singular-plural pair of prefixes which indicate persons: /mudigadi/ 'a defender', plural /badigadi/. (This pair was first recorded as a neologism in the speech of a twenty-three-year-old male informant who strangely bears the same surname as the author of the present work, in the not entirely irrelevant context of investigating manifestations of another prefix /ma-/ which indicates liquid masses, as in /matini/ 'alcoholic beverage'; /matini/ is commonly purveyed by a /mutenda/, plural /batenda/.)

Such analogic innovations are based on models which have long existed in Bantu. In Swahili, for example, a typical singular-plural pair is /m-zigo/ 'a load', /mi-zigo/ 'loads', and many other nouns have the same pair of prefixes. Another pair is illustrated by /ki-tasa/ 'a lock' and /vi-tasa/ 'locks'. A single stem occurring with all four of these yields the following forms:

m-ti	'a tree'	ki-ti	'a (wooden) stool'
mi-ti	'trees'	vi-ti	'stools'

Occurrences of this type make it difficult to say that a particular stem "belongs" in a particular noun class. Rather, a given stem "occurs," along with many other stems, in conjunction with a particular prefix or pair of prefixes, and perhaps also with other prefixes or pairs of prefixes as well. The classification of nouns is not inherent in noun stems as such, but is rather associated with the prefixes.

6.3. In any given Bantu language, most of the noun prefixes function as members of singular-plural pairs, though the pairing is evident only statistically, not on any formal basis; there is nothing that all singular prefixes or all plural prefixes have in common with each other. For some pairs, there is at least a partial semantic correlation. In many Bantu language grammars, accordingly, it has been considered convenient to say that a pair of prefixes, singular and plural, represents one "class" of nouns; in addition, there may be some "classes" with only one prefix, reflecting identity of singular and plural or the absence of numerical distinction. Following this type of statement, Swahili is generally said to have six noun classes. In the following outline of these classes, /Ø-/ is an allomorph of a prefix which appears as /ji-/ before monosyllabic stems and as /j-/ before some vowel-initial stems; /N-/ represents a complex of morphophonemic alternations affecting the beginning of stems; and allomorphs occurring before vowel-initial stems are not indicated, though in most cases they differ from the forms given here, generally by simple morphophonemic rules. The usual gross outline of the Swahili noun-class system, then, is this:

			Singular	Plural	
m-,	wa-	:	m-tu	wa-tu	'person'
m-,	mi-	:	m-zigo	mi-zigo	'load'
Ø-,	ma-	:	tofali	ma-tofali	'brick'
ki-,	vi-	:	ki-tasa	vi-tasa	'lock'
N-,	N-	:	ndizi	ndizi	'banana'
u-,	N-	:	u-bao	mbao	'plank'

On the surface, there are clearly several duplications in the above forms. Most of these duplications disappear, however, when more than simply the noun prefix is considered. Certain noun prefixes remain identical, but differences show up in other morphemes which, in a pattern of grammatical agreement, refer to these nouns. Compare the following sentences, in which the same noun forms appear, with the addition of verbal forms which in every case mean 'is/are lost'; the first syllable of each verbal form is a subject prefix referring to a noun of the class in question, singular or plural as the case may be:

Singular	*Plural*
m-tu a-mepotea	wa-tu wa-mepotea
m-zigo u-mepotea	mi-zigo i-mepotea
tofali li-mepotea	ma-tofali ya-mepotea
ki-tasa ki-mepotea	vi-tasa vi-mepotea
ndizi i-mepotea	ndizi zi-mepotea
u-bao u-mepotea	mbao zi-mepotea

On the basis of these sentences, the first two singular noun forms can be said to belong to different classes, although the noun prefixes themselves are identical. A difference also appears between the singular and plural with nouns for which there is a single prefix /N-/. On the other hand, the two /N-/ plurals turn out to be identical also in respect to the subject prefixes used with them. The last two singulars pair with plurals that are identical in all respects. Working from the subject prefixes, the second and sixth singular forms in the above are identical, but the nouns differ in their prefixes. Similarly, the second plural and the fifth singular have identical subject prefixes, but the noun prefixes differ.

Bantu noun classes must be distinguished and defined, therefore, not simply by noun prefixes, but in addition by morphemes such as the subject pronoun prefixes illustrated above, which stand in agreement or "concord" with noun prefixes. It is the combination of noun prefix and concordial morphemes that is significant.

6.4. The complete identity of two plurals in the above Swahili examples introduces a further problem. If a "class" is defined in terms of a singular-plural pair, then two of the Swahili classes (the last two pairs) are partially identical. Furthermore, each singular and each plural prefix and concord set has to be individually described in any case; there is no formal similarity running through all singulars or all plurals. No matter how the material is organized, eleven sets of forms must be separately identified and described. The only merit in pairing the forms is semantic, statistical, or pedagogical.

When a number of Bantu languages are compared with each other, further complications arise in treating a "class" as consisting of a singular and a plural form. For example, the Swahili nouns with the prefix /u-/ are cognate with nouns in other languages which have two different prefixes, frequently /lu-/ and /bu-/. It is only those nouns which have cognates using /lu-/ that are semantically singular, and that have plurals using /N-/. Nouns which have cognates using /bu-/ are typically abstracts, for which enumeration is irrelevant. Thus, on a comparative basis, Swahili /u-/ reflects two prefixes, one of which pairs with a plural and the other of which does not.

Further, in Swahili the plural corresponding to /u-/ is /N-/. In some other Bantu languages there is a parallel pairing of /lu-/ with /N-/, but there are also a number of languages in which the singular /lu-/ pairs with the plural /ma-/. Most of the common singular-plural pairs are well-nigh universal in Bantu, but in some cases there is a fair amount of irregularity. Only individual singular prefixes and their concordial morphemes, and individual plural prefixes and their concordial morphemes, can consistently be compared for the Bantu languages as a whole. And then, of course, one can readily add on the same level those prefixes and concordial morphemes for which there is no counterpart because number is irrelevant.

As a result, it has become traditional—starting with Bleek over a century ago—to speak of noun "classes" in the Bantu languages in general, and often in individual Bantu languages as well, in terms of separate prefixes and their concords, whether singular or plural or neutral. On this basis, the Swahili forms given above can be described in terms of eleven different noun classes. From the comparative point of view, twelve classes are represented; the last singular, /u-/, reflects two different Bantu classes, while the last two plurals, both /N-/, reflect only one Bantu class.

Swahili, like other Bantu languages, has a few additional sets of forms that must be considered part of the noun class system. Verbal infinitives share some of the grammar of nouns, including the capability of having certain modifiers. The infinitive prefix is /ku-/. In addition, three prefixes are used to form locative demonstratives; although these do not appear as the only prefix with any noun stems, they share many of the functions of the more obvious noun and concordial prefixes. These three prefixes are /pa-/ (indicating explicit location), /ku-/ (indicating general location), and /m-/ (indicating location inside). If these are treated as additional classes, Swahili has a total of fifteen classes, reflecting sixteen in Bantu as a whole.

6.5. Carl Meinhof (1899, 1932) presented the first outline of the class system of a reconstructed proto-Bantu, based, of course, on a comparison of the individual class systems of several languages. He followed Bleek's numbering system, and added a number of classes that do not appear in the languages with which Bleek had worked. The list begins with the most obvious and widely attested classes, such that the odd numbers are singular classes and the even numbers plurals, generally plurals of the immediately preceding singulars; for example, the reflexes of Meinhof's classes 7 and 8 constitute typical singular-plural pairs in a majority of Bantu languages. After so listing the classes that commonly appear in singular-plural pairs, the numbering continues for the classes that have no numerical significance. Since Meinhof's day, a few classes have been added to the list that have been found in only a few languages, and some refinements in reconstruction have been achieved.

In order to avoid changing the established numbering system, some classes recognized since Meinhof have been listed as subdivisions of his classes. Clement Doke added classes 1a and 2a. Desmond T. Cole later added 2b and 8x. Class 6a, added by the present author, is not distinguishable in form from 6 within Bantu itself; as will be shown in another connection, however, it must be recognized as a distinct class in a late stage of pre-Bantu, and even within Bantu it is identifiable on distributional and semantic grounds—6 is a plural paired with the singular 5, while 6a is numerically neutral, indicating liquid masses.

On page 165 is an adaptation of Cole's outline of the Bantu noun prefixes, listing the proto-Bantu reconstructed forms, and sample reflexes from four languages which illustrate all of the classes except 21. This chart does not follow the usual representation of vowels. Cole and Malcolm Guthrie (differing from Meinhof only in the choice of a diacritic) write the seven vowels of proto-Bantu ("common Bantu" for Guthrie) as on the left below; the symbols used here are those on the right:

į	ų	i	u
i	u	e	o
e	o	ε	ɔ
	a		a

The traditional symbols are reasonable from some points of view. About sixty percent of the Bantu languages have only five vowels, and it is most commonly the two highest front vowels and the two highest back vowels that have coalesced in the historical development from proto-Bantu. Thus /i/ in a contemporary language may reflect both */į/ and */i/, and /u/ may reflect both */ų/ and */u/. There are exceptions, to be sure, but this is the common type of development. The Cole-Guthrie representation has the advantage of using similar symbols for different prototypes of single vowels in many contemporary languages. On the other hand, there are some contemporary Bantu languages (not many, but LoNkundo is an outstanding example) in which there are seven vowels represented as on the right above; for such languages, that representation of proto-Bantu vowels seems preferable. Cole may (and does) dislike seeing SeTswana (his second native language) represented as it is here (and in the written language itself); others can have an equal aversion to seeing LoNkundo written with five vowels and two uses of a çedilla. For our present purposes, which ultimately envision the consideration of far more than the Bantu languages, the system on the right above is chosen.

A Bantu language name, as used by speakers of the language, is itself a noun with a class prefix, usually of class 7, but not uncommonly of class 11 or class 5. The commonest references to some Bantu languages (Swahili, Shona, Zulu, etc.) omit the prefix, but the commonest references to others include the prefix and give no indication of division between prefix and stem (Kikongo, Luganda, Lonkundo, Lingala, etc.). Some writers have attempted to be consistent by always omitting the prefix (Swahili, Shona, Zulu, Kongo, Ganda, Nkundo, Ngala); some others have written the prefix in all cases (Kiswahili, Chishona, Isizulu, Kikongo, Lonkundo, Lingala). Indices have appeared in which the prefix is indicated after citing the stem, e.g., Swahili (ki-). The convention used here is, with a few exceptions, to write the full form with prefix, and to capitalize both the prefix and (internally) the stem (KiSwahili, ChiShona, IsiZulu, KiKongo, LuGanda, LoNkundo, LiNgala); alphabetization by the stem rather than prefix is recommended for index purposes, so that the name can be readily located no matter how it is cited. Exceptions to this practice are made for a few of the best known language

The Bantu Noun Prefix System

Class	*PB	IsiZulu	SeTswana	LuGanda	LoNkundo
1 sg	mo-	um-	mo-	omu-	bo-
1a sg	Ø	u-	Ø-	Ø-	Ø-
2 pl	va-	aɓa-	ba-	ava	ba-
2a pl	va-			va-	baa-
2b pl	vɔ-	oo-	bo-		
3 sg	mo-	um-	mo-	omu-	bo-
4 pl	me-	imi-	me-	emi-	be-
5 sg	le-	i-	le-, le*-	e*-	li-
6 pl	ma-	ama-	ma-	ama-	ba-
6a nt	ma-	ama-	ma-	ama-	ba-
7 sg	ke-	isi-	se-	eki-	e-
8 pl	vi-			e vi-	bi-
8x pl	li-	izi-	li-		
9 sg	ne-	iN-	N-	eN-	N-
10 pl	li-ne	iziN-	liN-	eN-	N-
11 sg	lo-	u-	lo-	olu-	lo-
12 sg	ka-			aka-	
13 pl/nt	to-			otu-	to-
14 sg/pl/nt	vo-	uɓu-	bo-	o vu-	
15 nt	ko-	uku-	xo-	ku-	o-
16 nt	pa-	pha-	ʃa-	wa-	
17 nt	ko-	ku-	xo-	ku-	o-
18 nt	mo-		mo-	mu-	
19 sg/pl	pi-				i-
20 sg	ɣo-			ogu-	
21 sg	ɣi-				
22 pl	ɣa-			aga-	
23 nt	ɣe-	e-, o-		e-	

names which are rarely cited with the prefix: Swahili, Shona, Zulu, Xhosa, and a few others. In the northwestern Bantu area, some language names have no overt prefix: Bulu, Kaka, etc.

6.6. The foregoing chart lists only the forms of prefixes as they appear before stems which have an initial consonant. Many of these prefixes, in many languages, have different allomorphs before stems which have an initial vowel; for the most part, the rules for morphophonemic alternation are simple or even obvious. These, and certain other allomorphs, are omitted simply to permit a better overall view of the total system, if only in a gross way.

Only noun prefixes are included in the chart, not any of the concordial morphemes which must actually be used to help distinguish some of the classes. Each class is identified as typically singular (sg), plural (pl), or neutral (nt), or combinations of these in cases where different languages have different uses.

Classes 1a and 2a (or 1a and 2b for some languages) reflect a distinction that is on a different level from other distinctions between classes. Nouns used in 1a and 2a/2b are typically kinship terms, personifications, and proper names. The concords used with these classes are the same as those for 1 and 2, which themselves are almost exclusively personal. The plurals 2a and 2b are very nearly in complementary distribution among the Bantu languages; a given language will have only one of them as the plural of 1a, except that both are attested in U-Mbundu.

As noted above, classes 6 and 6a are identical in the Bantu languages, though they may be distinguished semantically in that 6 is the plural of 5 while 6a is neutral, indicating liquid masses. A formal distinction between 6 and 6a is found in Tiv, which is fairly closely related to Bantu as a whole.

Classes 8 and 8x are very nearly in complementary distribution; only a few languages have reflexes of both. Class 8x does not appear in western Bantu. However, class 10 may be analyzed as a combination of 8x and 9, and in this combination 8x has reflexes throughout Bantu.

6.7. Typical singular-plural pairs among these classes are 1-2, 3-4, 5-6, 7-8, and 9-10. Beyond these, 11-10 is a common pair, but 11-13 and 11-6 are also found. 12-13 is common, but plurals of 12 in other classes, especially 14, are also attested. It should be noted that the order of 12 and 13, generally accepted at present, is the reverse of Meinhof's original order. The present numbering uses an odd number for a plural, but places the plural after the two singulars with which it most commonly pairs.

There are some typical, but by no means completely consistent, semantic correlations with these classes. 1-2 include most personal nouns, and sometimes a few other animate nouns, but rarely inanimates. 3-4 include names of trees and other plants, but also a variety of inanimates. 5-6 are quite miscellaneous, but in many languages noun stems usually found in some other pair of classes may also be used in 5-6 with an augmentative significance. 7-8 are also miscellaneous, but in some languages have a diminutive significance (and in some others augmentative!) for noun stems usually found in other classes. 7 also includes nouns indicating manner or style, and 8 may be used adverbially with much the same meaning. 9-10 typically include most animal names, but also a variety of in-animates, and frequently a few personal nouns. 11 is sometimes used for long, thin objects (and as such may be called attenuative), and sometimes for abstracts. 12 and 13 are frequently diminutives. 14 is used as a plural in some languages, and is also commonly abstract; in at least one language, stems indicating grains or fruits are used in class 14 to indicate the beverages fermented (or distilled?) from them—thus inspiring Cole to label this use of 14 "alcoholative."

Class 15 is ordinarily the verbal infinitive, which may function as a noun in some of its uses. 16, 17, 18 are a special group of locative classes. In some lan-guages, these are not reflected as basic noun prefixes at all, but appear only in the concordial system. The prefixes may appear before and in addition to other prefixes, with nouns referring to places. In a few Bantu languages, and in many non-Bantu Niger-Congo languages, reflexes or cognates of */pa-/, */ko-/, */mo-/ function somewhat like prepositions. Generally, 16 refers to near or explicit lo-cation, 17 to remote or general location, and 18 to location inside. In non-Bantu Niger-Congo languages, present progressive verbal constructions often involve locative forms; in many Bantu languages, comparable constructions use the in-finitive. This suggests the question of whether classes 15 and 17, which are iden-tical in both noun prefix and concords, are actually different classes. For Bantu, they must be kept distinct because, in precisely the present progressive verbal construction in question, in a few languages, a double prefix is used, which is analyzed as the locative of 17 before the infinitive of 15.

Class 19 is diminutive; when used as a singular, it takes its plural from one of the common plural classes. In Kikongo, the plural has the prefix of class 8, but with reduplication of the stem accompanied by shortening of a long stem vo-wel; e.g., /mbéele/ 'knife', /fi-mbéele/ 'small knife', pl. /bi-mbéle-mbele/.

Classes 20-23 are rare. Class 20 is usually augmentative, sometimes diminu-tive. Class 21 is usually augmentative and pejorative; it has no concords of its own, but uses class 5 concords. Class 22, found only in LuGanda, is the plural of 20 and of some nouns in 5. Class 23 is another locative, which in at least some languages appears in combination with the prefix of many other classes; in Zulu, for example, it replaces the initial vowel characteristic of all classes, but is still followed by the essential part of the appropriate class prefix. Thus this is not a "class" in the same sense as the other classes, though it partakes of some of the same characteristics.

Two of the languages used for illustrative purposes, IsiZulu and LuGanda, show in most classes a vowel preceding what appears to be the reflex of the proto-Bantu prefix. In these and other languages, such additional vowels are of sec-ondary origin; the selection of the vowel is generally phonologically conditioned by the vowel of the following prefix. A semantic distinction based on the presence or absence of such a vowel (which has been called a "preprefix," an "augment," or simply an "initial vowel") is attested in a few languages. In other languages, the vowel is used in some constructions but not in others. The vowel at least appears to be historically a separate morpheme.

There are numerous instances in Bantu languages of a single noun form which includes two, or even three or four, different class prefixes in sequence. In such cases, a stem with one prefix is taken as a "base," and to this entire base a further prefix is added; such a form may then again be treated as a base to which still another prefix is added.

6.8. In the chart above, an asterisk after a prefix indicates the presence of morphophonemic alternations at the beginning of the following stem. In class 5 in SeTswana, such alternations are present in some stems, but not in others. Where an expected alternation does not appear, analogic regularization seems to have taken place. In some dialects, however, the consonant in the class 5 singular form is extended to the plural in 6, while in other dialects the reverse extension has been made. If there is alternation in 5, the underlying stem-initial consonant appears in 6; forms in 6 show a greater variety of consonants, and the alternations in 5 have resulted in some neutralizations. Judging from the examples cited by Cole (1955, pp. 83-84) the alternations apply only to certain voiced consonants. Stem-initial /b/, /l/, and /j/ have the alternants /ts/ and /tš/, apparently the former before unrounded vowels and the latter before rounded vowels and /w/; /r/, /g/, and /h/ have parallel alternants /s/ and /š/; and stems with initial vowels have alternants beginning with /k/. (Similar alternations of voiceless consonants as well are found in other morphologic contexts; all of them seem downright weird to the uninitiated.)

In LuGanda, class 5 nouns have double consonants after the prefix; again the underlying stem-initial consonant appears in the plural form in 6 (see Cole 1967, pp. 17-18). In Shona, there is also a morphophonemic alternation in nouns of class 5, but the prefix has no other overt form. The alternations apply to certain voiceless consonants attested in class 6 plurals. The result of the alternation in 5 is a set of consonants that appears nowhere else in the language. Stem-initial /p, t, k, c, tʂ/ have, respectively, the alternants /ɓ, ɗ, g, j, dʐ/, and in a few cases /pf/ has the alternant /bv/. (tʂ and /dʐ/ are affricates with labiodental release.)

A large number of Bantu languages, however, have no morphophonemic alternation of consonants after the prefix of class 5, and the prefix itself has a zero allomorph before consonants in many languages. In Swahili, a reflex of the proto-Bantu prefix, in the form /ji-/, appears before monosyllabic stems with an initial consonant; e.g., /ji-we/ 'stone', pl. /ma-we/. /ji-/ also appears before consonant-initial stems usually found in other classes but used in 5 with an augmentative significance; in such cases, it is treated as part of the base of the noun, and the class 6 plural prefix is added to the entire singular form rather than replacing the singular prefix; e.g., from /mbwa/ 'dog' (classes 9 and 10): /ji-bwa/ 'big dog', pl. /ma-jibwa/. Elsewhere, the class 5 prefix is zero before a consonant, as in /nanasi/ 'pineapple', pl. /ma-nanasi/ and many similar pairs.

6.9. It is the rule rather than the exception in Bantu to find morphophonemic alternations in the class prefixes conditioned by a following stem-initial vowel. The types of alternation found in Swahili are typical.

The prefixes of classes 1 and 3 are both /m-/ before a consonant. These may also appear as /m-/ before /u/ and /o/; in written Swahili, however, *mu-* or *mw-* is used before *u*, and *mw-* before *o*, and many speakers, at least among those for whom Swahili is not a native language, reflect these forms in pronunciation. Before /i, e, a/, these prefixes regularly have the alternant /mw-/, which clearly reflects the proto-Bantu form. Some speakers also use /mu-/ before the consonant /h/. The written Swahili forms of nouns in classes 1 and 3 with vowel-initial stems are illustrated by the following:

mw-alimu	'teacher'	mw-aka	'year'
mw-ele	'sick person'	mw-ezi	'moon, month'
mw-itaji	'one who calls'	mw-ili	'body'
mw-okaji	'baker'	mw-oko	'baking'
mu-unda	'creator'	mu-undi	'shin'

The prefix of class 2 before consonants is /wa-/. The same form appears before vowels in most cases; it is sometimes reduced to /w-/ before /a/, and sometimes fuses with /i/ to yield /we.../. The prefix of class 4 is regularly /mi-/ before vowels as well as before consonants. Thus the plurals of the above nouns are:

wa-alimu / w-alimu	mi-aka
wa-ele	mi-ezi
wa-itaji	mi-ili
wa-okaji	mi-oko
wa-unda	mi-undi

The prefix of class 5, as noted above, appears as /ji-/ before consonants in a few restricted cases; otherwise it has a zero allomorph. Before stem-initial /i/, and occasionally before other vowels, the form /j-/ is found; the zero allomorph is usual before other vowels. In class 6, /ma-/ appears before vowels other than /i/; it fuses with /i/ to yield /me . . ./. Examples are:

embe	'mango'	pl.,	ma-embe
j-ino	'tooth'	pl.,	meno

The prefix of class 7, /ki-/ before consonants, has the alternant written *ch-* ([č], which might be analyzed as /ky/) before vowels in the vast majority of cases. The prefix of class 8, /vi-/ before consonants, has the similar alternant /vy- /before vowels. In a few words, /ki-/ and /vi-/, with a fully syllabic vowel, appear before vowels; historically, a stem-initial consonant in these words was lost after the development of the prevocalic allomorphs of the prefixes. Examples of classes 7 and 8 with vowel-initial stems are:

ch-akula	'food'	pl.,	vy-akula
ch-uma	'piece of iron'	pl.,	vy-uma
ki-azi	'sweet potato'	pl.,	vi-azi

Bantu classes 11 and 14 have merged in Swahili. The prefix is /u-/ before consonants, with the alternant /w-/ before vowels. E.g.,

| u-shanga | 'bead' | u-zuri | 'beauty' |
| w-embe | 'razor' | w-ema | 'goodness' |

In coastal forms of Swahili, the N- of classes 9 and 10 is, at least for many speakers, realized as aspiration of a stem-initial voiceless stop. This is not indicated in written Swahili, however, and in other areas the prefix has a zero allomorph with such stems. In all forms of Swahili, N- also has a zero allomorph before voiceless fricatives and before nasals in disyllabic or longer stems. That a reflex of a reconstructed */ne-/ is present here must be accepted on faith for the following examples in isolation; it could be proven only by a lengthy and probably confusing interlude showing the consistency of concords, and such proof had best be delayed for the moment. Examples of the zero allomorph (or unwritten aspiration in the first four cases) of Swahili N- are as follows; ng' represents /ŋ/:

pembe	'horn'	shuka	'loin-cloth'
tembo	'elephant'	hiari	'choice'
chui	'leopard'	mende	'cockroach'
kuku	'chicken'	nazi	'coconut'
fimbo	'stick'	nyama	'meat'
simba	'lion'	ng'ombe	'cow'

N- has the alternants /m/ and /n/ combining with the voiced consonants /b, d, j, g, v, z/ to yield /mb, nd, nj, ng, mv, nz/, with non-syllabic nasal before disyllabic and longer stems. In addition, N- combines with /w/ as /mb/, with /l/ and /r/ as /nd/, and presumably with /y/ as /nj/ (no cases are known to me). As a result, if a noun begins with /mb/, it is impossible to tell whether the noun stem has initial /b/ or /w/ unless the stem is attested in another class or as a verb. Similarly, /nd/ is ambiguous; the stem-initial consonant might be /d/, /l/, or /r/. This is obvious for nouns with the singular in class 11 (prefix /u-/) and the plural in 10; but for nouns in 9 and 10 there is not always external evidence available. Examples of these combinations are:

mboga	'vegetable'	(9-10, cf. boga 'pumpkin' in 5)
mbao	'planks'	(10; sg. u-bao, 11)
mbati	'hut poles'	(10; sg. u-wati, 11)
ndizi	'banana'	(9-10; stem not identifiable)
ndevu	'beard'	(10; sg. u-devu, 11, 'a hair of beard')
ndimi	'tongues'	(10; sg. u-limi, 11)
njugu	'peanut'	(9-10)
nguruwe	'pig'	(9-10)
mvua	'rain'	(9-10)
nzige	'locust'	(9-10)

Syllabic (and stressed) /m/ or /n/ appears as the alternant of N- before monosyllabic stems beginning with any consonant. E.g.,

nta	'wax'	mvi	'gray hair'
mbwa	'dog'	nchi	'country'

Finally, the alternant of *N*- before vowel-initial stems is /ny-/. Class 11 monosyllabic stems retain the singular prefix /u-/ in the plural, and /ny-/ is prefixed to this as if it were a stem-initial vowel. E.g.,

ny-umba	'house'	(9-10; cf. ch-umba 'room', pl. in 8)
ny-uki	'bee'	(9-10; cf. u-ki 'honey', *14)
ny-embe	'razors'	(10; sg. w-embe, 11)
ny-imbo	'songs'	(10; sg. w-imbo, 11)
ny-uta	'bows'	(10; sg. u-ta, 11)

Two types of nouns in classes 9-10 do not follow the above pattern at all, but have a zero prefix no matter what their initial consonant is. One of these types is adopted words, like /baisikeli/ 'bicycle'. The other type includes a number of kinship terms, such as /baba/ 'father' and /rafiki/ 'friend'. It is nouns of this type which in some other Bantu languages are found in classes 1a and 2a or 2b. These nouns require some of the concords of classes 1 and 2 (personal), which is typical of 1a and 2a or 2b in other languages. However, concords of classes 9 and 10 are used at least with demonstratives. Another reason for not recognizing these nouns as belonging to 1a and 2a or 2b in Swahili is that 2a and 2b in other languages have overt prefixes similar to that of class 2.

6.10. The Bantu languages have often been described as having "alliterative concord". Such a description is understandable in the light of sentences like the following in Swahili:

> ki-kapu ki-kubwa ki-moja ki-lianguka.
> basket   large   one   fell
> 'One large basket fell.'

A plural counterpart of this is:

> vi-kapu vi-kubwa vi-tatu vi-lianguka.
> 'Three large baskets fell.'

The situation is not always so simple, however, as just repeating the noun prefix for the appropriate class with every modifier or other referent. In fact, the concord system appears rather complicated if class 1 is considered. The variety of concordial affixes is illustrated in the following:

Attributive:	m-tu m-moja	'one person'
Associative:	m-tu w-a Utete	'a person from Utete'
Demonstrative:	m-tu yu-le	'that person'
Relative:	m-tu ali-y-ekuja	'the person who came'
Subject:	m-tu a-likuja	'a person came'
Object:	nili-m-tafuta	'I looked for him'

Using this class, with its variety of concordial affixes, as a starting point, many writers of Bantu language grammars have provided forbidding or at least impressive charts of noun and concord prefixes, with six or even more columns

(adding columns for certain allomorphs before vowels), and as many lines as there
are noun classes. Unfortunately, the diversity found in class 1 is just as deceptive
as the uniformity found in classes 7 and 8. Further, the difference between such
allomorphs as the demonstrative concord /yu-/ and the relative concord /y-/ in
the above, which is determined simply by whether the following phoneme is a
consonant or a vowel, is of quite a different order from the difference between,
for example, the attributive concord /m-/ and the subject concord /a-/. Many
of the apparent non-identities among the affixes in the entire system can be accounted for by simple morphophonemic statements.

Using still another class as a starting point, a simpler formulation of the noun
and concord affixes begins to emerge. Paralleling the examples given above for
class 1 are the following in class 3:

Attributive:	m-shale m-moja	'one nail'
Associative:	m-shale w-angu	'my nail'
Demonstrative:	m-shale u-le	'that nail'
Relative:	m-shale nina-w-otaka	'the nail that I want'
Subject:	m-shale u-lianguka	'a nail fell'
Object:	nina-u-taka m-shale	'I want (it) the nail'

Here only two basically different prefixes appear: /m-/ as the noun prefix
and attributive concord, and /u-/ (before consonants, with the allomorph /w-/
before vowels) in all other cases. The same pattern appears in several other classes. For Swahili, an economical outline of the noun and concord affix system can
be presented in two columns, with special notes required for just two classes. A
similar two-column outline is possible for other Bantu languages as well; special
statements are regularly required for class 1, but the irregularity in Swahili class
11/14 is not typical of Bantu as a whole. Adding here classes 15-18, the complete Swahili outline is as follows:

	A	B
1:	m-	u-, yu-, a-, m-
2:	wa-	wa-
3:	m-	u-
4:	mi-	i-
5:	Ø-—ji-	li-
6:	ma-	ya-
7:	ki-	ki-
8:	vi-	vi-
9:	N-	i-
10:	N-	zi-
11/14:	u-, m-	u-
15:	ku-	ku-
16:		pa-
17:		ku-
18:		m-

In class 1, the concord /u-/ is associative (and always appears as /w-/, since it occurs only before a vowel); /yu-/ is demonstrative/relative; /a-/ is subject; and /m-/ is object.

In class 11/14, /m-/ is attributive, though /u-/ is occasionally used with abstracts derived from *14. The concords for 11/14 are thus identical with those for 3.

Statements have already been made concerning the allomorphs of the noun prefixes before vowels, except for class 15. The noun (infinitive) prefix of class 15, and all concords used as subject or object, appear in the forms given above before consonants, and also before the initial vowel of a verb stem, except that /m-/ in 1 and 18 appear as /mw-/ before /i, e, a/. In all other uses, the concords have different but similar allomorphs before vowels. In 1, 3, 11/14, /u-/ appears as /w-/ before vowels; similarly, in 4, 9, /i-/ appears as /y-/. In 7 and 8, as in the identical noun prefixes, /ki-/ and /vi-/ have the allomorphs /ch-/ and /vy-/. In 15 and 17, /ku-/ appears as /kw-/, and in 18 /m-/ appears as /mw-/. In all other cases (1 /yu-/, 2 /wa-/, 5 /li-/, 6 /ya-/, 10 /zi-/, 16 /pa-/), allomorphs before vowels consist of only the initial consonant of the prefix; thus /y-, w-, l-, y-, z-, p-/.

For most concords, the allomorphs before consonants and before vowels can be conveniently illustrated in demonstrative and associative phrases like the following; those on the left are 'that ...' or 'those ...', and those on the right are 'my...':

1:	mw-alimu yu-le	mw-alimu w-angu	'teacher'
2:	w-alimu wa-le	w-alimu w-angu	'teachers'
3:	m-shale u-le	m-shale w-angu	'arrow'
4:	mi-shale i-le	mi-shale y-angu	'arrows'
5:	shoka li-le	shoka l-angu	'axe'
6:	ma-shoka ya-le	ma-shoka y-angu	'axes'
7:	ki-su ki-le	ki-su ch-angu	'knife'
8:	vi-su vi-le	vi-su vy-angu	'knives'
9:	rafiki i-le	rafiki y-angu	'friend'
10:	rafiki zi-le	rafiki z-angu	'friends'
11:	u-bao u-le	u-bao w-angu	'plank'

6.11. It has already been noted that the concord prefixes here labelled "attributive" are identical with the noun prefixes except in class 11/14, for which Swahili is not typical of Bantu as a whole. These concords, under "A" in the chart in the preceding section, have sometimes been called "primary" concords; the set under "B," which might be termed "referential," have been called "secondary." The primary concords are used in Swahili with adjective and numeral stems. The same usages are typical of Bantu as a whole, although some Bantu languages (e.g., LoNkundo) have no adjectives; comparable modification of a noun is expressed by the associative construction with a noun indicating quality, or by a relative construction. In some languages, a few stems with numerical meaning unexpectedly take the secondary concords, and more often some numerals take no concord at all, but are invariable. In Swahili, the numerals for 'one' through 'five', and also 'eight' and the word for 'how many', take regular concords. But the forms for 'six', 'seven', 'nine', and 'ten' take no concord; the first three of these are adopted from Arabic. Multiples of ten are also adopted from Arabic and are invariable.

It has already been noted that, under certain conditions, the noun prefixes of classes 5, 9, and 10 all have zero allomorphs. The same is true, of course, for the identical primary concords. Thus there may be nouns and even noun phrases with no overt indication of their class membership; indeed, with only primary concords, 9 and 10 are always identical. The conditions for a zero allomorph of the class 5 prefix and for zero allomorphs of the class 9 and 10 prefixes, however, are not the same. Given the appropriate conditions in either the noun stem or the stem of the modifier, 5 may be distinguishable from 9/10 on the basis of one word in the phrase. In the phrases on the left below, an adjective stem /-kubwa/ 'large' is used; the class to which each phrase belongs is not demonstrable, except for speakers who use an aspirated /k/ in 9/10. But in the phrases on the right, using an adjective stem /-dogo/ 'small', there is a difference between 5 and 9/10:

| 5: | shoka kubwa | shoka dogo | '. . . axe' |
| 9/10: | nyumba kubwa | nyumba ndogo | '. . . house' |

With secondary concords, however, the three classes are always distinct; compare the examples in the preceding section.

As already noted, the secondary concords (or special forms of them for class 1) are used as verbal subjects and objects, and as such appear in their full forms before the initial vowel of a verb stem. Elsewhere, the secondary concords are used with demonstrative, interrogative, associative, and relative morphemes, and with a stem meaning 'all'. A variety of these is illustrated in the following, using class 6 as a sample:

ma-shoka ya-le	'those axes'
ma-shoka ya-pi	'which axes?'
ma-shoka y-angu	'my axes'
ma-shoka nina-y-otaka	'the axes I want'

In the last two of the above, /-a-/ is the associative morpheme and /-o-/ is the relative morpheme, which has other uses as well.

One further detail is significant. The secondary concords appear in a few types of forms as suffixes rather than prefixes. The commonest such occurrence is in another set of demonstrative forms, in which the demonstrative morpheme itself consists of /h/ plus the vowel of the appropriate concord. In this set, the concord for class 18 has the full form /-mu/. The demonstrative morpheme in question means 'this'; a further development is a set of demonstratives, indicating 'this' or 'these' already mentioned, which has the further suffix /-o/, before which the expected allomorphes of the concords before vowels are used; /w/ has a zero alternant before /o/. These demonstratives are summarized in the following:

1:	mw-alimu hu-yu	mw-alimu hu-y-o	'teacher'
2:	w-alimu ha-wa	w-alimu ha-o	'teachers'
3:	m-shale hu-u	m-shale hu-o	'arrow'
4:	mi-shale hi-i	mi-shale hi-y-o	'arrows'
5:	shoka hi-li	shoka hi-l-o	'axe'
6:	ma-shoka ha-ya	ma-shoka ha-y-o	'axes'
7:	ki-su hi-ki	ki-su hi-ch-o	'knife'
8:	vi-su hi-vi	vi-su hi-vy-o	'knives'
9:	rafiki hi-i	rafiki hi-y-o	'friend'
10:	rafiki hi-zi	rafiki hi-z-o	'friends'
11:	u-bao hu-u	u-bao hu-o	'plank'
16:	ha-pa	ha-p-o	'right here'
17:	hu-ku	hu-k-o	'around here'
18:	hu-mu	hu-m-o	'in here'

6.12. Special rules must be stated for concords with some types of nouns indicating animates. The first type is nonpersonal animates. Two of these, the words for 'animal' and 'insect', appear in classes 1 and 2 in Swahili; otherwise these are personal classes. A few appear in classes 7 and 8. Classes 9 and 10, however, contain the large majority of terms for animals, birds, fish, and reptiles. All such nouns take the concords of the personal classes 1 and 2. E.g.,

ki-faru m-dogo a-likuwa hapa	'a small rhinoceros was here'
tembo m-dogo a-likuwa hapa	'a small elephant was here'
tembo wa-tatu wa-likuwa hapa	'three elephants were here'

A few nouns indicating persons with physical defects appear in classes 7 and 8. These take the concords of classes 1 and 2. But some personal nouns in classes 7 and 8 are diminutives using stems commonly found in other classes; these take the concords of classes 7 and 8. E.g.,

ki-pofu yu-le	'that blind person'
ki-toto ki-le	'that baby'
(cf.: m-toto yu-le	'that child')

A number of nouns indicating kinship appear in classes 9 and 10. These take the concords of classes 9 and 10 with all modifiers, but the concords of classes 1 and 2 for subject and object. E.g.,

rafiki y-angu a-likuja	'my friend came'
rafiki z-angu wa-likuja	'my friends came'

A few personal nouns appear in classes 5 and 6. These do not all agree with each other in the concords most commonly used, and even a single noun may be irregular, using concords of class 1 in the singular but 10 in the plural, or of 9 in the singular and 2 in the plural.

The use of class 1 and 2 concords with nonpersonal animates, mostly from classes 9 and 10, is widespread in Bantu. Many Bantu languages, however, are more regular than Swahili in respect to the other types of nouns mentioned here. Since Swahili is spoken by vast numbers of people whose first language is something else, but often Bantu, there is a good deal of variation in some of the uses. It is significant, however, that kinship terms very often present special grammatical problems in Bantu; it will be noted that this is also true of many other Niger-Congo languages.

6.13. In a number of Bantu language grammars, there are references to "personal pronouns" in connection with verbs or with expressions of possession (which represent only one of many uses of the associative construction). The implication seems to be that morphemes or sets of morphemes meaning 'he/she, him/her, his/her' and 'they, them, their (personal)' belong with first and second person pronoun forms, and that referents to non-personal nouns have some kind of a secondary status. Actually, of course, the referents for personal nouns, singular and plural, are nothing more than the concords for nouns of classes 1 and 2. If there is to be any dichotomy, it should be between first and second person morphemes on the one hand and all class concords, including those for classes 1 and 2, on the other. Actually, first and second person morphemes can also be treated with the noun class and concord system. There are no first and second person noun prefixes, to be sure, and first and second person concepts are hardly expected with attributives or demonstratives. But there are subject and object forms, and forms used after the associative morpheme (indicating possession). Further, there are independent referents for first and second person singular and plural, and also for nouns of all classes, which must be treated in a uniform way. (The latter have been called "self-standing" by many writers, though why one would choose this awkward calque, from the German *selbstandig*, when the term "independent" is available, is something of a mystery; with less semantic justification, these have also sometimes been called "emphatic.") In the light of these similarities, although the parallelism is not perfect, it would seem more elegant to include first and second person forms in the concord system.

In the first person in Swahili, identical forms are used for subject and object: singular /ni/, plural /tu/. In the second person singular, the subject form is /u/ and the object form is /ku/. In the second person plural, the subject form is /m/; the object form may be /wa/ (the class 2 concord), or it may be either /wa/ or /ku/ (the second person singular form) plus a suffix /-ini/, with which final /a/ in the verb coalesces to yield /-eni/. In the following, the forms on the left mean '... came'; those on the right mean 'he looked for ...':

1s:	ni-likuja	ali-ni-tafuta
2s:	u-likuja	ali-ku-tafuta
1pl:	tu-likuja	ali-tu-tafuta
2pl:	m-likuja	ali-wa-tafuteni (etc.)

In use after the associative morpheme, Swahili has concords for the first and second persons singular and plural, and for classes 1 and 2, but not for the remaining noun classes. For all other classes, irrespective of number, the concord of class 1 (otherwise singular only) is used; this is discussed further in the next section. Four of the six forms in question are easily identifiable; they are the final syllables of the following:

mtoto wa-ngu	'my child'
mtoto wa-ko	'your (sg.) child'
mtoto wa-ke	'his/her child'
mtoto wa-o	'their child'

For the first and second plural, the corresponding forms must be analyzed as */-itu/ and */-inu/ respectively. With the first vowel of these forms, the /a/ which is the preceding associative morpheme fuses to yield /e/:

mtoto wetu	'our child'
mtoto wenu	'your (pl.) child'

Independent referents are typically reduplicated forms in Bantu, from the secondary concords for the noun classes. In Swahili, the forms for the second person plural and for classes 1 and 2 require minor morphophonemic statements. The forms are:[1]

1s:	mimi	1pl:	sisi
2s:	wewe	2pl:	ninyi
1:	yeye	2:	wao
3:	uu	4:	ii
5:	lili	6:	yaya
7:	kiki	8:	vivi
9:	ii	10:	zizi
11:	uu		

6.14. As noted above, after the associative morpheme Swahili uses the class 1 concord for all other classes except 2. This usage is illustrated in the following, in which /-ke/ refers back to nouns of four different classes (3, 4, 9, 10 respectively), two singular and two plural:

m-ti u-le na majani ya-ke	'that tree and its leaves'
mi-ti i-le na majani ya-ke	'those trees and their leaves'
nyumba i-le na mlango wa-ke	'that house and its door'
nyumba zi-le na milango ya-ke	'those houses and their doors'

In many Bantu languages, however, there are appropriate concords for each noun class in this construction. The merger of all of these in Swahili might possibly be cited as an example of how the complexities of Bantu structure have been simplified in Swahili—perhaps by way of pidginization or as a presumed

---

[1] In KeRezi, only the personal independent pronouns have been recorded; they are:

1s	mimi	1pl	wiwi
2s	yuyu	2pl	yiyi
C1.1	hihi	C1.2	hehe

result of Arabic influence. A similar merger of the corresponding forms, however, is reportedly found in some other Bantu languages for which there can be no reasonable hypothesis of foreign—or at least non-Bantu—influence. It may also be noted, in the light of all that has been said above, that Swahili has retained all of the major characteristics of Bantu, and is in no sense a bastardized language. The fact is that this particular usage is in the nature of the case quite uncommon, and would quite naturally be susceptible to analogic leveling.

At the same time, some Bantu languages display the full array of forms appropriate to this construction. To friends and acquaintances who, with genuine interest but little information, ask "Aren't those African languages you work with awfully primitive?", one might well reply, "Well, in Shona there are 256 ways of saying 'its' or 'their'!" Theoretically, that is, a noun of any class (of which Shona has nineteen, but duplications reduce the number of actually different concords to sixteen) may be associated with a concordial referent for a noun of any class. Any such form must begin with a concord of the class of the noun possessed. This is followed by the associative morpheme /a/. The possessor noun is then referred to by its appropriate concord, and, in all classes except 1, the form ends with a morpheme /o/. One such combination is the last word in the following phrase:[2]

>   tuvana nembwa dz-a-tw-o   'the little children and their dogs'

Here the first word is in class 13, with the prefix /tu-/, a plural with diminutive significance, superimposed on a class 2 plural form /vaná/ 'children' (sg., class 1 /mwaná/). The form /nembwá/ is a combination of /na/ 'and' and /ɪmbwá/, which could be either class 9 or class 10, 'dog' or 'dogs'. In the last word, /dz-/ is the class 10 concord, indicating that the plural 'dogs' was intended. /-tw-/ is the concord for class 13, referring to the possessor noun, the little children.

Different combinations are shown in the following:

>   imbwa navana v-a-dz-o   'the dogs and their pups'
>   buve nadandadzi r-a-r-o   'the spider and its web'

In the first of these, class 2 (/vana v-/ 'children, young') is associated with class 10 (/imbwa . . . -dz-/ 'dogs'). In the second, class 5 (/dandadzi r-/ 'web') is associated with class 5 (/buve . . . -r-/ 'spider'). Similarly, any class can be associated with itself or any other class, using the concords for the noun possessed and for the possessor, in that order. As might be expected, some of the combinations are not likely to occur very often, but all of them are possible.

A system such as this is likely to strike the beginner as being virtually impossible to learn. It should be remembered, however, that one does not learn 256 forms. One learns nineteen noun classes and their concords—and even in doing so, after learning the first ten, the concords for the rest can be safely guessed at

---

[2] Shona examples are taken from Fortune (1955), in which tone is unfortunately not marked. Similar examples have been independently elicited and frequently constructed by the present author, but the tones are not remembered for some words, and other words in these examples were never heard.

by analogy. Then, by analogy with a few examples like the above, any of the possible permutations can be put together with no need for further memorization.

6.15. In almost all of the foregoing, Swahili has been the language of illustration. Naturally, there are many details which are language-specific. Swahili, for example, has no reflexes of classes 12 and 13, which are fairly common elsewhere in Bantu. For classes 1 and 3, Swahili has the prefix /m-/, whereas /mu-/ is far more widespread among the Bantu languages. At the same time, the kinds of morphemic and morphophonemic problems which it has been necessary to discuss for Swahili are typical of noun class and concord systems throughout Bantu. One of the few respects in which Swahili is really atypical is that it is not a tone language. Tone, however, presents few problems in the Bantu noun class and concord systems. For the most part, in a given language, the noun and concord prefixes all have the same tone, far more commonly low than high. Subject concords may have high tone in some verbal constructions, but this is a function of the verbal construction, not of the concords themselves. In some languages, however, certain concords for classes 1 and 9 have low tone while all other concords have high tone. This irregularity seems to have been characteristic of proto-Bantu, in that a parallel irregularity for the same classes is found in Tiv (see Greenberg 1963, p. 35).

Tone may nevertheless be of crucial importance in another respect. In Shona and other languages in the south-central Bantu area, noun prefixes are low. There is, however, a morpheme of tonal replacement, high replacing low, which occurs with noun prefixes as an "identifier". Thus for every noun which has an overt prefix, there is a second form which differs minimally in tone. For nouns which do not have an overt or syllabic prefix, the identifier is /í-/. E.g., in Shona:

mùndà	(3)	'a field' :	múndà	'it is a field'
chìgárò	(7)	'a chair' :	chígárò	'it is a chair'
ngúrùvè	(9)	'a pig' :	íngúrùvè	'it is a pig'

6.16. As noted in 6.9 above, morphophonemic alternants of class and concord prefixes before vowels must be noted in perhaps every Bantu language. Many of these are the sort of alternation that would not be surprising anywhere in the world—/w-/ for /u-/, /y-/ for /i-/, and instances of /C-/ for /CV-/. A wider variety of more unexpected alternations of the class 5 prefix with stem-initial consonants has also been noted, in 6.8 above. In a number of languages, including those in which the prefix has a full form /li-/ or /di-/ or /ri-/ before consonants, an alternant /j-/ appears before vowels; this is presumably from */ly-/, becoming */dy-/ and then /j-/. (In Nsungli in Cameroon, heard only on tape but unmistakably clear, the class 5 prefix before voiceless consonants is a voiceless trill; the voicelessness, with its relaxation, must be interpreted as low tone !)

The manifestations of /N-/ in classes 9 and 10 merit a further word. The morphophonemic alternations found in Swahili are not widespread. In a number of languages, this /N-/ (whether or not anything precedes to distinguish the two classes in the noun and primary concord) appears as a nasal homorganic with any following consonant, voiceless or voiced. The nasal may or may not be syllabic. After the nasal, alternations of some stem-initial consonants are common, as found in Swahili: /b/ for /w/, /d/ for /l/, and the like. These are not always recoverable, but are sometimes identifiable if the stem is found also in other classes, particularly in languages which use classes 11 and 10 as a singular-plural pair. Such homorganic nasals are found in languages as geographically extreme as LoNkundo, KiKongo, Zulu, and LuGanda. In Shona, no nasal appears before voiceless fricatives and aspirates, but there are certain morphophonemic alternations with the stem-initial consonant. With voiceless stops, */Np/ is actualized as /mh/, */Nt/ as /nh/, and */Nk/ as /k/.

The situation in KiKongo has been discussed from the viewpoint of phonemic analysis in 3.22. It was there seen that there are phonetically two kinds of nasal-oral sequences. One of these is analyzed as /NC/, and the other as /N'C/. The first type includes such phenomena as aspiration or affrication of the oral component, and morphophonemically some consonants are neutralized. Occurrences of /NC/ in KiKongo are all manifestations of the /N-/ of class 9 or 10, or of the first person singular object concord; both of these are reconstructed as */ne/ for proto-Bantu. Occurrences of /N'C/, on the other hand, are all manifestations of the prefix of class 1, the prefix of class 3, or the object concord of class 1; all of these are typically identical in Bantu, and are reconstructed as */mo-/. Thus, although the phonemic analysis of the phonetic data in KiKongo is justifiable in its own right as the most economical interpretation, it now becomes clear that one would arrive at it most quickly against a background of some acquaintance with Bantu noun class and concord systems.

6.17. A brief overview of the noun class and concord system of another Bantu language, one of the more distantly related to Swahili, may help to reinforce this introduction. The language chosen is LoNkundo. The data are taken from Hulstaert (1938), but have been independently checked under rather unusual circumstances—the informant was a young American woman, about twenty-two years of age, who had been bilingual in LoNkundo and English until she was about thirteen, but had not used LoNkundo since; she was extremely reluctant to act as an informant in the usual sense of providing utterances for imitation or transcription, but gave every evidence of native competence in her enthusiastic approval or unhesitating rejection of utterances read (or misread) to her from Hulstaert's transcription.

In the prefixes which generally have initial /m/ in the Bantu languages (1, 3, 4, 6), LoNkundo has initial /b/. Further, there is a restricted vowel harmony in LoNkundo, which affects the form of a number of prefixes. The prefixes of five noun classes end with /o/ or /ɔ/, and of two with /e/ or /ɛ/, depending on vowel harmony; /o/ and /e/ appear if the next vowel is /i/, /e/, /u/, /o/, or /a/; /ɔ/ and /ɛ/ appear if the next vowel is /ɔ/ or /ɛ/. E.g., in classes 3 and 4 (and with low tone unmarked): /bo-tswó/ 'a night', pl. /be-tswó/; but /bɔ-kɔlɔ/ 'a day', pl. /bɛ-kɔlɔ/.

In all classes except 2, 6, and 15, the final vowel of a prefix does not appear before vowel-initial stems. The low tone of the prefix is also elided before a stem-initial vowel having low tone. With a stem-initial vowel having high tone, however, the low tone of the prefix is retained; the stem-initial vowel has a low-high sequence. E.g., in classes 1 and 2: /w-asi/ 'a fisherman', pl. /ba-asi/; but /w-ĕkoli/ 'a student', pl. /ba-ékoli/.

The following are the noun prefixes of LoNkundo; alternant forms before vowels are discussed below:

	-C	-V
1:	bo- / bɔ-	w- / b-
2:	ba-	ba-
3:	bo- / bɔ-	w- / b-
4:	be- / bɛ-	by-
5:	li-	l- / j-
6:	ba-	ba-
7:	e- / ɛ-	Ø-
8:	bi-	by-
9:	N-	nj-
10:	N-	nj-
11:	lo- / lɔ-	jw- / l-
13:	to- / tɔ-	tsw- / t-
15:	o- / ɔ-	o- / ɔ-
19:	i-	y-

In class 1, the prefix before vowels is normally /w-/. In nouns not derived from verbs or from nouns in other classes, and in a few nouns described as irregular, it is /b-/ before /o/ or /ɔ/. In class 3, /w-/ is regular before /i, e, ɛ, a/ and, /b-/ before /u, o, ɔ/. Perhaps the rules for classes 1 and 3 are actually the same; no counterexamples are given. In class 5, /l-/ appears before /i/, and /j-/ before other vowels. In class 11, /jw-/ appears before /i, e, ɛ, a/, and /l-/ before /u, o, ɔ/. The conditions for /tsw-/ and /t-/ in class 13 are basically the same; however, many words in 13 are diminutives, and in these /tsw-/ appears before all vowels.

For the first ten classes, consecutive odd and even numbers are regular singular-plural pairs. Class 6 also includes liquid masses. Class 10 also pairs with the singular class 11. Class 15 is the verbal infinitive class. Class 19 singular pairs with 13 plural; this pair of classes contains only a few nouns other than diminutives of nouns that appear also in other classes. (One, in true KeRezi fashion, is /i-máto/, from the reanalyzed plural /to-máto/ 'tomato'.) In diminutives with consonant-initial stems, the first syllable of the stem is reduplicated; the reduplicated syllable has phonologically conditioned tonal alternants.

6.18. For the singular-plural pair 11-10, Hulstaert readily recognizes the nasal prefix in 10; it is /m-/ or /n-/, homorganic with the following consonant; e.g., /lo-kásá/ 'a leaf', pl. /n-kásá/ (phonetically /ŋ-/). For 9 and 10, however, he peculiarly ignores the regular nasal prefix and analyzes all nouns as having no prefix. There are, to be sure, a number of adopted words in 9 and 10 which actually have no prefix, like /sapáta/ 'shoe, shoes'. But in indigenous words, the initial nasal is obvious. Pairs from 11 and 10 show that /N-/ conditions some morphophonemic alternations, but Hulstaert does not discuss them in full. Examples include /lo-lém/ 'a tongue', pl. /n-dém/, and /lo-foso/ 'a hide', pl. /m-poso/; for most consonants, however, there is no alternation.

Mention was made above of adopted words. In Bantu in general, foreign words are commonly taken into classes 9 and 10. In languages in which class 5 has no overt prefix, however, foreign words may be taken into 5, and used with the prefix of 6 in the plural. If the first syllable of the foreign word is sufficiently reminiscent of a prefix in the adopting language, the word is likely to be taken into the class for which that prefix is appropriate, singular or plural, and the pairing prefix is then also used with the reanalyzed stem, as in the case of the pair /i-máto, to-máto/ cited above. English has done the converse of this with its bastardized plural of *chimpanzee*; the language of origin is unknown, but definitely Bantu, and the plural should probably be *bimpanzee*.

6.19. Segmentally, there is only one set of concords in LoNkundo. In all classes except 1, 9, and 10, the concords are identical with the noun prefixes. In class 1, where variation is to be expected, the subject concord is /a/, and /o/ or /ɔ/ serves for all other concordial situations. The concord for 9 is /e/, and for 10 is /i/. Tonally, however, a distinction is made between primary (attributive) and secondary concord; primary concords have high tone, while secondary concords have low tone. Primary concords actually appear only before the first five numerals; higher numerals take no concord, and LoNkundo has no class of adjectives. There are three forms for 'one', and two of these irregularly (or perhaps conditioned by the first tone of the numeral stem) take concords with a low-high sequence. Examples of nouns with numerals are:

bo-nto ɔ-mɔ̌ / bo-nto ɔ̌-mɔ̌kɔ / bo-nto ɔ́-mɔ̌nkɔlɔ́   'one   person'
           be-támbá bé-fé   'two trees'
           ba-tóko bá-sáto   'three spoons' (6)
           t-ŭka tó-nɛi   'four baskets'
           nj-óngo í-tâno   'five hoes'

Hulstaert does list a seemingly different set of forms for object concords. However, these are derivable by a phonologic rule. The consonant /b/ is elided intervocalically within a word, and commonly also in word-initial position after a word ending with a vowel, at least in rapid speech. An unambiguous example is found in a class 11 and 10 pair. The stem for 'hoe', cited above, has an initial vowel, attested also in the singular /l-ŏngo/. Also in these classes, however, is a singular form /lɔ-ɛu/ 'lip', in which the pre-vocalic form of the prefix does not appear. The stem has an initial /b/, as shown by the plural /m-bɛu/. Now, in the object concords, the only differences from other concords are precisely in those which begin with /b/; the initial /b/ does not appear. And object concords occur only after vowels; clearly they are merely the intervocalic forms of the normal concords. In class, 8 /bi/ does occur as an object concord, though /i/ is an optional alternant; it is a general phonologic rule that the loss of /b/ before /i/ is optional.

Hulstaert does what a great many grammarians and beginning students of Bantu languages have done; he refers to the object concords as "infixes". This is obviously based on a comparison of forms like the following from Swahili:

nilitafuta ki-tabu	'I looked for a book'
nili-ki-tafuta	'I looked for it'

The object concord appears within a verb form, just before the stem, and after all other obligatory morphemes (in the above, the first person singular pronoun /ni/ and the marker for past action /li/). The object concord does not appear in the first of the above sentences, but in the second it is "put in." However, the term "infix" has always been a technical term for a morpheme which occurs between phonemes within another morpheme; infixes are common in languages of the Philippines, as in Bontoc /f-um-ikas/ 'he is becoming strong', in which /-um- is an infix within the monomorphemic stem /fikas/. The object concords of Bantu languages do not appear within another morpheme, but between morphemes in a word. They are not infixes, but prefixes the position of which, if they appear at all, is after all other prefixes and just before the verb stem.

6.20. As stated at the beginning of this chapter, this has not been intended as a treatise on comparative Bantu, though a good deal from the field of comparative linguistics has been referred to and even assumed. Most of the morphologic features that have been treated can be, and have been, subjected to comparative study, so that equating a noun class in one language with a class in another has far more than mere typological justification. As one goes beyond the limits of Bantu in the Niger-Kordofanian family, there is less obvious cognation in the morphemes that enter into noun class and concord systems, until among the most distantly related languages very little can be found which is specifically reminiscent of Bantu. At the same time, noun class and concord systems as such are by no means restricted to Bantu, and this introduction to such sustems within Bantu will serve as a useful point of reference in investigating the nominal morphology of other branches of the Niger-Kordofanian family.

Chapter 7

Functional and Vestigial Noun Class Systems

7.1. Prior to Greenberg's inclusion of the Kordofanian languages with the Niger-Congo languages in a larger family, it was clear that, within Niger-Congo, the earliest division was that which separated the ancestor of the present Mande languages from the parent Niger-Congo stock. The Mande languages of today appear to show no trace of a noun class system comparable to that of, for example, the Bantu languages. At least some languages in all of the other branches of Niger-Congo, however, have or give evidence of once having had noun class sytems displaying some striking similarities to those found in Bantu. Given that much evidence, it was reasonable to raise the question whether Proto-Niger-Congo had a noun class system which was lost in the Mande branch, or whether such a system was a later innovation in the non-Mande branch (see Welmers 1958). Greenberg's present classification, however, posits an even earlier bifurcation which separated Kordofanian from all of Niger-Congo. And many of the present Kordofanian languages have noun class systems remarkably reminiscent of Bantu. Independent innovation or borrowing of such a complex element of morphologic structure seems incredible; it is surely more reasonable to suppose that Proto-Niger-Kordofanian had a noun class system to begin with.

In some West African languages, there are a number of noun prefixes which distinguish singulars and plurals, and which have some semantic correlation, but which do not participate in concordial relationships such as those described in the preceding chapter for Bantu. Some investigators have referred to systems of this type as "embryonic" or "rudimentary" noun class systems (see Westermann and Bryan 1952, p. 91). The implication of such terminology seems to be that a language may well start with no noun class system at all, and develop one little by little, perhaps by borrowing or "grammatical contamination", as has been suggested. The unreasonableness of such a hypothesis has frequently been noted. A far more believable reconstruction of linguistic history is that the languages in question have lost some of the more complex characteristics of a system more like that of Bantu, and should rather be characterized as having "vestigial" or "decadent" noun class systems. A highly complex system may, to be sure, have become as complex as it is with the help of analogic developments; but independent development or borrowing of essential features of such a system is highly improbable.

Greenberg (1963, pp. 150-53) has pointed out some plausible instances of possible correspondences between specific Kordofanian noun prefixes and Bantu noun prefixes, or affixes or pronouns in other Niger-Congo languages. By no means all of the noun class affixes in the Niger-Kordofanian languages, however, can be presumed to be of extremely ancient origin. At best, hypothetical reconstructions can be suggested for only a few such affixes; the variety of noun class systems in contemporary languages may well reflect a considerable amount of innovation throughout their history. Yet the similarities among the various noun class systems found in Africa today, apart from the specific morphemes involved, are so noteworthy, and the differences so interesting, that one is tempted to ask whether we cannot at least determine what the Proto-Niger-Kordofanian noun class system was like. It is the purpose of this chapter to describe the nominal morphologies of selected languages or language groups. In addition to discussing grammatically functional noun class sytems in other than Bantu languages, attention will be given to apparent vestiges of an earlier noun class system in several languages in which the relevant morphemes have little or no grammatical function. Incidental to this discussion, however, it may be possible and interesting to say something about the typology of nominal morphology in Proto-Niger-Kordofanian, even if we cannot reconstruct much of its morphemic detail.[1]

7.2. Even in the Mande branch of Niger-Congo, a look at the morphology of Loma might tempt an investigator to see an isolated parallel with noun classification in some non-Mande languages. Most Loma nouns have a singular definite suffix /-i/, but some have the suffix /-gi/; one is reminded of different affixes for different classes in other languages, and one might even want to point to a similarity between the Loma suffix /-gi/ and the proto-Bantu class prefix */ke-/, which appears as /ki-/ in many Bantu languages. There is quite a different historical explanation, however, for the Loma suffixes. Loma has no final consonants; Kpelle, which is fairly closely related, has one, /-ŋ/. For most of the Loma nouns which take the definite suffix /-gi/, there is a Kpelle cognate with a final /-ŋ/ in the stem. This suggests that, in Loma, the consonant in the suffix /-gi/ belongs historically to the noun stem, and that the definite suffix is historically */-i/ for all nouns; there is no noun classification reconstructible for an earlier stage of the language. Apparently as the result of an independent development, Loma seems to favor the suffix /-gi/ with adopted words, even with those which have final vowels in the languages of origin; such words were presumably taken into Loma after the loss of the final consonant, when /-gi/ came to be recognized as a suffix.

This is not to say that the Mande languages show no possible cognates of any of the morphemes involved in class systems in other languages. There are a few likely instances of cognation, but the morphemes do not serve to differentiate groups of nouns in Mande. At the level of noun phrases, there are also other parallels between the Mande languages and languages with noun class systems, but in the forms of nouns as such Mande appears to have lost all characteristics of noun classification. In any case, the absence of noun class systems in the Mande languages has, of course, no bearing on questions of genetic relationship or reconstruction. The Mande languages without noun classes remain as much Niger-

[1] The substance of this chapter, but from the historical viewpoint, is published as Welmers 1971a.

Kordofanian as English without grammatical gender or case distinctions remains Indo-European and even Germanic.

7.3. The Kordofanian languages have prefix-marked noun class systems. For the most part, the prefixes are consonantal. There are a number of singular-plural pairs, and they show some semantic correlations closely paralleling those found in Bantu. One pair of classes is personal; although the prefixes do not resemble the Bantu prefixes of classes 1 and 2, similar affixes and pronouns are found elsewhere in Niger-Congo. Another pair of classes includes terms for trees and plants; in this case the prefixes, generally /w-/ and /y-/, are identical with the prevocalic forms of the secondary concords for Bantu classes 3 and 4, which also include terms for trees and plants. There is also a formal similarity with Bantu in the classes which include terms for fruits. In addition to the paired classes, there is also a liquid mass class with the prefix /ŋ-/; there is evidence of a correspondence between Kordofanian /ŋ/ and Niger-Congo /m/, so that this prefix may ultimately be related to Bantu /ma-/ for liquid masses.

It is not clear from Greenberg's listing whether there are any duplications among Kordofanian classes; it is possible, as in Bantu, that one plural serves for more than one singular. Greenberg at least lists each singular as pairing with a separate plural, and on this basis Kordofanian has no less than twenty-five classes —twelve pairs and the liquid mass class.

Kordofanian also has concord indicated by prefixes with the appropriate words. Little information is available on the form, or the extent of the function, of concords. It is known, however, that concords are used with an associative morpheme /a/, which is identical with the Bantu form.

If Kordofanian and Bantu as a representative of Niger-Congo are indeed as distantly related as Greenberg believes, it would seem at this point that proto-Niger-Kordofanian had the same kind of class system. Evidence from other Niger-Congo languages, however, complicates the picture. What does seem reasonable is that a few proto-Niger-Kordofanian class affixes can be identified—specifically those for classes (by the numbering used for Bantu) 3, 4, 5, and 6a; Greenberg's inclusion of 6 is less convincing.

7.4. In some languages of the Kwa branch, singular-plural distinctions are also marked by prefixes, which in most cases consist of a vowel or a syllabic nasal. There are few traces of concord, but the prefix systems themselves call for comparison with the more complex noun class and concord systems of the Bantu and other languages.

In Fante, there are two prefixes which frequently have a plural reference. The first of these, a syllabic nasal homorganic with the following consonant, also indicates liquid masses, as /m̀bógyá/ 'blood', /ǹsú/ 'water', /ǹgú/ ([ŋ̀gú]) 'oil'. At this point, a comparison of this syllabic nasal with the Bantu prefix */ma-/ for liquid masses may seem specious, but evidence from a number of other languages will make such a comparison significant. The second prefix which frequently has a plural reference is /à-/ or /è-/, the choice of vowel depending on a pervasive pattern of vowel harmony. This prefix is also used for masses and abstracts, as /àbír/ 'time', /èbùró/ 'corn', /àwìrèhú/ 'sadness'. In addition, this prefix is also used with singular reference with some noun stems.

The prefix /ì-/ or /ì-/, the choice of vowel again depending on vowel harmony, has singular reference for a large number of semantically miscellaneous non-personal nouns. This prefix appears only in clause-initial position; it is dropped if anything at all precedes the noun. Corresponding plurals are formed with the nasal prefix for some nouns, and with /à-/ or /è-/ for others. Thus:

ìhén	'a vehicle',	pl.:	ǹhén
idúa	'a tree',	pl.:	ńdúa
ìdán	'a house',	pl.:	àdán
ìkúr	'a sore',	pl.:	èkúr

Another prefix, /ɔ-/ or /ò-/, has singular reference in most cases, but is also used for some non-pluralizing abstracts. Most personal nouns have this prefix, though by no means all nouns with this prefix are personal. This prefix also appears only in clause-initial position. Again, corresponding plurals are formed with either of the two plural prefixes. Examples are:

ɔbɔdɔm	'a dog',	pl.:	m̀bɔdɔm
òbènyín	'a man',	pl.:	m̀bènyín
ɔhɔ'hú	'a stranger',	pl.:	àhɔ'hú
òkú'sí	'a rat',	pl.:	èkú'sí

A third type of singular has no prefix, or perhaps a zero prefix; once more, both types of plural occur:

dá	'a day',	pl.:	ǹdá
búùkùú	'a book',	pl.:	èbúùkùú
kètsí	'a thorn',	pl.:	àkètsí

And finally, as noted above, the prefix /à-/ or /è-/ may have singular as well as plural, mass, and abstract reference; both types of plural occur, the second resulting in homophony with the singular. E.g.,

àbúá	'an animal',	pl.:	m̀buá
èkùtú	'an orange',	pl.:	èkùtú

Other Akan dialects, such as Akwapem Twi and Asante, show some variation in the selection of prefixes with particular noun stems, but the overall pattern of prefixation and pluralization is closely similar. An interesting detail in other dialects is the use of two different prefixes with the same stem apart from pluralization; in addition to the liquid mass /ǹsú/ 'water', there is a noun /èsú/ 'a lake'.

Fante displays virtually no evidence of concord in noun modifiers, and none in the pronominal system. Only one adjective has a different form with plural than with singular nouns:

ìdán kèsí	'a large house',	pl.:	àdán ákèsí

All numerals above 'one' also have the prefix /à-/ or /è-/, appearing after plural nouns with either plural prefix; but the numeral 'one' is /kúr/, with zero prefix. In other Akan dialects, there is a further trace of concord in pronouns; /ɔ-/ or /o-/ is a personal singular pronoun, while /ɛ-/ or /e-/ is impersonal. In Fante, /ɔ-/ or /o-/ is the only third person singular pronoun.

Fante (and the rest of Akan) thus has four prefixes, if zero is included, which may have singular reference, and two (one homophonous with one of the singulars) which may have plural reference. There is no regular singular-plural pairing; any of the four singular prefixes may be paired with either of the plurals. Some of the prefixes also correlate with such categories as mass and abstract. Comparing the Fante prefixes with specific Bantu prefixes and concords produces little by way of convincing results, but the following are some of the most likely instances of actual cognation:

ɔ-, ò-	:	1, 14
ì-, ì-	:	5
Ø-	:	? (may be secondary in Akan)
à-, è- (sg.)	:	?
à-, è- (pl.)	:	2, 6
N- (pl.)	:	10
N- (mass)	:	6a

There are a very few cases in Akan of prefixes having high tone. Two of these are in the demonstrative forms /ɔ́nú/ 'that (one)' and /íyí/ 'this (one)'. Another is in the word /ńdɛ́/ 'today'. Perhaps these are conditioned by morphologic subclassification. In one other case, /ḿpúà/ 'banana, bananas', a nasal prefix atypically has both singular and plural reference; but this word appears only in the Fante dialect.

There are also a few suffixes in Akan nouns, but they have a more clearly derivational function, and do not suggest an underlying noun class system in the way that the prefixes do. A suffix /-fú/ derives, from non-personal noun stems or from verb stems, personal nouns which are for the most part plural, typically indicating members of a class or occupation; such nouns normally have the prefix /à-/ or /è-/. A few nouns with this suffix are singular, normally with the prefix /ɔ́-/ or /ò-/; plurals of these are formed with /à-/ or /è-/. A suffix /-nyí/ (the Fante form) derives corresponding singulars from many of the same stems, but also from a few plurals with /-fú/; such singulars have the prefix /ɔ-/ or /ò-/. Examples of these formations are:

ɔfàrí-ˈnyí 'fisherman', pl.: àfàr-fú (presumably from a verb /fàr/, perhaps an old form of /fà/ 'take')

ɔsɔ́-ˈfú 'minister, priest', pl.: àsɔ́-ˈfú (from /sɔ̀r/ 'perform a religous ceremony')

ɔpú-fú-ˈnyí 'sailor', from pl.: àpú-fú (from /ìpú/ 'the ocean'

There is also a suffix /-núm/ in the plurals of some kinship terms, of the demonstrative /íyí/ 'this', and of the noun /òbí/ 'someone'; pluralization in the prefix also is not found in all combinations. E.g.,

ònúá	'brother',	pl.:	ènúá-núm
yìŕ	'wife',	pl.:	yìŕ-núm
òbí	'someone',	pl.:	òbí-núm

A suffix /-í/ or /-i/, with a lexically conditioned allomorph consisting of the immediately preceding vowel with high tone, derives nouns indicating the time, place, or circumstances under which something happens; the preceding stem must be a verb, but that may be preceded by a noun which is logically either the subject or the object of the verb; everything preceding the suffix has low tone replacing whatever stem tones are involved. Examples are:

àhèn-gìnà-í	'seaport, airport', from /ìhén/ 'vehicle', /gìná/ 'stop'
àbù-gwì-í	'calm, contentment', from /àbú/ 'liver', /gwì/ 'cool off'
àdì-sà̰-á̰	'evening', from /àdí/ 'things', /sà̰/ 'die away'
ètìr-dì-í	'malaria', from /ètír/ 'head', /dì/ 'eat, consume'

These derivational suffixes have been brought into the picture in part to give a fuller outline of Akan nominal morphology, and in part because suffixes do enter into noun class systems in some languages, so that the question is worth raising in the case of Akan. In Akan, however, what are undoubtedly vestiges of a once functional noun class and concord system appear only as prefixes; the suffixes are in a different category.

7.5. In some other Kwa languages—for example Yoruba and many of its closest relatives, and Igbo and Efik—possible vestiges of a noun class system have frequently not been recognized at all. These languages have no affixal pluralization of nouns, no concord, and very little else immediately reminiscent of functional noun class systems. There are significant features in the structure of these languages, however, which are by all odds best explained in terms of vestigial noun class systems.

In these languages, verb roots are typically monosyllabic with an initial consonant: CV, or in the case of Efik and some other languages also CVC. By far the commonest type of noun formation, however, is with an initial vowel or syllabic nasal, VCV or VCVC. Thus in Yoruba typical verbs and nouns are:

rí	'see'	ilé	'house'
lọ	'go'	ẹja	'fish'
rà	'buy'	òbẹ	'knife'

Nouns such as those on the right have commonly been interpreted as monomorphemic noun roots. There is no pluralization and nothing resembling concord. However, the very difference between the canonic forms of verbs and nouns suggests, particularly in the light of the functional prefix systems of many other Niger-Kordofanian languages, that the initial vowels of nouns are prefixes.

This suggestion is greatly strengthened by occasional instances of the same consonant-vowel sequence, with related meanings, appearing with different initial vowels in different nouns. Thus Yoruba /ewé/ is 'a leaf, leaves', but /ìwé/ is 'paper, book, education', the semantic link being what even we in English call a "leaf" of paper. Here a root /-wé/, which originally appeared with one prefix to mean 'leaf,' has been given a different prefix to form a new noun with a related meaning. Similarly, in Igbo /m̀pì/ is 'horn of an animal', while /òpì/ is 'wind instrument, musical horn'.

Further reinforcement is found in the fact that nouns may be derived from verbs by the addition of an initial syllabic. Thus Yoruba has a verb /rò/ 'think', and a derived noun /èrò/ 'thought, thinking', and a number of comparable pairs. Igbo has a verbal infinitive, which itself has nominal uses, formed by a prefix /í-/ or /ì-/, and a number of nouns derived from verbs by other prefixes; e.g.,

í'má	'know'	àmá	'knowledge'
í'rí	'eat'	ńrí	'food'
ìbù	'sing'	ábù	'song'
í'té égwú	'dance'	òté 'égwú	'dancer'

Efik has numerous cases like the verb root /kpá/ 'die' and the derived nouns /ŋkpá/ 'death' and /àkpá/ 'a bequest'. If an added initial syllabic can form a noun from a verb as in the cases cited, then it must be a prefix. By analogy, the initial syllabic typical of almost all nouns may be interpreted, at least at the derivational level, as a prefix, even though in many cases the prefix and noun stem are completely inseparable morphologically. The variety of prefixes, and the traces of associating different meanings with different prefixes, are unmistakably reminiscent of noun class systems. In the languages in question here, the noun prefixes have no grammatical function, but their ultimate derivation from a functioning noun class system is virtually an undebatable hypothesis.

Such observations are, however, much more than an exercise in speculative reconstruction. They have to do with morpheme structure, and they shed light on certain restrictions in some languages. In Yoruba, for example, the vowel /u/ does not appear in noun prefixes, though the other six vowels do; in Akan, there is also no prefix /ù-/ or /ù-/. Further, the tone of Yoruba noun prefixes may be low or mid, but not high. In Igbo, all vowels occur as noun prefixes, as well as a homorganic nasal; there are really only four vocalic components in prefixes, since alternations between two vowels in four pairs are determined by vowel harmony. Each of the four vowel prefixes and the nasal prefix appear with high or low tone. In many cases, there is no way of ascertaining whether the same vowel with high and with low tone represents one or two prefixes, but there are a few details of derivational significance which, from a comparative point of view, are nothing short of exciting. The word for 'tree' and the names for many trees have the prefix /ó-/ or /ó-/, with high tone. The prefix which derives personal agent nouns from some verbs and verb-object phrases is identical before a verb stem with low tone, but it has low tone, /ò-/ or /ò-/, before a verb stem with high tone; by contrast with the prefix for tree names, this personal prefix may be analyzed as having low tone in its underlying form. The parallelism with some concords of classes 3 and 1 in some Bantu languages, and in proto-Bantu, is stunning. Also in Igbo, a number of abstracts, including several derived from verbs, have the vowel /ụ/ or /u/ in the prefix (compare Bantu class 14), though the tone is not entirely predictable.

In Efik, pluralization is found with a small class of adjectives. With the noun unchanged in form, /úsàn/ 'dish', compare /óbúfá úsàn/ 'a new dish' and /mbúfá úsàn/ 'new dishes'. Not all adjectives have the same singular and plural prefixes; compare /ákánì èkùrì/ 'an old axe' and /ŋkánì èkùrì/ 'old axes'. These adjectives precede the noun in Efik, which is unusual—though not unparalleled—in Niger-Kordofanian. In Igbo, a number of apparently comparable forms are analyzed as nouns. In Efik, however, they are definitely adjectives; nouns have no plural forms, and condition different tonal alternations in a following noun. Although this Efik pattern is hardly typical, it still suggests a noun-class system lurking in the background.

7.6. In many of the Gur languages, there are functional noun class systems, with singular-plural distinctions and at least some concord, but with a basically suffixal rather than prefixal typology. In Senari, for example, there are three singular and three plural noun classes, with regular singular-plural pairing, and two classes indicating masses. The classes are most conveniently identified by morphemes which may be called "identifiers"; they mean 'it is a . . .' or 'they are . . .'.[2] Examples illustrating each class are:

kɔ́rɔ́ wi	'it's a canoe'	kɔ́rɔ́béle pɛlɛ	'they are canoes'
kpa ʔa ki	'it's a house'	kpaya yi	'they are houses'
ŋèlè li	'it's a bell'	ŋègéle gɛlɛ	'they are bells'
	kárà ti	'it's meat'	
	sìmɛ̀ pi	'it's oil'	

In the *wi* class, some nouns have a final syllable which does not appear before the corresponding plural suffix /-béle/; these syllables may be considered suffixes, but there is a variety of them—seven different suffixes recorded in a total of eleven nouns—so that no characteristic singular suffix can be cited. A few noun stems have irregular alternants in the plural. But most nouns in this class have no suffix; the full singular form is used before the plural suffix. This class includes personal nouns, some animal names, perhaps a few other nouns of indigenous origin, and all identifiably adopted nouns. With the identifier /wi/ and the sub-

---

[2] Morphemes of this type in various languages have sometimes been called "stabilizers", though it can hardly be said that they "stabilize" anything; they serve rather to identify a noun as the answer to a question or the topic under discussion. In some Bantu languages, a syllable is added to what would otherwise be a monosyllabic word, following a general pattern of avoiding monosyllabic words in some form classes; the added syllable has no meaning, but serves merely to make the otherwise monosyllabic word viable. For such a phenomenon, the term "stabilizer" is well chosen.

ject concord /u/ and object concord /ú/, compare Bantu */o-/ (usually /u-/ or /w-/) as a class 1 (singular personal) concord; indeed, the /m/ of the corresponding noun prefix */mo-/ appears to be an innovation within Bantu, leaving */o-/ as the pre-Bantu noun prefix also, paralleling also /o-/ in many Kwa languages. The corresponding plural class in Senari, with the identifier /pɛlɛ/, has a regular noun suffix /-béle/. With these and the subject and object concords /pe/ and /bé/, compare the Bantu class 2 prefix and concord */ʋa-/.

In the *ki* class, with the exception of a very few irregular nouns, all nouns have a suffix, either /ʔ/ or /g/ plus a vowel. The choice of consonant is lexically determined, with about equal numbers of nouns having each. The vowel of the suffiu is identical with the final vowel of the stem in the case of /e, ɛ, a, e, o/; after /i/, /i/ is recorded as the suffix vowel in some nouns, but /e/ in others; similarly, after /u/, /u/ is recorded in some nouns, but /o/ in others. Some stems occur in both this and the *li* class, each with its corresponding plural; for such nouns, the *ki-yi* classes are augmentative and the *li-gɛlɛ* classes are diminutive; for example, /yáwéʔe/ 'a large animal', /yáwéle/ 'a small animal'. With the *ki* class suffixes and identifier, and also the concords *gi* and *gí*, compare the Bantu class 7 prefix and concord */ke-/. The corresponding plural class in Senari, with the identifier /yi/, has a regular noun suffix consisting of /y/ plus the appropriate vowel; for a few nouns, a plural identifier /di/ and suffix /rV/ is recorded as an optional alternant. There is no convincing parallel for this plural class in Bantu.

In the *li* class, all nouns have a suffix, which is /l/ plus vowel after oral vowels, and /n/ plus vowel after nasalized vowels. With this suffix, the identifier, and the concords /li/ and /lí/, compare the Bantu class 5 prefix and concord */li-/. The corresponding plural class in Senari, with the identifier /gɛlɛ/, has a regular noun suffix /-géle/. With these and the concords /ge/ and /gé/, compare the Bantu class 6 concord */ɣa-/; in pre-Bantu, */ɣa-/ was almost surely the noun prefix as well.

In the *ti* class, all nouns have a suffix, which is /r/ plus vowel. This class indicates solid masses. Concords were not recorded. Very possibly this class corresponds to Bantu 13, in which the prefix is */to-/, and which includes mass nouns in a number of languages.

In the *pi* class, all nouns have a suffix, which is /m/ plus vowel; because of general phonotactic restrictions in the language, the vowel is /ɛ/ where /e/ would be expected, and /ɔ/ where /o/ would be expected. This class indicates liquid masses. Compare the Bantu class 6a prefix */ma-/, which reconstructs in the same form for pre-Bantu. Eight of the nine Senari classes thus have clear parallels—correspondences is hardly too strong a word—in Bantu.

As suggested in the above, there is pronominal concord with the noun classes. For each noun class there is a corresponding subject, object, possessive, relative, and interrogative concord. Except for most of the subject and object concords, these were not recorded, but are known to exist and to show formal similarities to the class identifiers.

Senari has no attributive concord. Attributive constructions, however, appear to be largely a form of compounding of a noun stem (without suffix) and a verb stem; the combination belongs in one of the noun classes, but not necessarily that of the noun, and in some cases a choice of two or three classes is optional. In my earlier treatment of Senari (Welmers 1950a), I did indeed refer to stems occuring in attributive constructions as "adjectives", but this should be considered in the light of the fact that there was a grand total of one week in which to analyze as much of the language as possible and type the manuscript for a description of the phonology and most of the morphology. In any case, concord might at least be expected with the first five numerals, but does not appear.

7.7 Suppire is very closely related to Senari, though the two languages are not mutually intelligible; contrary to my impression in 1949, however, there is a chain of mutually intelligible dialects, discovered in 1957 on a visit to a small village about where the language boundary was thought to be, where American missionaries who had learned Senari and others who had learned Suppire found they could all understand conversation in the local dialect, and were understood, though the missionaries could not communicate with each other in the languages they had learned.

The noun class system of Suppire is closely similar to that of Senari, as would be expected, but there are some interesting differences. The semantic correlations of the classes are far more obvious and consistent in Senari. In many cases, cognate stems fall into one class in Senari, but into another class in Suppire. (This has also been noted to a lesser extent among dialects of Senari.) The *wi* class in Suppire is somewhat more regular than in Senari; most nouns have no suffix, but a number have a suffix consisting of /w/ plus a vowel, which is delightful from a comparative point of view; a very few have a suffix consisting of /ŋ/ plus vowel, which otherwise belongs in the *ki* class. In the *ki* class, the common suffixes are /-gV/ and /-ŋV/; the choice between these is lexically determined, not conditioned by the absence or presence of nasalization; there are also a few nouns with /-ˀV/, and several with no suffix. In the *li* class, many nouns have the suffix /-V/ identical with the stem-final vowel); others have /-rV/ or /-lV/, lexically determined, after oral vowels, and /-nV/ after nasalized vowels. The plural corresponding to the *li* class has the identifier /tyia/, and there is considerable irregularity in the plural suffixes. The *li* class has the suffixes /-dV/ and /-nV/, determined lexically, and the *pi* class has the suffixes /-mV/ and, in one recorded case, /-bV/. All of this suggests more irregularity in the system of noun suffixes in proto-Senufo than is now found in Senari, but a fairly regular and simple concord system. Some other Gur languages display similar or even greater irregularity in noun suffixes.

A number of sets of forms involving concord were recorded for Suppire (after all, in spite of having to crack the perversely complicated morphotonemics of the language, I did have four weeks rather than just one; see Welmers 1950b). These are tabulated in the six columns below. Column (1) lists the identifiers. Column (2) gives the concords for subject, object, and possessive; these are identical in their phonemic shape, but the object and possessive concords condition certain morphotonemic alternations—and not the same ones, either! Column (3) lists remote demonstratives, 'that, those', which appear before nouns; the noun also has a definite suffix. Column (4) lists demonstrative copulative particles, used like the identifiers after a noun, with the meaning 'that is a . . ., those are . . .'. Column (5) lists attributive interrogatives, used after nouns with the meaning 'which . . .?'. Column (6) lists independent or nominal interrogatives, meaning 'which one (s)?' with reference to a noun of the appropriate class. For most of the classes, the concordial element in all of these forms is clearly identical with or closely similar to the identifier. In the *wi* class, however (and wouldn't you know that that is where irregularity would show up?), /ŋ/ or /ŋg/ appears in addition to /u/ as a concord morpheme.

(1)	(2)	(3)	(4)	(5)	(6)
wi	u	ŋ́gé	úŋgé	ŋ́ŋere	ŋ̀ŋere
pia	pi	m̀pí	pímpía	mpere	pimpere
ki	ku	ŋ̀ke	kúŋke	ŋ̀kere	kùŋkere
yi	i	ǹyé	ínyé	nyere	inyere
li	li	ǹné	línné	ǹnere	lìnnere
tyi	tyi	ǹtyí	tyíntyíá	ntyere	tyintyere
ti	ti	ǹté	tínté	ǹtere	tùntere
pi	pu	m̀pí	pímpé	m̀pere	pìmpere

In connection with Bantu noun class and concord systems, it was noted that each singular and each plural class must be treated separately, since neither all singulars nor all plurals have any common recurrent feature. The regular pairing of singular and plural classes in languages like Senari and Suppire makes it possible to use the term "class"—as I orginally did, though that was before I knew anything about Bantu—for a singular-plural pair. A detail in the above tabulation gives some support to such a treatment; in the last two columns, the singular and neutral forms are characterized by concords with low tone, while the plural forms are characterized by concords with mid tone.

7.8. Very similar noun class systems are found in the other Senufo languages in the northern Ivory Coast, Dyimini and Palara. At the southwestern extreme of the Senari-speaking area, however, there is a remarkably divergent dialect. In the course of a dialect survey conducted by the Mission Protestante in 1957, we decided on the basis of lexical similarity to consider it a dialect of Senari; although we had no opportunity to make a carefully controlled study, it appeared that the speech of that area would by and large be mutually intelligible with the major dialects. Only two singular noun classes were recorded, however, the *wi* and *ki* classes, and neither of the neutral classes; everything other than the *wi* class has collapsed into the *ki* class. The status of plurals is not recalled, but we certainly got the impression that the dialect barely made it into the category of noun class languages.

Before leaving these fascinating languages and pleasant memories, an aside is in order on field techniques and native awareness of language structure. The work on Senari was done after two or three weeks of work on Suppire, and at least the essentials of the class system of Suppire had been recognized. The impression at that time was that Suppire and Senari were merely different dialects of a single "Senufo" language. As we sat down to begin work on Senari, I told the observing missionaries, in English, that I wanted first to check for noun classes. The senior missionary, who had made some haphazard effort to learn the language, asked what I meant, and I explained that I was looking for something a little like the genders of French. He immediately replied that there was nothing like that in the language. I asked him how he knew, and he said he had asked our informant. Before I could stop him, he addressed the informant in French and asked again if there were noun genders in Senari. The informant, who had probably had little more than a year of formal education, said no; he was certainly right in recognizing that there was no grammatical difference between the words for 'man' and 'woman'. I managed to get the subject dropped, and started work. I first elicited two nouns which I had found to be in the *wi* class in Suppire, with the identifier, and then two I trusted would be in the *li* class; they were as expected. I then asked for a noun I expected to be in the *ki* class. It was, but before ever saying it the informant said, in French, "Oh, now I see what you mean. Yes, we have five things like genders in my language!" He clearly regarded singular-plural pairs as single genders, which is entirely understandable, but the remarkable thing is that he was completely aware of this structural characteristic of his own language, and didn't have to stop to count classes. In other respects as well, he showed a remarkable *Sprachwissenschaftsgefühl*.

7.9. Bariba is a Gur language by no means closely related to the Senufo languages, but with a remarkably similar noun class system (see Welmers 1952a). There are six singular or neutral classes and four basically plural classes, two of which include some mass nouns and a few singulars. The classes are most conveniently referred to by their independent pronominal concords.

The *wi* class includes all singular personal nouns, and a few impersonal nouns. Stems found basically in this class have no suffix, but stems from other classes may take a suffix /gi/ indicating a person or owner, and then fall into this class. In all other classes, apart from one minor morphophonemic alternation, there are identical concords for the subject of the "consecutive" verbal construction and for object. In this class alone, these concords are different: subject /ù/ and object /nùn/—shades of Bantu! Impersonal nouns in this class do not have plural counterparts; they include words for 'the sun', 'the moon', and 'fire'. Personal nouns pair with a plural *bà* class, and are formed with a suffix /bu/; e.g., /sesu/ 'sister', pl. /sesubu/.

In the singular *gé* class, most nouns end with a back vowel, but in most cases the final vowel functions as part of the stem. There are a few irregular plurals, but over half the nouns in this class have plurals in the *ni* class, with a noun suffix /nu/; e.g., /bòo/ 'water jar', pl. /bòonu/. The remaining nouns in the *gé* class have plurals in the *si* class, with a noun suffix /su/; e.g., /booro/ 'owl', pl. /boorosu/. The *ni* and *si* classes also include a number of mass nouns, and a few singulars.

The singular *yé* class is the largest class; it includes a number of animal names, but also many inanimate nouns. Nouns in this class generally have final /a/, which in most cases functions as part of the stem in that it is retained before modifiers. This class pairs regularly with a plural *yí* class. Singulars with final single /a/ have plurals with final /i : /bɔra/ 'a stick', pl. /bɔri/. Singulars with final double /aa/ have plurals with final /ɛɛ/: /waā/ 'a snake', pl. /wɛɛ/ (an exhaustive treatment must also include statements concerning tone). Singulars ending with other vowels have a plural suffix /-bà/: /fɔrɔtɔ/ 'a bag', pl. /fɔrɔtɔbà/. There are also a few irregular plurals: /guwā/ 'a chicken', pl. /guwē/.

The *té* class is regular; all nouns in it have the suffix /-ru/. Plurals are in the *ní* class with the suffix /-nu/. E.g., /bíréru/ 'a basket', pl. /bírénu/.

There is a *pí* class which was discovered and reported to me by letter some months after my one month of research on Bariba; I have no record of speciifc nouns in this class, and even the independent pronominal concord form has not been verified.

The *mé* class, with syllabic /-m/ as the noun suffix, includes (shall we all say it in unison?) liquid masses; e.g., /nim/ 'water', /gum/ 'oil'. As in many languages, "liquid masses" include some nouns like 'sand' and 'dirt' (in Senari, also the word for 'population, inhabitants'); a more general description of such nouns is that they indicate substances which take the shape of the container into which they are poured—even a population is contained by natural obstacles such as mountains, rivers, and swamps, and by neighboring populations. In Bariba, the *mé* class includes also the word for 'language', /bàrùm̄/. The appearance of the liquid mass suffix as a syllabic /m/ in Bariba (and several other languages) strengthens the case for recognizing the homorganic nasal prefix for liquid masses in Akan as a reflex of the same affix.

There is attributive concord in Bariba. Noun suffixes of the shape /-CV/, and in a few cases /-V/, are dropped before modifiers, and at least some modifiers can safely be called adjectives. Some adjectives are clearly derived from verbs, and some have corresponding nominal forms; in the latter case, the evidence suggests that the nominal forms are derived from the adjectives rather than vice versa. Most attributive adjectives use the appropriate noun suffix; e.g.,

gé	:	gùnɔ̄	'a bird'	gùnɔ bakɔ	'a big bird'
yé	:	duma	'a horse'	dum baka	'a big horse'
té	:	bíréru	'a basket'	bíré bakaru	'a big basket'
ní	:	bírénu	'baskets'	bíré bakanu	'big baskets'
sí	:	sirūsu	'pots'	sirū bakasu	'big pots'
mé	:	yam	'space'	yam bakam	'a big space'

Some adjectives, or at least words used attributively in much the same way, have a class of their own, singular and plural, which remains the same after all nouns. Such forms are recorded in the *gé* and *té* classes: /píbu/ 'small', /tɔkɔ̄rū/ 'old'. There are also a few invariable adjectives with forms which are not characteristic of any class, as /tereré/ 'narrow'.

Attributive concord also appears with the numeral for 'one', of which the stem is /teè-/, but not with higher numerals. The fact that a few nouns in the *ní* and *sí* classes are singular is attested by the following; in the second, the noun stem has a final /m/ which does not appear before the noun suffix, and which has the alternant /n/ before /t/:

ní	:	gbèzɛnu	'cucumber'	gbèzɛ teènū	'one cucumber'
sú	:	tasu	'yam'	tan teèsū	'one yam'

The attributive concord suffixes, as noted above, are identical with the noun suffixes. As suggested by the independent pronominal concords by which the classes have been identified, concords with other than adjectives and the numeral 'one' have different forms. The secondary concords are used to form largely monosyllabic subjects, objects, possessives, relatives, and demonstratives—and probably, though not recorded, interrogatives.

The foregoing establishes, of course, that the distinction between primary concord and secondary concord noted for Bantu in the preceding chapter is far more widespread. The full extent of it is not known, but its appearance in both Bantu and Gur suggests that it is quite an ancient distinction.

7.10. Languages of the Adamawa-Eastern branch of the Niger-Congo family are not considered in any detail here, for lack of anything but the most minimal personal experience with them. Greenberg (1963, 1966), however, notes that the Adamawa languages in particular, and at least some of the Eastern languages, have pairs of singular and plural noun classes marked by suffixes, like the Gur languages just discussed.[3] He points out numerous parallels with Bantu noun prefixes in both the form and the semantic correlates of Adamawa-Eastern suffixes. At least some forms of concord are also attested. Although some Adamawa-Eastern languages have no pluralization and few other vestiges of a class system—in some cases apparently fewer than, for example, Yoruba—an original class system is definitely established for the branch as a whole, and extensive and functioning class systems remain in a number of contemporary languages.

7.11. The prefixal noun-class systems of the Bantu and many other languages, and the suffixal systems of many of the Gur and Adamawa-Eastern languages, thus show a number of remarkable similarities in function and form. It may still seem mysterious, to be sure, that prefixal and suffixal systems could have a common historical origin. In spite of the similarities, to say nothing of a significant number of lexical similarities as well, not everyone is convinced that the prefix-marked class languages and the suffix-marked class languages discussed in the foregoing sections are genetically related at all. Perhaps it will be easier to accept this possibility after examining two very closely related languages, perhaps even dialects of the same language, which display a somewhat similar difference in structure. These languages or dialects are Jukun (Wàpã) and Jukun (Dìyī).

---

[3] When writing Welmers 1971a, I had forgotten and did not happen to notice Greenberg's discussion; I there stated my erroneous impression that the Adamawa-Eastern languages show evidence primarily of prefixes.

There are no functional noun classes in either Wàpã or Dìyī. There is no morphologic pluralization. There is no clear-cut pattern of deriving nouns from verbs by affixes, as has been noted for several other languages. Yet there are affixes which hint strongly at a vestigial noun class system, in somewhat the same way as has been argued for Yoruba and some other languages. The remarkable thing is that the affixes are prefixes in Wàpã but suffixes in Dìyī; further, they show no obvious resemblance to each other, nor any parallelism in their occurrence with particular noun stems.

In 4.18-19, a number of nouns were cited from Wàpã, each of them beginning with a vowel which appears only in phrase-initial position. The vowel is /a-/ (with mid tone) for the large majority of such nouns, but /à-/ (with low tone) for some. No word in any morphologic class other than nouns begins with one of these vowels (though numerals begin with /á-/). There are some nouns of two or more syllables that do not have an initial vowel, but the structures /aCV/ and /àCV/ are clearly basic to the language. Verb stems are uniformly monosyllabic, with the structure /CV/ (a single verb /víni/, indicating completion of an action, is undoubtedly adopted from Pidgin *fini* 'finish'). These facts alone make it apparent that /a-/ and /à-/ in nouns can be analyzed as prefixes, though they have no grammatical function. Although the vocalic component appears only in phrase-initial position, the two prefixes are differentiated after mid or high tone by the retention of the low tone of /à-/, as noted in 4.19. What appears after the prefix is the noun root.

In Dìyī, there are a great many cognate roots, but only a very few nouns consist of such a root alone. (The ones which do are typically kinship terms, whose equivalents in a Bantu language might well belong in class 1a with a zero prefix.) In 4.20, two suffixes were recognized. The first of these has the allomorph /-rà/ after oral vowels, and /-nà/ after nasalized vowels. Examples with obvious Wàpã cognates are:

Wàpã	*Dìyī*	
abà	bàrà	'bag'
akyi	kirà	'mashed food'
adyí	dyírà	'word, matter'
àbǎ	bǎnà	'stone'
atã	tãnà	'house'
akǎ	kǎnà	'charcoal'

The second suffix recognized in Dìyī consists of low tone, realized after mid or high tone as the terminus of a falling glide, without lengthening of the preceding vowel; this suffix has no overt realization after low tone, but may be recognized as present in the deep structure of most monosyllabic nouns with low tone (excepting possibly a few kinship terms). Nouns with cognate roots in Wàpã are plentiful; e.g.,

Wàpā	Dìyī	
àdyí	dyí'	'dirt'
adyé	dyé'	'fish'
adyu	dyi'	'year'
aza	za'	'guinea corn'
anè	nè	'hoe'
abè	bè	'money'

A small number of nouns have a suffix consisting of /r/ plus the final vowel of the stem, with low tone. All nouns recorded with this suffix also have stems with low tone. E.g.,

Wàpā	Dìyī	
adì	dìrì	'body'
akù	kùrù	'chief'
atsè	sèrè	'bundle'

Finally, a very few nouns appear to have miscellaneous suffixes in Dìyī. The suffixes described up to this point were identified as such on purely internal grounds; these, of which the following are the only recorded examples, were analyzed as suffixes only after comparison of the Wàpā data:

Wàpā	Dìyī	
àdŭ	dŭŋà	'sheep'
anú	níŋà	'arrow'
asò	sìkà	'beans'
ake	kebà	'bone'

Some nouns in both Wàpā and Dìyī have bases of two or more syllables. Many of these are probably compounds or adopted words. For the most part, such nouns do not have suffixes in Dìyī. However, there are a few compounds like the following, in which only the first member loses its suffix:

tãnà 'house', kirà 'mashed food': tãkirà 'kitchen'

There are some tenuous traces of suffixation in the derivation of nouns from verbs, somewhat more in Wàpā than in Dìyī. A few nouns appear to be related to verbs, but have a different final vowel. Two of these are compounds with /bu/ 'thing, possession' as the first component. Thus, in Wàpā, /tsa/ is a verb meaning 'do, perform'; the derived noun is /butso/ 'work'. That this is a case of derivation is more evident when the Dìyī forms are compared: /sa/, /buso/. Again in Wàpā, /dyi/ is a verb meaning 'eat'; the derived noun is /budyu/ 'food'. In this case, Dìyī does not show the vowel change: /dyi/, /budyi/. For the function of /bu-/ in these nouns, compare Wàpā /atyī/ 'head', /butyī/ 'hat'.

In both Wàpā and Dìyī, there are many phrases which consist of a verb with a cognate object, as /ŋgo/ 'be tough', Wàpā /ŋgo ŋgó/ 'be angry'. In at least one such phrase a derivation by vowel change is found in Wàpā, and by vowel change and suffix in Dìyī. This is, in Wàpã, /da/ 'hit', /da do/ 'be sick'; in Dìyī, the verb /na/ 'lie down' is used instead, and the phrase is /na dorà/.

The only vestige of concord is that numerals in both Wàpã and Dìyī have a prefix /á-/. After nouns, the vocalic component of this prefix does not appear, but its tone is retained after low or mid; cf. 4.19.

There is no convincing case of a noun affix resembling a class affix in other languages which have been discussed. Yet the very existence of such affixes with nouns, but nothing comparable with verbs, suggests that we are dealing here with a vestigial noun class system. Kutep, which seems to be one of the closer relatives of Jukun on the basis of lexical evidence, has a fuller and functional noun class system, prefix marked, rather similar to the Bantu systems. Yet within Jukun, we find the vestiges of noun classes marked by prefixes in one language or dialect, but by suffixes in the other.

7.12. Some light may perhaps be shed on this phenomenon from a still more closely related language, Tigong, for which sufficient examples have been cited in 4.25. The name of this language, as used by its own speakers, was transcribed, perhaps not entirely accurately, as [mémbē]; it has been referred to as Mbembe, but there is quite a different language also called Mbembe some distance to the southwest. Westermann and Bryan (1952, pp. 141-142) cite a few forms from what they call Mbembe, which are clearly from the same language as our Tigong, though possibly from a different dialect. They state that noun plurals are formed "by change of final vowel, . . . by change of tone, . . . and by various other means (never, however, by Prefix)." In our data, however, a very few nouns in the singular have a vowel prefix, but virtually every plural has a prefix, which is usually /è-/ (with the next-to-highest tone in a discrete level system with four levels), but in a few cases /è'-/ with a tone falling from the next-to-highest level to low). At least as many plurals are formed with prefix alone as in any other way. Vowel changes and tone changes are also involved in many plurals, but we find no "various other means", though our data are not extensive. Vowel substitution most commonly takes the form of a front vowel in the plural replacing a back vowel in the singular, though a number of other replacements are also recorded, most of them in only one noun each. The commonest tonal replacement is a tone one step higher in the plural than in the singular; a second type is a tone one step lower in the plural than in the singular; and in some nouns the plural and singular have the same tone. (For examples, see 4.25.)

It would seem the most likely hypothesis that the vowel and tone replacives in Tigong plurals are morphophonemic alternations conditioned by suffixes which no longer appear overtly. In some cases, it is possible that the plural rather than the singular represents the base form. If this hypothesis is valid, then the ancestor of modern Tigong at one time had a number of singular and plural types comparable to noun classes, with at least some types or classes marked by both prefix and suffix. This would presumably have been the case also in Jukun, which is rather closely related; from such a system, Wàpã lost all suffixes except for a few traces in nominalizations, and Dìyī lost all prefixes (though numerals retain a prefix). Regular phonologic change—the simple loss of all final or initial syllables or vowels—is probably the simplest explanation of the present situation.

Perhaps this is a good point at which to mention a detail which is particularly fascinating, though by itself it is hardly enough to prove anything. In Kru, which is a long distance away from these languages in Liberia, a number of plurals have a front vowel corresponding to a back vowel in the singular. One of them (and the only one I recall from extremely limited exposure to languages of the Kru group) is the word for 'tree', singular /tú/ and plural /tí/. The plural form, of course, is like the extremely widespread *ti* as the root for 'tree' throughout most of Niger-Congo. Let us suppose that the vowel alternation in Kru had to do with a suffix or suffixes once present. Let us further suppose that the suffixes were historically the same morphemes as those reflected in common Bantu prefixes used with the same root: singular *mùtì*, plural *mìtì* in many languages, with the concords *u* and *i*. Now, the *m* of these Bantu prefixes is thought by some Bantuists, and by myself, to be an innovation within Bantu; thus the original morphemes were more like *u* and *i*, simply vowels. As suffixes in Kru, they would have yielded forms like **tí-u* and **tí-i* (the tone of the suffix is unknown, of course). Then, by assimilation to the vowel of the suffix, the forms would have become **tú-u* and **tí-i*, and finally, as today, /tú/ and /tí/. Some people may feel that this detail is too tenuous to bother with. It may help to note that, several months after writing the foregoing, I learned (from the Rev. John Duitsman, personal communication) and am now able to add that suffix-marked class systems are attested in the Kru languages, and that in one of them, Kwaa, the word for 'tree' is singular /tì'/, plural /tìì/! Descriptively—which is our major concern here— the nominal systems of these languages at least seem far more rational, and are more readily subject to satisfactory analysis, in the light of the functional noun class systems of other languages than they would be without such light.

7.13. One might now ask whether both prefixes and suffixes appear as class markers in any languages that have actually functioning noun class and concord systems. The answer certainly appears to be affirmative if we consider a group of Gur languages including Gourma. The Gourma examples given here are taken from Zwernemann (1967, pp. 75-97), and tone is not marked for all of them; however, from some six days of field work on Gourma in 1948, from which I now have no notes, I can confirm that forms such as these are typical.

Gourma has at least six singular and six plural classes, plus a class for liquid masses. One pair of classes is personal, and other classes include augmentative and diminutive references, like so many other Niger-Kordofanian class languages. Each class is marked by a prefix and a suffix. The prefix and suffix are identical in several cases, and similar to each other in the rest. For example, the singular personal class has a prefix *ó-* and a variety of suffixes, most of them ending with *-ó*. Thus, with a suffix *-ló*, there is *ó-nì-ló* 'a man'. In the corresponding plural class, the commonest pattern is a prefix *bi-* and a suffix *-ba;* the plural of *ó-nì-ló* is *bí-nì-bá*. (One wonders if the root in this pair could not be analyzed as *-nil-*, with loss of *l* before consonant-initial suffix, and whether a comparable analysis could not be applied to many other nouns, simplifying the affix system considerably.) In form as well as reference, of course, these affixes are reminiscent of the Bantu classes 1 and 2, and of personal affixes in many other languages.

Another singular class has a prefix *ó-* and a suffix *-ó;* the corresponding plural has *i-* and *-i*. E.g., *ó-tàm-ó* 'a horse', plural *i-tàm-i*; compare Bantu classes 3 and 4. Another singular class has a prefix *bu-* and a suffix *-bu*; the corresponding plural class has a prefix *i-* and a suffix *-i* or *-di*. E.g., *bu-ti-bu* 'a tree', plural *i-ti-di*, with the familiar root *ti* for 'tree'. With the same root, there are also *ku-ti-gu* 'forest', plural *ti-ti-di*, and *ke-ti-ga* 'a small tree', plural *mu-ti-mu*. In the liquid mass class, the prefix is *mi-* and the suffix *-ma*, as in *mi-nyi-ma* 'water'.

André Prost has suggested a somewhat different analysis of these data (see Zwernemann 1967, p. 95). He says that Gourma nouns as such consist of stem and suffix only (as in other Gur languages), and that what has here been called a prefix is rather a concordial pronoun prefixed to the noun form, indicating definiteness. It would not be the first language by any means in which nouns are commonly cited in a definite form; this has been noted in Mende, and it is often done in Kpelle when an informant is asked to repeat a noun—and one can imagine the frustration of early untrained learners when they asked for an equivalent of 'rice (cooked)' and heard something resembling English *bah* (/ɓá/), then asked to have it said again and heard something like English *my* (/m̀ái/); the informant was merely talking about 'the' rice already mentioned! Perhaps the status of the apparent prefixes in Gourma cannot be definitely settled at present, but it remains a fact that Gourma nouns are cited in forms like those given above, and I do not recall recording, even in a variety of fairly simple sentences, any form with suffix only.

Incidentally, the amount of segmental redundancy in a language such as Gourma may have a significant effect on the ease of acquiring competence in comprehension. After six days in Fada N'Gourma, I found it possible to understand a remarkable amount of bargaining conversation overheard in the market; in Kpelle, with virtually no segmental redundancy at the morphologic level, it took perhaps six months to reach the same degree of competence.

In Togo, there are several small languages which Westermann long ago labelled "Togo Restsprachen", or "Togo Remnant Languages" (see Westermann and Bryan, 1952, p. 96). The implication of this label was that these languages presumably reflect a "remnant" of Bantu origin or influence from a very long time ago. The Bantu-like class systems of many of them are striking. In at least one of these languages, Kebu, there are four plural classes which have both prefix and suffix (Westermann and Bryan 1952, p. 101). The four corresponding singular classes have only a suffix in three cases, but prefix and suffix in the remaining one. There are, however, alternations between the stem-initial consonant in the singular and plural if the singular has no overt prefix, which suggests that an original prefix conditioning such an alternation has been lost. The data, taken from Westermann and Bryan, include such pairs as *pii* 'a child', plural *ebibə; kutukə* 'forehead', plural *utugbɔ; vuturi* 'stomach', plural *efutuir; gbɛwo* 'throat', plural *akpɛɛ.*

No specific information is available on concord in the Gourma group of languages nor in Kebu; it is known, however, that there is full pronominal concord in Gourma, and a good deal of other concord in other of the so-called Togo remnant languages. Greenberg includes the latter in the Kwa branch, which adds significance to the evidence previously cited from other Kwa languages, which have noun prefixes.

7.14. A remarkably intricate noun class and concord system is found in Fula, in the West Atlantic branch of Niger-Congo. Greenberg (1963, p. 25) recognizes sixteen singular (including neutral?) classes and six plural classes. David Arnott (1960), describing eastern forms of Fula from Nigeria, Dahomey, and Niger, recognizes a total of twenty-five classes. The classes are suffix marked, but singular-plural pairs also show alternation in stem-initial consonants. E.g.,

pul-lo 'a Fula', pl.: ful-ɓe
gor-ko 'a man',   pl.: wor-ɓe

In each class, there are up to four different allomorphs of the class suffix, the choice among them being lexically determined; the sets of allomorphs, which Arnott calls "grades", differ in their initial consonants (or lack of such). A group of four such allomorphs must be considered as belonging to one class because they are accompanied by identical concords. In a few cases, there are sub-allomorphs of one grade, under phonologic conditioning. In one class, for example, Arnott lists the four grades as -*re*~-*de*, -*re*, -*de*, and -*nde*. For a noun followed by modifier, he cites the following as examples of the possible combinations; for modifier as well as noun, the choice of grade is lexically determined:

leemuu-re mau-nde   'a big orange'
loo-nde hes-re   'a new jar'
jii-re wor-de   'a male squirrel'

In addition to this complication (multiplied by twenty-five, of course), each class is characterized by one of three types or "categories" of initial consonant in the noun. Consonants must be characterized as stops, fricatives, or nasals. In the singular personal class, for example, the noun begins with a stop. In the corresponding plural, it begins with a fricative. Of the twenty-five classes listed by Arnott, initial stops are found in eleven, initial fricatives in six, and initial nasals in eight. In the "nasal" category, actually only *mb, nd, nj, ŋg* show nasality; the counterparts for voiceless consonants are realized as voiceless stops, identical with those in the "stop" category.

Further, the initial consonant of a verb is determined by the class of the subject noun; it is either a fricative or a nasal. There is also a full system of other concords—subject, object, possessive, independent referent, relative, associative, interrogative, anaphoric, and demonstrative—which resemble one or another of the suffix grades.

Some other northern West Atlantic languages show very similar noun class and concord systems, though that of Fula is undoubtedly the most complex. For purposes of the present discussion, the important point to note is that the initial consonant alternation in nouns, attributives, and verbs is very possibly the remnant of a set of prefixes, so that the ancestor of these languages would also have had a noun class system marked by both prefixes and suffixes.

In at least some of the southern West Atlantic languages—which, to be sure, some scholars do not agree are as closely related to Fula etc. as Greenberg's classification may suggest, though the time depth within West Atlantic must be considerable—there are prefix-marked noun class systems much more reminiscent of Bantu. Even in the 1850's, this resemblance had been noted and considered highly significant (see Bleek 1858, table opp. p. 191, pp. 204-5). W. A. A. Wilson (1962) recognizes sixteen classes in a group of these languages, and there is full concord. In Temne and Baga Koba, animate nouns take concords of the personal classes, irrespective of their own class prefixes—a phenomenon widely attested also in Bantu. This and a detail in the associative construction are so strikingly like the situation in some Bantu languages that, when Wilson's article appeared, I felt constrained to call it to the attention of my then colleague Professor A. C. Jordan. I did so by reading the relevant discussion in Wilson's sections on "Concord systems" and "Genetive construction", without identifying the languages and without citing the examples, but citing the specific associative morphemes of Baga Koba. I then asked Professor Jordan if he knew what language was being discussed; without hesitation, he replied, "Of course—that's my language [Isi-Xhosa]!"

Greenberg also notes a few instances of prefixes rather than suffixes in some languages in the Eastern section of the Adamawa-Eastern branch of Niger-Congo. In Mondunga, most classes are suffix-marked, but there is one singular-plural pair which is prefix-marked; the prefixes are *li-* and *ma-*. In this particular instance, without a body of data but in view of the location of Mondunga, I would not make an issue of these prefixes without checking on the possibility that they appear in words for which both singular and plural forms have been adopted from a neighboring and very possibly dominant Bantu language.

Actually, in some Bantu languages there are instances of suffixes as well as prefixes in at least some classes. In the extreme northeastern Congo, the language or dialect names Nyanga-li and Gbati-ri show suffixation, and the language name Li-kari-li shows both prefixation and suffixation. In-depth studies of comparative Bantu, including particularly the northwestern Bantu languages, are beginning to reveal considerable evidence of traces of suffixation.

At this point, therefore, it appears that prefixes alone, suffixes alone, or both prefixes and suffixes are no strangers to Niger-Kordofanian noun-class systems. Although systems with prefixes only or with suffixes only are the most common, there is evidence of both prefixes and suffixes in every branch of Niger-Congo which has noun classes at all. Historically, it would appear that such a system would be the most likely candidate for a prototype; the systems more commonly found today would then be simplifications by a total loss of all prefixes or all suffixes—and of both in the case of Mande. Before settling on such a conclusion, however, the peculiarly mixed system of Tiv must be accounted for.

7.15. Tiv is one of the non-Bantu languages most closely related to Bantu, and the Tiv noun classes can with little difficulty be equated with specific Bantu classes. Greenberg (1963, p. 35) has pointed out, indeed, that Tiv agrees with many Bantu languages in one very striking detail: in both, certain manifestations of the class-marking morphemes for classes 1 and 9 have low tone, but in all other classes the tone is high. (A similar distinction for a personal and a non-personal noun prefix has been noted in Igbo, 7.5 above.) In outlining the Tiv system here, the traditional Bantu class numbers will be used. The illustrative forms are taken from Abraham (1940b), though they are retranscribed in some respects. For the sake of convenience, Bantu class prefixes and concords are cited in forms commonly found in Bantu languages today, rather than in the hypothetical reconstructed forms.

Abraham recognizes eleven noun classes in Tiv, though dividing one class into two because it includes both singulars and plurals would yield twelve. Of the eleven different classes, one has a zero affix; five are marked by prefixes only; two are marked by suffixes only; and three are marked by both prefix and suffix. Rather than using nominal affixes to identify classes, a concordial morpheme for each class is used, which appears in a concordial copula. Concords differing only in tone in some classes appear also in demonstratives; Abraham uses one of the demonstratives to refer to the classes.

Class 1, with the noun prefix commonly *mu-* in Bantu, has the concord morpheme *ngù* in Tiv. Nouns in this class have a zero affix in Tiv, though there are traces of limitations of the initial phoneme of the stem. The subject and object concords are *á* and *ûn*, very similar to the widespread *a* and *mu* or syllabic *m* in Bantu; in both, this is the only class in which subject and object concords differ. (Compare the same situation with Bariba /ù/ and /nùn/, 7.9 above.) This class includes but is not restricted to singular personals.

Class 2, the regular plural of class 1, has the noun prefix *ba-* in Bantu, and the concord *mbá* in Tiv. The noun in Tiv is marked by a prefix, either *ù-* or *mbà-*. The alternation between these two is at least partially conditioned by the initial phoneme of the stem and by semantic category. Examples for classes 1 and 2 are:

tòr	'a chief',	pl.:	ùtòr
ànyàm	'a leopard',	pl.:	mbàànyàm

Class 3, with the noun prefix *mu-* in Bantu like class 1, has the concord *ngú* in Tiv, like the class 1 concord except that its tone is high rather than low. For many nouns, the prefix is *ú-*; for some others it is zero, though Abraham mentions what he believes to be an archaic prefix *é-* which is occasionally heard. There are some constraints on the tones of stems in this class.

Class 4, the regular plural of class 3, has the noun prefix *mi-* in Bantu, the concord *ngí* and the noun prefix *i-* in Tiv. Examples for classes 3 and 4 are:

úwér	'a month',	pl.:	íwér
kón	'a tree',	pl.:	íkón

Class 5, with the prefix *li-* in Bantu, is identical with class 4 in Tiv: concord *ngí*, noun prefix *í-*. It is distinguished here only to include the singular nouns in the class.

Class 6, the regular plural of class 5, has the noun prefix *ma-* in Bantu; in Tiv it has the concord *ngá* and the noun prefix *á-*. A class 5 and 6 pair is:

í'jí   'an egg',   pl.:   á'jí

In Bantu, liquid masses are also considered to belong to class 6. A class 6a for liquid masses has already been proposed (6.5); this was done on the basis of the near-Bantu evidence from Tiv, in which a liquid mass class is quite distinct from the class which forms plurals from 5. Tiv class 6a has the concord *má* and a noun prefix and suffix, both *m*; the prefix is syllabic, but Abraham does not make it clear whether the suffix also is. Examples of 6a are:

ṁgérém   'water'   ṁkúrém   'oil'

Class 7, with the noun prefix *ki-* in Bantu, has the concord *kí* in Tiv. Nouns in this class are marked with a prefix *í-* and a suffix -γ, which is perhaps syllabic. A hypothetical derivation of these affixes from a prefix **ki-* and a suffix **-ki* seems entirely plausible.

Class 8 in Tiv serves as the plural for some but not all nouns in class 7. Plurals for class 7 in class 6 are also common. Class 8, with the noun prefix *bi-* in Bantu, has the concord *mbí* in Tiv. Nouns are marked with a prefix *í-* and a suffix -v, which is perhaps syllabic. A hypothetical derivation of these affixes from a prefix **bi-* and a suffix **-bi* seems entirely plausible. A class 7 and 8 pair is:

ítyóγ   'a head',   pl.:   ítyóv

Class 9, with various manifestations of a nasal prefix in Bantu nouns, and with the Bantu concord *i*, has the concord *ngì* in Tiv, with low tone as previously noted. Nouns in this class have the prefix *ì-*. Plurals of class 9 nouns appear in either class 4 or class 6. An example of each combination is:

ìjì	'a fly',	pl.:	í'jí
ìcàmêγ	'a shea tree',	pl.;	átsá'mêγ

Class 14, with the noun prefix *bu-* in Bantu, has the concord *mbú* in Tiv. Nouns in this class have the suffix *-v*, which is perhaps syllabic. Abraham desribes nouns in this class as "collective", by which he may mean to include abstracts, a typical reference for this class in Bantu. There are also a few singulars in this class; at least one has a plural in class 4. An example of this class is:

ángév   'illness'

Class 15, with the prefix *ku-* in Bantu, has the concord *kú* in Tiv. Nouns in this class have the suffix -γ, again perhaps syllabic; Abraham mentions also what he believes to be an archaic prefix é- which is occasionally heard. In a very large number of Bantu languages, this is typically the infinitive class; infinitives are nominalizations of verbs. In some languages, however, class 15 includes also a small number of other nouns. In Tiv, this class includes only such other nouns. Some nouns in this class form their plurals in class 4, some in class 6, and some in class 8. Examples are:

> gbóɣ 'a stick', pl.: ígbóɣ (4, suffix retained)
> kpáɣ 'a camwood tree', pl.: ákpá (6)
> húrúɣ 'tree (sp.)', pl.: íhyúrúv (8)

Since mention has been made of infinitives, it may be added that Tiv has a verbal form which Abraham describes as a "verbal noun", which shares some of the syntactic uses of infinitives in Bantu and other languages. It is formed with a suffix -n. It is dubious, however, whether this form belongs in the noun class system as Bantu infinitives clearly do.

7.16. The Tiv concord morphemes mentioned in the preceding discussion are used in, or in some classes themselves constitute, copulas. With certain tonal differences, they are used also in demonstrative forms. However, a partially different set of concords is used for attributives (numerals only; there are no adjectives in Tiv), associative, subject, and object. In this set, the initial ng- of the copula concord is missing in classes 1, 3, 4, (5), 6, and 9. This finds an almost perfect parallel in Bantu, in which the noun prefixes for classes 1, 3, 4, and 6 have an initial m-, and class 9 is characterized by a nasal; but in secondary concords in these classes, initial m- and nasality do not appear. This is not to say that Tiv ng- corresponds to Bantu m- and/or a nasal; on the contrary, as will be seen, they must have different origins. It is still significant, however, that concords for these classes in both Tiv and Bantu, as well as the noun prefixes in Tiv (except for class 1, which has zero), consist of a vowel only.

Many characteristics of the Bantu noun class and concord system, therefore, can clearly be reconstructed for a pre-Bantu stage before the divergence of Tiv. Yet Tiv, with sporadic partial agreement in only a few peripheral Bantu languages, differs strikingly from most Bantu languages in marking nouns in some classes with prefixes only, in some with suffixes only, and in some with both. Tiv, of course, differs also from languages which use suffixes only, and from those which use both prefixes and suffixes in all classes.

A variety of Niger-Kordofanian nominal systems has now been outlined, showing everything from highly functional and complex class and concord systems to minimal vestiges of noun classification. It may now be interesting to depart from the subject of synchronic language structures as such, and raise once more the question of the typology of the Proto-Niger-Kordofanian noun class system; it is obvious that there must have been one. Following the established principle of comparative and historical linguistics, it is necessary to postulate a type of

system which most reasonably, after the application of typical phonetic or analogic or other changes, could result in the variety of systems existing today.

Until comparatively recently, it is probably safe to say, it has generally been
assumed that the typical Bantu prefix system was characteristic of proto-Bantu,
and that any traces of suffixes were the result of sporadic independent developments in isolated languages or subgroups. Indeed, the fullest and most regular
manifestation of noun classes and concords seems to have been considered the
most faithful representation of the original system—an assumption which ignores
the very real possibility of analogic regularization and also analogic extension.
The existence of suffix marked and prefix and suffix marked class systems in
West Africa was, in fact, one obstacle to accepting the hypothesis that languages
with such systems were genetically related to Bantu at all. In particular, it would
be difficult to justify a hypothesis of a historical shift from all prefixes to all suffixes, or vice versa. On the other hand, if we assume an original system with both
prefixes and suffixes in all classes, it is not inconceivable that some languages
would have dropped the original prefixes and others the original suffixes. For a
language such as Tiv, however, it is not particularly appealing to assume that the
prefixes of some classes were lost, but the suffixes of some other classes, while
both prefixes and suffixes were retained in still other classes.

It would seem more reasonable to postulate the most complicated or irregular
type of system for the proto language, and to assume that analogic regularization
accounts for the more homogeneous systems found in today's languages or language groups. Thus, starting with a system similar in type to that of Tiv, the application of analogic regularization, in various directions, could have resulted in
any of the more regular systems—all prefixes, all suffixes, or all both. Thus the
type of noun class system found in Tiv would be the key to, and typologically
would reflect, the Proto-Niger-Kordofanian system. That, indeed, was my hypothesis until I came to this very point in writing a preliminary version of this chapter, and I have stated it on more than one occasion in class lectures in past years.
Consideration of one detail of distribution in Tiv, however, which was alluded to
above, suggest a different reconstruction.

In Tiv, as typically in Bantu, there are some noun classes for which the sec-
ondary concords consist of a vowel only, rather than of consonant plus vowel.
These are classes 1, 3, 4 (and 5 in Tiv), 6, and 9—but very significantly not 6a in
Tiv. Further, in the light of Tiv, many other non-Bantu languages in the Benue-
Congo branch, and the typical situation in languages in other branches, the pre-
Bantu prefixes of classes 1, 3, 4 and 6 may be reconstructed as consisting of a vowel alone rather than the modern Bantu consonant-vowel; the *m*- typical of Bantu
is considered a Bantu innovation. To be sure, not every scholar accepts this reconstruction. Talmy Givón (personal communication) objects that, while loss of
an initial consonant is common enough, innovation of an initial consonant is unparalleled. The initial *m*- of class 6a (liquid masses), however, is attested through-

out Niger-Congo, and even strongly hinted at in Kordofanian. There are only extremely sporadic appearances of initial *m-* in class 6 outside Bantu, probably explainable as reflecting independent mergers of classes 6 and 6a; in 1, 3, and 4, initial *m-* is unique in Bantu, and may be considered a diagnostic criterion for recognizing a language as Bantu; initial *b-* in languages such as LoNkundo is a still later secondary development. How initial *m-* in class 6a alone would be retained almost universally, but in other classes lost everywhere except in Bantu, seems even more difficult to explain than the innovation of *m-* in Bantu. The initial *ng-* in the Tiv copula and demonstrative concords for classes 1, 3, 4, and 6 may reflect merely an aversion to initial vowels in such forms, or perhaps should be compared with the initial γ- of Meinhof's reconstructions of the class 1, 3, and 4 noun prefixes; in any case, it has nothing to do with Bantu *m-*, because *m-* appears in Tiv class 6a.

At least prior to the development of the present form of the Tiv class system, then, the affixes for classes 1, 3, 4, and 6 consisted of a vowel alone. Now, it is precisely in these classes in which Tiv nouns do not have a suffix—along with 5, which has merged with 4 in form, and 9, for which a similar argument could be developed. An original vowel suffix in just these classes was then lost, while an original CV suffix is retained in reduced form showing loss of final vowel: -γ in 7 and 15, -*v* in 8 and 14 (and in a few nouns in 2 as well), -*m* in 6a. It may well be assumed, therefore, that all classes in Tiv once had suffixes as well as prefixes.

But what of the classes in Tiv in which nouns have a suffix but no prefix? These are 14 and 15. In 15, Abraham refers to what he calls an archaic prefix *é-* which is occasionally heard. Although he does not mention such a prefix for class 14, it may well exist in similar archaic forms. Now, in contemporary Tiv, only the three vowels in extreme articulatory positions, *i-*, *u-*, and *a-*, occur in word-initial position. If *e-* ever did occur, or even does in the speech of elderly people, it has otherwise been lost. Although the origin of a prefix *é-* in these classes (and also in some nouns in class 3) has no ready explanation, the fact remains that Abraham recorded it, and its non-existence in contemporary Tiv is completely explicable on phonotactic grounds.

We may conclude, therefore, that at some stage in pre-Bantu before the divergence of Tiv, nouns in all classes had both prefixes and suffixes. This leaves us with only three types of noun-class system—all prefixes as in the vestigial systems of many Kwa languages, all suffixes as in some Gur languages, and both in all classes, as in other Gur and Kwa languages and, significantly, in pre-Bantu. As already suggested, it is this last type of noun-class system that can, if postulated for Proto-Niger-Kordofanian, most readily explain the origin of the all-prefix and all-suffix systems. The loss of prefixes or suffixes, or of initial and final vowels as in Tiv, may well have been the result of regular phonetic change, quite possibly independently in various language groups, rather than analogic change; this is also the more comfortable hypothesis. In Proto-Niger-Kordofanian, therefore, we may postulate a noun-class and concord system in which nouns in all classes were marked by both prefix and suffix, the suffix probably at least a partial echo of the prefix. If there was a distinction between primary and secondary concord, it seems most likely that primary concord was marked by suffixes, but secondary concord by prefixes.

From the point of view of entering upon new or more detailed investigations of almost any Niger-Kordofanian languages, the foregoing is, whatever its historical validity, also a useful framework by way of preparing the investigator for the types of phenomena he may expect to find in nominal systems. In many cases, the presentation of data and analyses in the light of this framework will be maximally illuminating.

Chapter 8

Nonclass Noun Systems

8.1. Vestiges of an original noun class system have been identified in a number of languages in which such a system is no longer grammatically functional, or at best functions only at the derivational level. Some such languages display other phenomena in their noun systems which remain to be discussed. Within Niger-Congo, the Mande languages show nothing at all comparable to the class and concord systems which have been treated in the preceding two chapters, but their noun systems have other characteristics which must be described. Features of noun systems in languages in the Nilo-Saharan, Afro-Asiatic, and Khoisan families must also be given some attention.

Morphological and syntactic distinctions in a number of these languages fully justify the recognition of what linguists would normally call different "classes" or "sub-classes" of nouns. In discussing the languages of Africa, however, it seems best to restrict the term "class" to the use made of it up to this point, with reference to languages which have a system of singular-plural distinctions and usually at least some concord, more extensive than the two-way or three-way division of nouns in languages with gender or other kinds of distinction. In nonclass languages as so delimited, grammatically different sets of nouns can as well be called "categories," "types," or, where appropriate, "genders." If, for example, one were to discover in an African language a morphological distinction between nouns referring to animate beings and nouns referring to inanimate objects and concepts, one would not likely call it a "noun-class" language, though one might well speak of the classification of nouns in the language. A distinction between animate and inanimate nouns would be one of the phenomena to be treated in this chapter.

Actually, just such a distinction has been noted—on the basis of only a few hours of investigation, to be sure—in Ndoro, a Benue-Congo language of Cameroon. Some of the languages presumably most closely related to Ndoro have typical functional noun class and concord systems. In Ndoro, an original noun class system has apparently, by coalescences and realignments, developed into a noun system which can be considered typologically different. It has been observed that, in the Bamileke group of Bantu languages farther south in Cameroon, the Bantu noun class and concord system, already considerably reduced, seems to be moving in the same direction—toward a reorganization of the noun classes in terms of two categories, animate and inanimate (see Hyman and Voeltz, 1971, p. 57). Even after such a reorganization, it may be possible to recognize reflexes of the original system, but we would seem to be dealing with a significantly different kind of nominal morphology.

8.2. A two-way distinction in the noun system is also characteristic of the Mande languages. In the case of Mande, the two categories of nouns may be labelled "free" and "relational."[1] A free noun is a noun whose stem alone may constitute a complete noun phrase. A relational noun is a noun which may be used only with an expressed possessor. By and large, these categories reflect the distinction between alienable and inalienable possession. Free nouns refer to what may be obtained or disposed of at will, or to that for which possession is irrelevant. Relational nouns refer to what cannot be obtained or disposed of at will—short of patricide and the like, or mutilation. Relational nouns are primarily kinship terms, words for parts of the body, and words for place relationships; included also are one's name, deserved pay for services rendered, footprints, odor, and similar things inseparably associated with their possessor. The formal criterion for assigning a noun to the relational category, however, is the fact that a possessor must be expressed.

The rigidity of this criterion may be illustrated by relating an early and unduly stubborn effort on my part to eliminate a possessor of a relational noun. I described a rather macabre imaginary scene in which someone's hand had been accidentally severed by an axe along a forest path, and is left lying there. Later two men come by, and one of them notices the hand and asks in horror, 'What's that?' How does the other reply, 'a hand'? The response in Kpelle must be /nǔu yée/ 'a person's hand'. The only recorded exception to the obligatory expression of a possessor in Kpelle is in a proverb-like utterance meaning 'Every mother loves her children'. This does not mean, however, that it is otherwise impossible to speak of 'a mother', a woman who has one or more children, without specifying whose mother she is. The stem for the relational noun 'mother' is /lee/. A corresponding free noun is constructed with a tonal replacive, low replacing the stem tone of the relational noun, and compounding that form with the word for 'person': /lèe-nǔu/ 'a mother'. In the case of 'child', the relational noun stem is /lóŋ/ 'son/daughter, offspring', and a corresponding free noun is formed by reduplication (not a widespread process in Kpelle): /lólóŋ/ 'a child'.

There are a few instances of noun stems found in both categories with semantic differences. In a number of Mande languages, the stem for 'skin', a relational noun, is also used as a free noun with the meaning 'paper', extended also to 'something written or printed (letter, book, etc.)' and to 'education'. A few relational nouns referring to place may also be used adverbially without an expressed possessor; the physical 'back' and 'face' may be so used with reference to motion 'back (to a place)' and 'forward'.

8.3. In most Mande languages, free and relational nouns are distinguished not only by the optional versus obligatory expression of a possessor, but also by the way in which possession is expressed. In Bambara, for example, a morpheme /ká/ is used between the possessor and a possessed free noun, but this morpheme does not appear with a possessed relational noun. Thus:

---

[1] The term "relational", suggested to me in private conversation by Prof. Talmy Givon, seems preferable to the term "dependent" which I have previously used.

à ká fàni   'his cloth'
à lén   'his child'

In Kpelle and Loma, a difference in the expression of possession is found for the first and third persons singular only. Compare the following Kpelle forms:

í pέrɛi	'your (sg.) house'	í pɔ́ɔ	'your (sg.) possession, yours'
kú pέrɛi	'our house'	kú pɔ́ɔ	'ours'
ká pέrɛi	'your (pl.) house'	ká pɔ́ɔ	'yours (pl.)'
'tí pέrɛi	'their house'	'tí pɔ́ɔ	'theirs'
But:			
ŋá pέrɛi	'my house'	ḿpɔ́ɔ	'mine'
ŋɔ̀ pέrɛi	'his/her house'	'pɔ́ɔ	'his/hers'

For relational nouns, the first person singular possessive pronoun is a homorganic nasal with high tone; the third person consists of prefixed low tone, a morpheme with many other uses centering around the idea of 'previous reference' (cf. 5.13). Westermann and Melzian (1930, p. 13) recognize different first and third person singular possessive pronoun forms, but treat them as if they are mere alternatives for any noun, the forms given above for relational nouns presumably being some kind of contraction. In slow and careful speech for the benefit of learners, the forms used with free nouns are sometimes heard with relational nouns until it is clear that the hearer has understood; but the reverse is never true.

8.4. Intersecting each of these two categories, there is in some if not all of the Mande languages a secondary formal distinction between personal and non-personal nouns. This distinction involves, in part, forms which have been assumed by many to be mere plurals, but which in fact require a far more subtle interpretation. What has been assumed to be pluralization in Kpelle has more than once been described as a generally regular pattern with a few miscellaneous exceptions (see Westermann and Melzian 1930, p. 15; Westermann and Bryan 1952, p. 44). The fact is that the forms and usages in question neatly divide free nouns into personals and nonpersonals on certain grounds, and relational nouns into personals and nonpersonals on other grounds.

Nonpersonal free nouns, other than those which are not countable in any case, occur in their stem form before numerals and similar words. They also occur with a suffix /-ŋà/, always with reference to more than one item, but not "plural" in the usual sense of merely more than one. An anecdote may be the best introduction to the concept in question. Working with two informants together, I once tried to elicit an equivalent for 'There are sweet potatoes on the veranda', hoping to find a word for 'veranda'. I was familiar with the word for 'sweet potato', /kwíɛŋ/. One of the informants quickly responded with a sentence in which he used /kwíɛŋ-ŋà/ for 'sweet potatoes'. The second informant objected, and said /kwíɛŋ/ alone was appropriate. The first informant argued, "No, the man said 'sweet potatoes'; that is plural." The second replied, "But if you say /kwíɛŋ-ŋà/, it means that there is one potato here, another there, another over there, and perhaps some on this side. I think he meant that the potatoes were together in a basket or a pan. That is /kwíɛŋ/." The first informant, having learned another little lesson on the noncongruity of linguistic structures, concurred. Clearly, the stem by itself refers not merely to one item, but also to several items treated as a unit, while the form with /-ŋà/ refers in some way to a number of items treated individually and separately. The stem by itself is not specifically singular, but rather generic; the form with /-ŋà/ implies individuation, which assumes but does not confine itself to plurality.

Perhaps further illustration will be useful. The sentence /ŋá tɛ́ɛ kàa./, word-by-word 'I chicken saw', may equally well be used after I have seen one chicken or after I have seen a number of chickens, which may but need not have been in a flock. /ŋá tɛ́ɛ-ŋà kàa/, however, specifically implies that I saw two or more chickens here and there, but probably didn't notice all that I might have. Similarly, /ŋá tɛ́ɛ-ŋà yà/ 'I bought some chickens' implies that I was selective, not buying all that were for sale.

Personal free nouns, on the other hand, have forms that function much more like plurals in the usual sense, and they are not formed in the same way. There are relatively few personal noun stems, and the word for 'chief' is not one of them —it refers to the office rather than the human occupant of it, a phenomenon paralleled in many noun-class languages in which the word for 'chief' is not in the personal class. Such stems are used before numerals and similar words, as impersonal free noun stems are. In other contexts, however, the stem form is specifically singular, and there is a corresponding plural form which must be used with reference to more than one person. These plurals end in /-à/, but there are also irregular morphophonemic alternations in the stem. The major pairs are:

nũu	'person'	nũa	'people'
surɔ̃ŋ	'male person'	sinâ	'males'
nɛnî	'female person'	nɛ̃yâ	'females'
lóloŋ	'child'	nîa-pèlɛi	'children'

In the light of the reference of /-ŋà/ with impersonal free nouns to individuation, it might also be said that these "plurals" are individuated, but that a plurality of persons is necessarily considered as a number of individuals. For those who would like to make ideological hay while the sun shines on this detail of Kpelle structure, it may be added that, in Kpelle culture, there would seem to be less rather than more emphasis on individuality or individualism than there is in Western European and American cultures.

In addition to personal free noun stems, there is a large number of compound personal free nouns, of which the final component in the singular is /nũu/ 'person', with the regular tonal replacive of low for stem tone typical of compounds. Such compounds have plurals ending with /ɓèla/, which is interpreted as being derived from a stem with unknown tone which does not appear except in such compounds. Thus, from a phrase /tíi kɛ́/ 'do work' (noun plus verb):

tíi kɛ́-nũ̀u	'a workman'	tíi kɛ́-ɓèla	'workmen'

For compounds of this type, it is the plural form which is used before numerals and similar words other than 'one'.

A special type of compound personal free noun is a noun indicating tribal affiliation. Singulars of such compounds are also formed with /nǔu/ 'person', but plurals are formed with the otherwise impersonal suffix /-ŋà/; e.g.,

> tõâ-nǔu   'a Loma person'   tõâ-ŋà   'Loma people'

Impersonal relational nouns appear only in their stem forms; there is nothing parallel to either individuation or pluralization. Many such nouns, of course, are exclusively singular for a single possessor in any case—'head, tail, back, top, underside' etc.; however, the stem form is also used in reference to the many heads etc. of more than one person or animal. In the case of body parts which are paired or quadrupled, specific reference to more than one is expressed by a numeral—'my two feet, the dog's four feet', etc. (It occurs to me, though the circumstance has never arisen in my experience, that one might conceivably want to refer to an indefinite number of the feet of, for example, a centipede. My intuition, to whatever extent it approximates that of a native speaker and for whatever it is worth, would require me to use the impersonal individuating suffix /-ŋà/.)

Personal relational nouns, like personal free nouns, have plural forms, which are also used before numerals. These are constructed with a suffix /-nì/, which shows a regular morphophonemic alternation in combination with stem-final /ŋ/. The major pairs are:

> í lîa   'your older sibling',   pl.:   í lîa-nî
> í lêγe   'your younger sibling',   pl.:   í lêγe-nì
> í lóŋ   'your child',   pl.:   í lònii

(Irrelevant to Kpelle structure as such, it may be of interest to note the possible cognation of this suffix /-nì/ with a personal plural class prefix *ny-* attested in Kordofanian.)

Within the category of relational nouns, personals and impersonals are further distinguished in constructions in which the expressed possessor is a noun. Impersonal relational nouns follow a noun possessor with no morpheme intervening, but personal relational nouns must have a pronominal possessor—for the third person singular, prefixed low tone; e.g.,

> ǹɛnîi tí kɔ́ɔ   'that woman's foot' (the-woman that foot)
> ǹɛnîi tí ǹóŋ   'that woman's child' (the-woman that her-child)

With free nouns, a pronominal possessor is used with both personal and impersonal nouns after a noun possessor:

> ǹɛnîi tí ŋɔ̀ surɔ̂ŋ   'that woman's husband (man)'
> ǹɛnîi tí ŋɔ̀ siγei   'that woman's cloth'

In connection with the semantics of relational nouns, it may be noted that the usual expressions for 'husband' and 'wife' are the free nouns for 'man' and 'woman'. There is, however, also a relational noun which may be used with a person of either sex as possessor, 'spouse'. Formal criteria are better than semantic criteria.

8.5. The closing sentence of the preceding section may also be considered the theme of this section. It has been mentioned that impersonal relational nouns in the Mande languages include primarily body parts and place relations. Place relations typically include the inside of something, the top, edge, underside, vicinity, area above, and so on. Many words of this type are by far most commonly used after another noun in complement position after a verb. E.g., with translations that do not reflect the morphologic categories of Kpelle:

a tíi kêi 'taai sù	'he's working in town'
a tíi kêi 'pérɛi kɔlɛ	'he's working near the house'
a tíi kêi 'pérɛi ŋá	'he's working on top of the house'
a tíi kêi 'pérɛi mù	'he's working in (under the ceiling beams of) the house'

The words that end these sentences, and a number of other words like them, are paralleled by locative prepositions or prepositional phrases in English. Observing only this, students of one or another Mande language have sometimes called such words "prepositions." With a greater sophistication born of knowing Latin etymologies, most authors of works on Mande languages have called them "postpositions," because they appear after rather than before the noun with which they belong. Two very important points are generally overlooked, and overlooking them has seriously impeded the progress of would-be learners of a number of Mande languages.

The first point is that a number of these so-called "postpositions" also function as ordinary human or animal body parts. For example, Kpelle /'pérɛi pôlu/ may generally be translated as 'behind the house, on the other side of the house', but /pôlu/ is also a body part: /ḿpôlu a sôlii/ 'my back hurts'. Similarly, /'pérɛi lá/ is often the equivalent of 'at the house', but it refers more specifically to 'at the door of the house'; /lá/ refers to an opening, and is also a body part: /ńá a sôlii/ 'my mouth hurts'. One may be surprised at the further use of this /lá/ in /ǹyái lá/ 'at the river'; /lá/ here refers to the opening made by a path through the forest or underbrush to the water's edge.

The second point commonly overlooked is that almost all of the words in question, even those not thought of as body parts in the strict sense, may also, with a possessor, be used as the subject or object of a sentence—that is, in any typical nominal usage. E.g. (with some irrelevant morphophonemic alternation):

ɓá káa ǹeɣii sù	'there's cooked rice in the pot',
and: ǹeɣii su è lìɓi	'the insideof the pot got dirty',
ŋá 'su wâa	'I washed the inside of it'

Such semantic overlaps between body parts in the restricted sense and place relations, and the freedom of usage of phrases ending with the words in question, clearly establish that such words are ordinary relational nouns. In the case of such a noun phrase used as a complement after a verb, the preposition-like relationship is not inherent in the relational noun at all, but rather in the position of the noun phrase after the verb. In a sentence like /a tíi kêi 'taai sû/ 'he's working in town', it is nothing more than the syntactic position of /'taai sù/ that relates it to the action; a more faithful representation would be 'he is doing work (at) the-town's inside'.

A number of such relational nouns are commonly used as verbal objects, not only in Kpelle but in any Mande language; a few are found only in this usage. Since the possessor of a relational noun is identical in form with the object of a verb, such nouns have commonly been interpreted as part of the verb—somewhat like the prepositional prefixes of verbs in Germanic, presumably—and what precedes has been taken as the object of the verb rather than the possessor of a relational noun. In Kpelle, for example, the relational noun /sù/ 'inside' (with a predictable alternant /su/) is used as the object of a verb /kula/ 'remove'; the combination /'su kúla/ is literally 'take out its inside', but in fact means 'explain it'. In a combination like /m̀ɛnii tí su kúla/ 'explain that matter', the common interpretation, undoubtedly based on the structure of the English translation, is that the constituents are /m̀ɛnii tí/ 'that matter' and /su kúla/ 'explain'. The interpretation insisted on here is rather that the constituents are /m̀ɛnii tí sù/ 'the inside of that matter' and /kula/ 'remove'. Like many such combinations, this one is somewhat "idiomatic"; that is, its specific meaning cannot be confidently predicted from a knowledge of the meanings of the separate constituents. An exact grammatical parallel, however, is /ǹeɣii tí su wáa/ 'wash the inside of that pot', in which the identification of the constituents is reflected also in translation. In Mende, all such combinations of relational noun object with verb are written as single words, as if the combination is a verb of which the preceding possessor is the object. Such a distortion of the grammar certainly serves no useful purpose in writing for native speakers, and is downright misleading to the unsophisticated learner of the language. Although recent treatments of Mende (e.g., Innes 1963) avoid such naivete, it unfortunately remains true that too many so-called grammars of African languages are little more than grammars of English translations of utterances in this or that language.

In the case of a relational noun which is used only as the object of a verb, it is understandable that the analysis is not immediately apparent. Such a case is the Kpelle relational noun /sɔlɔ/ as object of the verb /ɓó/; /'sɔlɔ ɓó/ means 'receive it', but /sɔlɔ/ is not found in any other combination and no independent meaning can be assigned to it, while /ɓó/ appears elsewhere with the meaning 'break open, leak', which hardly seems applicable to this combination. Yet the superficially attractive interpretation of the combination as a one-word verb is indefensible. For one thing, there are no other three-syllable verbs in the language. More importantly, tone plays an important role in the verbal morphology of Kpelle—unlike Mende and Loma. In this combination, only /ɓó/ is affected by the tone rules for verbs; /sɔlɔ/ has its own independent tone like any noun.

A completely analagous argument has been applied to the analysis of similar combinations in Mano and Dã, languages as distantly related to Kpelle as is possible within Mande.

For Mende and Bambara, I have heard arguments to the effect that some morphemes cannot be interpreted as relational nouns, but do indeed fall into a class of "postpositions." In the case of Mende, it has been said that formal distinctions between body parts and postpositions can be defined. I am not sufficiently acquainted with either Mende or Bambara to categorically state that all such forms are relational nouns, as they clearly are in Kpelle, but it seems clear that their analysis as relational nouns has not been adequately explored. It may be, of course, that these and possibly other Mande languages do have a separate morphological class of postpositions, but such an analysis should not be accepted on superficial grounds. In any case, a distinction between what is here labelled free and relational nouns seems to be basic to Mande noun systems.

8.6. The typological difference between noun systems in the Mande languages and noun class and concord systems in other Niger-Kordofanian languages is not, of course, to be construed as implying that these languages are unrelated. Negative evidence of this sort proves nothing at all about relationship. There are, in fact, a number of details in noun-class languages, and in languages which show clear vestiges of noun-class systems, which parallel features of the noun systems found in Mande. In Bantu, for example, kinship terms are frequently a recognizably special type of noun, appearing in classes 1a and 2a rather than in 1 and 2 as other personal nouns do. Locative nouns such as words for 'inside' and 'top' are commonly restricted to class 9. Classes 16, 17, and 18 also demonstrate a special treatment of locatives. Paired body parts may typically be found in class 15. Such restrictions suggest that the distinction reflected by free and relational nouns in Mande is no stranger to Niger-Kordofanian.

In itself, this is nothing sensational. Distinctions of some sort between, roughly, alienable and inalienable possessions are common in languages all over the world. In private conversation, Kenneth L. Pike has noted a remarkable similarity between Mande and Mayan in this respect. When working with languages believed on other grounds to be related, however, it is useful to observe and even to seek parallel usages of this sort.

In Jukun (Dìyì) there are two sets of pronominal possessive forms, the uses of which distinguish a number of (but apparently not all) kinship terms from other nouns. Compare the following sets of possessive phrases:

bè ḿ	'my money'	zò ḿ	'my friend'
bè bú	'your (sg.) money'	zò ú	'your (sg.) friend'
bè bá	'his money'	zò á	'his friend'
bè bí	'our money'	zò í	'our friend'
bè bu ní	'your (pl.) money'	zò ní	'your (pl.) friend'
bè bu bé	'their money'	zò bé	'their friend'

The possessive forms on the right are clearly the simpler set. They are segmentally identical with the verbal subject pronouns, but include a morpheme of high tone replacing stem tone—the stem tone is low in the first two, but mid in the rest. The possessive forms on the left show no distinction in the first person singular. The second and third persons plural clearly show a linking morpheme /bu/; the remaining forms are unquestionably to be analyzed as this same /bu/ combining with the appropriate pronoun. The morpheme /bu/ may be a noun referring to 'thing' or 'possession'; in a construction with the identifier /á/, compare /á bu bé/ 'it is theirs'.

The possessive forms on the right above are recorded only with nouns meaning 'father, mother, husband, wife, sibling, friend', not as might be expected with a form in the same semantic category, 'older brother'. Further, there are other forms meaning 'father' and 'mother' which are not used with these possessives; the following alternatives are recorded:

títá bu bé	*and*	tá be	'their father'
nǎ bu bé	*and*	yè bé	'their mother'

The first of each of these pairs appears to be more common, and also more informal. There is evidence that the second connotes more respect; Jukun Christians insist on /tá í/ 'our Father' in reference to God.

In expressions of possession and other association with nouns rather than pronouns, /bu/ is commonly used, and apparently is permissible in all cases. E.g.,

tǎnà bu títá m̀	'my father's house'
wǔzà bu pèrè ní	'that person's sibling'
(cf.: wǔzà á	'his sibling')

There are some combinations, however, in which /bu/ may readily be omitted. These do not involve kinship terms, but do appear to involve especially close relationships; e.g.,

busõ wudyi	'buffalo meat'
yô kà	'the inside of town, in town'

Thus, although the distinction between something like alienably and inalienably possessed nouns is far less developed in Dìyī than in the Mande languages, there are clear cases of such a contrast.

8.7. It has been noted that, in the Mande languages, the stem form of impersonal nouns has a generic reference, not specifically singular or plural, but that it is possible to express individuated pluralization. Personal nouns, on the other hand, are singular unless plurality is specified. A similar contrast is found in a number of other languages which, though they display vestiges of a noun class system, do not have affix-marked singular and plural forms.

My first experience in teaching Yoruba was with a native speaker who, through no fault of his own, knew even less about languages in general than I knew about his language in particular. The first several hours of instruction were devoted to drills designed to teach accuracy in the recognition and reproduction of tonal contrasts. The drill material consisted of very short sentences, one of the first of which was /mo rí ajá/, with the gloss 'I saw a dog'. After having said it for the students to repeat several times, the informant sidled up to me and whispered, "You know, that doesn't really mean 'I saw a dog'; it means 'I saw dog.'" My reply was, "I know what you mean, but unfortunately 'I saw dog' is not an English sentence. Let's leave it as it is, because if I asked you what you had seen, and you had actually seen a dog, you would undoubtedly say /mo rí ajá/." There could hardly be a more explicit demonstration of the generic character of simple nouns in Yoruba. If it is felt necessary to specify singularity, the numeral 'one' can be used. Such non-personal nouns can also, however, be preceded by the third person plural pronoun to form phrases like /àwọn ajá/; as in Mande, however, such phrases express not merely pluralization but individuation. If one had seen three dogs together, he would still in all probality say /mo rí ajá/; /àwọn ajá/ refers to some dogs out of a larger possible number.

The pronoun /àwọn/ is also used before personal nouns. Although the distinction is not as clear in Yoruba as it is in the Mande languages, such phrases are often preferred in contexts where their impersonal counterparts are considered quite unnecessary; the reference seems to be much closer to simple pluralization than is the case with impersonal nouns.

In the case of Igbo, a distinction must first be made between inanimate and animate nouns. Inanimate nouns are generic; in almost any context, /éféré/ may refer to 'a dish' or 'dishes', or 'the dish' or 'the dishes'. An individuated plural can be expressed by adding /ńdí/: /éféré ńdí/ 'certain dishes', /éféré ńdí à/ 'these (selected) dishes'.

Nonpersonal animate nouns may be used with modifiers specifying plurality, such as numerals higher than 'one'. Otherwise, however, an unmodified noun in this category is specifically singular; /ọ́ hụ̀rụ̀ éwú/ is only 'he saw a goat'. Pluralization is expressed by /ụ́mụ̀/ before such a noun: /ụ́mụ̀ é'wú/ 'goats'. This /ụ́mụ̀/ is also the word for possessed offspring: /ụ́mụ̀ yá/ 'his/her children, its young'; the corresponding singular is /ŋwá/: /ŋwá 'yá/ 'his/her child, its (one) young'. In construction with a non-personal animate noun, /ŋwá/ indicates a single young specimen: /ŋwá e'wú/ 'a young goat'. But /ụ́mụ̀ e'wú/, the apparent plural, does not specify age; it is merely a plural.

A few personal nouns behave somewhat similarly, but there is a significant distinction in that only the plural may be used with a modifier specifying plurality. The singular forms of two of these are unquestionably derived from phrases beginning with /ŋwá/ 'child', but this has become an integral part of these words, and their plurals are expressed by /ụ́mụ̀/ before them:

| ŋwó'ké | 'man, male', | pl.: | ụ́mụ̀ ŋwó'ké |
| ŋwáànyì | 'woman, female', | pl.: | ụ́mụ̀ ŋwáànyì |

In two other cases, the singular may optionally be preceded by /ŋwá/; again the plural is formed with /úmù/. In these, the word /ọ́byà/, with no separately identifiable meaning, is also optional. These are:

òkóró (ọ́byà)~ŋwá 'ókóró (ọ́byà)   'young man',
    pl.: ụ́'mụ́ 'ókóró (ọ́byà)
àgbọ́'ghọ́ (ọ́byà)~ŋwá 'ágbọ́'ghọ́ (ọ́byà)   'young woman',
    pl.: ụ́'mụ́ 'ágbọ́'ghọ́ (ọ́byà)

Three words for 'child' (unpossessed) are also derived from phrases beginning with /ŋwá/, with elision of the first syllable of the second word in the underlying phrases. The corresponding plurals are full phrases beginning with /úmù/:

ŋwátà   pl.:   úmù ńtà
ŋwátàkị́rị́   pl.:   úmù ńtàkị́rị́
ŋwá'ká   pl.:   úmù á'ká

There are a few similar phrases beginning with /ŋwá/ which show no elision; these also pluralize with /úmù/. All of these refer to young people. E.g.,

ŋwá ákwụ́kwọ́   'student',   pl.:   úmù ákwụ́kwọ́

Another plural formation applies to a few other personal nouns. For these, unlike the types described above, the singular form is used with modifiers specifying plurality. If such a modifier is not present, plurals of these are expressed by the morpheme /ńdí/ before the noun; compare the use described above of /ńdí/ after an inanimate noun to form an individuated plural. The personal nouns recorded of this type are:

ṁmádù   'person'   pl.:   ńdí ṁ'mádù
ókéènyè   'old man'   pl.:   ńdí ókéènyè
ókíìbìrì   'old woman'   pl.:   ńdí ókíìbìrì

Although /ńdí/ is used also with inanimate nouns (but after them, not before), its underlying reference is personal. In noun phrases, including nouns with relative modifiers, a word /ónyé/ is used for 'a person', and /ńdí/ is its suppletive plural. E.g.,

ọ́rụ́   'work':   ónyé ọ́'rụ́   'workman',   pl.:   ńdí ọ́'rụ́
ónyé 'byárá   'the person who came',   pl.:   ńdí 'byárá

Apart from noun class systems, therefore, the Mande distinction between individuated non-personal nouns and pluralized personal nouns is reflected also in other branches of the Niger-Congo family.

8.8. The Afro-Asiatic languages display a type of nominal morphology quite different from what has been described for the Niger-Kordofanian languages. Typical of Afro-Asiatic languages is a two-gender system, reflected in the forms of nouns and in pronominal referents for them, and considerable complexity and irregularity in noun pluralization. Each of the genders includes a semantically miscellaneous assortment of inanimate nouns, but almost without exception nouns referring to male persons or animals belongs in one gender, and nouns referring to female persons or animals in the other; the latter distinction justifies the labels "masculine" and "feminine."

Saho will be taken as a representative of the Cushitic languages (see Welmers 1952b). For masculine singular nouns, the independent pronominal referent is /úsuk/ 'he, it'; for feminine singular nouns it is /íse/ 'she, it'. A third person plural pronoun, of which the independent form is /úsun/ 'they', is used only with reference to personal nouns. Comparable "plural" forms of impersonal nouns use singular pronominal referents, and thus fall into the singular genders.

A word in Saho may be stressed on any syllable except the last, or may have no stress. Nouns with stress are regularly masculine. Nouns without stress and with a final consonant are usually masculine; there are some exceptions, most of them recognizably adaptations from Arabic feminine nouns. Nouns without stress and with a final vowel are regularly feminine; in a few apparent exceptions like /abba/ 'father', the presence of the final vowel is conditioned by the preceding double consonant.

Nouns that are stressed (and therefore masculine) and have a final vowel have a subject form in distinction from a general form; the subject form is unstressed, and the final vowel of the general form is replaced by /i/. E.g.,

| ᴳáre | 'house': | ᴳari naba | 'the house is big' |

Intersecting the distinction of genders, nouns fall into three categories on other formal grounds. First, there are, in each gender, mass nouns which have only one form. E.g.,

| gádda (m.) 'wealth' | dite (f.) 'darkness' |

Second, there are generic nouns, which in their stem form indicate an unspecified quantity. From these, unit forms are derived by suffixation, indicating a single specimen. There are two unit suffixes, /-to/ and /-ta/. With a few exceptions for each, /-to/ is used if the last vowel of the stem is /a/, and /-ta/ if the last vowel of the stem is anything else. Before either of these suffiues, /y/ is added after a stem-final vowel. Unit forms appear in either gender; the choice cannot be predicted from the gender of the stem or in any other way. In a few cases, both a masculine and a feminine unit form are derived from the same stem, indicating sex differences where appropriate, but also other differences. Examples of generic nouns and unit derivatives are:

basal	(m.)	'onions'	basálto	(m.)	'an onion'
biršiq	(m.)	'melons'	biršiqto	(f.)	'a melon'
ganga	(f.)	'twins'	gangáyto	(m.)	'a twin'
hado	(f.)	'meat'	hadoyta	(f.)	'a piece of meat'
barya	(f.)	'slaves'	baryáyto	(m.)	'a male slave'
			baryayto	(f.)	'a female slave'
barbare	(f.)	'pepper'	barbaréyta	(m.)	'a pepper'
			barbareyta	(f.)	'a pepper plant'

Third, there are unit nouns which have singular and plural forms. If such nouns are listed in groups, such that all nouns in each group show the same relationship between their singular and plural forms, there are over thirty groups of unit nouns, plus a number of idiosyncratic nouns including some with suppletive plurals. With the exception of the latter, however, these nouns show four major types of pluralization: by internal vowel replacement, by suffixing /-it/, by suffixing /-a/, and by infixing /-á-/. To a large extent, the choice among these four types is determined by the structure of the singular, but there are a number of nouns, particularly with plurals of the first two types, for which the choice is lexically determined. Plurals with the suffix /-a/ are feminine (and grammatically singular except for personals). All other plurals are masculine (also grammatically singular except for personals), and with the exception of a few nouns in one subtype the plural forms are stressed on the next-to-last syllable.

Internal vowel replacement is the predominant plural formation for singular forms that have two or more vowels before the last (but not necessarily final) consonant, the last of which is /a/, for singular forms with one vowel which is inherently short, and for other singular forms with final /a/ or /o/. The replacive vowel is most commonly /o/, but there are some cases in which it is /u/, /i/, or /e/; under most circumstances the choice is lexically determined. The following examples include only nouns with two or more vowels before the last consonant in the singular, the last of them /a/, and with the last consonant also final; /e/ is not attested as a replacive vowel in this type:

arat, árot	'bed'
mabrad, mábrod	'file'
sáḥsaḥ, sáḥsoḥ	'roasting pan'
araḥ, áruḥ	'road'
waraqat, waráqit	'piece of paper'

Although the last of these is, in its singular form, adopted from Arabic (and, incidentally, feminine), the plural is not Arabic. The same is true of the pair /faras, fáaris/ 'horse', which also shows a lexically conditioned vowel lengthening in the plural.

For singulars which have two or more vowels before the last consonant, the last of them not necessarily /a/, and which also have a final vowel, internal vowel replacement operates in the same way, but in addition the final vowel of the singular does not appear in the plural. For this restricted type, the replacive is usually, but not entirely regularly, /o/ for /a/, and /o, u, i, e/ for themselves; in the latter cases, the replacement as such has a zero effect. Examples are:

maḥádo,	máḥod	'spear'
wagaba,	wágob	'lip'
lakota,	lákot	'goatskin bag'
yangula,	yángul	'hyena'
Ɡebina,	Ɡebun	'bride'
kimbiro,	kímbir	'small bird (sp.)'
bakkéla,	bákkel	'rabbit'
masangale,	masángel	'side'

If the singular ends with a consonant cluster followed by /a/ or /o/, internal vowel replacement actually takes the form of infixing the vowel between the consonants of the cluster, and dropping the final vowel. E.g.,

sarba,	sárob	'lower leg'
qábre,	qábur	'grave'
bírta,	bírit	'piece of iron'
gúnde,	gúned	'log'

If the singular has only one vowel, inherently short, and a final consonant, internal vowel replacement again takes the form of infixation, between the vowel and final consonant. There are only a very few such formations; e.g.,

bab,	báob	'door'
sar,	sáur	'goatskin water bag'

Other pluralizations which may be assigned to the same general type involve reduplication of the last consonant of the singular. Any vowel may appear before the final reduplicated consonant in the plural, though again it is most commonly /o/; it is only partially predictable. Most singulars with this type of pluralization have final vowels, but a few are monosyllables with final consonants; the latter have plurals which, unlike all other masculine plurals, are unstressed. These nouns refer predominantly, though not exclusively, to body parts and kinship terms. Examples are:

lafa,	láfof	'bone'
gaba,	gábob	'hand'
illa,	íllal	'spring'
boodo,	bóodad	'hole'
rado,	rádod	'animal hide'
angu,	ángug	'breast'
inti,	íntit	'eye'
af,	afof	'mouth'
nef,	nefof	'face'
kor,	koorar	'saddle'

The second type of pluralization is by suffixing /-it/. All singulars that pluralize in this way have a final vowel. If the singular is masculine, as most of them are, the suffix /-it/ replaces the final vowel. In the five recorded cases in which the singular is feminine, the suffix replaces the final vowel in one, follows it in two, and appears after an alternant form of the stem in two. The plurals (stressed) are masculine in all cases. Examples are:

m. s.:	alfénta,	alféntit	'lid'
	dísti,	dístit	'pan'
	síile,	síilit	'picture'
f. s.:	maxadda,	maxáddit	'pillow'
	mallada,	malladáit	'razor'
	ḥaḍa,	ḥóḍit	'tree'

The third type of pluralization is with a suffix /-a/; these plurals, unlike all others, are feminine. To a large extent but not without exception, the singulars which pluralize in this way differ in their segmental structure from singulars which take the first two types of pluralization. For example, a majority of the singulars with plurals in /-a/ have two or more vowels and a final consonant, but the last vowel is not /a/; if it were, pluralization by vowel replacement would be typical. Some other singulars have structures which permit any of the first three types of pluralization; the choice is lexically determined. Alternations in the stem are common. Examples are:

qaalib,	qaaliba	'pipe'
gulub,	guluuba	'knee'
rimid,	rimiida	'root'
akat,	akoota	'rope'
bádna,	badaana	'corpse'
sariddo,	sariida	'cedar (?)'
dik,	diika	'extended family'
gádi,	gadua	'wadi'
káre,	karua	'dog'
sído,	siida	'skin rug'

The fourth type of pluralization is by infixation, usually with some additional alternation. The infix is /á/ or /áa/ in most cases; it is inserted between two consonants of a medial cluster, or in a few cases after or before a single medial consonant. This type of pluralization resembles a type found also in Arabic, and some of the singulars are clearly adopted from Arabic. They do not all, however, appear to be instances of adopting both the singular and plural forms. Examples are:

muftah,	mufátih	'key'
maqdet,	maqádet	'sickle'
xaatim,	xawátim	'ring'
bismar,	bisáamir	'nail'
zambil,	zanáabil	'basket'
qamiš,	qamáiš	'shirt'
badiila,	badáil	'shovel'
faanus,	foánus	'lamp'
kofyet,	koáfi	'cap'
miskin,	misaakin	'poor man'

A small subtype of plurals with infix are exceptionally feminine, and also have a suffix /i/ or /e/, which in a few cases is the same as the ending of the singular. Examples are:

kursi,	kuraasi	'chair'
kondoḍ,	kondaaḍi	'boil'
mos,	moosaasi	'knife'
bakal,	bakooli	'kid'

Within the framework of these four types of pluralization, there is a fairly large number of nouns which display some lexically determined irregularity apart from the plural affix. In addition, there is a fairly small number of nouns whose plural forms do not fit into any of these four types in any way. For some of these, the singular and plural forms are partially similar; in other cases the plural is suppletive. Examples are:

sarena,	sára	'garment'
áwka,	irri	'boy'
saga,	láa	'cow'

8.9. In the Berber branch of the Afro-Asiatic family, the complications of noun morphology are somewhat similar.[2] Before discussing gender and pluralization, however, it is of interest to note that kinship terms form a special class of nouns. In two striking respects, their behavior resembles that of kinship terms in the Mande languages. Such a similarity must not, to be sure, be taken as evidence of linguistic relationship; the typological similarities are of a sort that might crop up in languages elsewhere in the world, and there are also grammatical differences that should not be overlooked.

Most kinship terms in Berber begin with a consonant, while other nouns begin with a vowel, or with a feminine prefix followed by a vowel. Kinship terms are not marked for gender. Possessive pronouns used with kinship terms are different from those used with other nouns; for at least some pronouns, the same is true in the Mande languages, but for impersonal as well as personal relational nouns. Further, for kinship terms alone, a redundant third person possessive pronoun is used when a noun possessor is expressed; in Mande, this is true of personal but not impersonal relational nouns, though it is also true of all free nouns. E.g., Berber /baba/ 'father' takes the possessive suffix /-s/ 'his', and is linked to /uryaz/ 'man' in the phrase /baba-s n-uryas/ 'the man's father'. (Mande has prefixed pronouns, the reverse word order, and no marker of the possessive construction.)

As in Cushitic, masculine and feminine genders are morphologically and syntactically distinguished in Berber. In addition to designating female sex, the Berber feminine gender may indicate a diminutive. In addition, a masculine noun may be generic in meaning, with a derived feminine noun indicating a unit of the genus; in Saho, as has been noted, the generic-unit distinction does not correlate with gender, but there is a comparable derivative formation. With very few exceptions, masculine nouns begin with a vowel—/a/ in about eighty percent of the cases, /i/ in most of the rest, and /u/ in a relatively few. The initial vowel is analyzed as a prefix. Feminine nouns begin with a feminine prefix /t-/ followed by one of the same vowels, with about the same relative frequency. (These are the

---

[2] The following treatment of Berber noun morphology is based on a preliminary outline kindly prepared by Prof. Thomas G. Penchoen, using data from Tamazight. The statistics are based on a lexicon by Abes. I have attempted to refine the analysis in a few details, and take full responsibility for any respects in which I have beclouded rather than clarified the situation.

only vowel phonemes in the Berber languages; there is also a shwa whose occurrence is predictable.) Most feminine nouns, especially those derived from corresponding masculine forms, also have a suffix /-t/ in the singular, though not in the plural. Thus typical masculine-feminine pairs are as follows; the specific forms in this section are from Tamazight, and the predictable shwa is indicated by a period:

aɣyul	'male donkey'	taɣyult	'female donkey'
axam	'tent'	taxamt	'small tent'
iz.m	'lion'	tiz.mt	'lioness'

There are, of course, many nouns in each gender without conterparts in the other; e.g., masculine /alud/ 'mud', feminine (without suffix) /tig.mmi/ 'tent circle'.

Four mechanisms—apart from the automatic absence of the feminine suffix /-t/ in plurals—are found in the formation of plurals from singulars. These are prefix vowel alternation, suffixation, vowel alternation in the stem, and tense-lax alternation in consonants. The vast majority of nouns show both prefix vowel alternation and suffixation, but there are also other combinations of two of the four mechanisms, and also combinations of three and of all four. In addition, each of the mechanisms has two to several surface manifestations, though some of the distinctions might be collapsed by morphophonemic statements. Thus the permutations are very numerous. In terms of surface forms, 86 different plural formations are attested in a corpus of 433 masculine nouns, and 53 in a corpus of 209 feminine nouns. Many of the formations appear in only one noun, and only a few in more than ten. Yet there is much more regularity than such a statement suggests; one combination alone accounts for 169 of the 433 masculine nouns, and one for 75 of the 209 feminine nouns. The amount of regularity, as well as the possibilities of variety, will be evident from a brief summary of the four mechanisms found in the formation of plurals.

In the total corpus of 642 nouns, the singular prefix vowel is /a/ in 505 cases, /i/ in 111, and /u/ in 26. If the singular prefix vowel is /a/ or /i/, the plural prefix vowel is /i/ in the vast majority of cases, /a/ in a few, and /u/ in only one. If the singular prefix vowel is /u/, the plural prefix vowel is regularly /u/ as well. These facts have been described in terms of "alternations" of /a/ to /i/, /a/ to /u/, and /i/ to /a/, plus "no alternation" for each of the three vowels. It seems preferable, however, to group together all appearances of the predominant /i/ in the plural, all appearances of the much less frequent /a/, and all appearances of /u/; all but one of the last are regular, corresponding to /u/ in the singular.

Most Tamazight nouns end with a consonant, and the vast majority take a suffix in the plural. For such consonant-final nouns, the masculine plural suffix (if used at all) is regularly /-n/; the feminine plural suffix is regularly /-in/. Thus the most common plural formation is with the prefix vowel /i/ and the suffix appropriate to either gender. This combination is found with over forty percent of all nouns. An example for each gender is:

axam,	ixam.n	'tent'
taxamt,	tixamin	'small tent'

A number of other nouns may be analyzed as having final vowels in the singular, and one of three plural suffixes in each gender: masculine /-w.n/, /-y.n/, /t.n/, feminine /-win/, /-yin/, /-tin/. In most such cases, however, it would seem preferable to analyze the /w/, /y/, or /t/ of the apparent plural suffixes as belonging to the stem, and as having dropped when no suffix follows; this analysis is supported by the fact that these consonants do not appear word-finally after vowels except as the result of relatively recent secondary developments; and this analysis is virtually required in the many cases where these consonants appear also before the feminine suffix /-t/. In such cases, then, the plural suffixes are the regular /-n/ and /-in/. This would account for a number of sets like the following:

am.ksa,	im.ksaw.n	'shepherd'
tam.ksawt,	tim.ksawin	'shepherdess'
uṣka,	uṣkay.n	'harehound'
tuṣkayt,	tuṣkayin	'female harehound'
anu,	anut.n	'well'
tanutt,	tanutin	'small well'

There are, however, some cases in which this analysis cannot be made, because the expected consonant does not appear in a feminine singular form. For such cases, it would appear that the three plural suffixes for each gender, as cited above, must be posited as distinct from the normal /-n/ and /-in/.

Some nouns, all masculine and having a final consonant in the singular, appear to have plural suffixes /-an/, /-aw.n/, or /-iw.n/. In these cases, however, the vowel of the apparent suffix can more conveniently be treated as a manifestation of vowel alternation as described below, in which case the plural suffixes as such would be regular.

Interlocking with the three-way distinction of plural prefix vowel and the variety of possible suffixes or the non-use of a suffix, is a third mechanism found in plural formation: vowel alternation. Plurals with suffixes, as described above, may also have vowel alternation; plurals without suffixes invariably do. Vowel alternation, if it appears at all, must appear either after or before the last consonant of a stem; there may then also be alternation of an earlier vowel. The alternation may be between any vowel in the singular and any other vowel or zero in the plural, or between zero in the singular and any vowel in the plural; a wide variety of combinations is found, but the commonest occurrences are /a/ or zero after the last consonant in the plural, and /u/ before the last consonant. A few of the many possibilities of vowel alternation are illustrated in the following singular-plural pairs:

akurdi,	ikurdan	'flea'
axbu,	ixba	'hole'
an.bgi,	in.bgaw.n	'guest'
acniḍ,	icnaḍ	'mat'
asɣur.t,	isɣurut.n	'ululation'
afrag,	if.rgan	'hedge'
ag.nsu,	igunsan	'tent interior'
asaka,	isuka	'ford'
aɣbalu,	iɣbula	'spring'
agadir,	igudar	'wall'
azlaf,	izlufa	'reed'
tadist,	tidusin	'stomach'
tislit,	tislatin	'fiancee'
tuɣm.st,	tuɣmas	'tooth'
tadawt,	tidiwa	'back'

In a few nouns (17 in the corpus), in addition to suffixation or vowel alternation or both, but not independently of both, pluralization is characterized by an alternation of tenseness and laxness in the second consonant of the root. If the consonant involved is final in the singular, the alternation is between a lax consonant in the singular and a tense consonant in the plural. If the consonant involved is not final in the singular, the opposite alternation appears. A few examples are:

aṣaḍ,	iṣaṭṭ.n	'calamity'
ad.r,	id.rran	'acorn'
afus,	ifass.n	'hand'
asif,	isaff.n	'river'
iɣil,	iɣall.n	'cow'
af.ttal,	if.tlan	'cuscus'
as.kkur,	isukran	'partridge'

In addition to gender and number distinctions, one further aspect of Berber noun morphology is worthy of note. For any noun, singular or plural, there are two forms (which happen to be identical for a few types of nouns) with different grammatical functions. Following the terminology long used in describing the Semitic languages, these are known as the "absolute state" and the "construct state"; in both their form and their function, however, there are striking differences between Berber and Semitic. The term "construct" has to do with "constructions"; the construct state is used when a noun is used in a particular grammatical construction. In Berber, unlike Semitic, a construct appears after another word in certain constructions, and is distinguished from the absolute by a difference at the beginning of the noun.

In Tamazight, the difference between the absolute and construct forms is in the vowel prefix. If both the singular and the plural vowel prefixes of the absolute are known, the prefix of the construct is predictable. For the predominant type of masculine noun, with the prefix vowel /a/ in the singular and /i/ in the plural, the construct prefix vowels are /u/ singular and /i/ plural. For the corresponding type of feminine nouns, the construct prefix vowel (after the feminine prefix /t-/) is zero in both singular and plural. If the absolute prefix vowel is /i/ in both singular and plural, the construct prefix vowel is usually /i/ for masculine nouns but zero for feminine, but in some cases /yi/ for masculine and /i/ for feminine. Otherwise—in the less common types of nouns—masculine constructs begin with a semivowel before the prefix vowel, yielding /yi/, /wu/, /wa/, and feminine constructs are identical with absolutes. For purposes of illustration in following paragraphs, only three nouns will be used; the corresponding absolute and construct forms are:

aryaz	:	uryaz	'man'
tam.ṭṭuṭ	:	tm.ṭṭuṭ	'woman'
axam	:	uxam	'tent'

Four uses of the construct may be distinguished, though perhaps the first three may be considered subtypes of one usage in the underlying structure. First, the construct is used with the second noun of a noun-noun phrase, in which the first noun is the head. If the second noun is vowel-initial (including most masculines), it may optionally be preceded by a preposition-like morpheme /n/; if the second noun is consonant-initial, /n/ is obligatory. This usage rather resembles that of an Indo-European genitive case, or a Niger-Kordofanian associative construction:

> axam (n) uryaz   'the man's tent'

Second, the construct is used after numerals. In this combination, /n/ is never used with a vowel-initial noun, but is obligatory before a consonant. This usage could be considered the same as the first if numerals may be treated as a subclass of nouns. Examples are:

> yun uryaz   'one man'
> yut n tm.ṭṭuṭ   'one woman'

Third, the construct is used after prepositions. It is possible that prepositions may also be treated as a subtype of noun in the underlying structure, so that the following example would basically mean something like 'he went-to place of tent':

> idda ɣ.r uxam   'he went to the tent'

Fourth, and apparently in quite a different category of usage, the construct is used for a noun subject when it follows the verb—its usual position. E.g.,

> idda uryaz   'the man went'

8 10. In the Semitic languages, there is a similar gender distinction, there are comparable complications in noun pluralization, and there is a distinction between an absolute and a construct state. Although Arabic is spoken by far more people than any other single language on the African continent, it is not usually thought of as being an African language, and is not chosen here for purposes of illustration. Among the Ethiopian Semitic languages, noun morphologies quite similar to that of Arabic are found. Tigrinya is fairly typical.[3] By comparison, Amharic has a considerably simplified system of noun pluralization, using only suffixes.

Tigrinya shows only a few traces of a gender distinction marked morphologically in the noun itself; the distinction nevertheless exists, as shown by obligatory agreement of a noun with masculine and feminine forms of certain modifiers and pronoun substitutes. The typical Semitic (and probably proto-Afro-Asiatic) feminine suffix /-t/ is found with a few types of derived nouns and a few personal nouns, and also with some adjectives. An example is:

käfati	'a man who opens'	käfatit	'a woman who opens'

Besides indicating female sex, the feminine may have diminutive, pejorative, or affectionate significance.

The construct state is also a relatively minor problem in Tigrinya. There are a few phrases, largely in the context of religion, which show an archaic construct form ending in /ä/. In other cases, the construct is distinguished from the absolute only for nouns whose absolute forms have final /i/—and even then the use of the construct form is optional. The construct is used only in noun-noun phrases such as those representing the first of four uses in Berber. It is the first rather than the second noun in the phrase, however, that takes the construct form. This is typical of the Semitic languages. In the following examples, using nouns for which the absolute forms are /lam/ 'cow' and /kälbi/ 'dog', only the third, an optional alternative of the second, shows a distinct construct form:

lam ḥawwáy	'my brother's cow'
kälbi ḥawwáy	'my brother's dog'
kälb ḥawwáy	'my brother's dog'

There is also an alternative to the above, not using a construct form in any case, but using a morpheme /nay/ which, at least for present purposes, may be called a preposition. The modifying phrase may either follow or precede the head noun. Thus:

kälbi nay ḥawwáy	'my brother's dog'
nay ḥawwáy kälbi	'my brother's dog'

Like the Cushitic and Berber languages already discussed, and like most other Semitic languages, Tigrinya shows an exuberant proliferation of plural formations. Before going into detail, a general comment about Semitic word structure is in order. Word roots have generally been analyzed as consisting of consonants only; the commonest roots have three consonants, but some have only two, and some

---

[3] Data on Tigrinya—with which I once had some direct acquaintance—are taken from Leslau 1941.

four or more. Accompanying a root, there may be a variety of sequences of vowels, with or without an additional consonant before or after the root, or both. A root is treated as a discontinuous morpheme consisting of consonants only. Everything else in a word, apart from inflectional prefixes or suffixes, is treated as another discontinuous morpheme. Thus a typical word consists of two intercalated discontinuous morphemes. For example, a root consisting of three consonants may be found in one word with a shape such as CaCaC, and in another word with a shape such as ʔiCCiC. Particularly in the verbal system of Semitic languages, each nonroot morpheme has a definable meaning. The same is not so clearly true for nouns, but a great many nouns have plural forms differing from singulars in that which is intercalated with a constant series of consonants. Such forms may be analyzed as having consonantal roots, which may be accompanied by either a singular or a plural nonroot morpheme; indeed, some nouns, derived from consonantal verb roots, can only be so analyzed. There is some correlation between the use of particular singular and particular plural nonroot morphemes, but by no means complete regularity. In fact, a given noun may have two or more plural forms, used optionally or in some cases with a distinction in details of meaning. The situation with respect to pluralization in Tigrinya is not fully systematized here, but illustrations of some of the major patterns are given.

First, a number of nouns have plurals formed only by suffixation, with no difference in the internal non-root morpheme. The usual plural suffix is /-at/ after a final consonant or /-tat/ after a final vowel. E.g.,

| säb, | säbat | 'man' |
| ʔabbo, | ʔabbotat | 'father' |

An archaic plural suffix /-an/ appears with some nouns used primarily by well-educated speakers. In addition, some singulars ending in /-a/ or /-ay/ have corresponding plurals ending in /-ot/, and some singulars ending in /-i/ or /-ay/ have corresponding plurals ending in /-o/. Examples of these formations are:

gwasa,	gwasot	'shepherd'
tästay,	tästot	'cow'
käfati,	käfato	'one who opens'

Among the intercalated non-root plural morphemes, one is CäCaCəC. In a number of forms, this corresponds to a singular CäCCäC, and in some to CəCCəC; there are also pairs with three consonants in the singular which infix /w/ in the plural. E.g.,

mänbär,	mänabər	'seat'
qəlsəm,	qälasəm	'arm'
qamis,	qämawəs	'shirt'

Some nonroot morphemes include an additional consonant before the root; perhaps this may be considered automatic if the first vowel of the morpheme precedes the root, since the consonant is always a glottal stop, and there are no word-initial vowels. A plural ʔaCCaC appears in a number of cases like the following, the last of these including a suffix:

färäs,	ʔafras	'horse'
bərki,	ʔabrak	'knee'
səm,	ʔasmat	'name'

A somewhat similar ʔaCaCəC is attested in the following:

nabri,	ʔanabər	'leopard'
bäggə,	ʔabagə	'sheep'

The same sequence plus a suffix /-ti/ is found in:

kälbi,	ʔakaləbti	'dog'

And a somewhat similar form is illustrated by:

ʔadgi,	ʔaʔdug

Variations on another theme are illustrated by the following:

barya,	bärayu	'slave'
ḥaläqa,	ḥalaqu	'chief'
mərak,	mərakut	'calf'

Some pluralizations are generally grouped along with the various "internal" plurals so far illustrated, presumably because of their relative infrequency, though they appear to be varieties of suffixation, all including a final /-ti/. Examples are:

käsasi,	käsasti	'accuser'
ḥəṣan,	ḥəṣawənti	'baby'
gäza,	gäzawətti	'house'
səraḥ,	səraḥətti	'task'

Finally, some plurals show reduplication of an internal consonant in the singular form, or the separation by a vowel of a double consonant in the singular. E.g.,

tämän,	tämamən	'snake'
märäṣṣan,	märäṣaṣən	'mirror'
gwàräbet,	gwàräbabətti	'neighbor'

8.11. Although it was only relatively recently that the relationship of the Chadic languages to Cushitic, Berber, and Semitic (and ancient Egyptian) was widely recognized, an almost monotonously similar typology of nominal morphology can be found in Chadic. A gender distinction, a type of construct, and a proliferation of plural formations is found, for example, in Hausa.[4]

---

[4] I am indebted to Mr. Russell G. Schuh for the following outline of Hausa noun morphology. The final wording of the descriptive statements is mine, but all credit for the organization is his. This outline is clearly an improvement on any published treatment, and extends far beyond my own past and limited competence in the language, which at present is virtually restricted to checking suspected slips of the pen with an informant.

There is a fairly good correlation between the segmental form of singular nouns and their gender in Hausa. Nearly all feminine singulars end in /a/, and all singulars which do not end in /a/ are masculine. There are, however, a number of masculine singulars ending in /a/; some of these are recognizably adopted words, and some others are in all probability historically plurals. There is no gender distinction in the plural; the morpheme indicating identification with plural nouns and the construct ending are identical with those for masculine singulars, though plurals do require plural agreement in pronouns and demonstratives. The following illustrate the construction of identification; high tone is unmarked in examples in this section, and the morphemes indicating identification regularly have the opposite tone from the immediately preceding syllable:

m. sg.:	gidā nè	'it's a compound'
f. sg.:	rìgā cè	'it's a gown'
pl.:	rīgunà nē	'they are gowns'

A construct form has a suffix /-n/ for masculine singular and all plural nouns, and /-r/ (almost surely from an original */-t/) for feminine singulars. With shortening of final long vowels in closed syllables, the constructs of the nouns used above are illustrated in the following:

gidan sarkī	'the chief's compound'
rìgar sarkī	'the chief's gown'
rīgunàn sarkī	'the chief's gowns'

A superficial survey of Hausa plurals suggests that there are well over twenty-five types. Most if not all of these can be analyzed as involving suffixation, but there are also frequent occurrences of internal vowel replacement or insertion, and of consonant reduplication—mechanisms which have been noted also for Cushitic, Berber, and Semitic. Careful analysis reveals a considerable correlation between the segmental and tonal shape of the singular and the choice of plural formation, and some correlation with derivational types and semantic groups. Six basic types of pluralization can be distinguished, most of them with two or more sub-types, and there are a few miscellaneous unclassified plurals. The first three of the types described below are productive, in the sense that new words taken into the language will be assigned plurals of one of these types; of the non-productive types, however, (6) below is one of the commonest plural formations in the language, even though it is not used for newly acquired nouns.

1) Plurals in -ōC'ī, in which C' is a repetition of the last consonant of the singular. The singular is usually disyllabic, with the tones high-low, and with final /à/. This is the commonest plural formation for adopted words. The plurals have high tone throughout, and the final vowel of the singular does not appear. The following examples include three highly typical pairs, the third of which illustrates a regular pattern of palatalization before front vowels, as well as one pair with a final vowel other than /à/ in the singular, and one with a trisyllabic singular:

hanyằ,	hanyōyī	'road'
k'ōfằ,	k'ōfōfī	'doorway'
mōtằ,	mōtōcī	'automobile'
zākì,	zākōkī	'lion'
tàmbayằ,	tambayōyī	'question'

2) Plurals in -uCằ, in which C is either /n/, /k/, /w/, or a repetition of the last consonant (or in some cases two consonants) of the singular (C'). Plurals in /-unằ, -ukằ, -uwằ/ are formed from most disyllabic singulars with the tones low-high, and from many disyllabic singulars with the tones high-low and a final vowel other than /a/. There is some dissimilatory restriction in the choice of C in the plural ending; it is not /n/ if the last consonant of the singular is /n/; it is not /k/ if the last consonant of the singular is a velar, and it is not /w/ if the last consonant of the singular is /m/. Otherwise the choice of C is lexically determined. In addition, some of these plurals—nearly all if C is /w/—show repetition or doubling of the last consonant of the singular. Plurals in /-uC'ằ/ are formed from a number of trisyllabic or longer singulars, or from a few singulars of the shape CVCCV, where CC is not a double consonant. In all of the subtypes, plurals have high tone throughout except for the final vowel. Again, the final vowel of the singular does not appear in the plural; yet there is no particular motivation for analyzing the final vowel of the singular as a suffix. In the last subtype, /-uC'ằ/ replaces the final VCV or CV of the singular, sometimes with reduplication of the last consonant or two consonants of the singular. The available options within this general type of plural result in a considerable variety of surface forms of pluralization. Examples are:

-unằ:	rìga,	rīgunằ	'man's gown'
	hancì,	hantunằ	'nose'
	damì,	dammunằ	'bundle (as of grass)'
	jìkī,	jikunkunằ	'body'
-ukằ:	zaurè,	zaurukằ	'entrance hut'
	zàncē,	zantukằ	'conversation'
	cùtā:	cūtuttukằ	'disease'
-uwằ:	gàrī,	garūruwằ	'town'
	k'ayằ,	k'ayāyuwằ	'thorn'
	k'anè,	k'annuwằ	'younger brother'
-uC'ằ:	gàtarī,	gāturằ	'axe'
	māgànī,	māgungunằ	'medicine'
	shagàlī,	shagulgulằ	'celebrating'
	àlkāwàrī,	alkāwurằ	'promise'
	tafkì,	tafukằ	'pond, lake'
	hargì,	haruggằ	'sword fastener'

3) Plurals in /-ai/, /-ū/, /-ī/. These are grouped together on the basis of tone; all plurals with these endings have low tone throughout except for the ending

itself. Many singulars with these plural forms, and apparently all in the case of
/-ū/, are trisyllabic; many of these are adopted words. Nouns with plurals in
/-ai/ and /-ī/ also include a number of terms for domestic or small wild animals.
Nouns indicating instrument or place of action, derived from verbs and having
a prefix /ma-/, regularly form their plurals with /-ai/. Again, consonant reduplication or doubling appears in some cases; in the case of trisyllabic singulars, this
applies to the second or to the last two consonants. Examples of this type
are:

-ai:	jàkī,	jàkai / jàkkai	'donkey'
	birì,	bìrai	'monkey'
	àbōkī,	àbòkai	'friend'
	lōkàcī,	lòkàtai	'time'
	littāfì,	lìttàttàfai	'book'
	madūbī,	màdùbai	'mirror'
-ū:	takàrdā,	tàkàrdū	'paper'
	màganà,	màgàngànū	'speech'
-ī:	tàbarmā,	tàbàrmī	'palm leaf mat'
	ɓàrāwò,	ɓàràyī	'thief'
	k'ātò,	k'àttī	'huge'
	sābō,	sàbbī / sàbàbbī	'new'

4) Plurals in /-ū/ or in /-ī/ or /-ā/, differing in tone from the above. With
one exception, plurals of this type have the same tones as the corresponding singulars, except for the final vowel which is always high. A few nouns assigned to
this type could also have been included in 3) above, since the "same" tones are
low to begin with. Plurals in /-ī/ and /-ā/ in this type are in complementary distribution: the plural has /-ī/ if the singular ends in a non-front vowel, and /-ā/ if
the singular ends in a front vowel. Singulars include a rather small number of
disyllabic forms, mostly with the tones high-low; among these are several personal
nouns which—if one may include 'woman, wife' and 'stranger, guest' on cultural grounds and 'husband' perhaps with tongue in cheek—seem to share something of a deprecatory significance. Also included are trisyllabic or longer derived
singulars with a prefix /ma-/, indicating agents (cf. 3 above); these all have
singulars ending in /-ī/ and plurals in /-ā/. No consonant reduplication or doubling
is attested in this type of plural. Apart from the derived nouns, the pattern for
which is productive, the following examples may be exhaustive for this type of
plural:

-ū:	yātsà,	yātsū	'finger'
	māshì,	māsū	'spear'
	māyè,	māyū	'sorcerer'
	shēghè,	shēgū	'bastard'
	sà	'bull' } shānū	'cattle'
	sānìyā	'cow'	

-ī / -ā:	bāwằ,	bāyī	'slave'
	kằzā,	kằjī	'chicken'
	bằk'ō,	bằk'ī	'stranger, guest'
	zằbō,	zằbī	'guinea fowl'
	arnē,	arnā	'pagan'
	mijì,	mazā	'husband'
	màcè,	mātā	'woman, wife'
(Agent:)	magìnī,	magìnā	'mason'
	marùbùcī,	marùbùtā	'scribe'

5) Plurals in /-àkū/, /-àkī/, /-ànnī/, /-aC'ī/. The first of these, /-àkū/, has an optional alternant /-àikū/. With either /-àkū/ or /-àkī/, the plural has low tone throughout except for the final syllable; however, /-àkī/ also appears with reduplication and doubling of the last consonant of the singular, and this combination has the tones /-àCCakī/, preceded by high. Singulars corresponding to these plurals are disyllabic, mostly of the shape /CāCā/ (high-high), in which the second consonant is a resonant. The third subtype, /-ànnī/, also has disyllabic singulars, but with other tones, mostly low-high. With singulars which have three consonants, this has an alternant with /è/ inserted before the last consonant, and the ending /-anī/. The sub-type /-aC'ī/ has singulars with three (or more) consonants and usually high tone throughout; the plurals show vowel insertion, and consonant reduplication in two of the three known cases. Thus, in respects which hardly seem relevant, there is complementary distribution among all of these subtypes, except between the first two. For some of the subtypes, the following examples are probably exhaustive:

-akū:	rānā,	rằnàkū / rằnàikū	'sun, daytime'
	zānā,	zằnàkū / zằnàikū	'grass mat'
-àkī:	gōnā,	gònàkī	'farm'
	kwānā,	kwằnàkī	'day'
-àCCakī:	gāwā,	gāwàwwakī	'corpse'
	kāyā,	kāyàyyakī	'load'
	k'ārā,	k'àràrrakī	'complaint, noise'
	kunyā,	kunyàyyakī	'plowed row'
-ànnī:	gwàfā,	gwàfànnī	'forked post'
	fùrē,	fùrànnī	'flower'
	wằsā,	wằsànnī	'play, game'
	watằ,	wàtànnī	'moon, month'
-èCanī	gàrmā,	garèmanī	'large hoe'
	fartanyằ,	farètanī	'small hoe'
	màlàfā,	malèfanī	'straw hat'
-aC'ī:	k'aryā,	k'aràirayī	'lie'
	tarwaɗā,	tarèwaɗī	'catfish'
	shāwarằ,	shāwàrwarī	'advice'

6) Plurals in -àCV̄, in which C is /y/ or the last consonant of the singular, and V̄ is /ē/, /ā/, or /ū/, the choice depending on the segmental and tonal shape of the singular. This is a very common type of pluralization, accounting for many disyllabic singulars and none other than disyllabic. If the singular has the tones high-high, and if the first syllable has a long vowel or a short vowel followed by NC or a double consonant, the plural ending is /-àyē/. If the singular has the shape CVCV̄ with the tones high-high, the plural ending is /-àC'ē/. If the singular contains a cluster other than NC or a double consonant, and has the tones high-high, the plural ends in /-àCē/, in which /à/ is inserted before the last consonant and C is the last consonant of the singular. If the singular has the shape C̄VCV̄ with the tones high-low, the plural ends in /-C'ā/, in which C' is a doubling of the second consonant of the singular. If the singular has the shape C̄VCCV̄ and the tones high-low, the plural ends in /-àCā/, in which C is the last consonant of the singular, and /à/ is inserted before it. If the singular is either C̄VCV̄ or C̄VCCV̄ with the tones high-low (like the preceding two sub-types, but with some evidence of different historical development reflected in morphophonemic irregularities), the plural ends in /-àCū/, in which C is the last consonant of the singular and /à/ is inserted before it. In all plurals of this type, the tones are high-low-high. Examples are:

-àyē:	zōmō,	zōmàyē	'rabbit'
	sūnā,	sūnàyē	'name'
	bangō,	bangwàyē	'wall'
	k'yallē,	k'yallàyē	'piece of cloth'
-āC'ē:	k'asā,	k'asàshē	'land, country'
	gidā,	gidàjē	'compound'
	wurī,	wuràrē	'place'
	wuk'ā,	wuk'àk'ē	'knife'
-àCē:	birnī,	birànē	'walled city'
	kaskō,	kasàkē	'small clay bowl'
	farkē,	fatàkē	'itinerant trader'
-C'ā:	zōbě,	zôbbā	'ring'
	rēshě,	rêssā	'branch'
-àCā:	sirdì,	siràdā	'saddle'
	gunkì,	gumàkā	'idol'
-àCū:	dūtsě,	duwàtsū	'stone'
	kuncì,	kumàtū	'cheek'
	gwīwà,	gwiyàyū	'knee'
	idồ,	idànū	'eye'

All of the preceding may give the impression of being remarkably exhaustive. There are in addition, however, a few more minor types of pluralization, and a few unclassified plurals, including one known suppletive. Even within the types outlined above, there are instances of morphophonemic alternation which have not been noted; some of these are regular, accounted for by phonologic rules, but some are restricted to the lexical items in which they occur. Thus the data cited from Cushitic, Berber, Semitic, and Chadic display characteristics exceedingly common in Afro-Asiatic languages: two genders, noun forms of a "construct" type, and complex pluralization featuring suffixation, vowel insertion, consonant doubling (or fortition) and/or reduplication, and sporadic morphophonemic irregularities. As might be expected, some languages show extensive simplification.

8.12. For sheer complexity or irregularity in nominal morphology, however, it is hard to beat a number of Nilo-Saharan languages. Because of very limited direct experience and the paucity of extensive descriptions by others that can be confirmed as reliable, no adequately representative treatment is attempted here. The nature of the problem can be suggested by two typical statements of others. Of Maasai, Tucker and Mpaayei (1955) say, "There are many ways of forming the plural, and although Hollis has listed nouns into 'classes' according to their plural formation, these 'classes' admit of a bewildering number of 'exceptions'. There is only one safe rule for beginners, viz. learn the plural of each noun as you come to it." And of Ateso, Hilders and Lawrence (1956, p. 3) observe, "To form the plural the ending of the noun is changed. This change may consist of the omission of the last syllable, the addition of another syllable or syllables, or the alteration of the last syllable or syllables. E.g., (omission) *amukat* 'shoe', pl. *amuk*; (addition) *ekek* 'door', pl. *ikekia*; (alternation) *apese* 'girl', pl. *apesur* .... These changes in the endings of nouns are so irregular that it is not worthwhile trying to formulate rules for the formation of plurals."

Some years ago I had the opportunity to work for some time with data from Nuer, tape-recorded and transcribed, giving the various forms of a few hundred nouns. In addition to a singular-plural distinction, there were forms that appeared to function somewhat like the case forms of Indo-European languages. In the singular, one form is used for subject and object, another in other constructions, and a third (in appropriate cases) as a vocative. In the plural, only forms corresponding to the first two of these were found. The forms—a great many of them of the structure CVC, in which V may be single, double, or a cluster —differed from each other in their vocalic nucleus, often in tone, and sometimes in final consonant. Attempting to classify the variations in form, on the basis of only two or three of the available five forms, resulted in recognizing at least seventy-five types, no one of them representing more than a handful of nouns. There appeared to be no reasonable hope of grouping numbers of these types together in any rational way.

The internal changes in Nuer and some other languages are very likely developments from suffixes in an earlier period of the languages' history. Suffixation appears quite commonly in the nominal morphology of other Eastern Sudanic languages. Gregerson (1970) suggests a historical relationship between suffixation for pluralization in Nilo-Saharan and the noun class systems of Niger-Kordofanian. If such an ultimate relationship exists, however, it sheds little light on the complexities of suffixation and its historical developments in Eastern Sudanic as far as synchronic description is concerned.

The nominal morphology of Sapiny (Sebei) is described in a dissertation (Montgomery 1966) written under my supervision, and the general outlines of it were checked by myself not only from transcription but also from tape recordings and with a native speaker. Nouns in Sapiny show a two-way formal distinction: between singular and plural, and between what Miss Montgomery calls "thematic" and "paradigmatic" forms. For any noun, all forms contain a root, which is defined as consisting of segmental phonemes only; tones are analyzed as belonging to separate morphemes accompanying the root and affixes of any form. A thematic form may consist of only a root and an accompanying tone, or it may have any of several combinations of one or more thematic suffixes; a root alone and an accompanying tone may be called a "stem." A paradigmatic form has one of several suffixes in final position; they include demonstrative and possessive suffixes, a zero nominative suffix for one class of nouns, and a "general" case suffix. In most constructions, the thematic form and the paradigmatic form with the general case suffix are optional alternatives. There is no significant correlation between the choice of thematic and/or paradigmatic suffixes in singular and plural forms.

The significance of the definition of a stem as a root with an accompanying tonal morpheme can be seen in one type of pluralization. There are some cases in which neither the singular nor the plural thematic form has any suffixes, but in which they differ in tone; there is no predictable tone sequence for the plural, as might be supposed from the following two examples, nor for the singular. The appearance of stem only in both singular and plural is by no means a predominant type of pluralization, but it is attested in some cases like these (with mid unmarked):

sarùr,	sarúr	'tail'
kɔ̀yey,	kɔyéy	'bride price'

There are a few instances of internal vowel alternation between singular and plural forms, but in the vast majority of cases the root is the same in the singular and plural, as well as in thematic and paradigmatic forms. A case of internal alternation is:

pe'ñ,	pàñ	'piece of meat'

A small group of kinship terms may be used with the demonstrative and possessive paradigmatic suffixes, but not with the general case suffix. For these, therefore, there are not two optional forms as there are for other nouns. These nouns also take no thematic suffixes.

Thematic suffixes appear in four successive positions after a root; any number of these positions may be filled depending on the root in question and on whether or not a paradigmatic suffix is also used. In most of these positions, in singular and plural forms, there are two or more possible suffixes. In some cases, the choice of suffix in a particular position is lexically determined; there are also, however, co-occurrence restrictions among the suffixes. If the first position is filled, the second position must also be filled if no paradigmatic suffix is used, or the fourth position must also be filled if a paradigmatic suffix is used. Except for the group of kinship terms mentioned above and one other group of nouns, the fourth position must be filled if there is a paradigmatic suffix. An example of a noun form with every suffix position filled is the following:

tàr-y-à-nt-e-t   'termite'

1 2 3 4 P

Singular nouns (exclusive of the kinship terms) fall into seven classes in terms of the combinations of thematic suffixes which occur with and without paradigmatic suffixes. There is some subclassification, depending largely on the choice of suffix in a particular position. Without including all of the details, the following will give some idea of the nature of the system (or lack of system). Vowels are long unless otherwise indicated.

(1) No T(hematic suffix) without or with P(aradigmatic suffix):

por	: pòrtə	'body'
supén	: supentə	'young female goat'
mŭ's	: mŭstà	'corpse'

(2) No T without P, T4 with P:

wok	: wòkèt	'forest'
rokər	: rokərét	'cliff'
tərtáy	: tərtayet	'kind of magic'
kat	: kàtĭt	'neck'

(3) T4 without or with P:

cəkè	: cəket	'granary'
pàkuli	: pàkùlit	'bowl'
kənti	: kəntit	'horn'

(4) No T without P, T1 and T4 with P:

sarùr	: sarùryèt	'tail'
capas	: capasyet	'arm clamp'

(5) T2 without P, T4 with P; a subclass also has T1 both without and with P:

lɔnà	: lɔnet	'shield'
werɔ	: werit	'boy'
kɔrkɔ	: kɔrket	'woman'
tùlwà	: tùlwèt	'hill'
warwà	: warwet	'goat'

(6) T2 without P; T2, 3, 4 with P:

kùcə	: kùcɔntét	'lamb, kid'
ŋùŋúyɔ	: ŋùŋúyɔntet	'mosquito'

(7) T1, 2 without P; T1, 2, 3, 4 with P:

tolyə	:	tolyɔ̀ntet	'bell'
tàryà	:	tàryàntet	'termite'
cepsəkeyɔ́	:	cepsəkéyɔntet	'diviner'

The last of the above examples includes also a prefix /cep-/. There is also a prefix /kǐp-/; both of these derive personal nouns; in another dialect they are male and female. In addition, there are nominalizing prefixes /kə-, /ka-/, /ko-/, /ki-/ deriving nouns from verbs.

Plural nouns fall into similar classes depending on the choice of thematic suffixes. In all positions, suffixes for plural forms differ from those for singular forms. Mass nouns are formally plural. A brief outline of the plural classes follows:

(1) No T without or with P:

mo	:	mòkà	'calves'
pé	:	pekə	'water'

(2) No T or T1 or T2 and 3 without P; T4 with P:

àr	:	àrèk	'ashes'
sarúr	:	sarurák	'tails'
tukǔn	:	tukúk	'things'
tipín	:	tipík	'girls'
lèkoy	:	lèkok	'children'
kàynəy	:	kaynək	'names'

(3) No T without P; T4 with P, but differing from the above in that T4 is a short rather than a long vowel:

lok	:	lokǐk	'tears'
tàrìt	:	tàrìtĕk	'birds'

(4) No T or T3 and 4 without P; T3 and 4 with P:

kutúŋ	:	kutuŋwĕk	'knees'
mĕlil	:	mĕlilwĕk	'leopards'
nətwé	:	nətwék	'spears'

(5) T1 without P, T1 and 4 with P:

tulon	:	tulonək	'hills'
aywən	:	aywənok	'axes'
cəkèn	:	cəkènǐk	'granaries'

(6) T1 or T2 without P, T1 or T2 and T3 and T4 with P:

àrəs	:	arəsyĕk	'roads, clans'
latyos	:	latyòsyĕk	'neighbors'
yewún	:	yewúnwĕk	'hands, arms'

(7) T2 without P, T2 and T4 with P:

pǔnút	:	pǔnutĕk	'age sets'
lwelkut	:	lwèlkùtĕk	'antelopes'

(8) T1 and T2 without P; T1, 2, and 4 with P:

| còrònut | : | còrònùtĕk | 'friends' |
| sɔkwonút: | : | sɔkwonutĕk | 'ceremonies' |

There are, thus, several classes of singular noun forms and several classes of plural noun forms. Significantly, however, there is no appreciable correlation between singular and plural classes, except for one type of verbal noun. That is, there is no way of predicting the plural from the singular, nor vice versa. Theoretically, there are fifty-six possible combinations of singular and plural classes, and in fact a great many of these combinations are attested; it is difficult to say that any combination is impossible, since the very small number of nouns in some of the classes is sufficient to prevent all possible combinations from occurring.

The tones or tone sequences occurring with noun forms are conditioned by an exceedingly complex set of factors. There is lexical tone, in the sense that the identity of the noun root is one of the factors conditioning the tones of the entire form. The different combinations of suffixes also enter into determining the tone sequence. There are also morphotonemic alternants conditioned by adjacent words. And finally grammatical function may condition different tone sequence; in particular, a sort of case distinction is marked by tone, in that most noun forms have different tones depending on whether they function as subject or object. For example:

| cǐle pɔntét | 'he's looking at the old man' |
| cǐle pɔntet | 'the old man is looking at him' |

Although it is possible to isolate various factors that condition the tones of noun forms, the permutations are so numerous that it is hardly more economical to make structural statements than merely to list the sequences that occur in isolation, in different environments, and in different constructions.

In the above classifications of singular and plural forms, it may be noted that alternatives seem to form the basis for subclassification in some cases, but for distinguishing classes in other cases. There might thus be some refinement of the classifications. No matter how the data are organized, however, Sapiny clearly has an unusually complex system of noun morphology (and the verb morphology is even worse!), quite different in type from anything found in Niger-Kordofanian or Afro-Asiatic, but showing at least some similarity to complexities in other Nilo-Saharan languages.

8.13. Dho-Luo displays considerably more phonological conditioning in its noun morphology.[5] In addition to a number distinction, Dho-Luo also has a

---

[5] Work on Dho-Luo was begun in 1970 in a course in Field Methods. Additional data have been collected by Mr. Leon Jacobson, and the initial grouping of nouns by their plural formations was done by him. The irregular availability of our informant, Mr. John Ochieng, has stood in the way of checking all of the data in detail and testing the forms in larger and more varied contexts.

distinction between absolute and construct forms, similar in function to the distinction typical of Afro-Asiatic languages.

The available Dho-Luo data are in some respects tentative, and known to be incomplete, as far as tone is concerned. In forms cited in isolation, a distinction between low and nonlow is usually clear, but we have not been able to distinguish two different nonlow levels. In initial position in a sentence, however, high and mid in a noun can readily be distinguished before a mid tone. For many of the nouns recorded, no convenient or plausible sentence could be found, so that the tones in such a context have not been tested. For this reason, low tone is indicated in the examples in this section, high tone is indicated in only a few forms where it has been recorded before mid, and in other cases nonlow tone (presumably mid in some cases, high in others) is left unmarked. Further, it is known that the tones of nouns may vary in different contexts, but not all the conditioning factors have been isolated. The examples cited here are, therefore, either forms in isolation or initially in a sentence in the case of absolutes; for constructs, they are the forms that appear before a first person singular possessive pronoun. The possessive pronoun has the segmental shape /-a/ after a consonant, and /-na/ after a vowel; its tone is non-low after low, but low after non-low. Examples of forms from which the constructs are abstracted are:

| kità | (kit-) | 'my stone' |
| kitɛnà | (kitɛ-) | 'my stones' |

Dho-Luo nouns fall into three major definable types, in addition to which there are some quite irregular nouns. Within the three major types, a few nouns also show an alternation between the two harmonic sets of vowels in singular and plural forms. A few forms with suffixes have also been recorded with violation of vowel harmony (as /kitɛ-/ above); it is possible that these are errors in transcription, since the contrasts between short /i/ and /ɪ/ and between short /u/ and /ʊ/ are not always easy to recognize. There are also tonal alternations between singulars and plurals in many cases; these have not been studied in detail, but it appears that they are largely lexically determined.

In the first type of noun, plurals are formed with a suffix /-e/ or /-ɛ/, depending on vowel harmony. There are several subtypes defined by the last consonant of the singular form. The singular construct is fairly regular, and the plural construct is identical with the plural absolute. For nouns of this type, accordingly, only three forms will be listed: the singular absolute, plural absolute, and singular construct.

The first subtype includes nouns with a final voiceless consonant in the singular (absolute), or (in two recorded cases) a final vowel preceded by /r/. The plural suffixes /-e/ or /-ɛ/ appear after the final consonant or replacing the final vowel. In all recorded cases, the plural suffix has nonlow tone, but this may not be significant. On the basis of a limited number of nouns of this subtype, the singular construct seems normally to be identical with the absolute; one ex-

ceptional consonant alternation and one (dubious) alternation in vowel length
and tone are recorded. Examples are:

lɛp	lɛpɛ	lɛw-	'tongue'
làk	leke	làk-	'tooth'
yùwòth	yuwothe	yùwòth-	'armpit'
aùrà	aùre	?	'river'
àthɛɛ̀rɔ̀	athèère	àthɛ̀rɔ̀-	'bow'

The second subtype includes nouns with a final vowel preceded by a voiced
stop. The final vowel might be treated as a suffix (the sort of analysis which has
been applied to Sapiny), but there seems to be no great motivation for such an
analysis. In the plural, the corresponding voiceless stop appears, followed by
the plural suffix replacing the final vowel of the singular. The singular construct
is formed by replacement of voiced by voiceless stop, with the deletion of the vowel
of the absolute, except for one recorded case in which the construct and absolute
are identical. Examples of this subtype are:

kìdi	kítɛ́	kit-	'stone'
lùɛ̀dɔ̀	lùɛ̀tɛ̀	luɛt-	'hand'
òguùdu	òguùte	òguùt-	'hat'
kʊdhɔ	kùthɛ̀	kʊth-	'thorn'
cògo	coke	cok-	'bone'
àjuɔ̀gà	àjuòkɛ̀	àjuɔ̀gà-	'doctor'

Grouped together in a third subtype are nouns whose singulars have final
/r/, a few with final /yɔ̀/, and a few with a final vowel. In the plural, /c/ replaces
/r/ or /y/ and follows a final vowel, and the plural suffix appears after /c/. In the
singular construct, two cases are recorded with final /r/ as in the absolute, but
different in tone, and two cases with /c/ replacing /r/. Examples are:

bùr	bùcè	bur-	'hole'
wɔr	wɔcɛ̀	wɔr-	'shoe'
àkuùr	àkuce	àkuùc-	'pigeon'
ɔ̀ŋèèr	ɔ̀ŋɛcɛ	ɔ̀ŋɛɛc-	'monkey'
ɔ̀tɔɔyɔ̀	ɔ̀tɔɔ̀cɛ	?	'hyena'
tuo	tuocè	tuo-	'sickness'

The fourth subtype includes nouns with singulars having final /c/. In the
plural, /y/ replaces /c/ in three recorded cases, followed by the plural suffix.
Other nouns with singulars having final /c/ belong in other major types. The
singular construct also has /y/ replacing /c/. Examples are:

wìc	wiye	wìy-	'head'
kwàc	kwaye	kway-	'leopard'
bùndìc	bùndɪyɛ	bùndɪy-	'belly'

The fifth subtype includes nouns whose absolute singulars have as their last
(and usually final) consonant /l/ or a nasal (/m, n, ny, ŋ/), or an orally released

nasal (/mb, nd, nj, ŋg/) before a final vowel. Plurals of such nouns have the corresponding (or identical) orally released nasal followed by the plural suffix. Singular constructs must be defined in terms of the last consonant of the absolute singular. If that consonant is /l/, /m/, /n/, or /ŋ/, the construct has the corresponding orally released nasal in final position in almost every case; there are two recorded cases of constructs with final nasals without oral release. If the last consonant of the absolute is /ny/, the construct also has final /ny/, but may differ in tone from the absolute. If the absolute ends with an orally released nasal followed by a vowel, the construct and absolute are identical. Examples of this subtype are:

duɔl	duɔ̀ndɛ̀	duɔnd-	'voice'
dììl	——	dììnd-	'body'
ràbòlò	ràbònde	ràbònd-	'banana'
cʊmà	cʊmbɛ	cùmb-	'piece of iron'
kɔɔm	kɔ̀mbɛ̀	kɔɔm-	'chair'
rɔ́mbɔ́	ròmbè	rɔ́mbɔ́-	'sheep'
thunò	thùndè	thùnd-	'breast'
pààny	pànjɛ̀	paany-	'country'
cɔ̀ɔ̀ŋ	cɔ̀ngɛ̀	cɔ̀ɔ̀ŋg-	'knee'
wàŋ	wàŋgɛ̀	wàŋ-	'eye'
bùŋgu	buŋgɛ	bùŋgu	'forest'

In several of the above subtypes, there seems to be a common element of fortition of the last consonant of the absolute singular in the plural and construct forms—voiceless for voiced, /c/ for /r/ or /y/, an orally released nasal for /l/ or a nasal. In only one subtype, in which /y/ replaces /c/, is there clearly lenition. That fact might suggest that that subtype belongs with the second major type described below; the form of the plural suffix, however, is a counterargument.

The second major type of noun has a final voiceless stop in the absolute singular (as do some nouns in the first type, first subtype). In the plural, the corresponding voiced stop appears, and the plural suffix following it is usually /i/, though /e/ is recorded in a few cases. The singular construct usually ends with the voiced stop, but in three recorded cases (all of them, and only these, happen to be body parts) with the voiceless stop. The plural construct has the voiced consonant in all but two cases, and a suffix /e/. Examples of this type are, with the fourth form being the plural construct:

guòk	guogi	guog-	guoge-	'dog'
ruàth	ruedhi	ruadh-	ruedhe-	'bull'
nyuɔ̀k	nyuogi	nyuɔg-	nyuoge-	'he-goat'
nyèèt	nyeede	nyèèt-	nyeede-	'rib'
gòòk	googe	gòòk-	googe-	'shoulder'
ŋùt	ŋùdì	ŋùt-	ŋùtè-	'neck'
ɔ̀ɔt	ùùdì	ɔ̀ɔd-	uute-	'house'

The third major type of noun in Dho-Luo takes a plural suffix /-ni/, with nonlow tone. Singular absolutes of this type are with few exceptions forms of two or three syllables, with a final vowel. In the plural, there appear to be no contrasts in vowel quality before the suffix /-ni/; however, the preceding consonant has a voiced release with non-low tone. On the assumption (not fully proven as yet) that this is an automatic transition from a consonant to /n/, this release is not indicated in the exampels below. A few plurals show a vowel alternation, and in one recorded case the plural has a voiceless consonant corresponding to a voiced consonant in the singular. The singular construct is based on the absolute without its final vowel, with orally released nasals in final position replacing /l/ and nasals in the absolute. The plural construct shows the same consonant alternations, and has a suffix /-e/, in most cases with the same tone as the preceding syllable. Examples of this type are:

àgulu	àgùlni	àgund-	àgunde-	'pot'
òbudho	òbùdhni	òbudh-	òbudhe-	'pumpkin'
ɔ̀kùmbo	ɔ̀kùmbni	ɔ̀kumb-	ɔ̀kumbe-	'elbow'
àgwata	àgwètni	àgwàt-	àgwete-	'calabash'
àdɪta	àdìtni	àdɪt-	àdìte-	'basket'
pàla	pèlni	pànd-	pende-	'knife'
luɛ̀dɔ̀	luɛ̀tni	luɛt-	luɛ̀tè-	'hand'

Finally, there are some nouns which can only be listed as irregular. There is some partial similarity with other nouns as far as consonant alternations are concerned, particularly in the construct forms, but in every case there is a unique irregularity between singular and plural, including one case of complete suppletion. The recorded irregular nouns are:

dhɪàŋ	dhòk	dhɛ̀r-	dhòg-	'cow'
dɪ̀ɛl	dièk	dɪɛnd-	dièg-	'goat'
yàath	yɛn	yàadh-	yɛnd-	'tree'
nyàkɔ̀	nyìrì	nyàr-	nyig-	'girl'
nyàthɪ	nyɪthɪndɔ̀	nyàthɪ-	nyɪthɪnd-	'child'
lɪ̀ɛl	lɪètè	lɪɛnd-	liète-	'mound'
kognò	koke	kòk-	kòke-	'fingernail'
guɛ̀nɔ̀	guɛn	guɛnd-	guɛnde-	'chicken'
wìnyɔ	wìɪny	wɪnj-	wìɪnje-	'bird'
yìè	yɪɛdhi	yiè-	?	'boat'
wendo	wèlò	wendo-	wènd-	'guest'
dhàkɔ̀	moon	dhàke-	mond-	'woman'

Although the foregoing is by no means a complete analysis of the nominal system of Dho-Luo, and may contain some errors in transcription, some patterning is clear, and the major area for further investigation is the complexities of morphotonemics. Although the system is somewhat different from, and not as complicated as, that of Sapiny, there are also distinct typological similarities.

In particular, the recognition of thematic and paradigmatic suffixes in Sapiny seems the more valid in the light of the Dho-Luo system, and the function of tone in the two languages may be more similar than has been definitely established so far. Further detailed investigation of these and more distantly related Nilo-Saharan languages may reveal other manifestations of some of these structural characteristics.

8.14. For total lack of personal experience with any of the Khoisan languages, a treatment of their noun systems is not included here, except to note the well-known fact that many of them have a functional gender system distinguishing masculine, feminine, and common, as well as a number system including dual forms as well as singular and plural. To what extent the gender system includes more than physical sex is a question not answered in the most readily available brief observations about these languages.

Chapter 9

Adjectives and Un-Adjectives

9.1. Many works on African languages, including some that might be expected to be among the most reliable, show a remarkable lack of linguistic sophistication in their treatment of noun modifiers. The term "adjective" may be applied to any form which is reflected by an English adjective in translation, without reference to its derivation or grammatical function in the language being described. Ward (1933, pp. 42-43), for example, lists eight "adjectives" in one class for Efik, and twenty-four in another class. The classes are distinguished by the morphotonemic alternations they condition with a following noun. Her first class is valid; it includes only adjectives which end with low tone. In her second class, however five more forms which end with low tone are included. These should be analyzed as nouns; they condition the morphotonemic alternations typical of the associative construction in noun-noun phrases. Three of these five show a derivation by reduplication; by analogy with these, six others which show a similar derivation but end with high tone can as well, and probably should, be analyzed as nouns. As far as morphotonemics is concerned, the remaining thirteen forms in Ward's second class could also be analyzed as nouns, but considerations of usage favor considering them adjectives like those of the first class.

Working from quite a different grammatical model, Carrell (1970, pp. 44-45) lists a few "adjectives" in her sample lexicon of Igbo. Some of them are indeed best classed as adjectives, but a special transformational rule of "adjective shift" applies to two others. This rule simply has the effect of making these two forms function like nouns; if they had merely been analyzed as nouns to begin with, the rule would have been unnecessary. It appears that they were analyzed as "adjectives" primarily on semantic grounds, though it might also have been observed that they rarely if ever occur independently, and are not themselves modified. At most, it would seem better to analyze these (and several forms with similar uses) as belonging to a sub-type of noun rather than a subtype of adjective.

Green and Igwe (1963), like many writers on other languages, include some quantitative and demonstrative forms in their class of "adjectives" in Igbo. The quantitatives—two words meaning 'all' and the attributive form for 'two'—could at least as appropriately be classed as numerals. The demonstratives are distinguished by other distributional considerations. Three forms are described as adjectives with cognate verb roots.

These are indeed adjectives, but there are also five more, and not all of them are cognate with verb roots. Green and Igwe do not mention the type of noun which others have called "adjectives". (They do also include two monosyl-

labic "adjectives" which are not recognized at all by informants with whom I
have worked.)

Lest the foregoing be interpreted as nothing more than negative and perhaps
petulant criticism, it should be observed that investigators who may at least
be described as more suspicious have also made some statements about "adjectives" that fall short of adequacy. My article on Senari (Welmers 1950a) includes
a section entitled "The Morphology of Adjectives". Two types of forms labelled
"adjectives" are recognized: those not used in verbal constructions, and those
used in verbal constructions. Included in my list of the latter are four forms described as "verb stems used as adjectives." To my knowledge at present, there is
really no justification for distinguishing adjectives used as verbs from verbs used
as adjectives; they all appear to be verbs, perhaps of a sub-type defined by their
use attributively after a noun stem. Similar treatments lacking in rigidity are
to be found in my articles on Suppire and Bariba (Welmers 1950b, 1952a) though in
the latter there is a stronger case for recognizing a separate class of adjectives,
since attributive forms are not identical with verb roots. Perhaps I could plead
the pressure of time as an excuse for inelegant analysis. More significantly, it
should be recognized that the status of forms used as noun modifiers in these
languages, and of related forms, is intrinsically difficult to define. There are also
difficulties, though not just the same ones, in the case of Igbo, Efik, and many
other languages. The problem remains, however, that few writers have carried
their analysis beyond the point of assuming that a word is an adjective merely
if it seems to have a meaning such as 'small', 'red', or 'a lot of'—the last of which,
of course, is not an adjective in English either.

In LoNkundo, where the grammar of noun modifiers is less difficult to pene-
trate, Hulstaert (1938, p. 19) does not hesitate to say that there are no qualificatives. In other languages, there are forms with qualificative meaning which
are used to modify nouns, and which constitute a separate form class, but all
of which may be derived from verbs; they may be called "adjectives", of course,
though perhaps "adjectivals" is a preferable term. In still other languages, a
class of non-derived forms may be found which an legitimately be called adjectives. It is important to note, however, that in almost all Niger-Congo languages
which have a class of adjectives, the class is rather small, and many concepts
expressed by adjectives in European languages are expressed by other kinds of
constructions using nouns or verbs or both. The purpose of this chapter is to illustrate how a class of adjectives may or may not be defined in a variety of Niger-
Congo languages, and also how some concepts expressed by adjectives in English
are articulated.

9.2. In Kpelle, there are a number of qualificative adjectivals, used attributively after nouns, which are derived from verbs. Many of the verbs from which
the commonest adjectivals are derived are inceptive in meaning: 'become big',
'get dirty', and so on. The adjectivals are also used in a predicative construction
referring to present state, which is unlike any verbal construction, and in an adverbial construction.

In only one known case, an adjectival is identical with the stem of the verb from which it is derived. This is /kétɛ/ 'big'; my early transcriptions include some others, but at that time I was not hearing vowel length contrasts in final position consistently. A verbal and an attributive use are illustrated in the following:

è kètɛ	'it got bigger'
pérɛ kétɛ	'a big house'

Otherwise adjectivals are derived by suffixation. The suffix is segmentally /-ɔ/ after /ŋ/, and otherwise /-ɔ/, /-ɛ/, or /-a/ depending on the final vowel of the stem. The suffix has high tone after high or mid, but low tone after low. Combinations of final single and double vowels followed by this suffix involve some morphophonemic rules; for stems with mid tone, the realizations are as follows:

Ci-ɛ́	:	Ciɛ́	CVCi-ɛ́	:	CVCiɛ	Cii-ɛ́	:	Ciɛ́ɛ
Ce-ɛ́	:	Ceɛ́	CVCe-ɛ́	:	CVCéɛ	Cee-ɛ́	:	Ceɛ́ɛ
Cɛ-ɛ́	:	Cɛɛ́	CVCɛ-ɛ́	:	CVCéɛ	Cɛɛ-ɛ́	:	Cɛɛ́
Ca-á	:	Caá	CVCa-á	:	CVCáa	Caa-á	:	Caá
Cɔ-ɔ́	:	Cɔɔ́	CVCɔ-ɔ́	:	CVCɔ́ɔ	Cɔɔ-ɔ́	:	Cɔɔ́
Co-ɔ́	:	Coɔ́	CVCo-ɔ́	:	CVCɔ́ɔ	Coo-ɔ́	:	Coɔ́ɔ
Cu-ɔ́	:	Cuɔ́	CVCu-ɔ́	:	CVCúɔ	Cuu-ɔ́	:	Cuɔ́ɔ

For the first and last forms in the second column, the variants /CVCéɛ/ and /CVCɔ́ɔ/ are sometimes heard. The high tone of the suffix is realized with the last vowel of the stem also in the case of disyllabic stems with final /ŋ/. Some examples of stems and derived adjectivals, in attributive use, are as follows:

kpanaŋ	:	tíi kpanáŋɔ	'difficult work'
sêlɛŋ	:	ɣɛli sêlɛŋɔ	'a hanging vine'
liɓi	:	leɣi liɓiɛ	'a dirty pot'
wiɛ	:	kpîri wiɛ́ɛ	'a heavy load'
táma	:	nǔu támaa	'a lot of people'
lélɛ	:	pérɛ lélɛɛ	'a fine house'
kpɔlu	:	'kwêi kpɔlúɔ (/kpɔlɔ́ɔ)	'ripe bananas'

What may be analyzed as another type of derived adjectival, used attributively after a noun, consists of a verb stem with a morpheme of tonal replacement: low tone replaces stem tone, with the regular alternant high-low after mid.[1] In a few cases, this is an alternative to the adjectival with a suffix described above, but in most cases either one or the other is the only possibility. Some examples are:

waa	'wash'	:	siɣe wâa	'clean cloth'
kpela	'become mature'	:	nɛnî kpèla	'a mature girl'
yɔɔ	'become dry'	:	kɔi yɔ̂ɔ	'dry firewood'
kpɔlu	'become ripe'	:	'kwêi kpɔ̀lu	'ripe bananas'

---

[1] In Welmers 1969b, these phrases are treated as a type of noun compound.

The last of these examples is an alternative for the last of those in the preceding paragraph.

Adjectivals derived by suffixation, and the stems of those derived by tonal replacement (without the tonal replacive) are used in a predicative construction which differs from ordinary verbal constructions. The logical subject or topic of such a predicative is, in form, like the object of a verb (or the possessor of an impersonal relational noun). The form has a suffix /-ì/, which is also found in some verbal constructions, including one which indicates present action. A contrast between a verbal construction and an adjectival predicative is illustrated in the following:

a kétɛ̀ì	'it is getting bigger'
'kétɛ̀ì	'it is big'

The negative corresponding to such predicative constructions uses the verb stem in all cases; the construction is the past negative, usually translatable by 'be' with an adjective in the case of verbs referring to state or condition. Some examples of affirmative adjectival predicatives and their negative counterparts are:

'tíi ɲí kpanáŋɔ̀ì	'this work is difficult'
('tíi ɲí fé kpanaŋ ní)	
ǹeɣii tí liɓíɛ̀ì	'that pot is dirty'
(ǹeɣii tí fé liɓi ní)	
'tí támaaì	'there are a lot of them'
('tí fé táma ní)	
ǹélɛɛì	'it's fine'
('fé lélɛ ní)	
'kɔii ɲí yɔ̂i	'this firewood is dry'
('kɔii ɲí fé yɔɔ ní)	
'kpɔlúɔ̀ì (/ 'kpɔlɔ́ɔ̀ì)	'it is ripe'
('fé kpɔlu ní)	

Finally, adjectivals derived by suffixation, and the verb stems from which adjectivals are derived by tonal replacement, are used in an adverbial construction. This is a "marked complement" after a verb, which is a complement beginning with the morpheme /à/. The adjectival or verb stem has prefixed low tone, which in general is a morpheme indicating previous reference. Nouns, without prefixed low tone, may also be used in such complements; a contrast between the two is illustrated by the following:

'kɛ́ à ɓóa	'do it with a knife'
'kɛ́ à ǹélɛɛ	'do it well'

Such adverbials are common after /káa/ preceded by an object. In form, /káa/ is a singular imperative meaning 'see'; in this use, however, the number of persons addressed is irrelevant, and the combination with a marked complement is the common expression of description. An example with a noun, an adjectival, and a verb stem from which an adjectival may be derived by tonal replacement, are:

'káa à ɓóa	'it is a knife'
'káa à ǹiɓíɛ	'it is dirty'
'káa à 'kpɔlu	'it is ripe'

The last two of these examples are thus similar to, or indistinguishable from, the predicative usage discussed above, as far as meaning is concerned. The predicative usage is generally preferred, but both are heard.

Corresponding expressions of description for other than the present use the verb /kɛ́/, intransitively. Thus:

è kè à ɓóa	'it was a knife'
è kè à ǹiɓíɛ	'it was dirty'
è kè à 'kpɔlu	'it was ripe'

Here, however, there is generally a clear distinction in meaning between such descriptive sentences with adverbial complements and the use of an ordinary verbal construction. The descriptive sentences refer to a state which used to obtain, while the verbal constructions refer to a process. Compare the following pairs:

è kè à 'kɛ́tɛ	'it was big'	è kɛ̀tɛ	'it got bigger'
è kè à ǹyɔɔ	'it was dry'	è yɔɔ	'it got dry'

Adjectival derivation can hardly be described as productive in Kpelle, but on occasion I have suggested a form, in an attributive construction, which I had been unable to elicit by translation, and found it accepted even though native speakers said they would not have thought of using it.

Some other qualificative concepts are expressed by forms classified as "ideophones", which will be discussed in another context.

9.3. In Jukun, qualificatives are also derived from verbs, and their verblike character is conspicuous. They occur after a morpheme /à/, following a noun. The same construction with a verb which has no subject is a relative whose subject is the antecedent noun; the same construction with a verb which does have a subject is a relative whose subject is other than the antecedent noun. Qualificatives differ from ordinary verbs, however, in that they are reduplicated. The following examples from Dìyī illustrate these three possibilities:

pèrè à bi kéré ní	'the person who came here'
(cf.: pèrè ní bi kéré	'the person came here')
tórà à ku to ní	'the trap he had set'
(cf.: ku to tórà	'he set a trap')
tukpa à kìkyè	'clean cloth'
(cf.: tukpa kyè ra	'the cloth is clean')

The segmental form of the reduplicating syllable in qualificatives is not entirely predictable. For some verbs, the stem syllable is prefixed without change.

For other verbs, the reduplicating syllable consists of the initial consonant of the stem followed by a different vowel—in the limited number of forms recorded, /i/ appears in three and /o/ in one. Tonally, however, the reduplicated forms are regular and reveal an interesting pattern. Verb stems have either mid or low tone, never high. The tones of a reduplicated qualificative depend on the tone of the verb stem, and also on whether the verb is intransitive or transitive. For intransitive verbs with low tone, the qualificative has the tones low-low. For transitive verbs with low tone, the qualificative has low-high with the first syllable and mid-low with the second. For intransitive verbs with mid tone, the qualificative has the tones mid-mid. For transitive verbs with mid tone, the qualificative has the tones high-mid. These four types are illustrated by the following:

Stem low, intransitive:

fǎ	'be hot'	:	zàpè à fìfǎ	'hot water'
kyè	'be clean'	:	tukpa à kìkyè	'clean cloth'
mbù	'be white'	:	tukpa à mbùmbù	'white cloth'
tù	'be difficult'	:	buso à tùtù	'difficult work'

Stem low, transitive:

syì	'boil'	:	zàpè à syǐsyi`	'boiled water'
kì	'split'	:	yìnà à kǐki`	'split wood'
pě	'roll up'	:	tukpa à pěpē`	'rolled up cloth'
wǒ	'roast'	:	busô à wǒwõ`	'roasted meat'

Stem mid, intransitive:

| wom | 'be dry' | : | yìnà à wõwom | 'dry wood' |
| ŋgo | 'be tough' | : | busô à ŋgoŋgo | 'tough meat' |

Stem mid, transitive:

hwa	'carve'	:	yìnà à hóhwa	'a pointed stick'
wa	'drink'	:	zàpè à wáwa	'drinking water'
pē	'put out to dry'	:	tukpa à pḗpē	'clothes out to dry'
mbya	'make, fix'	:	bà à mbímbya	'something repaired, something manufactured'

It can be seen from the above that, for transitive verbs, the qualificative is usually translatable by a passive. In one case, however, it meaning is stative: /zàpè à wáwa/ is water that is drinkable, not water which has been drunk.

In negative counterparts of the above, the distinction between intransitive and transitive is retained. For intransitive verbs, the negatives are regular verbal relatives, without reduplication of the verb stem. For transitive verbs, the reduplicated form is used in the same negative construction. E.g.,

zàpè à fǎ á mbá	'water that is not hot'
yìnà à wom ra á mbá	'wood that has not dried'
yìnà kǐki` á mbá	'wood that is not split'
tukpa à pḗpē á mbá	'clothes that have not been put out to dry'

There is one recorded word which appears in the same construction which is not reduplicated and not derived from a verb; this is found in the following:

fì à kwàkì   'a big leopard'

Unfortunately, no negative or predicative was recorded corresponding to this.

There are a few peculiar phrases of an agglutinative type which do not fit any major pattern, but which certainly cannot be called adjectival. An example is /fì pǎ pèrè/, literally 'leopard catch person', which is a common expression simply designating a leopard.

With few exceptions, therefore, qualificatives in Jukun are derived from verbs, and are used in a construction which is basically a relative clause. There is no class of adjectives independent of verbs, unless the form /kwàkì/ is so classified; but even that form appears in what is basically a relative clause.

9.4. In Akan also, though for different reasons, it is legitimate to question whether there is a class of adjectives. Derivations from verbs are not involved. Christaller (1875) refers to "adjective nouns", observing that many of them are also used as substantive nouns, though he also calls the words in question "qualifying adjectives", and seems to begin with a semantic rather than a structural definition. In 1943, I distinguished adjectives from other classes in Fante on the syntactic level, but not on the morphological level (see Welmers 1946). Morphologically, they belong to or are derived from a general class of non-verbal stems. Syntactically, they are differentiated from nouns in that they may be followed by an adverb, and from adverbs in that they may appear in sentence-initial position (if followed by a demonstrative). It thus seems possible to recognize a class of adjectives, but it must be emphasized that they share many of the grammatical properties of nouns. Thus the following phrases have a nominal function:

kèsí bí	'a big one'	ní 'féw	'its beauty'
kèsí nú	'the big one'	ní 'dín	'its hardness'

In a predicative usage, the distinction between adjectives and nouns is, at best, not well established. There is a verb, or possibly two homophonous verbs, /yè/, meaning 'be (described as)' and 'make'; the analysis as one verb parallels the similar uses of the Kpelle verb /ké/, which in fact may possibly be cognate. Before a noun and with the meaning 'be', /yè/ takes subject pronouns with low tone; with the meaning 'make', it takes subject pronouns with high tone. /yè/ is also used before adjectives, obviously with the meaning 'be', but in this use it takes subject pronouns with high tone. Thus the predicative sentence with an adjective is like the usage meaning 'make' with a noun, unlike the expression for description. It remains true, however, that both nouns and adjectives appear in an identical environment. The following sentences illustrate this problem:

ɔ̀ yè kyéw	'it is a hat'
ɔ́ yè kyéw	'he makes hats'
ɔ́ yè hyìw	'it is hot'

Some adjective stems combine with nouns to form compounds, for which there are distinctive tone rules. Compounds of two noun stems are also common, however, and the same rules apply to them. Thus the crucial criterion for distinguishing nouns and adjectives appears to be that an adjective may be followed by an adverb while a noun cannot; the phrase /kὲsí dúdú/ 'too big' proves /kὲsí/ to be an adjective rather than a noun. A more subtle distinction is that a noun may be used by itself at the beginning of a sentence, as a verbal subject; an adjective at the beginning of a sentence must (as a noun may) be followed by a demonstrative.

In Fante, I have recorded only one adjective that has different singular and plural forms. (Christaller cites two more for Twi, but I am not aware of these in Fante.) Strangely, but perhaps not significantly, this is the third language cited in this chapter in which the expression for 'big' is in some way unique. The Fante case is:

    ìdán kὲsí   'a big house'   àdán ákὲsí   'big houses'

Some adjectives appear only in a stem form, or in a form consisting of a stem with a prefix. Other adjectives appear only in a reduplicated form, usually with full reduplication of the stem. A few typical forms are:

kὲsí	'big'	pùrɔ̀mpùrɔ̀m	'prosperous'
tùrɔ̀m	'flat, level'	tùntúm	'black'
m̀bìréw	'weak'	múmún	'green'

Other adjectives appear in two or three forms. One form is the stem, usually a monosyllable; this is the usual form in predication, it may be used in a compound noun, and it may be used attributively. In predication, the stem has low tone in many and perhaps all cases. The other forms, generally used attributively and sometimes with an intensive meaning, are reduplicated and triplicated. In the triplicated forms, the second sylable is lengthened. Some speakers seem to prefer the triplicated to the reduplicated forms. Thus there are sets like the following:

fὲw	féféw	féfééféw	'beautiful'
dìn	díndín	díndínńdín	'hard'
tìn	tíntín	tíntínńtín	'long'

Although a class of adjectives may thus be recognized in Akan, a number of qualificative ideas are also expressed by verbs with an inceptive meaning. A present state is expressed by a completive construction; attribution takes the form of a relative clause, in which the verb has a different tone sequence characteristic of subordinate clauses. E.g.,

òébìr	'it is (has become) black'
ìtám áà óé'bír	'black cloth (cloth which has become black')
ɔ̀áfùná	'he is (has become) tired'
bènyín áà ɔ́á'fúná	'a tired man'

9.5. Qualificative attributives in Yoruba are reduplicated forms derived from verbs or also used as verbs. This, however, is only one aspect of the use of reduplicated forms, and such forms cannot simply be called adjectives. Reduplication of verb stems (most of which are monosyllabic) is productive in Yoruba, but by no means all reduplicated forms are attributive or can be used attributively. A statement covering other uses will shed light on the attributive construction.

A topicalized word or phrase in Yoruba appears at the beginning of a sentence, and is followed by a morpheme /ni/ indicating identification, which has an alternant form before vowels other than /i/ which is here represented as /l'/. A verb may be topicalized by using its reduplicated form in this position. E.g.,

jíjẹ l'ó jẹ išu náà	'actually, he *ate* the yams'
(cf.: ó jẹ išu náà	'he ate the yams')
lílọ l'ó lọ	'actually, he *went*'
(cf.: ó lọ	'he went')
gíga l'ó ga	'actually, he's *tall*'
(cf.: ó ga	'he's tall')

Beyond this point, however, it is necessary to distinguish between transitive and intransitive verbs—or perhaps between verbs indicating action and verbs indicating state. For each type, it is possible to use the reduplicated form of a verb after a noun, but the underlying structure of the resultant phrases is quite different. With a transitive verb, the phrase indicates the action designated by the verb, and the noun is the object of that action. With an intransitive verb indicating state, the phrase has the structure of a noun and an attributive. E.g.,

išu jíjẹ	'the eating of yams'
igi gíga	'a tall tree'

Verbs indicating state differ in other respects from verbs indicating action. In the simple construction of a subject pronoun and a verb stem, a verb indicating action refers to past time, but a verb indicating state refers to present time. This difference is reflected in the translations of the sentences above. It is only from intransitive verbs indicating state that reduplicated forms are derived which have an attributive function after nouns.

In the few forms cited thus far, the reduplicating syllable consists of the initial consonant of the stem followed by the vowel /i/ with high tone. This is the predominant pattern. The following are some typical attributives of this type; the stem, which is in all respects a verb, is everything after the first syllable:

gígùn	'long'	títọ́	'straight'
gíga	'tall'	mímú	'sharp'
mímọ	'holy'	gbígbun	'crooked'
títóbi	'big'		

There are some common attributives, however, which violate this pattern, like the following:

kpúkpọ̀	'a lot of'	ńká	'big'
dáadáa	'good'	kékeré	'small'
kúkúrú	'short'		

Of these, /ńlá/ may well be derived from */lílá/ by typical morphophonemic rules. A further irregularity appears in /kékeré/, in that the verb from which it is derived has the tones high-high: /kéré/. Full reduplication of the stem is shown in /dáadáa/, as attested by an alternant form often heard, /dáradára/, with /dára/ as the alternant of the verb stem. I have heard the regular formation /kpíkpọ̀/, which is reported to be normal in some dialects.

There is also a small number of attributives which show reduplication, but for which the corresponding verbs have the same reduplicated forms; e.g.,

iwé tuntun   'a new book'   ó tuntun   'it is new'

Included in this group are the three primary terms for colors, usually translated 'white', 'black', and 'red', but designating much larger ranges as suggested by the glosses below. (This is a very common primary division of the spectrum in West Africa.) The pattern of reduplication is also different in these forms. In four of the following cases, the reduplication includes tone and nasalization, and the reduplicating vowel may be considered /u/. The glosses given here reflect the attributive use, but all appear also in verbal uses:

funfun	'light colored'	tuntun	'new'
dúdú	'dark colored'	tútù	'cold, wet, fresh'
kpukpa	'bright colored'		

In the case of /tútù/ the tone is irregular; in its verbal use, the form has mid-low: /tutù/. The attributive form may reflect a contraction from a regular reduplication */títutù/.

A great many qualificative concepts are also expressed by ideophones in Yoruba. These, however, constitute a special grammatical class, paralleled in countless languages of Africa, which is reserved for separate treatment.

Older treatments of Yoruba, and school instruction in the language, provide a striking example of the blind application of English (or Latin) grammatical categories to a language with quite a different structure. Words are assigned to classes not on the basis of their form or function in Yoruba, but on the basis of the English classes to which their English equivalents (at least in terms of semantic features) belong. Only one of many instances of this is that the stems from which reduplicated attributives are derived are themselves called "adjectives", even though, for example, /ga/ must be translated 'be tall', not simply 'tall'. Speakers of Yoruba will naturally go on speaking their language as its structure requires, but efforts to teach its grammar probably do more to obscure than to illuminate, and learners are thoroughly confused.

9.6. As mentioned at the beginning of this chapter, Igbo does have a class of adjectives. It is highly restricted and symmetrical, and is characterized by a peculiar semantic feature. Before defending this analysis, the class will be defined and described.[2] Igbo has eight adjectives, semantically four pairs of antonyms. These are:

úkwú	'large'	ǹtà	'small'
ọ́hụ́'rụ́	'new'	ócyê	'old'
ọ́má	'good'	ọ́jọ́'ọ́	'bad'
ọ́cá	'light colored'	ójí'í	'dark colored'

Any of these adjectives, used after a noun, implies that the noun is a member of a category which is large, new, and so on. In some cases this feature of category membership is not conspicuous or crucial, but phrases with contrasting meaning show that it is present. Attribution with the same meaning apart from this category membership is expressed by a relative clause using the verb /í'dí/ 'be described as' and a noun related to the adjective. For example, /ùwé ójí'í/ is 'black (or dark blue etc.) clothing', but of a particular type or for a particular function, as a uniform. This is used with a noun meaning 'person' to form the phrase /ónyé 'úwé ójí'í/, specifically 'a police officer'. But 'dark clothing' in general is /ùwé 'dí ójí/.

A comparison of the phrases cited above suggests that the adjective /ójí'í/ may be a derived form, and indeed it is. For four of the eight adjectives, there are related nouns; for each of these the stem (without the vowel prefix) is also a verb, which is used only with the related noun as a cognate object, and which may be considered the underlying root. With the verbs cited in the infinitive form, and glosses for the adjectives only, the four sets are:

Verb	Noun	Adj.	
í'má	ḿ'má	ọ́má	'good'
í'jọ́	ń'jọ́	ọ́jọ́'ọ́	'bad'
í'cá	òcá	ọ́cá	'light colored'
í'jí	òjí	ójí'í	'dark colored'

The four adjectives in the above sets are used only attributively. Predication is expressed by either /í'dí/ or the underlying verb (yielding different shades of meaning) with the related nouns. With such predications used as relative clauses, a noun may thus be modified in three ways. E.g.,

ákwụ́kwọ́ ọ́má	'a good book' (worthwhile or well written)
ákwụ́kwọ́ 'dí ḿ'má	'a fine book' (at least in appearance or manufacture, not necessarily in content)
ŋwáànyị́ 'márá ḿ'má	'a beautiful woman'

For the other four adjectives, there are no related verbs from which they can be considered to be derived, and identical forms are used after /í'dí/ only to express predication. Apart from these forms, there are good reasons to say that /í'dí/ in the meaning 'be described as' (it also means 'be located at') can be fol-

---

[2] This material is treated from a somewhat different viewpoint, but with the same conclusions, in Welmers and Welmers 1969.

lowed only by a noun. For this reason, the four forms in question here are interpreted as adjectives when used attributively, but as homophonous nouns when
used predicatively. The category membership implied by the adjective is again
evident in the following pair:

òròmá ńtà	'a lime' (cf.: òròmá 'orange')
ŋkú'mé 'dį́ ńtà	'a small stone'

It must still be demonstrated that the eight forms here called adjectives do
indeed constitute a separate class, rather than being, for example, a special type
of noun. It is clear from the above discussion that the eight forms do constitute
some kind of a set. For three of them, a detail of tonal behavior demonstrates
that they are distinct from nouns. Crucial phrases are such as the following:

ákwų́kwǫ́ ǫma	'a good book'
ùwé ǫcá	'white clothing' (e.g., a nurse's uniform)
éféré úkwú	'a large plate' (e.g., a dinner plate as opposed to a salad plate or saucer)

If a noun with the tones high-high is used after another noun (in an associative
construction), a downstep must accompany the second syllable, in contrast with
the absence of downstep above. E.g.,

éwú	'goat':	ánų́ é'wú	'goat meat'

The other five adjectives have tonal sequences which do not undergo alternation even in nouns. But the other evidence cited above is sufficient to group
them with these three in a special class for which "adjective" is a justifiable label.
Adjectives are not used in an associative construction.

A number of other Igbo words are commonly called adjectives, and it is now
necessary to exclude them from this class, or to show cause why they should be
assigned to other classes. Among such words, numerals can readily be excluded;
they are used attributively after nouns, but also in an associative construction
with ordinal meaning. Thus:

úlò àtǫ́	'three houses'	ú'lǫ́ ('ŋké) 'atǫ́	'the third house'

The words /ùfǫ́dú/ 'some' and /òbúlà/ 'any' are clearly nouns; they are used
after other nouns, but only in an associative construction. The words /ótù/ 'one',
/ǫ́'gú/ 'twenty', and /ńnù/ 'four hundred' are not numerals, but neither are they
adjectives; they are nouns used before other nouns in an associative construction,
identifiable by characteristic tonal alternations. The word /ǫtútú/ 'a lot of' may
be grouped with these; it is used in the same way, although its tones are such
that the diagnostic tonal alternation is not possible.

Two demonstratives, /áhù/ 'that' and /à/ 'this', constitute a special class;
they are the only forms so far considered that can occur after a numeral. Two
words for 'all', /dúm̀/ and /ní'ílé/, constitute still another class; they can be used
after numerals, and also after demonstratives. The word /ná'ání/ 'only' can also

be so used, but in addition it may be used before a noun; it is probably best considered a type of adverb.

Several words which designate qualities, and which have commonly been called adjectives, are actually nouns, although there are some restrictions in their use. These include the following, here glossed as if they were adjectives:

ógólógó	'tall long'	ńtịńtị	'a small amount of'
óbódóbó	'wide'	ńtàkịrị	'a small amount of'
m̀bádám̀bá	'wide'	ǹnúkwú	'large'
ŋ̀kpóŋkpó	'short (animate)'	ágá'dị	'aged'
óbéré	'small'	ŋ̀kpìsị	'short'

These are used before nouns, and superficially give the impression of modifying such nouns in a modifier-head construction. E.g.,

ógólógó ósísí	'a tall tree'
óbódóbó ụ́zọ̀	'a wide road'

However, the diagnostic tonal alternation for the associative construction with two nouns appears with the only one of these for which it is possible; as in the second of the following, final low tone becomes high before low:

ŋ̀kpìsì ósísí	'a short stick'
ŋ̀kpìsị́ ùdọ̀	'a short (length of) rope'

Thus the words in question are interpreted as nouns, and here are head nouns in an associative construction. Strange as it may seem from the viewpoint of translation, the phrases above have the structure 'a tallness of tree', 'a wideness of road', 'a shortness of stick/rope'. As might be expected, the words in question are called "adjectives" in many treatments of Igbo and in schools, but it is significant that speakers of Igbo who have not studied the "grammar" of their language in school readily recognize the nominal rather than adjectival character of these words. There are, indeed, some uses in which their nominal character is more obvious, though these are not very common. It is quite possible, for example, to say /ógólógó 'yá/ 'its height'. Interpreted as nouns, these words also fit into the statement previously made that only a noun may appear after /ị́'dị́/ in the meaning 'be described as', in absolute or relative constructions.

There are admittedly restrictions in the use of these nouns. Except after /ị́'dị́/, it seems to be impossible to use any of them unmodified. Included in this is the fact that they cannot be used alone after the verb /ị́'bú/ 'be identified as'; most nouns can be so used, but cannot be used after /ị́'dị́/. A few nouns, however, can be used after both, and the distinction is illuminating for the present analysis. Compare the following:

ọ́ bụ̀ ụ́lọ̀	'it is a house'
ọ́ bụ̀ ọ́kụ́	'it is fire'
ọ́ dị̀ ọ́kụ́	'it is hot' (i.e., describable in terms of fire, but not actually flame)

ọ́ dị̀ ógólógó   'it is tall' (i.e., describable in terms of
                       tallness, but not actually the quality
                       of tallness itself)

It may be desirable to set up subclasses of nouns or to define a semantic feature, such that /úlọ̀/ is "concrete" while /ógólógó/ is "nonconcrete", and /ọ́kụ́/ may be either.

A number of other words may be used after the verb /í'dí/ or after verbs related to them and from which they may be taken as derived. These are also analyzed as nouns. Examples are:

ọ́ dị̀ ụ̀tọ́ / ọ́ tọ̀rọ̀ ụ̀tọ́   'it is delicious'
ọ́ dị̀ m̀pé / ọ́ pèrè m̀pé   'it is small'
ńrí 'dị́ ụ́tọ́ / ńrí 'tọ́rọ́ ụ́tọ́   'delicious food'
óċé 'dị́ m̀pé / óċé 'péré m̀pe   'a small chair'

Because of their qualificative meaning, these have also commonly been called "adjectives". They cannot, however, be used attributively after nouns; the attributives in the above examples are relative clauses. These do not appear in most other typical nominal constructions either, but one other is attested and is is sufficient to establish that these also are nouns. A "nonconcrete" noun not so far cited is /ézígbó/ 'a true specimen, real'; it is typically used in an exclamatory sense. The following show it used with an obvious noun, and with one of the nouns in question here:

ọ́ bụ̀ ézígbó m̀'mánụ̀   'it's real palm wine !'
ọ́ dị̀ ézígbó 'ụ́tọ́   'it's really delicious !'

Finally, there are a few expressions for colors which are reduplicated phrases of a unique type, but clearly derived from nouns. They are used after the verb /í'cá/ 'be bright, shine, be colored', and corresponding relative clauses are used attributively. The underlying nouns in the following are two names of species of trees from which dyes are made, and two words (from different dialect areas) for 'blood':

úhyé: ákwúkwọ́ 'cárá úhyé 'úhyé   'a brownish-red book'
èdò: ákwúkwọ́ 'cárá èdó èdò   'a yellow book'
ọ̀bàrà: ákwúkwọ́ 'cárá ọ̀bàrá ọ̀bàrà   'a (bright) red book'
m̀mé: ákwúkwọ́ 'cárá m̀mé 'm̀mé   'a (bright) red book'

Igbo thus provides an outstanding example of the need for caution in labeling words "adjectives." There definitely is a class of adjectives, to be sure, but most words one would at first think of calling adjectives are nouns or belong to other smaller form classes, while adjectives are a limited and distinctive class.

9.7. The existence of a class of adjectives in Efik was established in another connection in 5.20, and alluded to at the beginning of this chapter. The class is not large, but it has nothing of the symmetry or semantic uniqueness characteristic of Igbo adjectives. As in Igbo, tone is crucial to the definition of adjectives;

in the case of forms with final low tone, adjectives differ from nouns in an associative construction in the tonal alternations which they condition. Efik adjectives also differ from nouns in that they have a singular-plural contrast. An attributive adjective precedes a noun, an unusual word order in Niger-Congo languages, though not unparalleled—in Ijo, modifiers of all types precede nouns.

Ward (1933, pp. 42-43) had noted differences in tonal alternations, and attributed them to two classes of "adjectives". Her first class includes only actual adjectives with final low tone. Her second class includes some forms with final low tone which are better analyzed as nouns, and a number of forms with final high tone which, as far as tonal alternations are concerned, could be either adjectives or nouns. Having failed to discover the actual basis for distinguishing adjectives from nouns, she raises the question of why there should be two types of morphotonemic alternation, and quotes a suggestion by M. D. W. Jeffreys that her Class 1 Adjectives "come from Sudanic root verbs." Since the derivation of adjectivals from verbs has been noted in other languages, this suggestion is worth mentioning here. Actually, I see no particular evidence for such a hypothesis, although a few adjectives are clearly derived from verbs within Efik itself. There is no extensive or productive pattern of adjective derivation; the following recognizable instances, established as adjectival rather than some other type of derivation by tonal behavior or the existence of singular and plural forms, are insufficient to establish rules for prefixation or tone in derived adjectives:

tíbé	'begin, happen'	:	ùtíbè, (pl. ?)	'remarkable'
dyɔ́k	'be bad'	:	ìdyɔ́k, ǹdyɔ́y	'bad'
ɣ̀àn	'expand'	:	àɣán, ǹɣán	'long, far'

With her characteristic humility, integrity, and good sense, Ward adds that she "has been concerned with the existing facts of the language and has not touched on the historical side of the question". She is hardly to be castigated for not pressing the descriptive analysis to a rigidly defensible solution, though such a procedure would have explained the differences in morphotonemic alternation without recourse to historical speculation.

9.8. Given the opportunity for far more extensive exposure to some Gur languages, the status of forms that may at least be described as adjectivals might be far more satisfactorily established. The limited evidence available, however, is sufficient to demonstrate that cautious analysis is in order, and that words cannot blindly be labeled "adjectives" simply because they happen to have a qualificative meaning.

In Suppire (see Welmers 1950b) forms with a qualificative meaning are used after the stem of a noun, without the noun class suffix (if any). Some examples are:

kéré-gɛ́	'farm'	:	kéré bóʔá	'a big farm'
kàkɔ̂	'lizard'	:	kàkɔ̂ bóʔá	'a big lizard'
su-go	'mortar'	:	su bílèère	'a small mortar'
bo-ro	'bag'	:	bo bílèère	'a small bag'

The first of the nouns above belongs to the *ki* class and the second to the *wi* class; the form meaning 'big' which is used after their stems is the same in both cases. Similarly, the third of the nouns above belongs to the *ki* class, and the fourth to the *li* class; the form meaning 'small' which is used after their stems is the same in both cases. The phrases on the right above do belong to noun classes, but the class is determined by the qualificative rather than by the noun stem. The qualificatives themselves consist of stem and class suffix: /bó-ʔá/ in the *ki* class and /bílèè-re/ in the *li* class. Each qualificative so used belongs to a specific class; the recorded examples are all in either the *ki* class or the *li* class, and the appropriate corresponding plural forms also occur; it is dubious whether forms in other classes are to be found in the language.

In spite of the restriction in class membership, the data strongly suggest that the forms in question are nominal, and that they combine with the stems of other nouns to form a type of compound noun, the class of which is determined by the class of the second member, which is the modifier rather than the head. Unfortunately, no information is available on other possible combinations of two nouns (e.g., a combination of 'house' and 'wood' for 'a frame house') which might verify this analysis or suggest that the qualificatives in question belong to a form class of their own. Other evidence, however, suggests that the solution may not be as simple as the available forms make it seem.

Corresponding to at least some of the qualificatives which are used as illustrated above, there are alternative attributive forms which are used after the indefinite singular form of nouns—the stem with its class suffix. These attributives have a prefix /nu-/ or /ni-/ (the alternation is probably phonologically conditioned), with morphophonemic alternations at the beginning of the stem. The recorded cases of corresponding qualificatives used after a noun stem and after the indefinite form of a noun are:

faʔa	:	nuvaʔaga	'light'
fógó	:	núvogo	'hot'
tǎgá	:	nintã	'good tasting'
tyènè	:	nintyɛnɛ	'good, nice'
?	:	númpíŋɛ́	'soft'

Further, a majority of the recorded qualificatives are derived from verbs, or are at least cognate with verbs whatever the underlying root may be. Verbs appear in two forms, which for present purposes may simply be labelled "stem" and "present"; the present seems to be derived from the stem by a complex set of derivational patterns, though in at least some cases the stem also may be derived from an underlying root which does not appear by itself. Cases of related verbs and qualificatives are as follows; all of the qualificatives here are in the *ki* class:

Stem	Present	Qualif.	
dugo	dudui	dugogo	'(be) heavy'
fà?ai	fà?àgà	fa?a	'(be) light'
nyíŋέ	nyíŋílí	nyiŋɛ	'(be) cold'
lyɛ	lyàgɛ	lyágá	'(be) old'
tǎ	ńtǎá	tǎgá	'(be) good tasting'
tyùgò	ǹtyùgòlì	tyùgògò	'(be) deep'

For qualificatives which are not related to verbs, verbs with related meanings are recorded. For the first two of the following sets with the qualificative having an independent stem, the qualificative is in the *ki* class; for the other two, it is in the *li* class:

Stem	Present	Qualif.	
pèì	pèrì	bó ?á	'(be) big, fat'
wyɛri	wyɛgɛ	fógó	'(be) hot'
tyέrέ	ntyégέ	bílèère	'(be) small'
nyɔ	nyɔ̀gɛ	tyɛ̀nὲ	'(be) good, nice'

Unfortunately, the data elicited or happened upon in Senari (see Welmers 1950a)—which is not far beyond the bounds of mutual intelligibility with Suppire—are not sufficiently parallel with the Suppire data to confirm or refute a hypothesis of a closely similar structure in respect to forms with qualificative meaning. There is some evidence, however, of significant differences.

Three forms referring to the primary colors are recorded in Senari, only in a predicative usage. This usage is not recorded for any other words, and predication for other words with a qualificative meaning is clearly verbal. All of this may well be paralleled in Suppire; comparable sentences were not recorded. It is not known how attribution is expressed for these color terms; it may be by a kind of relative construction. For what they are worth, the three sentences which merely exist in the blue for lack of other data are:

ki wo vigeni	'it is light-colored'
ki wo wo?oni	'it is dark-colored'
ki wo nyi?ɛni	'it is bright-colored'

Otherwise, one can start with a pattern of qualificatives used after noun stems which is somewhat similar to that of Suppire. Again, the class of the combination depends on the class of the qualificative. A striking difference, however, is that at least some qualificatives may appear in two or three different classes, largely independently of the class of the modified noun. Restriction to one class is illustrated by /kpɔ?ɔ/ 'big, fat' in the *ki* class; this may seem natural in view of the fact that the *ki* class may have an augmentative force, but an interesting counter-example will be noted later:

kpàsa	(*wi*)	'mat'	:	kpàsa kpɔ?ɔ	'a big mat'
kpa?a	(*ki*)	'house'	:	kpa kpɔ?ɔ	'a big house'
ŋèlè	(*li*)	'bell'	:	ŋè kpɔ?ɔ	'a big bell'

The qualificative meaning 'small' is found most frequently in the *li* class as /pílé/; this may also seem natural in view of the fact that the *li* class may have a diminutive force, but actually a form /pígé/ in the *ki* class may also be used, with no apparent difference in meaning. After a noun in the *wi* class referring to an animate, a *wi* class form is used with the specific meaning 'infant'; only the plural /píbéle/ is recorded. E.g.,

kpàsa	(*wi*)	'mat'	:	kpàsa pílé kpàsa pígé	'a small mat'
súgu	(*ki*)	'mortar'	:	sú pílé sú pígé	'a small mortar'
ŋèlè	(*li*)	'bell'	:	ŋè pílé ŋè pígé	'a small bell'
dèká	(*wi*)	'cat'	:	dèká píle dèká pígéle dèká píbéle	'a small cat' 'small cats' 'kittens'

The qualificative meaning 'sick' has forms in three classes: /yáa/ (*wï*), /yáʔa/ (*ki*), /yála/ (*li*). Any of the three may be used after a noun belonging to the *wi* class, but the *wi* class form is not used after nouns of other classes. It is interesting that the distinction between augmentative and diminutive is neutralized in such combinations. The noun /yáwéʔe/ (*ki*) refers to 'a large animal', while /yáwéle/ (*li*) is 'a small animal'. When the stem /yáwé-/ is used before a qualificative, the qualificative may appear in either the *ki* or *li* class, but the distinction has no reference to size. Thus:

dèká	(*wi*)	'cat'	:	déká yáa dèká yáʔa dèká yála	'a sick cat'
yáwéʔe (*ki*) yáwéle (*li*)		'animal'	:	yáwé yáʔa yáwé yála	'a sick animal'
fídyɛ̀nɛ̀	(*li*)	'bird'	:	fídyɛ̃ yáʔa fídyɛ̃ yála	'a sick bird'

For Senari as well as Suppire, such combinations suggest that qualificatives may be nominal, though there is a freedom of class membership in Senari that is not found in Suppire. Even more consistently than in Suppire, however, Senari qualificatives are related to verbs. Only two qualificatives are recorded for which there is no related verb form. One of these is /yáa, yáʔa, yála/ 'sick', for which no parallel is recorded in Suppire. The other is /pílé, pígé/ 'small'; in Suppire, the cognate qualificative also has no related verb form. One Senari qualificative with related verb is cognate with a Suppire verb, while two are cognate with Suppire independent qualificatives. (A question not raised before, and unanswerable from available data, is whether only those qualificatives which have no related verb form are free as to class membership; it seems a strong possibility.)

Further, in Senari the qualificative forms are identical with the corresponding verb stems, rather than apparently derived as in Suppire. All such Senari qualificatives and identical verb stems have mid tone throughout. In four recorded cases, the identical verb is transitive:

dyia	'shatter; shattered'
kabi	'break in two; broken in two'
sulu	'tear; torn'
wari	'heat; hot'

In the eight remaining recorded cases, the identical verb is intransitive:

faʔa	'(be) light'	lubo	'(be) heavy'
kpere	'(be) short'	nyɔ	'(be) good'
kpɔʔɔ	'(be) big, fat'	tɔnɔ	'(be) tall'
lɛ	'(be) old'	tyara	'(be) young'

It was noted in Suppire that verbs have two forms, stem and present. In general, the same is true in Senari. However, there is no present for the eight intransitive verbs above. Present development is expressed with a particle /m̀ba/, not otherwise recorded. E.g.,

u m̀ba tɔnɔ   'he is becoming tall'

The foregoing comparison of qualificatives in Suppire and Senari thus reveals a great deal of similarity, and also some interesting differences considering the close relationship of the languages. It would require more data and analysis to define the status of qualificatives satisfactorily in terms of the total structure of the languages, but it is clear that one must be most suspicious in respect to a class of "adjectives." There are many unanswered questions, but actually it is surprising how much pattern emerges from a limited amount of data, gathered almost incidentally in a short period devoted largely to the considerable complexities of the phonology, morphophonology, and the morphology of the nominal and verbal systems. The experience also points up a highly significant principle of field work: rather than gethering a mass of data and hoping to make sense of it later, the investigator should proceed with analysis on the spot, while informants are available to fill in gaps in the data and to provide additional information so that the analysis can be made more comprehensive.

9.9. The following statement represents a fairly reasonable way of treating certain forms in Bariba (see Welmers 1952a), though I would approach the problem somewhat differently today: "An adjective, in Bariba, is a word which has a form used attributively after nouns. Some adjectives have an additional form that may be called nominal, some have a Stative form and verbal forms." It is significant that I added, "Meaning is no criterion: the meaning 'sweet' is expressed by a verb /dorā/, 'become sweet', Stative /do/, which cannot be an adjective because it has no attributive form." More significant, however, is the consideration that at least many of the attributive forms in question are best treated as derived. It would seem preferable to speak of "adjectivals" rather than "adjectives"; they may be said to constitute a class (or three classes) of words, but this is by no means co-extensive with a class of roots. By way of orientation for the following discussion, a few details discussed in previous chapters may be repeated here. Bariba has four tone levels: top /'/, high (unmarked), mid /ˉ/, and low /'/. There are noun classes identified by the initial consonant of a concordial demonstrative (singular): y-, t-, g-, w-, m-, s-, n-, p- (the last reported but not recorded). Most singular classes have characteristic plural counterparts.

Bariba attributives are of three types: invariable, class-bound, and class-inflected. For nouns in some nouns classes, the class marking suffix does not appear before an attributive. For nouns in other classes, a final vowel is treated as a suffix in some cases, and does not appear before an attributive, but is treated as part of the stem in other cases. In at least one class, the m-class, the suffix /m/ is retained before an attributive.

Seven invariable attributives are recorded; for these there is no singular-plural distinction. They are miscellaneous in form and meaning. A phrase consisting of a noun with one of these attributives must belong to some class, but unfortunately the class membership is not recorded. One of these was recorded with two different tone sequences; one undoubtedly represents an error in copying. The invariable attributives are:

dɔ ~ dua	'male'	pikó	'a little'
goma	'raw'	tereré	'narrow'
gbãrã	'high'	sɛ̃ɛ̃sɔ	'difficult'
kaà (kàā ?)	'white'		

Of these, the last is derived, though not by any productive pattern. There is a corresponding stative verbal form /sɛ̃/, which is apparently the underlying root; other verbal forms are based on the consecutive, which is /sɛ̃sĩã/. The form /pikó/ is apparently also derived, though not from a verb, and again not by any productive pattern; in the second class of attributives described below, an apparently related form /píbu/ appears, with the meaning 'small'. It is quite possible that further analysis would lead to the conclusion that all of these forms are a type of noun, used in an associative construction with the preceding noun. Data of a kind not elicited would be required to prove or disprove such a hypothesis.

Class-bound attributives are those which have their own class, irrespective of the class of the preceding noun—a phenomenon paralleled in Suppire and Senari as noted in the preceding section. These attributives have plural forms like nouns in the same classes. Five are recorded in the t-class only; two are recorded in the g-class only; and one is recorded in both of these classes, independently of the class of the preceding noun. The regular suffixes of the t-class are singular /-ru ~ -rū/ with phonologically conditioned alternation, and plural /-nu/. The three g-class forms all end in /-bu/ in the singular; this is by no means characteristic of nouns in the g-class, which normally has no suffix. Plural nouns in the g-class have either /-nu/ or /-su/ as suffix, under lexical conditioning. The plural forms of the attributives were undoubtedly heard, but are not recorded. The following are class-bound attributives:

binu (pl.)	'some, a few'	yàkàbū	'small'
dabīrū	'much, many'	píbu	'small'
kpirìrū	'short, small'	kpirìbū	'short, small'
gorū	'dead'		
tɔ̀kɔ̄rū	'old'		
kìnèrū	'male' (of certain animals)		

Of these, two are derived from verbs; the stative, consecutive, and attributive forms for these are as follows:

dabī	dabiā	dabīrū	'(be) much, many'
gō	gbi	gorū	'die; (be) dead'

An effort was made to elicit predicative constructions involving meanings paralleling each attributive, but related verbal forms were not found for any others. As in the case of invariable attributives, further analysis may lead to the conclusion that these are a type of noun.

A considerably larger number of attributives are class-inflected. That is, they have forms for all classes, depending on the class of the preceding noun. The following illustrate this type of attributive in the singular:

y-class:	duma	'horse'	:	dum baka	'a big horse'
t-class:	kpèrū	'stone'	:	kpèè bakaru	'a big stone'
g-class:	boo	'goat'	:	boo bakɔ	'a big goat'
w-class:	dɔ̌ɔ̌	'fire'	:	dɔ̌ɔ̌ bakɔ	'a big fire'
m-class:	yam	'space'	:	yam bakam	'a big space'
s-class:	tasu	'yam'	:	tam bakasu	'a big yam'
n-class:	gáánu	'thing'	:	gáá bakanu	'a big thing'

The final vowel /a/ is characteristic of the y-class, though it is not always treated as a suffix. Similarly, the final vowel /ɔ/ or /o/ (a variation whose conditioning has not been defined) is characteristic of the g-class and the w-class. This analysis is substantiated by the following set, in that a different vowel, /i/, appears before the CV suffix in other classes; the nouns are as above with one exception:

dum̀ kpìkā	'a white horse'
kpèé kpìkìrū	'a white stone'
boó kpìkō	'a white goat'
(no appropriate noun in the w-class)	
werem̀ kpìkīm̀	'white soap'
tam̀ kpìkìsū	'a white yam'
gáá kpìkìnū	'a white thing'

(These include examples of morphotonemic alternation; final high has the alternant top before low.) The stem of attributives of this type may be defined as what precedes a CV suffix.

Somewhat less than half of the recorded class-inflected attributives appear to be derived; in several cases the derivation involves reduplication. The stative, consecutive, and attribute stems of related sets are as follows:

bɔ̄ ~ bɔ̄bū	bɔ̄biā	bɔɔ̀bɔā-	'(be) hard'
bɔrū	bɔriā	bɔrùbɔrū-	'(be) fat'
dḕū̃	dḕḕyā	dɛǹdɛ̃-	'(be) long'
sō ~ sōsū	sosiā	soɔ̀suā-	'(be) bitter'
sūɛ̀rī	sūɛ̀rā	sṳ̀ā̃-	'(be) red'
sum̄	sṳ̀yā	súm-	'(be) hot'
tāū	taàyā	taàtaā-	'(be) tough'
?	wɔ̄kù	wɔ̄kū-	'(be) black'

The following class-inflected attributives, on the other hand, are recorded without related verbal forms being elicited; these differ in their final tones from the preceding:

baka-	'big'	kpaà-	'new'
bèku-	'fresh'	kpikī-	'white'
bùra-	'good'	ni-	'female'
dangi-	'strong'	sìnùǹgi-	'thick'
ge-	'good'	yíre-	'cold'
gbebu-	'dry'		

While invariable and class-bound attributives may perhaps be analyzable as types of nouns, the same can hardly be the case for class-inflected attributives. These, at least, seem to constitute a real class of adjectives, some of which are derived but more of which are not. At the same time, even some of these have forms which seem to function as nouns in certain constructions. For some, predication is expressed by such a form before a particle /sã/ 'it is', or before the stative form /mɔ̀/, a suppletive stative of the verb /kō/ 'do, make, be'. E.g.,

ya kpaà sã	'it is new'
ya dam mɔ̀	'it is strong'

Other attributives, including representatives of all three types, are found only in the attributive use after a noun.

The numeral 'one' is class-inflected like adjectives, with some morphophonemic alternations which seem to be unique to this word. The forms are:

y-class:	tiā	w-class:	turō
t-class:	teèrū	s-class:	teèsū
g-class:	teū	n-class:	teènū

All higher numerals, however, are invariable in form. In Suppire and Senari, discussed in the preceding section, all numerals are invariable. From points of view other than class concord, numerals are treated in the following chapter.

9.10. From many points of view, and particularly in terms of pedagogical usefulness, one of the most sensible treatments of qualificative constructions in an African language is to be found in E.O. Ashton's *Swahili Grammar* (Ashton 1944). There are two chapters, 10 and 25, covering the topic "Adjectival Concepts". The latter of these conveniently groups together a number of constructions translatable into English by adjectives, but clearly not grammatically adjectives in Swahili; these include the associative construction, relatives, nouns in apposition, and the use of a form meaning 'having'. The rationale for this treatment is found at the beginning of the earlier chapter: "In Swahili there are few words may be termed 'Adjectives'. There are, however, many ways of expressing an adjectival concept." This, of course, takes English adjectives as a point of departure; but the organization of the Swahili data clearly distinguishes what may legitimately be called "adjectives" from other ways of translating English adjectives.

Like most—but not all—Bantu languages, Swahili does have a class of adjectives. Ashton distinguishes two types of form in chapter 10: roots and stems taking the adjectival concord, and uninflected loan words. The cautious statement is made that "These two categories of qualifiers approach nearest to the conception of 'Adjective' in English." Ashton lists fifty stems (if /nane/ 'eight' is added to her list; the omission appears to have been inadvertent) which take class prefixes identical with those of nouns except for class 11/14, and which are used attributively after nouns. She notes that this usage "virtually converts the 'Adjective' stem into a noun in apposition", and indeed adjectival forms can also be used independently as nouns, though with implicit reference to an unexpressed noun. Adjective stems may be distinguished from noun stems, however, in that they are not restricted in class membership, but take concords determined by the class of the noun referred to. Some adjectives appear to be derived from verbs as /-bivu/ 'ripe' from /ku-iva/ (*/ku-biva/) 'ripen'. In other cases, verbs appear to be derived from underlying adjectives, as /ku-nenepa/ 'get fat' from /-nene/ 'fat'. Most adjective stems, however, are exclusively adjectival.

Included in the list of adjectives are the stems for 'one' through 'five', 'eight', and 'how many?'; these take the same concords as qualificative adjectives. A formal distinction between numerals and other adjectives could be made on the basis of the fact that the stem for 'one' takes only singular class concords, and the others take only plural class concords, while qualificative adjectives take both singular and plural concords. This seems to be a rather trivial distinction, however.

Some uninflected adopted words, largely if not exclusively from Arabic, are used attributively like class-inflected adjectives, but are invariable in form. They include the words for 'six', 'seven', and 'nine', and multiples of 'ten'. The word for 'ten', though Bantu in origin, is also uninflected; this is typical of the Bantu languages in general.

The general principles and specific prefixes of attributive or primary concord in Swahili have been outlined in 6.10-12. The following illustrate the usage
for all classes:

1:	mtu mkubwa	'an important person'
2:	watu wakubwa	'important people'
3:	mzigo mkubwa	'a large load'
4:	mizigo mikubwa	'large loads'
5:	shoka kubwa	'a large axe'
6:	mashoka makubwa	'large axes'
7:	kikapu kikubwa	'a large basket'
8:	vikapu vikubwa	'large baskets'
9:	ngoma kubwa	'a large drum'
10:	ngoma kubwa	'large drums'
11:	ubao mkubwa	'a large plank'

The following illustrate uninflected adjectives (both adopted from Arabic):

1:	mtu hodari	'a clever person'
3:	mti hodari	'hard wood'
7:	chumba safi	'a clean room'
8:	vyumba safi	'clean rooms'

Actually, a few stems adopted from Arabic are now used with adjectival
concords. These include /-dhaifu/ 'weak' and /-kaidi/ 'obstinate'. As might be
expected, these usages are somewhat limited; not all classes are represented.

Most adjectives may form the basis for a derived abstract noun in class 11/14.
E.g.,

-zuri	'fine'	:	uzuri	'beauty'
hodari	'clever, brave':		uhodari	'bravery'

Ashton describes her list of inflected adjective stems as "more or less exhaustive". There are some in addition to those she lists, but it is still true that
the class of adjectives is by no means as large as the class of nouns or verbs. At
the same time, it is by no means as restricted a class as has been noted in a number
of non-Bantu languages in the Niger-Congo family. Without going into detail,
it may simply be noted that a great many Bantu languages have a comparable
class of adjectives, not very large but showing a variety of qualificative meanings.

Some writers have treated the Swahili forms in question as nouns, but must
still distinguish them from other nouns by the freedom of class membership, and
also by the fact that primary concord for class 11/14 is not the same as the noun
prefix. Quite a different structure must be recognized in phrases consisting of
two nouns each of which has its own class membership. This is not an extremely
common construction in Swahili, but well established. For example, /mbwa/
'dog' (9-10) combines with /mwitu/ 'forest' (3) in the phrase /mbwa mwitu/ 'a
wild dog'. It is quite legitimate to recognize the noun-like characteristics of what

are generally called adjectives in Swahili, but it is also important to note the characteristics peculiar to them.

9.11. Some languages, however, including some Bantu languages, get along very nicely without any qualificative adjectives. One such language is LoNkundo (Hulstaert 1938, p. 19). As noted in 6.19, LoNkundo has primary concords, distinguished from secondary concords only in that they have high rather than low tone, which are used only with the numeral stems for 'one' through 'five'. Ideas which one might expect to be expressed by "adjectives" are expressed in other ways, most significantly by nouns which, with a special exception noted below, have their own class membership. Such nouns, like other nouns, may be used after a copula /-le/ to express predication. To express attribution, they are used in an associative construction with a head noun. For example, the following use a class 7 head noun /etóo/ 'garment' and a class 3 qualificative noun /wɛ̆lɔ/ 'whiteness':

etóo ele wɛ̆lɔ	'the garment is white'
etóo éâ wɛ̆lɔ	'a white garment'

The latter of these may be more meaningfully represented by the gloss 'a garment associated with whiteness'.

Most nouns with qualificative meaning so used seem to appear in classes 3-4, but some are found in other classes. The last of the following examples is in classes 19-13:

bɔlɔ́tsi,	bɛlɔ́tsi	'goodness'
bɔnéne,	bɛnéne	'bigness'
bobé,	bebé	'badness'
wɛ̆lɔ,	byɛ̆lɔ	'whiteness'
bŏlɔ́,	byŏlɔ́	'strength'
bŭwé,	byŭwé	'shortness'
isîsí,	tosîsí	'smallness'

In predications, such words appear in the singular if the subject noun is singular; they may appear in either the singular or plural if the subject noun is plural. Thus:

etóo ele wɛ̆lɔ	'the garment is white'
bitóo bile wɛ̆lɔ	'the garments are white'
bitóo bile byɛ̆lɔ	

In the associative, there is a special and peculiar usage for some qualificative nouns. There are dialectal variations in this usage, but the most widespread and thus obligatory pattern applies to four nouns, of which the regular class 3 singular forms are:

bɔlɔ́tsi	'goodness'	bɔnéne	'bigness'
bobé	'badness'	botálé	'length'

These four nouns take the noun prefix of the head noun in the construction if
that noun is in class 2 or 6 (for both of which the prefix is /ba-/). They nevertheless
remain independent nouns, with which they must be in an associative construction, but they enter into a form of concord with the head noun. Thus:

banto bǎ balɔ́tsi	(2)	'good people'
bǎna bǎ babé	(6)	'bad children'
basukú bǎ banénɛ	(6)'	'large hats'
bayá bǎ batálé	(6)	'tall palm trees'

Apart from these limited and special exceptions, qualificative nouns retain
their own class membership in the associative. The four cited above are used only
in the singular (3), even after a plural head noun. The noun /isîsí, tosîsí/ 'smallness' is used only in the plural (13) after a plural head noun. Other qualificative
nouns may be used in either the singular or the plural after a plural head noun.
Thus:

betámbá (4) byǎ bɔnénɛ (3)	'large trees'
yǒmba (19) yǎ bɔlɔ́tsi (3)	'a good thing (abstract)'
tǒmba (13) tswǎ bɔlɔ́tsi (3)	'good things (abstract)'
jǒi (5) jǎ isîsí (19)	'a small thing'
baói (6) bǎ tosîsí (13)	'small things'
etóo (7) éâ wĕlɔ (3)	'a white garment'
bitóo (8) byǎ wĕlɔ (3)	'white garments'
bitóo (8) byǎ byĕlɔ (4)	

A fuller discussion of associatives in a number of languages is reserved for the
following chapter. Even with what has been said on the subject up to this point,
however, it is clear and highly important that the final words in the phrases cited
above are nouns, and not adjectives as the English translations might suggest.
The formula for all of them is 'a thing associated with a quality', and the words
expressing quality are nouns.

9.12. A number of grammars of African languages have been consulted apart
from any personal experience with the languages they describe. Almost all of
them speak of "adjectives." In the case of Bantu languages, the descriptions are
usually sufficiently clear to make it possible to determine what the situation is
in respect to expressions of quality. For non-Bantu languages, however, the descriptions very commonly betray a great deal of confusion on the subject, usually
stemming from the tacit assumption that the equivalents of English adjectives
will be adjectives in other languages. It is rarely possible to extract a satisfactory
description of qualificative expressions from such grammars. To be sure, even
my own hasty treatments of some languages have fallen well short of adequacy
in this respect, but at least they display a reasonable freedom from unwarranted
assumptions. This area of analysis, at least for Niger-Congo languages, is by no
means the easiest to explore. But the message derived from the discussions above
is loud and clear: be suspicious of "adjectives"; some of them are not.

Chapter 10

Other Noun Modifiers; Conjunction

10.1. There have been numerous references in preceding chapters to "associative" constructions in a variety of languages. It was impossible to avoid the subject; it was crucial for describing the functions of tone in some languages, for distinguishing adjectives from nouns in some languages, and for describing concord in some languages. No attempt was made, however, to describe the full range of the manifestations and usages of such constructions. They constitute an important aspect of noun modification in a variety of Niger-Kordofanian languages, and must now be surveyed from that point of view. The starting point will be the Bantu languages, in most of which an associative construction is conspicuous.[1]

The beginning student of a Bantu language meets phrases like the following (from Swahili) at an early stage:

kisu cha Hamisi	'Hamisi's knife'
nyumba ya mtu yule	'that person's house'
mkono wa mtu yule	'that person's hand'

In each of these phrases, the second word consists of a concord appropriate to the class of the preceding noun, plus a morpheme /-a/. The beginner is likely to refer to such constructions as "possessive", and to /-a/ as a "possessive" morpheme. Indeed, a number of treatments of individual Bantu languages have unfortunately used just that term, and have then been forced into tortuous and confusing explanations of the identical construction with meanings that have nothing to do with possession. A number of more sophisticated writers have resorted to the term "genitive," and indeed the usages of an associative construction are rather closely parallel to the uses of the genitive case in languages such as Latin. Personally, however, I prefer to reserve the term "genitive" for inflected noun forms in languages with case systems. A similar preference seems to have been felt by E. O. Ashton (1944, p. 7), who calls the morpheme /-a/ in Swahili "the -A of relationship". For both the morpheme and the construction, and their counterparts in countless other languages, I have chosen to use the term "associative". Something of the variety of semantic aspects of association expressed is illustrated by the following:

---

[1] The material in 10.1-5 is treated from a somewhat different point of view in Welmers 1963a.

material:	nyumba za mawe	'houses made of stone'
contents:	chupa ya maji	'a bottle of water'
place of origin:	mtu wa Utete	'a person from Utete'
place of use:	saa ya mkono	'wrist-watch' (clock for the arm)
time of use:	chakula cha asubuhi	'breakfast' (food for morning)
function:	miti ya kujengea	'sticks for building'
quantity:	chakula cha kutosha	'enough food' (food assoc. with be-enough)
possession:	kisu cha Hamisi	'Hamisi's knife'

In Swahili and most other Bantu languages, pronominal association is expressed with the same morpheme /-a/. Four of the Swahili pronominal forms are monosyllabic, and form one word with what precedes. The first and second person plural pronominal forms are reconstructed as */-itu/ and */-inu/ respectively; the associative /-a/ combines with the initial vowel of these as /-e/. The Swahili forms in question are:

-angu	'my'	-etu	'our'
-ako	'your (sg.)'	-enu	'your (pl.)'
-ake	'his, her, its'	-ao	'their'

As noted in 6.13-14, Swahili does not use pronominal referents or concords after the associative morpheme for classes other than 1 and 2; the form for class 1, /-ke/, is used for all other classes, both singular and plural. In many other Bantu languages, however, a chart like the above would have to be extended to include forms for every noun class.

In some Bantu languages, there is a second associative morpheme /ka/, usually with quite restricted uses.[2] One example of its use is to be found in Lo-Nkundo, where it is used for personal pronominal association, but not for association with nouns or with concords for classes other than 1 and 2. The following examples do not indicate a pervasive vowel elision at word boundaries, and use the fullest pronoun forms; the full form /-ká-/ is found with the singular pronominal referents, but before the vowel-initial plural forms the alternant /-k-/ appears:

bekélé bekáṁ	'my eggs'
etóo ekáwĕ	'your (sg.) garment'
bikálá bikándé	'his/her cups'
bolaki ŏkísó	'our teacher'
bokúné ŏkínyó	'your (pl.) younger brother'
bitóo bikíyɔ́	'their garments'

For other classes, the associative /-a/ is used with independent referents which function as nouns; the same associative construction is used with all nouns. The

---

[2] The LoNkundo data are taken from Hulstaert 1938. For examples from other Bantu languages, I am indebted to Professor Desmond T. Cole (private communications).

independent referents have a stem /-kɔ́/, with a class prefix; Hulstaert is not entirely clear at this point, but the prefixes appear to be the same as those for
primary concord with numerals, having high tone. As noted in the preceding
chapter, Lonkundo uses nouns having a qualificative meaning in the associative
construction, often paralleling adjectives in languages such as Swahili. Nominal
association, including pronominal reference to classes other than 1 and 2, is illustrated by the following:

bitóo byǎ bolaki	'the teacher's garments'
botámbá óâ bɔnénɛ	'a large tree'
byili byǎ bɔ́kɔ́	'its (3) leaves'
byili byǎ békɔ́	'their (4) leaves'
bekóo byǎ bíkɔ́	'their (8) colors'

A somewhat similar restricted use of the associative /-ka/ is found in Zulu;
it is used only before personal nouns of Class 1a, which includes largely proper
names and a few kinship terms. This is illustrated by the first of the following;
in the second, a counter-example, the associative /-a/ fuses with the initial vowel
of the following word, /umuntu/, as /o/; tone is not indicated here;

izinja zikaɓaɓa	'my father's dogs'
izinja zomuntu	'the person's dogs'

Tswana uses a morpheme /-xa/, a reflex of */-ka/, in the same circumstances
as Zulu, but only in addition to /-a/, in the combination /-axa/. Mwela uses
either /-a/ or /-ka/, interchangeably, in almost all combinations.

In some western and northwestern Bantu languages. e.g., Bušɔɔŋ and Ngombe, neither /-a/ nor /-ka/ appears in any readily identifiable overt form in associative constructions. The possibility of such a morpheme disappearing historically is thus recognized even within Bantu; it is quite possible, however, that these
languages retain some trace, perhaps tonal, of an associative morpheme that is
not apparent from the available evidence.

In Bantu languages that make extensive use of an associative morpheme,
it is important to recognize not only the constructions in which such a morpheme
occurs, but also the relationships normally indicated without such a morpheme.
The associative /-a/ (or /-ka/) is not used in constructions of noun plus modifying
numeral or noun plus demonstrative. Numerical attribution is expressed simply
by a noun followed by a numeral, the numeral normally having a concord prefix
to agree with the noun. In languages which have a class of adjectives (such as
Swahili), the same is true for adjectives. Ordinal numerals, however, are expressed by numerals in their citation form (class 9) in an associative construction
after a noun. Compare the following in Swahili:

visu vitatu	'three knives'
kisu cha tatu	'the third knife'

An associative construction without an expressed antecedent noun may be
used as an adverbial complement with a variety of references; these usages in

Bantu, with striking parallels in languages not at all closely related, will be discussed in connection with adverbials at a later point.

10.2. It would not be particularly surprising, of course, to find close parallels to the Bantu associatives in languages fairly closely related. Actually, such constructions, and even the specific morphemes that mark them, appear to be traceable to proto-Niger-Kordofanian, and are reflected in a variety of ways in languages of many branches of the family. Specifically in a Kordofanian language, it is reported that a noun possessor is introduced by a concord referring to the possessed noun, plus a vowel /-a/ functioning as an associative morpheme (Werner Winter, private communication). The extension of this construction to relationships other than possession has not been defined, but in all likelihood exists.

Within the West Atlantic branch of Niger-Congo, a fantastically close parallel to some of the southern Bantu languages is found. W. A. A. Wilson (1962) has described the situation in Temne, Landuma, and the Baga languages, and, virtually every detail could be repeated verbatim, with translated examples, for Zulu or Xhosa. Wilson does not mention numerical attribution, but adjectival and demonstrative attribution involve immediate sequence, as in Bantu. Such sequences involve personal class concord for impersonal but animate nouns, as in many Bantu languages. Wilson's statement on this is:

> As is known, there are in Temne two types of concord, depending on whether the noun is animate (denoting a person or animal) or inanimate. In the latter case, the concord is purely grammatical, all dependent words being in the same class as the noun that controls them; if the noun is animate, then the dependent words are in class 1 (singular) or class 2 (plural), irrespective of the class of the noun. Two examples suffice to show this:
>
> | ạbil ạbana | 'a big boat' |
> | ạbok ubana | 'a big snake' |
>
> The notional concord illustrated in the latter example does not operate in all members of the [language] cluster. In Baga Maduri and Baga Sitemu there is no difference between animate and inanimate nouns in the concord they require; in Baga Koba the concord operates just as in Temne. In Landuma, however, there is a mixed system, in which most dependent words show class concord even with animate nouns, but pronouns show notional concord, thus:
>
> | abil ŋŋe, inəŋk ŋi lɛ | 'this boat, I have seen it' |
> | abok ŋŋe, inəŋk kə lɛ | 'this snake, I have seen it' |
> | oteem uwe, inəŋk kə lɛ | 'this old man, I have seen him' |

Even the mixed concord referred to can be found in Bantu; in the last set of examples, /kə/ is the personal pronoun object. These examples also illustrate the immediate sequence (with concord) of demonstrative attribution.

In the associative construction, however, there is an associative morpheme /-a/. In all the languages illustrated below except Temne, the noun prefix itself is /da-/, so that an additional /-a/ is absorbed (unless it is betrayed by tone, which Wilson does not mark). In Temne, however, the noun prefix is /rạ-/ in this instance (with other alternants under some circumstances); the associative /ra-/ with a different vowel, is /r-/ from the concord plus the associative /-a/. Wilson refers to the associative construction as "genitive"; his total statement is:

As Houis (*Bull. IFAN*, 1935, p. 848) has pointed out, there is a general similarity in the genitive construction throughout the cluster. The regent noun is followed by a concordant linking syllable which precedes the genitive noun or pronoun; the linking element is written as a separate word; in the examples we mark it with a hyphen. In BK [Baga Koba] the vowel of the linking element is lost before another vowel, but in the other languages we find two adjacent vowels in such contexts.

Temne:	rabomp ra-ɔḅay	'the chief's head'
Landuma:	dawomp da-obe	'the chief's head'
Baga Maduri:	daboomp da-ka-obe	'the chief's head'
	daboomp da-wana	'the cow's head'
Baga Koba:	dabomp di-ibɛ	'the chief's head'

It will be noticed that in BMd there is an additional linking syllable /-ka/- when the genitive noun is personal. We have no example of the construction in BS [Baga Sitemu].

Among other West Atlantic languages, Fula at least appears to show nothing like the Temne, Landuma, and Baga patterns. But in the latter, the use of an associative /-a/ in most circumstances, but of /-ka/ with personal nouns, is almost identical with the pattern of usage in Southern Bantu.

10.3. Among the Mande languages, some dialects of Mandekan have a morpheme /ká/ which is used in one of two types of possessive construction, showing a detail of parallelism with Bantu usage in spite of striking differences. The Mande languages as a whole distinguish "free" nouns (those which can be used without an expressed possessor) and "relational" nouns (those which require an expressed possessor; these are largely inalienable possessions—kinship terms, body parts, and place relations such as something's 'inside'). In the dialects in question, /ká/ is used to link possessor and possession when the possession is a free noun, but not when the possession is a relational noun:

ń ká bón	'my house'	ḿ bólo	'my hand'
kɛ́ ká bón	'the man's house'	kɛ́ bólo	'the man's hand'
a ká fani	'his cloth'	a dén	'his child'
muso ká fani	'the woman's cloth'	muso dén	'the woman's child'

Although this precise distinction is not found anywhere in Bantu, there is nevertheless a partial parallelism in the restriction of usage of /ká/. Relational nouns in Mande form a set somewhat like that of Bantu classes 1a and 2a, particularly in including kinship terms. In Southern Bantu, the use of /-ka/ (or /-xa/) is defined in terms of distinguishing such nouns from all others; in Mandekan likewise, the use of /ká/ is similarly defined in terms of the distinction between relational and free nouns. The actual surface manifestations are, to be sure, quite different: southern Bantu uses /-ka/ only with a restricted set of possessors; Mandekan uses /ká/ with all except a restricted set of possessions. Even the word order (possessor first in Mandekan, possession first in Bantu) is reversed. Yet the association of /ka/ with such a highly restricted distinction in nouns is unmistakable in both.

In Mandekan, reference has been made only to constructions expressing possession, not to a broader range of nominal association. Possession is distinct from other aspects of association throughout the Mande languages, but, as in Bantu,

numerical, adjectival, and demonstrative attribution are distinct from both, and
are expressed by immediate sequence (and with no concord, of course, since
Mande has no noun class system). In Kpelle, for example, immediate sequence is
shown in the following:

| 6oli feerɛ | 'two goats' | 6oli kɛtɛ | 'a big goat' |
| 6oli náaŋ | 'four goats' | ṁolii tí | 'that goat' |

Pronominal and nominal association, however, use the opposite word order, modifier-head. Pronominal possession consists simply of pronoun plus noun in Kpelle, though in the first and third persons singular there is a distinction in pronoun
forms used with free and relational nouns (paralleling the Bambara usage above
and the Bantu peculiarities of classes 1a and 2a). Thus:

ŋá pérɛi	'my house'	ṁpôlu	'my back'
í pérɛi	'your house'	í pôlu	'your back'
ŋɔ̀ pérɛi	'his house'	ʼpôlu	'his back'

In the case of noun possessor (as opposed to other nominal associative constructions), the possessive pronoun follows the noun possessor before free nouns; immediate sequence is found before impersonal dependent nouns; but the appropriate pronoun is used before personal dependent nouns (kinship terms)—an even
more selectively striking parallel to Bantu classes 1a and 2a:

ʼkâloŋ ŋɔ̀ pérɛi	'the chief's house'
ʼkâloŋ pôlu	'the chief's back'
ʼkâloŋ ɦee	'the chief's mother'

(In the last of the above, /ɦee/ is 'his mother', using the stem /-lee/ with prefixed
low tone.)

Nonpossessive nominal association in Kpelle takes the form of what has been
described as compounding; the range of associations so expressed is similar to
that expressed by the associative /-a/ in Bantu. Several Mande languages show
some type of tonal alternation in such compounds. In Kpelle, members of the
compound after the first have low tone, no matter what their independent tone
may be; this low tone has a regular alternant high-low after mid. Thus:

telâŋ-wùlɔ	'peanut oil' (wúlɔ 'oil')
kwí-tɔ̀li	'coconut' (kwí 'foreigner'; tɔlî 'palm kernel')
samu-kâla	'turtle shell' (kala 'shell')
kóli-kàloŋ	'section (of town) chief' (kâloŋ 'chief')

The lowering of tone in the second member of a compound is a morpheme, a replacement of stem tone by low. Historically, the most likely assumption is that
a morpheme composed of a segmental phoneme or sequence, which had low tone,
has disappeared except for this tonal trace. The segmental shape of such a morpheme was most likely just a vowel. There is no particular reason why this vowel
should have been /a/ in Kpelle; but neither is there any reason why it could not

have been. In fact, there is excellent evidence for the loss of /a/ in Kpelle, with retention of low tone, in the case of a different morpheme, a pronoun; compare:

| Mandekan: | à nyín | 'his tooth' |
| Kpelle: | ǹyíŋ | 'his tooth' |

Mande compound nouns may thus very well be derived from noun phrases using an associative construction like those with /-a/ in Swahili illustrated in 10.1 above though with inverted word order.

10.4. In a number of quite disparate languages assigned to the Kwa branch of Niger-Congo, there are also tonal manifestations of nominal association. In Akan, as in all the other languages cited so far, numerical, adjectival, and demonstrative attribution are expressed by immediate sequence. A vestige of concord appears in the following examples from Fante:

| ìdán kèsí | 'a big house' | ìdán 'kúr | 'one house' |
| àdán ákèsí | 'big houses' | àdán é'núm | 'five house' |

Pronominal and nominal association, as in Mande, invert the Bantu word order. The Akan system is simpler than the Mande in that there is no distinction involving kinship terms or other nouns which might be compared to Bantu classes 1a and 2a. Relevant possessive constructions are:

ní 'dán	'his house'
mí 'ná ní 'dán	'my mother's house'
ɔ̀hín nú ní 'dán	'the chief's house'

Like Mande, however, Akan also has a noun-noun construction that is generally described as compounding. Strikingly, it is also marked by a lowering of tone. In the case of Akan, however, it is the first rather than other members of a compound that has low tone replacing stem tone. E.g.,

| ǹkàtì-ǹgú | 'peanut oil' | (ǹkátí | 'peanuts') |
| àbè-ǹgú | 'palm oil' | (àbɛ́ | 'palm nuts') |

It is possible, therefore, that Akan also has retained only the tone of a morpheme that once consisted of a vowel with low tone. Such a reconstruction seems even more convincing in the light of evidence from other languages.

Yoruba, Igbo, and Efik use the same word order as Bantu in possessive and other associative constructions. In Yoruba, the distinction between attributive and associative constructions is as sharp as it is in Bantu—and, as in Bantu, it is the associative construction that displays an additional morpheme. Yoruba attributive numerals above 'one' have a prefix /m-/, reminiscent of plural agreement, and perhaps an actual vestige thereof. The numeral 'one' has lower-mid tone, reflecting the loss of a preceding vowel with low tone. Illustrations of Yoruba attributives are:

ilé kān	'one house'	ilé yǐ	'this house'
ilé méjì	'two houses'	ilé títóbi	'a big house'
ilé mẹwǎ	'ten houses'	aṣọ kpukpa	'red cloth'

In associative constructions with two nouns, both possessive and other than possessive, the nouns are joined by a morpheme consisting of mid tone. If the first noun ends with a mid tone, or if the second noun begins with a mid tone, this morpheme generally has a zero form, without lengthening of the preceding vowel. Between high and low tones, a pause at the mid level is not always descernible. Joining a sequence of two low tones, the morpheme is normally realized as mid tone replacing low with the first of the two vowels. This seems to leave few environments for the morpheme to have an overt realization; it is most significant, however, that the presence of this morpheme is betrayed by the absence of vowel elision, which is typical of other sequences. E.g.,

ilé⁻Òjó	'Ojo's house'
ònà⁻kpákpá	'the way to the field'
ònā Èkó	'the road to Lagos'
ilé ọkùnrin náà	'the man's house'
ilé ọkùnrin náà	'the man's house'
(cf.: fọ̀sọ, *fọ aṣọ	'wash clothes')

Pronominal association operates in much the same way, except that what appears to be the associative morpheme has the form low tone for the first and second person singular pronouns. This has very widespread parallels, however: in Jukun the same two pronouns and no others have low tone; in Tiv the same two pronouns and no others condition lower tone in one verbal construction; and many other Niger-Congo languages, including Bantu, have low tone for the first and second singular but high tone for the third (though the plural system may be unlike that of Yoruba). The final vowel of the noun is always lengthened in pronominal association; this seems superficially to differ from nominal association, but it actually does not—what follows the "linking" tone is a consonant, and in the occasional cases where that is true in nominal association, vowel lengthening is also found. Yoruba pronominal association is illustrated by the following:

ilé'mi	'my house'	ilé⁻wa	'our house'
ilé'rẹ	'your (sg.) house'	ilé⁻yín	'your (pl.) house'
ilé⁻rẹ̀	'his house'	ilé⁻wọn	'their houses'

A clearer case could hardly be cited for internally reconstructing an associative morpheme which, in an earlier stage of Yoruba, took the form of a vowel with mid tone. There is ample evidence in contemporary Yoruba for loss of a vowel with retention of its tone in a number of combinations.

In discussing the functions of tone and the identification of a class of adjectives in both Igbo and Efik, an associative morpheme consisting of high tone in the underlying structure (and presumably accompanying a vowel in an earlier stage of the languages) has already been identified in 5.19-20 and 9.6-7. In these languages also, it has been observed that numerical and adjectival attribution are expressed by immediate sequence, and are quite distinct from nominal association. It has even been noted that, in Igbo, just as in Bantu, ordinals are expressed by the associative construction with numerals, as in:

> ụ́'lọ́ ('ŋ́ké) 'átọ́   'the third house'
> (cf.: ụ́lọ̀ àtọ́   'three houses')

Tonal evidence for one of the two Igbo demonstratives, however, suggests that they appear in the associative construction. With /áhụ̀/ 'that' there could be no overt realization of the associative morpheme in any case; before /à/ 'this', however, a final low tone in a noun becomes (downstep-)high, an alternation typical of the associative construction. Thus:

> ụ́lọ̀ áhụ̀   'that house', but: ụ́'lọ́ à   'this house'

On the other hand, in Igbo and Efik, like Mande and Akan but unlike Bantu and Yoruba, pronominal possession is expressed without using the associative construction; the tonal alternations typical of the associative are not found in the following Efik examples (a comparison with LoNkundo may be in order, in which /-ka/ rather than /-a/ is used in precisely these contexts):

> úfɔ̀k mì   'my house'   úfɔ̀k ńỹìn   'our house'
> úfɔ̀k fò   'your (sg.) house'   úfɔ̀k m̀bùfò   'your (pl.) house'
> úfɔ̀k ésyĕ   'his house'   úfɔ̀k ḿmɔ̀   'their house'

In Igbo, pronominal possession for the first and second person plural is expressed with independent pronoun forms which are nominal in function; the construction is clearly associative in the first person, though the tones of the second form cannot be diagnostic:

> ụ́'lọ́ 'ányị̀   'our house'   ụ́lọ̀ únù   'your (pl.) house'

For the other four pronouns, however, monosyllabic forms are used which are like the independent pronoun forms, but the associative construction, which would be betrayed by tonal alternations, is not used. E.g.,

> ụ́lọ̀ ḿ   'my house'   ụ́lọ̀ yá   'his house'
> ụ́lọ̀ gị́   'your (sg.) house'   ụ́lọ̀ há   'their house'

After a verbal noun (used in the incompletive and future conconstructions), however, the tonal alternations characteristic of the associative construction are found, as attested by the form of a verbal noun otherwise ending with high-low tone. Thus:

> ọ́ gà èwépụ̀ ḿmà   'he's going to take out a knife'
> ọ́ gà èwé'pụ́ 'yá   'he's going to take it out'

Igbo and Efik thus show a well-defined associative morpheme and construction in nominal association, distinguished from numerical and adjectival attribution. With the highly restricted classes of demonstratives and pronouns, however, there is less complete agreement with many other languages. Pronominal association implies the special category of possession, and the function of demonstratives is also semantically unique, so it is not surprising that inconsistencies in the system would appear with just these types of morphemes.

10.5. Among the Benue-Congo languages other than Bantu and its closest relatives, Jukun is about as unlike Bantu in superficial respects as a language can get. There is no class system in the usual sense, though vestiges of a class system were described in 7.11; there is no pluralization or concord. Jukun has a morpheme /à/ which may very well be cognate with the associative /a/ of Bantu languages, but it is not used in typically associative constructions. It rather functions as a relative marker, as in the following:

> pèrè à bi kéré ní   'the person who came here'
>   (cf.: pèrè ní 'the person', ku bi kéré 'he came here')
> pèrè à fì pǎ (ku) ní   'the person the leopard caught'
>   (cf.: fì pǎ ku 'the leopard caught him')

One combination, however, shows a closer resemblance to Bantu usage. This is the construction of /à/ with a reduplicated verb stem, functioning as an adjectival, which was described in 9.3. This may be compared to the use of an infinitive, which is nominal, in the associative construction in Bantu. E.g.,

> Jukun: zàpè à fìfǎ   'hot water'
>   (cf.: fǎ 'become hot')
> Swahili: chakula cha kutosha 'enough food'
>   (cf.: kutosha 'to suffice')

Ordinary nominal association in Jukun, as well as pronominal possession, involves an entirely different morpheme /bu/. The range of usage, however, is quite similar to that of associatives in Bantu. This morpheme appears in Wàpã as a noun meaning 'thing'; in Dìyī the corresponding noun is apparently a derivation from this, /bwa'/, but the form /bu/ is used to indicate association. As noted in 8.6. this form combines with three pronouns which consist of a vowel only to yield /bú/ 'your (sg.)', /bá/ 'his, her, its', and /bí/ 'our'; the form is not used at all with /m̄/ 'my'. Examples of its use are:

> tété bu bé   'all of them'
> wǔnà bu pèrè ní   'the man's brother'
> yàkě̌ bu tanà   'the back of the house'
> yô bu parà   'the inside of the pot'

As also previously noted, /bu/ is optional in some combinations, apparently primarily when the first noun is personal or locative. Thus, beside the third of the above examples, /yàkě̌ tanà/ was also recorded, though not frequently. Paralleling the last of the above, the phrase /yô kà/ 'the inside of town' must have been heard hundreds of times, but never with /bu/.

The use of a noun meaning 'thing' in associative constructions, with or without another associative morpheme, is not peculiar to Jukun. In Igbo, /ŋkè/ 'thing' is so used in three ways. It is usually used between a noun and a numeral

in ordinal expressions, which are associative; after a noun which ends with high
tone, a numeral alone would be ambiguously cardinal or ordinal in reference.
In simple associatives, /ŋkè/ indicates that the following noun (or possessive
pronoun) is in contrast with other possibilities. It is also used if the preceding
noun is modified so that the associated noun is separated from it. E.g.,

ọŋwá 'ŋké 'átọ̀	'the third month'
ócé ŋkè ńnà ḿ	'my *father*'s chair'
ócé 'dị̌ ọ́hụ́'rụ́ ŋkè ńnà ḿ	'my father's new chair'

Somewhat similarly, the possessive construction in Kpelle may use a relational noun /-wɔ/ between possessor and possession. This noun seems basically to
refer to one's 'share' of something; it is also used, however, to indicate that the
possessor is in contrast with other possible possessors. E.g.,

í wɔ mii-sɛ̂ŋ	'your share of the food, *your* food'
kú wɔ lɔii	'our country (as opposed to others)'

10.6. It was noted in Chapter 8 that languages in all branches of the Afro-
Asiatic family, and some Nilo-Saharan languages, have noun forms labelled "construct." Such forms enter into combinations with semantic ranges very similar
to those of associative constructions in Niger-Kordofanian. In most cases, however, the grammar is interestingly different, and both types of construction differ
also from the use of a genitive case in a language such as Latin. In all three, the
order head-modifier is typical (though not universal, as has been noted for Mande
and Akan, and as is well known in the case of Latin). In most languages with
construct forms, it is the head noun which has a special form; in languages with case
systems, it is the modifier; in languages with associatives, it is neither—the nouns
are rather linked by an additional morpheme. Such an additional morpheme is
found also in Berber, but a construct form is nevertheless required.

In Dho-Luo, there are two alternative possibilities, one using a construct
form and the other more closely resembling a Niger-Kordofanian associative,
using a morpheme /mar/ after the first or head noun. Thus the following pairs
are interchangeable:

diɛndà	∼	dìɛl marà	'my goat'
àgund dhakɔ	∼	àgulu mar dhakɔ	'the woman's pot'

10.7. Among those noun modifiers which are typically excluded from the associative construction in Niger-Kordofanian languages are demonstratives. In
some languages, demonstratives are ludicrously simple; there are two invariable
forms, often monosyllabic, the one meaning 'this' or 'these' and the other meaning 'that' or 'those', with references pretty much as in English. In many more
languages, the demonstratives seem perfectly straightforward at first, but turn
out to involve some subtleties that are not easy to discover.

In Kpelle, the demonstratives /ŋí/ 'this, these' and /tí/ 'that, those' are used
after the specific form of a noun or noun phrase. E.g.,

| pérɛ | 'a house' | 'pérɛi ŋí | 'this house' |
| 'pérɛi | 'the house' | 'pérɛi tí | 'that house' |

There is, however, a third demonstrative, rarely used after a noun, but otherwise used like /ŋí/ and /tí/ with reference to a noun; it seems to have a more general reference, not contrasting an item near at hand or farther away. E.g.,

lé ɓe ŋí	'what is this?'
lé ɓe tí	'what is that?'
lé ɓe ní	'what is it?'

There are also independent or nominal forms of these demonstratives: /nyíŋi/ 'this one, these', /nyíti/ 'that one, those', and /nyíni/ 'it'. Indefinite reference is expressed by a form /'ta/ 'some, a certain', which has some different uses and appears to be a noun.

Akan has two demonstratives with definite reference and one with indefinite reference. They are /yí/ 'this', /nú/ 'that, the', and /bí/ 'some, a certain'. The form /nú/ is also a third person singular pronoun form; in Fante, it is regularly reduced to [ń]. There is no other noun form to indicate definiteness or specificity. The demonstratives have independent or nominal forms /íyí/, /ɔ́nú/, and /òbí/, the last of these restricted in meaning to a personal reference, 'someone'; 'something' is expressed with a noun meaning 'thing': /àsém bí/.

Somewhat similar systems, with minor differences in details of usage, are found in a number of languages. These are, however, by no means the only possibilities. Efik, for example, has a three-way distinction in definite demonstratives, as illustrated by the following:

ébwá ɛ́mì	'this dog'
ébwá órò	'that dog (relatively near)'
ébwá ókò	'that dog (relatively far)'

In Efik and other languages with this type of system, the second demonstrative is commonly used to refer to something in the possession of or near the person addressed, while the third refers to something away from both the speaker and the person addressed. In Efik, the same forms are used nominally:

ɛ́mì ɛ́dì ébwá	'this is a dog'
órò ɛ́dì ébwá	'that (near you) is a dog'
ókò ɛ́dì ébwá	'that (over there) is a dog'

CiBemba has commonly been said to have a four-way distinction in demonstratives: 'this' near the speaker, 'that' near the person addressed, 'this' near both (as 'this room' in which we are), and 'that' away from both. Such a four-way distinction seems entirely reasonable and may appear in some other languages, but a linguistically sophisticated native speaker of CiBemba (Steven P. C. Moyo, personal communication) has made it claer that there is actually a five-way distinction; one distinction has apparently been ignored because recognizing it requires recognizing vowel length and/or tone! The five demonstratives, with class 1 concord, are:

ù-nó	'this' immediately adjacent to or on the speaker
ù-yú	'this' nearer the speaker than the hearer
ù-yóò	'this' equally near or relevant to both
ù-yó	'that' immediately adjacent to or on the hearer
ù-lyà	'that' away from both.

A different kind of distinction appears to be the focus of a contrast in Hausa. Proximity and remoteness are differentiated as in many languages, but in addition there are forms for each which indicate something newly introduced into the conversation and something previously referred to. (Since the latter distinction involves only a contrast in tone, it has been ignored by many who have studied or worked on Hausa.) The following contrasts are found, with explanations believed to represent the semantic distinctions quite closely:

gídán nàn	'this compound (in which we are, or near us)'
gídáǹ nán	'the compound previously mentioned'
gídán càn	'that compound (at a distance)'
gídáǹ cán	'that other compound mentioned earlier'

The form /gídán/ is a masculine construct; /gídáǹ/ is also used by itself as a sort of definite form, not sharply different in usage from the second phrase above. Corresponding to these demonstratives, there are independent nominal forms which may, however, also be used before a noun much like the above forms are used after a noun. In these forms, the feminine construct ending of the first part assimilates to the consonant beginning the last part, resulting in identity with the masculine in the case of the near demonstratives. The forms are:

Masc.	*Fem.*	
wánnàn	wánnàn	'this (newly mentioned)'
wànnán	wànnán	'the one previously mentioned'
wáncàn	wáccàn	'that (newly mentioned)'
wàncán	wàccán	'that other one'

10.8. Languages with noun class systems and concord add a new dimension to demonstratives; class concord is required. In the Bantu languages in general, secondary concords are used. These have been fully illustrated for Swahili in 6.10-11; for purposes of the present discussion, it should particularly be noted that the concords are prefixed for the remote demonstratives, but suffixed for the near demonstratives and for those indicating previous reference. The demonstrative morpheme in the first case is /-le/; for the other two types, /hu- ∼ hi-∼ha-/ is used, and an additional suffix /-o/ specifies previous reference. Thus, using classes 3 and 4 for examples:

ule	'that'	huu	'this'	huo	'the aforesaid'
ile	'those'	hii	'these	hiyo	'the aforesaid'

These forms can all be used independently. Attributively, they may be used either before or after a noun. Before a noun, the first two sets do not have the sharp distinction in reference to proximity; either may usually be translated simply by 'the'. Both imply previous reference or knowledge, but the third set makes previous reference more explicit, and generally seems to refer to something mentioned very shortly before.

Demonstratives for the three locative classes (16, 17, 18) are nominal, and are commonly used as adverb-like complements. The semantic references of the three classes operate independently of the demonstrative distinctions, but in a way that is easily confusing to the beginner. If a speaker of Swahili is asked how to say 'here', he will almost invariably reply with /hapa/ (near demonstrative, class 16). If he is asked how to say 'there', the response will almost always be /kule/ (remote demonstrative, but class 17). Yet every now and then, in conversation, he will say /pale/ (class 16) for 'there', and /huku/ (class 17) for 'here'. The class 18 forms /mle/ and /humu/ are also heard, to say nothing of the previous reference demonstratives for all three classes: /hapo, huko, humo/. The secret to understanding this apparently mixed up system lies in the more specific meanings associated with the three classes. Class 16 (/pa-, -pa/) refers to location in a specific place; the reason /hapa/ is generally given as the first equivalent for 'here' is simply that 'this place' has a tendency to be a very specific place. Class 17 (/ku-, -ku/) refers to location in a general area; the reason /kule/ is generally given as the first equivalent for 'there' is simply that 'that place' or 'over there' is more readily associated with general rather than specific location. But the opposite associations are also possible, and one can also express the meaning of class 18, 'location inside'. A chart of the permutations is as follows, with specific glosses after the chart:

	16	17	18
Remote:	pale	kule	mle
Near:	hapa	huku	humu
Prev. Ref.:	hapo	huko	humo

For remote reference, the three class forms are approximately 'right there, there as opposed to another there', 'over there', and 'in there'. For near reference, they are 'right here', 'around here somewhere', and 'in here'. For previous reference, 'just where we were talking about', 'around where we were talking about', and 'in where we were talking about'.

In short, the apparent simplicity of demonstrative systems in some languages when one first begins is often deceptive. In addition to proximity and remoteness, one must consider locations relative to the speaker and hearer, new versus previous reference, and generality versus specificity (distinguished by classes rather than demonstratives in Swahili)—and possibly other parameters not clearly recognized in some languages. For those who may have occasion to teach an African language to students with a weak background in grammar of any kind, it may be added that an astonishing number of adult native speakers of English are not im-

mediately aware that 'these' is the plural of 'this' and that 'those' is the plural
of 'that'!

10.9. The remaining type of attributives typically excluded from associative constructions is numerals. A class of numerals very commonly includes other quantitative stems with meanings such as 'all', 'some', and 'how many?'. The grammar of numerical—or, more generally, quantitative—attribution as such rarely presents any serious problems. A few details must be mentioned, however, and an outline of some representative systems of numeral structure will be given.

Words with numerical meaning are not necessarily numerals. In Igbo, the words translated as 'one', 'twenty', and 'four hundred' are nouns; in Yoruba, the same is true for 'twenty', 'thirty', and 'two hundred'. Such nouns appear before other nouns in an associative construction; the relevant phrases can be represented by glosses such as 'a unit of . . .', 'a score of . . .'. Numerals, on the other hand, appear after nouns, in immediate sequence when counting is referred to. For example, in Igbo only the last of the following involves a numeral:

ótù	'one'	:	ó'tú 'ákwá	'one egg'
ọ́'gụ́	'twenty'	:	ọ́gụ́ 'ákwá	'twenty eggs'
ńnù	'400'	:	ń'nú 'ákwá	'four hundred eggs'
àtọ́	'three'	:	àkwá 'átọ́	'three eggs'

The same kind of contrast is found in Yoruba also:

| ogún | 'twenty' | : | ogún⁻ọ̀bẹ | 'twenty knives' |
| eéjì | 'two' | : | ọ̀bẹ méjì | 'two eggs' |

In Igbo, additions to 'twenty' follow the noun phrase for 'twenty . . .'. Thus:

| ọ́gụ́ 'ákwá nà isé | 'twenty-five eggs' |
| ọ́gụ́ 'ákwá nà irí nà ótù | 'thirty-one eggs' (+ 10 + 1) |

Multiples of twenty involve the kind of problems of the structure of numeral systems which is the topic of the next sections.

10.10. Straightforward decimal systems, with no extensive adopting of words for numerals from other languages, do not seem to be particularly common in Africa. Perhaps the best example is Akan, with examples here from Fante. The simple numerals up to ten are:

kúr	'one'	èsìắ	'six'
èbìén	'two'	èsón	'seven'
èbàásắ	'three'	àwɔ̀kwí	'eight'
àná	'four'	àkúrún ∼ àkúnú	'nine'
ènúm	'five'	ìdú	'ten'

Expressions for 'eleven' through 'nineteen' are phrases combining 'ten' with whatever is added. The structure of these phrases is similar to that of noun plus numeral, so that it may seem as if multiplication rather than addition is being expressed, except that the plural form for 'ten' is not used. There is a special form for 'one' in the combination meaning 'eleven', using a morpheme */bì/ which appears also in 'two' and 'three' above, but the other numerals are as above except for regular tonal alternations. These phrases are:

dú bá'ákŭ	'eleven'	dú ésí'ǎ	'sixteen'
dú ébí'én	'twelve'	dú é'són	'seventeen'
dú ébá'ásǎ	'thirteen'	dú áwɔ́'kwí	'eighteen'
dú á'ná	'fourteen'	dú á'kúrún	'nineteen'
dú é'núm	'fifteen'		

Multiples of ten are expressed by compounds consisting of the plural of 'ten' and the multiple; alternants of 'two' and 'three' are used, without the morpheme */bì/ mentioned above. The forms for 'twenty' and 'thirty' end with low tone in phrase-final position, but in high tone when another word follows. The form for 'forty' adds a final /n/ when another word follows; in many Akan dialects, 'four' is /ànán/ to begin with. Apart from the prefix characteristic of these compounds, 'forty' through 'seventy' differ only in tone from 'fourteen' through 'seventeen'; 'eighty' and 'ninety' show a distinctive vowel assimilation. These compounds are:

èdùènù	'twenty'	èdùèsìǎ	'sixty'
èdùàsǎ	'thirty'	èdùèsón	'seventy'
èdùànán	'forty'	èdùàwɔ̀kwí	'eighty'
èdùènúm	'fifty'	èdùɔ̀kúrún	'ninety'

Additions to multiples of ten are phrases like those for additions to 'ten'. E.g.,

èdùènú ébí'én   'twenty-two'   èdùànán á'ná   'forty-four'

There is a new unit for 'one hundred', /ɔhá/. Multiples of a hundred are expressed by this word, permissibly in its singular form but commonly in the plural, /àhá/, followed by a numeral; in terms of tonal alternations, these phrases resemble those for addition to multiples of ten, but this time multiplication is involved. Similarly, there is a new unit for 'one thousand', /àpím/, which is multiplied in the same way, using the plural form /m̀pím/. Examples of such multiples are:

àhá é'núm   'five hundred'   m̀pím é'són   'seven thousand'

If a numeral lower than ten is added to one hundred or one thousand, it must be preceded by /ńnà/ 'and', to avoid confusion with multiplication. In all other combinations, /ńnà/ is permissible, but it is also common simply to pause after the thousands and hundreds. Thus:

ɔhá ńnà àwɔ̀kwí	'108'
àhá ébí'én ńnà èdùèsón ∼ àhá ébí'én, èdùèsón	'270'
m̀pím ébí'én, àhá á'ná, èdùènúm ébá'ásǎ	'2,453'

10.11. Swahili has a straightforward decimal system, but it is marked by extensive adoption of numeral words from Arabic. Only the forms for 'one' through 'five', 'eight', and 'ten' are indigenous. The basic units, in their counting forms, are:

moja	'one'	ishirini	'twenty'
mbili	'two'	thelathini	'thirty'
tatu	'three'	arobaini	'forty'
nne	'four'	hamsini	'fifty'
tano	'five'	sitini	'sixty'
sita	'six'	sabini	'seventy'
saba	'seven'	themanini	'eighty'
nane	'eight'	tisini	'ninety'
tisa	'nine'	mia	'hundred'
kumi	'ten'	elfu	'thousand'

Additions to multiples of ten are introduced by /na/ 'and'; higher combinations are marked by pauses after the thousands and hundreds. E.g.,

elfu mbili, mia nne, hamsini na tatu   '2,453'

The numerals 'one' through 'five' and 'eight', when used attributively, take class concord; the remaining numerals do not. In numerals higher than ten, the same forms require concord even though they appear at the end of the numeral phrase. Thus:

watu watano	'five people'
miaka miwili	'two years'
miaka ishirini na miwili	'twenty-two years'

The counting forms listed above are class 9 noun forms.

10.12. LuGanda has what is basically a decimal system, but the forms for 'hundred' and 'thousand' are derived from 'ten' by a change of class. Within every set of ten or its multiples, 'one' through 'five' operate in the same way; there is some system, though not complete consistency, above five. In their counting forms, 'one' through 'five' are in class 9; 'six' through 'nine' are in class 3; 'ten' is in class 5. These forms are:[3]

èmû	'one'	mùkáàgá	'six'
bbírì	'two'	mùsánvú	'seven'
ssátù	'three'	mùnáánâ	'eight'
nnyǎ	'four'	mwèndâ	'nine'
ttáànó	'five'	kkúmì	'ten'

[3] I am indebted to Beatrice F. Welmers for the transcription of LuGanda numerals with full indication of tone. In spite of the amount of publication on LuGanda, some of it very good, no comprehensive treatment of the numerals with tone indicated was found.

In attributive use, only 'one' through 'five' require concord. 'Six' through 'ten' are invariable, which makes it possible to use their stems in other classes for tens, hundreds, and thousands. This sets up a sharp division between 'one' through 'five' on the one hand, and higher numerals on the other hand, as multipliers. For 'twenty' through 'fifty', a class 6 plural of 'ten' is used, /àmàkúmì/; the multipliers take class 6 secondary concord (not primary as might be expected from usage in many other Bantu languages). For 'sixty' and 'seventy', tens are not separately expressed; class 10 forms of 'six' and 'seven' are used. For 'eighty' 'ninety', and 'one hundred', class 7 forms of 'eight', 'nine', and 'ten' are used. Thus the multiples of ten through a hundred are:

àmàkúmì àbírì	'twenty'	ǹkáàgá	'sixty'
àmàkúmì àsátù	'thirty'	ǹsánvú	'seventy'
àmàkúmì ànâ	'forty'	kìnáánâ	'eighty'
àmàkúmí àtáànó	'fifty'	kyèndâ	'ninety'
		kìkúmí	'one hundred'

In the first four of the above, the 'tens', /àmàkúmì/, are redundant in most contexts, and are not expressed; the class 6 forms of the multiples are distinctive. There is one exception; in modifying a noun which is already class 6, forms like /àbírì/ could refer either to the noun or to the otherwise unexpressed tens. To distinguish 'twenty' from 'two' etc. after a Class 6 noun, /àmàkúmì/ must be used. Thus:

èmìsótà àbírì	'twenty snakes (4)'
èmìsótà èbírì	'two snakes'
àmàggí àbírì	'two eggs (6)'
àmàggí àmàkúmì àbírì	'twenty eggs'

'One hundred', as noted above, is class 7. The first five multiples of a hundred use the corresponding class 8 plural form with concordial multipliers. Again, the hundreds are redundant except after a class 8 noun. 'Six hundred' through 'one thousand' are expressed by class 11 forms of 'six' through 'ten'. The multiples of a hundred are:

èbìkúmì bìbírì	'200'	lùkáàgá	'600'
èbìkúmì bìsátù	'300'	lùsánvú	'700'
èbìkúmì bìnâ	'400'	lùnáánâ	'800'
èbìkúmì bìtánò	'500'	lwèndâ	'900'
		lùkúmì	'1,000'

The first five multiples of a thousand use the class 10 form of 'ten' (the usual plural of class 11) with concordial multipliers. 'Six thousand' through 'eight thousand' are class 14 forms of 'six' through 'eight'; 'nine thousand' is the class 9 form of 'nine'. Thus:

ènkúmì bbírì	'2,000'	kàkáàgá	'6,000'
ènkúmì ssátù	'3,000'	kàsánvú	'7,000'
ènkúmì nnyâ	'4,000'	kànáánâ	'8,000'
ènkúmì ttáànó	'5,000'	kkèèndâ	'9,000'

So far, the entire numeral system has been based on the first ten digits, with the device of class membership to distinguish digits, tens, hundreds, and thousands. Now a new unit is introduced: /mùtwáàlò/ 'ten thousand'. This is a normal class 3 form, and pluralizes in class 4, /mìtwáàlò/. Multiples are expressed by the usual concordial multipliers.

Additions to ten are introduced by /nà/ 'and', but additions to multiples and derivatives of ten, and to ten thousands, are introduced by /mù/, which may be a concordial morpheme of class 18. Thus at least ten and perhaps eleven classes figure in the structure of numeral forms, in addition to which 'one' through 'five' require concord with a head noun. If an example like the following is fully understood, the entire system is not difficult to master; here the noun is in class 6, plural of class 5, the form for 'eighty' is in class 7 because that is its invariable class, and the form for 'one' is in class 5 to agree with the singular form of the initial noun:

àmàggí kìnáánâ mù lìmû   'eighty-one eggs'

This is a convenient place to add a completely irrelevant but amusing detail of historical linguistics. The class 5 singular form meaning 'egg' in LuGanda is /èggí/; LuGanda is spoken in what was formerly a British protectorate. The Herero form for 'egg' is /ei/; Herero is spoken in what was for many years German Southwest Africa. That these words were adopted from English and German respectively seems almost transparent—but they were not; both are traceable through demonstrable phonetic changes to the same proto-Bantu form.

10.13. Like Swahili, Hausa has a fairly straightforward decimal system with heavy adopting from Arabic. In particular, the multiples of ten are taken from Arabic. The basic forms are:

dáyá	'one'	àshìrín	'twenty'
bíyú	'two'	tàlâtín	'thirty'
úkù	'three'	àrbàʔín	'forty'
húɗú	'four'	hàmsín	'fifty'
bìyár	'five'	sìttín	'sixty'
shídà	'six'	sàbàʔín	'seventy'
bákwài	'seven'	tàmânín	'eighty'
tákwàs	'eight'	tàsàʔín ~ càsàʔín ~ tìsʔín	'ninety'
táȓà	'nine'		
gómà	'ten'	dàrí	'one hundred'

For 'two hundred', a new unit, /mètán/, is commonly used. For 'three hundred' through 'five hundred', phrases of Arabic origin are fairly common. For all multiples of a hundred, however, simple sequences of /dàrí/ and the appropriate digit may be used. For 'one thousand', /dúbú/ is the commonest form, but /zámbàr/ and the Arabic /àlfín/ are also heard. The second of these is common in the multiple for 'two thousand'.

Additions to 'ten' are introduced by a morpheme /shâ/, which is nowhere else used for 'and' or 'plus', but confined to the phrases for 'eleven' through 'nineteen'. Additions to all higher units are introduced by /dà/, the usual word for 'and'.

Although the Hausa numeral system is thus decimal with few problems, there is evidence from other Chadic languages of a system in which numerals above five are based on additions of five and the lower numbers. This, as will be seen, is very common in the Niger-Congo languages of West Africa.

10.14. Kpelle clearly shows the use of 'five' as a base for 'six' through 'nine', but in other respects has a decimal system, with adopted words for 'hundred' and 'thousand'. The counting forms through ten are:

táaŋ	'one'	m̀ɛi 'ta	'six'
'feerɛ	'two'	m̀ɛi feerɛ	'seven'
'saaɓa	'three'	m̀ɛi saaɓa	'eight'
ǹáaŋ	'four'	m̀ɛi náaŋ	'nine'
ǹɔɔlu	'five'	puu	'ten'

All but the first and last of these appear with prefixed low tone, which in general indicates previous reference. The form for 'one' above is used only in counting; in attribution and in phrases where one is added to ten or a multiple of ten, a form /tɔnɔ/ is used. The absence of prefixed low tone with 'ten' is significant for the nature of counting, and counting multiples of ten is very common in measuring rice by the pint (= pound), or in counting oranges. Basically, the counting goes 'a unit, two of them, three of them, . . ., nine of them, a ten', and then the counter adds, /'puu tɔnɔ/ 'one ten of them'. That is filed away for future reference, and the counting is repeated exactly as above, through /puu/ 'a ten', to which is then added, /'puu feerɛ/ 'two tens of them'. The same procedure is repeated up to a hundred, for which the form /ŋɔ̀ndɔ/, adopted from English 'hundred' is used.

In the forms for 'six' through 'nine' given above, the first word is from a relational noun /-mɛi/, referring to the area over something; it will here be represented by 'superior'. The form /'ta/ in 'six' elsewhere means 'some, a certain'. The previous reference in /m̀ɛi/ is to the preceding 'five'. Thus the forms are reflected by 'a superior of it (five), two of its superiors, three of its superiors, four of its superiors'.

In attributive use, the prefixed low tones used in counting do not appear. Further, 'five' must be expressed in the combinations for 'six' through 'nine'. Thus:

pérɛ tɔnɔ	'one house'	pérɛ lɔɔlu mɛi 'ta	'six houses'
pérɛ feerɛ	'two houses'	pérɛ lɔɔlu mɛi feerɛ	'seven houses'
pérɛ saaɓa	'three houses'	pérɛ lɔɔlu mɛi saaɓa	'eight houses'
pérɛ náaŋ	'four houses'	pérɛ lɔɔlu mɛi náaŋ	'nine houses'
pérɛ lɔɔlu	'five houses'	pérɛ puu	'ten houses'

Additions to ten are introduced by a morpheme /káu/, which is not used elsewhere in the meaning 'and' or 'plus'; it is homophonous with, and may be the same morpheme as, a relational noun meaning 'kernel'. Multiples of ten are simple sequences of /puu/ and the appropriate lower digit. The following examples use prefixed low tone because there is no expressed noun:

'puu káu lɔ́ɔlu	'fifteen of them'
'puu feerɛ	'twenty of them'
'puu saaɓa kau lɔ́ɔlu mɛi 'ta	'thirty-six of them'

In addition to the adopted form /ŋɔ̀ndɔ/ 'hundred', it is reported that elderly people once used /-ŋuŋ/ 'head' in the same meaning. The reference was to a 'head' or cluster of palm nuts; at a rough glance, the pile of palm nuts that can be removed from a single cluster is suggestive of about a hundred. In 1946-1948, no informant could cite any higher unit than a hundred, but under the necessities imposed by Bible translation, and specifically at the suggestion of intelligent informants who happened to know the word, the form /wála/ 'a thousand' has been adopted from Mandekan; the "Mandingo" speakers of Mandekan in Liberia, mostly traders, were about the only people who had occasion to talk about thousands—especially thousands of dollars.

Although the numeral system of a language such as Kpelle may seem awkward, it can be mastered. American currency is used in Liberia, but until recently (with the gradual adoption of /dâla/ 'dollar' and /kwɔ̂ta/ 'twenty-five cents'), as a hangover from earlier days, currency was counted in the terminology of sterling. Value equivalents date from the time when a pound was $4.00 and a shilling 20c; Kpelle has special terms for the equivalents of 5c, 10c, and 15c. With practice, it has proven possible to learn to snap back with the Kpelle sterling terminology and numerals for amounts like the price of ninety-eight pounds of rice at seven and one-half cents per pound—in about three seconds:

pâu tɔ̀nɔ, sêleŋ puu káu lɔ́ɔlu mɛi 'ta, éetĭ.

10.15. Jukun also shows a use of five as a base numeral. In addition, twenty forms the base for multiplication, so that the system is vigesimal. The form for 'twenty' is related to the word for 'body', and in multiples the phrase explicitly refers to the body of a person. In some other languages as well, 'twenty' is expressed by a phrase referring to something like 'the whole person', presumably with reference to the physical digits. 'Five', however, is rarely if ever expressed with a recognizable word meaning 'hand'; 'ten', to my knowledge, is never expressed as 'two hands'; and I know of no language in which the numeral system refers explicitly to the feet. Yet the reference to the totality of physical digits in connection with twenty is significant. Of course, the association of the fingers with counting is obvious, perhaps in every culture. Verbalizing such an association is not common, but it is understandable; it is not, as the remarks of some observers seem to suggest, evidence of a "primitive" culture or a low level of mental evolution.

The precise derivational processes forming numerals on the base five in Jukun is obscure and irregular, but there are clearly some relationships between numerals below and above five. In Dìyī, the numeral 'ten' is strangely anomalous. Dìyī has a few words with final /m/, but /ádup/ 'ten' is the only known word in the language with any other final consonant. It hardly seems likely that it is of foreign origin, though it may perhaps have been adopted from Efik /dwòp/. In counting, all numerals begin with a prefix /á-/; in attributive use after a noun, the vowel of this prefix does not appear, but its tone is retained after mid or low. The Dìyī and Wàpã forms through ten are as follows:

Dìyī	Wàpã	
ázū	ázū	'one'
ápìnà	ápyìnà	'two'
ásara	átsara	'three'
áyēna	áyēna	'four'
ásōna	átswãna	'five'
ásyìdyī	átyìdyē	'six'
ásyìpì	átsǔpyì	'seven'
ánìni	átsǔtsa	'eight'
átâni	átsǔyō	'nine'
ádup	ádzwe	'ten'

Additions to ten are introduced by different morphemes in the two dialects or languages, as follows:

Dìyī	Wàpã	
ádup kpã́ zū	ádzwe wǎ'zū	'eleven'
ádup kpã́ sara	ádzwe wǎ'tsara	'thirteen'

Forms for 'twenty', and further additions and multiplications, are as follows:

ádì zū	ádì zū	'twenty'
ádì zū kpã́ pìnà	ádì zū wǎ'pyìna	'twenty-two'
ádì zū kpã́ dup	ádì zū kyà'dzwe	'thirty'
ádì pèrè'pìnà	ádì pà'pyìnà	'forty'
ádì pèrè'sōna	ádì pà'tswãna	'one hundred'
ádì pèrè'nìni	ádì pà'tsǔtsa	'one hundred sixty'
ádì pèrè'dup	ádì pà'dzwe	'two hundred'

Counting higher than two hundred was not thoroughly investigated. In Dìyī, another expression for 'hundred' was recorded, /kùsá (górò)/ 'a gourd-full (of kola nuts)', which can also be multiplied. This is not generally accepted, however, in counting persons. In Wàpã, /àsyùkú/ 'a bag (-full)' is used for a hundred kola nuts, but not for other objects.

Attributively, the form /zū/ 'one', without its prefix, is used for 'some, any, a certain'. With the tone of the prefix retained after low or mid, and frequently reduplicated as /ázūzū/, it has the specific numerical meaning 'one'.

10.16. Igbo also shows some evidence of the use of five as a base for the next higher numerals, though again in an obscure pattern. The derivation of the various forms for 'nine', used in different dialects and sometimes alternatively by the same person, are unknown, but may originally have alluded to one missing from ten. Igbo also uses twenty as a base for higher multiplication. As previously noted, however, the Igbo words for 'one' and 'twenty' are nouns, not numerals. Twenty is multiplied up to nineteen times, and then there is a new unit meaning 'four hundred'. The numeral 'two' has different forms for counting and attribution; the latter is seen in the phrase for 'forty' below. In counting, the basic units, patterns of addition, and patterns of multiplication are summarized in the following:

ótù	'one'	ìrí nà ótù	'eleven'
àbụ́'á	'two'	ìrí nà ìsé	'fifteen'
àtọ́	'three'	ọ́'gụ́	'twenty'
ànọ́	'four'	ọ́'gụ́ nà àtọ́	'twenty-three'
ìsé	'five'	ọ́'gụ́ nà ìrí	'thirty'
ìsíì	'six'	ọ́gú náàbọ̀	'forty'
àsáà	'seven'	ọ́gú náàbọ̀ nà ìrí nà ótù	'fifty-one'
àsá'tọ́	'eight'	ọ́gụ́ 'írí	'two hundred'
ìtèná'ánị ∼ ìtéghéíté		ọ́gụ́ 'írí nà ìtèná'ánị	'three hundred
∼ ìtóó'lú	'nine'	nà ìrí nà ìtèná'ánị	ninety-nine'
ìrí	'ten'	ńnù̀	'four hundred'

Four hundreds can be multiplied like twenties; /ńnù̀/ is also grammatically a noun.

Atributively, numerals are used after a noun, with regular tonal alternations. The nouns /ótù/, /ọ́'gụ́/, and /ńnù̀/ are used before another noun in an associative construction. For figures higher than twenty, the remainder of the numerical expression follows the noun. Thus:

ó'tụ́ ḿ'mádù	'one person'
ṁmádù náàbọ̀	'two people'
ṁmádù àsá'tọ́	'eight people'
ṁmádù ìrí nà àsá'tọ́	'eighteen people'
ọ́gú ḿ'mádù	'twenty people'
ọ́gú ḿ'mádù nà ìrí	'thirty people'
ọ́gú ḿ'mádù ìrí nà ótù	'two hundred twenty people'

The last of the above may seem to be ambiguous; could not the 'one' refer to one person more than the 'two hundred people', rather than being added only to 'ten' to express 'eleven score of people'? Only the latter can be intended. To express anything from 'two hundred one' to 'two hundred nineteen', the noun must be repeated. Compare the following:

ọ́gú ḿ'mádù ìrí nà àsá'tọ́	'360'
ọ́gú ḿ'mádù ìrí nà ṁmádù àsá'tọ́	'208'

10.17. In Efik, the base five is more clearly and consistently used. 'Six' 'seven', and 'eight' are clearly combinations of 'five' with 'one', 'two', and 'three'; 'nine' contains the form for 'one', and apparently refers to one less than ten. There is a new unit for ten, and another new unit for fifteen; the stems for 'one' through 'four' are joined to these by /è/, which is probably a contraction of /yè/ 'and'. There is another new unit for twenty. Counting up to this point is as follows:

kyèt	'one'	dwòp-è-kyèt	'eleven'
ìbà	'two'	dwòp-è-bà	'twelve'
ìtá	'three'	dwòp-è-tá	'thirteen'
ìnàŋ	'four'	dwòp-è-nàŋ	'fourteen'
ìtyôn	'five'	èfít	'fifteen'
ìtyôkyèt	'six'	èfít-è-kyèt	'sixteen'
ìtyâbà	'seven'	èfít-è-bà	'seventeen'
ìtyâìtá	'eight'	èfít-è-tá	'eighteen'
ùsúk-kyèt	'nine'	èfít-è-nàŋ	'nineteen'
dwòp	'ten'	édíp	'twenty'

Any combination through 'nineteen' may be added to 'twenty' after the full form /yè/ 'and':

édíp yè kyèt	'twenty-one'
édíp yè ìtyôkyèt	'twenty-six'
édíp yè dwòp-è-bà	'thirty-two'
édíp yè èfít-è-nàŋ	'thirty-nine'

'Forty', 'sixty', and 'eighty', multiples of twenty, are derived from 'two', 'three', and 'four' by using a different prefix, /à-/ rather than /ì-/. (Compare the closely similar but more fully developed pattern in LuGanda, 10.12 above.) There is a new unit for one hundred, which may be multiplied by digits through nine (quite likely through nineteen among older people). Beyond '999', younger informants use the adopted form /tɔ́sìn/ for 'one thousand', and multiply it. These higher patterns are illustrated by the following:

àbà	'forty'
àbà yè dwòp	'fifty'
àbà yè èfít-è-bà	'fifty-seven'
àtá	'sixty'
àtá yè dwòp-è-tá	'seventy-three'
ànàŋ	'eighty'
ànàŋ yè èfít-è-nàŋ	'ninety-nine'
íkyê	'100'
íkyê yè àbà yè dwòp	'150'
íkyê ìbà yè àtá yè èfít	'275'

10.18. Five and twenty appear to be common bases also in the Gur languages, but there are some interesting differences among the known systems at higher

levels. In Bariba, 'one' follows class concord, but no other numerals do. The
counting forms through 'ten' are as follows:

tiā	'one'	nɔɔbâ tiā	'six'
yìru	'two'	nɔɔbá yìru	'seven'
yìta	'three'	nɔɔbá yìta	'eight'
ǹnɛ	'four'	nɔɔbá ǹnɛ	'nine'
nɔɔbù	'five'	ɔkuru	'ten'

There are new units for 'twenty' and 'thirty'. 'Forty' introduces a new
morpheme for 'twenty', multiplied by 'two'. Alternant forms of the same morpheme are multiplied by 'three' through 'five'; the multiplying forms of the
numerals 'two' through 'four' suggest that the first part of the full forms may
be a prefix—class 9? These forms are:

yɛndu	'twenty'	wàta	'sixty'
tɛnā	'thirty'	wɛnɛ	'eighty'
weeru	'forty'	wɔnɔbù	'one hundred'

Additions to 'ten', 'twenty', and 'forty' resemble those to 'five' as illustrated above. Additions to the remainder of the above units are introduced
by a morpheme /kà/. Thus:

ɔkurá tiā	'eleven'	tɛná kà yìta	'thirty-three'
yɛndá nɔɔbù kà yìru	'twenty-seven'	wàtá kà ɔkuru	'seventy'
werá àkuru	'fifty'	wɛnɛ́ kà ɔkuru	'ninety'

Additions to one hundred, up to nineteen, are introduced by /kà/. Then,
with a new structure for addition, twenty and higher combinations are added.
There is another new morpheme for 'twenty' in the combination 'one hundred
twenty' only. 'Two hundred' is a new unit. Thus:

wɔnɔbù kà ɔkuru	'110'	wɔnaà weerú kà ɔkuru	'150'
wɔnaà teèru	'120'	wɔnaà wàta	'160'
wɔnaà teèrú kà ɔkuru	'130'	wɔnaà wɛnɛ	'180'
wɔnaà weeru	'140'	goòbu	'200'

Just as a new form for 'twenty' is used when multiplying begins, so a new
form for 'two hundred' is used for its multiples. Thus:

goobá wɔnɔbù	'300'	nàtá kà wɔnɔbù	'700'
nɛɛru	'400'	nɛnɛ	'800'
nɛɛrá wɔnɔbù	'500'	nɛnɛ́ kà wɔnɔbù	'900'
nàta	'600'	nɔrɔbù	'1000'

The forms /goòbu/ 'two hundred' and /nɔrɔbù/ 'thousand' may perhaps be
derived from unique units for 'forty' and 'two hundred' multiplied by 'five'. If
so, a new unit would be expected for 'two thousand', which would enter into
comparable multiplications and additive phrases. The pattern of multiplying by
two through five, and no more, seems completely consistent.

10.19. In Senari, five again functions as a base for the next higher numerals, but not with as simple a pattern as in Bariba. The numerals through ten are:

nìbí	'one'	kɔrɔ́ni	'six'
sī	'two'	kɔrɔ́sī	'seven'
tãri	'three'	kɔrɔ́tãri	'eight'
sityɛrɛ	'four'	kpǎídyɛrɛ	'nine'
kagulò	'five'	kɛ́	'ten'

There is a new unit for 'twenty', which is multiplied by 'two' through 'four' and by 'six' through 'nine', but not by 'five'; there is a special form for 'one hundred'. There is a new phrase for 'two hundred', apparently adopted from Mandekan; but another morpheme for 'two hundred' is used for multiplying. Although sample forms were not recorded beyond about six hundred, this may well form the base for phrases up to 1,999; a new unit for 2,000 would be expected, though the system may revert to a decimal base after a thousand. The types of multiples recorded are as follows:

tòkò	'twenty'	tòkò èkɔrɔ́sī	'140'
tòkò èsī	'forty'	tòkò èkɔrɔ́tãri	'160'
tòkò ètãri	'sixty'	tòkò èkpǎídyɛrɛ	'180'
tòkò èsityɛrɛ	'eighty'	sìrà kélé	'200'
dàbàtà	'100'	sàlà sī	'400'
tòkò èkɔrɔ́ni	'120'	sàlà tãri	'600'

All additions to ten and higher numerals are introduced by /ní/, except that /dàbàtà/ is recorded as added without this morpheme. There is a different morpheme for 'ten' in additions to 'twenty' and higher numerals. Sample additions are:

kɛ́ ní nìbí	'eleven'
kɛ́ ní kpǎídyɛrɛ	'ninety'
tòkò ní sī	'twenty-two'
tòkò ní kpɔrɔ̀gɔ̀	'thirty'
tòkò èsī ní kpɔrɔ̀gɔ̀ ní kpǎídyɛrɛ	'fifty-nine'
tòkò èsityɛrɛ ní kpɔrɔ̀gɔ̀ ní kpǎídyɛrɛ	'ninety-nine'
dàbàtà ní kpɔrɔ̀gɔ̀	'110'
tòkò èkpǎídyɛrɛ ní kpɔrɔ̀gɔ̀ ní kpǎídyɛrɛ	'199'
sìrà kélé ní tòkò ètãri	'260'
sàlà sī ní tòkò èkɔrɔ́ni	'520'

10.20. Suppire is closely related to Senari, and the numerals up to ten are clearly cognate, though addition to five is differently formed. These numerals are:

niŋkī	'one'	bááni	'six'
syuŋini	'two'	báásyuŋini	'seven'
tããri	'three'	báátããri	'eight'
sìtyiere	'four'	báárítyiere	'nine'
kaŋkuro	'five'	kɛ́	'ten'

Numerals involving multiplication, however, are remarkably different from those in Senari. There is a unit 'twenty', which is multiplied only by 'two' and 'three'. There is then a new unit 'eighty', unparalleled in any other language discussed up to this point, which is multiplied by 'two', 'three', and 'four'. Between 'two eighties' and 'three eighties', there is a special form for 'two hundred', which is used only for adding 'one' through 'thirty-nine (20 plus 10 plus 9)'. Unfortunately this form was not recorded. After 'four eighties', there is a new unit for 'four hundred', also not recorded, though heard and used in some combinations. This is also multiplied, but in this rarified atmosphere the informant began to get confused. He said he was quite sure that there is another higher new unit; it probably has the value of 'two thousand'. The recorded multiples are as follows:

bényɛgɛ	'twenty'	ŋkúù syuŋini	'160'
bé syuŋini	'forty'	ŋkúù tãári	'240'
bé tãári	'sixty'	ŋkúù rítyiere	'320'
ŋkúù	'eighty'		

Addition is regularly introduced by /ná/:

kɛ́ ná syuŋini	'twelve'
bényɛgɛ ná báárityiere	'twenty-nine'
bényɛgɛ ná kɛ́ ná kaŋkuro	'thirty-five'
bé syuŋini ná kɛ́ ná bááni	'fifty-six'
ŋkúù ná bényɛgɛ	'100'
ŋkúù syuŋini ná bényɛgɛ ná kɛ́ ná báárityiere	'199'
ŋkúù rítyiere ná bé tãári ná kɛ́ ná báárityiere	'399'

$$(80 \times 4 + 20 \times 3 + 10 + 5 + 4)$$

You'd get confused too! Actually, if one can get away from thinking in a decimal system, this system is not particularly difficult to handle; there is very little irregularity in the patterns of multiplication and addition.

10.21. For sheer complexity or at least difficulty for the learner, however, it is hard to beat the Yoruba numeral system.[4] Even in counting up to ten, there are two sets of forms, though neither set is particularly difficult in itself. The simpler set—though not the one more commonly used—has prefixes consisting of a vowel with low tone. The second set has prefixes consisting of a double vowel with the tone sequence mid-high. This set is said to be a contraction of the noun /owó/ 'money' (originally referring to cowrie shells) with the numerals, but all that is left of the noun is its tones. Used attributively after other nouns, 'one' appears with no prefix; the remaining forms have a prefix consisting of /m-/ and a vowel with high tone. The tonal alternations in stems are regular; the first set must be considered basic to the others. The three sets are:

[4] Yoruba numerals are fully though less systematically outlined in Abraham 1958, pp. xxxii-xxxix. To a large extent, this forms the basis for a treatment by Armstrong (1962), which includes a suggested decimal system for Yoruba. For information on phonology and tonology, see 4.27.

̀v-	v́-	m̀v-	
̀òkan	oókān	kān	'one'
èjì	eéjì	méjì	'two'
̀ẹta	ẹ́ẹ́tā	mẹ́tā	'three'
èrin	ẹ́ẹ́rīn	mẹ́rīn	'four'
àrún	aárŭn	márŭn	'five'
̀ẹfà	ẹ́ẹ́fà	mẹ́fà	'six'
èje	eéjē	méjē	'seven'
̀ẹjọ	ẹ́ẹ́jọ̄	mẹ́jọ̄	'eight'
̀ẹsán	ẹ́ẹ́sǎn	mẹ́sǎn	'nine'
̀ẹwá	ẹ́ẹ́wǎ	mẹ́wǎ	'ten'

There are new units for 'twenty' and 'thirty'. 'Forty' and higher multiples of twenty, through nine twenties, combine an alternant form of 'twenty' (with subalternations conditioned by the following vowel) with the stem of the appropriate digit. All of these are nouns, used before another noun in an associative construction. The forms are:

ogún	'twenty'	ọgọ́rŭn	'100'
ọgbọ̀n	'thirty'	ọgọ́fà	'120'
ogójì	'forty'	ogójē	'140'
ọgọ́tā	'sixty'	ọgọ́jọ̄	'160'
ọgọ́rīn	'eighty'	ọgọ́sǎn	'180'

Odd multiples of ten, beginning with 'fifty', represent subtractions from the next higher multiple of twenty. A great deal of contraction has gone into these forms, but the end result is a regular pattern. These forms are also nouns. They are:

àádọ́tā	'fifty'	àádójē	'130'
àádọ́rīn	'seventy'	àádójọ̄	'150'
àádọ́rŭn	'ninety'	àádọ́sǎn	'170'
àádọ́fà	'110'		

The digits 'one' through 'four' are added to 'ten' or any of its multiples. The digit comes first, but its stem has an alternant with low tone in every case. Addition is then expressed by /lé l''/; /l''/ (the apostrophe is morphophonemic) is a regular alternant of /ní/ before vowels other than /i/. The combination of this with 'ten' involves further contraction, but the other combinations are regular. The attributive forms of these combinations, used after nouns as the simple digits are, begin with /m-/ followed by a vowel with high tone. This is true even for additions of 'one', which begin with /mọ́-/, though 'one' by itself has no prefix when used attributively. Some examples of these additions are:

oókàn l'àá	'eleven'
eéjì l'àá	'twelve'
ẹ́ẹ́tà l'àá	'thirteen'
ẹ́ẹ́rìn l'àá	'fourteen'

eéjì lé l'ógún	'twenty-two'
ẹẹ́tà lé l'ọ́gbọ̀n	'thirty-three'
ẹẹ́rìn lé l'ógójì	'forty-four'
oókàn lé l'âádọ́tā	'fifty-one'
eéjì lé l'ọ́gọ́sǎn	'182'

The digits from 'five' down to 'one' are subtracted from the next higher multiple of ten. Again the digit comes first, and its stem has an alternant with low tone. Subtraction is then expressed by /dín l''/. Thus:

aárùn dín l'ógún	'fifteen'
eérìn dín l'ógún	'sixteen'
eétà dín l'ógún	'seventeen'
eéjì dín l'ógún	'eighteen'
oókàn dín l'ógún	'nineteen'
oókàn dín l'ọ́gọ́sǎn	'179'

An irregularity is introduced in the combinations for '185' through '189'. These are additions to '180'. The form for 'nine twenties' come first. Addition is expressed by /ólé/. The following digit has the form used attributively, with /m-/ followed by a vowel with high tone. Although 'nine twenties' is used as a noun, these combinations are used attributively after a noun, without modification of prefix. A sample of these forms is:

| ọgọ́sǎn ólé márǔn | '185' |
| ọgọ́sǎn ólé méjè | '187' |

There is a new unit /igba/ for 'two hundred'. Combinations for '190' through '199' are subtractions of 'ten' down to 'one' from this unit. The form /igba/ comes first. Subtraction is expressed by /ódín/. The digit follows in its attributive form. The unit /igba/ is another noun, and like other nouns with numerical meaning is used before a noun in an associative construction. In the subtractive combinations, /igba/ still precedes the noun counted, and the rest of the combination follows. Examples of this group are:

igba ódín méwǎ	'190'
igba ódín métā	'197'
igba ọkùnrin ódín méjì	'198 men'

The foregoing carries the outline of the Yoruba numeral system only through 'two hundred'. All of the information is accessible in the sources cited, but the above treatment organizes the system in a new way, which quite clearly is also of pedagogical value. The system as such is best seen by starting with one through ten, then going on to twenty and its multiples (along with thirty), subtractions of ten from multiples of twenty, additions of one through four to all decimal combinations, subtractions of five down to one from the same, and finally the subsystems found in 185 to 200. For higher numbers, the same types of formation are found, although new multiples of twenty are used. Starting with 320, multiples

of twenty are subtracted from a new unit for 'four hundred'. Still higher, multiples of 'two hundred' are used. The interplay of addition, subtraction, and
multiplication is not entirely consistent, and continues to involve a great deal
of contraction. Details can be found in the sources cited.

While discussing this with a Nigerian who has spoken Yoruba from child-
hood, though as a language of second choice, the dry remark was made, "Any
Yoruba who knows some English tries very hard to avoid the Yoruba numeral
system." So what else is new? Actually, of course, any of the systems that has
been described is perfectly viable for the purposes for which it was used in African
cultures prior to extensive European influence. Items, especially cowrie shells
and kola nuts, were counted seriatim, which is not difficult to learn to do. There
was, however, little occasion to cite specific large numbers out of a counting context, or to practice arithmetic operations extensively. Even at that, arithmetic
is by no means impossible using these systems; the great difficulty is merely in
translating from one of them to ours or vice versa.

10.22. The foregoing sections have covered types of noun modifiers that are
common to languages in general—possessives, demonstratives, and numerals. In
many languages, possessives have been seen to be only a special usage of an associative construction. What such modifiers modify may be considered the head
or core of a noun phrase. Such heads, however, are themselves not always single
words. A few illustrations will suggest how they may be defined; problems of
analysis in individual languages are usually minimal.

In Igbo, it is convenient to treat phrases consisting of two (or occasionally
more) nouns in the associative construction as single nouns. This is particularly
true in the case of one type of combination in which the second noun is derived
from a verb. Such nouns, referring to actions, are derived in two ways, depending
on whether the origin is a monosyllabic verb stem or a verb base of two or more
syllables. In the former case, there is a prefix /ò-/ or /ọ̀-/, and the verb stem is
reduplicated, the reduplicating syllable taking a high vowel. In the latter case,
there is a nasal prefix with high tone preceding the verb base. These derived
nouns are rarely used except in the associative construction. Some examples are:

ị'ŋụ́	'drink'	:	ihé 'ọ́ŋụ́ŋụ́	'something to drink'
ị'tá	'bite, eat'	:	ihé 'ọ́tịtá	'a snack'
i'ré	'sell'	:	ihé 'óríré	'something for sale'
ị'mùtà	'learn'	:	ihé ḿmụ̀tá	'lesson, assignment'
ị'kúzí	'teach'	:	ónyé ŋ́kúzí	'teacher'

These, of course, themselves consist of a one-word noun (/íhé/, /ónyé/ in
these cases) with an associative modifier. The head of a noun phrase may also
consist of two or more words in other relationships. Again in Igbo, noun phrases
are derived from phrases consisting of verb and object, indicating the customary
performer of the action indicated. In such derivations, there is a prefix /ò-/ or
/ọ̀-/, followed by the verb stem with high tone (even if it has low tone lexically),
followed by a downstep (realized only before high tone, of course). This is a

tonally unique formation in Igbo, and must be defined as a tonally realized morpheme deriving such nouns. Some such derivations are:

í'té + égwú			'dance' :	òté 'égwú		'dancer'
í'ŋú	'drink',	m̀mányá	'booze' :	ǫ̀ŋú 'm̀mányá		'drunkard'
í'tí	'hit',	ìgbà	'drum' :	òtí ìgbà		'drummer'
í'rí	'eat',	ńrí	'food' :	òrí 'ńrí		'glutton'
í'bé + ákwá			'cry' :	òbé 'ákwá		'crybaby'
íbè	'cut',	ákwà	'cloth' :	òbé 'ákwà		'cloth-cutter'

Comparable agentive derivations are found in Kpelle, though with quite a
different structure. The object and verb appear in their usual order, but the verb
is compounded with /nũu/ 'person' (pluralized as /-ɓèla/) with the usual low tone
replacing stem tone with the final element. There are also similar combinations
in which the head noun, in final position, is not personal. Examples are:

siɣe sɔlɔ-nũu	'tailor' ('cloth sew-person')
tíi ké-ɓèla	'workmen' ('work do-people')
siɣe waa-kpôlo	'laundry soap' ('cloth wash-sodium')
kɔ́ kɔ́-sèŋ	'weapon' ('fight fight-thing')

Contrary to what the last of these might suggest, the derivation of one-word
nouns from verbs (or vice versa) is highly exceptional and by no means productive
in Kpelle. A few such derivations have been mentioned in connection with some
other languages, but the topic will not be systematically treated. In some languages, patterns of noun derivation are transparent and productive. Sporadic
and unproductive derivational patterns are also common. Derivation of nouns
from verbs by suffixation and addition of class prefixes is typical of Bantu;
it should be noted that the final vowel in forms like the Swahili /kifungo/ 'a fasten-
ing', from /kufunga/ 'fasten', is a suffix.

10.23. Appended to this discussion of noun modifiers, because there seemed
to be no better place to put it, is this section on nominal conjunction. In the
vast majority of African languages, there appears to be a single simple word for
'and', frequently a monosyllable, and one might wonder why attention should
be given to the subject at all. There is one crucial reason for doing so. The beginner is almost sure to assume that he can use the same word to join verbs or sentences, to express combinations like 'they were eating and drinking'. That
simply is not true in any African language to which I have had sufficient exposure
to find out. Verbal conjunction will be treated in connection with verbal systems,
but it must be emphasized here that, when the form of nominal conjunction has
been discovered, that is pretty much the end of it—the construction has little if
any additional use.

Disjunction, 'or', is likely to be somewhat more complicated or idiomatic.
A very few examples will suggest the possibilities. In Kpelle, 'or' is expressed
by a two-word phrase, /kpà máŋ/, which apparently means 'No, also . . .'. In
Igbo, it is expressed as /m'ǫ̀ bù/ 'but it may be'. In Fante, there is a simple con-

junction /ànáá/; this, however, may also be used as a question marker at the end
of a yes-no question.

One instance of nominal conjunction that is considerably more complicated
than a single word is worthy of note. This is found in Kpelle. One's first impression may well be that nominal conjunction is as simple in Kpelle as in most other
languages. Nouns appear to be joined simply by /'tà/. When pronominal referents are brought into the picture, however, it develops that /'tà/ is a third person
plural pronoun form, derived from the basic form /'tí/. The sentence /surôŋ 'tà
nɛnî 'tí pà/ 'a man and a woman came' is structurally 'man they-including woman
they came'. This is only one specialized example of a more complex structure.

After any conjunctive phrase used as the subject of a clause, the subject
pronoun with the verb must refer in person to the pair or group mentioned, and
must of course be plural. Thus 'you and I' or 'he and I' constitute 'we'; 'you
and he' or 'you and Sumo' constitute 'you (pl.)'; 'he and she' or 'he and Sumo'
constitute 'they'. If the conjunctive phrase includes pronominal reference, it
must itself begin with a corresponding plural pronominal referent, which may
be labelled a "conjunctive pronoun." This is followed by a noun, which may be
an independent pronoun form. If the phrase refers to only two persons, the noun
or independent pronoun must be singular. If the phrase refers to more than two
persons, an overtly plural noun may be used, or a plural independent pronoun,
which must then be followed by /-nì/. Thus the following combinations are possible:

kwà yá kú pà	'you (sg.) and I came' (we-including you-sg. we came)
kwà ǹya kú pà	'he/she and I came' (we-including him/her we came)
kwà Sumo kú pà	'Sumo and I came' (we-including Sumo we came)
kà ǹya ká pà	'he/she and you came' (you-pl.-including him/her you came, total of two)
kà Sumo ká pà	'Sumo and you came' (you-pl.-including Sumo you came, total of two)
'tà ǹya 'tí pà	'he/she and he/she came' (they-including him/her they came)
'tà Sumo 'tí pà	'he/she and Sumo came' (they-including Sumo they came)
kwà ká-nì kú pà	'you (pl.) and I came / you (sg.) and we came / you (pl.) and we came' (we-including you came, total more than two)
kwà 'tiá-nì kú pà	'they and I came / he/she and we came / they and we came' (we-including 3d person came, total more than two)
kwà Sumó-nì kú pà	'Sumo and we came' (we-including Sumo came, total more than two)

kà 'tiá-nì ká pà	'you (pl.) and he/she came / you (sg. or pl.) and they came' (you-pl. including 3d person came, total more than two)
kà Sumó-nì ká pà	'you (pl.) and Sumo came' (you-pl.-including Sumo came, total more than two)
'tà 'tiá-nì 'tí pà	'he/she and they came / they and they came' (they-including 3d person came, total more than two)
'tà n̂ûaī tí 'tí pà	'he/she/they and those people came' (they-including people those they came)

Sentences like the above can also be translated by sentences like 'Sumo came with us'; this is the only way to express accompaniment.

Chapter 11

Being, Having, and Verbs

11.1. "I tried for three years to find the verb 'have' in Ewe, and now you have it all figured out in fifteen minutes!" Those were the words, uttered with a mixture of frustration and delight, of a missionary on furlough several years ago. It was my first work on Ewe, with my now distinguished colleague and beloved friend Gilbert Ansre, then a graduate student, as informant. The work was undertaken in order to help the missionary in question in learning the language; she had spent three years floundering on the field, and was unable to construct even simple sentences. As usual, I had begun by eliciting and transcribing the equivalents of about twenty common, concrete nouns, noting particularly such tonal distinctions as were apparent in their citation forms. I then proceeded to elicit the same nouns in the frames 'There's . . . over there' and 'There's . . . here', in order to compare the tones of nouns with something that might be invariable. The next frames I used were 'I have . . .' and 'you have . . .', This procedure produced simple sets like the following:

gà	'money'
gà lè àfímè	'there's money there'
gà lè àfìì	'there's money here'
gà lè àsínyè	'I have money'
gà lè àsíwò	'you have money'

It was immediately apparent that the expressions for location and the expressions for possession were similar. Having had prior experience with a similar situation, I made a judicious guess and asked how one would say 'my hand'. The response was, /nyě ásí/. Although the order of elements was different, it was obvious that the same morphemes were involved as in the expression for possession. So I observed that apparently an expression for possession is merely a special case of an expression for location; if you want to say 'I have so-and-so', you express it as 'So-and-so is in my hand'. It was, of course, a fortunate coincidence that I happened to choose the particular frames I did for what was supposed to be primarily a test for tone, but it was a dramatic fifteen-minute demonstration to one who had never dreamed of expressing 'have' by anything other than a verb.

Naturally, the foregoing does not answer all the questions that can be asked even about the few sentences cited. An obvious question has to do with the different structures of 'my hand', /àsínyè/ and /nyě ásí/. It turns out that there are two formations for pronominal possession in Ewe. The formation illustrated by the first of the above is regular for kinship terms (shades of Bantu la and similar patterns in Mande and other branches of Niger-Congo). The formation illustrated by the second of the above is regular for alienably possessed nouns. For body parts (for which I happen to have very little evidence), the second formation appears to be the usual one, though perhaps the first is an optional alternative. The first formation, however, is used for a body part in a locative construction. In this formation, the first and second person singular possessive pronouns follow the possessed noun; all other possessive pronouns precede. In the second formation, all pronouns precede the noun; the first and second person singular pronouns precede it immediately, but a morpheme /ʃé/ is used after all other pronouns and after nouns.

Another question is the status of the form /lè/. One might first assume that this is "the verb 'to be'." But there is another pitfall to be avoided. All that is clear from the few examples cited is that it means 'be-located-at'; there is no justification for assuming that Ewe, like English, would use the same verb to express description or identification as it uses to express location. Actually, the same form is used in some expressions of description, before words which very likely constitute a class of adjectivals. To express identification, however, a different form is used, /nyé/; e.g.,

ésia nyé gà   'this is money'

It is even questionable whether /lè/ is a verb at all, and the same question can be asked about /nyé/. These forms may perhaps be classified as verbs, but if so they are peculiarly defective verbs. They do not appear in the usual tense-aspect constructions characteristic of verbs like 'buy' or 'see'. It would perhaps be safer to describe them as copulas.

Ewe thus illustrates a situation that is exceedingly common in Niger-Congo, and undoubtedly in languages all over the world. It is that four types of predication, which happen to be expressed by the verbs 'be' and 'have' in English, are frequently non-verbal or marginally verbal, and involve semantic distinctions we are not used to expressing overtly. These types of predication are: identification, description, location, and possession. These, and their relationship to ordinary verbal predication, are the subject of this chapter.

11.2. An unusual distinction between identification and description is found in Akan. Identification in this case does not refer merely to identifying, but to being identical with. One element in the predication is a noun; the other is frequently a pronoun or a demonstrative, but may be another noun. Being identical with is expressed by /ní/. Thus in Fante,

mí'kyéw ní yí   'this is my hat'
mé'gyíá ní ɔ́nú   'he is my father'

In such sentences, the point is that the noun exhausts the definition of the other element in the predication. Simple identifying merges with description, expressed by /yè/; e.g.,

ɔyè kyéw   'it's a hat'

The point here is that, although the object in question is identified as a hat, 'it' does not exhaust the category of hats; there are many other hats in the world.

The forms /ní/ and /yè/ are members of a small set of what I have described as "stative verbs" (Welmers 1946, p. 54). There are perhaps no more than nine or ten such stems. They differ from other verbs in that they are highly restricted in their use with verbal affixes which mark tense and aspect distinctions, and in that they take subject pronouns with low rather than high tone. Most of them, including /ní/, occur with none of the verbal affixes; some may occur alone or with the future affix; /yè/ may occur with the future affix and also with the completive affix. There is a homophonous regular verb /yè/ 'do, make', which is used with all affixes and which takes subject pronouns with high tone; it is apparently this verb rather than /yè/ 'be described as' which is used with adjectivals (cf. 9.4). There is no negative corresponding to /ní/; being identical with is neutralized with being described as in the negative, and /yè/ is used for both.

Again rather unusually, both location and possession are expressed in Akan with the same stem, another stative verb, /wɔ/. In the negative, this has the suppletive allomorph /ní/, homophonous with the affirmative /ní/ 'be identical with'. Thus:

ɔwɔ síká	'he has money'
ɔwɔ dán nú nú mù	'he is in the house'
ònní síká	'he doesn't have money'
ònní dán nú nú mù	'he isn't in the house'

Another resemblance between expressions for location and possession was noted in Ewe, but in that case it was easy to see how possession is merely a special case of location. Here, however, there is identity of construction, not merely a special application. Technically, that is, there is ambiguity, as far as the verbal predication is concerned, as to whether location or possession is being expressed. Actually, however, there can be no confusion. What follows the stative verb unambiguously refers to one or the other; one cannot possess a place, and one cannot be located at an object. Or to put it differently, it might be said that one does indeed possess a place, and there is really no verbal expression of location at all.

Another of the stative verbs in Akan, /tì/, also has to do with location, but in a more specific way, particularly in the meaning 'live at, stay at'. A possibly related regular verb /tìná/ is used with the verbal affixes.

11.3. The situation is somewhat similar in Igbo, but must be described in terms of a stative construction in which some verbs appear, rather than in terms of stative verbs as such. The stative construction is used only with monosyllabic verb stems, and with only a relatively few of them. For the most part, verbs which are used in the stative do not appear in the common "factative" construction in the same dialect. In some dialects, however, there is an alternant of the factative which is used with such verbs to express past time. Verbs used in the stative, however, may also appear in other constructions such as the incompletive, future, consecutive, and conditional. The stative is marked by low tone replacing stem tone. The factative is marked with the same tonal replacive, and in addition by a suffix consisting of /r/ plus the preceding vowel repeated, with low tone. The alternant formation for verbs used in the stative has the stem vowel doubled. That verbs used in the stative are not clearly a separate class as in Akan, however, is suggested by the fact that the factative construction, which refers to past time for verbs expressing action, refers rather to present or undefined time for other verbs expressing state or situation. For some verbs, indeed, northern dialects use the stative where southern dialects use the factative, with the same present or undefined meaning.

Identification—here meaning being identified as, as well as being identical with—is expressed in Igbo by the verb /í'bú/ (cited in the infinitive; the root is /-bú/). Thus, in the stative:

ọ́ bụ̀ ónyé ŋ́kúzí   'he is a teacher'

In dialects which do not have a factative form for verbs used in the stative, this sentence is ambiguous; it could also mean 'he was a teacher', and the latter could be specified only by adding a phrase referring to a past time. In dialects which do have an alternant of the factative for such verbs, the following is possible:

ọ́ bụ̀ụ̀rụ̀ ónyé ŋ́kúzí   'he was a teacher'

Description—being describable in terms of—is expressed by the verb /í'dí/. Except for a few special cases, this is not used with the same nouns that are used after /í'bú/, but only with nouns which are themselves descriptive in meaning— and which have commonly but erroneously been called adjectives; cf. 9.6. A special case—and there are probably a relatively few others—is illustrated by the following contrast:

ọ́ bụ̀ ọ́kụ́   'it is (identifiable as) fire'
ọ́ dì ọ́kụ́   'it is describable in terms of fire, it is hot'

The same verb /í'dí/ is also used to express location, but only for inanimate nouns, or optionally (with dialect or personal variations) for nouns indicating reptiles, insects, only small animals, or all non-human animates. For other animates, including humans in all cases, the verb /ínọ̀/ is used; in some contexts, this may have the sepcific meaning 'sit'. More than one of these verbs, however, is required for predications of location. The noun or phrase indicating the place is introduced by a morpheme whose basic form is /nà/; before a vowel, the vowel and tone of this morpheme are deleted (but in some dialects not the duration of the vowel); before a syllabic nasal with high tone, the alternant /ná/ appears; but before a place name beginning with a consonant (with rare exceptions from another language), the basic form /nà/ appears and cannot be considered derived. Examples of expressions for location are:

ọ́ dì n'ébé áhụ̀   'it is there'
ọ́ nọ̀ n'ébe áhụ̀   'he/she is there'
ọ́ nọ̀ nà Kánụ̀   'he/she is at Kano'

The status of /nà/ in these constructions is worthy of consideration. There is another form /nà/ which is used before a verbal noun to form an incompletive construction, usually translatable by a present progressive. This is analyzed as a stative verbal form from a root /-ná/, the tone of which is attested by its use in a present consecutive construction; this verb has no other uses, but the constructions are paralleled by future constructions which use the corresponding forms of the verb /í'gá/ 'go'. For example:

ọ́ nà àbyá	'he is coming'
há nà èrí ń'rí, ná àŋụ́ ḿ'mányá	'they are eating and drinking'
ọ́ gà àbyá	'he's going to come'

The surface phonetic realizations of /nà/ before a phrase indicating place (or time) and of /nà/ before a verbal noun differ in some respects. For both, the vowel quality is completely elided before a different vowel; but in the latter case the vowel duration is never lost, and the low tone remains (as the beginning of a glide) before a vowel with high tone. Nevertheless, it is tempting to posit an underlying relationship between the two. If future action has to do with 'going to' then present action may well be associated with 'being at'; compare the semantic similarity between English 'he is at work' and 'he is working'. The /nà/ of locative phrases cannot be analyzed as any kind of verbal construction in the present structure of Igbo, but the evidence is good for positing a relationship to the /nà/ of the incompletive. It will be seen that location and present action appear to show an underlying relationship in a variety of languages.

The Igbo expression for identification, using /í'bú/, figures heavily in the grammar of topicalization. The subject of a sentence may be topicalized (emphasized, contrasted, singled out for attention) simply by introducing it with /ọ́ bù/ 'it is'. Other elements in a sentence, except a verb, may also be topicalized by being transposed to the beginning of the sentence, introduced with /ọ́ bù/, and—crucially—followed by a morpheme /kà/. In topicalizing something other than the subject, particularly a locative or temporal complement, /ọ́ bù/ is occasionally omitted; question words, which will be treated more fully in a later chapter, but which also normally appear in a topicalized construction, are usually not introduced by /ọ́ bù/. The use of this phrase, of course, is simply a way of identifying the major topic of the sentence. E.g.,

ńnà ḿ zụ̀rụ̀ éwú écí	'my father bought a goat yesterday'
ọ́ bù ńnà ḿ zụ̀rụ̀ éwú	'it was my father who bought a goat'
ọ́ bù éwú kà ńnà ḿ zụ̀rụ̀	'it was a goat that my father bought'
ọ́ bù écí kà ọ́ zụ̀rụ̀ yà	'it was yesterday that he bought it'
(∼ écí kà ọ́ zụ̀rụ̀ yà)	
ònyé zụ̀rụ̀ yà	'who bought it?'
gí'nị̀ kà ọ́ zụ̀rụ̀	'what did he buy?'
(∼ ò bù gí'nị̀ kà ọ́ zụ̀rụ̀)	

(Before a question word, as in the last parenthesized alternative, the subject pronoun has low tone, itself an indicator of something hypothetical, implicitly a question.)

Possession is expressed in Igbo by a verb /íˈŋwé/; the present state of possession is expressed by the factative. Thus:

    ó ŋwèrè éˈgó   'he has money'

It is deceptive, however, to assume that the verb /íˈŋwé/ simply means 'have'. In constructions other than the factative, a more basic meaning 'receive, obtain' is obvious. E.g.,

    ọ́ nà èŋwé éˈgó kwà ízù   'he gets money every week'

11.4. In terms of the types of construction presently under consideration, there is no distinction between identification and description in Yoruba; description involves specific verbs such as 'be big'. Identification, including topicalization, is expressed by a morpheme /ni/, with the allomorph /n'/ before /i/ and /l'/ before other vowels. For example,

         ilé ni   'it's a house'
         ilé ni mo rí   'it's a house I saw'
         ilé l'ó rí   'it's a house he saw'
         (cf.: ó rí ilé   'he saw a house')

In topicalizing a subject, a subject pronoun must be used after /ni/. In reference to an explicitly plural subject, the third person plural pronoun may be used, but the singular is also possible. In reference to a first or second person subject, the third person singular subject pronoun is used; that is, any independent pronoun is treated like an ordinary (third person) noun. E.g.,

    bàbáˈmi'ra ewúrẹ́   'my father bought a goat'
    bàbáˈmi l'ó ra ewúrẹ́   'it was my father who bought a goat'
    àwọn ni wọ́n ra ewúrẹ́   'it was they who bought a goat'
      (~ àwọn l'ó ra ewúrẹ́)
    èmi l'ó ra ewúrẹ́   'it was I who bought a goat'

An unusual phenomenon in Yoruba is that an entire sentence can be topicalized by adding /ni/ at the end. This gives something of the force of 'The point is that . . .'. E.g.,

    ó ra ewúrẹ́ ni   'the point is that he bought a goat'

As noted in 9.5, a reduplicated form of a verb may be topicalized in the same way; e.g.,

    lílọ l'ó lọ   'actually, he went'

It has been noted that location and possession are expressed in the same way in Akan, and that location and present action appear to be related in Igbo. In Yoruba, all three of these appear to be related. This will not be immediately

apparent from the following examples, but a strong case can be made for the hypothesis of an underlying relationship:

ó wà n'íbẹ̀	'he is there'
ó l'ówó	'he has money'
ó ń lọ	'he is going'

Each of the above contains a form which is clearly or probably derivable
from an underlying /ní/. The full form appears in expressions of location and
possession before a word with an initial consonant; there are relatively few such
cases, but the following is an example:

ó ní bàtà	'he has shoes'

This /ní/ is not to be confused with the quite different morpheme indicating identification, which is /ni/ with mid rather than high tone. Both have similar allomorphs before vowels, but the allomorphs of /ní/ must be represented as /n''/
before /i/ and /l''/ before other vowels; the following vowel always has high tone,
which is a replacive since only mid and low tone occur with word-initial vowels
otherwise. (I am quite aware of a more sophisticated analysis which treats [n]
and [l] as allophones of one phoneme, but I consider it inconvenient here; by this
analysis, the allomorphs of /ní/ and /ni/ would have to be described a little differently, but the descriptions would be mutually convertible.) In expressions
of present action, the form /ń/ appears (a homorganic syllabic nasal in the surface
phonology, with high tone), always followed by a consonant. This is not as obvious an allomorph of the same /ní/, since /ní/ occurs in the surface phonology in
expressions of location and possession; but an underlying relationship seems extremely likely, particularly in view of the analogous situation described above
for Igbo.

Locative predication is expressed by a verb /wà/, which has a suppletive allomorph /sí/ in negative constructions, followed by /ní/. The verb /wà/ may be
used without a locative complement in the meaning 'exist, be on hand'; in response to a question about someone's welfare, a common reply is /ó wà/, perhaps
best reflected by 'he's around'. (A verb /bẹ/ is also used in the present construction to mean 'exist, be alive'.) A locative complement follows /wà/ just
as it follows other predicates; for example,

ó wà n'íbẹ̀	'he is there'
ó ń šíšẹ́ n'íbẹ̀	'he's working there'

It is not difficult to consider /ní/ in such combinations verbal; the above could
be represented by 'he exists and is-at there' and 'he is working and is-at there'.

Possession is expressed by /ní/ alone, as illustrated by a few examples in the
preceding paragraphs. If /ní/ can be considered to have the semantic range 'be
at, be with', the relationship between location and possession is clear.

Present action is expressed by /ń/ before a verb, and an ultimate relationship
between this /ń/ and /ní/ has already been suggested. As in Igbo, the underlying
idea of present action appears to be 'be-at . . .-ing'.

The interrelationships between location, possession, and present action can be summed up in the following citations from Yoruba, Igbo, and Fante. Spaces left blank could of course be filled in, but the constructions involved are irrelevant to the point at issue here. Note the occurrences of /ní/ in Yoruba, /nà/ in Igbo, and /wɔ̀/ in Fante:

Yoruba	Igbo	Fante	
ó wà n'íbí	ọ́ nọ̀ n'ébé à	ɔ̀ wɔ̀ há	'he's here'
ó l'ówó		ɔ̀ wɔ̀ sìká	'he has money'
ó ń lọ	ọ́ nà àgá		'he's going'

11.5. 'Being' and 'having' present special problems in Kpelle also, but in different ways. First, the usual expression for location is illustrated by the following:

'káa nãa	'he/she/it is there'
pérɛ káa nãa	'there's a house there'

In form, /káa/ is a singular imperative of the verb meaning 'see', and the above sentences could be represented by 'see him/her/it there' and 'see a house there'. But /káa/ must be interpreted as having a specialized, fossilized function in such locative expressions, since the plural imperative form is not used when speaking to more than one person. What follows /káa/ is a noun or noun phrase, the head of which is frequently a relational noun indicating place. E.g.,

'káa ǹeɣii sù	'it is in the pot'
(cf.: ǹeɣii su wáa	'wash the inside of the pot')

Present action may be expressed in a closely similar way. There are two alternative constructions, used quite interchangeably with no recognizable difference in meaning. They are:

a pâi ~ 'káa pâi	'he/she is coming'

In the first of these, /a/ is a combination of the third person singular pronoun whose underlying form is /è/, and a construction marker indicating present action, elsewhere attested as /a/. In both alternatives, /pâi/ is from the verb /pá/ 'come', with a suffix /-ì/. It is significant that, for some verbs, this form clearly functions as a relational noun with locative meaning in other combinations. From the verb /láa/ 'lie down, sleep', for example:

a láaì ~ 'káa láaì	'he's (in the process of) lying down'
kú láaì káa nãa	'there's a place for us to sleep there'

The suffix /-ì/ is thus attested as having a locative meaning, and it is an easy step to recognizing the expressions for present action as meaning something like 'he is-at lying down'. Once more, location and present action appear to be related in the underlying structure.

This in turn forms the basis for the description of expressions of possession. Possession of a free noun is expressed by the same /káa/ followed by a possessed form of the word for 'hand', /-yée/, with the same locative suffix /-ì/. E.g.,

sɛŋ-kâu káa ńyéeì	'I have money'
sɛŋ-kâu káa ńâŋ yéeì	'my father has money'
`káa ńyéeì	'I have it'

Possession is thus a special instance of location; the above can be represented by something like 'money is-at my hand-place' etc. The suffix /-ì/ is used in only a very few combinations with other relational nouns, but its locative function is clear in such expressions for possession. It was this construction in Kpelle which provided the clue to the analysis of expressions for possession in Ewe (cf. 11.1 above).

Expressions for possession of relational nouns are also locative, but use a different locative complement. The concept of alienable vs. inalienable possession finds expression in this distinction. One can be thought of as holding an alienable possession—even by extension something too large to carry, as a cow—in one's hand; it was obtained, and can be disposed of. The same is not true of inalienable possessions; they simply exist. The locative complement used is /m̀à/, literally 'its surface, its edge'. E.g.,

ńêγe-ni feerɛ káa m̀à	'I have two younger siblings'

(lit., 'my two younger siblings are-at its-surface', or 'my two younger siblings exist')

ńyée feerɛ káa m̀à	'I have two hands'

(cf.: γâla káa m̀à   'God exists')

Expressions for description or identification are of two types. The first, with an implication more of description than of identification, uses /káa/ once more, but followed by a marked complement—a noun or noun phrase introduced by the complement marker /à/ (which in other combinations, as will be noted in a later chapter, closely reflects the widespread associative morpheme /a/). As noted in 9.2, a form of an adjectival can also be used in such marked complements, as an alternative to an adjectival predicative construction. E.g.,

γâla káa à kú nâŋ	'God is our father'
`káa à ɓóa	'it's a knife'
`káa à ǹélɛɛ (∼ ǹélɛɛì)	'it's fine'

Another construction, with more of an implication of identification and used only with demonstratives, involves a morpheme /ká/, which has nothing to do with the verb /káa/ 'see', and which is in no sense verbal. In this construction, the noun precedes and the demonstrative follows /ká/. E.g.,

ɓóa ká tí	'that's a knife'
ŋá ɓóai ká ŋí	'this is my knife'

Thus location, present action, possession, and description all use or may use the form /káa/. In every case, the reference is to a present situation. Other time and aspect references may also be expressed, but with the verb /kɛ́/ 'happen, be' (also transitively 'do, make'). With reference to present time, the noun located, acting, possessed, or described is the object of /káa/; with other references, it is the subject of /kɛ́/ E.g.,

è kɛ̀ nãa	'he/she/it was there'
ɓóa è kɛ̀ nãa	'there was a knife there'
è kɛ̀ ɲeɣii sù	'it was in the pot'
è kɛ̀ pâi	'he/she was coming'
ɲêɣe-ni feerɛ 'tí kɛ̀ m̀à	'he had two younger siblings'
è kɛ̀ à kóraŋ lɛ́lɛɛ	'it was a good year'
è kɛ̀ à ɲ́lɛɛ	'it was fine'
a pâi kɛ̂i à ɲ́lɛɛ	'it will be fine'

Expressions for identification using /ká/ and a demonstrative were noted above. There is still another expression for identification, not commonly used with a noun except as an answer to a question such as 'What is that?', but forming the basis for topicalization.[1] The key morpheme is /ɓé/, with an allomorph /ɓe/ (with mid tone) in final position and before demonstratives. A simple answer to a question asking identification may be:

mɔlɔŋ ɓe	'it is rice'

Question words are only occasionally used, in very short questions, in other than a topicalized construction. Some examples are:

lé	'what?':	a lé kɛ̂i	'what is he doing?'
mí	'where?':	ɓa lìi mí	'where are you going?'

Otherwise, question words come at the beginning of a sentence, and are followed by the topicalizing morpheme /ɓé/. In the following, if the question word refers to an object or complement of a verb, note that there is a back-reference to it, or a recapitulation of it, in the last part of the sentence:

lé ɓe tí	'what is that?'
lé ɓé a 'kɛ̂i	'what is he doing (it)?'
'kpɛ̂ ɓé í 'kàa	'who did you see (him)?'
ɣɛɛlu ɓe	'how much is it?'
mɔlɔŋ ɣɛɛlu ɓé 'káa nãa	'how much rice is there there?'
mí ɓé Sumo a lìi nãa	'where is Sumo going (there)?'

A typical answer to the first of the above is likely to be of the type /ɓóa ká ŋí/ 'this is a knife'. In general, none of the above questions is likely to be answered with a sentence using /ɓé/. This is likely to lead a learner of the language to conclude that /ɓé/ has something to do with questions as such. But it is by no means

---

[1] The following material is treated in detail in Welmers 1964.

restricted to questions. If frequently occurs in statements, but as an indicator of topicalization. E.g.,

tíi ɓé a 'kɛ̂i	'it's work that he's doing (it)'
Sumo ɓé ŋá 'kàa	'it's Sumo that I saw (him)'
'taai sû ɓé Sumo a lîi nãa	'it's into town that Sumo is going (there)'
nãa ɓé è lì naa	'it's there that he went (there)'

The appearance of /ɓé/ in most question-word questions merely demonstrates, therefore, that such question words are normally topicalized. In topicalizations in general, /ɓé/ may be used after a noun or noun phrase (including independent pronoun forms), or a question word. It may be used after a noun that might otherwise appear in a marked complement (introduced by /à/), but not after a full marked complement (with /à/). It is not used after an adjectival from a marked complement, nor after a verb. Recapitulation of what is topicalized is typical, and must be more fully treated.

After a topicalized subject, there is a recapitulating subject pronoun, agreeing in person and number with the subject, in most verbal constructions; two significant exceptions will be noted. Subject pronouns combine with verbal construction markers; before third person singular forms consisting of or beginning with /a/, /ɓé/ is reduced to /ɓ-/. What follows is in each case a complete sentence with a pronoun subject. E.g.,

ńyá ɓé ŋaâ pá	'I'm the one who has come'
kúa ɓé kwaâ pá	'we're the ones who have come'
ǹya ɓaâ pá	'he's the one who has come'
Sumo ɓé é 'kɛ́	'it is Sumo who should do it'
Sumo ɓa 'kɛ̀	'it is Sumo who does it'

In the past, there is no (or a zero) construction marker; the subject pronouns appear in their basic forms. In the present, there is a construction marker /a/, but the verb stem has a suffix /-ì/ which is unique to this construction and thus sufficient to mark it. In these two constructions, there is no recapitulating subject pronoun. It thus appears that the important thing to indicate after a topicalized subject is the verbal construction; where this must have an overt form, the pronoun goes along for the ride, but where the construction marker does not have to appear the pronoun is also unnecessary. Thus:

lé ɓé kɛ̀	'what happened?'
Sumo ɓé pà	'it was Sumo who came'
'tia ɓé pà	'it was they who came'
'tia ɓé pâi	'it's they who are coming'
'nya ɓé wúru téeì	'it's he who's cutting sticks'

A topicalized object is recapitulated by an object pronoun with the verb, agreeing in person and number with the object. Where number is irrelevant,

since nouns generally have a generic rather than numerical significance, a singular
pronoun is used. Again, what follows /ɓé/ is thus a complete sentence, with a
pronoun object. E.g.,

lé ɓé è 'kɛ̀	'what did he do (it)?'
'kpɛɛ̂ ɓé í 'kàa	'who did you see (him)?'
'tia ɓé ŋá 'tí kàa	'they're the ones I saw (them)'
kúa ɓé 'tí kú kàa	'we're the ones they saw (us)'
wúru ɓé kú 'tèe	'it's sticks that we cut (it)'
'tíi ŋí ɓé Sumo a 'kɛ̀	'it's this work that Sumo does (it)'

In cases where the subject and object pronouns have the same person and
number reference, one might wonder whether ambiguity is not possible; could
not either pronoun be taken as recapitulating what is topicalized? Such a possibility would seem to be restricted to third person reference. In the singular,
no ambiguity is possible in most constructions. In the past and present, as noted
above, a recapitulating subject pronoun is not used; thus if there is a subject
pronoun after /ɓé/, it must be the object that is topicalized; e.g.,

ǹya ɓé 'kàa	'it is he who saw him'
ǹya ɓé è 'kàa	'it is he whom he saw'

In most other constructions, /ɓé/ has the allomorph /ɓ-/ before a third person singular construction after a topicalized subject, but not after a topicalized object.
Thus the following contrast:

ǹya ɓaâ 'káa	'it is he who has seen him'
ǹya ɓé aâ 'káa	'it is he whom he has seen'

In one construction, however, there is ambiguity if the subject and object person
are both third person singular; this is the hortative. Further, there is ambiguity
in all cases if the two pronouns are both third person plural. Thus:

ǹya ɓé é 'káa	{ 'it is he who should see him' { 'it is he whom he should see'
'tia ɓé 'tí 'tí kàa	{ 'it is they who saw them' { 'it is they whom they saw'

In practice, of course, such ambiguous sentences are quite unlikely to occur;
normally either the subject or the object would be identified more specifically
than by mere pronouns. A noun before the subject pronoun would indicate that
the object is topicalized; a noun in place of the object pronoun would indicate
that the subject is topicalized.

A locative complement may be topicalized, and is recapitulated in the complement position by /nãa/ 'there'; this is used even if the topicalized element
means 'here'. E.g.,

nãa ɓé ŋá lì nãa	'there is where I went (there)'
ɓɛ́ ɓé ŋá 'kàa nãa	'here is where I saw him (there)'
'taai sù ɓé ŋá lì nãa	'it was into town that I went'

Locative complements are commonly like the one in the last example above, a possessed relational noun referring to place (in this case, 'the town's inside'). What precedes and possesses the relational noun may be topicalized by itself. In this case, it is recapitulated by a possessive pronoun with the relational noun in complement position. E.g.,

'taai ɓé ŋá lì 'sù   'it's the town that I went into'
(cf.: 'sù 'its inside')
'pérɛi tí ɓé è kɛ̀ ǹá   'it's that house that he was at'
(cf.: ǹá 'its mouth, its opening, its doorway')

A noun or noun phrase from a marked complement may be topicalized, and is recapitulated by a word /là/. This itself functions as a marked complement; it is a portmanteau for the complement marker /à/ with a third person singular pronoun, with impersonal meaning. E.g.,

kâli ɓé è pà là   'a hoe is what he brought'
(cf.: è pà à kâli 'he brought (came with) a hoe')
ɓóa ɓé è 'tèe là   'a knife is what he cut it with'
(cf.: è 'tèe à ɓóa 'he cut it with a knife')
wúru ɓé 'ta konâ kpɛ̀tɛ là   'it's wood that they make mortars of'
(cf.: 'ta konâ kpɛ̀tɛ à wúru 'they make mortars of wood')

Temporal complements may have the same construction as locative complements, a noun indicating time plus a relational noun indicating 'inside', or they may be marked complements. When topicalized, however, only the construction paralleling a marked complement may be used, with /là/ recapitulating. E.g.,

ŋáloŋ tí ɓé kú pà là   'it was last month that we came'
(cf.: kú pà à ŋáloŋ tí ~ kú pà ŋáloŋ tí sù 'we came last month')
ŋáloŋ tí ɓé è pà là à moloŋ 'it was last month that he brought
rice' (cf.: è pà à moloŋ ŋáloŋ tí sù 'he brought rice last
month'; here, to avoid two marked complements in one sentence, the locative formation is used for the temporal complement)

It is possible to use /là/ twice in one sentence, once as a recapitulating element, and once as a regular marked complement, and clearly in that order. E.g.,

ŋáloŋ tí ɓé è pà là là   'it was last month that he brought it'
(cf.: è pà là ŋáloŋ tí sù 'he brought it last month';
cf. also: ŋáloŋ tí ɓé è pà là 'it was last month that he came')

By analogy with the above, /là/ is also used to recapitulate the temporal question word /yɛlɛ/ 'when?'. The words for 'today', 'yesterday,' and 'tomorrow', however, are topicalized without recapitulation. Thus:

yɛlɛ ɓé í pà là   'when did you come?'
wɛ́ɛ ɓé ŋá pà   'it was yesterday that I came'

This discussion of topicalization in Kpelle began with the observation that a noun (or independent pronoun) may be identified simply by using /ɓé/ after it. Such sentences are simply apocopated topicalizations; they identify the topic without saying anything further about it.

Verbs and adjectivals are not topicalized in Kpelle. There are, however, adverbs with restrictive or emphatic meaning which serve a somewhat similar function. In English, topicalization of any element in a sentence very commonly takes the form of contrastive stress; the glosses given in the foregoing are convenient for avoiding ambiguity in writing, but are not the most natural ways of expressing such ideas in speech. English-speaking learners of African languages are almost irresistibly tempted to sprinkle their speech with English contrastive stresses and varieties of intonation, destroying tonal contrasts in the process. The foregoing should demonstrate that an African language has the equipment to express all the subtle nuances of emphasis that we are used to, without resorting to our conventions of stress and intonation.

11.6. Description, location, and possession were not fully investigated in the Gur languages with which I have worked, and there is not a great deal in the literature which is clearly reliable. Identification in Senari and Suppire was discussed in connection with the noun class sytems of those languages in 7.6. There is a form indicating identification, used after a noun, for each class, singular and plural. Suppire (and probably Senari as well; the subject was not investigated) has a second set of forms indicating identification of something at a distance. The two types are illustrated by the following:

ŋkùù wi	'it's a chicken'	ŋkùù úŋgé	'that's a chicken'
sugo ki	'it's a mortar'	sugo kúŋké	'that's a mortar'
boro li	'it's a bag'	boro línné	'that's a bag'
kárá ti	'it's meat'	kárá tínté	'that's meat'
súmɔ́ pi	'it's salt'	súmɔ́ pímpé	'that's salt'
síkaa pia	'they are goats'	síkaa pímpíá	'those are goats'
baya yi	'they are houses'	baya ínyé	'those are houses'
bɔɔrí tyia	'they are bags'	bɔɔrí tyíntyíá	'those are bags'

These forms indicating identification apparently do not enter into constructions of topicalization. The only relevant construction recorded appears to be a case of a topicalized object, which is simply put at the beginning of a sentence so that the order is object-subject-verb rather than the normal subject-object-verb. E.g., in Senari:

> karà wò tyaa   'it's meat we want'
> (cf.: wò karà tyaa   'we want meat')

A few expressions of location are recorded in Senari. They use a morpheme /i/ which is clearly not verbal, since all verbs have initial consonants. This morpheme can apparently be preceded by either an independent pronoun or a subject pronoun, or of course a noun. Thus the following alternatives appear:

    wòlò i ná ~ wò i ná   'we are here'

    An expression of possession is recorded in Senari, using a verb /ta/, the underlying meaning of which is 'obtain'. With kinship terms, however, this is not used. In the following, /ò/ appears to be an alternant of the locative copula /i/ in negatives; /i/ is a negative marker. The phrase /mì má/ appears to be a possessive pronoun with a noun indicating place, but the specific type of location, of any, is not known. This sentence seems to have the structure 'a child is-at my-? not':

    pìà ò mì má í   'I don't have a child'

    Even these very limited data are sufficient to suggest that all of the concepts in question—identification (and topicalization), description, location, and possession—are nonverbal, or at least only marginally verbal.

    In Bariba, a morpheme /wâ/ is recorded with the meaning 'exist, be located at', which is apparently not a verb; I have no record of sentences in which it is used. Otherwise, only identification was recorded in Bariba, and my notes show glosses of the type 'there's a goat', 'there's some money'; difficulty in communicating with informants may have affected the situation, and I suspect that simple identification is closer to the meaning. Although Bariba has a suffix-marked class sytem rather similar to that of Senari and Suppire, noun classes do not enter into the expression for identification. The single morpheme has allomorphs, however, which are conditioned by the final vowel of the noun and, if the noun ends with high tone, by its morphotonemic class. After nouns with final high tone in the smaller of two morphotonemic classes, the identifying morpheme has low tone; after all other nouns, it has top tone.[2] After final /i, e, ɛ/, the forms /yá ~ yà/ appear; after final /u, o, ɔ/, the forms are /wá ~ wà/; after final /m/, the form is /á ~ à/. After a final single /a/, the form with top tone is an added /á/; the form with low tone has no added vowel, but the final tone becomes falling. With a final double /aa/, only the top tone form is attested; it takes the form of top replacing top or high tone, and rising tone replacing mid; no noun is recorded with final /aà/ and final low tone. All of these allomorphs have nasalized suballomorphs after nasalized vowels. Some examples of identification in Bariba are:

gobi yá	'it's money'		boo wá	'it's a goat'
wii yà	'it's straw'		bɔ̃ɔ̃ wǎ	'it's a dog'
guwā	'chicken'	:	guwāá	'it's a chicken'
yasa	'cloth'	:	yasaá	'it's cloth'
duma	'horse'	:	dumâ	'it's a horse'
yaa	'animal'	:	yaá	'it's an animal'
naā	'cow'	:	naǎ	'it's a cow'

11.7. In a number of Bantu languages, identification is expressed by a tonal replacive accompanying the noun class prefix if it is a full syllable, or otherwise

---

    [2] This was erroneously labelled "high," though transcribed correctly, in Welmers 1952a, p. 88.

an added vowel. In Shona, for example (and the same pattern is found in many
other languages in that part of Bantuland), nouns by themselves have prefixes
with low tone, or nonsyllabic prefixes in the case of classes 5, 9, and 10. To express identification, high tone replaces low tone; if there is no tone to replace,
/í-/ is prefixed, which undoubtedly is the same replacive with an underlying */ì-/
reflecting the original forms of the class prefixes in question. There are also some
instances of tonal alternation in noun stems; I have no record of the rules for such
alternations, but tonal alternations in Shona are, in general, restricted and simple.
Here low replaces high in a monosyllabic stem, and high replaces the first of two
or more lows in a stem; these may be the only statements required.[3] The following
illustrate identification with nouns of classes 1 through 10:

mùnhù	'a person'	múnhù	'it is a person'
vànhù	'people'	vánhù	'they are people'
mùtí	'a tree'	mútì	'it is a tree'
mìtí	'trees'	mítì	'they are trees'
bhúkù	'a book'	íbhúkù	'it is a book'
màbhúkù	'books'	mábhúkù	'they are books'
chìgàrò	'a chair'	chígárò	'it is a chair'
zvìgàrò	'chairs'	zvígárò	'they are chairs'
ngùrùvè	'a pig, pigs'	íngúrùvè	'it is a pig, they are pigs'

There are other noun classes in Shona for which expressions of identification
are similarly formed. With class 1a and (including?) independent pronoun forms,
however, a morpheme /ndí/ is used as a prefix for identification.

To express identification with reference to anything other than present time,
a verb is used, the infinitive form of which is /kùvá/; in some cases, this is also
translatable as 'become'. E.g.,

| ndìnózòvá mámbò | 'I'm going to be chief' |
| ndìnódà kùvá mámbò | 'I want to be chief' |

Location is expressed by a morpheme /rí/, with the regular subject concords
as prefixes, followed by a locative noun. Locative nouns are formed by the
prefixes of classes 16 (/pa-/, of specific location), 17 (/ku-/, of general location)
and 18 (/mu-/, of location inside), superimposed on the full noun form with its
own prefix (if any). E.g.,

bhúkù rírí pàtáfùrà	'the book is on the table'
bhúkù rírí kùchìkórò	'the book is at school'
chìgàrò chírí mùùmbá	'the chair is in the house'

Location in other than present time is expresssed by forms of a verb /kùngà/,
which elsewhere means 'be like', with a "participial" construction using /rí/;
in this construction, first and second person subject forms have high rather than

---

[3] The data for Shona is taken from Stevick and Machiwana 1960. My own competence has
deteriorated beyond the point of assuring comprehensive statements.

low tone, the subject concord for class 1 is /á-/ rather than /ú-/, and low replaces the stem tone of /rí/. This appears to be comparable to what I normally call a "consecutive" construction; however, /rí/ is not a normal verb in other respects, since it requires the auxiliary /kùngà/ to express what would normally be found in a verb construction without an auxiliary. Examples of location in other than present time are:

> bhúkù rángá rírì pàtáfùrà   'the book was on the table'
> tìnóngà tírì kùchìkórò   'we will be at school'

Shona provides another striking example of expressing present action in a way closely similar to that of expressing location. Continuous action in other than the present is also expressed in the same way. In either case, an infinitive (which is nominal, in class 15) is used after /rí/ rather than a locative noun. With the constructions illustrated above, compare:

> tìrí kùfúndá chìMànyíkà   'we are studying ChiManyika'
> tàngá tírì kùfúndá chìMànyíkà   'we were studying ChiManyika'
> tìnóngà tírì kùtámbá   'we will be playing'

In Shona as in the Bantu languages in general, the prefix and all concords for classes 15 and 17 are identical. In a strictly synchronic treatment of comparative Bantu, the two classes must nevertheless be distinguished, because the locative class 17 prefix may be superimposed on the infinitive class 15 prefix in some languages to form a locative noun referring to action. However, an underlying relationship and near identity between expressions of location and present action has been noted in a number of other Niger-Congo languages; it would appear that the association of the two has its roots in proto-Niger-Congo, since it is found both in Mande and in non-Mande languages. In Bantu languages which at present permit the superimposition of class 17 upon class 15, infinitives have come to be treated as action nouns with no suggestion of location; classes 15 and 17 have become separate classes by the intrusion of a distinction between action and location. In languages such as Shona, however, the construction for present action (and continuous action in other than the present) strongly suggests that the infinitive simply is a locative, and that classes 15 and 17 should not be distinguished in modern Shona, and probably not in Bantu as a whole prior to relatively recent times.

Shona has a morpheme used as a nominal conjunction, 'and', which has the allomorphs /nà/ (only before nouns of class 1a and exceptionally in a few other cases), /nè/ (elsewhere before underlying low tone, but a following low is replaced by high, and a following disyllabic noun with low-high takes the tones high-low), and /né/ (elsewhere before underlying high tone); this is usually written with the following word. E.g.,

> bàbá nàmái   'father and mother'
> mìchèrò nèmúríwó   'fruit and vegetables'
> mùríwó nényámà   'vegetables and meat'

Actually, this may be divisible into two morphemes, /n-/ and the associative morpheme, which has the same vocalic and tonal alternants, and which by this analysis appears in other combinations as well. This is in itself an attractive analysis, but is not particularly relevant to the present discussion. The combination in question is also used to express accompaniment:

tàéndà nàbàbá   'we went with father'

The same morpheme (or morpheme sequence) is also used with subject concords to express possession, though with different tonal rules (high after low, low after high). Thus the morpheme appears to impinge on the category of verbs, but it does so in a very defective way. The underlying idea appears to be that the possessor 'is with' what is possessed. E.g.,

ndìné nyámà   'I have meat'
váně vàná váìrí   'they have two children'
ndìné mùsóró   'I have a headache'
tìné mùríwó nèmíchèrò   'we have vegetables and fruit'

To express possession in other than the present, the verb /kùvá/ is used (as in expressions of identification; see above) with the regular conjunctive forms of the same morpheme. Here, still more clearly, possession is 'being with'. E.g.,

ndìnózòvá nèmúríwó   'I will have vegetables'

Expressions of location comparable to 'there is . . . (there)' are expressions of possession, the possessor being the subject concord of one of the locative classes. E.g.,

kúně vàná váìrí   'there are two children'
                         (there or in existence)
páně nyámà   'there's meat here'
múně nyámà   'there's meat inside this'

11.8. Swahili, as an example of another Bantu language, shows a number of similarities with Shona in the types of construction under consideration, but also some differences. First, identification is expressed by a morpheme /ni/ rather than by tonal replacement as in Shona; Swahili, of course, is not a tone language, but other Bantu languages use similar syllabic forms. To express the corresponding negative, /si/ is used. In each case, the noun completing the identification follows. If the subject is an independent pronoun or a demonstrative, /ni/ may be omitted, and the resultant construction is simple parataxis. The last of the following examples is a delightful saying to be graciously used when your wife asks if she may buy a new dress (or when your husband says you certainly may not):

ni kisu   'it's a knife'
hiki (ni) kisu   'this is a knife'
hiki si kisu   'this isn't a knife'
mimi (ni) Hamisi   'I am Hamisi'
mimi ni nyama; wewe ni kisu   'I'm the meat; you're the knife'

If the subject identified is a first or second person pronoun, independent pronoun forms may be used as above. Alternatively, and when emphasis or contrast is not involved, subject pronoun forms may be used, without /ni/. The first person singular subject pronoun also happens to be /ni/, but there is no ambiguity because the following noun is personal. E.g.,

ni mpishi	'I'm a cook'
u mpishi	'you're a cook'
tu wapishi	'we are cooks'
m wapishi	'you are cooks'

To express description with adjectives, the same /ni/ may be used with some adjectives, particularly if the reference is to an irrevocable quality. Alternatively, however, concord morphemes may be used instead of /ni/; these are not verbal subject concords, since the class 1 form is /yu/ rather than the verbal subject form /a/. For adjectives generally referring to a temporary state, only the concord morphemes are used, not /ni/. E.g.,

Hamisi ni mrefu	
Hamisi yu mrefu	'Hamisi is tall'
chungwa hili ni bovu	
chungwa hili li bovu	'this orange is rotten'
yu dhaifu	'he is weak'
sahani zi safi	'the plates are clean'

The above constructions may refer to other than present time if it is not necessary to specify time. If such specification is necessary to avoid ambiguity, and to express other than temporal ideas which are normally expressed by a verb, the verb /kuwa/ is used (compare Shona /kùvá/) in place of /ni/ or the concord marker. This verb has regular negative forms also, so that /si/ does not appear before the noun to express the corresponding negatives. E.g.,

nilikuwa mpishi	'I was a cook'
Hamisi atakuwa mrefu	'Hamisi is going to be tall'
sahani zikiwa safi, . . .	'If the plates are clean, . . .'

In relatives and a few other unusual constructions, a stem /li/ is used in place of /kuwa/; for identification, /ni/ may optionally be used after it. In the following, /a-/ is a subject concord, and /-ye/ is a concord used in relatives:

| aliye (ni) mpishi | 'he who is a cook' |

To express location, predicative forms of the concords for the locative classes (16, 17, 18: specific, general, inside) are used. These are combinations of the concords with a morpheme /-o/, forming /po/, /ko/, and /mo/. Concordial prefixes refer to the subject; again these are not verbal, since the class 1 form is /yu-/.

These combinations are followed by one of a few specifically locative words, or by a noun with the general locative suffix /-ni/. With the first three of the following examples, the corresponding Shona sentences cited in the preceding section may be compared; the construction is rather different, but the locative distinctions are the same:

kitabu kipo mezani	'the book is on the table'
kitabu kiko shuleni	'the book is at school'
kiti kimo nyumbani	'the chair is in the house'
mlango uko wapi	'where is the door?'
yumo nyumbani	'he is in the house'

If the place has already been referred to, as in a question, these predicative forms may be used by themselves; e.g.,

vikombe vimo sandukuni?	'are the cups in the box?'
vimo	'they are (inside)'

To express location in other than the present, forms of /kuwa/ and /li/ are used as for identification and description. The predicators /-po/, /-ko/, /-mo/ may be used after these, or may optionally be omitted if what follows makes the nature of the location sufficiently clear. E.g.,

alikuwa (yuko) kule	'he was there'
atakuwa (yupo) hapa	'he will be here'
kilikuwa kimo sandukuni	'it (7) was in the box'

When the verb /kuwa/ is used directly before a noun, an adjective, or an expression of place, it approximates the range of usage of English 'be' more closely than anything that has been described in other languages discussed so far. It may refer to identification, description, or location. It is still most important to note, however, that it is not used with reference to the present situation; with such reference, the three concepts must be treated separately.

Swahili, like Shona, has a nominal conjunction, 'and'; in Swahili, it has the invariable form /na/. This is used with regular verbal subject concords to express possession. As Ashton (1944, pp. 98-99) clearly and perceptively points out, however, more than mere possession is involved; the emphasis is on association. In some cases, the possessor and possession may appear in the reverse order from what is expected; what is expressed is merely an association between the two. The use of subject concords with /na/, and also the fact that the negative formation with /na/ is the same as with verbs, suggests, as was noted also for Shona, that this form impinges on the category of verbs. Again it is defective, however. Among other things, it does not take the usual verbal object concords. Rather, concords combined with a morpheme /-o/ are used after /na/; for class 1, the special form /-ye/ is used. The last of the following examples shows the reverse of the expected order:

nina kisu	'I have a knife'
ana watoto wawili	'he has two children'
ana njaa	'he is hungry' (is-with hunger)
sahani hizi zina taka	'these plates are dirty'
wanacho	'they have it, they have one (7)'
wanayo	'they have it, they have one (9)'
kina Hamisi	'Hamisi has it' (it is-with Hamisi)

As in Shona, the concords of the locative classes may be used as subjects of /na/ to express location:

kuna visu	'there are knives' (there in general or in existence)
pana nyoka	'there's a snake' (right there, as when pointing)
mna visu	'there are knives in it'

With reference to other than the present, the verb /kuwa/ is used once more, followed by /na/:

alikuwa na kisu	'he had a knife'

The situation with regard to possession, therefore, is closely similar in Shona and Swahili. In connection with Shona, it was mentioned that /nà/ and its alternants could be analyzed as a sequence of morphemes, /n-/ and the associative morpheme. This analysis becomes more significant in the light of what is found in Swahili but not in Shona. The /n-/ of /na/ may be identified with the /ni/ which expresses identification and description, and /na/ may be seen as having the underlying meaning 'be described as associated with'. It is also used as a nominal conjunction, and as such is not predicative in the surface structure, but its underlying predicative character is clear. Compare also the /ní/ expressing identification in Yoruba (11.4 above), and the analysis of the conjunctive /nà/ in Igbo as apparently being ultimately related to a form analyzed as verbal but defective in usage (11.3 above).

11.9. The foregoing sections have illustrated how, in a variety of languages, predications referring to identification, description, location, and possession are frequently non-verbal; if verbal predications are used, they are restricted in some way, or at least differ significantly from their English counterparts. In almost any language, such expressions require special treatment, most conveniently before the verbal system of the language is described. It is for this reason that such predications have been outlined here, prior to a discussion of verbs and verbal systems. The way has now been prepared to go on to the latter. The remainder of this chapter is devoted to a discussion of verb roots and verbal bases; the following chapter will illustrate how such roots and bases enter into a variety of grammatical constructions.

Implicit in this division of the subject matter is the recognition of a distinction between derivation and inflection. It is quite true it that is difficult if not impossible to give a rigid and satisfactory formal definition of this distinction, but it has nevertheless frequently been found useful. What is relevant here is that, in all the languages to be considered, there are morphemes marking distinctions in such categories as tense, aspect, and mode, which operate somewhat similarly; there are also, of course, pronominal morphemes. Such morphemes may, at least in a loose way, be classed as inflectional; in some languages, they may be considered agglutinative. In only some of the languages to be considered, such inflectional morphemes may be used with lexical units which themselves consist of more than one morpheme. The formation of these lexical units may be viewed as derivational.

A root is, in general linguistic usage, a single morpheme. For the most part —because a distinction has rarely been found necessary in the languages with which I have dealt—I have tended to use the terms "root" and "stem" interchangeably, and will undoubtedly continue to do so. The term "base," however, may be assigned a specific meaning; it is a form composed of more than one morpheme to which inflectional morphemes may be attached as they also are to a root or stem. A base may theoretically be composed of two or more roots otherwise used independently, of such a root and one or more bound morphemes, or combinations of such ingredients.

In most of the Niger-Congo languages of West Africa, it is unnecessary to make any distinction at all between verb roots (or stems) and verbal bases. Inflectional morphemes occur only with monomorphemic lexical units. Inflection may, to be sure, involve internal modification as well as external affixation, but it is nevertheless analyzable as inflection. (In the case of Senari and Suppire, I did tentatively propose the term "present base" for what must be analyzed as an inflected form [Welmers 1950a, p. 139; 1950b, p. 522]. I would now correct that to "present stem", and use "root" or "non-present stem" for what I called simply "stem". The formations in question are complex, which probably had something to do with my failure to achieve a consistent terminology. In the case of Bariba, where the situation is even more complex, I successfully dodged the issue by referring simply to verb "forms" [Welmers 1952a, p. 93].) Morphemically complex verbal bases are found in Igbo and closely related languages, and sequences that might be thought to be complex verbal bases must be considered for Jukun and Yoruba; Efik also has complex verbal bases, but of types quite different from the other languages mentioned. Otherwise, within Niger-Congo, such bases are found primarily in Bantu. The following treatment does not go beyond the Niger-Congo languages, but quite clearly the same kind of approach is appropriate to languages of other families as well.

11.10. A skeleton outline of the derivation of Igbo verbal bases appears in 5.18, where their tonal structure is significant for an outline of Igbo tonology. A fuller statement of their morphemic composition is now in order.[4] To the def-

---

[4] What follows is, with few changes, the substance of the last part of Welmers 1970a.

inition of a verbal base given in my earlier treatment must be added one detail
in connection with tone.

A verbal base is defined, for Igbo, as that part of the infinitive form which
follows the infinitive prefix, excluding two morphemes (described as the additive
and applicative extensions) which may occur after other clearly inflectional affixes,
but with no more than the first syllable having low tone. Such verb bases may
consist of one or more syllables. In bases of more than one syllable, the first is
itself a verb root, which with very few exceptions occurs independently as a monosyllabic verb base. The few exceptions display no system; they appear to be merely
a few sporadic cases of bound roots, appearing only in combination with other
morphemes to form bases. It is the syllable or syllables after the first in a base
which concern us.

Ida C. Ward's *An Introduction to the Ibo Language* was published in 1936.
Miss Ward's field of specialization was phonetics. As she herself explicitly states,
however, the study of tone inevitably led her farther into the field of grammar
than she had anticipated. In her discussion of two-syllable verb bases (she cites
a few three-syllable bases, but makes no statements about them), she distinguishes
between what she calls "compound verbs" and "verbs with meaning suffixes"
(pp. 127ff.). A "compound verb" is a base consisting of two verb roots, each of
which occurs independently as a monosyllabic verb base. A "meaning suffix" is
a morpheme which appears in second position in a two-syllable verb base, but
which does not occur independently as a monosyllabic verb base, yet which adds
something to the meaning of the preceding root. She recognizes the possibility
that what she calls "meaning suffixes" may be bound verb roots, or at least
may originally have been verb roots; and she observes, rightly, that the distinction between the two formations is irrelevant to the grammar of Igbo in so far
as she treats it. Miss Ward's remarkable intuition in matters of language analysis,
however, makes the question of the validity of her "meaning suffixes" as a separate class of morphemes well worth pursuing.

Some examples of two-syllable verb bases in which each syllable is attested
as an independent verb root are as follows:

gá	'go',	fè	'cross, pass over'	:	gáfè	'go across'
byá	'come',	fè	(as above)	:	byáfè	'come across'
kwà	'push',	cí	'be stopped up'	:	kwàcí	'push shut'
mé	'do, make',	cí	(as above)	:	mécí	'close, shut'
mé	'do, make',	ghé	'be open'	:	méghé	'open'
tí	'hit, beat',	wá	'split open'	:	tíwá	'shatter'
wè	'take, pick up',	pù	'exit'	:	wépù	'take out'
kwọ́	'scoop up',	pù	(as above)	:	kwọ́pù	'scoop out'
wú	'pour',	nyé	'give'	:	wúnyé	'pour in, on'
tụ́	'throw',	fù	'get lost'	:	tụ́fù	'throw away'

Examples of two-syllable verb bases in which the second syllable is not attested as an independent verb root, but is one of Ward's "meaning suffixes", are:

With /-tá/, indicating action performed in the direction of the subject or speaker, or in his interest:

zú	'buy'	:	zútá	'buy and bring, buy for oneself'
wè	'take, pick up'	:	wètá	'bring'
mù	'study'	:	mùtá	'learn, master'
dọ́	'pull'	:	dọ́tá	'attract, be attractive to'
ŋwé	'obtain, get'	:	ŋwétá	'receive'

With /-cá/, indicating action performed to completion or to the exhaustion of the object:

rí	'eat'	:	rícá	'eat all of, eat up'
hú	'see'	:	húcá	'get a good look at, inspect'
gụ́	'count, read'	:	gụ́cá	'read all of, finish reading'

With /-sị́/, indicating action performed up to a stopping point or to temporary completion:

| rí | 'eat' | : | rísị́ | 'finish eating' |
| kwụ́ | 'stand' | : | kwụ́sị́ | 'stop' |

With /-cí/ (not the independent root meaning 'be stopped up'), indicating action performed as a replacement of another action:

zú	'buy'	:	zụ́cí	'buy as a replacement'
nọ̀	'be at, sit'	:	nọ̀cí	'take the place of'
lụ́	'marry'	:	lụ́cí	'remarry (as a widower)'

With /-hyè/, indicating action done in a wrong way or by mistake:

| gá | 'go' | : | gáhyè | 'go the wrong way' (obj. 'road') |
| kwú | 'speak' | : | kwúhyè | 'speak disrespectfully of'; with object 'mouth':) 'make a slip of the tongue' |

With /-wá/ (not the independent root meaning 'split open'), indicating action taken up or initiated (not just begun):

| gá | 'go' | : | gáwá | 'get going' |
| gụ́ | 'count, read' | : | gụ́wá | 'get at reading' |

In some three-syllable bases, the second and third syllables are not readily analyzable as separate morphemes, but are bound to each other; further, these combinations do not appear as independent verb bases, and thus belong with Ward's "meaning suffixes". Examples are:

With /-gídé/, indicating continuation of an action:

| nọ̀ | 'be at, sit' | : | nọ̀gídé | 'stay' |
| rụ́ | 'work' | : | rụ́gídé | 'keep on working' |

With /-ghárị̂/, indicating action performed at random, aimlessly, or in other than a straight line:

| gá | 'go' | : | gághárị̂ | 'walk around, stroll' |
| lé | 'look' | : | léghárị̂ | 'look around, turn one's head' |

In other three-syllable bases, the second syllable, as in two-syllable bases, may be either an independent root or a bound morpheme. The third syllable, however, is only very rarely an independent verb root. Monosyllabic bound morphemes of the type illustrated above are common in this position. Only a few independent roots may occur in third position; only /gá/ 'go' indicating action away from the speaker or subject, and /fè/ 'pass by' indicating action past or over a place, have been recorded, though it would not be surprising to find also /pụ̀/ 'exit' indicating action out of a place. Significantly, these form a semantic group with the bound morpheme /tá/ indicating action toward the speaker or subject. Examples of three-syllable bases of this type are:

wè	'take, pick up',	dà	'fall',	with	/tá/:
		wédàtá	'bring down'		
wè	'take, pick up',	pụ̀	'exit',	with	/tá/:
		wépụ̀tá	'bring out'		
mé	'do, make',	/kọ́/ indicating action done together,	/tá:/		
		mékọ́tá	'do together, bring together'		
ké	'tie',	cí	'be stopped up',	with	/sị́/:
		kécísị̂	'tie up, fasten up completely'		
dà	'fall',	sá	'spread',	with	/sị́/:
		dàsásị̂	'fall apart and scatter all around'		

The same patterns apply to bases of more than three syllables; the first syllable must be an independent verb root, the second may be either an independent root or a bound morpheme; any syllable thereafter must be a bound morpheme or one of the very few directional verb roots mentioned above in final position.

Igbo verb bases may thus be composed of morphemes of two definably different types in terms of distribution. Independent monosyllabic roots may occur alone to constitute verb bases. They may also occur in either first or second position within a longer verb base. With only a few exceptions, they may not occur after the second position, and those which do must be in final position. On the other hand, certain bound morphemes, Ward's "meaning suffixes," may not occur in first position in a base of two or more syllables, but may occur in any position after the first.

The bound morphemes in question, which occur as parts of verb bases, may now be given a label more formal than "meaning suffixes", namely "base formatives." Most base formatives, like verb roots, are monosyllabic, but a handful of disyllabic morphemes (or at least unanalyzable disyllabic forms) are included in this class. Some thirty such base formatives have been identified in Igbo. Semantically, they indicate motion or direction of various sorts, completion, in-ception, and comparable modifications of the action indicated by the preceding independent root or roots. No claim is made that every morpheme involved in Igbo verb bases has been unambiguously identified, since the status of a morpheme met for the first time may not be immediately established, but it is clear that a morpheme class of "base formatives" can be recognized as distinct from verb roots.

The morphotactics of Igbo base formatives in bases containing more than one have not been investigated. It is clear, however, that there are certain restrictions on their co-occurrences and order.[5]

11.11. In my treatment of Jukun (Welmers 1968b), I referred to "open" and "closed" verb phrases consisting of two verb roots. I distinguished the two types by noting that an object may follow the first verb in an "open" phrase, but only the second in a "closed" phrase. An example of each in Dìyī is:

> zè kúnà bi   'bring a knife'   (zè 'take', bi 'come')
> ku wǎ zu be 'he saved them' (wǎ 'pull out of the way', zu   'go a-way')

The first type of sequence is a serial verb construction, to be discussed in the following chapter. There seems to be no reason why the second type could not be called a complex base rather than a phrase, though I see no strong motivation for doing so. There are no inflectional suffixes whose position might force the interpretation of the sequence of two roots as a unitary base.

Such sequences, however, must be carefully distinguished from sequences of two syllables which are verb-noun; the distinction is not always immediately apparent. If the morphemes can be identified by independent uses in other contexts, of course, the question is settled immediately. Otherwise, the form of the second syllable may betray its classification. In the sequence /na nâ/ 'sleep', for example, the second syllable can only be a noun because of its tone; a verb root can have only a level tone, and the structure of /nâ/ is /ná-/ plus a nominal suffix consisting of low tone. Judging from a few similar cases, /nâ/ is a noun derived from /na/ 'lie down'; its high tone is part of the derivational pattern. On the other hand, the status of /ndè/ in the phrase /ki ndè/ 'cry out' cannot be so simply determined; it is not independently attested, and could be either a verb or a noun as far as its tone is concerned. There is always, however, a diagnostic criterion, which in this case demonstrates that /ndè/ is a noun. Negative constructions are characterized by the use of a pronoun form, recapitulating the subject pronoun, which appears immediately after the verb; there is also a negative morpheme at the end of the clause. In the following examples, the position of the recapitulating pronoun form /bé/ demonstrates that /zu/ is a verb and /nâ/ is a noun (which had already been established on other grounds), and also that /ndè/ is a noun:

> be wǎ zu bé ku mbá   'they didn't save him'
> be na bé nâ mbá   'they didn't sleep'
> be ki bé ndè mbá   'they didn't cry out'

[5] A detailed treatment of this subject for a closely related language is found in Clark 1971.

11.12. The situation in Yoruba is somewhat similar. Speakers of Yoruba may cite, and a dictionary may list, countless two-syllable sequences and uncritically call them "verbs." The vast majority of them are two-verb sequences in which the first verb requires an object; the two verbs appear in immediate sequence only if the object is topicalized, or for purposes of citation. Thus /gbájọ/ is not "a verb" meaning 'collect', as demonstrated by the following:

> ó gbá wọn jọ   'he collected them'

A great many more such sequences consist of a verb and a noun, in which the initial vowel of the noun is elided. Thus /kparí/ is not a "verb" meaning 'finish', but a phrase whose component parts are /kpa/ 'cut off' and /orí/ 'head'; finishing something in Yoruba is expressed as cutting off its head. This is demonstrated by the fact that the sequence may be followed only by a possessive pronoun, not an object pronoun. Thus 'finish it' is /kparí-rè/ (compare /orí-rè/ 'his ∼ her ∼ its head', not */kparí⁻/, in which the final mid tone would be an object pronoun.

There are, however, some verb-verb sequences, proven to be such by the fact that they take object pronouns. E.g.,

> wọn ba-dè'   'they waylaid him' (ba 'hide', dè 'wait for')
> wọn ba-tì'   'they took refuge with him' (ba 'hide', tì 'lean on')

As in Jukun, such verb-verb sequences might possibly be interpreted as complex verb bases, though again there are no inflectional suffixes whose position might force such an analysis. There is evidence, however, that native speakers of Yoruba tend to think of these as phrasal rather than joined as single words. They can readily be analyzed as serial verb constructions in which the first verb happens to be intransitive.

In most cases, as the two examples above, the two verbs in such sequences can be separately identified. There are a few instances, however, in which the second syllable is not attested except in a sequence. If the syllable has lowered mid or rising tone, it must be from a noun whose elided prefix has low tone. Otherwise, if such a sequence cannot be used with either a possessive or an object pronoun, there is no way to tell whether the second syllable is verb or noun. Even where a pronoun may be used, I have known native speakers to be unsure (in the case of one sequence unfortunately not recorded) which to use.

11.13. Efik has a limited number of types of derived verb bases, none of which is composed of two independent verb roots. Some of these involve suffixation to monosyllabic roots, and account for a number of two- and three-syllable bases in the language. There are, however, many other two- and three-syllable bases which cannot be analyzed as derived from monosyllabic roots. In fact, the most obvious derivational patterns are strangely restricted.[6]

First, a verb with intransitive meaning may be derived from a transitive verb by suffixing a vowel (usually the same as the vowel of the root) with high

---

[6] The following is outlined in Welmers 1968a, pp. 159-60 and 141-44.

tone. This pattern is recorded only with roots having final /p/, /t/, or /k/; with
the vowel suffix, these stops have their usual intervocalic (and ambisyllabic) alternants, here interpreted as /b/, /r/, and /g/. Examples of this formation are:

fɔ́p	'bake, burn'	:	fɔ́bɔ́	'be burnt'
byàt	'destroy, ruin'	:	byàrá	'become spoiled'
nwák	'crush'	:	nwágá	'get crushed'
syák	'split in two'	:	syágá	'(get) split'
wàk	'tear'	:	wàgá	'get torn'
bók	'gather up'	:	bógó	'assemble'
nùk	'bend'	:	nùgó	'get bent'

Second, the same derivational pattern is found without the derived root being
intransitive. One case is recorded in which the root has final /m/. E.g.,

kpép	'teach, learn'	:	kpébé	'imitate'
kɔ̀t	'grow' (intrans.)	:	kɔ̀rɔ́	'add to, supplement'
kèm	'equal, fit'	:	kèmé	'be able'
yét	'wash' (things)	:	yéré	'wash' (body parts)

In addition to the form /kɔt/ cited in the above, there is a form /kɔrì/ with the
same meaning, clearly related; there are a few other such pairs, but they appear
to be free or perhaps dialect alternants rather than derivations.

Third, some three-syllable bases are derived from monosyllabic roots by suffixing a vowel, the choice of which does not seem to be fully predictable, followed
by /-re/, all with high tone. From the few recorded cases, there does not seem to
be any restriction in the ending of the root; after a root with a final vowel, the
suffix has an alternant with initial /m/. The derived bases in this case have a
reversive meaning; they refer to undoing the action referred to by the root. E.g.,

kɔ́ŋ	'hang out' (clothes)	:	kɔ́ŋɔ́ré	'take down'
dyán	'add'	:	dyánáré	'subtract, deduct'
fík	'press down'	:	fígéré	'loosen up'
kɔ̀p ∼ kɔ̀bì	'hook, hang up'	:	kɔ̀béré	'unhook, take down'
dé	'go to sleep'	:	déméré	'wake up'

Fourth, some roots with final /k/ only refer to a single action or an action
performed by one subject; parallel forms with final /y/ (or in one case /ŋɔ́/) refer
to multiple actions or actions performed by several subjects. E.g.,

wàk	'tear' (e.g., one sheet of paper):
wày	'tear' (e.g., many sheets of paper)
dwɔk	'sprinkle' (e.g., a single plant):
dwɔy	'sprinkle' (e.g., all the flowers)
twàk	'jab, set' (as a stick in the ground):
twày	'hammer lightly and repeatedly'
syák	'split in two' (of one object):
sáy	'split in two' (of several objects)

dyɔ́k	'be bad' (with singular subject):
dyɔ́y	'be bad' (with plural subject)
kpɔ̀k	'crow, hoot' (of rooster, owl, perhaps others):
kpɔ̀y	'set up an incessant barking' (of dog only)
dwɔ́k	'throw away' (a single object):
dwɔ́ŋɔ́	'throw away' (many objects)
(with no single-action counterpart recorded):	
kóy	'bail out' (a boat; usually with plural subject)

The restrictions in the phonologic shapes of roots in some of these types of derivation, and in particular the restriction of the last to roots with final /k/, suggest that what are treated here as roots may themselves be morphologically complex. There is no other evidence that this is the case, however. In fact, it is possible that pairs such as /kɔ̀t ~ kɔ̀ri/ and /kɔ̀p ~ kɔ̀bí/ cited above may historically have been other manifestations of the multiple action derivation; a suffix */-i/ would be posited, and the statement made that root-final /k/ plus this suffix is realized as /y/.

In quite a different category from the derivations cited so far, Efik also has verb bases derived by reduplication. Reduplication has two completely different functions. With verbs having an inceptive meaning, the reduplicated base refers to the state resulting from the process, rather than the process itself. With other verbs, the reduplicated base has a contrastive force. The form of reduplication is the same in each case. Segmentally, a syllable is prefixed to the root which consists of the initial consonant of the root plus a harmonizing vowel (/e/ before /i/, /o/ before /u/, otherwise the root vowel). Tonally, the reduplicating syllable is low before a root with high tone, and downstep-high before a root with low or low-high tone; low-high in the following root becomes low throughout. In relative and negative constructions, however, there is a different form of reduplication; the unreduplicated root is used with the appropriate relative or negative suffix, and then the root is repeated in full. Examples of inceptive-stative pairs are:

dɔ́ŋɔ́	'get sick'	:	dɔ̀dɔ́ŋɔ́	'be sick'
tyɛ̆	'sit down'	:	tétyɛ̀	'be seated'
nă	'lie down'	:	nánà	'be lying down'
dá	'stand up'	:	dàdá	'be standing'
bìt	'get wet'	:	bébìt	'be wet'

Reduplicated statives appear to be used primarily if not exclusively in the present and past. The following include an example of a negative with root repetition:

ɛ́'tétyɛ̀ k'ísɔ̀ŋ	'he's lying on the ground'
ɛ́kɛ́'tétyɛ̀ k'ísɔ̀ŋ	'he was lying on the ground'
(cf.: ɛ́kétyɛ̀ k'ísɔ̀ŋ	'he lay down on the ground')
ìkétyɛ̀gétyɛ̀	'he wasn't lying down'

Contrastive reduplication is illustrated by the following; the inclusion of negatives or relatives with root repetition is almost inevitable in order to get clear-cut examples. The verb roots used in the following are /dép/ 'buy', /tɔ́/ 'cultivate, grow', /byàt/ 'spoil', and /ɣ̃àm/ 'sell':

ŋkédèdép byâ émì. ŋkɔ́'tɔ́gɔ́tɔ́.
    'I bought these yams; I didn't grow them.'
ìkábyàtkébyàt énàŋ úkwàk ésyĕ. áká'ɣ̃áɣ̃àm.
    'He didn't wreck his bicycle; he sold it.'
ákánì mótò émì ŋkáɣ̃àmdéɣ̃àm ɔ́'fɔ́n ákàn óbúfá émì ŋké'dépdédép.
    'The old car I sold is better than the new one I bought.'

Reduplication as a form of verb base derivation is attested in several other West African languages, but not with such specific functions as in Efik. Other derivations such as those illustrated in the foregoing for Igbo and Efik do not seem to be at all common. The types of derivation in Igbo and Efik are not very similar, and neither has a great deal in common with Bantu.

11.14. Typical of the Bantu languages as a whole is the derivation of verbal bases from verb roots by suffixes which are commonly known as "verbal extensions". Formally, these are somewhat similar to the base formatives described for Igbo in 11.10 above. They are rather different in their semantic characteristics, however, and Igbo does have a close counterpart to one of the Bantu verbal extensions which does not function as a base formative. Prior to discussing the Bantu extensions in detail, it should be noted that verbs in Bantu are commonly cited in the infinitive form, or sometimes without the infinitive prefix; the citation form ends with /a/ in all but a very few cases. Thus, some Swahili verbs as usually cited are:

kutafuta	'look for'
kupenda	'like'
kununua	'buy'

Not only is /ku-/ in these forms a prefix; the final /-a/ can also be shown to be a suffix, though it is not always recognized as such. There are certain verbal constructions which have other final vowels, using the same roots. No specific meaning can be assigned to /-a/, but it is obligatory in conjunction with certain prefixes. The roots of the above verbs are, respectively, /tafut-/, /pend-/, and /nunu-/; probably the major reason they are rarely cited in this way is that they cannot be pronounced in isolation within the phonologic rules of the language.

Verbal extensions are suffixes which occur immediately after the verb root —often with complex morphophonemic alternations involving the final consonant of the root and the extension itself—before the final suffix /-a/ or other vowel. Citations of the forms of extensions commonly include the suffix /-a/. A common form of a causative extension, for example, is usually cited as /-isa/. Actually, the extension itself is /-is-/, and the final vowel is an inflectional suffix.

Something like ten different verbal extensions are attested in a number of Bantu languages. Fortune (1955, p. 200) lists thirteen for Shona, but some of these are duplicates, listed separately because of different shades of meaning associated with the same extension. Rather easily definable meanings are assignable to some of the extensions, such as passive, causative, reflexive, reciprocal, and reversive. Terms for others—and the terminology may vary from writer to writer—do not so readily convey the ideas expressed. Some examples from Swahili will illustrate a number of extensions with the root /fung-/ 'fasten'; the infinitive prefix is not used here, but the suffix /-a/ is, with hyphens marking off the extensions:

Passive:	fung-w-a	'be fastened' (agent implied)
Causative:	fung-ish-a	'cause (someone) to fasten'
Reversive:	fung-u-a	'unfasten'
Applicative:	fung-i-a	'fasten for (someone)'
Stative:	fung-ik-a	'be fastened' (no agent implied), 'be fastenable'

Other terms more or less commonly used for some of the above are "conversive" for my "reversive", "prepositional" or "applied" (and accasionally "benefactive") for my "applicative", and "neuter" (as well as "potential" with reference to one of its implications) for my "stative".

The above examples do not show anything of the morphophonemic alternations involved with extensions; they are relatively simple in Swahili, but deserve explanation. In several of the extensions, some of the alternant forms show vowel harmony: /e/ if the preceding vowel is /e/ or /o/, and /i/ otherwise; the same pattern is found in many other Bantu languages. The Swahili passive extension has the form /-w-/ after roots with a final consonant. After final /a/ or /i/, it is /-w-/ or /-liw-/, optionally with some verbs, but sometimes lexically conditioned. After final /e/, it is similarly /-w-/ or /-lew-/. After final /u/ it is /-liw-/, and after final /o/ it is /-lew-/. There are a few roots consisting of a single consonant; after such, both /-iw-/ and /-ew/- are attested. After verbs adopted from Arabic which do not use the suffix /-a/, the alternants require a few additional statements which need not be included here. The ordinary allomorphs are illustrated by the following:

kat-a	'cut'	:	kat-w-a
twa-a	'take'	:	twa-liw-a
ti-a	'put'	:	ti-w-a ∼ ti-liw-a
poke-a	'receive'	:	poke-w-a ∼ poke-lew-a
chuku-a	'carry'	:	chuku-liw-a
ondo-a	'take away'	:	ondo-lew-a
l-a	'eat'	:	l-iw-a
p-a	'give'	:	p-ew-a

The causative extension is somewhat more complicated. Combinations of certain root-final consonants with this extension suggest an underlying form */-y-/.

Root-final /p/ combines with this to form /fy/; final /t/ yields /s/ in some cases and /sh/ in others; final /k/ yields /sh/; final /w/ yields /vy/; final /n/ yields /ny/; and final /l/ yields /z/. The extension is also /-z/ after a root-final vowel. It is normally /-ish-/ or /-esh-/ after other consonants, but throughout the system there are some lexically conditioned irregular formations. A few examples are the following; morpheme cuts cannot always be illustrated:

pit-a	'pass'	:	pish-a
ruk-a	'jump'	:	rush-a
lew-a	'be drunk'	:	levy-a
lal-a	'sleep'	:	laz-a
som-a	'read'	:	som-esh-a
imb-a	'sing'	:	imb-ish-a
tuli-a	'be quiet'	:	tuli-z-a

The applicative extension has alternants /-i-/, /-e-/, /-li-/, /-le-/, the choice of which is conditioned very much as for the passive extension.

There are some verbs in Swahili (and other Bantu languages) which in form and meaning appear to consist of a root and an extension, but for which the root alone does not appear in the language at present. There are also attested cases of false etymologies involving such forms.

Other extensions in Swahili may be more briefly mentioned.[7] One is a "static," /-am-/ ~ /-m-/ (after consonants and vowels respectively), indicating a stationary condition or inactivity. E.g., /kwa-a/ 'stumble, be stopped by a sudden obstacle': /kwa-m-a/ 'become jammed'. Another is a "contactive" or "tenacious," /-at-/ ~ /-t-/; it would seem from the examples that "intensive" might be a better term, though some languages have an intensive in addition to this. E.g., /kam-a/ 'squeeze': /kam-at-a/ 'take forcible hold of, arrest'. There is a rare "inceptive" /-p-/ (attested after vowels only), from roots which appear elsewhere in the language, but not as verbs. E.g., /nene/ (adj.) 'thick, stout': /nene-p-a/ 'get fat' (of persons). And finally there is an "associative," frequently called "reciprocal," which is widespread in Bantu, /-an-/ (after both consonants and vowels). E.g., /ju-a/ 'know': /ju-an-a/ 'be mutually acquainted'.

Depending on the root with which an extension is used, and its meaning, the precise semantic force of the extension is not the same in all cases. The situation is relatively straightforward in Swahili, but considerably more subtle in some other languages.

Most significantly, more than one extension may appear in a single base. Two are fairly common; in at least some languages, as many as four with some verbs do not seem unduly awkward. Bases with as many as seven extensions have been reported, but such forms, while technically grammatical, are probably not easily used in speech. The composition of a Swahili base with applicative

---

[7] For the less common extensions, I rely on Ashton 1944 to supplement my rather limited competence. I cite the forms of the extensions, however, in a more consistent way.

and passive extensions is illustrated by the following set of sentences; with both, note the unusual relation of the subject and object to the verb:

Juma alipik-a chakula	'Juma cooked food'
Juma alinipik-i-a chakula	'Juma cooked food for me'
chakula kilipik-w-a na Juma	'food was cooked by Juma'
nilipik-i-w-a chakula na Juma	'food was cooked for me by Juma'
	(lit. 'I was cooked-for food by Juma')

The applicative does not always refer to action performed on someone's behalf; it merely brings a person into relationship with the action. Compare the following:

baba yangu alikuf-a	'my father died'
nilif-i-w-a na baba yangu	'my father died (with direct effect on me)' (lit. 'I was died-to by my father')

A combination of associative, causative, and passive is illustrated by the following set:

pat-a	'get'
pat-an-a	'agree' ('get together'!)
pat-an-ish-a	'reconcile'
pat-an-ish-w-a	'be reconciled'

Some descriptions of Bantu verbal extensions treat the causative as having rather an intensive meaning with some roots; others recognize two homophonous extensions. The latter is probably the more satisfactory, since what appears to be and has been described as a "double causative" is semantically a causative intensive. Actual double causatives from intransitive verbs are also possible. Similarly, in some languages there appear to be two successive uses of the applicative in one form, and this combination has been called a "double prepositional." It would probably be preferable to recognize this combination as a single extension different from the applicative, an "extensive"; it refers to action done a lot or "all over the place." It can be combined with the applicative, so that the latter appears to be used three times, to refer to such extensive action performed for someone.

The morphotactics of extensions in succession may be complicated. Pairs such as the applicative and causative may appear in either order, with different meanings. A few restrictions are clear, however. The passive and the stative can only be the last extension in a base. The reciprocal may be followed by the applicative, causative, or stative, but not by others. At the present state of our knowledge, perhaps the best that can be said is that a great deal depends on the semantics of individual roots.[8] The use of most of the extensions is by no means productive, and in some languages is quite restricted. There are relatively few

---

[8] This is the opinion of Mr. Livingstone Walusimbi (personal communication) after a fairly extensive study of extensions in LuGanda and some other Bantu languages.

extensions in the northwestern Bantu languages, and in some of them perhaps no extensions at all. There is some evidence, however, that the use of verbal extensions goes back to pre-Bantu times, as the following section will suggest.

11.15. It has been noted that, in spite of the operation of a similar derivational process, the verbal extensions of Bantu do not find a real parallel in the base formatives of Igbo. There is in Igbo, however, a close parallel to one of the Bantu extensions, the applicative. Even its form, /-r/ plus a repetition of the preceding vowel, is reminiscent of Bantu forms with /l/ or /r/. It is not, however, simply attached to a verb root to form an extended base. It rather occurs after a root or after certain inflectional suffixes. E.g.,

í'kpọ́	'to call'
ọ́ gà àkpọ́ ńnà yá	'he will call his father'
ọ́ gà àkpọ́rọ́ 'gí ńnà yá	'he will call his father for you'
kpòọ́ ńnà gí	'call your father'
kpòọ́rọ́ 'ḿ ńnà gí	'call your father for me'
ọ́ 'kpọ́ọ́lárá 'ḿ ńnà yá	'he has called his father for me'

The derivational suffixes used with verb roots in Efik, on the other hand, show more semantic similarity to Bantu verbal extensions, though no great formal similarity. The derived bases of Efik include intransitives from transitives, which are similar to statives in Bantu. The Efik reversives in /-V́ré/ have their semantic parallel in Bantu, and perhaps a formal parallel as well; compare the Shona reversive extension /-ur-/. And the Efik forms indicating action performed on a number of objects or by a number of subjects may be compared with Bantu bases with the extensive extension.

From the viewpoint of speakers of English, it is interesting that, outside the Bantu languages, there is no recorded passive formation in Niger-Congo. What in other languages is expressed by a passive without an agent may be expressed by an active construction with a third person plural subject, or in some languages with an impersonal singular subject, or by a stative construction. Other ideas expressed by Bantu extensions, such as the causative and applicative, are usually expressed by combinations of verbs; still others, such as the intensive and extensive, tend to be expressed by adverbial complements.

11.16. By way of appendix to this chapter, an observation will be made about a curious case of convergence between unrelated languages; the major significance of this point is perhaps to assure students of African languages that earlier investigators of those languages have not been totally naive. The observation has to do with expressions for obligation ('I have to do it' and the like) in Yoruba and Efik.

In the relatively early days of my acquaintance with Yoruba, I elicited sentences expressing obligation, and recorded the following, without a common contraction:

mo ní l'átī lọ	'I have to go'

Frankly, I didn't believe it. I recognized /ní/, which elsewhere means 'have, possess', as in /mo ní bàtà/ 'I have shoes'. I also recognized /l'átī/ as a form used after other verbs in the meaning 'in order to'. So 'I have to go' (itself a strange idiom in English) is 'I possess in order to go' in Yoruba?? I was convinced that my informant had been guilty of a gross translationism, giving my English words individual equivalents one at a time. It developed, however, that that actually is the ordinary construction used by everybody in Yoruba. Could it still have been originally a calque? The likelihood of that diminished to approximately zero when I began work on Efik.

Efik has an infinitive form, with the prefix /ńdí-/. Efik also has a verb /ỹéné/ 'get, acquire', which is used in the completive construction for 'have'. And in Efik you say:

         ḿmé'ỹéné ńdíkǎ   'I have to go'

Ajabu ![9]

---

[9] Over a year after writing this section, it was learned that these expressions actually may be —necessarily independently in Yoruba and Efik—calques after all. According to Mr. Baruch Elimelech (private communication), Yoruba speakers with whom he has worked report that elderly people, whose contact with English has been minimal, use an apparently indigenous Yoruba expression /gbọdà/ meaning 'have to'; the informants believe that the currently more common expression is a translation from English.

Chapter 12

Verbal Constructions in Niger-Congo

12.1. There is a great deal more structural similarity between the following two clauses, from widely separated and only distantly related languages, than meets the eye:

Swahili:	tukisema, . . .	'If we speak, . . . '	
Kpelle:	kwà lòno . . .	'If we speak, . . . '	

Each of these clauses contains four morphemes. In the Swahili clause, these can be very simply identified by a comparison of other clauses using different pronouns, different tense-aspect-mode references, and different verb bases. The first morpheme is a pronoun, /tu-/. The second is a marker of what may for the time being be called "conditional," /-ki-/. The third is a verb root which is also the base, /-sem-/. The fourth is a suffix which appears with the conditional and with many other, but not all, verbal constructions, /-a/. The analysis of the Kpelle clause is not so immediately apparent, but strikingly similar. First there is a pronoun, the basic form of which can be established as /kú/. This combines with a morpheme /-à/ which, in combination with another morpheme still to be defined, signals the conditional construction. There is a verb root, the basic form of which can be established as /lóno/, with high tone. And finally there is a morpheme definable as low tone replacing stem tone, which appears in the conditional and some other constructions; both /-à/ and this replacive are required to make the construction conditional. In neither language is there anything like a conjunction corresponding to English 'if'; the construction is conditional by virtue of the particular morphemes used with the verb base. In both Swahili and Kpelle, the construction can be represented by the formula P-C-V-A: Pronoun - Construction marker - Verb base - Affix with verb base. The same formula is valid for a great many more verbal constructions in both languages, and for much of the verbal systems of countless Niger-Congo languages throughout the family. It is hardly to be expected, of course, that this formula is predominant in every language, or for every construction in a given language; at the same time, it is so pervasive that it is worthy of statement by way of introduction to verbal systems.

(For the most part, the verbal systems of Niger-Congo languages are best described in terms of a uni-dimensional list of "verbal constructions" rather than in terms of a bi-dimensional or multi-dimensional grid with intersecting categories such as tense, aspect, and mode. There may be ways of expressing two dimensional parallelisms such as simple vs. progressive action in the past and in the future (as 'he worked, he was working; he will work, he will be working'), but (as in English also) these distinctions typically do not involve combinations of morphemes

343

as a verbal form, but rather auxiliaries and similar secondary constructions. Even the affirmative-negative contrast is usually asymmetrical; there are typically more affirmative than negative constructions, and not all negatives are formed in the same way or in terms of a single, simple transformation applied to affirmatives. In the Bantu languages, the unidimensional character of the system is so conspicuous that many grammarians, having applied the term "tense" to forms with obvious reference to past, present, and future time, have felt compelled to extend that label to other forms with similar morphological composition, so that one hears such incongruous combinations as "the subjunctive tense" and "the conditional tense." To be sure, the Bantu languages, unlike almost all other Niger-Congo languages, ultimately have categories such as passive, causative, and stative intersecting the basic system of verbal constructions. As noted in the preceding chapter, however, these involve the derivation of verb bases; the almost totally unidimensional system of verbal constructions is then applied to these derived bases just as to simple verb roots.

In a wide variety of languages, two important types of verbal construction may be distinguished. The first type may be called "primary constructions"; these contain only one verb base, plus inflectional morphemes of definable classes —construction markers and affixes with the base. The second type is "auxiliary constructions"; these contain two verb bases, one of which may be considered an auxiliary and the other the "main" verb, though grammatically the auxiliary rather than the main verb takes primary inflectional morphemes. In some languages it is useful to speak also of "expanded constructions"; these include, for example, primary constructions with the addition of adverbial modifiers not otherwise freely used, combinations which fill in gaps in the list of primary negative constructions.

The term "verbal construction" is thus designed to avoid the confusions and complications inherent in distinguishing categories such as tense, aspect, and mode. Some constructions, to be sure, may have specific reference to time, such as past; others may have specific reference to mode, such as conditional. But the forms or constructions of Niger-Congo languages do not fall into neat sets with different types of morphological structure. For each construction, of course, the semantic reference must be defined, and in many cases familiar labels are adequate to suggest the function of given constructions. In many other cases, however, there has been widespread misuse of labels, and apparently widespread misunderstanding of usage. Accordingly, before saying adything about the verbal system of any one language in depth, some observations are in order about the types of verbal constructions found in a variety of languages, and how they have typically been treated or mistreated.

12.2. Most traditional grammars of languages throughout the world begin their discussion of verbs and verbal morphology with "the Present Tense." And in field work, or in a course in Field Methods, many a student who should be fairly sophisticated about languages and linguistics can be caught, very early in his elicitation of the equivalents of English verbal predications, asking how one would say 'I build a house'. Before anything can be said about verbal constructions in African languages, it must be pointed out that 'I build a house' is not an English sentence, and if an African informant gives an alleged equivalent we really have no idea what it actually means. One can say 'I build houses', or perhaps even 'I build a house at ten-fifteen every Monday morning', both of which express customary action. Or one can say 'I am building a house', which expresses continuing action in the present time. But 'I build a house' is in itself totally meaningless. On the other hand, 'I see a house' is perfectly legitimate, and refers to the present time. English has, in general, two types of verbs. One refers to what may be called "private" actions—actions of which only the actor is the proper judge. For such verbs, like 'see, feel, have, be, think, hear, smell, believe', the stem of the verb, with the inflectional ending /-z/ $\sim$ /-s/ $\sim$ /-əz/ in the third person singular (the so-called "present") indicates present time. The second type of verb refers to "public" actions—actions which can be observed by someone other than the actor as well as by the actor himself. For such verbs, like 'work, sing, sleep, walk', the so-called present does not refer to present time as such, but rather to customary action; the actual present is expressed by the 'be . . . -ing' construction. This distinction must be fully recognized, since many African languages have quite distinct constructions to indicate customary and present continuing action; and if they do not, the lack of such a distinction should be noted.

Having straightened that much out in English, one might well elicit an equivalent of 'I am building a house', and the response can legitimately be said to express continuing action in the present. It does not follow, however, that the construction illustrated can immediately be labelled "present". In all probability, if there are no further modifiers or complements, it will by itself be interpreted as referring to the present. It may well be, however, that precisely the same construction can be used with a modifier or complement referring specifically to another time, such as 'last year', and in that case the construction refers to continuing action in the past. In such a situation, the construction might better be labelled "continuative". Such is the case in Yoruba; compare the following:

ó ń šišẹ́   'he's working'
ó ń šišẹ́ l'ánǎ   'he was working yesterday'

Yoruba has a customary construction distinct from the continuative. In Igbo, on the other hand, continuing action irrespective of time, and customary action, are all expressed by the same construction. The only thing that can be said to be in common to all uses is the fact that there has not as yet been an end to the action; it either is going on at present, was or will be going on at a time mentioned, or goes on regularly. Accordingly, a more appropriate label in the case of Igbo is "incompletive". This construction (an auxiliary type) is illustrated by the following:

ọ́ nà àrụ́ ọ́'rụ́	'he is working' ∼ 'he works'
ọ́ nà àrụ́ ọ́'rụ́ ùgbú à	'he is working now'
ọ́ nà àrụ́ ọ́'rụ́ écí	'he was working yesterday'
ọ́ nà àrụ́ ọ́'rụ́ kwà ụ́bọ̀cì	'he works every day'

Many languages, like Yoruba, do distinguish a present or continuative construction from a customary construction; the latter usually has specific reference to the present. An adverbial complement or an auxiliary is found in some languages to express the idea of 'used to', but more commonly simple and customary action in other than the present are not distinguished at all. Kpelle has a specifically present construction, and also a customary; e.g., with a verb whose root is /kɛ́/ 'do'.

| a tíi kêi ∼ 'káa tíi kêi | 'he is working' |
| a tíi kɛ̀ | 'he works' |

Swahili has two different constructions covering the range of present and customary, but they are not always sharply distinguished in usage. Apparently the original distinction was between continuative and customary; the two constructions are sometimes referred to as "Present Definite" and "Present Indefinite". The first has a construction marker /-na-/; the second has a construction marker /-a-/, which conditions morphophonemic alternations with the preceding pronoun. Thus:

| ninafanya kazi | 'I am working' |
| nataka ndizi | 'I want bananas' |

For at least some speakers, the distinction between these two constructions is maintained in that the former, if used with the verb /taka/ 'want', implies a more immediate need; e.g., if one is distressingly thirsty, he would more likely say:

| ninataka maji | 'I want water' |

Not everything that we think of as referring to present time is expressed by a present or a continuative construction in many Niger-Congo languages. First, a number of languages distinguish two types of verbs, in general "stative" and "active;" stative verbs usually include equivalents for most of the "private" verbs of English. For statives, a reference to present time may use the same construction that refers to past time if an active verb is used; or more accurately, the construction is timeless for stative verbs—a modifier may indicate that the reference is to past time. In Yoruba, the construction in question is the simplest construction in the language, consisting of only a pronoun and a verb root; this may be analyzed as having a zero construction marker, but Yoruba has no affixes with the verb base in any case. This construction is commonly known as "past", but the reference is obviously not always to past time. A better label might be "factative"; the construction expresses the most obvious fact about the verb in question, which in the case of active verbs is that the action was observed or took place, but for stative verbs is that the situation obtains at present.[1] Thus:

ó lọ	'he went'
ó fẹ́ owó	'he wants money'
ó fẹ́ owó l'ánǎ	'he wanted money yesterday'
ó dára	'it's fine'

Igbo also uses a factative construction in a similar way. In the case of Igbo, the factative is formed by low tone replacing stem tone for a monosyllabic base (with minor modifications for one type of longer base), plus a suffix consisting of /r/ plus the preceding vowel repeated, also with low tone. Thus:

ọ́ byàrà	'he came'
ó ŋwèrè é'gó	'he has money'
ọ́ cọ̀rọ̀ é'gọ̀	'he wants money'
ọ́ cọ̀rọ̀ é'gọ̀ écí	'he looked for (∼ wanted) money yesterday'
ọ́ tọ̀rọ̀ ụ̀tọ́	'it is delicious'

A second type of nonmatch between what we think of as present time and verbal constructions in many Niger-Congo languages has to do with verbs which, in those languages, have a basically inceptive meaning—e.g., 'get sick, ripen, mature, age'. With such verbs, reference to the present situation ('be sick, be ripe, be mature, be old') is typically expressed by a "completive" construction—commonly, on the background of our Latin-English terminological tradition, called "perfect" or "the Perfect Tense." E.g.,

Fante:	ɔ́áfùná	'he is (has become) tired'
(cf.:	ɔ̀rìfùná	'he is getting tired'
and:	ɔ́ábá	'he has come')
Kpelle:	aâ kpɛɛ	'it is all gone'
(cf.:	è kpὲɛ	'it got used up',
and:	aâ 'kpɛɛ	'he has finished it')

Kpelle has a rather unusual application of the use of the completive which deserves a report on the circumstances of an interesting discovery. I had noted from my very early elicitations that 'see', with reference to the present, is expressed by a completive. But I had no explanation for this fact. Then one late afternoon my two informants and I went for a walk, with a shotgun and some hopes of bringing home some precious protein. On a quiet forest path, they suddenly stopped me; one of them pointed toward a tree branch ahead and above me, and whispered in English, "There's a monkey." With my inexperience in the sights of the rain forest (later fairly well overcome), I saw nothing but branches and leaves. With a minimum of motion and sound, both informants tried for some

---

[1] The term "factative" was first proposed and defined for a construction with a similar range of usage in Igbo, in Welmers and Welmers 1968b, pp. 75-6.

time to tell me just where to look. Finally the monkey moved slightly, and I was able to distinguish him from his background. Without saying a word, I quietly cocked my shotgun and slowly raised it. At that point, one of my informants whispered to the other (yes, tones can be distinguished in a whisper), "/aâ 'káa"/, which I knew in the meaning 'he sees it', but which is completive in form. The informants and some of their friends had meat for dinner, and I had a rewarding bit of intelligence: the Kpelle verb /káa/ does not simply mean 'see', but rather 'catch sight of', and 'he sees it' is expressed as 'he has caught sight of it'.

12.3. In many languages there is a single construction which has explicit and exclusive reference to past action; for such languages it is quite legitimate to speak of a "past" construction. It has already been noted, however, that some languages use a single construction to refer to past time for active verbs and present time for stative verbs; for such languages, a term like "factative" may be preferable, and the grammar may very properly make no reference to a "past tense" as such. On the other hand, there are a number of languages which have more than one construction referring to past time. Some Bantu languages distinguish a "near past" (particularly with reference to action performed earlier on the same day) and a "remote past" (or perhaps better a "general past"). Such a distinction is reported in LoNkundo (see Hulstaert 1938, pp. 55, 189-90). Misinterpretations of language data in terms of such a distinction will be noted presently, but it seems clear that Hulstaert has presented the correct analysis for LoNkundo, since he explicitly describes a completive in distinction from a "today past" (*verleden vorm van heden*) and an "earlier past" (*verleden vorm van te voren*); his analysis was, in fact, confirmed by a former student of mine who had spoken LoNkundo as a child. The two past constructions of LoNkundo are distinguished only by tone (and the distinction is thus ignored by most speakers of English learning the language). There is some evidence that what is suffixed to the verb base in each of these constructions is two morphemes, one indicating past time and the other indicating the degree of remoteness; these would then be subtypes of one construction, not two totally distinct constructions in a unidimensional list. Thus, from a verb whose root is /kìs/ 'sit down':

ákìsàkí	'he sat down (today)'
ákìsákí	'he sat down (earlier)'

Not every report of a distinction between "near past" and "remote past", however, can be taken at face value. Abraham (1940b, pp. 47-48) appears to describe such a distinction for Tiv, but it is clear on the basis of the data he himself presents that the distinction is rather between a completive and a simple past. He describes what he calls the "Special Form" of verbs, with two "varieties"; the two forms merely show a morphotonemic alternation conditioned by the choice of subject pronoun, and the term "special" seems to have no positive significance, but appears to have been chosen merely for lack of a more specifically meaningful label. This form (or forms) is said to be used "when an act has occurred *recently*," and Abraham's first examples all include a word /áshén/ 'recently'; e.g.,

áshén m̀ kìmbí   'I recently paid'

Abraham does go on to say that such a word is not essential, and that the verbal construction by itself refers to action "as recent as a few minutes ago or a few days ago," but that if a specific past time is referred to, even yesterday, the "past tense" is used. Yet, in spite of his repeated emphasis on the recentness of action supposedly expressed by this construction, just two pages later he cites a sentence using the same construction in which the idea of an immediate past is by no means in focus:

tóhó ú mé'ndé   'the grass has sprouted'

Surely the grass in this case need not have sprouted within the past few minutes or even the past few days; the point is that it is now in a state which is the result of a past action—a typical reference of a completive rather than a recent past. Had the illustrative sentence been 'the grass has dried', the situation would be even clearer; the drying process might have been pretty well complete as much as two or three months ago, but the point is simply that it is dry now. In all further citations of the same construction, Abraham translates with the English "perfect," which is clearly a more faithful representation than a past with recentness specified.

A similar misinterpretation of the usage of constructions has been applied to LuGanda, in which three degrees of remoteness in the past have been seen by some: immediate (today), near (roughly yesterday), and remote (earlier). The first of these, however, cannot be used in an equivalent of 'I did it this morning' if one is speaking in the late afternoon, i.e., after some time has elapsed; on the other hand it can be used with reference to something that happened at an unspecified earlier time if the focus of attention is on the resultant present situation. Nothing could more precisely define a completive. Fortunately, the best works on LuGanda at least call it a "perfect" or "perfective"; I have avoided the latter labels merely because the word 'perfect' no longer has its older meaning of 'complete', and the construction in question has nothing to do with being 'flawless' or 'sinless'. The LuGanda completive and recent past both use a form of the verb which is commonly known as the "modified stem;" it is the root plus an inflectional ending, required in certain constructions, which appears rather commonly in Bantu in forms like /-ile/, but which in LuGanda and some other languages conditions a complicated set of morphophonemic alternations. E.g., using a root /kól-/ 'work', the three constructions are:

ŋkózè	'I have worked'
nàkózè	'I worked (recently)'
nàkólà	'I worked (earlier)'

Three degrees of past actually do appear to be distinguished, however, in KiKongo. Using the best techniques of elicitation and comparison I could think of, I have recorded forms distinguishing immediate past (today), near past (yesterday or perhaps a little more general), and remote past (earlier), all in distinction from a completive. The first of these was suspect for a while; I thought it might refer to 'I was doing it' or 'I have been doing it'. But specific sentences recorded, such as the first of those below, simply do not yield themselves semantically to the idea of continuous action in other than the present; although I did not acquire great fluency in KiKongo, I also recorded the immediate past in conversations about such topics as going to the market and buying things earlier in the day. The immediate past is nevertheless formally the completive with a suffix consisting of /ng/ plus the preceding vowel repeated, with high tone; the same or a homophonous suffix appears also in the customary. In a pattern strikingly similar to that of LuGanda, the immediate and near past, as well as the completive, use the root with an inflectional suffix which in this case has the form /-idi/; there are other alternants largely conditioned by the final consonant of the root and by vowel harmony. The four KiKongo constructions are illustrated with a verb whose root is /suumb/ 'buy'; only high tone is marked here:

nsuumbidingí nkóombo	'I bought a goat (today)'
yásuumbidí nkóombo	'I bought a goat (yesterday)'
yasúumba nkóombo	'I bought a goat (earlier)'
nsuumbidi nkóombo	'I have bought a goat'

12.4. A good deal has already been said about "completive" constructions; there does not seem to be any Niger-Congo language that lacks something of the sort. The reference, as already suggested, is to the present effect of an action: 'he has become tired (and therefore is tired now)', 'he has eaten (and is therefore full or at least not about to eat again)', and the like. Obviously, the action or process that has such a present effect is normally something in the past, and very commonly (though by no means necessarily) something in the recent past; hence the rather common and unfortunate confusion of such a construction with the idea of recent past. In one striking instance, however, a completive was recorded in which the present effect is actually the result of a future action; at least, this seems a better way to describe the situation than by hedging about the speaker being so sure that the action would take place that he thought of it as already completed. The language was Kpelle once more; the situation was a mock court case staged by informants who should have been signed to contracts as dramatic and comedy actors on the spot. The defendant was accused of stealing a bag of rice; the evidence was largely circumstantial and not unequivocally confirmed by impartial witnesses; the defendant had no good alibi, but might have been innocent. The judge pontifically pronounced the defendant guilty and imposed a fine. At that point the defendant arose and made a stirring announcement (the Kpelle words are forgotten, but not the completive construction): "I have appealed to the District Commissioner!" The action was still in the future, but the "complete" effect was dramatically in the present.

For most languages, it may seem like nit-picking to observe that the completive construction may refer to two kinds of present effect, but in a few other languages there are two distinct constructions reflecting just such a contrast. First, the present effect may be the immediate situation, as in 'I have eaten (and am therefore full)', or 'the clothes have dried (and are therefore dry)'. Second, however, the present effect may have to do with the totality of experience, as in 'I have eaten palm oil stew (at one time or often, but not necessarily recently, and at the moment I may be—and am—starved for some)', or 'I have played all of Beethoven's piano sonatas (though that was almost forty years ago, it is nevertheless part of my experience)'. In most languages, these two ideas are not differentiated in the verbal system as such, but only—if it is considered necessary to avoid ambiguity—by adverbial complements or explanatory additions. The corresponding negatives are often expressed by complements, in Niger-Congo languages as well as in English, as in 'I haven't done it yet' vs. 'I've never done it'. If a language does incorporate such a distinction into the verbal system, the first of the two constructions may be called "completive", and the label "experiential" is suggested for the second.

Kpelle is such a language. The completive and experiential use different construction markers; in both constructions the verb root has its stem tone (zero affix). E.g.,

ŋaâ 'kpɛtɛ	'I have fixed it (and it works)'
ŋà 'kpɛtɛ (à tȃi támaa)	'I have fixed it (many times; but it keeps breaking down)'

In the following parallel pair of examples, note that English uses different verbs to express this contrast:

aâ lí Dukɔɔ	'he has gone to Monrovia (and is away now)'
à lí Dukɔɔ	'he has been to Monrovia'

Christian missionaries, undoubtedly the largest category of non-Africans who attempt to use African languages, would do well to pay attention to such a contrast. It would be disastrous to say that our sins are forgiven because /Yîsɛ aâ saa/ 'Jesus has died (and is dead)', rather than /Yîsɛ à saa, kélɛɛ aâ ṁu síɣe/ 'Jesus has had the experience of dying, but has (and is) risen'. Fortunately, most missionaries find the past construction handier, and it is perfectly adequate for this situation.

And unfortunately, not all missionaries do pay attention to such a contrast. It is found also in LoNkundo, though it is not clearly recognized by Hulstaert (1938, pp. 42-43, 191-92). He cites two paradigms for what he calls "present completed tense (situation)" (voltooid tegenwoordige tijd (toestand)), which he describes as referring to today and earlier respectively. Such an analysis may well have been suggested by the fact that the two forms differ only in tone, and in somewhat the same way that the recent (today) and remote (earlier) past constructions described in 12.3 above differ from each other. The two constructions are illustrated by the following with the root /kìs/ 'sit down':

àôkìsà   'he has sat down (today?)'
áókìsà   'he has sat down (earlier?)'

My experience with Kpelle made me wonder whether the distinction was not rather between completive and experiential, neither of which is necessarily tied in with either recent or remote time. Although I had no access to an African native speaker of LoNkundo, I was fortunately able to check with the student referred to in 12.3 above. She considered LoNkundo her first language, and had spoken it constantly, along with English in her missionary family circle, until she was about thirteen. Eight or nine years later, she refused to act as an informant in the usual sense, but would gleefully applaud my efforts (if they were accurate) to produce intelligible utterances on the basis of Hulstaert's generally excellent description. I laboriously put together two sentences, both of which would be meaningful, with a description of the situations in which I thought each might be used, to illustrate the difference between a completive idea and an experiential idea. The emphasis was on the minimal contrast in tone. Having set the stage with descriptions of contrasting situations, I produced the two sentences to see if they matched the situations. With unrestrained delight, the student said, "That's exactly right! And you know, my parents have spoken LoNkundo for twenty-five years and have never recognized that difference!"

Who knows how many other languages have unreported and unnoticed distinctions of this sort?

12.5. Although written from more of a philosophical than a linguistic viewpoint, the following statement may serve as a legitimate warning by way of introduction to verbal constructions referring to the future: "The linear concept of Time, with a Past, Present and Future, stretching from infinity to infinity, is foreign to African thinking, in which the dominant factor is a virtual absence of the Future. By our definition, Time is a composition of events, and since the Future events have not occurred, the Future as a necessary linear component of Time is virtually absent. Such is either *potential Time*, with certainty of its eventual realization, or *No-Time*, lying beyond the conceptual horizon of the people." (Mbiti 1969, p. 159.) On the basis of evidence or informant testimony long forgotten, I observed that an apparent "future" construction in Jukun, particularly Dìyí, referred to an action that will, can, or may take place, and noted, "No levity is intended in referring to the common observation that when an African says 'I will do it' (even in English), it means that perhaps he will and perhaps he won't. His frequent failure to 'keep a promise' may be more of a linguistic ambiguity than a moral fault." (Welmers 1968b, p. 159.) It may be difficult to pinpoint the reference of a given construction as focusing on potentiality or futurity, but it should not be surprising that our translations may well fall short of precisely representing such constructions in African languages.

The difference between two ways of referring to the future in English must also be recognized. We normally think of the "future" as being expressed by sentences like 'he will do it'. Actually, we probably more commonly say 'he's going to do it', and few of us are aware of the semantic difference between the two sentences. It has nothing to do with desire or with motion, as the words might suggest. Rather, the 'will' future generally refers to an action incidental to a broader purpose, and often an action just decided on. The 'going to' future refers to more of a predetermined action. Thus, if one leaves the house with the primary intention of mailing some letters, he would say, 'I'm going to mail these letters'; but if he leaves with some other purpose, and incidentally notices some letters ready to be mailed, he would say, 'I'll mail these letters (while I'm at it)'. This rather unusual and subtle distinction is rarely found in other languages; we may use the 'will' future in glosses for the sake of convenience (it takes less space in type), but for the most part our 'going to' future is a better representation of future or future-like constructions in other languages.

It should also be noted that we sometimes use the present to express future action in English, particularly with the verb 'go' ('he's going tomorrow'), often with 'come', and occasionally with other verbs. The use of 'can' with future reference is also common ('I can do it next week'). In all such cases, a more consistent use of future constructions can be expected in other languages.

With these warnings and reservations, one or more future or future-like constructions can be recognized in any known African language. In some cases, there is a single future construction paralleling other constructions in formation. In Swahili, for example, the future construction marker is /-ta-/, and its parallelism with other construction markers is evident from the following:

a-ta-kwenda	'he's going to go'
a-li-kwenda	'he went'
a-me-kwenda	'he has gone'
a-na-kwenda	'he's going'

There are two future constructions in Yoruba. Both are used by many speakers, but the first appears to be more common; the second may be more typical of some dialects, and may be archaic in others, but no semantic distinction is known. The subject pronouns required by these two constructions differ in three cases; partial similarity to the first set is found also in some other constructions which refer to other than the known past or present. The two futures are illustrated by the following:

n ó lọ ∼ mo máa lọ	'I'm going to go'
yó lọ ∼ ó máa lọ	'he's going to go'
wọn ó lọ ∼ wọ́n máa lọ	'they're going to go'
a ó lọ ∼ a máa lọ	'we're going to go'

In Akan, the future construction marker is unquestionably derived from the verb for 'come', the root of which is /bá/. As a construction marker, it has four alternant forms, /bέ ∼ bé ∼ bɔ́ ∼ bó/, conditioned by vowel harmony and the unrounded or rounded quality of the next vowel. Thus:

òbébá	'he's going to come'
òbédìdí	'he's going to eat'
òbɔ́kɔ́	'he's going to go'
òbósùró	'he's going to be afraid'

Although the future construction marker is derived from the verb meaning 'come', it has no more reference to motion in this direction than English 'going to' as a future marker has to do with motion away. Similar derivatives of /kɔ́/ 'go' are also used as a type of construction marker in Akan, most commonly but not exclusively if /kɔ́/ has been used as a regular verb earlier in the sentence. This has specific reference to motion away in order to perform the action. If /bá/ 'come' is used as a main verb, the derived construction marker may also be used later in the sentence with specific reference to motion in this direction rather than futurity; in fact, it may be used before a past form. E.g.,

mìkédì gùá	'I'm going shopping'
ɔkɔrì hɔ́ kédáì	'he went there to sleep'
ɔbáà há bédáì	'he came here to sleep'

The use of a verb meaning 'come' as an auxiliary in future constructions is widespread; 'go' is also attested as a future auxiliary, but less commonly. In Kpelle, the present of /pá/ 'come' is used before a form of the main verb with a suffix /-ì/, which is a kind of verbal noun with an underlying reference to place (cf. 11.5). E.g.,

a pâi 'kêi ∼ 'káa pâi 'kêi	'he's going to do it'

In the complex known as Jukun, two patterns are found. In Wàpã, /bi/ 'come' is used in the present construction as an auxiliary before the main verb in its stem form. In Dìyī, two future construction markers are used, /á/ and /bá/, the former apparently more frequently, but with no known distinction in meaning or usage between the two. Thus:

Wàpã:	ku ri bi ya	
Dìyī:	kwá ya ∼ kú bá ya	'he's going to go'

In Igbo, /gá/ 'go' is used in the stative construction as an auxiliary before a verbal noun to express the future:

ọ́ gà àbyá	'he's going to come'

In 5.21, a distinction was noted in Efik between a "neutral past" construction and two "contrastive past" constructions, one focusing attention on something preceding the verb and the other on something following the verb. Efik also distinguishes between neutrality and contrast in the future, but there is only one contrastive future; what is contrasted can be determined only by the context, usually a question which is being answered. The neutral future has a construction marker /-yé'-/, after which the verb base has its lexical tone. The contrastive future has a construction marker /-dì-/ (with an alternant /-dì-/ after

low tone for some speakers, and perhaps regularly in some dialects), after which the verb base has high-low tone. The form /-dî-/ is sometimes heard with a long vowel; it is in all probability derived from the verb /-dí-/ 'come' and an archaic infinitive prefix /ì-/ (the regular Efik infinitive prefix is /ndí-/). Thus the contrastive future is only a step away from being an auxiliary construction. Of the following two examples, the first would be a typical statement with no reference to anything previously said; the second is an appropriate answer to a question such as 'What are you going to buy?', focusing attention on the object:

> ńyé'dép m̀bòró ⎫
> ńdîdêp m̀bòró ⎬   'I'm going to buy bananas'

As in the past, there may be degrees of remoteness in the future. LuGanda distinguishes two degrees: a near future for action expected to take place within about a day, and a remote future for action expected to take place only later. In addition, there is a third future which apparently has an indefinite reference ('sometime'). The near future uses a construction marker /-náà-/. The remote future uses a construction marker /-lí-/. The indefinite future is an auxiliary type, using the stem of the verb /jjá/ 'come' (which with the preceding pronoun is not otherwise an independent verbal construction) with the infinitive of the main verb. Thus:

> ànáàgéndá   'he's going to go (within a day)'
> àlígéndá   'he's going to go (later)'
> àjjá kúgéndá   'he's going to go (sometime)'

KiKongo appears to have very nearly the same distinctions as LuGanda. The near future has a morpheme /sì-/ before the subject pronoun, no construction marker after the pronoun, and high tone with the first vowel of the verb (or at least for the verb in the examples below). The remote future uses the same morpheme /sì-/ before the pronoun, and a construction marker /-á-/ after the pronoun, after which the first vowel of the verb has low tone. (My informant suggested the term "indefinite future" for this construction, but it is mutually exclusive in usage from the clearly "near future". I would prefer to reserve the term "indefinite" for the third future, which may be used in place of either of the first two.) The indefinite future uses a construction marker (or possibly an auxiliary, though I am not aware of other uses of it) /-ená-/ (in some dialects /-ná-/), after which the first vowel of the verb has high tone. Thus:

> situsúumba nkóombo   'we're about to buy a goat'
> sitwásuumba nkóombo   'we're going to buy a goat (later)'
> twenásúumba nkóombo   'we're going to buy a goat (sometime)'

It is possible that such distinctions, or other distinctions which may be found in other languages, reflect unrecognized subtleties of reference to the degree of probability or potentiality; the quotation at the beginning of this section should not be dismissed as mere fanciful philosophizing.

12.6. Verbal constructions such as those discussed up to this point are referred to by Ashton (for Swahili, 1944, pp. 35ff.) as "the primary tenses" (though she fully recognizes that not all of them are primarily temporal in reference). There is little if any formal justification for drawing a line at this point and referring to all other constructions as "secondary"; Ashton's distinction appears to reflect little more than a recognition of Latin indicatives as opposed to other moods. In fact, in many if not most Niger-Congo languages, some of the constructions discussed in the preceding sections are not "primary" in the sense defined in 12.1 above, but rather "auxiliary". On the other hand, most languages have other constructions which are equally primary in formation, and which may also appear as independent rather than subordinate predications.

Perhaps the commonest of these is a construction which has almost universally—but unfortunately, in my considered opinion—been called "subjunctive". It is not that I have any violent objection to terminology derived from the grammar of Latin; it's not bad at all—for Latin. Nor do I have any zeal for the proliferation of grammatical terminology for its own sake. I seek only terminology—language-specific when necessary—which will meaningfully reflect the categories and usages of the languages with which I work. For the most part, the so-called "subjunctive" in Niger-Congo languages matches the Latin subjunctive in only one use, and in most languages that is its major or only use. It is not primarily "subjoined" or used in subordinate clauses (which the term "subjunctive" is meant to suggest). On the basis of its usage in the languages in question, I have settled (after some vacillation in my early works) on the label "hortative." To be sure, some students complain that "hortative" is no more meaningful to them than "subjunctive". The term—and the construction for which it is used—has to do with urging or suggesting; it is related to 'ex*hort*'.

Once more there is a problem, for many people, with English equivalents of utterances in other languages. In the first person plural, a hortative may readily be translated by the construction found in 'let's do it'. But how is a similar reference to action expressed, for example, in the third person singular? The most likely response is 'let him do it'; but that does not have a hortative meaning in contemporary informal English, but rather a permissive meaning—'permit him to do it', which is usually not included in the range of a Niger-Congo hortative without some modification. 'Let him do it' was hortative in older English, as in the Biblical 'Let him who is without sin cast the first stone', and is still so used in formal and somewhat stereotyped expressions such as 'Let everyone join in song on this festive occasion', or 'Let us pray'. Since this literary and formal usage is taught in African schools where English is used, informants are likely to give equivalents such as 'let him do it' for a hortative in their own languages; they do not mean it as permissive, but that is what it means to us. More accurate equivalents in contemporary English are 'he should do it' (with 'should' having weak stress, or otherwise it is obligatory, an equivalent of 'ought to'), 'have him do it', or 'he'd better do it'. In most languages, the first person singular of the hortative is used primarily or exclusively in questions ('should I do it?'

or 'shall I do it?') or after verbs like 'tell' ('he told me I should do it' = 'he told me to do it'). The latter combination is also the commonest or only circumstance under which second person hortatives are used; in isolation, there is usually an imperative in place of the hortative, at least in the singular, which commonly has no subject pronoun.

The hortative in Jukun was described in 5.14 in connection with a discussion of morphemes of tonal replacement; high tone replaces the stem tone of subject pronouns, which are low in two cases and mid in the rest. The second person plural hortative functions as an imperative; e.g., /ní ya/ 'Go!'. To express a singular command, the hortative may be used, or alternatively the verb stem by itself; e.g., /ú ya/ or simply /ya/ 'Go!'; it is quite possible that the hortative is a more courteous or gentle way of telling one person to do something.

In Kpelle (also discussed in 5.14), the hortative also has high tone replacing the stem tone of subject pronouns. The stem tone is low in one case and high to begin with in all others, but the stem form of subject pronouns is not used with a verb without an affix (which may be a replacive). The second person hortatives are not used in isolation. A singular imperative is expressed by the verb stem alone, or occasionally with a subject pronoun /ɓe/. The plural imperative has a subject pronoun with mid tone; e.g., /ka lí/ 'Go!'

The Kpelle hortative—or what might perhaps better be analyzed as a different but homophonous construction—is also used to express actions after the first in a series; this will be treated in a later section.

In Igbo, the hortative has an introductory morpheme /kà/, which may be considered a particle or a conjunction. (In another usage, the same or a homophonous /kà/ can be replaced by a noun, but it can hardly itself be considered a noun.) This is followed by the subject, and then the verb base with a vowel suffix; the form of the suffix is generally conditioned by the final vowel of the base, and, with a few lexically conditioned exceptions, is zero after a base of two or more syllables with a final vowel other than /i/ or /u/. What follows /kà/ is identical with a conditional construction, but there is little motivation for positing an underlying relationship. Examples of the hortative, with the verb base identified for each, are:

gá:	kà ànyị́ gáá	'let's go'
mé:	kà ó méé 'yá	'he should do it'
mécí:	kà ó mécíé úzọ̀	'he should shut the door'
méghé:	kà Óbì méghé úzọ̀	'Obi should open the door'

Igbo has a distinct imperative construction. The same vowel suffix is used, but the imperative differs from the hortative in tonal structure. For a base of two or more syllables beginning with high-low, the lexical tones are used. Otherwise, the first syllable of the base has low tone replacing stem tone, and all other syllables have high tone. The replaced tone is itself low for bases with low tone, and in this case the base and suffix have the same form as in the hortative, but only because the replacive required for the imperative happens to have a zero effect. There is no subject pronoun for a singular imperative; to form a plural, /nù/ is used after the verb—a unique manifestation of the second person plural. Imperatives corresponding to the hortatives cited above are:

gàá	'Go !'
mèé 'yá	'Do it !'
mècíé ụ́zọ̀	'Shut the door !'
mèghé nù̀ ụ́zọ̀	'Open (pl.) the door !'

In Swahili, the hortative ("subjunctive") has no (or a zero) construction marker before the verb base, but has the suffix /-e/ rather than the /-a/ which is common to a large number of verbal constructions. Compare the following:

a-li-nunu-a nyama	'he bought meat'
a-nunu-e nyama	'he should buy meat'

Again there is a distinct imperative. In the singular, no subject pronoun is used; the verb has the suffix /-a/ unless there is an object concord, in which case the suffix is /-e/. In the plural, the verb has the suffix /-e/, followed by a plural indicator /-ni/; note the striking parallel with Igbo. E.g.,

nunua nyama	'Buy meat !'
inunue	'Buy it (9) !'
nunueni nyama	'Buy (pl.) meat !'

It was mentioned above that a hortative may be used after a verb such as 'tell'. An example from Igbo (in which the verb 'tell' has an irregular imperative without suffix) will be sufficient to illustrate this common pattern:

gwá 'yá kà ó mécíé ụ́zọ̀	'tell him to (that he should) close the door'

The situation after a verb meaning 'want' requires special treatment. In the Bantu languages in general, and in some but by no means all West African languages, there is an infinitive form of the verb. This is generally used in equivalents of sentences like 'I want to do it', in which the person wanting and the person performing the desired action are the same. If those persons are different, however, as in 'I want him to do it', the hortative is used; that is, one says 'I want that he should do it'. In Igbo, for example:

á cọ̀rọ̀ m̀ í'mé yá	'I want to do it'
á cọ̀rọ̀ m̀ kà ó méé 'yá	'I want him to do it'

In Yoruba, there is no generally recognized infinitive. In constructions like the first of the above, however, the vowel of the verb meaning 'want' is lengthened; this unquestionably reflects an older infinitive prefix with the following verb base, probably with the form *$/í-/$ (which I understand still exists in Itsekiri). Thus the Yoruba pattern may be considered the same as that of Igbo and many other languages; e.g.,

mo fę́ę́ lọ (*mo fę́ ílọ)   'I want to go'
mo fę́ kí wọ́n lọ   'I want them to go'

In languages which do not have an infinitive form, it appears that the hortative is typically used in both types of expressions, whether the performer of the desired action is different from or the same as the person wanting. E.g.,

Dìyī:	m̀ ri syō m̀ ya	'I want to go'
	m̀ ri syō kú ya	'I want him to go'
Kpelle:	ŋa ŋ̀wêlii ŋá lí	'I want to go'
	ŋa ŋ̀wêlii é lí	'I want him to go'
Bariba:	na kí̂ n tasu dɔɔ̄rā	'want to sell yams'
	na kí̂ ù tasu dɔɔ̄rā	'I want him to sell yams'

Very commonly, a hortative is used after another verb to express permission, necessity, purpose, and the like. Efik, for example, uses a hortative after /yàk/ 'permit', /nà/ 'be necessary', and /màn/ (not separately identified, but introducing a purpose clause). The Efik hortative is characterized by high-low replacing stem tone with the verb. E.g.,

ìkâ	'let's go'
yàk étìŋ íkɔ̀	'let him speak'
m̀'má ńyàk éỹɔ̀ŋ úfɔ̀k	'I let them go home'
ánà ŋ́kpêp ŋ̀wèt	'I have to study'
ákánà ŋ́kpêp ŋ̀wèt	'I had to study'
ńnàm útóm màn m̀bɔ̀ òkúk	'I'm working to earn money'

In Bariba, the hortative is used after a morpheme /ko/ to form the regular expression for future action; it is possible that this is ultimately derived from an expression something like 'let me do it'. E.g.,

ko n tasu dūē   'I'm going to buy yams'

In Bariba, as in Kpelle, an identical construction is used to express actions after the first in a series.

12.7. Reference was made in 12.2 above to a distinction in some languages between stative and active verbs. In addition, some languages have a distinct stative construction. Such a construction is frequently restricted to a limited number of verbs, particularly verbs like 'stand up', 'sit down', 'lie down', for which the present construction refers to the process of getting into the position referred to, but the stative refers to being in that position. In Kpelle, the stative uses the same construction marker as the present, but the verb root has a suffix /-nì/ rather than /-ì/. E.g.,

a tɔɔ̂i ~ 'káa tɔɔ̂i   'he's getting to his feet'
a tɔɔ̂ni ~ 'káa tɔɔ̂ni   'he's on his feet'

In Igbo, the stative is used only with a limited number of monosyllabic verb roots; it is characterized by low replacing stem tone with the verb root. The following are the commonest; the last two are statives followed by a verbal noun, forming the auxiliary-type incompletive and future constructions:

ọ́ bù ìtè	'it is (identified as) a pot'
ọ́ dì m̀'má	'it is (describable as) good'
ọ́ dì n'ébé à	'it is (located at) here'
ọ́ nọ̀ n'ébé à	'he/she is (located at) here'
ó jì é'gó	'he has (with him) money'
ó sì Ọ̀nìcà	'he is-from Onitsha'
ó bì Ọ̀nìcà	'he lives-in Onitsha'
ọ́ nà àbyá	'he is (in the process of) coming'
ọ́ gà àbyá	'he is going to come'

In northern dialects, statives are more commonly used, especially with verbs (or verb phrases) having a descriptive meaning, which in other dialects are used in the factative (cf. 12.2 above). Some examples, with the nonnorthern forms in parentheses, are:

ó ŋwè é'gó	(ó ŋwèrè é'gó)	'he has (owns) money'
ó pè m̀pé	(ó pèrè m̀pé)	'it is small'

In Bariba, stative forms are recorded for a number of verbs, largely with inceptive meaning. The formations are apparently rather irregular. Some examples comparing the hortative (which is the form from which other verb forms are most readily derived) with the stative are:

tīīrā	:	tīīrī	'become / be black'
taàyā	:	tāū	'become / be tough'
yasiā	:	yasū	'become / be wide'
yemiā	:	yēm̄	'become / be cold, damp'
sǔyā	:	sum̄	'become / be hot'
kīǎ	:	kí̵	'want'
sē	:	yǒ̵	'stand up'

Equally irregular and even suppletive forms, best analyzed formally as statives, are used in place of the continuative for the common verbs 'go', 'come', and 'do'.

Swahili has a construction which, while not restricted to a small number of verbs, is unusual in its formation. It is formed with a morpheme /hu-/ before the base, and the common suffix /-a/ after the base. No subject concords are used with this construction; a pronominal subject is expressed by an independent pronoun form, used like a noun. This construction is described by Ashton (1944, p. 38) as occurring "in contexts which imply habitual or recurrent action, apart from time." The emphasis, however, is not on the habitual or customary nature of the action, but rather on the inevitable naturalness of it; the construction is much more of a stative. Thus, when one says:

ng'ombe hula nyasi	'cows eat grass',

one is not referring so much to the daily habit of cows as to "the nature of the beast." Ashton observes that this construction is commonly found in proverbs and aphorisms—precisely the kind of idiom that commonly refers to the state of affairs.

12.8. Another idea frequently expressed by a simple and independent verbal construction rather than by clausal syntax is "hypothetical." In Efik, the construction marker for the hypothetical is /kpV́-/, in which the vowel is determined by vowel harmony; the reference is to action which would take place. Past hypothetical action is expressed by adding the past construction marker /kV́'-/, or alternatively by using a reduplicated form of the verb base. E.g.,

ŋkpé'dép m̀bòró	'I would buy bananas'
ŋkpé'ké'dep m̀bòró ⎤	
ŋkpédèdép m̀bòró ⎦	'I would have bought bananas'

As might be expected, such constructions are commonly used with another clause; for the above, for example, 'but I don't / didn't have money'. They are also used in contrary-to-fact conditions. In Efik, the conditional clause is introduced by the word /èdyékè/, which seems to function like a noun; it is followed by the hypothetical in a relative construction, formed with a suffix /-dé/. The conclusion is a hypothetical as illustrated above. The clauses may appear in either order. E.g.,

èdyékè ŋkpé'ŷénédé òkúk,	'If I had money, I would
ŋkpé'dép m̀bòró	buy bananas'
ŋkpé'ké'dép m̀bòró, èdyékè	'I would have bought bananas
ŋkpé'ké'ŷénédé òkúk	if I had money'

In Swahili, a present and a past hypothetical with similar uses are formed by the construction markers /-nge-/ and /-ngali-/ respectively; the latter may well be a combination of the former with the past construction marker /-li-/. These constructions are used in both the conditional clause and the conclusion in contrary-to-fact conditions; the conditional clause may optionally be introduced by the word /kama/. The temporal distinction is not rigidly observed by all speakers, but the constructions recognized as standard are:

(kama) ungekitafuta,	'if you would look for it,
ungekiona	you would find it'
(kama) ungalikitafuta,	'if you had looked for it,
ungalikiona	you would have found it'

In Kpelle, a construction with similar uses has a special meaning when used in isolation, which led me to label the construction "desiderative"; it expresses an action which the subject wishes would take place or had taken place. It is formed with a suffix /-ì/ after the subject pronoun, and low tone replacing stem tone with the verb. In contrary-to-fact conditions, it is used in both clauses with nothing added. There is no distinction between present and past. E.g.,

èi pà   'I wish he would (/had) come', 'if only he would (/had) come'
èi pà, ŋâi lì   'if he would come, I would go', 'if he had come, I would
                    have gone'

In Igbo, the hypothetical construction is derived from the future. The future uses the stative of the verb /í'gá/ 'go' and a verbal noun. A stative with past reference is formed by doubling the vowel of the verb root and adding the factative suffix which consists of /r/ plus the preceding vowel repeated; the entire form has low tone. The hypothetical is formed with this form of /í'gá/ followed by a verbal noun. Used by itself, there is no distinction between present and past; e.g.,

        ọ́ gàárà àbyá   'he would (have) come'

In contrary to fact conditions, this hypothetical construction is used only in the conclusion. The condition is introduced by the phrase /á sị̀ nà/ 'if one says that', followed by an ordinary verbal construction which in most cases has a clear reference to present or past time. E.g.,

á sị̀ nà ọ́ nà àrụ́ ọ́'rụ́,   'if he were working, he
  ọ́ gàárà èŋwé é'gó   would have money'
á sị̀ nà ọ́ rụ̀rụ̀ ọ́rụ́,   'if he had worked, he
  ọ́ gàárà èŋwé é'gó   would have (had) money'

12.9. Most languages also have a "conditional" construction which is used only in subordinate clauses; in the Igbo sentences above, /á sị̀/ 'if one says' is such a construction. A comment about English uses will help in explaining conditionals in Niger-Congo languages. We ordinarily think of a conditional clause as a clause introduced by 'if'; by contrast, we think of a clause introduced by 'when' as temporal. Thus we group clauses such as 'when he came' and 'when he comes' together, in contrast with 'if he comes'. Another grouping, however, is entirely logical. Of the three clauses, 'when he came' refers to a known time in the past. On the other hand, both 'when he comes' and 'if he comes' refer to something which has not yet happened, and technically we are not positive of the time in either case. The difference between these two clauses in English is that 'when he comes' implies that his coming is fully expected, while 'if he comes' implies that it is dubious; 'if he should come' expresses an even lower degree of expectability. Such degrees of expectability are not obligatorily distinguished in many languages; the same expression may be translatable as 'when he comes' or 'if he comes'. In a random sampling of English translations of Kpelle conditionals by two informants, 'when' and 'if' were used by each with approximately equal frequency, but not with the same distribution by the two. Such conditional constructions are used in most Niger-Congo languages with nothing like a conjunction corresponding to our 'if'; the construction alone is the condition. In Kpelle and some other languages, a lower degree of expectability, regularly reflected by 'if' in translations, may be specified by introducing a conditional with another conditional, of a verb which may be translated as 'be'.

The Kpelle conditional uses a construction marker /-à/ combined with pronouns, and low tone replacing stem tone with the verb. The first of the following examples has one conditional, and the second has two:

à pà, ŋa pâi lîi	'when/if he comes, I will go'
à kɛ̀ à pà, ŋa pâi lîi	'if he comes, I will go'

The Igbo conditional, as noted in 12.6 above, is identical with what follows /kà/ in the hortative; the verb has a vowel suffix, with allomorphs including zero under definable conditions. A low degree of expectability may be expressed by introducing a conditional with /ọ́ bụ́rụ́ nà/ 'if it is that'. E.g.,

ó méé 'yá, į̀ gà àhụ́ 'yá	'when/if he does it, you'll see it'
ọ́ bụ́rụ́ nà ó méé 'yá, į̀ gà àhụ́ 'yá	'if he does it, you'll see it'

The Efik conditional, formed by low tone replacing stem tone with subject pronouns (and with resultant ambiguities resolved by using nominal independent pronoun forms), seems inherently to express a lower degree of expectability than is the case in many other languages. It is a higher degree of expectability that is optionally expressed by something added; the conditional of a verb /má/, not otherwise attested in a meaning that seems appropriate to this combination, introduces another conditional to give a rough equivalent of 'when'. Thus:

èté fò èdí, ńdîkût ɛ̀ỹé	'if your father comes, I'll see him'
èté fò àmá èdí, ńdîkût ɛ̀ỹé	'when your father comes, I'll see him'

In Swahili, a single construction using a marker /-ki-/ and the common suffix /-a/ is used as a condition, and also in a way that seems quite different to us, paralleling the English participle in a sentence like 'I saw him coming'. On the basis of the latter usage, this has frequently been called the "participial tense" (!). A semantic link between the two uses can be seen in the idea of 'when'. E.g.,

ukimtafuta, utamwona	'when/if you look for him, you will find him'
nilimwona akinitafuta	'I saw him looking for me'

The same construction, which might perhaps better be labelled "simultaneous" to reflect its range of usage, is used after forms of the verb /kuwa/ 'be' to express continuous or customary action in other than the present. E.g.,

alikuwa akinitafuta	'he was looking for me',
	'he used to look for me'

Swahili has two other constructions used in subordinate clauses only, which may be called "concessive," paralleling English clauses introduced by 'although'. One of these, using the construction marker /-nga-/ and the suffix /-a/, expresses a concession of something actual. The other, using the construction marker /-japo-/ and the suffix /-a/, expresses a concession of something suppositional; the construction marker is a derivation from the verb /kuja/ 'come' and a relative form with a sense like 'whenever'. These two concessives are not always sharply distinguished. Examples are:

angafanya kazi, hana fedha   'although he works, he doesn't have money'
ajapofanya kazi, hangekuwa   'even if he were to work, he wouldn't have
   na fedha   money'

I know of no case outside the Bantu languages where a concessive idea is incorporated into a basic verbal construction.

12.10. A great many languages have a special verbal construction used to refer to actions after the first in a sequential series. Such a construction may be labeled "consecutive." (In some languages, as noted in the following section, a second type of verb sequence must be recognized. If such a sequence requires a special verbal construction, the label "sequential" is suggested. The two terms should therefore not be used interchangeably.) A consecutive may be used after any construction referring to the first action; in itself, the consecutive has no reference to time, aspect, or mode—the reference of the first verb applies throughout the sequence.

In Kpelle, the consecutive is identical in form with the hortative (cf. 12.6 above); high tone replaces stem tone with subject pronouns, and the verb has no (or a zero) affix. The two ideas converge in sentences in which the second action may be interpreted as the purpose of the first. E.g.,

è lì ŋɔ̀ kpâlaŋ ŋá é tíi kɛ́   'he went to his farm and worked (/ to
  (cf.: è tíi kɛ̀ 'he worked')   work)'
a pâi lìi ŋɔ̀ kpâlaŋ ŋá é tíi kɛ́   'he's going to go to his farm and work'
'tí lì à sɛŋ-kâu 'tí manaŋ   'they took money and bought cassava and
  yá, 'tí ŋ́ili 'tí m̀ii   cooked and ate it'

In informal narrative, especially in folk stories, the same construction may also be used to refer to the first action in the series as well as later actions; the reference is assumed to be to past time. In a series including several actions, a sentence-terminal pause may occur, and the next construction may still be a consecutive.

Kpelle has quite a distinct construction, and a peculiar one by comparison with other constructions in the language, to express an action simultaneous with one previously mentioned. The logical "subject" of the simultaneous action is expressed as the object of the verb /kɛ́/ in its stem (= singular imperative) form; elsewhere, transitively, this verb means 'do' or 'make'. This is followed by the main verb, with low tone replacing stem tone. E.g.,

è kɛ̀ ɣélɛ̀i 'he was laughing'; è kɛ̀ wɔlɔ̂i 'he was crying': è kɛ̀ ɣélɛ̀i 'kɛ́
  wɔ̀lɔ 'he was laughing and crying (at the same time)'
'tí ɓá m̀ii 'they ate'; kú tíi kɛ̀ 'we worked': 'tí ɓá m̀ii, kú kɛ́ tíi kɛ̀ 'they
  ate and we worked'

In expressions of location (including possession; cf. 11.5), it has been noted that the verb /kɛ́/ is used (intransitively) with reference to anything other than the present. In the simultaneous construction alone, this is replaced by the verb /ɓó/, whose range of meaning elsewhere includes 'appear'. E.g.,

ŋâŋ káa nãa   'my father is there';   ŋâŋ è kɛ̀ naa   'my father was there':
'tí lì 'pɛ́rɛi mù, ŋâŋ kɛ́ ɓò nãa   'they went into the house, and my father
was there'

tɛ́ɛ káa ɲéeì   'he has a chicken';   tɛ́ɛ è kɛ̀ ɲéeì   'he had a chicken':
nɛnî tɔ̀nɔ è sìɣe 'pɛ́rɛi mù, tɛ́ɛ kɛ́ ɓò ɲéeì   'a woman came out of the house
carrying a chicken'

In using constructions like the Kpelle consecutive and simultaneous, it is
most important to note that there is nothing like a conjunction joining verbs or
sentences. Nouns may be conjoined, often in ways similar to English (cf. 10.22),
but it is rare to find a language in which verbs are conjoined; the constructions
themselves indicate a following or simultaneous action. Simultaneous constructions do not appear to be widespread in Niger-Congo languages, but consecutive
constructions are frequently found; in some languages, consecutive and simultaneous action are not grammatically distinguished, and the label "consecutive"
may be taken as referring simply to consecutive verbs in a sentence, not necessarily to consecutive actions in time.

Swahili has a consecutive with the construction marker /-ka-/ and the suffix
/-a/, used primarily though not exclusively with the first verb in the past. E.g.,

nilikwenda sokoni, nikanunua   'I went to the market and bought ba-
   ndizi   nanas'
   (cf.: nilinunua ndizi   'I bought bananas')

The same construction marker /-ka-/ may also be used with the suffix /-e/, which
with no construction marker forms the hortative. This combination expresses
purpose. E.g.,

nitakwenda sokoni, nikanunue   'I'm going to go to the market to (/and)
   ndizi   buy bananas'

In both Kpelle and Swahili, a subject pronoun is required with the consecutive even if the two or more actions are performed by the same subject. This
is not true in all languages. In Igbo, the consecutive with the same subject consists of a verb base with vowel suffix (with the usual allomorphs, including zero,
that have been mentioned in several other contexts), with no subject pronoun.
E.g.,

ó bàrà n'úlọ̀ mécíé úzọ̀   'he went in the house and shut the door'
   (cf.: ó mècìrì úzọ̀   'he shut the door')

If a new subject is introduced for an action after the first, it may consist of a subject pronoun with low tone. If it is a noun subject, the verb has a prefix /à-/
or /è-/ (depending on vowel harmony); if high tone follows, the tone of the prefix
has the alternant downstep-high after high. Actions performed by different subjects, and so expressed, may be simultaneous. E.g.,

ànyị̀ làrà ụ̀lọ̀, m̀ sáá ˈáhụ   'we went home and I took a bath'
  (cf.: á sàrà m̀ àhụ́   'I took a bath')
ànyị̀ làrà ụ̀lọ̀, Òkóyè èsíé   'we went home and Okoye cooked (food)'
ń'rí
  (cf.: Òkóyè sìrì ńrí   'Okoye cooked')
ànyị̀ làrà ụ̀lọ̀, ńnà m̀ ˈárụ̀wá   'we went home and my father
  ọ́'rụ́ yá, ǹné ˈm̀ ˈésíé   got at his work, my mother
  ń'rí, m̀ déé ákwụ́kwọ́   cooked, and I wrote a letter'
  (cf.: ńnà m̀ rụ̀wàrà ọ́rụ́ ˈyá   'my father got at his work'; ǹné ˈm̀
  sìrì ńrí   'my mother cooked'; é dèrè m̀ ákwụ́kwọ́ 'I wrote a letter')

The auxiliary verb /ná/ is used in the stative, followed by a verbal noun, to form
the incompletive. The consecutive may be used with /ná/ and a verbal noun to
express simultaneous actions with an incompletive reference; e.g.,

há nà èrí ń'rí, ná àŋụ́   'They are (/were) eating and drinking and
  m̀'mányá, ná àkpá ŋ́kàtá   chatting'
  (cf.: há nà àŋụ́ m̀'mányá   'they are drinking (booze)';
  há nà àkpá ŋ́kàtá   'they are conversing')
m̀mụ́ nà àkwádébé ń'rí, Òkóyè   'I'm getting food ready, and Okoye is
  àná èwépụ̀tá éféré   getting out dishes'
  (cf.: Òkóyè nà èwépụ̀tá éféré   'Okoye is getting out dishes')

The consecutive is not ordinarily used after an imperative; more than one imperative may appear in sequence. The consecutive is used in some other constructions of a subordinate nature, which are not relevant to the present discussion.
In addition to the consecutive, Igbo has sequential constructions which will be
distinguished and discussed in the following section.

12.11. Common to a large number of West African languages is a syntactic
phenomenon generally known as "serialization," sometimes referred to as "serial
verbs," and rather naively called by some "split verbs." The uses of consecutive
constructions as described in the preceding section are not instances of serialization in the proper sense of the word. Some languages distinguish two types of
verb sequence, one of them using a consecutive as described above for verbs
after the first, and the other using some other construction in at least some combinations. Special forms used in the second type of sequence may be called "sequential"; "serialization" is a good, distinctive label for the entire sequence.

Serialization has attracted the attention of a number of graduate students
in linguistics in recent years, and several unpublished papers have been written
on the subject from the viewpoint of transformational-generative grammar. All
of the writers agree that an adequate treatment is difficult and perhaps impossible within the framework of current grammatical models. None of the writers
has been entirely satisfied with his own treatment of the subject. I will not presume to suggest a competing treatment, but will only outline the data from some
languages in as clear and systematic a way as possible.

Merely defining the problem, or stating the circumstances under which serialization appears, is difficult enough. An example from Igbo will be used as a starting point:

ó bù íbú àgá á'hyá   'he's carrying a load to market'

The first verb form in this sentence is /bù/, the stative of the verb /í'bú/, which has the basic meaning 'have on one's head'. The second verb form is /àgá/, the verbal noun of /í'gá/ 'go'. The entire sentence may be represented by 'he has a load on his head going to market'. The question is, what is distinctive about a sentence like this as opposed to a sentence in which the consecutive is used?

For Igbo, it may be an adequate definition to say that the above type of construction is used, rather than an incompletive and a consecutive, if the first verb is one of those verbs that normally appears in the stative with reference to present time. Efik, however, also has two different constructions, and an examination of a large body of data reveals differences in usage or meaning that are strikingly similar to the differences in the Igbo constructions; yet Efik has no special subclass of verbs with a distinctive use apart from these sequences.

Another suggestion that may be made is that the actions in this case are inevitably simultaneous. That may be true, but it does not seem to be distinctive. In both Igbo and Efik, the consecutive may refer to a simultaneous action, and the inevitability of the simultaneity is a rather tenuous notion.

It has frequently been observed that serial costructions seem to be used for actions that are particularly closely related to each other. Indeed, in many cases, as the above example illustrates, the serialized verbs may be translated by a single English verb and a preposition, and in some cases simply by a single verb. The close interrelationship of the actions enters into my own earlier descriptions of such sequences in both Igbo (see Welmers and Welmers 1968b, pp. 161-64) and Efik (see Welmers 1968a, pp. 68-84). I have never been entirely satisfied with those descriptions, however; again, close interrelationship appears to be a rather tenuous concept.

Perhaps a more satisfactory approach would be in terms of the subject or subjects involved. If a consecutive is used, it may of course have the same subject (whether expressed or not, depending on the language) as the first verb. A new subject, however, may also be introduced with a consecutive; if it is, the relationship between the actions is not seriously altered. For example, a consecutive would be used in Igbo in the equivalent of either 'he returned home and cooked' or 'he returned home and I cooked'; in either case, there was a returning home and then a cooking, and the identity or nonidentity of the subjects is incidental to the sequence of the two actions (or even their simultaneity in other sentences). On the other hand, a sequential must be used in the equivalent of 'he is carrying a load to market', as illustrated above; if one person has a load on his head and another goes to market, the situation described is totally different—the load never gets to market. Serialization, in short, seems to involve actions that can be associated with each other only if they are performed by the same subject.

In Igbo, as noted above, it is also true that the first verb must be selected from the subclass for which the stative is used to express present time. Two basic types of serialization must be distinguished. In the first, verbs after the first are in the verbal noun form. Normally, if the first verb is in the stative, the reference is to present time; if the first verb is in the incompletive, the reference is to customary action. In one common combination, however, the first verb is in the stative and the reference is nevertheless to customary action. Some speakers also use the first verb in the future in this type of serialization, with reference to future action; an instance of this is included in the examples below, with an asterisk to indicate that it is not universally accepted. Examples of this first type of serialization are as follows, with parenthesized glosses reflecting the structure in more detail:

> há nò n'ócé àkpá ŋ̀kàtá   'they're sitting and chatting'
> ('they sit on chairs holding conversation')
> ó jì ńcà àsá á'ká   'he's washing his hands with soap'
> ('he has soap washing hands')
> gí'ní kà í jì ḿmà ḿ èmé   'what are you doing with my knife?'
> ('what is it you have my knife doing?')
> ébé 'ólé kà į́ nyà úgbọ́ àgá   'where are you driving to?'
> ('which place is it you propel vehicle going?')
> ọ́ nà ányà ígwè àgá ú'gbó yá   'he rides a bicycle to his farm'
> ('he propels iron going-to his farm')
> ọ́ nà é'kpú 'ókpú àrú ọ́'rú   'he wears a cap at work'
> ('he wears cap doing work')
> ó nà éjì ánụ́ èté ófé 'tọ́rọ́ ụ́tọ́   'she cooks delicious meat soup'
> ('she has meat cooking soup which is delicious')
> gí'ní kà í nà éjì ŋ̀kè áhụ̀ èmé   'what do you use that for?'
> ('what is it you have that thing doing?')
> *gí'ní kà į́ gà éjì ŋ̀kè áhụ̀ èmé   'what are you going to do with that?'
> ('what is it you will have that thing doing?')

The exceptional usage in which the stative with the first verb refers to customary rather than present action is in expressions of manner; these will be treated in chapter 14 in another context.

The second type of serial construction uses the consecutive form for verbs after the first.[2] It is thus like the ordinary use of the consecutive after another verb, as described in the preceding section. With the first verb, the stative refers to past time; in some dialects, a special form for these verbs, specifically referring

---

[2] We have also (Welmers and Welmers 1968b) recognized the verb base without suffix as an alternative for the consecutive. This may be acceptable for some speakers, but it is possible that this represents an error in our early transcriptions; because of the phonetic realization of vowel sequences, the presence of the vowel suffix characteristic of the consecutive is often difficult to detect—and indeed, it has a zero allomorph with some bases. At best, the base alone is apparently not widely used.

to past time, may be used. Other constructions are obvious in their reference.
Examples are:

    há nọ̀ n'ócé kpáá ŋ́kàtá   'they sat and chatted'
        ('they sit on chairs and-hold conversation')
    ó bù íbú gáá á'hyá   'he carried a load to market'
        ('he has-on-head load and-goes-to market')
    há sò anyị́ gáá 'Ábá   'they went to Aba with us'
        ('they accompany us and-go-to Aba')
    ó yì ùwé 'márá m̀'má gáá óméré   'she wore a pretty dress to the party'
        ('she wears dress which is beautiful and-goes-to party')
    ì gághị́ èŋwé íké í'jí ósísí   'you won't be able to fix that
        mézíé ŋ̀kè áhụ̀   with a stick'
        ('you will-not have strength to-have stick and-fix that')
    kà ọ́ nyàá ú'gbó m̀ gáá 'Ábá   'he should drive my car to Aba'
        ('he should propel my vehicle and-go-to Aba')
    ọ̀ nyághị̀ úgbọ́ byá   'he didn't drive here'
        ('he didn't-propel vehicle and-come')

12.12 The stituation in Efik is quite similar to that in Igbo, including the
fact that the verb form used as a sequential in one type of serialization is also
used as a consecutive. Five types of serialization must be distinguished.

    First, imperatives or hortatives may be used in sequence with no special
sequential forms. E.g.,

    dá íkwâ dí   'bring a knife'
        ('take knife come')
    mén òkpókóró dí   'bring a table'
        ('lift table come')
    dá íkwâ émì sìbé únàm   'cut the meat with this knife'
        ('take knife this cut meat')
    nám útóm émì nọ̀ mî   'do this work for me'
        ('do work this give me')
    ádâ édî   'he should bring it'
        ('he-should-take he-should-come')
    ńyòm ánâm útóm ónọ̀ fî   'I want him to work for you'
        ('I-want he-should-do work he-should-give you')

    Second, after an infinitive (which has the infinitive prefix /ńdí-/), verbs in
series have a prefix /ǹ-/. E.g.,

    dómó ńdídá òkúk ǹdí   'try to bring money'
        ('try to-take money and-come')
    ńyòm ńdínám útóm ǹnọ̀ fî   'I want to work for you'
        ('I-want to-do work and-give you')
    ńdwàk ńdídúk mótò ŋ̀kǎ   'I intend to go by car'
        ('I-intend to-enter car and-go')

The third type of sequential is used after a verb in the present or past contrastive construction with the contrasted item preceding the verb (or, in the case of a few question words only, optionally following the verb). After such a verb, the sequential consists of the subject pronoun repeated and the verbal base. By way of contrast with other sequentials, it should be noted that in this one the subject pronouns have their stem tone, which is high in some cases and low in others, and the verb base also has its lexical tone; further, there is no downstep after the pronoun. Examples of this type are:

ànyè áká'dá m̀bòró émì édí   'who brought these bananas?'
('who took banana this he-come?')
ǹsò útòm ké àká'nám ɔ̀nɔ̀ ɛ̀ɣé   'what kind of work did you do for him?'
(' what work is-it you-did you-give him?')
ǹsò ké édá édí   'what are they bringing'
(' what is-it they-are-taking they-come?')

The fourth type of sequential is used only after the future contrastive construction. In the first person singular, the sequential has the prefix /ǹ-/, interpreted as the first person subject pronoun with low replacing stem tone. In all other persons, the more common usage appears to be that the sequential has the prefix /ì-/; alternatively, however, the appropriate subject pronoun may be used, with low replacing stem tone. In addition, the verbal base in this sequential has the tones high-low, which are also characteristic of the future contrastive which precedes. Examples of this type are:

íkwâ émì kpɔ́t ké ńdîdâ ŋ̀kâ   'this knife is all I'm going to take'
(' knife this only it-is I-will-take I-go')
ǹsò ké édîdâ ìdî (∼ . . . èdî)   'what is he going to bring?'
(' what is-it he-will-take subj.-come?')

The third sequential above is also used after the general present and past negative constructions, and the fourth after the general future negative. These negatives are, in form, derived from the contrastive constructions which require these sequentials.

The fifth type of sequential is used after other verbal constructions. These include the noncontrastive constructions, and the present and past contrastive with the contrasted item (other than a question word) following the verb. After these, the sequential has a subject pronoun with high tone replacing stem tone, followed by downstep (realized only before high tone, of course). For a pronoun whose stem tone is high and a verb whose base tone is low or low-high, this sequential is the same as a sequential of the third type; but in other cases, the two differ in the tone of the pronoun, or in the presence of downstep, or both. Examples of this type are:

ákádà òkúk ɛ́'dí   'he brought money'
(' he-took money he-come')

ìyé'dép únàm í'sɔ́k fì   'we're going to buy meat for you'
  ('we-will-buy meat we-deliver-to you')
ánàm útóm ɔ́nɔ̀ mî   'he's working for me'
  ('he-is-doing work he-give me')
ànàm útóm ɔ́nɔ̀ mî   'you're working for me'
  ('you-are-doing work you-give me')

In the light of this last sequential construction, it is clear that the neutral past construction is itself a sequential, though apparently with a slight irregularity. The first verb is undoubtedly from the root /mà/ 'fulfill, accomplish', and its low tone appears after a pronoun with low tone. After a pronoun with high tone, however, it has the exceptional tone downstep-high, apparently by assimilation to the preceding and following high tones. Thus:

ìmà í'dí   'we came'   ('we-accomplish we-come')
ḿ'má ń'dí   'I came'   ('I-accomplish I-come')

A special variety of the last three of the types of sequentials described above involves actions in which coming or going is involved. The first verb is often but not necessarily a verb of motion. In the sequential form, in the construction marker position, /dí/ (from the verb 'come') is used if the action involves coming, and /kV́/ (with a harmonizing vowel, but from the verb /kǎ/ 'go') is used if the action involves going. Otherwise, the three sequentials are as described above, with one exception: the fourth type, used after the future contrastive and future negative, does not have the expected high-low tone sequence after the pronoun, but rather high followed by the lexical tone of the base. An example of each of the three sequentials in question is as follows; the last, using the neutral past, would probably not be acceptable to a speaker of Efik in the context of the preceding questions, but it is perfectly appropriate as an answer to the question 'What did he do?':

ànyè ákákǎ ùrwà ékédép ùdyá   'who went to the market and bought food?'
  ('who went-to market he-go-buy food?')
ànyè édîkǎ ùrwà ikédép ùdyá   'who's going to go to the market and buy food?'
á'má ákǎ ùrwà éké'dép ùdyá   'he went to the market and bought food'

This all started with the observation that there are two types of verb sequence in Efik. All of the above illustrate only one of them: serialization. Although the equivalents of some of the examples above would have to be expressed by a consecutive in Igbo, they all fit pretty well into the definition of serialization given in the preceding section; they involve actions which can be associated with each other only if they are performed by the same subject. It is frightfully embarrassing not to be able to make an airtight case for this point in connection with the Efik data; unfortunately, I do not seem to have in my materials any examples of expressions for successive or simultaneous actions with different subjects. I am reasonably certain, however, that they would fit generally into the

second kind of verb sequence which can now be described. What is certain is
that, in this kind of sequence, the actions are far more independent of each other;
semantically, the kind of situation described is such that a change of subject
would not be surprising. In this second kind of sequence, which may be called
"consecutive" although simultaneity of action may be included, the first verb
can be in any construction other than the imperative, hortative, or infinitive—
that is, any construction taking the third, fourth, or fifth type of sequential as
described above. A verb after the first has a form identical with the fifth type of
sequential; that is, as in Igbo, the consecutive and sequential are not distinguishable in some—in fact, most—cases. What is significant, however, is that they
must be distinguished with certain constructions. In the first of the following
examples, the second verb has the same form as if the construction were serialization; in the second, however, the consecutive is distinctive:

á'má ɔ́kpɔ̀rì ísɔ̀ŋ, ɛ́'yét ɔ̀fɔ̀ŋ   'he swept the floor and washed the clothes'
ànyè ɔ́kɔ́kpɔ̀rì ísɔ̀ŋ, ɛ́'yét ɔ̀fɔ̀ŋ   'who swept the floor and washed the
                                               clothes?'

In this consecutive construction, the second verb, always followed by a third,
is frequently /ỹùŋ/, which has the rather unusual meaning 'do something in addition'. The first of the above sentences, for example, can be so expanded:

á'má ɔ́kpɔ̀rì ísɔ̀ŋ, óỹùŋ   'he swept the floor and also did the
   ɛ́'yét ɔ̀fɔ̀ŋ   wash'

Independent forms of /ỹùŋ/ can also be used, followed by a consecutive; e.g.,

ŋ́kpé'kóỹùŋ ŋ́kǎ dó   'and I would have gone there', 'I would also have gone there'   ('I-would-have-done-something-in-addition I-go
there')

One of the most delightful anecdotes in the annals of African language studies[3]
centers on just such a sentence as this. The late Ida C. Ward, like anyone else in
the field of African languages, was often asked, "Aren't those African languages
you work on terribly primitive?" Her gentle but effective reply was, "Well,
in one West African language I could give you the pluperfect subjunctive of the
verb 'and'!" By the same token, it might be added, Efik has another verb meaning 'about', still another meaning 'to (a person)' or 'toward (a place)', and—
like virtually every other West African language—a verb meaning 'than'. These
appear commonly after the first verb in a serial construction.

There are a few minor irregularities in this area of Efik syntax that have
not been included; the foregoing is judged sufficient to illustrate the overall structure.

12.13. Akan (with examples here from Fante) is one of the very few languages
in which a kind of verbal and clausal coordinating conjunction is found. Nouns
may be conjoined by /nà/ or /ńnà/ 'and'. The same conjunction is also used be-

---

[3] Reported to me by Miss Margaret A. Bryan.

tween verbs and clauses, sometimes translatable as 'and' but frequently requiring the translation 'but'. (In still another use, /nà/ frequently introduces
questions.) There are also conjunctive phrases, including /nà m̀'bóm/ 'but even,
but yet' and /nà sù/ 'and also, and yet'; in other environments, 'also' is /sú/ with
high tone. Verbs or clauses so conjoined express quite independent actions, and
a new subject may be introduced after the first. The reference may be to either
consecutive or simultaneous actions. After a verb referring to a present situation
or action (and perhaps also a future in some cases), an explicitly later action
is expressed by a verbal construction with the marker /-a-/. This construction
is not used independently; one is tempted to call it a consecutive, but perhaps
this label should be avoided in the light of its use also in serial constructions as
discussed below. Some examples of verbal and clausal conjunction are:

sìnà dùrúbá nú nà pàm tém nú	'thread the needle and mend the cloth'
ìtúm̀ kìnkán nà kyìréw m̀fàntí à	'can you read and write Fante?'
mìní wú bókó, nà mìpè déè mídi'dí wié	'I'll go with you, but I want to eat first'
mèésùã̀ m̀fàntí m̀fí é'bíèn, nà sù mìntúm̀ m̀kásà	'I've studied Fante for two years, but I still can't speak (it)'
mí 'núá kúr tì fié, nà kúr nú sú tì m̀kìràn	'one of my brothers lives at home, and the other ('the one also') lives in Accra'
mùrúkɔ hɔ́ nà màabá	'I'm going there, and I'll be right back ('I'm coming')'

In addition to and apart from the above, serialization is exceedingly common in Fante. As in other languages, it may be noted that, in serial constructions,
the actions or situations seem to be more closely related. Again, however, the
significant feature seems to be that it is impossible to introduce a new subject.
Two types of serialization may be distinguished, depending on whether or not a
stative verb is included in the series.

If all verbs in a series are active, there is construction agreement throughout
the series—a past follows a past and so on. The agreeing construction for a first
verb referring to a present situation or action uses the marker /-à-/, and this is
occasionally found after a future also. Subject pronouns are sometimes repeated,
especially with forms with /-à-/, with no obvious rationale for their inclusion or
omission. In sentences referring to motion, verbs after the first may also be
marked by derivatives of /kɔ́/ 'go' or /bá/ 'come' (derivatives of the latter also
constitute a future construction marker). Examples of serialization with active
verbs are as follows; verb roots are set apart by hyphens to show the construction
agreement:

mì-fí-ì m̀kìràn bà-à há ('I left Accra came here')	'I came here from Accra'

mì-nàntíw-ì pá-à ní 'dán hṹ   'I walked past his house'
   ('I-walked passed-by his house's body')
ɔ̀kyí nú ó-kwìà tìn hén 'dán   'the river flows past our house'
   ('river the it-cuts goes-along our house')
ɔ́-sɔ̀r mà mì   'he prays for me'
   ('he-prays gives me')
mà yéń-kɔ́ ńkɔ́-búr   'let's go swimming'
   ('give we-should-go should-go-swim')
ɔ̀-bà-à há bɔ́-tɔ́-ɔ̀ ǹdìémbá   'he came here to do some shopping'
   ('he-came here come-bought things')
mìrì-nántìw à-kɔ̀ ní 'fíé   'I'm walking to his place'
   ('I-am-walking and-go-to his home')
mìbɔ́-kɔ́ mààkɔ́-búr   'I'm going to go swimming'
   ('I-will-go I-and-go-swim')

One recorded sentence with a superficially similar structure does not show
construction agreement. This may be interpreted as an instance of apocopation
rather than serialization, from something like 'I enjoyed the fact that I have
stayed here'. The verbs are, respectively, past and completive:

mì-pé-ɛ̀ màá-tìná wɔ̀ há   'I enjoyed staying here'

Stative verbs appear in their root form in serial constructions; time and other
construction references are expressed only by an active verb in the sentence. The
commonest statives used in serial constructions are /wɔ̀/ 'be located at' after an
active verb, and /dì/ 'take, use' before an active verb. In the imperative, hortative, and negatives, the active verb /fà/ 'take' is used in place of /dì/; derivatives of it may be prefixed to the following verb. In addition, /fí/ 'come from,
go from, leave', used as an active verb in the first of the above examples, is used
as a stative after another verb. Examples of serialization with statives (and /fà/)
are as follows:

wɔ́-tɔ̀n èdìbán wɔ̀ hɔ́   'they sell food there'
   ('they-sell food be-at there')
mì-yé-ɛ̀ ègwúmá wɔ̀ ǹkìràn   'I worked in Accra'
   ('I-did work be-at Accra')
yè-yé-ɛ̀ kúr wɔ̀ bìríbíárá hṹ   'we agreed about everything'
   ('we-were one be-at everything's body')
ɔ̀-dì sí'kán kwíá-à nám nú   'he cut the meat with a knife'
   ('he-take knife cut meat the')
nà íyí wɔ̀-dí yɛ̀ íbèn àdí   'what is this used for?'
   ('Q this they-take do what thing?')
sɛ̀ ì-dì kèté'ké fì tákɔ̀ràdí   'if you take a train from
 rí-kɔ̀ ǹkìràn à, í-kwìà mù   Takoradi to Accra, you pass
wɔ̀ kùmáásí   through Kumasi'

('if you-take train leave Takoradi going-to Accra *cond.*, you-cut inside
be-at Kumasi')

fà ìgùá nú fé-sì pún nú   'put the chair at the table'
ní ń'kyén
('take chair the take-put table the its vicinity')

fá bùrà   'bring it' ('take come')

mìn-ní ǹ-túm̀ ǹ-fá m̀-bá   'I can't bring it'
('I-am-not not-able not-take not-come')

The verbs /kyìn/ and /sìn/ 'surpass' are apparently also used as statives
after another verb; my records happen to include only examples in which an active and a stative verb would have the same form, but my memory, though fal-
lible, tells me the root would be used in all combinations. Somewhat similarly,
a few other invariable forms with construction markers are used, independently
of the construction of the preceding verb. These include /ké-pìm/ 'go up to, until' ('go-reach'), and /bé-yέ/ 'approximately' ('will-be'). E.g.,

mú hō̃ yὲ dìn kyìn nù   'I'm stronger than he is'
('my body is strong surpass him')

mìbé-tìná hɔ́ képìm bíò   'I'm going to stay there until tomorrow'
('I-will-stay there go-reach tomorrow')

ɔ́á-kɔ̀ béyέ dàpén   'he's been gone about a week'
('he-has-gone will-be week')

From the point of view of the usage of serial constructions, it is worth noting
that expressions referring to ability are serializations in Fante; note the sentence
glossed 'I can't bring it' above. This is not common in other languages.

12.14. Construction agreement in serialization is not found in all languages.
In Yoruba and Nupe, for example, a construction marker appears overtly only
once in a serial construction. There is evidence, however, that construction a-
greement is not far below the surface. In Yoruba, the verb 'come' is /wá/ in
most constructions, but has the suppletive form /bò/ in the present. In a serial
construction, the latter, though without the present construction marker, is required after a present. Compare the following:

ó mú ọbẹ 'he picked up a knife'; ó wá 'he came':
ó mú ọbẹ wá 'he brought a knife'
ó m̀ mú ọbẹ 'he's picking up a knife'; ó m̀ bò 'he's coming': ó m̀ mú
ọbẹ bò 'he's bringing a knife'

The Nupe equivalent of the last sentence ends with a verb whose root is /bé/
'come'. In this sentence, however, this verb undergoes tonal alternation and has
the form /bě/. This tonal alternation is normal after low tone, but the preceding
tone here is not low. The alternation can best be explained by positing the present

construction marker, which does have low tone, in the underlying structure; it is deleted only after triggering the tonal alternation.[4] The sentence is:

> Òjó è lă èbi bě   'Ojo is bringing a knife'

Otherwise, serialization in Yoruba and Nupe consists simply of stringing verbs one after another. Except in one combination noted below, only the first verb is marked (if at all) for construction. The various serial constructions that occur seem to reflect a puzzling variety of underlying structures, but the surface manifestations are fairly straightforward. One significant detail, however, is that there are some verbs which are used only in serial constructions, not independĕntly. One of these is /fi/, with a meaning like 'take, use' in the combinations in which it occurs, used before another verb. In the same usage is /bá/ 'accompany'. Another such verb is /sí/, used after a verb of motion, or after /fi/, with a meaning like 'arrive at'. Since these verbs and the noun phrases which follow them are commonly translated by English prepositional phrases, these verbs are frequently called "prepositions." Another such bound verb is /tún/ 'do something again', used before another verb to express repeated action. Since this is generally reflected in translation by 'again', it is frequently called an "adverb." Even when two independent verbs are used in a series but are translated by a single verb (as /mú . . . wá/ 'bring' in examples above, there is reluctance to recognize that each is a verb in its own right; such combinations are frequently called "split verbs," and their alleged unitary nature is triumphantly pointed out when the object of the first is preposed in a topicalized construction, leaving the two verbs in immediate sequence—as if topicalization were primary rather than derived. All of this may say something about the grammar and lexicon of English, but it does not permit justice to be done to the structure of Yoruba.

There is, to be sure, something unusual about the usage of the above-mentioned /tún/. If it is immediately followed by a verb with no object, any construction marker other than that of the present precedes /tún/ as expected, but the present construction marker exceptionally precedes the following verb rather than /tún/. Further, if /tún/ is used before a verb-object combination, the order of verb and object is reversed; actually, this may be alternatively explained by saying that the noun phrase becomes the object of /tún/, and that another verb follows with the same object in the underlying structure, deleted in the surface structure. There is thus only one unusual detail about /tún/, and there are no counterexamples using other forms which would give reason to call /tún/ anything other than a verb.

Some typical examples of serialization in Yoruba are given below. There is no (or a zero) construction marker in the factative (translated as a past in these

---

[4] For this analysis and example I am indebted to Mr. Isaac George (private communication), whose native language is Nupe. Actually, Mr. George notes that the morphotonemic alternation involved here is more widespread than this example suggests, and may require other explanations in other cases; he nevertheless feels that the explanation given is correct for this type of sentence.

cases), but markers for other constructions would appear before the first verb only, except for the one case mentioned above and included here. Other problems of deep structure will be left for others to work out.

wọ́n se išu jẹ	'they cooked yam and ate it'
('they cooked yam eat')	
wọ́n ti mú owó wá	'they have brought money'
('they have taken money come')	
ó ń fi ọ̀bẹ ge išu	'he's cutting the yam with a knife'
('he is using knife cut yam')	
ó ń fi ọ̀bẹ s'íbẹ̀	'he's putting the knife there'
('he is taking/using knife arrive-at there')	
ó bá mi lọ	'he went with me'
('he accompanied me go')	
ó ti tún lọ s'ójà	'he has gone to market again'
('he has repeated go arrive-at market')	
ó tún ń lọ	'he's going again'
('he repeat is going' !)	
ó ń tún ɛmu mu	'he's drinking (booze) again'
('he is repeating alcoholic-beverage drink')	
ó ń tún‾ še	'he's doing it again'
('he is repeating-it do')	
wọ́n jẹ išu tán	'they ate up all the yam'
('they ate yam be-gone'; cf.: ó ti tán 'it's all gone')	

One important type of verb sequence has been omitted in the above, because it has a significantly different structure. This uses a form /sì/, which appears only in sequences, and which may possibly be analyzed as a conjunction rather than a verb. It is not preceded by construction markers, but it is preceded by a subject, which may be the same subject repeated or a new subject. The first verb following /sì/ is preceded by a construction marker (except for the factative, of course). This is the Yoruba formation for introducing an additional action, consecutive or simultaneous, as opposed to referring to actions which require the same actor (serialization, as above). E.g.,

ó ti š'išẹ́‾rẹ̀ tán, ó sì ti	'he has finished his work,
jẹ-un	and has also eaten'
('he has done-work-his be-done, he also has eaten-thing')	
mo ń š'išẹ́, Òjó sì ń jẹ-un	'I'm working, and Ojo is eating'

Particularly in the light of the Yoruba verbs which are used only in serial constructions, one may wonder if the construction markers of Yoruba (like /ti/ and /ń/ in the above examples) may not also be considered verbs used initially in a serial construction. Such an analysis is particularly tempting in the case of /ń/ (cf. 11.4, where a suggestion of a verbal derivation of this marker is made). For other construction markers, there does not appear to be any convincing evidence for such an interpretation. It would be a more attractive hypothesis if construction markers themselves appeared in a number of serial combinations, but such combinations are at best highly restricted; indeed, a special status for /ń/ may be reinforced by the fact that it actually does appear after another construction marker.

12.15. Similar manifestations of serialization could be cited from several other languages; Jukun, for example, seems to be particularly enthusiastic about stringing verbs one after another, in much the same way as is done in Yoruba. A representative selection has by now been presented, however, of the ways in which distinctions are made between actions necessarily associated with a single subject and actions which may be performed by different subjects. But the subject of serialization must not be dropped without observing that Gilbert Ansre's caveat has not been overlooked (see Ansre 1966, pp. 29-32). He notes, as others had before him, that serialization in Ewe usually involves construction agreement, as in Fante (12.13 above), but that such agreement is not present for all of the presumed verbs involved in serialization. To account for the exceptions, he sets up a morpheme class of "verbids"—morphemes which happen to be homophonous with verb roots (in all cases except one, for which there is no parallel verb, but which might be interpreted as a conjunction in any case), but which do not follow the usual rules in serial constructions. He cites an apparently comparable situation in Akan, with reference only to /wɔ́/ 'be located at', though he might have included a few others. The occurrence in Yoruba of forms analyzed as verbs, but which appear only in serial constructions, might seem to strengthen the case for such an analysis. I will not presume to re-analyze the Ewe data without a much deeper competence in the language than I have ever had, but would point out that the Akan and Yoruba data can be satisfactorily explained without recourse to such a device. In Akan, the verbs in question are attested as stative rather than active verbs on other grounds, and the analysis presented above defines their special use in serial constructions on that basis. In Yoruba, the recognition of a few bound verbs appears to be adequate; they have no special uses in contrast with other verbs in serial constructions. Is it possible that the "verbids" in question in Ewe may also be a special class of verbs with distinctive uses elsewhere, on the basis of which their apparently atypical use in serial constructions could be explained? If not—if they are unique only in this usage—then Ansre would seem to have made a most perceptive observation for Ewe, which might possibly apply to other languages as well, though it does not seem necessary for Akan or Yoruba, or for the other languages that have been treated here.

12.16. In the foregoing survey of verbal constructions in Niger-Congo, an effort has been made to assign meaningful labels to verbal constructions, reflecting their meaning and use, rather than simply to take over the familiar but often inaccurate and misleading labels of English, Latin, and Greek. The inadequacy of traditional labels has not escaped the notice of others, and a word about alternative treatments is in order.

Some writers have, for at least some verbal constructions, used a distinctive morpheme such as the construction marker as a label. Thus Ashton (1944) refers to certain Swahili constructions as "the -ME- tense" (completive), "the -TA-tense" (future), "the -NGE- tense" (present hypothetical), and so on. There is a certain admirable sophistication about thus avoiding questionable or obscure labels, but there are also disadvantages in this practice. Unless one already knows Swahili fairly well, it is not easy to find information in Ashton's grammar about how some type or time of action, such as conditional or past, is expressed. One can only page through the various discussions of the "tenses" until one happens upon the desired one. In other languages, this labelling technique may be complicated by tone, particularly if (as is by no means uncommon) two constructions differ only in tone; in lecturing or language teaching, it is awkward to introduce tonal distinctions in a phrase that is mostly English. And finally, in many languages distinctive morphemes which can be cited are not always so readily identifiable.

For some constructions in Igbo, Ward (1936) uses a similar labelling device. To her credit, she chooses this device specifically for two constructions for which no well-known labels would be accurate. One is "the Na-form", which has often uncritically been called "present", and which has been called "incompletive" in foregoing references to Igbo; /nà/ is an auxiliary in the stative construction, followed by a verbal noun. The second construction in question is Ward's "the Ra-(Suffix) form", often uncritically called "past", for which I have used the term "factative". Ward's label in this case is less elegant; as she herself points out, the suffix consists of /r/ plus a repetition of the preceding vowel; she does not include in her description of the construction, though she indicates in her examples, the distinctive tone of the construction.

For Efik, Ward (1933, esp. pp. 61-69) largely confines herself to traditional labels; fortunately, most of them are reasonably satisfactory for Efik, but there is one glaring exception. Ward follows an earlier student of Efik, Hugh Goldie, in speaking of "the Aorist." To begin with, few students of African languages today have the vaguest notion of what that term is supposed to mean—and for that matter, it is pretty meaningless to many students of Greek. What is worse, however, is that Goldie had used the term for any construction that includes nothing more, segmentally, than a subject pronoun and a verb base; he did not recognize tone in Efik, which is somewhat comparable to not recognizing noun cases in Latin or Greek. Ward unfortunately perpetuates the term, in spite of the fact that she recognizes a number of "tone variations" and proceeds to list five tonally different paradigms (and she missed a sixth) to which she gives subordinate labels like "Narrative" and "Conditional" which, although not all as accurate as they might be, at least represent an effort to say something meaningful—and none of which is in any sense like a Greek aorist. It is regrettable that Ward did not simply scrap the term "aorist," or at most relegate Goldie's confusion to a footnote. One still gets the abominable impression from Ward's treatment that tonal distinctions are somehow secondary to consonant and vowel distinctions. Actually, six minimally different tone sequences occur with a subject pronoun and a verb base if the inherent tones of both are other than low; if inherent low tones are involved, there is neutralization between some pairs of sequences. For the third person singular pronoun and the verb meaning 'buy', the constructions are as follows:

édép :   Present contrastive for something preceding the verb; also sequential after some constructions (the third type described in 12.12 above)

éʼdép :   Sequential after most constructions (the fifth type described in 12.12 above); also completive for third person pronouns only

édèp :   Present contrastive for something following the verb, or neutral if the context does not permit contrast

èdép :   Conditional

édêp :   Hortative

èdêp :   Sequential after future contrastive and negative (alternatively /ìdêp/ for all persons other than first singular; the fourth type described in 12.12 above)

(Since tone is not marked in Efik orthography, and since the vowels /ɛ/ and /e/ are not distinguished, the spelling *edep* represents no less than twenty phonologically different forms; the form intended is predictable from the context in only a limited number of cases.)

12.17. Some matters have been omitted or have received only passing mention in the foregoing discussion. One of these is negatives; little more has been said than to note that negative systems rarely parallel affirmative systems fully, and that in many languages some affirmative constructions do not have any corresponding negative in the basic verbal morphology. Examples of these phenomena will be given in connection with a treatment of the total verbal systems of some specific languages in the following chapter.

Another matter that has received minimal attention is subject pronouns—or concords in the case of noun-class languages. In fact, the impression has undoubtedly been given that such forms are part of the predicate of a sentence, although it would be expected that they should be treated in a rigid syntactic analysis as part of the subject noun phrase. There are good practical reasons, however, for considering them under the heading of verbal constructions. In most Niger-Congo languages, a subject pronoun or concord is required even after an expressed noun subject. Further, subject pronouns and following construction markers are frequently combined as single syllables by morphophonemic rules; in many languages, a construction marker may be a tonal replacive operating on the subject pronoun. By and large, it is simplest to treat subject pronouns or concords with verbal constructions, and then to note the circumstances and ways in which such morphemes may be omitted. Their omission or apparent omission in some languages may be briefly noted.

In Akan, subject pronouns are omitted after a noun subject unless the noun subject is topicalized. Topicalization may be signalled by nothing more than the use of a noun subject, but the conjunctive /nà/ is frequently also used initially in the sentence.

In Jukun, a subject pronoun after a noun subject may be—and usually is—omitted in all constructions except the hortative. The hortative is marked by high tone replacing stem tone with the subject pronoun, and a third person pronoun with this high tone is required after an expressed noun subject. E.g.,

ku sa víni	'he finished it'
Áŋgyú sa víni	'Angyu finished it'
kú sa víni	'he should finish it'
Áŋgyú kú sa víni	'Angyu should finish it'

In Igbo, a subject pronoun must be omitted after a noun subject except in a hypothetical (interrogative) construction. In the hypothetical, low tone replaces stem tone with a pronoun, including the plural independent pronouns used as subjects, and a third person pronoun with low tone is required after a noun subject. E.g.,

ó mèrè yà	'he did it'
Òkóyè mèrè yà	'Okoye did it'
ò mèrè yà	'did he do it?'
Òkóyè ò mèrè yà	'did Okoye do it?'

This is by no means all there is to the situation in Igbo, however. In some constructions, there is a vowel prefix before the verb base after a noun subject, including the plural independent pronouns, which does not appear after a singular pronoun subject. The prefix is /á'-/ or /é'-/ in the negative, and /à-/ or /è-/ (with the alternants /'á-/, /'é-/ between two high tones) in the completive and consecutive. Singular pronouns have low tone in the negative and consecutive, but high tone followed by downstep in the completive. E.g.,

ọ̀ byá'ghị̣	'he didn't come'
há á'byághị̣	'they didn't come'
ó 'méélá 'yá	'he has done it'
Òkóyè èméélá 'yá	'Okoye has done it'
ànyị̣ 'éméélá 'yá	'we have done it'

In Yoruba, one is likely to get the impression from the orthography and from older treatments of the language that subject pronouns are omitted after noun subjects. Unless deleted or absorbed by something else in the environment, however, a noun subject must be followed by a high tone, with no lengthening of the final vowel of the noun subject. This high tone must certainly be interpreted as a manifestation of the third person singular subject pronoun /ó/. E.g.,

ó lọ	'he went'
bàbá'mi ' lọ	'my father went'

This high tone does not appear overtly if the noun subject ends with high tone, or if the incompletive construction marker /ń/ follows; in these cases it may be considered to be absorbed by the adjacent high tone. Nor does a high tone appear before the negative morpheme /kò/—precisely where the third person singular pronoun has a zero allomorph.

In very recent discussions of Yoruba, this high tone reflex of a subject pronoun has unfortunately been described by some students as indicating "concord." This represents a gross misunderstanding of what is ordinarily meant by "concord." Concord implies a choice between two or more (usually many more) forms conditioned by the particular noun class referred to. Thus /a-/ is the subject concord for Class 1 in Swahili, /u-/ for Class 3, /ki-/ for Class 7, and so on. There is no such choice in Yoruba—and there are no functional noun classes. In fact, Yoruba does not even require a concordial choice between singular and plural after a noun subject. The same high tone is used not only after all nouns, but after independent pronouns of all persons and both numbers. This still reflects the third person singular pronoun /ó/, since that pronoun can be used in constructions such as relatives with reference to any noun or independent pronoun. With reference to the surface structure, this high tone in Yoruba may be called "subject high tone"; in the underlying structure it is the pronoun /ó/, which by definition is non-concordial.

Finally, a word about word order and object pronouns. In the Mande languages and in at least those Gur languages with which I am acquainted, the regular nontopicalized order in simple sentences with a subject and an object is subject-object-verb. In other Niger-Congo languages, the usual order is subject-verb-object. In most cases, the order is the same whether the object is a noun or a pronoun. In the Bantu languages, however, an object concord appears as a prefix immediately before the verb base, after construction markers. In Swahili, for example, compare the following:

nilitafuta kisu	'I looked for a knife'
nili-ki-tafuta	'I looked for it (7)'

Unfortunately, object concords in this position have frequently been mislabeled "infixes". Subject concords in initial position are obviously prefixes, and construction markers after them have unhesitatingly been called prefixes as well, presumably because they are obligatory in the constructions in which they are used, and do appear before the verb base. Apparently the optional use of an object concord in place of (or even in addition to) a noun object is thought of as "insertion," and this is then confused with "infixation." The term "infix" should be restricted to a morpheme which appears within the bounds of, and interrupting the segmental sequence of, another morpheme. Its use with reference to a morpheme "inserted" or appearing optionally between morphemes within a word is unwarranted.

In conclusion, African language studies have too commonly—and sometimes still are—characterized by an uncritical and often naive imposition of classical grammatical categories and terminology in structures to which they are quite foreign. In both description and labeling, it is past time to bring the era of linguistic imperialism to an end, and make a more consistent effort to capture what is really going on in African languages. This is not to say, of course, that the only acceptable grammatical terminology is that suggested or approved by the present author, who is entirely prepared to use the terminology of other scholars and even non-specialists if such terminology is appropriately meaningful, but who is not about to call something a "subjunctive tense" when it is neither subjunctive nor a tense.

Chapter 13

Verbal Systems

13.1. A number of details in the verbal systems of several specific languages have been treated in various contexts in preceding chapters. In connection with tonal systems, functions of tone, subject and object pronouns or concords, and the derivation of adjectivals, problems and procedures in analysis and description have been discussed which may apply to almost any part of a language's grammar, its verbal system included. With a more specific focus on predications in the last two chapters, there has been a discussion of nonverbal and marginally verbal predications, the derivation of verbal bases, and the kinds of constructions into which verbal bases enter. It is the purpose of this chapter to illustrate some manifestations of inflection in verbal systems, and to show how the various structural phenomena that have been discussed up to this point are realized in the total verbal system of a few selected languages.

It was noted in the preceding chapter that a verb base in Swahili—and the same is true for the Bantu languages in general—has a suffix /-a/ in many constructions, but a suffix /-e/ in some; a suffix /-i/ also appears in constructions not mentioned up to this point. In addition, in a great many Bantu languages (e.g. LuGanda; cf. 12.3) there is a suffix which in many cases combines with the final consonant of the base according to morphophonemic rules which, for some languages, are quite complex. This suffix, which is commonly used in a completive construction, and in some languages in a few other constructions such as a recent past, seems for Bantu as a whole to have the underlying form */-ile/.[1] The combination of a base with this suffix has been referred to by such terms as "the modified stem" and "the perfect stem," terms which are quite appropriate if, as so frequently happens, the boundary between the base and the suffix is obscured by morphophonemic combinations. In most cases, however, the derivation of the resultant forms from a definable base and suffix can be stated in terms of reasonably straightforward rules. The situation in SeTswana will be taken as an example.[2]

---

[1] This formation is completely regular in KeRezi. It gives a stative force to verbs with inceptive meaning. E.g.,

mob-a	'move, start out': mob-ile 'be movable'
sen-a	'become aged': sen-ile
aj-a	'become skilled': aj-ile
juven-a	'become mature (of a male)': juven-ile
nub-a	'become mature (of a female)': nub-ile

[2] SeTswana data taken from Cole 1955. I use /ɛ/ and /ɔ/ for his ê and ô respectively. The absence of tone marks is not relevant here; verbs fall into two tone classes and follow tonal paradigms for the various constructions, while the forms given here are not in full constructions.

After a verb root with no extension, the completive suffix has the regular form /-ilɛ/ in most circumstances. It has an alternant /-nɛ/ after a root-final /n/. There are a few verb roots consisting of only a single consonant or cluster; after such, the form of the suffix is not completely predictable, and the combination must be stated for each. E.g.,

rɛk-a	'buy, barter'	:	rɛk-ilɛ
bu-a	'speak'	:	bu-ilɛ
bin-a	'dance'	:	bin-nɛ
nɔn-a	'become fat'	:	nɔn-nɛ
f-a	'give'	:	f-ilɛ
j-a	'eat'	:	j-elɛ
nw-a	'drink'	:	nolɛ ~ nw-elɛ
šw-a	'die'	:	šulɛ ~ šw-ilɛ

After derived bases with the durative extension /-ay-/ or /-y-/, the same regular form /-ilɛ/ is used, but the /y/ of the extension is elided. (An alternation between /a/ and /ɛ/ as the last vowel of the base has to do with the base itself and is irrelevant to the occurrence of the suffix.) E.g.,

tsamay-a	'go, walk'	:	tsama-ilɛ
apay-a	'cook'	:	apɛ-ilɛ

After derived bases with most other extensions—with the important exceptions of the causative and passive—Cole recognizes what he describes as a "contracted" form of the completive suffix, with the alternants /-yɛ/, /-ye/, and /-e/. As the data appear to me, it would seem preferable to recognize two distinct forms: /-yɛ/ or /-ye/ (the vowel alternation determined by regular dissimilation rules) with some extensions, and /-e/ with others. The form /-ye/ appears clearly after the reciprocal extension /-an-/. Less obviously, but by regular morphophonemic rules, /-yɛ/ or /-ye/ appears after extensions ending in /-l-/ (including the applicative and reversive); */ly/ regularly becomes /ts/. Thus forms with /-yɛ/ or /-ye/ are:

lekan-a	'be equal'	:	lekan-ye
kɔpan-a	'meet'	:	kɔpan-ye
rɔbal-a	'go to sleep'	:	rɔbɛtse
rɛkɛl-a	'buy for'	:	rɛkɛtse
apol-a	'undress'	:	apotsɛ

The form /-e/ of the completive suffix clearly appears after the positional extension /-am-/. It appears also after the contactive extension /-ar-/, the vowel of which then has the alternant /ɛ/. E.g.,

khubam-a	'kneel'	:	khubam-e
palam-a	'climb, ride'	:	palam-e
tšhwar-a	'grasp, catch'	:	tšhwɛr-e
fular-a	'turn around'	:	fulɛr-e

After the causative extension (which itself has several surface manifestations, derivable from two alternants /-is-/ and -y-/), the completive suffix has the form /-itsɛ/, which Cole analyzes as a combination of /-ilɛ/ and the alternant /-y-/ of the causative extension, with */-ilyɛ/ becoming /-itsɛ/. There are thus two manifestations of the causative extension in completive forms. This analysis also strongly suggests what one might have guessed from the beginning, that /-ilɛ/ is itself a combination of two suffixes, /-il-/ and /-ɛ/, neither of which appears without the other, but which may be separated by another suffix. In the causative base before /-itsɛ/, final /s/ and /tsh/ are retained without alternation; final /ts/ usually has the alternant /d/ but is sometimes retained; final /ny/ combines with the suffix to yield /ntsɛ/. E.g.,

rɛkis-a	'sell'	:	rɛkis-itsɛ
tšhos-a	'frighten'	:	tšhos-itsɛ
ntsh-a	'take out'	:	ntsh-itsɛ
bots-a	'ask, question'	:	bod-itsɛ
tlats-a	'fill'	:	tlad-itsɛ
gɔts-a	'kindle'	:	gɔts-itsɛ
fɛny-a	'conquer'	:	fɛntsɛ

By phonologic analogy with completive forms from bases derived by verbal extensions, a few verb roots also use the completive suffix alternants /-yɛ/ or /-ye/, /-e/, and /-itsɛ/ rather than the regular /-ilɛ/. A case of this is:

bɔn-a	'see'	:	bɔn-ye

Cole also lists a number of irregular forms, which he says can be explained on the basis of the historical phonology of the language, though the explanations are too involved to be included in his grammar. For the most part, the irregular forms do not seem to involve highly unexpected morphophonemic alternations. Their very presence, however, may be of considerable interest in the light of the situation in some non-Bantu languages which will be considered.

The passive verbal extension, unlike all the other verbal extensions, does not appear before the completive suffix, but combines with its various forms in a way parallel to the formation of /-itsɛ/ as described above. The passive /-w-/ appears before the final vowel of the completive suffix, adding force to the analysis of the latter as itself composite. Before /-w-/, /ts/ has the alternant /tš/, and /m/ has the alternant /ng/. Examples of passive completives are:

rɛk-a	'buy, barter'	:	rɛk-ilɛ	:	rɛk-il-w-ɛ
j-a	'eat'	:	j-elɛ	:	j-el-w-ɛ
men-a	'fold'	:	men-nɛ	:	men-n-w-ɛ
gagol-a	'tear'	:	gagotsɛ	:	gagotš-w-ɛ
thus-a	'help'	:	thus-itsɛ	:	thus-itš-w-ɛ
bots-a	'ask, question'	:	bod-itsɛ	:	bod-itš-w-ɛ
fɛny-a	'conquer'	:	fɛntsɛ	:	fɛntš-w-ɛ
palam-a	'climb, ride'	:	palam-e	:	palang-w-e

In the Bantu languages in general, verb bases without the completive suffix are usually preceded by a construction marker; in some cases, zero or a zero allomorph of a construction marker may be included. Completive forms, however, are usually not preceded by a construction marker. Subject concords, however, may include one or two alternants that do not appear in other constructions. The restriction of such special forms to only a few cases, and the nature of the forms themselves, make it unattractive to analyze them as portmanteau forms including a completive construction marker; they are more readily described simply as conditioned by the use of the completive suffix.

13.2. In most non-Bantu Niger-Congo languages, there appears to be nothing paralleling this widespread Bantu phenomenon of an inflectional suffix other than a vowel. The Senufo languages, however, do have a distinction between two stem forms of verbs, and at least in Suppire there are some tantalizing similarities in form. The morphological situation is far more complicated than in Bantu; one can only list a number of classes of verbs—eleven plus some irregulars in Suppire —in terms of the relationship of the two forms to each other. The usage is also different; the derived form is used in the present rather than the completive, and also (at least in Senari; I have no relevant evidence for Suppire) in the imperative. Still, when one finds the commonest pattern in Suppire illustrated by pairs such as /dire/ and /dirìlì/ 'pull on', or /tùgo/ and /tùgòli/ 'carry'—and sees somewhat similar patterns in /pi/ and /pìni/ 'soften' and in /pèì/ and /pèrì/ 'become fat' — well, one has to wonder.

Verb forms used in constructions other than the present and imperative appear in most cases to be monomorphemic roots, and for most classes of verbs the present is formed by suffixation. In one class, however, the root and present forms are the same, and in some classes the ending of the present replaces the final part of the other form, suggesting that the latter may also, for these verbs, be a root plus suffix. A number of individual verbs show lexically conditioned morphophonemic alternation in what precedes the present suffix. And in a small number of verbs, the present form also has a prefix consisting of a homorganic nasal. Except for a few verbs which must be specially listed, the tones of the present form are predictable from the tones of the root. A few examples of each class are as follows:

No present suffix (but nasal prefix in a few cases):

wíí	wíí	'look at'
tɔri	tɔri	'count'
tyìrì	ǹ-tyìrì	'sneeze'

Present with suffix /-li/:

káá	káá-lí	'roast'
kùri	kùrù-li	'bend'
turu	n-tuu-li	'pass by'

Present with suffix /-ni/:

nɔ	nɔ̀-ni	'arrive'
tye	tyi-ni	'find out'
tyī	tyì-nì	'weave'

Present with suffix /-ri/:

kúó	kúó-rí	'draw (water)'
kɔri	koo-ri	'chase'
tà-ʔai	tà-ri	'cook'

Present with suffix /-ge ~ -gɛ ~ -ga/ (choice of vowel generally predictable):

bère	bèrè-ge	'become short'
nyɔ	nyɔ̀-gɛ	'become good'
lyɛ	lyà-gɛ	'become old'

Present with /-gɛ/ (and probably other alternants) replacing /-ri/ or /-rɛ/; only the following are recorded:

wyɛ-ri	wyɛ-gɛ	'become hot'
ká-rí	ŋ́-ké-gɛ́	'go'
tyé-rɛ́	ń-tyé-gɛ́	'become small'

Present with /-rV/ replacing /-gV/; only the following:

du-go	du-ro	'become heavy'
tí-gí	ń-tí-rí	'go down'

Present with /-rui/ replacing /-go/:

du-go	du-rui	'go up'
mú-gó	mú-rúí	'open'

Present with only or final vowel of root repeated as suffix:

sú	sú-ú	'pound'
kea	kea-a	'eat (meat)'
kú	ŋ́-kú-ú	'die'

Present with first vowel of root repeated, replacing a different vowel in a vowel sequence:

bbìà	bbìì	'drink'
kua	kuu	'finish'
tyuo	n-tyuu	'fall, drop'

Present with /i/ replacing final vowel of root:

fé	fí	'run'
firìle	firìli	'drag'
tyùùgo	tyùùgi	'rub'

Irregular:

dyie	dyi	'enter'
ppu	ppùa	'tie'
pa	ma	'come'

The present construction in Suppire uses a construction marker /ná/ before the present form. An object comes between the construction marker and the verb, which undergoes morphotonemic alternation in many cases. E.g.,

kó ʔà :	pi ná ŋkó ʔàli	'they are dancing'
pèì :	u ná pèrì	'he's getting fat'
wyɛri :	ku ná wyɛgɛ	'it's getting hot'
nyà :	mi ná baga nyáà	'I see a house'

A construction marker /á/ (before low or high tone, /â/ before mid) is used before the verb root in a completive construction. E.g.,

ku á tyùgò	'it is (has become) deep'
ku â nyɔ	'it is good'
u â nɔ	'he has arrived'

So much of the brief period of work on Suppire was devoted to the complexities of morphotonology and morphology that little more of the verbal system was recorded. It is known, however, that there are several major constructions similar to the completive, with a construction marker before the verb root. Negatives were recorded for some constructions, in each case with /mɛ́/ after the verb. Quite clearly, the significant feature of the Suppire verbal system is the derived forms used in the present.

13.3. Senari is rather closely related to Suppire; there is excellent evidence that ancestral forms of the two were entirely mutually intelligible, if not identical, as recently as six hundred years ago. Senari also has a variety of formations used in the present and imperative verbal constructions. For some verbs, the formations are clearly parallel to those found in Suppire. The remarkable thing, however, is how diverse the two systems are. Senari does not have a reflex of the commonest present suffix of Suppire, /-li/. On the other hand, Senari has a number of verbs whose present is formed by a tonal replacive. The nasal prefix found occasionally with present forms in Suppire is missing in Senari. And most strikingly, no class of verbs in either language seems to be made up predominantly of cognates from a single class in the other; in many cases, individual verbs seem to have gone their own perverse ways in the two languages. Nor does either language appear to reflect in its present system a historical process of regularization or simplification. A survey of the types of present formation in Senari is as follows:

Root and present identical:

kpúmɔ́	kpúmɔ́	'hit'
tyóró	tyóró	'count'
tugo	tugo	'carry'

Low-high replacing low-low, or high replacing low, in present:

dèmè	dèmɛ́	'help'
kùrù	kùrú	'bend'
lì	lí	'eat'

Low-mid replacing low-low or high-high in present :

sɔ̀lɔ̀	sɔ̀lɔ	'pass'
tyèrè	tyère	'sneeze'
dyíé	dyìe	'enter'

Present with only or final vowel of root repeated as suffix; high tone replacing low:

dyíé	dyíé-é	'wash'
kà	ká-á	'eat (meat)'
kù	kú-ú	'die'

Higher vowel replacing lower vowel in present, and repeated as suffix; high tone replacing low:

pɛ́	pé-é	'sweeep'
syɔ	syo-o	'buy'
fǎ	fó-ó	'run'

Higher vowel replacing lower vowel in present; final high tone replacing low:

dya	dye	'shatter'
kòlògò	kòlògú	'roll'
sáŋgá	sáŋgí	'do'

Present with suffix /-gV/ (too few examples to establish a rule for choice of vowel):

nya	nya-gi	'look at'
tǔ	túŋ-gú	'fight'
tɔ̌	tóŋ-gó	'close, bury'

Present with suffix /-rV/; the following are the only cases recorded:

fã	fã-ri	'build'
kó	kó-rí	'draw (water)'
kú	kú-rú	'chew'

Present with /-rV/ replacing /-gV/ or /-ʔV/; high tone replacing low:

lú-gú	lú-rú	'go up'
tì-gì	tí-rí	'go down'
sɔ-ʔɔ	sɔ-ri	'cook'

Irregular:

pã̃	ma	'come'
kárí	syé	'go'
pie	pĭ	'do, make'

The present form is used by itself as a singular imperative, or may be preceded by /ta/ or /a/, which are unique forms if they are subject pronouns. A pronoun /ya/ is used in the plural imperative. E.g.,

kùrù	:	lí kùrú	'bend it (li-class)'
nya	:	ya kpagì nyagi	'look (pl.) at the house'

The present form is used after subject concords without a construction marker (unlike Suppire) in the present construction. E.g.,

yɔ́	:	wóle yóó	'we're dancing'
tyànà	:	wi mɛnɛ tyàná	'he's spinning rope'
dyíé	:	pe fànì dyíéé	'they're washing clothes'

A construction marker consisting of a syllabic nasal homorganic with the following consonant, with low tone, is used in a construction which includes a completive meaning, but which in at least some cases seems to refer to the recent past; it is recorded in one sentence with the word for 'yesterday'. The verb root is used in this construction. If the subject is first or second person singular, the construction marker may optionally be omitted; this results in identity with the present only for verbs which have identical root and present forms (and there is some suspicion of a tonal difference with the pronoun, which was not recorded). E.g.,

mǐ kɔlɔ	'I coughed / I'm coughing'
pe ǹ lɔgì kpa	'they have drunk the water'
mɔ tyèrè	'you (just) sneezed'
wi ŋ̀ kù	'he has died'
wi ŋ̀ kárí tyà ʔànù	'he went yesterday'

A more remote past construction uses the marker /mà/ with the verb root. This construction may also be used with the word for 'yesterday'; what difference there may be in meaning between this and the last example above is not known. It is established, however, that this construction is always used when the reference is to a more remote past event. E.g.,

pe mà kárí	'they went'
wɔ̀le mà pã̄ tyà ʔànù	'we came yesterday'
mǐ mà ú tórógó	'I sent it (wi-class)'

Three construction markers are recorded, used with the verb root, with future reference: /à/, /dyà/, and /yà/. The distinctions in reference among these three are not known, though there is some evidence that /à/ indicates an immediate future. Any of these construction markers may be followed by /kɔ́/; the modification that this gives to the meaning is also unknown. Distinctions relating to probability or desire, as well as to degrees of futurity, may be involved.

Other morphemes, which may be construction markers or auxiliary verbs, are similarly used to form a hortative, and to express ability and desire. Again, my records are fragmentary. A conditional construction marker /gá/, used with the verb root, is attested.

A few sequences of verbs were recorded, suggesting a consecutive or a form of serialization. Unfortunately, the only cases recorded happen to be with verbs for which the root and the present are identical, so that the choice or permissible sequences of forms are unknown. No pronoun is used, however, for verbs after the first in a sequence if the subject is the same.

In spite of the paucity of material elicited, Senari provides a good illustration of the way in which negative systems do not perfectly match affirmative systems. All recorded negatives have a negative morpheme /í/ at the end of the sentence—not merely after the verb, but also after an adverbial complement. (I would not, however, want to bet on the same /í/ appearing in a negative hortative.) A present negative also has /ò/ (rather than nothing) in the construction marker position before the present form of the verb. A past negative, apparently including the references of both of the affirmative constructions described above, with a syllabic nasal and with /mà/, has /gá/ in the construction marker position. Future negatives are recorded with the same construction markers as in the affirmatives. E.g.,

kárí:	mǐ ò syé í	'I'm not going'
	mǐ gá kárí tyà ʔànù í	'I didn't go yesterday'
	mǐ à kárí í	'I'm not going to go'
	mǐ yà kárí nyì ʔèna í	'I'm not going to go tomorrow'

It may be more impressive to someone who has had experience with a number of African languages than to a novice, but the significant thing about the foregoing is that, in spite of the serious limitations of the data, everything points to a typical Niger-Congo verbal system. The construction markers are just where they belong, and indicate a unidimensional system of constructions. There is not much by way of differentiation of affixes with the verb base, but the present form suffixation and morphophonemic alternations may be attributable to earlier suffixes; the parallelism (one can hardly say cognation, of course) with the one form in Bantu languages which has a suffix consisting of more than a single vowel is striking. Something like a consecutive or serialization is present, and there is the typical lack of parallelism between affirmatives and negatives. In the short time available, the analysis was by no means completed, but it was clearly off und running in the right direction.

13.4. Some aspects of the verbal morphology of Bariba—particularly the status of endings and tone in forms of the verb, and the occurrence of rather irregular stative forms for some verbs—have already been discussed (cf. 5.23, 12.7). A verb may have, apart from the stative, as many as seven different forms, used in different constructions, though for most verbs the forms used in two or more constructions are the same. The recognized variables permit twenty-five permutations, and twenty-three different classes of verbs are attested. Although the allomorphics and morphotonemic alternations are quite complex, any verb form can ultimately be analyzed as a root plus a suffix. This is an unusually extensive use of suffixes in a verbal system, particularly in light of the fact that, with a few highly restricted exceptions, each construction is unambiguously marked by other obligatory morphemes, so that the suffixes and the resultant proliferation of verb forms are actually redundant.

Subject pronouns (first and second persons) and concords for all noun classes have the same forms in all verbal constructions except one, the hortative, which serves also as a consecutive. In the latter construction, a set of pronouns and concords is used which differs in all cases except the second person forms. In this set, the subject concords for noun classes generally end in /ù/. The general subject pronouns and concords all have high tone. The two sets are as follows:

Class	Singular		Class	Plural	
1s	na	n	1pl	sa	su
2s	a	a	2pl	i	i
w-	u	ù	w-pl	ba	bù
y-	ya	yì ~ yù	y-pl	yi	yì
t-	ta	tù	n-pl	nu	nù
g-	ga	gù	s-pl	su	sù
m-	mu	m̀			
s-	su	sù			
n-	nu	nù			

Six primary affirmative constructions are recognized. These are illustrated below for a verb which has the maximum number of distinct froms, and in an order reflecting the order of descriptive statements required to define those forms most efficiently. Problems of communication with informants made it difficult to determine the precise meaning of some constructions. What is here called "experiential" may quite possibly be a completive. The informants' description of circumstances in which this construction would be used, given in Yoruba and then translated into English, or sometimes given in broken French, suggested a meaning like 'I have often done it', and I originally labelled the construction "frequentative." It seems unusual to have an experiential among the primary constructions and a completive in a derived set, but that is the best analysis possible at present. The primary affirmative constructions are:

Hortative	:	su tasu dūūrē	'let's plant yams'
Past	:	na tasu dūūrā	'I planted yams'
Incompletive:		na tasu duurù mɔ́	'I am planting yams'
Customary	:	ná rà tasú dùùrè	'I plant yams'
Experiential :		na tasu dūūrū rē	'I have (often) planted yams'
Imperative	:	a tasu dūūrūō	'plant yams (sg.)'

It will be noted that only the customary has a morpheme in the usual construction marker position; the two top tones in this example and in others below are regular alternations of high before low. Two of the other constructions have another morpheme after the verb, like an additional suffix. The past is frequently followed by a morpheme /kɔ̀/, the force of which is not known.

There are negatives corresponding to the first five of the above; the negative hortative in the second person is used in place of a negative imperative. There is a special verb form in the past negative only—the seventh of the possible different forms. There is also a negative construction marker, but it is not the same for all forms; it is /kú/ for the hortative, /kù/ for the customary, and /ǹ/ for the past, incompletive, and experiential. The primary negative constructions are:

Hortative	:	su kú tasu dūūrē	'let's not plant yams'
Past	:	ná ǹ tasu dūūrê	'I didn't plant yams'
Incompletive:		ná ǹ tasu duurù mɔ́	'I'm not planting yams'
Customary	:	ná kù rà tasú dùùrè	'I don't plant yams'
Experiential :		ná ǹ tasu dūūrū rē	'I have never planted yams'

Bariba is one of the few Niger-Congo languages known to me which may be said to have a bidimensional—and in fact a tri-dimensional—system of verbal constructions. Any of the above may be modified by the addition of a morpheme /rǎ/, with an allomorph /dǎ/ after a nasal, which must be the last morpheme before the (object and) verb. With some constructions, this morpheme seems to refer to past time. With the past, there is some evidence of a completive force, but again it was impossible to pin-point the meaning. In other cases, particularly the hortative and imperative, it was impossible to determine whether the presence of this morpheme reflected any modification in meaning at all. Informants readily accepted its use, however, with each of the above affirmative and negative constructions. Examples for which the semantic distinctions seem best established (and some of these may not be entirely accurate) are:

Incompletive:	na rǎ tasu duurù mɔ́	'I was planting yams'
	ná ǹ dǎ tasu duurù mɔ́	'I wasn't planting yams'
Customary :	ná rà rǎ tasú dùùrè	'I used to plant yams'
	ná kù rà rǎ tasú dùùrè	'I didn't often plant yams'
Experiential :	na rǎ tasu dūūrū rē	'I often used to plant yams'
	ná ǹ dǎ tasu dūūrū rē	'I never used to plant yams'

Another set of constructions based on the above, both without and with /rǎ/ ∼ /dǎ/, is a set of conditionals. No conditional would be expected corresponding to the hortative or imperative, but all of the others are recorded. In conditionals, low tone replaces the high tone of the subject pronoun, and this is immediately followed by a construction marker, /ǹ/ in the affirmative and /kù/ (in place of the non-conditional negative morpheme) in the negative. E.g.,

Past	:	ù ǹ tasu dūūrā	'if he (has) planted yams'
		ù kù tasu dūūrê	'if he didn't plant yams'
Incompletive:		ù ǹ tasu duurù mɔ́	'if he is planting yams'
		ù kù tasu duurù mɔ́	'if he isn't planting yams'

A future is conspicuously absent from the primary constructions described up to this point. Future action is expressed by an auxiliary construction using /ko/ plus a hortative in its consecutive use, with some special statements required. Before /ko/, a first or second person singular pronoun may be omitted; the pronoun before the following consecutive is sufficient to indicate the person. After other personal pronouns and /ko/, the pronoun before the consecutive form is omitted in the first and second person plural, and /ù/ appears in place of /bù/ in the third person plural. For non-personal nouns, subject concords are used regularly. Futures with personal subjects are:

(na) ko n dī	'I'm going to eat'
(a) ka a dī	'you (sg.) are going to eat'
u kó ù dī	'he's going to eat'
sa ko dī	'we're going to eat'
i ko dī	'you (pl.) are going to eat'
ba kó ù dī	'they're going to eat'

Desire, ability, and probably some other ideas are also expressed by auxiliaries with a hortative, without the irregularities in pronoun usage found in the future. E.g.,

na kí n dī	'I want to eat'
sa kí su dī	'we want to eat'

Statives are used with no construction marker and nothing after the verb in the affirmative, and with /ǹ/ marking the negative. For verbs having statives used in an incompletive meaning, the incompletive seems to be rarely used, but seems to have a kind of customary meaning, which may or may not be different from the force of the ordinary customary. E.g.,

Past	:	u dūīā	'he went to sleep'
		u nā	'he came'
Incompletive:		u duià mɔ́	'he's going to sleep'
		u naà mɔ́	'he comes (now and then?)'
Stative	:	u dò	'he is asleep'
		u ǹ dò	'he's not asleep'
		u sīsī	'he's coming (on his way)'
		u ǹ sīsī	'he's not coming'

Perhaps the very uncertainty of the precise semantic references of some of the Bariba verbal constructions—the result of too short a time for analysis, with informants who were unimpeachably cooperative, cheerful, and intelligent, but with whom it was difficult to communicate at the level of precise definition—will underscore the range of possibilities that must be considered, and the caution which must be exercised in linguistic field work.

13.5. The Kpelle verbal system shows substantial superficial differences from even closely related languages, but close typological similarities to systems throughout Niger-Congo. The first step is to isolate the primary constructions—those which do not include an auxiliary or an adverbial complement. These are illustrated by the following sentences, using the same subject and the same verb root in so far as possible:

Imperative	:	kula	'Get out!'
Past	:	è kùla	'he went out'
Hortative	:	é kúla	'he should go out'
Present	:	a kulâi	'he's going out'
Stative	:	a seêni	'he's seated' (imper.: see)

Customary	: a kûla	'he goes out'
Conditional	: à kùla	'when/if he goes out'
Experiential	: à kula	'he has been out'
Completive	: aâ kula	'he has gone out (and is out)'
Desiderative	: èi kùla	'(if only) he would go out'
Past Neg.	: 'fé kula ní	'he didn't go out'
Hort. Neg.	: 'fé kùla	'he shouldn't go out'
Pres. Neg.	: 'fé kulâi	'he isn't going out'
Stat. Neg.	: 'fé seêni	'he isn't seated'
Cust. Neg.	: 'fa kùla	'he doesn't go out'
Desid. Neg.	: 'fêi kùla	'(if only) he wouldn't go out'

A subject pronoun is obligatory in an affirmative verbal construction, even after a noun phrase functioning as the subject of the sentence. The apparent absence of a subject pronoun in the singular imperative may be interpreted as a zero subject pronoun; indeed, there is an optional—though not frequently used—singular imperative which does use an overt subject pronoun. The root forms of the subject pronouns are:

I	:	ŋá	we	: kú
you (sg.)	:	í (~ɓé)	you (pl.)	: ká
he/she/it	:	è	they	: 'tí

That these, rather than some other set of forms described below, are indeed the root forms of the subject pronouns will be evident when those forms are introduced. Two roots must be recognized for the second person singular, though in some dialects only the first, /í/, appears. In most of the southwestern Kpelle area, the first combines with certain following morphemes, and the second, /ɓé/, with others. The second is also the form used optionally though infrequently as the subject of a singular imperative, with mid replacing stem tone. The first, and the root forms for the other persons, appear by themselves only in the past affirmative construction.

In most verbal constructions, the subject pronoun is followed or accompanied by a construction marker, with fairly simple morphophonemic rules governing the combinations. The various combinations that occur may be summed up in a chart; the first column lists the roots, and each of the other columns is headed by a representation of the construction marker:

	Root	H	M	-a	-à	-aâ	-ì
1s :	ŋá	ŋá		ŋa	ŋà	ŋaâ	ŋâi
2s :	í	í	(ɓe)	ɓa	ɓà	ɓaâ	îi
3s :	è	é		a	à	aâ	èi
1pl:	kú	kú		kwa	kwà	kwaâ	kûi
2pl:	ká	ká	ka	ka	kà	kaâ	kâi
3pl:	'tí	'tí		'ta	'tà	'taâ	'tîi

In the last four of the seven columns, it is immediately apparent that all the forms end in the same way; whatever the recurrent partials are, they may clearly be interpreted as morphemes, and the combined forms are obviously not the root forms of the pronouns. The second column differs from the first only in the tone of the third person singular form. Applying the principle of maximum differentiation, the forms in the first column, which show a greater variety (in tone) are taken as the root forms rather than those in the second. The forms in the second column are derived by replacing the tone of the root with high tone. This replacement has a zero effect in five of the six cases, but is identified as present on the basis of the third person singular form. Similarly, in the third column, the tone of the root is replaced by mid tone; these two second person forms are used only in the imperative. In the first, second, and last columns, the first form of the second person singular root is used; in the remaining columns, the second form is used. In the last column, the construction marker is a vowel suffix added to the root with no change in the root. In the preceding three columns, the final /u/ of the first person plural root becomes /w/ before the construction marker. Comparably, a rule not evident in the surface forms states that a final /i/ becomes /y/ before the same construction markers. This rule is negated in the third person plural forms because */ty/ is not a permissible cluster, as /kw/ is. The rule does apply in dialects which use only the first form of the second person singular root; the corresponding forms are /ya/, /yà/, and /yaâ/. Final /a/ and /e/ in the remaining pronoun roots are dropped before these construction markers.

In spite of the label, it cannot be said that each construction marker uniquely marks a single construction. The marker /-a/ is used in the present, the stative, and the customary; the marker /-à/ is used in both the conditional and the experiential. Each of these might, of course, be considered a set of homophonous construction markers, but in any case the contrasts between the constructions also involve morphemes accompanying the following verb root.

Before discussing verb roots and their affixes, it should be noted that an object noun phrase, including a pronoun object, may occur between the construction marker and the verb. Certain adverbials of time may also occur in this position, and before the object if there is one. For example:

a kulâi	'he is going out'
a 6óa kulâi	'he is getting out a knife'
a 'tí kulâi	'he is getting them out'
a nâa kulâi	'he is now going out'
a nâa 6óa kulâi	'he is now getting out a knife'

Parenthetically, it may be observed here that many verbs in Kpelle are used either intransitively or transitively. The verb used in the above examples, in intransitive use, has the basic meaning 'exit', including both 'go out' and 'come out'. In transitive use, it means 'remove': 'take out, bring out, pull out, put out', etc. Even a verb which would seem to be necessarily transitive, like 'cut', may have an intransitive use; a rope may 'get cut' by friction, without an active

agent. Some semantic ranges are unexpected; one verb used intransitively means
'jump', and transitively 'throw'—the cover definition is 'move or cause to move
from one place to another without touching the surface between'. Other verbs,
however, are necessarily transitive; the verbs for 'eat', 'drink', 'cook', 'sew',
'see', and many others require an object, though their English counterparts do
not. Still other verbs, like 'come', 'go', 'sleep', 'laugh', are always used intransitively.

In the list of constructions illustrated above, it will be noted that what appears to be the verb root occurs with four different tone marks (including the
absence of a mark), and in a few cases with a suffix. In some constructions—
specifically those illustrated with the forms /kùla/ and /kúla/—all verbs in the
language are identical in tone. In most of the remaining constructions, however,
a verb may have one of four tones, depending on the identity of the verb root.
For example, in the completive four lexical tones appear in contrast:

High throughout	:	aâ píli	'he has jumped'
Mid throughout	:	aâ kula	'he has gone out'
High-low	:	aâ pêlaŋ	'he has gotten down'
Mid-fall	:	aâ tuâŋ	'he has moved over'

To illustrate the identity of tones in some other constructions, the corresponding
pasts are as follows:

è pìli	'he jumped'
è kùla	'he went out'
è pèlaŋ	'he got down'
è tùaŋ	'he moved over'

The low tone found in the past construction is thus clearly a characteristic
of the construction itself, since it is identical for all verbs. The various tones found
in the completive, on the other hand, are characteristic of individual verb roots.
These may be called the "root tones" of the verbs in question. No two verb roots
differ minimally in their root tones. (In northeastern dialects, where /r/ and /l/
have merged as /l/, there is one instance of a minimal pair; the southwestern forms
are /ɣíli/ 'cook' and /ɣíri/ 'tie'.) Thus, in constructions like the past, in which
all verbs are identical in tone, all verbs remain in contrast with each other. The
root tones are nevertheless lexical tones, each one an integral part of some verb
roots.

The segmental shape of a verb root is CV, CVV, CVCV, or any of these plus
a final /ŋ/. CV(ŋ) roots can have only one of the first two tones, high or mid;
CV roots are all high with one exception, and more CVŋ roots are high than mid.
For other segmental shapes, verbs with high or mid tone far outnumber those
with high-low or mid-fall. A very high proportion of roots with high-low and
mid-fall have final /ŋ/, for no obvious reason. A few representative examples of
verb roots with each root tone are as follows:

pá	'come'	soŋ	'catch'
lɔ́	'enter'	see	'sit down'
ɓóŋ	'sting'	saa	'die'
káa	'see'	kpaaŋ	'be busy'
láa	'lie down'	pala	'weave'
píli	'jump'	wɔlɔ	'cry'
ɣέlε	'laugh'	fεli	'beg of'
kɔ́ri	'look for'	kula	'exit'
kéreŋ	'burn'	ɣeleŋ	'fry'
kɔ̀ɔŋ	'measure'	koôŋ	'fly'
nîa	'forget'	tuâŋ	'move over'
sêlεŋ	'hang'	tisô	'sneeze'

Some of the tonal variety noted in the various verbal constructions can, as has been suggested, be attributed to characteristics of particular constructions. Thus, for example, forms have been cited to show that the completive uses the verb root with its root tone, while the past has a low tone replacing the root tone of the verb. There are also, however, instances of morphotonemic alternations which make the data seem somewhat more complicated than it actually is. First, by no means restricted to the verbal morphology but perfectly regular in the language, low tone has the alternant high-low after mid (cf. 5.5). This alternation appears in a number of verbal constructions; e.g.,

	è kùla	'he went out'
	è ɓóa kùla	'he got out a knife'
	è kâli kùla	'he got out a hoe'
But:	è kɔni kûla	'he got out a stone'

In the illustrations of verbal constructions at the beginning of this section, all of the cases in which the form /kûla/ appears are instances of this same morphotonemic alternation; in each case, a mid tone precedes, and if a tone other than mid preceded the form would be /kùla/. E.g.,

	a kûla	'he goes out'
	'fa kûla	'he doesn't go out'
But:	a ŋalêŋ kùla	'he takes out thorns'
	'fa nǔu nyíŋ kùla	'he doesn't extract teeth'

A similar morphotonemic alternation, similar in that the sequence mid-low does not occur, is found in verbs with mid tone when followed by a suffix, the tone of which is low. The tones of the verb root (mid) plus suffix (low) are mid-high-low; adding the suffix to a verb with the tones mid-fall yields the same tones. Thus:

| kula | 'go out' : | a kulâi | 'he is going out' |
| tisô | 'sneeze' : | a tisôi | 'he is sneezing' |

But verbs with other root tones add the suffix with no alternation in tone. The second of the following examples includes an additional morphophonemic alternation. For any verb with a final /ŋ/ in the root, the final /ŋ/ has the alternant /n/ before the suffix /-ì/, and the suffix appears with a double vowel. Thus:

píli	'jump'	:	a pílii	'he is jumping'
pêlaŋ	'get down'	:	a pêlanii	'he is getting down'

One further morphotonemic alternation makes it necessary to subdivide verb roots with mid tone into two groups (cf. 5.9). A verb root is initially identified as having mid tone on the basis of such forms as the singular imperative (where nothing precedes the verb) or the completive without an object (where low tone precedes). In the past negative, all verb roots with mid tone appear with that tone unaltered; thus the past negative is also diagnostic for identifying the tone of a verb root as mid. But in other constructions—the imperative, hortative, experiential, and completive—all verb roots with mid tone appear with that tone unaltered only if the preceding tone is low — or if, as in the imperative without an object, nothing precedes. In the same constructions, however, if the tone preceding the verb is mid or high, only some verbs with mid root tone—about a third of the total—retain that mid tone unaltered. The remaining verbs with mid tone— only in the four constructions listed, and only after mid or high—have high tone as an alternant of mid. The following examples use two mid-tone verbs, /kula/ 'exit, remove', and /kpɛtɛ/ 'get rich, fix'; the first of these shows the alternation in question, but the second does not:

é kúla	'he should go out'
kú 'kpáwɔi kpɛtɛ	'let's fix the bridge'

These morphotonemic statements have now reduced the seemingly formidable variety of forms which may follow a subject pronoun and construction marker to only four types. One of these is the verb root by itself, with its root tone and no suffix (in the imperative, hortative, experiential, completive, and past negative). The second is the verb root with low tone replacing root tone (in the past, customary, conditional, desiderative, hortative negative, customary negative and desiderative negative). The third is the verb root with a suffix /-ì/ (in the present and present negative). The fourth is the verb root with a suffix /-nì/ (in the stative and stative negative). Additional morphemes found only in negative constructions will be discussed in the following section. In both affirmative and negative constructions, however, low tone replacing root tone, the suffix /-ì/, and the suffix /-nì/ may be grouped together as one set of verbal affixes. Just as the subject pronoun root by itself may be considered to have a zero construction marker following it, so the verb root by itself may be considered to have a zero affix. This makes it possible to state the formation of affirmative verbal constructions in the formula suggested in 12.1: P-C-V-A, in which either C or A, but not both, may be zero.

13.6. All of the primary negative constructions in Kpelle, included in the list at the beginning of the preceding section, share a morpheme /fé/. By analogy with uses of /káa/ discussed in 11.5, /fé/ must be analyzed as a verb in the underlying structure, and all of the negative verbal constructions are basically auxiliary constructions. Apart from uses with verbs, compare the following:

'káa nãa	'he is there'	'fé nãa	'he isn't there'
'káa ńyéeì	'I have it'	'fé ńyéeì	'I don't have it'
ńóŋ káa m̀à	'I have a child'	ńóŋ fé m̀à	'I have no child'

What precedes /fé/ in the above and also in negative verbal constructions is formally an object. But just as the verbal function of /káa/ has been shown to be fossilized (in that the plural pronoun of an imperative is not used when addressing more than one person), so the verbal function of /fé/ is also fossilized. This is the more true in that /fé/ combines with some of the verbal construction markers found also in affirmative constructions. Further, there is a detail of irregularity in object pronouns preceding /fé/ which is not paralleled elsewhere in the language. The first person singular object pronoun has a zero allomorph, so that the form /fé/ by itself implies a first person singular object; the expected form is */m̀fé/ ([m̀vé]). In northeastern dialects, the first person singular object pronoun is as expected, but the second person singular has a zero allomorph—a rather unusual opportunity for interdialectal misunderstanding.

Although all of the primary negative constructions use /fé/, they do not perfectly parallel the affirmative constructions in either variety or form. First, as far as variety is concerned, there is no negative imperative; a negative command is expressed by a negative hortative in the second person. Negatives corresponding to the experiential and completive are expansions of the past negative by the addition of adverbs which appear elsewhere only in questions. E.g.,

'fé tá kula ní	'he hasn't ever gone out'
'fé nîi kula ní	'he hasn't gone out yet'

A semantically negative conditional is an expansion of an affirmative construction by the insertion of a morpheme /wàla ~ là/. It uses the construction marker /-à/ which appears also in the affirmative conditional. The verb root may have low tone replacing root tone, as in the affirmative conditional, or alternatively it may have its root tone; in the latter case, the combination in question has the form of an expanded experiential, but it seems preferable to call it an expanded conditional with the statement that the tonal replacive is optional after /wàla ~ là/. Thus a semantically though not formally negative conditional is:

à wàla kula ~ à wàla kùla
   ~ à là kula ~ à là kùla   'if he doesn't go out'

In form, the construction marker (combined with /fé/) and verbal affix of affirmative constructions are found in parallel negative constructions only in the customary and desiderative. In the present and stative negatives, the construction marker /-a/ of the affirmative does not appear; this may be considered a case of a zero construction marker, or alternatively a deletion of /-a/ in the presence of the unambiguous verbal suffix. In the hortative, the verb root has the low tone replacive in the negative, in contrast with root tone in the affirmative. Conversely, in the past the verb root has its root tone in the negative, in contrast with the low tone replacive in the affirmative, but an additional morpheme /ní/ occurs after the verb; this may be considered a suffix, though written as a separate word.

In the primary negative constructions, then, an object with /fé/ replaces the subject of affirmatives; an object pronoun is not used after a noun object. Beyond this, however, negatives cannot be derived from affirmatives by a simple transformational rule. Rather, negatives independently show the same formulaic structure as affirmatives; the remainder of each is a construction marker and a verb root with affix.

The occurring permutations of construction markers and verbal affixes are summarized in the accompanying chart. Horizontal rows indicate the occurrences of each construction marker; vertical columns indicate the occurrences of each verbal affix. After putting together a construction from this chart, of course, the lexical tone of the verb selected must be introduced, an object and/or an adverb may be added before the verb, and then the morphotonemic and other morphophonemic rules summarized in the foregoing discussion must be applied in order to arrive at the surface structure.

	Zero	Low replacive	/-ì/, /-nì/	/-ní/
Zero		Past	Pres. Neg.	Past Neg.
		Hort. Neg.	Stat. Neg.	
High	Hortative			
Mid	Imperative			
/-a/		Customary	Present	
		Cust. Neg.	Stative	
/-à/	Experiential	Conditional		
/-aâ/	Completive			
/-ì/		Desiderative		
		Desid. Neg.		

13.7. Uses of the Kpelle hortative as a consecutive were discussed and illustrated in 12.10. An auxiliary construction expressing simultaneous action was also discussed in that section; it uses the imperative form of the verb /kɛ́/, transitively 'do, make', with an object, followed by the verb root with low tone replacing root tone. A sequence of conditionals was noted in 12.9, expressing a low degree of expectability reflected in translation by 'if'; the first conditional in the sequence is /à kɛ̀/. These uses and constructions are noted again here for the sake of completeness.

All other verbal constructions are of the auxiliary type, in which the main verb has the suffix /-ì/ of the present or /-nì/ of the stative. The interpretation of /-ì/ as forming a kind of locative verbal noun was discussed in 11.5; /-nì/ may be considered to have a similar function. As noted there, the imperative form of the verb /káa/ 'see' with an object is used as an auxiliary to form an optional alternative to the present and stative. To express continuing action or state with reference to other than present time, /kɛ́/ (with a subject) is used in a variety of primary constructions as an auxiliary. In the simultaneous construction, the auxiliary is /ɓó/. In 12.5, it was noted that the verb /pá/ is used in the present, before the main verb with the suffix /-ì/, to form a future. These auxiliary constructions are illustrated in the following:

'káa kulâi	'he is going out'
'káa seêni	'he is seated'
è kɛ̀ kulâi	'he was going out'
è kɛ̀ seêni	'he was seated'
à kɛ̀ kulâi	'if he is going out'
à kɛ̀ seêni	'if he is seated'
. . . 'kɛ́ ɓò kulâi	'. . . and he was going out (at the same time)'
a pâi kulâi (∼ 'káa pâi kulâi)	'he's going to go out'

In addition to these, a verb root with the suffix /-ì/ is used after a few other auxiliaries. One of these is the verb /pɔri/ 'be equal, be able'; e.g.,

ŋa pɔ̂ri 'kêi	'I can do it'
fé pɔri ní 'kêi	'I wasn't able to do it'
à pɔ̀ri 'kêi	'if he can do it'

The only other such construction I can recall uses the verb /lɛɛ/ 'stay, remain' (transitively 'leave') as an auxiliary to express action still going on. In several primary constructions, this seems to be a reasonably straightforward combination. One of its uses, however, is rather unusual; /lɛɛ/ is used as an auxiliary before a future to express action which is or was still going to take place, and which therefore has or had not yet taken place. Using /lɛɛ/ in the consecutive (after a past, for example) indicates that something happened and that something else was still going to happen, and therefore had not yet happened; this is the standard way of saying that one thing happened before something else happened. Examples of these uses are:

è lὲε tíi kêi	'he was still working'
à lὲε tíi kêi	'if he is still working'
à pâi lεêi tíi kêi	'he will still be working'
è lὲε pâi kulâi	'he hadn't gone out yet'
	('he was still going to go out')
è ŋɔ̀ tíi kélee kὲ	'he did all his work before he went out'
é lέε pâi kulâi	('. . . and he was still going to go out')
a pâi ŋɔ̀ tíi kélee kêi	'he'll do all his work before his father
ǹâŋ é lέε pâi serîi	gets there' ('. . . and his father will
nãa	still be going to arrive there')
à ŋɔ̀ tíi kélee kὲ	'if he does all his work before you get there'
í lέε pâi serîi nãa	

13.8. The affirmative verbal constructions of Igbo have been adequately treated in various contexts in preceding chapters. A brief summary of them, using only monosyllabic bases with high tone in order to avoid problems in morphophonemics which have been treated, will serve as an introduction to the subject of negation. First, the following examples of primary constructions will serve to illustrate their ingredients, which include prefixes, tonal replacives, and suffixes; for some constructions, forms with singular subject pronouns and forms with noun subjects must be distinguished:

Infinitive:	í'rí	'to eat' (object obligatory)
Imperative:	rìé ńrí à	'eat this food'
Stative:	ọ́ bụ̀ ńrí	'it is food'
Factative:	ó rìrì ńrí	'he ate'
Conditional:	ó ríé ń'rí	'when/if he eats'
Consecutive:	ọ́ làrà ụ́lọ̀ ríé ń'rí	'he returned home and ate'
	ọ́ làrà ụ́lọ̀ m̀ ríé ń'rí	'he returned home and I ate'
	ọ́ làrà ụ́lọ̀, Òkóyè èríé ń'rí	'he returned home and Okoye ate'
Completive:	ó 'ríélá ń'rí	'he has eaten'
	Òkóyè èríélá ń'rí	'Okoye has eaten'

For verbs used in the stative, a construction referring to past time may be considered a type of factative; it differs from the factative cited above in that the vowel of the root is repeated. E.g.,

| ó bììrì Àbá | 'he lived (used to live) in Aba' |

The hortative is formally an expansion of the conditional; it consists of a morpheme /kà/ plus the conditional. E.g.,

| kà ó ríé ń'rí | 'he should eat' |

The incompletive and future are auxiliary constructions using the stative of the verbs /í'ná/ (otherwise unattested) and /í'gá/ 'go' respectively, followed by a verbal noun. E.g.,

> ọ́ nà èrí ń'rí   'he is eating'
>
> ọ́ gà èrí ń'rí   'he's going to eat'

Negatives in Igbo are remarkably restricted in form, though entirely adequate in usage. There is no negative infinitive or consecutive. Corresponding to all of the other affirmative constructions, two negative constructions and two auxiliary constructions do all of the work. First, there is a unique negative imperative, formed by a vowel prefix with high tone followed by downstep, and a suffix /-la/ with the same tone as the final tone of the verb base. E.g.,

> é'rílá ńrí à   'don't eat this food'

Second, there is a "general" negative corresponding to either the stative or the factative. The incompletive and future affirmatives use an auxiliary in the stative; the corresponding negatives simply use this general negative with the auxiliary. The general negative uses singular subject pronouns with low tone, or a vowel prefix with high tone followed by downstep after a noun subject. There is also a suffix, segmentally /-ghị/, whose tone is conditioned by preceding tones. E.g.,

> ọ̀ bụ́'ghị ìtè   'it isn't a pot'
>
> ò rí'ghị ńrí   'he didn't eat'
>
> Okóyè é'ríghị ńrí   'Okoye didn't eat'
>
> ọ̀ ná'ghí èrí ń'rí   'he isn't eating'
>
> ọ̀ gá'ghị èrí ń'rí   'he isn't going to eat'

The completive is negated by a perfectly regular general negative, but with something added to the verb base. Any verb base is compounded with the root of /íbè/, which seems to be the verb meaning 'cut', although the semantic relationship is not entirely clear; it is possible that the syllable /bè/ should be analyzed as a base formative, especially since it may occur after other base formatives. In any case, speakers of Igbo (unless they have been brainwashed by the linguistic imperialism of the school system) unquestioningly recognize the syllable /bè/ as part of the verb base, not part of a negative suffix. Thus:

> ò ríbèghì ńrí   'he hasn't eaten'

A semantically negative conditional is expressed by the affirmative conditional construction /ọ́ bụ́rụ́/ 'if it is', followed by the conjunctive /nà/ 'that' and a general negative construction. E.g.,

ọ́ búrụ́ nà ò rí'ghị́ ńrí   'if he didn't eat'
ọ́ búrụ́ nà ọ̀ ná'ghị̀ èrí ń'rí   'if he isn't eating'
ọ́ búrụ́ nà ò ríbèghì̀ ńrí   'if he hasn't eaten'

Finally, a semantically negative hortative is expressed by a formally affirmative hortative of a verb /íghàrà/, which is also used in other constructions and has a meaning something like 'refrain from, avoid', followed by an infinitive or occasionally by a consecutive. E.g.,

kà ọ́ ghàrá í'rí ńrí   'he shouldn't eat' ('he should re-
(∼ kà ọ́ ghàrá ríé ń'rí)   frain from eating')

13.9. In both Kpelle and Igbo, as noted in the foregoing sections, there is something unusual about the negation of imperatives and hortatives. The same is true in many other languages, and strikingly so in Efik. Another unusual feature of the Efik verbal system has been hinted at before, particularly in 12.12 in connection with the variety of sequential forms. For a part of the verbal system, there is a bi-dimensional grid of constructions, in which distinctions between "neutral" and "contrastive" intersect other distinctions. These features justify a summary of the Efik verbal syst m, to bring together all of what has been referred to in other contexts and to add a few details.

First, the constructions for which there is no neutral-contrastive distinction may be listed. The root /dép/ 'buy' will be used in illustrations of independent constructions, and /sók/ 'deliver to' for sequentials. Both require an object.

The infinitive is formed with a prefix /ńdí-/; the sequential infinitive is formed with a prefix /ǹ-/. There is no negative infinitive. E.g.,

ńyòm ńdídép m̀bòró ǹsók fî   'I want to buy bananas for you'

The imperative is the verb root with no pronoun in the singular, but with the regular subject pronoun /è-/ in the plural. Imperatives may be used in sequence. There is no negative imperative; negative commands are expressed by the negative hortative. E.g.,

dép m̀bòró sók mî   'buy bananas for me'
èdép m̀bòró èsók mî   'buy (pl.) bananas for me'

The affirmative hortative is marked by high-low tone replacing the lexical tone of the verb base. Affirmative hortatives may be used in sequence. The negative hortative is marked by low tone replacing the stem tone of subject pronouns, and a construction marker /-kù-/; the verb base has its lexical tone. This is unlike any other negative formation in Efik. A sequential for the negative hortative has the same pronoun and verb base forms, but omits the construction marker. Without a subject pronoun, the negative hortative functions as a negative imperative singular; the second person plural form functions as a negative imperative plural. In sequence, the second person singular subject pronoun is /ù-/ rather than the usual harmonizing vowel with low tone. E.g.,

ɛ́dêp m̀bòró ɔ́sɔ̀k mî	'he should buy bananas for me'
òkûdép m̀bòró ɔ̀sɔ́k mî	'he shouldn't buy bananas for me'
kûdép m̀bòró ùsɔ́k mî	'don't buy bananas for me'

The conditional is marked by low tone replacing stem tone with subject pronouns; the verb base has its lexical tone. This is the same as the sequential for a negative hortative. I have no evidence for a sequential with a conditional, but I would be astonished if it is not identical; sequentials typically have the same pronoun and verb base forms as the preceding verb, but omit a construction marker if there is one. In the example below, the first verb is known to be correct, and I will stick my neck out as far as the second is concerned. Since the low tone replacive with pronouns results in identity between second and third person forms, an independent pronoun may be used to specify the person. A negative condition is expressed by a relative construction which does not belong here in the outline of the verbal system. An affirmative condition is:

| ɛ̀ÿé ɛ̀dép m̀bòró ɔ̀sɔ́k mî | 'if he buys bananas for me' |

The completive occupies the position among the remaining constructions which one would expect to be occupied by a neutral present. This is true in respect to form, and also in the light of other considerations. Like other neutral constructions, past and future, the completive is characterized by downstep preceding the verb base (only after a high tone and if the verb base tone is also high, of course). If contrast must be expressed—as is frequently true in answer to a question in the completive—the constructions which otherwise refer to present time are used. Further, there is no neutral-contrastive distinction in the negative, and one negative serves for both completive and present reference; if it is necessary to specify a completive reference, an adverb /káŋá/ '(not) yet', used only with negatives, is added, usually at the end of the sentence. For present reference, the construction which formally is contrastive for something following the verb is also used in a neutral sense—i.e., when it is not necessary to express contrast. There may at one time have been a distinction between a completive and a neutral present, since the completive is somewhat irregular, at least in the dialect under consideration here, and appears to reflect a mixed paradigm. In the first and second persons, singular and plural, there is a construction marker consisting of /m/ plus a harmonizing vowel (for details see 2.2) with high tone. Downstep follows this construction marker, preceding the verb base, if the subject pronoun is first person singular (which has high tone) or second person plural (which has low). There is no downstep if the subject pronoun is second person singular or first person plural (both of which have low tone). In the third persons, singular and plural, there is no construction marker; the forms consist of a subject pronoun (which has high tone) followed by downstep and the verb base. The verb base has its base tone, which of course involves the deletion of the preceding downstep if that tone is low or low-high. E.g.,

ḿmé'dép m̀bòró	'I have bought bananas'
èmẹ́'dép m̀bòró	'you (pl.) have bought bananas'
èmédép m̀bòró	'you (sg.) have bought bananas'
é'dép m̀bòró	'he has bought bananas'

The completive can now be considered, at least formally, among the constructions which show a neutral-contrastive distinction, and will be treated as if it were simply a neutral present. These constructions, along with negatives, are illustrated in the chart that appears below, with three different subject pronouns. The constructions are divided into three groups depending on the form of the sequential appropriate to each; a number assigned to each group refers to the type of sequential described in 12.12. The term "Contr.-pre" refers to constructions which indicate that something preceding the verb, or in a few cases a question word following it, is contrasted. The term "Contr.-post" refers to constructions which indicate that something following the verb, other than a question word, is contrasted.

		Past	Present	Future
Neutral :	I:	ḿ'má ń'dép	ḿmé'dép	ńyé'dép
	he:	á'má é'dép	é'dép	éyé'dép
	we:	ìmà í'dép	ìmédép	ìyé'dép
			5	
Contr.-post :	I:	ńkédèp	ńdèp	
	he:	ékédèp	édèp	
	we:	ìkédèp	ìdèp	ńdîdêp
				édîdêp
Contr.-pre :	I:	àmì ńké'dép	àmì ńdép	ìdîdêp
	he:	è̃yé éké'dép	èỹé édép	
	we:	ǹỹìn ìké'dép	ǹỹìn ìdép	
			3	4
Negative :	I:	ńké'dépké	ńdépké	ńdîdêpkè
	you:	úkú'dépké	údépké	údûdêpkè
	others:	íké'dépké	ídépké	ídîdêpkè

As noted in 12.12, the neutral past is a serial construction; the second word is a sequential. With the exceptions noted above, the neutral constructions and the sequential appropriate to them are characterized by downstep preceding the verb base. The contr.-post constructions for past and present are characterized by low tone replacing the base tone of the verb; these, however, use the same sequential as the neutral constructions—the only instance in which the tone of the base in the sequential differs from that in the first verb. In the contr.-pre constructions for present and present negative, the verb base has its base tone, without a preceding downstep. This statement can be extended to include the past and its negative by analyzing the downstep in the latter as being part of the past contrastive marker /-kV'-/ (with harmonizing vowel). The sequential for this group of constructions also has base tone without downstep. The future contrastive and negative have high-low tone replacing base tone with the verb; the sequential also does, but has low tone replacing the stem tone of subject pronouns. There is a special set of subject pronouns for negatives; otherwise the negatives are identical with the contr.-pre and future contrastive constructions up to the negative suffix.

As also noted in 12.12, there is a consecutive construction identical with the fifth type of sequential, the use of which is not confined to the same group of constructions.

There are two other sets of constructions, derived from the above by the addition of a morpheme. A present and past hypothetical, using /-kpV́'-/ after the subject pronoun, was described in 12.8. There are also customary constructions corresponding to most if not all of the above. These are formed by adding /-sí-/ immediately before the verb base. E.g.,

ìsídèp m̀bòró	'we buy bananas'
ìké'sídèp m̀bòró	'we used to buy bananas'
ìmésídép m̀bòró	'we've been buying bananas'

All in all, during the four and a half months we spent in Efik-speaking territory, there was a brisk trade in bananas.

13.10. Jukun also has a unique negative formation for the hortative; in addition, other negatives show an unusual formation. Five primary affirmative constructions are recorded; some of the labels used here have not previously been used for Jukun. The formation of these constructions is fairly simple, and should be obvious from the following examples (from Dìyì):

Factative	:	ku bi	'he came'
Incompletive:		ku ri bi	'he is coming'
Potential	:	kwá bi ∼ ku bá bi	'he will come'
Conditional	:	ku ma bi	'when/if he comes'
Hortative	:	kú bi	'he should come'

That the first of the above is a factative rather than a past is evident from the fact that it expresses present time, if not modified, for verbs referring to situation rather than action. The incompletive may refer to past as well as present time, and at least for the verbs 'come' and 'go' may include a near future. The two forms of the potential may differ in meaning, but no difference is known. There is a minor peculiarity about the conditional; the first and second person singular subject pronouns, ordinarily /m̀/ and /ù/, combine with the construction marker to form /ma/ and /wa/ respectively, which differ only in tone from the same pronouns with the /-á/ of the potential. The second person singular forms of the hortative are used as imperatives; the subject pronoun may be omitted in the singular.

At least the first four of these constructions may be modified by the addition of a morpheme /ra/ after the verb and its object (if any). This is by all odds most common with the factative, and the combination expresses completed action. The force of /ra/ after the other constructions has not been accurately defined; with the incompletive, it may convey the idea of 'already'. The fact that /ra/ may be separated from the verb by an object suggests that it is not grammatically as closely associated with the verb as it would be if it were a suffix. Its use might be compared with serialization. However, no independent word in the language has initial /r/. There are also other difficulties with this interpretation which will be pointed out in connection with a negative construction. Whatever the origin or status of /ra/ may be, its use is illustrated in the following:

ku bi ra	'he has come'
ku tu tukpa ra	'he has washed the clothes'
tukpa kyè ra	'the clothes are clean'
ku ri bi ra	'he is (already?) coming'
ku ma bi ra	'when he comes (gets here?)'

A very few sentences are also recorded with a morpheme /rè/ or /rù/ (apparently allomorphs of one morpheme conditioned by the preceding vowel) immediately after the verb. It is possible that this indicates an action performed only once; however, I was unable to construct additional acceptable utterances with any consistency. Recorded examples include the following:

| ku zè rè zo' | 'he looked up' (lit. 'he picked up eyes') |
| ku wu rù | 'he died' |

The negative hortative, like the affirmative, has high tone replacing stem tone with subject pronouns. In addition, there is a construction marker /ká/ before the verb, and at the very end of the clause a form which is usually /àná/ but occasionally /mbá/. E.g.,

kú ká bi àná	'he shouldn't come'
(∼ kú ká bi mbá)	
kú ká tu tukpa àná	'he shouldn't wash the clothes'

Other negatives usually have /mbá/, but sometimes /àná/, at the end of the clause. In addition to this, there is nothing preceding the verb relevant to negation, but immediately after the verb there is a second pronoun form recapitulating the subject. This pronoun form has high tone replacing stem tone, and the third person form is /á/ rather than */kú/; these are thus not to be identified with the subject pronouns of the hortative. Examples of such negatives are:

ṁ bi ṁ mbá	'I didn't come'
ù bi ú mbá	'you didn't come'
ku bi á mbá	'he didn't come'
be bi bé mbá	'they didn't come'
be bi bé kéré mbá	'they didn't come here'
ku tu á tukpa mbá	'he didn't wash the clothes'

ku ri tu á tukpa mbá	'he isn't washing the clothes'
tukpa kyè á ra mbá	'the clothes aren't clean'
bá dyi-fò bé pùká Fíkyú	'they will not defeat the people of
ba kànà mbá	Fikyu in war'

Although such recapitulating pronouns are obligatory in negative constructions other than the hortative, their use is not confined to negatives. They are
sometimes optionally used in affirmative sentences, apparently sentences of only
a few types. One of these is sentences with /ra/ as described above. Another is
sentences with /kí/, which has a locative force. There is no apparent modification
in meaning associated with the use of recapitulating pronoun in such sentences.
E.g.,

m̀ ya m̄ ra	'Goodbye' (lit. 'I'm gone')
be byē bé ra	'they are ripe'
ku kà-sõ bi á bà bá	'he came back (returned came)
kí tanà	to his affairs at home'

The comparison of /ra/ with a verb in a serial construction was mentioned
above. It would be delightful to be able to analyze /kí/ as a verb meaning 'be
located at'. It would then be advisable, however, to analyze the negative morphemes /mbá/ and /àná/ as verbs also. But /kí/ and /mbá/ would then be the only
exceptions to the statement that a verb may have only mid or low tone, and
/àná/ would be the only verb with an initial vowel. Further, regular subject pronouns are sometimes used before a verb after the first in a series, but they are not
used before the forms in question here. The recapitulating pronouns, which may
be separated from these morphemes by other phrases, do not stand in anything
like a subject relationship to them. The analysis must rest as above: recapitulating pronouns are obligatory in negative constructions other than the hortative,
and optional in some affirmative constructions.

13.11. In at least some languages of the Kru group, negation in at least some
constructions involves a change in word order from the affirmative. A few hundred slips, with words, phrases, and short sentences transcribed in pencil, are the
only souvenir of a few days of work on Kwaa (popularly known as Bellleh) in
1947, with an informant whose English and Kpelle were barely minimal. This is
apparently the only work done on Kwaa until a few months prior to writing these
words; data from the current work is not yet available, but it is known that the
negative formation in question has been verified. The morphemic composition
of the relevant sentences is not entirely clear. Differences in tone may represent
the presence or absence of a negative morpheme. If, however, the tonal differences between the affirmatives and the negatives should turn out to be only morphotonemic alternations and not morphemic, then the only morphemic distinction between the two would be word order. The affirmatives have the order subject-verb-object; the negatives have the order subject-object-verb. My transcriptions (and I am not sure whether I intended the absence of a tone mark to
represent the preceding low continued or a lower mid) are as follows:

mà sà wɔ́	'I saw him':
mà wɔ́ sà	'I didn't see him'
mà tíbá wɔ̀	'I hit him':
mà wɔ́ tíbá	'I didn't hit him'
mà tɛ̀ màna	'I bought bananas'
mà maná tɛ̀	'I didn't buy bananas'

(Actually, I much prefer pineapples, but the word is usually an awkward compound.)

In Krahn (Gbaison dialect), there is also a reversal of word order in the negative, but in addition there is a negative morpheme /sé/.[3] (I am strongly suspicious of the phonemic status of [w] in what is here transcribed [gbw]; I would not be at all surprised if I could not even detect a bilabial glide.) E.g.,

ɛ́ gbwe i	'it is black' ('it black is'):
ɛ́ sé í gbwe	'it is not black' ('it not is black')
ī ble kwɔ	'I have rice' ('I have rice'):
ī sé kwɔ bli	'I don't have rice' ('I not rice have')

It is interesting how much can sometimes be extracted from data as highly restricted as the above. A comparison of the two pairs of sentences reveals that the forms translated 'is' and the forms translated 'have' are grammatically quite different. In the affirmative sentences, 'is' follows the remainder of the predicate, but 'have' precedes. Further, 'is' does not begin with a consonant; my memory of a few days of work on Bassa, which is quite closely related, in 1948, is that words in major form classes are all consonant-initial. Almost beyond a doubt, 'be (described as)' in Krahn is not a verb; 'have' probably is.

13.12. Throughout the Bantu languages there are ample additional examples of many of the phenomena that have been noted in the foregoing sections, including the imperfect match of negative and affirmative constructions, a unique negative formation for the hortative, and auxiliary constructions. A summary of the Swahili verbal system will illustrate such phenomena.

Not particularly relevant to the primary purpose of this discussion, but important in the total verbal morphology, is the status of the relatively few verbs whose roots consist of a single consonant, and also the roots /-end-/ 'go' and /-ish-/ 'finish'. The infinitive forms of some of these verbs are:

ku-j-a	'come'	ku-f-a	'die'
ku-p-a	'give'	kw-end-a	'go'
ku-l-a	'eat'	kw-ish-a	'finish'

In some but not all verbal constructions, the infinitive forms of these verbs are used where only the root would be expected. A full listing of the two sets of constructions is not given here, but examples are:

---

[3] Krahn data from John Duitsman, personal communication.

	But:	
	a-li-kuj-a	'he came'
	a-na-kuj-a	'he is coming'
	a-j-a	'he comes'
	a-j-e	'he should come'

For the most part, the morphemic composition of the primary affirmative constructions is apparent from the examples below. A few details, however, require explanation. In the customary, there is a construction marker /-a-/, which combines with the Class 1 subject concord to yield /a-/; compare the combination of the first person plural /tu-/ with this construction marker: /tw-a-/. The construction marker /-japo-/ is morphemically complex. The verb used in these examples is one of a very few for which an irregular singular imperative is usually used; the regular form is given in parentheses. With an object concord, the imperative suffix is regularly /-e/; the plural also uses the suffix /-e/, followed by the plural marker /-ni/. Apart from the stative, which requires separate treatment, the primary affirmative constructions are as follows:

Present	:	a-na-let-a kisu	'he's bringing a knife'
Customary	:	a-let-a visu	'he brings knives'
Past	:	a-li-let-a kisu	'he brought a knife'
Future	:	a-ta-let-a kisu	'he will bring a knife'
Completive	:	a-me-let-a kisu	'he has brought a knife'
Consecutive	:	a-ka-let-a kisu	'and he brought a knife'
Conditional	:	a-ki-let-a kisu	'if he brings a knife'
Concessive	:	a-nga-let-a kisu	'though he brings a knife'
Suppositional	:	a-japo-let-a kisu	'though he were to bring a knife'
Hypothetical	:	a-nge-let-a kisu	'if he should bring a knife'
Hortative	:	a-let-e kisu	'he should bring a knife'
Imperative	:	(let-a kisu), let-e kisu	'bring a knife'

The stative, discussed in 12.7, is not inflected for person; it has a prefix /hu-/ and the common suffix /-a/. There are also two complex constructions. One is a consecutive hortative, with the consecutive construction marker /-ka-/ and the hortative suffix /-e/. The other is a past hypothetical, with a construction marker /-ngali-/ which appears to be composed of the concessive /-nga-/ (or possibly the hypothetical /-nge-/) and the past /-li-/; the hypothetical construction listed above is often used with past as well as non-past reference, and the specifically past hypothetical is not commonly used at all. These two constructions are:

	a-ka-let-e kisu	'and he should bring a knife'
	a-ngali-let-a kisu	'if he had brought a knife'

A negative formation common to many of the above constructions uses a morpheme /ha-/ at the beginning of the verb form, preceding even the subject pronoun. This combines with the Class 1 subject concord /a-/ to form /ha-/, and with the second person singular pronoun /u-/ to form /hu-/. A suppletive form /si-/ is used in place of the combination of /ha-/ with the first person singular pronoun /ni-/. Apart from this which several negatives have in common, however, special statements must be made for each negative construction.

The present, customary, and stative are not distinguished in the negative. The negative for all of them has no construction marker, but uses the suffix /-i/. E.g.,

General   :   ha-let-i kisu   'he's not bringing a knife'

The past and completive use construction markers in the negative which are quite different from the affirmative construction markers: /-ku-/ in place of /-li-/, and /-ja-/ in place of /-me-/. The future negative, however, uses the same construction marker as the future affirmative. These constructions are:

Past   :   ha-ku-let-a kisu   'he didn't bring a knife'
Future   :   ha-ta-let-a kisu   'he isn't going to bring a knife'
Completive :   ha-ja-let-a kisu   'he hasn't brought a knife'

The hortative uses a different negative marker; it is /-si-/, used in the construction marker position after a subject pronoun. The suffix is /-e/ as in the affirmative. The negative hortative functions also as a negative for the imperative (with no subject pronoun in the singular), and for the consecutive; a merger of these constructions has been noted in other languages as well. E.g.,

Hortative   :   a-si-let-e kisu   'he shouldn't bring a knife'
                si-let-e kisu   'don't bring a knife'

The conditional is usually negated by using a conjunction /kama/ 'if' with the general negative. There is another negative form, however, which uses a morphemically complex construction marker /-sipo-/, the first part of which is the same as the negative morpheme in the hortative. This construction has a specialized meaning. E.g.,

Conditional :   kama ha-let-i kisu   'if he doesn't bring a knife'
                a-sipo-let-a kisu   'unless he brings a knife'

The hypothetical is negated in either of the two ways described so far, by /ha-/ before the subject pronoun or (the preferred usage) by the construction marker /-si-/ after the subject pronoun; in both types, the construction marker of the affirmative is also used. This formation applies also to the complex past hypothetical. E.g.,

Hypothetical: ha-nge-let-a kisu,   'if he were not to bring a knife'
              ∼ a-si-nge-let-a kisu

The concessive and suppositional are negated by auxiliary constructions. The auxiliary verb is /kuwa/ 'be'; it appears in the appropriate affirmative construction, commonly with a Class 9 (nonpersonal) subject. The immediate counterpart of the constructions listed above uses the general negative of the main verb, but other negatives (to say nothing of other affirmatives) may also be used. E.g.,

i-nga-wa ha-let-i kisu   'though he is not bringing a knife'
i-japo-kuwa ha-let-i kisu   'though he may not bring a knife'

The above are only two examples of a variety of auxiliary constructions in Swahili. The verb /kuwa/ 'be' is not used with reference to the present, but in any construction not referring to the present. It appears in a variety of constructions as an auxiliary, with the main verb also in a number of different constructions. Some examples are:

a-li-kuw-a a-me-let-a kisu   'he had already brought a knife'
a-li-kuw-a a-na-let-a kisu   'he was bringing a knife'
a-ta-kuw-a a-me-let-a kisu   'he will have brought a knife'
a-ki-wa a-na-let-a kisu   'if he is bringing a knife'
a-ka-wa a-na-let-a kisu   'and then he brought a knife'
i-nga-wa a-me-let-a kisu   'though he has brought a knife'

There are also other auxiliaries, most of them regular verbs, including such expected verbs as /kuweza/ 'be able' (followed by an infinitive) and /kutaka/ 'want' (followed by an infinitive for the same actor, or by a hortative for a different actor). In addition, /kuja/ 'come' is used as an auxiliary before the future, hortative, or infinitive to convey the idea of 'then' or 'later' in the future. Similarly, /kwenda/ 'go' is used before either the infinitive or the base without prefix but with the suffix /-a/ (the infinitive with its prefix dropped, if one prefers), to convey the idea of 'just now' in the completive, or 'then' in the past. And /kwisha/ 'finish' is used, also before the infinitive with or without prefix, to convey the idea of 'already'. The verb /kupata/ 'get' is similarly used, to indicate ability or opportunity. A defective verb /-ngali/ 'still be', preceded only by a subject pronoun, conveys the idea of action still going on; with reference to the past or future it is followed by an infinitive, but reference to the present it is followed by the conditional (referring to simultaneity) or by the completive of a verb with inceptive meaning. All of these auxiliary constructions can further participate in larger auxiliary constructions with /kuwa/, or in some cases with each other—semantic probability seems to determine the possible combinations. Just a few examples of these auxiliaries are:

a-ta-kuj-a a-ta-let-a kisu   'then he will bring a knife'
∼ a-ta-kuj-a ku-let-a kisu
a-me-kwish-a (ku-)let-a kisu   'he has already brought a knife'
a-ta-kuw-a a-me-kwish-a   'he will already have brought a knife'
  (ku-)let-a kisu
ni-na-tak-a a-let-e kisu   'I want him to bring a knife'
a-li-kuw-a a-ngali ku-let-a   'he was still bringing knives'
  visu
a-ngali a-ki-let-a visu   'he is still bringing knives'
You'd think he'd get tired of it eventually.

Chapter 14

Questions, Relatives, Subordination

14.1. English words like 'who', 'what', 'where', 'when', 'why', and 'how' have two distinct grammatical functions. First, they may be question words, as in 'What did he do?' Unless the question word is the subject, such questions require an auxiliary or a modal, and the order of the subject and the auxiliary or modal in a declarative sentence is inverted in the question. In American English, such questions have the same intonation as declarative sentences, not the intonation typical of questions to which the answer 'yes' or 'no' is appropriate. Second, these words may have a relative function, as in 'I don't know what he did'. In this use, the clauses which they introduce are grammatically nominal.

Learners of an African language, having learned an equivalent of 'What did he do?', recognize something in it as a question word, but then often assume that they can use the same word to construct an equivalent of 'I don't know what he did'; they are almost invariably wrong—what they are saying is the impossible 'I don't know what did he do?'. In almost all cases, equivalents of clauses like 'what he did' are nominal and include a relative clause as in English; but they are nominal by virtue of beginning with an explicit noun which is then modified by a relative clause, as 'I don't know the thing (that) he did'. Corresponding to most question words in many languages are ordinary nouns like 'person', 'thing', 'place', 'time', 'reason', and 'manner', which may be modified by relative clauses.

In languages which have a distinctive question intonation for yes-no questions, superimposed on or apart from tone, question-word questions typically have the same intonation as declarative sentences, as in English. This is true, for example, in the Mande languages and in Swahili. Question intonation may be used with question-word questions, but only with the implication that something previously said was not understood or was considered incredible; this also parallels English usage. In my transcriptions of African languages, I do not use a question mark at the end of a question-word question; a question mark is reserved for indicating an interrogative intonation if such exists. It was possibly the redundant use of question marks with question-word questions in Swahili that led the first two or three informants with whom I worked on the language to teach me to use question intonation where it was actually inappropriate.

From the viewpoint of analysis, and even more for purposes of language pedagogy, it is convenient to treat question-word questions and the corresponding nominals together. A pattern of topicalization (treated for some languages in Chapter 11; note particularly 11.5) often appears in the questions, and a pattern of relativization in the nominals. Topicalization is semantically natural to question words; when we say 'It is rice he bought.', we are contrasting 'rice' with all other possibilities, and in the same way, when we ask 'What did he buy?', we are asking 'what?' in contrast with all other possibilities. For relativization too, of course, applications of the pattern or patterns elsewhere in the language must also be noted. In treating such questions and nominals together, occasional exceptions to the predominant patterns, requiring special treatment, will also be conspicuous.

Of all the question words, in English and in the African languages under consideration here, only 'who?' and 'what?' are commonly used as verbal subjects, as in 'Who did it?' and 'What happened?'. Others among the nominals may occasionally occur as subjects, as in 'Why he did it is a mystery.', but these can be expected to follow the analogy of 'What happened is a mystery.'. The other question words, for the most part, function as objects or adverbial complements. The construction of relatives with antecedent subject and with antecedent object or complement must frequently be carefully distinguished.

Apart from the question words cited above, an equivalent of 'how many?' is usually a single question word functioning like a numeral; the corresponding nominal often differs from the other nominals. Similarly, an attributive 'which?' may be a simple question word, but the modified noun may appear alone in the corresponding nominal. On the other hand, equivalents of 'how much?', 'how far?', 'how heavy?', 'how big?' and the like are rarely simple question words, and usually present problems; for the most part, African languages do not have abstract general terms for 'amount', 'distance', 'weight', 'size', and so on, and do not ask questions about them.

Once more, the constructions under consideration will be surveyed in selected languages, with similarities and differences noted. For many of the languages on which I have done some work, insufficient time was available to cover the topic of questions and relatives fully. In almost all of them, however, a few pertinent questions and sentences were elicited, and patterns similar to those described in the following sections began to emerge. It is only relatively recently that the significance of handling these systematically as a set was realized. For three languages in which my present competence is inadequate, equivalents of the same set of English questions and nominals were provided by linguistically sophisticated informants for purposes of this chapter, and the analysis was discussed with them.[1]

14.2. In Kpelle, as noted in 11.5, question words typically appear in a topicalized construction, with recapitulation later in the sentence. In questions of minimal length, two question words and one interrogative phrase may appear without topicalization; these are noted as alternatives in the data below. One question word, /léŋ/ 'how?', is never topicalized; the same is true for the corresponding question word in Akan, /dén/, which is very probably a cognate. The

---

[1] The relevant data for Yoruba were provided by Mr. Isaac George; for LuGanda by Mr. Livingston Walusimbi; for Swahili by Mr. Fred Longan in consultation with Miss Enrica Marshall and other speakers of Swahili.

relevant types of questions in Kpelle are as follows; in the first two, the usually required recapitulating subject pronoun does not appear in the past:

'kpɛê ɓé 'kɛ̀.	'Who did it?'
lé ɓé kɛ̀.	'What happened?'
'kpɛê ɓé è 'kàa.	'Who did he see (him)?'
lé ɓé è 'kɛ̀.	'What did he do (it)?'
∼ è lé kɛ̀.	('He what did?')
nênɛ ɓé è ǹyà.	'Which one did he buy (it)?'
mî ɓé è lì nãa.	'Where did he go (there)?'
∼ è lì mî.	('He went where?')
ɣɛlɛ ɓé è lì là.	'When did he go (with it)?'
lé-mèni ɓé è 'kɛ̀ m̌à.	'Why did he do it (on it)?'
∼ è 'kɛ̀ lé-mèni m̌à.	('He did it on what matter?')
è 'kɛ̀ léŋ.	'How did he do it?'
ɓóa ɣɛɛlu ɓé è ǹyà.	'How many knives did he buy (it)?'
lé-ɓòa ɓé è ǹyà.	'Which knife did he buy (it)?'
lé-ɓòa-sìi ɓé è ǹyà.	'What kind of knife did he buy (it)?'
mɔlɔŋ pǎi ɣɛɛlu ɓé è ǹyà.	'How many pints of rice did he buy (it)?'
	(I.e., 'How much rice did he buy?')

For several of the above, the structure is obvious; for some, additional comments will be helpful. In a 'when?' question the recapitulating particle /là/ substitutes for a marked complement introduced by /à/, which is one of two constructions for a temporal complement. In a 'why?' question, the question word /lé/ 'what?' is compounded with the noun /mɛni/, which is often translatable as 'thing', not in the sense of a material object, but rather 'event, topic, affair, matter'. Thus /lé-mèni/ is 'what matter?, what reason?'. With the relational noun /m̌à/ 'surface, edge', /lé-mèni m̌à/ is 'on what matter?' or 'for what reason?'. Any noun may be compounded with /mɛni/ and followed by /m̌à/ to express 'because of . . ., for the sake of . . ., about . . .'. In questions asking 'which?' and 'what kind of?', /lé/ 'what' is compounded with any appropriate noun; in 'what kind of?', the last member of the compound is /sii/ 'tribe, type'. 'How much?' is expressed only in terms of a number of appropriate measures. Since there are no measures for distance, weight, or size, there are no real equivalents for 'how far?' and the like; one usually asks 'Is it far?', and any answer is naturally rather imprecise. But then, distance is pretty much a relative matter in a pre-westernized African society; there was a time when eighteen miles didn't seem an unduly long walk for me, but it would seem endless today.

A few types of question-word questions are not included in the above. First, /ɣɛɛlu ɓe/ by itself means 'How many (units of currency) is it?', or 'How much is it?', 'What's the price?'. When asking the price of a specific item, a non-topicalized descriptive expression is used. E.g.,

mɔlɔŋ pǎi tɔ̀nɔ káa à ɣɛɛlu.   'How much is one pint of rice?'

Second, the question word /nênɛ/ 'which one?' may be used in the minimal question /nênɛ ɓe/ 'Which one is it?'. To ask which of several an item is, the appropriate noun phrase is followed by the topicalizing morpheme /ɓé/ combined with a nonverbal predicative morpheme /à/ which is elsewhere used only in short expressions of location, followed by /nênɛ/. E.g.,

ŋɔ̀ pɛ́rɛi ɓà nênɛ.　　　　　'Which is his house?'
(cf.: Sumo à nãa.　　　　　'Sumo is there.')

Third, the question word /lé/ 'what?' may be used for 'why?' if there is nothing in the remainder of the question that could be interpreted as a recapitulating element. E.g.,

lé ɓé 'tí fé tíi kɛ̂i sâa.　　　　'Why aren't they working today?'

And fourth, when asking about the location of a person or thing, rather than a destination or the location of an action, there is a unique interrogative expression. What appears to be the imperative form of a verb /kɔɔ/ is used after a noun (phrase) or pronoun, the latter formally its object, in the meaning 'where is . . .?'. E.g.,

Sumo kɔɔ.　　　　'Where is Sumo?'
í nâŋ kɔɔ.　　　　'Where is your father?'
'kɔɔ.　　　　　　'Where is he/she/it?'

In nominals correspondings to most question words, ordinary nouns are used, modified by a relative clause. The nouns most commonly so used, in their specific forms with their roots given in parentheses, are as follows:

ǹṹui	(nṹu)	'the person' (for 'who?')
m̀ɛnii	(mɛni)	'the thing (nonphysical)' (for 'what?' and 'why?')
'sɛŋ	(sɛŋ)	'the thing (physical)' (for 'what?' and 'which one?')
ŋelei	(ɣele)	'the day, the time', or now more commonly:
tɑ̂iī	(tɑ̃i)	'the time' (for 'when?')
'perei	(pere)	'the way' (for 'how?')

Among the above, the adopted word /tɑ̃i/ 'time' is not preceded by prefixed low tone in the specific form; this is usual for words adopted from English. The same is true, however, for a form corresponding to 'where?'; the specific suffix is used with the adverbial /ɓé/ 'here' to yield /ɓéi/, which functions exactly like the nouns listed above. With a relative clause, this refers to location in general, not specifically to a place nearby; in fact, it is recapitulated by /nãa/ 'there'. In nominals corresponding to /lé/ compounded with a noun, the noun itself is used, in its specific form, followed by a relative clause.

The only exception to this pattern is in the nominal corresponding to 'how many?'. In this case, /ɣɛɛlu ɓé/ is used, after the modified noun, in the nominal as well as in the question. The rationale for this may be that /ɣɛɛlu/ is not inherently a question word at all, but a numeral meaning 'an unspecified number of'.

Then a sentence like 'An unspecified number of knives it is he bought.' is interpreted as expecting a response specifying the number.

A relative clause is a complete sentence nominalized by the addition of the specific suffix /-i ∼ -i/ to the entire sentence. The sentence so nominalized is itself complete by virtue of including a subject pronoun, an object pronoun, or a complement which refers back to (recapitulates) the antecedent noun. If the antecedent noun is the object of the main verb in the sentence, it precedes the verb as usual, and the relative clause follows the verb. In the sentences below, the two nominals with /yɛelu/ 'unspecified number' do not fit this pattern. The verb has the object 'it' in these two, and the nominal follows the verb, in apposition with 'it' and followed by the topicalizing /ɓé/ and then the relative clause. (Irrelevant to the structure under discussion, the verb /kɔ́lɔŋ/ 'know' appears in a construction unique to it and one other verb, not included in the treatment of the Kpelle verbal system in chapter 13, with a stative meaning.) These sentences parallel the questions cited above, with two added to illustrate the difference between /mɛni/ 'thing (nonphysical)' and /sɛŋ/ 'thing (physical)'. One pronoun is changed to avoid ambiguity; 'the person he saw' and 'the person who saw him' would be identical. In the parenthesized glosses, the separate word 'the' represents the final vowel, the specific suffix, in each sentence; the position of 'the' in the gloss indicates the beginning of the clause which is nominalized by that suffix.

fé ǹũui kɔ́lɔŋ è 'kɛ̀ī.   'I don't know who did it.'
('I-not the-person know the he it-did.')

fé m̀ɛnii kɔ́lɔŋ è kɛ̀ī.   'I don't know what happened.'
('I-not the-thing know the it happened.')

fé 'sɛŋ kɔ́lɔŋ è tòoī.   'I don't know what fell.'
('I-not the-thing know the it fell.')

fé ǹũui kɔ́lɔŋ è 'tí kàaī.   'I dont' know who saw them.'
('I-not the-person know the he them saw.')

fé m̀ɛnii kɔ́lɔŋ è 'kɛ̀ī.   'I don't know what he did.'
('I-not the-thing know the he it-did.')

fé 'sɛŋ kɔ́lɔŋ è ǹyaī.   'I don't know what (which one) he bought.'   ('I-not the-thing know the he it-bought.')

fé ɓéi kɔ́lɔŋ è lì nãai.   'I don't know where he went.'
('I-not the-place know the he went there.')

fé tã̀ī kɔ́lɔŋ è lì làī.   'I don't know when he went.'
('I-not the-time know the he went with-it.')

fé m̀ɛnii kɔ́lɔŋ è 'kɛ̀ m̀ã̀ī.   'I don't know why he did it.'
('I-not the-thing know the he it-did on-it.')

fé 'perei kɔ́lɔŋ è 'kɛ̀ làī.   'I don't know how he did it.'
('I-not the-way know the he it-did with-it.')

fé 'kɔ́lɔŋ ɓóa yɛelu ɓé è ǹyàī.   'I don't know how many knives he bought.'   ('I-not it-know knife indefinite-number it-is the he it-bought.')

fé m̀óai kɔ́lɔŋ è ǹyàī.   'I don't know which knife he bought.'
('I-not the-knife know the he it-bought.')
fé m̀óa-sìī kɔ́lɔŋ è ǹyàī.   'I don't know what kind of knife he bought.'
('I-not the-knife-kind know the he it-bought.')
fé 'kɔ́lɔŋ mɔlɔŋ pầi yɛɛlu ɓé è ǹyàī.   'I don't know how many pints
of (= how much) rice he bought.' ('I-not it-know rice pint indefinite-
number it-is the he it-bought.')

Relative clauses, of course, have many uses other than the above. A fairly
obvious example, in which the relative modifies the subject of a sentence, is as
follows:

ǹũui è wɛ́ɛ pàī è pà ŋɔ́nɔ sâa.   'The person who came yesterday came
again today.' ('The-person the he yesterday came he came again today.')

Three of the nouns modified by relative clauses illustrated above—those referring to place, time, and manner—are also used like subordinate clauses; there
are no subordinating conjunctions, and the constructions in question remain nothing more than noun phrases functioning as adverbial complements in sentence-
initial rather than the usual sentence-final position. An example of each is:

ɓéi è lì nãai, ɓía máŋ ɓa pɔ̀ri lìi.
'Where he went, you can go too.' ('The-place the he went there, you
also you can go.')
tầiī ŋá pà là ɓéi, fé 'káa ní.
'When I came here, I didn't see him.' ('The-time the I came with-it
here, I-not him-saw.')
'perei a tíi kêi làī, 'fé pâi 'kpɛêi sâa.
'The way he's working, he won't finish it today.' ('The-way the he-
is work doing with-it, he-not-is coming it-finishing today.')

The second of the above can be used only with reference to past time. Equivalents of other 'when' clauses are expressed by the conditional construction
(cf. 12.9). The use of an adopted word, the specific form of /tầi/ 'time', in such a
common construction is hardly what one would expect; yet, from a number of
different informants with whom I worked, and in a much greater number of informal conversations with people of all ages, I heard no alternative to this for almost all of the first two years of work on the language. No one could tell me what
might have been used before the word came into the language, which was almost
certainly within the lifetime of elderly people still living at the time. I tried using
/ŋelei/ 'the day', but it was not accepted except with reference to a specific day.
Finally, after almost two years, the mystery was solved. I spent a few hours listening to court cases brought before the district commissioner, in which everything said in Kpelle was translated into English. One participant, narrating his
side of the case being heard, began a sentence with a relative clause with no noun

antecedent, and nothing recapitulating an implicit antecedent; it was translated by an English past temporal clause. This turned out to be a universally acceptable usage, and no one seemed to notice when I adopted it. Apparently /tâı̃/ 'the time' is considered obligatory when speaking to someone whose native language is presumably English, though it is also very frequently used under other circumstances. This is an excellent illustration of the fact that, no matter how efficient and effective structured elicitation of language data may be, there are always likely to be some details which can be discovered only by overhearing speech which is not addressed to the investigator. The sentence in question, an alternative to the second above, was:

> ŋá pà ɓέi, fé 'káa ní.   'When I came here, I didn't see him.'

An expression of manner like that in the third example above may also have the force of 'since' or 'inasmuch as', especially with another reference to the manner in the main clause of the sentence. E.g.,

> 'perei è kpɔ̀ŋ là mǎı̃, 'perei nɔ́ ɓé ŋa pâi kpənîi là m̀ǎ.
> 'Since he helped me, I'm going to help him.'
> ('The-way he helped with-it on-me, the-way only it-is I-am coming helping with-it on-him.')

Equivalents of English relatives with '-ever' are expressed by a nonspecific noun followed by /kélee/ 'all' and then a relative clause, which still has the specific suffix. The form /ɓέi/, which has the specific suffix but is not derived from a noun, is used in 'wherever'. E.g.,

nṹu kélee è 'kě̄ı	'whoever did it'
sɛŋ kélee 'káa ŋ́yéeı̄	'whatever I have'
ɓέi kélee è lì nãai	'wherever he went'

After the noun antecedent of a relative clause, and immediately before the relative clause if a verb intervenes, a morpheme /nyı̋i/ or /yíi/ may optionally be used, apparently most commonly if the antecedent is nonspecific. One might be tempted to call this a relative pronoun, though it seems a little strange to drag such a category into the grammar when the one word to which it applies is never obligatory. A preferable interpretation is that it is an independent indefinite demonstrative, 'a one', in apposition with the preceding noun and functioning as the immediate antecedent of the relative clause. This is reinforced by its similarity in form to the independent definite demonstratives like /nyíŋı̃/ 'this one' (cf. /ŋí/ 'this' attributive), which may be analyzed as derived from /nyı̋i/. Examples of the optional use of /nyı̋i/ are:

> ŋá ǹṹui kàa nyı̋i è 'kě̄ı.   'I saw the person who did it.'
> sɛŋ nyı̋i kélee 'káa ŋ́yéeı̄   'whatever I have'

Although the term "relative clause" has sometimes been used in the foregoing discussion, it should be remembered that we are dealing simply with nominalized sentences which stand in apposition with a preceding noun, not with subordination in the usual sense of the word. Further, the equivalents of clauses of place, time, and manner are not subordinate clauses but transposed adverbial complements which are noun phrases. A verbal construction such as a conditional is by definition subordinate, even though it is not introduced by any kind of subordinating conjunction. Apart from such inherent subordination, there is no clear-cut case of clausal subordination in Kpelle. A few other expressions which might seem to involve subordination must, however, be considered.

A phrase /kpɛ́ni fêi/ can regularly be translated by 'because'. In structure, however, it is a complete sentence in its own right. The first word must be analyzed as a noun, with a meaning something like 'something done for nothing or in vain'. The second word is the usual negative predicator translatable as 'it is not'; compare /pérɛ fêi/ 'it is not a house'. In speech, /kpɛ́ni fêi/ is always preceded and followed by sentence-terminal pause. (In written Kpelle, it begins a new sentence, properly, but is followed by a comma; a period would technically be preferable.) An example of its use is:

ŋá pà ɓɛ́. kpɛ́ni fêi. í káa ɓɛ́.
 'I came here because you are here.' ('I came here. It is not without reason. You are here.')

Direct quotation is introduced by a form /-yɛɛ/, or more commonly /-yɛɛi/, apparently with the specific suffix, preceded by what may be either the object of a verb or the possessor of a relational noun. It is perhaps the imperative of a verb; with a third person singular object, it would mean something like 'quote him'. It is sometimes but not always preceded by sentence-terminal pause; it usually has the intonation of a nonterminal clause, represented in transcription by a comma. In any case, it appears to be an instance of parataxis rather than subordination. An example of its use is:

è m̀ò ǹyɛɛi, ŋa pâi.   'He said (it), "I'm coming".'

Indirect quotation is introduced by a phrase /à ꞌkɛ́ɛ/, translatable as 'that'. The same phrase is used with a hortative after it, with the force 'in order that'. The phrase itself appears to be a marked complement of the type in which an adjectival is used, which ordinarily has an adverbial force (cf. 9.2). The adjectival must be derived from a verb /kɛ́/, which has frequently been cited as intransitively 'happen' and transitively 'do, make'; intransitively, without an indication of who is addressed and without any other complement, it is also used in the meaning 'say'. The parallelism in the use of marked complements seems to be that, for example, just as one can do something 'well' (/à ǹélɛɛ/), so one can say something 'saying' (/à ꞌkɛ́ɛ/). What follows /à ꞌkɛ́ɛ/ then seems to be in appositional relationship to it. Examples of its use are:

è m̀ò à ꞌkɛ́ɛ a pâi ꞌkêi. 'He said (it) that he would (~ will) do it.'
è lì nãa à ꞌkɛ́ɛ é tíi kɔ́ri. 'He went there in order to look for work.'
è lɛ̀ɛ nãa à ꞌkɛ́ɛ ŋá ꞌtóli. 'He stayed there so I would call him.'

Other Mande languages, even those most distantly related to Kpelle, appear to be grammatically similar in respect to most of the usages described in the foregoing. In particular, conjunctive subordination seems to be marginal at best. Such subordination does exist in many other Niger-Congo languages, but at most it is restricted to a few types. Structures strikingly similar to that of Kpelle in many details are widespread.

14.3. In Igbo, there are two types of questions asking for substantive answers. Only one of these types will be treated at this point; the other will be noted after a discussion of relatives. The first type is question-word questions rather similar to those found in many other languages. Question words are normally topicalized (cf. 11.3); an optional alternative is found only in a very short question such as the following:

gí'nị bù áhà gị.	'What is your name?'
~ áhà gị ọ̀ bụ̀ gí'nị.	('Your name is it what?')

If a question word is the subject of a sentence, it appears in the normal subject position, and there is no evidence on the surface that it is to be considered topicalized. It may, however, be preceded by the phrase /ọ̀ bụ̀/ 'is it?' (the declarative form of which is /ọ́ bụ̀/ 'it is'), which signals topicalization of a subject. If a question word is other than the subject, it is followed by /kà/, which marks topicalization in such cases. It may be, but usually is not, preceded by /ọ̀ bụ̀/. Questions paralleling those given for Kpelle in the preceding section are as follows:

ònyé mèrè yà.	'Who did it?'
gí'nị mèrè.	'What happened?'
ònyé kà ọ́ hụ̀rụ̀.	'Who did he see?'
gí'nị kà ó mèrè.	'What did he do?'
ŋké 'ólé kà ọ́ zụ̀rụ̀.	'Which one did he buy?'
ébé 'ólé kà ọ́ gàrà.	'Where did he go?'
ŋgbé 'ólé kà ọ́ gàrà.	'When did he go?'
màkà gí'nị kà ó sì méé 'yá.	'Why did he do it?' ('For what is-it he used and-did it?')
~ ó mèrè yà màkà gí'nị.	('He did it for what?')
~ gí'nị mèrè ó sì méé 'yá.	('What happened which-he used and-did it?')
ótú 'ólé kà ó sì méé 'yá.	'How did he do it?' ('Manner which is-it he used and-did it?')
ḿmà òlé kà ọ́ zụ̀rụ̀.	'How many knives did he buy?'
ḿ'má 'ŋké 'ólé kà ọ́ zụ̀rụ̀.	'Which knife did he buy?'
ụ̀dị ḿ'má 'ŋké 'ólé kà ọ́ zụ̀rụ̀.	'What kind of knife did he buy?'
òsíkápá 'há ótú 'ólé kà ọ́ zụ̀rụ̀.	'How much rice did he buy?' ('Rice which-equals amount which is-it he bought?')

The question word /ònyé/ 'who?' is a unique form in Igbo. It is derived from /ónyé/ 'person'; the replacement of the first tone by low is paralleled by low tone with subject pronouns in a hypothetical construction which functions as a question. It is specifically singular, though the answer—unknown to the questioner, after all—may be plural. A specifically plural question asking 'who(-all)?' cannot be asked with this type of question.

A number of the questions above use a form of a question word /òlé/ after a noun. The word /òlé/ may be used either as a numeral, 'how many?', or as a noun in an associative construction meaning 'which'? ('the how-many-eth?'). In the 'how many?' question above, /òlé/ is unambiguously a numeral because there is no tonal alternation. In the 'which one?' and 'when?' questions, it is unambiguously a noun because the phrases have the tones of the associative construction; by themselves, /ŋkè/ 'thing' and /ŋgbè/ 'time' end with low tone. In the 'which?' and 'what kind of?' questions, /ŋkè/ is actually redundant, and /òlé/ would unambiguously be a noun without it; after a noun ending with high tone, however, the use of /ŋkè/ resolves an ambiguity because a numeral and a noun would undergo the same tonal alternation, though for different reasons in the underlying structure. In the 'where?' and 'how?' questions, the status of /òlé/ is ambiguous in the surface structure, but /ébé/ 'place' and /ótú/ 'manner' are nouns not normally counted, and the phrases are assumed to be associative.

In the 'how?' question and two forms of the 'why?' question, the last part of the question uses a serial verb construction (cf. 12.11). The first verb, from a root /sí/, is common in serial constructions in the meaning 'use'; elsewhere, the same or a homophonous verb means 'come from, start from'. The important point is that, in Igbo, one must 'use' a reason or a way of doing something in order to do it. (This is a remarkably close parallel with the use of a marked complement /là/ 'with it' in Kpelle in expressions referring to time and manner.)

The second form of the 'why?' question above does not use a serial verb construction. It seems rather to be a paratactic construction: 'He did it—for what?'. The word /màkà/ is one of the words in Igbo that can with some justification be called prepositions. Its range of meaning includes 'for the purpose of' and 'about', but always with the implication of interest or involvement in what follows. The third form of the 'why?' question appears to ask about the cause of something rather than its purpose; this distinction in meaning, however, is by no means rigidly observed, and the first and third forms of the question are considered interchangeable. With appropriate time references in the remainder of the question, it is also possible to begin with /g'íní nà èmé/ 'what is happening?' or /gí'ní gà èmé/ 'what will happen?'.

In the 'how much?' question, the noun glossed 'amount' is /òtù/ for some speakers, and the phrase is /òtú 'ólé/. After the relative form of the preceding verb, this may have the alternant /ótú/ as transcribed above for other speakers, and the word becomes indistinguishable from /ótú/ 'manner', and is indeed not recognized as being of different origin. Although this type of question is generally acceptable, questions using terms for measures (in the case of rice, /ìkó/ 'cup',

/ọ́bà/ 'calabash', or /àkpà/ 'bag' would be appropriate) are probably more common. E.g.,

        ìkó 'ósíkápá 'ólé kà ọ́ zụ̀rụ̀.   'How many cups of rice did he buy?'

In most nominals corresponding to the above questions, there is a noun modified by a relative clause. Several of the nouns so used have already appeared in the questions, modified by the numerical or nominal interrogative /òlé/. For 'person', 'thing', 'place', and 'time', Igbo has an interesting distinction between generality and particularity, shown in the first four pairs of the following relevant nouns:

ńdí	'people' (general, specifically plural)
ónyé	'person' (particular, specifically singular)
íhé	'thing' (general, nonphysical or physical)
ŋ̀kè	'thing' (particular, physical and singular)
ébé	'place' (general)
ŋ̀gà	'place, spot' (particular; not used by some)
ŋ̀gbè	'time' (general)
ógè	'time, occasion' (particular)
ótú	'manner' (see alternative below)
òtù ~ ótú	'amount'
ụ̀dị́ . . .	'kind of'

In nominals referring to reason, /íhé/ 'thing' is used, but the serial construction in the following relative clause restricts the meaning to reason. In nominals referring to number ('how many'), the interrogative /òlé/ is used after the noun—another striking parallel to Kpelle, in which this is also the only case in which a question and the corresponding nominal both use a question word. In nominals referring to 'which', again as in Kpelle, the appropriate noun is directly modified by a relative clause.

For the immediate purpose of this discussion, only affirmative relatives for the stative and factative constructions will be considered; actually, many speakers of Igbo go to considerable lengths to avoid using any other relative. With this restriction, there are two sharply distinguished types of relative clause. In the first, the subject of the relative clause is the same as the antecedent noun. There is nothing comparable to a relative pronoun; relativization is marked exclusively by tone. A final low tone in the antecedent noun is replaced by downstep-high. For most types of verb bases, the absolute stative and factative have low tone throughout; in the relative, the first tone of the verb form is replaced by downstep-high, and any additional syllables continue on the same high level. For one type of verb base, there is no stative, but the absolute factative has downstep-high followed by two or more low tones; in the relative, the first syllable of the verb form remains downstep-high, but the second has another downstep-high, and any additional syllables continue on the same high level (or, in some dialects, the second syllable is low and all remaining syllables high). E.g.,

ŋwáànyì byàrà	'a woman came':
ŋwáànyí 'byárá	'the woman who came'
ŋwáànyì hápụ̀rụ̀	'a woman went out'
ŋwáànyí 'há'pụ́rụ́	'the woman who went out'

In the second type of relative clause, the subject is different from the antecedent noun; the antecedent is the object or a complement in the underlying sentence which is relativized. Again there is nothing comparable to a relative pronoun, and in fact in a great many cases there is no overt indication of relativization except the word order (which is true also of the English 'the woman he saw'). In restricted circumstances, there is tonal replacement in the subject of the relative clause. A single initial low tone (followed by high) is replaced by high after high, and a final low tone is replaced by downstep-high (or simply high after low, of course). Both of these replacives appear in a form like the proper name /Òkóyè/, which as the subject of a relative clause, after high tone, is /Ókó'yé/. E.g.,

ọ́ hụ̀rụ̀ ŋwáànyì	'he saw a woman'
ŋwáànyì ọ́ hụ̀rụ̀	'the woman he saw'
Òkóyè hụ̀rụ̀ éwú	'Okoye saw a goat'
éwú Ókó'yé hụ̀rụ̀	'the goat Okoye saw'

Using such relative clauses, nominals corresponding to the questions cited above appear in the following:

à má'ghị̀ ḿ ónyé 'méré yá.	'I don't know who did it.'
à má'ghị̀ ḿ ńdí 'méré yá.	'I don't know who-all did it.'
à má'ghị̀ ḿ íhé 'méré.	'I don't know what happened.'
à má'ghị̀ ḿ ónyé ọ́ hụ̀rụ̀.	'I don't know who he saw.'
à má'ghị̀ ḿ ńdí ọ́ hụ̀rụ̀.	'I don't know who-all he saw.'
à má'ghị̀ ḿ íhé ó mèrè.	'I don't know what he did.'
à má'ghị̀ ḿ íhé ọ́ zụ̀rụ̀.	'I don't know what he bought.'
à má'ghị̀ ḿ ṇ̀kè ọ́ zụ̀rụ̀.	'I don't know which one he bought.'
à má'ghị̀ ḿ ébé ọ́ gàrà.	'I don't know where he went.'
à má'ghị̀ ḿ ógè ọ́ gàrà.	'I don't know (just) when he went.'
à má'ghị̀ ḿ íhé ó sì méé 'yá.	'I don't know why he did it.'
~ à má'ghị̀ ḿ íhé 'méré ó sì méé 'yá.	
à má'ghị̀ ḿ ótú ó sì méé 'yá.	'I don't know how he did it.'
~ à má'ghị̀ ḿ kà ó sì méé 'yá.	(see below)
à má'ghị̀ ḿ ṁmà òlé ọ́ zụ̀rụ̀.	'I don't know how many knives he bought.'
à má'ghị̀ ḿ ṁmà ọ́ zụ̀rụ̀.	'I don't know which knife he bought.'
à má'ghị̀ ḿ ụ́dị́ ṁmà ọ́ zụ̀rụ̀.	'I don't know what kind of knife he bought.'
à má'ghị̀ ḿ ótú ósíkápá ọ́ zụ̀rụ́ hà.	'I don't know how much rice he bought.'

In the 'when' nominal above, the particular /ógè/ is used. The implication
is that I know that he went, but I don't know the particular time. In other contexts or with another implication, /ŋ̀gbè/ can be used; in some situations the distinction is not rigidly maintained. Speakers who use the particular /ŋ̀gà/ 'place'
might well use it in the 'where' nominal above.

The alternative of the 'how' nominal uses the word /kà/ in place of the noun
/ótú/ 'manner'. There is every reason to believe, however, that /kà/ itself is not
a noun; a further comment in connection with conjunction appears below. No
distinction of meaning, such as between generality and particularity, has been associated with the choice between these two, and no further explanation of /kà/
can be suggested.

In the 'how much' nominal, the construction is 'I don't know amount (which)
rice (which) he bought equals'. The phrase whose independent form would be
/òsíkápá ọ́ zụ̀rụ̀/ 'the rice which he bought', itself a noun with a relative clause
modifier, is the subject of the stative /hà/ 'be equal to'. As such, its initial single
low tone is replaced by high after high, and its final low tone by high, as in the
sentence cited. (For those who say /òtù/ 'amount', the initial low tone of /òsíká-
pá/ remains low.) This is a rather complicated and awkward construction, and
once more a reference to a number of measures is probably commoner, as:

> à má'ghị́ ḿ íkó 'ósíkápá 'ólé   'I don't know how many cups of rice
> ọ́ zụ̀rụ̀.   he bought.'

Now the second type of question, an optional alternative for any of those
cited above, may be introduced. No one can be exposed to Igbo for very long before hearing the word /kèdú/. By itself it is the common greeting to one person.
A common response to it is /ọ́ dì ḿ'má/ 'it is fine'. Such an exchange is frequently
followed by something like the following, which is clearly a question: /kèdú màkà
ńdí'bé gị́/ 'how about your family?', in which /màkà/ seems to be a fairly close
equivalent of 'about'. Thus /kèdú/ in these usages seems to mean something like
'how's everything?'. But it may also be used before a noun, and if a speaker of
Igbo is asked to translate out of context the question /kèdú ákwúkwọ́ 'gị́/, which
asks something about 'your book', he is most likely to suggest 'where is your
book?' as an equivalent. The same question, however, can be asked if the book
in question is obviously in sight, and in such a case it might be answered by giving
its price, telling where it was purchased, saying that it's a fine book, or with almost any other information about it. Actually, /kèdú/ before a noun has the exceedingly general meaning of 'how about?'; it asks for whatever information the
person addressed considers the most appropriate. Now, when one asks 'how
about?' with reference to a place or time, for example, the answer is obviously
expected to specify a place or time. On this basis, any of the nouns modified by
relative clauses illustrated above can be used after /kèdú/, and the result is a
specific question. Any such question is simply /kédú/ 'how about?' followed by
a noun phrase; in each of the sentences cited above, /kèdú/ can be substituted
for /à má'ghị́ ḿ/ 'I don't know' (with a few regular morphotonemic changes) to

produce a question with the same meaning as one of the question-word questions previously cited. Such a question can ask 'who?' with specific reference to more than one person; it was noted above that there is no question word with such a reference. Thus:

kèdú ńdí 'méré yá.   'Who-all did it?'
('What about the people who did it?')

Again, relative clauses are naturally found in other uses, and nouns referring to place and time, modified by a relative clause, may be used as preposed adverbial complements functioning like subordinate clauses. E.g.,

ḿmà ọ́ zụ̀rụ̀ dị̀ ḿ'má.	'The knife he bought is fine.'
ébé ọ́ gàrà, í ŋwèkwàrà íké	'Where he went, you can go too.'
í'gá.	('Place which-he went, you have-also strength to-go.'
ọ̀gbè ḿ byàrà ébé à, à	'When he came here, I didn't see him.'
hụ́'ghị ḿ yá.	

A locative complement of the type /n'ébé ọ́ nọ̀/ 'at the place where he is' has an interesting secondary meaning. If the reference of the main clause of the sentence excludes a locative idea, such a complement means 'as far as he is concerned'.

So far the only relatives that have been discussed are based on the factative and the stative; the latter include the derived incompletive and future constructions. The only other constructions for which relativization is relevant are the completive and the general negative. These have a somewhat different formation. A relative whose subject is the same as the antecedent noun is introduced by /'ná/, and the following verb form has a prefix whose underlying form is probably /à/ or /è/, but which has an alternant with high tone by regular morphotonemic alternation. This is like an incompletive relative in form; the stative auxiliary of the incompletive is also /'ná/ in the relative, and the following verbal noun begins in the same way. Yet there is no clear justification for associating the completive and negative relatives with the incompletive. Examples are:

ńdí 'ná á'byághị́	'those who didn't come'
ńdí 'ná á'nághị́ àbyá	'those who aren't coming, those who don't come'
ńdí 'ná á'gághị́ àbyá	'those who aren't going to come'
ńdí 'ná á'byábèghị̀	'those who haven't (yet) come'
ńdí 'ná á'byálá	'those who have come (already)'
cf.: ńdí 'ná ábyá	'those who are coming'

Completive and negative relatives with a subject different from the antecedent noun have been recorded so rarely that there is some doubt about the transcription of tone and about homogeneity of dialect. A negative relative has been transcribed with /ná/ (without downstep) after the subject. A completive re-

lative also uses /ná/, before a second or third person singular pronoun but after
any other subject; the second or third person singular subject, or vowel prefix in
other cases, and the entire verb form, have low tone. Many speakers use a factative relative in place of a completive. Examples recorded are:

ńdí ḿ ná á'húghị	'those I didn't see'
ọ́rụ́ ná ọ̀ rụ̀àlà	'the work he has done'
ọ́rụ́ ḿ ná àrụ̀àlà	'the work I have done'

A few morphemes may be considered subordinating conjunctions, though the
uses of some of them seem to be developments from constructions that are not
basically subordinating. The clearest case is /nà/ 'that' followed by any declarative sentence. E.g.,

ọ́ gwàrà ḿ nà ọ́ gà àbyá.   'He told me he would come.'

There is a noun /íhì/ 'reason' which is commonly used in the phrase /n'í'hí à/
'for this reason, therefore'; what is transcribed /n'/ is a sort of preposition with a
general locative reference. The conjunction /nà/ appears in the combination
/n'íhì nà/ 'for the reason that' to mean 'because'. E.g.,

á byàrà ḿ ébé à, n'íhì nà	'I came here because you are
ị́ nọ̀ n'ébé à.	(~ were) here.'

The conjunction /mà/, when followed by a declarative sentence, is coordinating, with the meaning 'but'. When followed by a hypothetical construction
which requires a low tone pronoun, and which by itself functions as a yes-no
question, it has the meaning 'whether'. Thus the equivalent of 'I don't know
whether he will come' seems to have the structure 'I don't know, but perhaps
he will come'. The sentence is:

à má'ghị́ ḿ mà ọ̀ gà àbyá.

A morpheme /kà/, followed by the incompletive construction, has the force
of 'while' or 'as'. The same syllable is used after the verb /í'dí/ 'be described
as' and before a noun, with the meaning 'like'; /kà/ also substitutes for the noun
/ótú/ 'manner' before a relative clause, introduces the hortative construction, and
marks nonsubject topicalization. Now many different morphemes are involved
in these five uses is impossible to determine; a case might be made for semantic
similarity where the references are to 'while, as', 'like', and 'manner', and more
subtly for the use of /kà/ introducing the hortative, but hardly for topicalization.
The usage relevant at this point is illustrated by the following:

kà ọ́ nà àbyá, m̀mí'rí bìdòrò ízò.	'As he was coming, it began to rain.'
kà ị́ nà àsá éféré, á cọ̀rọ̀ m ị́'sá áhụ́.	'While you wash the dishes, I want to take a bath.'
á hụ̀rụ̀ ḿ yà kà ọ́ nà arụ́ ọ́'rụ́.	'I saw him (while he was) working.'

In the last of these, the object pronoun /yà/ may be omitted.

A morpheme /tútú/, followed by the consecutive with an obligatory subject (even if it is the same as the subject of the preceding clause) has the meaning 'before' or 'until'. There is no obvious interpretation of this as anything other than a conjunction, but some other derivation may be lurking in the shadows. It is usually preceded by a pause, and marks the beginning of a new series of tonal terraces (i.e., its pitch is higher than or the same as the last preceding high tone); perhaps it should be interpreted as beginning a new independent sentence. Examples of its use are:

ó sàrà àhú̩, tútú ò ríé ń'rí.	'He took a bath before he ate.'
á gà m̀ àhú̩ 'yá, tútú ò ríé ń'rí.	'I'll see him before he eats.'
ò mé'cíghí̩ ú̩zò̩, tútú m̀mí'rí 'ébídó ízò̩.	'He didn't close the door until it began to rain.'

(No, /àhú̩/ in the first two of the above is not the same word. In the first it is a noun meaning 'body'—bathing is washing the body. In the second, it is the verbal noun of of the verb /í̩'hú̩/ 'see'.)

Two significant differences in the structure of questions and relatives in Kpelle and Igbo may be noted. First, in Kpelle anything preposed in a sentence, including question words and the antecedents of relatives, must be recapitulated in what follows; Igbo shows nothing of this. Second, a relative in Kpelle is a sentence nominalized by a suffix which is also used with nouns; in Igbo, relatives are marked by tone with a sharp distinction between those whose subject is the same as the antecedent noun and those whose subject is different. Otherwise, the general structure and usage of question-word questions and related relatives, as well as the restricted or even marginal character of other types of subordination, are remarkably similar in the two languages, although they are extremely distantly related.

14.4. The relationship of question-word questions and parallel relatives will not be outlined in as full a way for Efik; suffice it to say that the situation is closely similar to that in Kpelle and Igbo. Question words are typically (but not invariably) preposed and topicalized, and parallel nominals for the most part use ordinary words for 'person', 'place', 'time' and the like, modified by relative clauses; such nominals for place and time are also used as preposed adverbial complements functioning like subordinate clauses. Among the nominals there is one unique form, referring to a thing, /sé/. This can hardly be analyzed as a noun; it would be the only noun that does not have a vowel or nasal prefix. Nor is there any reason to call it a relative pronoun; the clause that follows is fully marked as relative in itself. Its status seems to be more like that of the Kpelle indefinite demonstrative /nyîi/, or the Igbo /kà/ substituting for the noun /ótú/ 'manner'.

The structure and grammar of relatives in Efik, however, deserves separate treatment. First, an antecedent noun is almost always followed by a demonstrative. If it is definite, the demonstrative is /ɛ́mì/, which elsewhere means 'this' but has no reference to proximate location with a relative. If the antecedent is indefinite, the demonstrative is /ɛ́kè/, which elsewhere refers to possession, as in /ɛ́kè ǹỹìn/ 'ours'. Second, as in Kpelle but not Igbo, a relative clause in Efik whose subject is the same as the antecedent noun must have a subject pronoun. If this creates an ambiguity, as between 'the man who saw (it implied from previous mention)' and 'the man he saw', the latter is introduced by an independent pronoun form to indicate that the subject of the relative clause is different from the antecedent noun. These points, apart from the marking of relativization as such, are illustrated in the following:

ówó ɛ́mì ɛ́ké'dídé   'the person who came'

 (cf.: ówó ɛ́mì 'this person')

ówó ɛ́kè ɛ́ké'dídé   'someone who came'

ówó ɛ́mì èỹé ókó'kútdé 'the person he saw'

Affirmative and negative relativization are quite different; there is a second type of affirmative relativization similar to negative relativization, but it has a special reference to time relationships. The usual affirmative relativization is marked by a suffix with the verb of the relative clause, which is not necessarily at the end of the clause. If there is more than one verb in the relative clause (later verbs being consecutive or sequential), the relative suffix appears with the first verb only. The form of the suffix is /-dé/ or /-dè/; in some cases the choice between these is phonologically conditioned, but under restricted circumstances the two are in contrast, as will appear presently.

Mention has been made in several contexts of the existence in Efik of two types of contrastive constructions, in addition to neutral constructions. One contrastive refers to something preceding the verb, and other to something following the verb. Neutral constructions do not appear in relative clauses. Further, the distinction between the two contrastives is largely broken down in relatives. In absolute verbal forms, the two are distinguished in the past and present by the tone of the verb base, which is base tone if something preceding the verb is contrasted, and low tone if something following the verb is contrasted. (Of course, these two are identical in any case if the lexical tone of the base is low.) In relatives, only base tone is used with one minor exception. It is in the light of this that the tone of the relative suffix can be discussed.

After a base with high tone, the relative suffix always has high tone. After a future contrastive, in which the base has the tonal replacive high-low, the relative suffix always has low tone. After a base with low or low-high tone (in the past or present), the relative suffix has high tone if it is in sentence-final position. After a base with low or low-high tone, however, if something follows the verb with its relative suffix, both high and low tone are recorded with the negative suffix; if the suffix has low tone, a base with low-high tone is low throughout. This contrast strongly suggests that, in this restricted circumstance, a difference between something preceding and something following the verb being contrasted is now signalled by the tone of the relative suffix: high to contrast what precedes (which is required if nothing follows), and low to contrast what follows. This question will be taken up again later; for the present, the following sentences illustrate relative clauses in which the tone of the suffix is obligatorily high or low:

ówó émì éké'dídé	'the person who came'
únàm émì íké'dépdé m̀fín	'the meat we bought today'
únàm émì ìdîdêpdè m̀fín	'the meat we'll buy today'
únàm émì èkétèmdé	'the meat you cooked'
étó émì ékésìbédé	'the tree he cut down'

Whether the tone of the relative suffix after low or low-high when something follows is merely optional, or whether it does signal a difference between contrasting what precedes and what follows, is difficult to answer. At best, the usage of the Efik neutral and contrastive constructions are likely to seem subtle to a speaker of English. A major reason for this apparent subtlety is the fact that we so often express comparable distinctions in English by differences in intonation and by contrastive stress—which we do not represent in written English, nor readily control in an artificial translation situation. This is further complicated by the fact that English as taught and learned by speakers of Efik almost totally ignores these important aspects of spoken English, so that it is exceedingly difficult to discuss the distinctions of contrast—in either Efik or English—in terms that all parties concerned can understand. In relative clauses in particular, the focus of contrast is often irrelevant to the grammar of the main clause, and it is likely to be the main clause on which the speaker's attention is concentrated. It seems almost certain that a difference in contrast focus depending on the tone of the relative suffix is the historical origin of the present situation. The extent to which such a distinction is recognized at present is difficult to determine; it is quite possible that the first of the two sentences below is contrastive as translated, but that the second is neutral. In any case, it would certainly seem a pity if a language were to lose a delightful contrast like the following, for whatever it's worth:

únàm émì èkétèmdé ŋkpóŋ ékénèm étî étî.	'The *meat* you cooked yesterday was delicious.' (Of course, the less said about the turnips, the better.)
únàm émì èkétèmdè ŋkpóŋ ékénèm étî étî.	'The meat you cooked *yesterday* was delicious.' (Now that bilge we had today was something else again.)

Relative clauses in Efik are used in much the same ways as in other languages, but there is also one unusual usage. Efik has a conditional construction, which is used to express conditions like 'when he comes, if he comes', in which the outcome is still in doubt. There are also verifiable conditions such as 'if he is here, if he came', These are expressed by a word /èdyékè/ followed by a relative clause; /èdyékè/ is probably best interpreted as a single word in contemporary Efik, since the second vowel does not have the prominence that is typical of word-initial vowels, but it is undoubtedly derived from a noun phrase /èdí ɛ́kɛ̀/, meaning something like 'the indefinite circumstance'. Examples of such conditions are:

èdyékɛ̀ ɛ́dídé, . . .	'if he is coming (now), if he has come'
èdyékɛ̀ ɛ́ké'dídé, . . .	'if he came (in the past)'
èdyékɛ̀ ɛ́dîdîdè, . . .	'if he is going to come (according to a plan already established)'

There is another construction, with quite a different formation, which must also be considered a relative because it is used after the same types of nominals. This construction has an auxiliary /má/, with all subject pronouns having low tone; after the auxiliary, the verb form is like a contrastive for what precedes the verb, with no relative suffix, but uniquely with downstep preceding the subject pronoun (overtly present, of course, only before pronouns which have high tone). This second relative refers to something completed before the time reference of the main verb of the sentence. The contrast between the two types of relative is illustrated in the first two of the examples below; in both cases, the noun modified is /ìnì/ 'time', preceded by a contracted form of a preposition-like morpheme /ké/, which refers to general location in place or time. The second relative may also follow /ké/ directly; this and other uses are illustrated after the first two of the following:

ɔ́kɔ́tɔ̀ŋɔ̀ ńdíkǎ úfɔ̀k ŋ̀wèt, k'ìnì ɛ́ké'dídé mí.	'He started attending school when he came here.'
ɔ́kɔ́tɔ̀ŋɔ̀ ńdíkǎ úfɔ̀k ŋ̀wèt, k'ìnì àmá 'ɛ́ké'dí mí.	'He started attending school after he came here.'
ké àmá 'ɛ́késìm dó, édìm á'má ɔ́'tɔ́ŋɔ ńdídèp	'After he arrived there, it began to rain.'
ɛ́kédì èbyét ɛ́mì m̀má 'ŋ̀ká'nám útóm.	'He came to where I had been working.'

This second relative formation is the basis for all negative relatives, which, however, do not have the same implication of prior time. The auxiliary is followed by a regular negative form of a verb, again preceded by downstep and without a relative suffix. The auxiliary with its negative subject pronouns is, however, somewhat irregular. The first person singular form is /m̀mé/ instead of the expected */m̀má/; the second person singular form is /m̀mú/ instead of the expected */ùmá/ or */ùmú/; the form for all other persons is /m̀mí/ instead of the expected */ìmá/ or */ìmí/. Such a relative is used after /èdyékɛ̀/ to express a negative conditional; the relative by itself, with no antecedent, is an optional alternative. Examples of negative relatives are:

m̀mè ówó ɛ́mì m̀mí 'íké'dígé	'those who didn't come'
èdíwàk ŋ̀kpɔ́ ɛ́mì m̀mé 'ŋ̀kɔ́- fyɔ̀kké	'many things I didn't know'
m̀fyɔ̀kké ńták ɛ́mì èỹé m̀mí 'íké'dígé.	'I don't know why he didn't come.'

útóm ɛ́mì àfò m̀mú 'úkú'námké	'the work you (sg.) didn't do'
(èdyékè) m̀mé 'ńdígé, . . .	'if I don't come'
(èdyékè) èy̆é m̀mí 'íkpódùgó mí, . . .	'if he weren't here'
(èdyékè) èy̆é m̀mí 'ikpé'ké'dígé, . . .	'if he hadn't come'

14.5. The patterning of question-word questions and parallel nominals in Yoruba is again similar to that in the other languages dealt with up to this point, with one major exception: Yoruba has what may reasonably be called a relative pronoun which introduces a normal sentence to form a relative clause. Question words are preposed and topicalized; the marker of topicalization is /ni/, with the contraction /l'/ before vowels other than /i/. Questions like those cited for other languages are:

ta l'ó še'.	'Who did it?'
kí l'ó šẹ 'lè̩.	'What happened?'
ta l'ó rí.	'Who did he see?'
kí l'ó še.	'What did he do?'
elé wō l'ó rà.	'Which one did he buy?'
n'íbo l'ó lọ.	'Where did he go?'
n'ígbà wo l'ó lọ.	'When did he go?'
kí l'ó jɛ́ k'ó še'.	'Why did he do it?'
	('What is-it it permitted that he do it?')
báwo l'ó še še'.	'How did he do it?'
	('How is-it he did did it?')
~ ọ̀nà wo l'ó gbà še'.	('What way is-it he took did it?')
ọ̀bẹ mélǒ l'ó rà.	'How many knives did he buy?'
ọ̀bẹ wō l'ó rà.	'Which knife did he buy?'
irú ọ̀bẹ wō l'ó rà.	'What kind of knife did he buy?'
(báwo ni) irẹsì t'ó rà 'ti	'How much rice did he buy?'
(še) kpọ̀ tó.	(see below)

Three of the question words in the above are fairly obvious: /ta/ 'who?', /ki/ 'what?', and the attributive /mélǒ/ 'how many?'. In most of the others, there is a syllable /wo/, or a derivative of it, from an underlying form /èwo/ 'which?'. The deletion of the prefix vowel of /èwo/, with its low tone, results in the remaining syllable having lowered mid tone after high or mid, as in the phrases /elé wō/ 'which one?' and /ọ̀bẹ wō/ 'which knife?'; this is not distinctive after low tone, as in /ọ̀nà wo/ 'which road?, which way?' and /n'ígbà wo/ 'at which time?, when?'. There is further contraction in two forms, without lowered mid tone as expected. A noun /ibi/ 'place' contracts with /èwo/ in the form /n'íbo/ 'at which place?, where?'. The form /báwo/ 'how?' shows a similar contraction; the first morpheme, though it can hardly be analyzed as a noun, functions like a noun (compare the strikingly similar status of the Igbo /kà/, 14.3 above).

In the 'where?' and 'when?' questions above, the initial morpheme, /ní/ in its full form, with a preposition-like function referring to general location in place or time, is optional. It is required, however, in nonpreposed complements.

In the two 'how?' questions, a serial verb construction is required. Whatever /bá/ is, one 'does' it in the process of doing something else. In the alternative question cited, /ònà/ is the regular word for 'road, path', with the extended meaning 'way, manner'; the verb /gbà/ is the regular verb for 'take, follow' with reference to a road. One takes a road in doing something. This is the clearest example of the rationale of this type of construction, a parallel to which has been noted in Igbo.

Once more, the 'how much?' question gives the greatest difficulty. The morpheme /ti/ is homophonous with the marker of the completive construction, but it is difficult to interpret it as the same morpheme. It appears to include an interrogative force, since there is nothing else interrogative in the question if the optional (and apparently redundant) /báwo ni/ 'how is it?' is omitted; there is other evidence that it is indeed interrogative. The preceding high tone indicating a verbal subject marks /ti/ as the beginning of the predicate, so that /ti/ itself may be a verb with an interrogative meaning, 'be how?', appearing here in a serial construction. The question thus appears to have the structure '(How is it) rice which he bought is-how (does) is-plentiful is-enough?'. A remarkable parallel to /ti/ as an interrogative verb will be noted in LuGanda presently.

In the parallel nominals, a noun is typically modified by a relative clause, which is introduced by /tí/, contracted to /t'/ before a vowel. For the most part, the identity and nature of the nouns will be clear from the following examples; comments follow for others:

n kò mọ ẹni t'ó še'.	'I don't know (person) who did it.'
n kò mọ nǹkan t'ó šẹ 'lẹ̀.	'I don't know (thing) what happened.'
~ n kò mọ ohun t'ó šẹ 'lẹ̀.	
n kò mọ ẹni t'ó rí.	'I don't know who he saw.'
n kò mọ nǹkan t'ó še.	'I don't know what he did.'
~ n kò mọ ohun t'ó še.	
n kò mọ èyí t'ó rà.	'I don't know (this-one) which he bought.'
n kò mọ ibi t'ó lọ.	'I don't know (place) where he went.'
n kò mọ ìgbà t'ó lọ.	'I don't know (time) when he went.'
n kò mọ ìdí t'ó fi še'.	'I don't know (reason) why he (used) did it.'
n kò mọ bí ó ti še'.	'I don't know how he did it.'
~ n kò mọ ònà t'ó gbà še'.	('I don't know way which he took did it.')
n kò mọ iye ọbẹ (mélǒ) t'ó rà.	'I don't know (number-of) knives (how-many) which he bought.'

n kò mọ ọbẹ t'ó rà.	'I don't know which knife he bought.'
∼ n kò mọ ọbẹ wō t'ó rà.	
n kò mọ irú ọbẹ t'ó rà.	'I don't know what kind of knife he bought.'
n kò mọ bí ìrẹsì t'ó rà ti (še) kpọ̀ tó.	'I don't know how much rice he bought.'

There are two nouns for 'thing', /nǹkan/ and /ohun/. These are generally considered to be interchangeable. It seems likely, however, that there was originally a distinction between 'thing (general, physical or nonphysical)' and 'thing (specific, physical, singular)', as in Igbo. If so, the more general word was undoubtedly /ohun/. In talking about 'which one', the independent demonstrative /èyí/ 'this one' is used, rather than either word for 'thing', or /elé/ as in the question.

Once more, one 'uses' a reason in doing something, and one 'takes' a way. The first alternative for referring to manner, however, is different in construction. The morpheme /bí/ is not nominal nor even pseudonominal, since it is not followed by a relative clause. It appears to be a type of subordinating conjunction, and may be related to the /bá/ in 'how?' questions. It appears also in referring to 'how much'; the remainder of the last sentence above is like the parallel questions.

In referring to 'how many' in both Kpelle and Igbo, it was noted that the interrogative word for 'how many?' was used also in the parallel nominal. Yoruba has a noun /iye/ 'number' which makes /mélǒ/ redundant; yet /mélǒ/ may optionally be included before the relative clause. In talking about 'which', the interrogative /(è)wo/ may also optionally be included, although it too is redundant.

For many of the questions cited above, there are fuller alternatives which can now be understood in the light of the parallel nominals. The following are some examples:

ta l'ẹni t'ó še'.	'Who did it?' ('Who is the person who did it?')
kí ni nǹkan t'ó še.	'What did he do?' ('What is the thing which he did?')
kí ni ìdí⁻rẹ̀ t'ó fi še'.	'Why did he do it?' ('What is his reason he used did it?')
iye ọbẹ wō l'ó rà.	'How many knives did he buy?' ('Number-of knives which is-it he bought?')

Without going into detail here, it may be added that, in Yoruba as in the other languages discussed in the foregoing, there are very few morphemes that can clearly be analyzed as subordinating conjunctions. As in the other languages, subordinate expressions referring to place and time are preposed adverbial complements consisting of a noun and a relative clause. E.g.,

n'ígbà t'ó lọ, . . .	'when he went'
n'íbi t'ó lọ, . . .	'where he went'

14.6. There are similarities also between the Bantu languages and the languages already discussed in respect to question-word questions and parallel relatives. A major superficial difference is that the class concord system is involved in relativization, and also in some question words. The same phenomenon is attested, as might be expected, in noun class languages in the Gur branch of Niger-Congo; with varying degrees of restriction, it is probably characteristic of class languages in general. A more significant difference is that, at least in the Bantu languages for which convenient data are available, many question words are not topicalized.

The following are LuGanda equivalents for the same questions that have been cited in other languages; major morpheme boundaries within words (but not the final /-a/ of most verb forms) are indicated by hyphens:

àní é-y-à-kí-kòlá.	'Who did it?'
ky-á-bá kí-tyá.	'What happened?' ('It-happened it-is-how?')
~ kì-kí é-ky-á-bááwô.	('What happened-there?')
y-à-lábá ání.	'Who did he see?'
y-à-kólá kí.	'What did he do?'
kì-kí ky-è y-à-gúlà.	'Which one (~ What?) (7) did he buy?'
y-à-géndá wá.	'Where did he go?'
y-à-géndá ddí.	'When did he go?'
lw-á-kí y-à-kí-kòlá.	'Why did he do it?'
y-à-kí-kólá á-tyá.	'How did he do it?' ('He-did-it he-is-how?')
y-à-gúlà ò-bw-àmbè bù-mèká.	'How many knives did he buy?'
k-àmbè kí k-è y-à-gúlà.	'Which knife did he buy?'
k-àmbé k-á ngérí kí k-è y-à-gúlà.	'What kind of knife did he buy'?
y-à-gúlà ò-mù-céèré gw-énkáná wá.	'How much rice did he buy?' ('He bought rice, it measures where?')

Again, some of the question words are fairly obvious, but comments are required for others. In the second question, the subject of each of the two verbs is a class 7 concord, referring implicitly to a noun such as /è-kí-ntú/ 'thing'. The root of the second verb, apart from tone, is /ty-/ or */ti-/; the appearance of a verb /ti/ in Yoruba, noted above, with the same unusual interrogative meaning, is nothing short of exciting. (This may also have something to do, ultimately, with the fact that the Kpelle /lén/ and Akan /dén/ 'how?' are the only question words in those languages which are never topicalized; there may be a serial verb construction somewhere beneath the surface.)

In the alternative form of the second question, /kì-kí/ is a class-marked nominal form of an interrogative meaning 'what?, which?'. This form is in class 7; there are other forms with the prefixes of all other appropriate noun classes. The form /kí/, without indication of class, appears in several other questions after a verb or (somewhat unexpectedly) attributively after a noun. Nominal forms of /kí/, or a noun followed by /kí/, appear in initial position, and, if they function as other than the subject of the question, are topicalized. Topicalization is marked by a concord with the morpheme /-è/: /ky-è/ for class 7, /k-è/ for class 12, the latter in two of the above questions referring to the class 12 noun /k-àmbé/ 'knife'.

In the 'why?' question, /kí/ appears in an associative construction with a class 11 concord and the associative morpheme /-á/. This would appear to refer to an unexpressed class 11 noun meaning 'reason', but informants associate the semantic reference of /lw-á-kí/ with a class 9 noun, /è-nsóngá/. There is actually no identifiable noun to which the class 11 concord can refer; one can only say that class 11 in such a question refers arbitrarily to the reason asked about. A similar phenomenon will be noted below in connection with relatives. Another instance of the associative is found in the 'what kind of?' question; here /ngérí/ 'kind' is clearly associated with the class 12 /k-àmbé/, and it appears in all appropriate classes.

'How many?' is simply a root /-mèká/ appearing in concord with any plural noun—class 14 in this case.

Once more the 'how much?' question is expressed indirectly. The use of 'where?' seems to refer to 'up to where?' in a measuring container.

In the other languages which have been discussed, nominals paralleling questions like the above are typically nouns modified by relative clauses. It is easy to see that the same formation is not very far beneath the surface in LuGanda, but in the surface manifestation there is no overt noun in most cases. Relatives are marked for class, and the reference—to person, thing, place, etc.—is indicated by the class of the relative. A specific implied antecedent can be identified in some cases, but in other cases the reference is arbitrary.

A relative whose subject is the same as the antecedent does not have the initial vowel (apparently an indication of topicalization) which appears in the questions above. In relatives whose subject is different from the antecedent, there is a concordial relative form similar to, and sometimes identical with, the topicalizing forms described above. In the sentences below, both /-è/ and /-é/ appear as the relative morpheme; the tonal difference is conditioned by complicated tone rules. If the relative and the topicalizing morpheme do not follow different tone rules (a question I am not in a position to answer), they are at least distinguishable by something in the syntax; informants immediately recognize a difference. In relatives, there is no distinction between a general 'what?' and a specific 'which one?'; nor is there a distinction between 'which?' and 'what kind of?'. With these restrictions, relatives parallel to the questions cited above are as follows:

sí-mányî y-à-kí-kòlá.	'I don't know who did it.'
sí-mányî ky-á-bááwô.	'I don't know what happened.'
sí-mányî gw-è y-à-lábà.	'I don't know who he saw.'
sí-mányî ky-è y-à-kólà.	'I don't know what he did.'
sí-mányî ky-è y-à-gúlà.	'I don't know which one (∼ what) (7) he bought.'
sí-mányî gy-è y-à-gêndá.	'I don't know where he went.'
sí-mányî w-è y-à-géndèrá.	'I don't know when he went.'
∼ sí-mányî̀ lw-è y-à-gêndá.	(refers to 'what day')
sí-mányî ky-è y-à-vá á-kí-kòlá.	'I don't know why he did it.'
sí-mányî bw-è y-à-kí-kòlá.	'I don't know how he did it.'
sí-mányî mù-wêndó gw-à bw-àmbé bw-é y-á-gúlà.	'I don't know how many knives he bought.'
sí-mányî k-àmbé k-é y-á-gúlà.	'I don't know which (∼what kind of) knife he bought.'
sí-mányî mù-céèré gw-è y-à-gúlà bw-è gw-ènkánà.	'I don't know how much rice he bought.'

The object relative /gw-è/ may be class 1, 'who', or class 3, in which case it is 'what' with reference to a noun of that class. By itself, it refers only to class 1, and the implied antecedent is /ò-mú-ntú/ 'person'. If it were to refer to class 3, an antecedent noun would be obligatory unless clear from the immediately preceding context.

The object relative /ky-è/ is class 7, and is assumed to refer to /è-kí-ntú/ 'thing'. It appears in the above not only obviously as 'what', but also in the 'why' relative; the latter sentence has the structure 'I-don't-know what he-started-from he-did-it'. Similar constructions have been noted in other languages with reference to either reason or manner; one uses or takes or starts from a reason or manner in doing something.

The object relative /gy-è/, referring to place, is class 23. There is no noun inherently belonging to this class to which the relative can implicitly refer, but the class is itself locative; nouns in other classes can be made locative by preposing the class 23 prefix.

The object relative /w-è/, referring to time, is similar in structure to the other object relatives, but does not belong to any of the recognized classes. A verb used after it must have the applicative verbal extension; this is also attested in other sentences with temporal complements. In the alternative relative of time, /lw-è/ is class 11, and is assumed to refer to /ò-lù-nákù/ 'day'; the applicative extension is not used in this case.

The object relative /bw-è/, referring to manner, is class 14. There is no identifiable noun to which it may refer; the association of this class with manner is completely arbitrary. The class includes many abstract nouns. The same relative appears in the last sentence above, which has the structure 'I-don't-know rice which he-bought how it-measures'.

The sentences referring to number and choice use relative clauses modifying specific nouns, which may be in any class. The structures are: 'I-don't-know number associated-with knives which he-bought' and 'I-don't-know knife which he-bought'.

14.7. A major point that has been made in the foregoing sections is that, in the languages discussed, question words do not ordinarily function also as relatives, as they do in English. There have been occasional exceptions, particularly in the case of the attributive 'how many(?)', but the general pattern is that the equivalents of English relatives are nouns modified by relative clauses or, as in LuGanda, relative clauses with an unambiguous noun-class reference. LuGanda is completely consistent in excluding question words from relative usage. In Swahili, on the other hand, three question words—including 'how many?'—are regularly used also in relatives, and others may be. The Swahili equivalents of the questions cited for other languages are given below; the interrogative words or phrases which are not subjects appear here after the verb, but they may optionally occur in initial position.

nani a-li-i-fanya.	'Who did it?'
kitu gani ki-me-tokea.	'What happened?' ('Thing what-kind-of it-has-happened?')
~ ki-me-tokea nini.	('It-has-happened what?')
~ ki-me-tokea nini.	('It-has-happened what?')
a-li-mw-ona nani.	'Who did he see (him)?'
a-li-fanya nini.	'What did he do?'
a-li-nunua ki-pi.	'Which one (7) did he buy?'
a-li-kwenda wa-pi.	'Where did he go?'
a-li-kwenda lini.	'When did he go?'
a-li-i-fanya kwa nini.	'Why did he do it?'
a-li-i-fanya vi-pi.	'How did he do it?'
~ a-li-fanya-je	(see below)
a-li-nunua vi-su vi-ngapi.	'How many knives did he buy?'
a-li-nunua ki-su ki-pi.	'Which knife did he buy?'
a-li-nunua ki-su gani.	'What kind of knife did he buy?'
a-li-nunua mchele kiasi gani.	'How much rice did he buy?' ('He-bought rice measure what-kind-of?')

In the equivalent of 'Who did he see?', /-mw-/ is the class 1 object concord. Object concords are required with reference to classes 1 and 2 only, even if a noun object (or /nani/ 'who?' in this case) is expressed.

The question words themselves are almost completely transparent from the above examples. A root /-pi/ has the meaning 'which?', and is used with concords of all classes. Class 8, /vi-/, in addition to being a plural class, refers to manner; it forms adverbs of manner from adjective stems, but is so used also with some noun stems. In /wa-pi/ 'where'?, the prefix does not belong to any recognized noun class, but compare the LuGanda /wá/ 'where?'; 'which ones?' with reference

to the personal plural class 2, would be expected to have the same form, but is irregularly /we-pi/.

The phrase /kwa nini/ 'why?' is an adverbial of a type to be discussed in the
following chapter: an associative referring to class 15, the infinitive class. It may
be represented by '(action) associated with what?', 'reason' is implied.

The sentence /a-li-fanya-je/ is actually more of an equivalent of 'How did he
do?' or 'How did he get along?', referring to any action under discussion. This
particular verb does not take an object if the suffix /-je/ 'how?' is used. An object is required, however, with a verb referring to a more specific action. E.g.,

        a-li-i-tengeneza-je.   'How did he fix it?'

'What kind of?' is expressed by the invariable form /gani/ after a noun.
As in all the other languages discussed in preceding sections, 'how much?' is expressed indirectly, in the case of Swahili by asking what kind of measure or a-
mount.

After an expression such as /sijui/ 'I don't know', all of the above questions
seem to be acceptable without change in contemporary Swahili, as if they were
relatives. It is considered possible that this usage, which seems totally foreign
to Niger-Congo languages, first developed among people who spoke English fluently, in light of the dual interrogative and relative usage of the English words
in question. Grammatical adaptation of this sort is certainly not common, but it
is conceivable; the usage seems to be well established in Swahili. Proponents of
hypotheses of language mixture have little reason to feel smug about this detail;
they would do better to explain why this sort of thing does not happen far more
often.

Swahili does, however, also have a relative formation for all but one of the
parallel nominals. A nominal referring to reason does not use a relative, but is
identical with the question cited above. Relative clauses are formed by using
relative concords, which consist of the appropriate concordial prefixes and a morpheme /-o/, except that the relative for class 1 is commonly /y-e/ rather than /y-o/.
In the past construction used here, either a subject or a non-subject relative
concord appears immediately after the construction marker. The question word
/nani/ 'who?' as subject, and a noun with one of the attributive question words
/gani/ 'what kind of?' and /-ngapi/ 'how many?', are used as antecedents of relatives. In other cases, the class reference of the relative is sufficient to indicate
the semantic reference. "Sufficient" seems a strange word in light of the fact
that, as cited below, one relative is completely ambiguous; it may be interpreted
as referring to either place or time. A comment follows the examples. The nominals paralleling the questions cited above appear in the following:

        si-jui nani a-li-y-e-i-fanya.   'I don't know who did it.'
        si-jui ki-li-ch-o-tokea.   'I don't know what happened.'
        si-jui a-li-y-e-mw-ona.   'I don't know who he saw.'
        si-jui a-li-y-o-fanya.   'I don't know what he did.'

si-jui a-li-ch-o-nunua.	'I don't know which one (∼ what) (7) he bought.'
si-jui a-li-p-o-kwenda.	'I don't know where/when he went.'
si-jui kwa nini a-li-i-fanya.	'I don't know why he did it.'
si-jui a-li-vy-o-i-fanya.	'I don't know how he did it.'
si-jui vi-su vi-ngapi a-li-vy-o-nunua.	'I don't know how many knives he bought.'
si-jui ki-su a-li-ch-o-nunua.	'I don't know which knife he bought.'
si-jui ki-su gani a-li-ch-o-nunua.	'I don't know what kind of knife he bought.'
si-jui mchele ki-asi a-li-ch-o-nunua.	'I don't know how much rice he bought.'

In the second sentence above, the class 7 relative concord /ch-o/ is used for 'what'; in the fourth sentence, the class 9 concord is used with the same reference. Either is permissible with reference to a non-physical 'thing', and the class 5 /l-o/ may also be used.

The concord used with reference to place or time is class 16, /p-o/. This is otherwise a locative class, referring to a specific place. The ambiguous relative is normal usage. If it is felt necessary to specify either place or time, however, a noun can be used. The noun for 'place' is /mahali/, which is the only noun inherently belonging to class 16, even though it does not have the prefix /pa-/. The noun for 'time' is /wakati/, in class 11; nevertheless, when it is used as an antecedent of a relative, it takes the class 16 relative concord. Specific references to place and time are thus:

| si-jui mahali a-li-p-o-kwenda. | 'I don't know where he went.' |
| si-jui w-akati a-li-p-o-kwenda. | 'I don't know when he went.' |

Relative concords appear in the position illustrated above, immediately after the construction marker, only in the past, present, and future constructions, and in a negative noted below. The past and present construction markers, /-li-/ and /-na-/ respectively, are regular. In the future, however, the construction marker /-ta-/ has the alternant /-taka-/ before a relative concord. (Actually, /-taka-/ is the underlying form from which /-ta-/ is a derivative; it is undoubtedly the verb meaning 'want'.) E.g.,

m-tu a-li-y-e-kwenda	'a/the person who went'
m-tu a-na-y-e-kwenda	'a/the person who is going'
m-tu a-taka-y-e-kwenda	'a/the person who will go'
(cf.: a-ta-kwenda 'he will go')	

With relative concords in the same position, there is a negative construction not paralleled in nonrelative clauses. It apparently substitutes for the negative of the customary. It uses a morpheme /-si-/, which appears also in some other negatives, in construction marker position. E.g.,

| m-tu a-si-y-e-soma | 'a/the person who doesn't read' |

The affirmative customary, which in nonrelative clauses has the construction marker /-a-/, has no construction marker in a relative clause. Further, the relative concord appears after the verb as a suffix. E.g.,

m-tu a-soma-y-e	'a/the person who reads'
kengele i-lia-y-o	'a bell (9) that rings'
kengele zi-lia-z-o	'bells (10) that ring'

With all other verbal constructions, the relative concord is suffixed to a stem /amba-/, and the combination appears before the verb form. E.g.,

m-tu amba-y-e a-me-kwenda	'a/the person who has gone'
m-tu amba-y-e ha-ku-kwenda	'a/the person who didn't go'

If a relative clause modifies something other than the subject of the sentence, a noun subject appears after the verb rather than in its usual position before the verb. A verb may take an object concord in addition to a relative concord referring to the object. E.g.,

ki-su a-li-ch-o-ki-nunua Hamisi	'the knife which Hamisi bought'
vi-su a-li-vy-o-vi-nunua Hamisi	'the knives which Hamisi bought'

Class 1 and 2 relative concords are also used with reference to first and second person independent pronouns. The appropriate first and second person object concords are used if the relative clause modifies an independent pronoun as object. E.g.,

wewe ni-li-y-e-ku-ona	'you whom I saw (you)'

14.8. Although my notes on KiKongo are not sufficiently complete to provide an outline comparable to those given for several other languages, there is enough information to make some significant comments about question-word questions and relatives—comments which could not be made on the basis of treatments of the language which ignore tone. KiKongo is, of course, a Bantu language. There has been some loss of noun class prefixes, but the concord system operates pretty much as expected in almost every respect. There are, however, no concordial relative forms.

Several question words and phrases are recorded as appearing in initial position. A noun object may also be preposed. Immediately after either a question word or a noun object, a verb form which elsewhere has the tonal sequence high-low with the first two syllables begins with low-high instead. Initial high tone with a verb is retained, however, after a noun subject, after a yes-no question marker, and after certain morphemes that are probably best analyzed as conjunctions. Thus the tonal difference is morphemic, and high tone with the second rather than the first syllable of the verb form quite clearly indicates topicalization of what precedes. A verb form with initial low tone undergoes no change, so that topicalization is not overtly marked with such a verb form. Examples of such topicalization are:

náni wamóna.   'Whom did you see?'
     (cf.: wámona sé dyámi.   'You saw my father.')
masoká yanáta   'It was axes I took.'
     (cf.: yánata masoká.   'I took axes.')
masoká banáta.   'It was axes they took.'
     (cf.: banáta masoká.   'They took axes.')

The same shift of high tone from the first to the second syllable of a verb form, and merely word order if the verb form elsewhere begins with low tone, marks relativization if the subject of the relative is different from the antecedent noun. Thus the second and third examples of topicalization above are identical with nouns modified by relative clauses; the latter would simply be parts of longer sentences with their own main verbs. Another example is:

nzo yatúunga   'a/the house I built'
     (cf:. yátuunga nzo.   'I built a house.')

A relative whose subject is the same as the antecedent noun is also tonally marked, but in a different way. In most nonrelative verb forms that can be so relativized, the first syllable of the verb base has high tone, and preceding tones, if any, are low. (Forms with other tones can surely be relativized also, but I happen to have no examples, so the statement must remain incomplete.) In relatives, the first syllable of the base of such a verb form has low tone rather than high, and the preceding syllable, if any, has high tone. This is true also if there is no expressed antecedent. Thus:

muuntu wákala ye báana boole   'a man who had two children'
     (cf.: wakála ye báana boole.   'He had two children.')
i yáandi ukúsadisi.   'It is he who has helped you.'
     (cf.: ukusádisi.   'He has helped you.')
muuntu sedi sálu kya mbóte   'a man who has done good work'
     (cf.: sédi sálu kya mbóte.   'He has done good work.')
básuumbidi zinkóombo   'those who have bought goats'
     (cf.: basúumbidi zinkóombo.   'They have bought goats'.)

Fante, like Igbo and KiKongo, also has different tones with the verb in relative clause from those of a main verb. In Fante, however, this is characteristic of all subordinate clauses (cf. 9.4). Relative clauses are introduced by what can properly be called a relatlve conjunction, /áà/. Other subordinates using the same subordinate tones include clauses introduced by /déὲ/ 'that', and conditions. Conditions require a clause-final morpheme /à/, and are usually introduced by a conditional conjunction as well.

Chapter 15

Adverbials, Ideophones, Semantic Ranges

15.1. A great deal has already been said about adverbial complements, particularly in connection with relativization in the preceding chapter, but also in connection with adjectivals (cf. 9.2), demonstratives (cf. 10.8), and topicalization (cf. 11.5). The entire subject, however, has not been discussed in any systematic way to provide a framework into which the details already treated may be fitted. It is the purpose of the first part of this chapter to give a more general overview of adverbials, particularly in the Niger-Congo languages.

Most languages have a rather limited number of one-word adverbials referring to time and place, and even fewer referring to manner, means, or other categories. Temporal adverbs will be considered first, and an outline of the situation in Kpelle will serve as the basis for comments on other languages. In Kpelle, there are three temporal adverbs which share certain special characteristics: /wέɛ/ 'yesterday', /sâa/ 'today', and /tína/ 'tomorrow'. Like their English counterparts, these may have a nominal use, particularly as the subject of a sentence. They can hardly be said to be nouns, however; among other things, they take no noun affixes, and are never modified by a demonstrative or adjective. They may be topicalized, but the rest of the sentence does not include the recapitulating reference otherwise required with topicalizations. In adverbial use, they appear most commonly after the verbal construction marker or auxiliary but before an object and the verb, but they may also optionally be used in sentence-final position. E.g.,

è wέɛ tíi kὲ	}	'he worked yesterday'
è tíi kὲ wέɛ		
è sâa pà à mɔlɔŋ	}	'he brought rice today'
è pà à mɔlɔŋ sâa		

In addition to these, there are a few temporal adverbs which are not attested in any nominal use and are not topicalized, and which generally appear in the preverbal position, rarely in sentence-final position. All of these are mutually exclusive with the above and with each other. These include /nâa/ 'now, by now' (in specific contrast with the past; a more general expression for 'now' is a phrase), and /wɔ́lɔ/ 'long ago, at some time'. Also, /nîi/ '(not) yet' and /tá/ '(ne)ver' are used preverbally with the past negative to form negative counterparts of the completive and experiential constructions respectively (cf. 12.4); I have no record of these in other uses, but there may be such. Examples of these are:

446

à nâa 'kɛ́	'he has done it by now'
a nâa 'kɛ̂i	'he is now doing it'
è wɔ́lɔ 'kɛ̀	'he did it long ago'
à wɔ́lɔ 'kɛ́	'he has done it at some time'
'fé nîi 'kɛ́ ní	'he hasn't done it yet'
'fé tá 'kɛ́ ní	'he hasn't ever done it'

The adverb /ŋɔ́nə/ 'again' (with negatives also '(not) any more') is not strictly speaking temporal, but is conveniently treated in this connection. It may appear in either the pre-verbal or sentence-final position shown above. It may also be used in addition to one of the adverbs cited above. With another adverb in pre-verbal position, /ŋɔ́nə/ usually appears in sentence-final position, but may follow the other adverb immediately. It usually precedes but may follow /wɛ́ɛ/, /sâa/, or /tína/ in sentence-final position. In this variety of possible positions, /ŋɔ́nə/ may be added to almost any sentence of the types illustrated above, or may be used by itself. With a negative, one example of an adverb /lâa/ is recorded, in preverbal position, apparently with the similar meaning 'any more' or 'at all'; unfortunately, the sentence is grammatically obscure in other respects.

It cannot be expected, of course, that other languages will have exactly the same inventory of root adverbs, but comparable restrictions seem to be rather typical of the Niger-Congo languages. In some languages, even the distinction between 'yesterday' and 'tomorrow' is missing; in almost every case, of course, such a distinction is redundant because the verb has a past or future reference in itself, and a single form can serve for 'the day adjacent to today'. This is true in major (but not all) dialects of Igbo, where the word is /écí/. After an expression like 'he said he would do it', which does not restrict the reference of /écí/ unambiguously to either 'yesterday' or 'tomorrow', /écí/ may be modified by a relative clause to specify past or future reference. Thus:

ọ́ byàrà écí	'he came yesterday'
ọ́ gà àbyá é'cí	'he will come tomorrow'
ọ́ sìrị̀ nà yá gà àbyá écí 'gárá ágá	'he said he (same person) would come yesterday' ('the /écí/ which went a going')
ọ́ sìrị̀ nà yá gà abyá écí 'ná ábyá	'he said he would come tomorrow' ('the /écí/ which is coming')

On the other hand, some languages have single words for such time references as 'day before yesterday', 'day after tomorrow', and even days farther removed from today. Swahili has the forms /jana/ 'yesterday', /leo/ 'today', /kesho/ 'tomorrow', then a phrase /kesho kutwa/ 'day after tomorrow', but a single word /mtondo/ 'three days from today'. There is also a form /juzi/ 'within the past few days', often taken to mean specifically 'day before yesterday'. Outside of Niger-Congo, Hausa can cover an entire week with six single words and only one phrase:

shěkáràn jíyà   'day before yesterday'; then:

jíyà	'yesterday'	jíbí	'two days from today'
yâu	'today'	gátà	'three days from today'
gòbě	'tomorrow'	cíttà	'four days from today'

Kpelle has a few temporal adverbials with unique structures which can most conveniently be treated along with the adverbs cited above. Among these is /wɔ́lɔwɔlɔ/, a reduplicated form of the root /wɔ́lɔ/. It is used only in sentence-final position. With reference to the past, it means 'always' or, like the unreduplicated form, 'long ago'. With reference to the future, it means 'always, forever'. It is modified by a demonstrative in the phrase /wɔ́lɔwɔlɔ tí sù/ 'long, long ago' ('in that long-ago'). Another unique adverbial is /tua tína/ 'day after tomorrow'; the first word may be the verb root /tua/ 'pass the day', but its use in this phrase is not verbal. A third instance is the phrase /luníi mǎ/ 'right now', referring to the immediate past or future. The second word in this phrase appears to be the relational noun meaning 'surface, edge', often paralleled by 'on' in English, but the first word is not attested in any other combination, and is tonally unlike anything else in the language.

Somewhat similar unique formations are found in other languages also. The Igbo expression for 'now' is /ùgbú à/; this appears to be a noun with the demonstrative 'this', but /ùgbú/ does not exist apart from this phrase.

The position of adverbs in a sentence in Kpelle is not so typical of Niger-Congo languages in general. It is not common to find a temporal or any other adverb between the subject and predicate of a sentence. For the most part, adverbs appear in sentence-final position, or at least after the major part of the predicate, the verb or the verb and its object. Adverbs may also appear in sentence-initial position, even without being topicalized. In this position, they are usually followed by a pause, and call attention to the time referred to, particularly when the subject is changed from another time.

Kpelle has three locative adverbs with similar uses: /ɓέ/ 'here', /nãa/ 'there', and /mána/ 'over there, the other way'; the last of these is far less commonly used than the other two, and may primarily refer to a more remote location, and perhaps to a place mentioned before another place away from the speaker. These are the only one-word locative adverbs which may be topicalized. With the possible occasional exception of /nãa/, these are not used as verbal subjects; instead, a general word for 'place', /kwaa/, is used with a demonstrative: /'kwaai ɲí/ 'this place', /'kwaai tí/ 'that place'. A special use of /ɓέ/ was described in 14.2; with the specific suffix /-i/, but without the prefixed low tone which a noun would have in a similar use, it is modified by a relative clause to form a nominal referring to a place, without specific reference to proximate location. One would expect /'kwaai/ 'the place' in this usage, but it does not occur. All three of these locative adverbs are frequently compounded with the noun /pere/ 'path, road, way'; the compounds are nouns, but they may also be used as adverbial complements, often with no definable difference in meaning from the adverbs by themselves, but sometimes with the specific meaning of 'in this direction' etc. Unlike temporal adverbs, locative adverbs are not used in preverbal position. They appear immediately after the verb, before a temporal adverb or any other complement. Examples of their use are as follows:

è lì nãa	'he went there'
è pà ɓέ	'he came here'
ŋá ǹàŋ kàa nãa	'I saw his father there'
ŋá ǹàŋ kàa nãa sâa	'I saw his father there today'
~ ŋá sâa ǹàŋ kàa nãa	
è pà ɓέ à mɔlɔŋ sâa	'he brought rice here today'
~ è sâa pà ɓέ à mɔlɔŋ	

It was noted above that temporal adverbs may be used in sentence-initial position followed by pause. It is my impression that /nãa/ is also so used occasionally, but the derived compound nouns are more common in that use, followed by a demonstrative: /ɓέ-pèreī ŋí/ 'here', /nãa-pèreī tí/ 'there', /mána-pèreī tí/ 'over there'.

Only two other one-word locative adverbs are recorded (or remembered by me) in Kpelle. It is my impression that these are never topicalized or used in sentence-initial position; their position is otherwise like that of the three locative adverbs already discussed, immediately after the verb. One of these is apparently a single morpheme, but has a rather atypical vowel sequence: /síɣai/ 'toward the coast (southwest)', usually expressed as 'down' in Liberian English. The other is /ɣelêi/ 'up, upwards', which is the noun /ɣele/ 'sky, day' with the fairly uncommon locative suffix /-ì/. This suffix occurs with a few other nouns, but does not make them adverbs; for its apparent use with verb roots also, see 11.5. Although 'up' is the opposite of 'down' in English, I do not recall that /ɣelêi/ is ever used in the meaning 'away from the coast, inland', although of course the terrain rises in that direction; I associate /ɣelêi/ only with vertical height or ascent on a fairly steep hill. Details of the usage of items in small morphological classes like this are the sort of thing one often neglects to record fully, but my impression is that these two adverbs are used only with verbs of motion. Certainly a bird or an airplane, and God, are located at /ŋelei sù/ 'in the sky' (the structure of which will be noted in the following section), but one says /'tέ ɣelêi/ 'lift it up, lift it higher', and also metaphorically /í wóo tέ ɣelêi/ 'raise your voice, speak louder'.

Igbo has no locative adverbs at all. Even 'here' and 'there' are expressed by noun phrases, which in complement position are preceded by the preposition-like form transcribed as /n'/ before vowels: /n'ébé à/ 'at this place' and /n'ébé áhù̀/ 'at that place' respectively.

Efik, like many Niger-Congo (and other) languages, has a three-way contrast in locative adverbs. The three forms are clearly related to demonstratives which have both nominal and attributive uses. The pairs are:

mí   'here' : ɛ́mì   'this'
dó   'there (near the hearer)' : órò   'that (same)'
kó   'there (away from the hearer') : ókò   'that (same)'

In the Bantu languages, as outlined fully for Swahili in 10.8, comparable locatives are commonly demonstratives in the locative classes 16, 17, and 18. General location, specific location, and location inside are distinguished by the concordial morphemes for the three classes; the affixes with them distinguish near location, remote location, and location previously referred to. Without a modified noun, such forms are nominal; it is only in complement position after a predicate, as complements, that they can be called adverbial. They may also be used as verbal subjects and objects.

Many Bantu languages have adverbials consisting of a noun with a suffix /-ni/, discussed in the following section. Otherwise, the foregoing probably covers most of the types and restrictions of non-phrasal locative adverbials in Niger-Congo. Word order seems to be similar in most languages as well; locatives generally precede temporals after the predicate.

Other types of one-word adverbs tend also to be restricted in number, but there always seem to be a few of them—about a half dozen in Kpelle. The first to be noted is /máŋ/ 'also', which may be used after a noun or a temporal or locative adverb (with a temporal, only in sentence-final position), but not after a verb, and nowhere else that I recall. If used after an independent pronoun form (which is nominal), the phrase is in apposition with a subject pronoun. If a second action is mentioned, as in 'I washed the clothes and (also) cooked food', the consecutive construction is used, or the construction for simultaneous action, whichever is appropriate (cf. 12.10, 13.7); there is no way of emphasizing that the second action is additional except by adding an explanatory comment like 'I did a second thing also', which is rarely felt to be necessary. Uses of /máŋ/ are illustrated in the following:

è pà à mɔlɔŋ máŋ   'he brought rice too'
è mɔlɔŋ máŋ yà   'he bought rice too'
ǹàŋ máŋ è mɔlɔŋ yâ   'his father also bought rice'
ŋá mɔlɔŋ yâ, ŋ́yá máŋ   'I too bought rice'
ŋá mɔlɔŋ yâ wɛ́ɛ máŋ   'I bought rice yesterday too'

Adverbs with similar uses are found in many languages, but there are also other ways of expressing 'also'. Efik has an adverb /ŋ́'kó/ 'also' with uses similar to those of the Kpelle /máŋ/. As noted in 12.12, however, Efik also has a verb meaning 'do in addition', used in the consecutive before another consecutive referring to the added action. In Igbo, there is a verbal extension /-kwa/, with the tone of the preceding syllable, to express the idea of 'also'; it may refer to a nominal in the sentence, or to an adverbial complement, or to the verb itself, but not to a subject or object pronoun; its reference is usually clear from the context. Thus in the following sentence, depending on what had been said before, the reference may be to 'also my father', 'also yams', 'also yesterday', or even 'also ate' (e.g., in addition to cooking); note that the reference of 'also' or 'too' in the written English equivalent is equally ambiguous apart from context, but in spoken English is indicated by contrastive stress, for which there is no parallel in Igbo:

| ńnà ḿ rìkwàrà jí écí | 'my father ate yams yesterday too' |
| (cf.: ńnà ḿ rìrì jí écí | 'my father ate yams yesterday') |

The Kpelle adverb /nɔ́/ 'only, just' is used immediately before a verb or the topicalizing morpheme /ɓé/ with reference to what precedes, or immediately after the verb with reference to what follows. To express exclusive reference to a verbal subject, which never immediately precedes the verb, the subject must be topicalized. Exclusive reference to the verb itself is expressed by /nɔ́/ after the verb only if nothing follows in the same clause; the clause must be followed by another, with the verb in the consecutive. This has the special meaning shown in the last example below. Exclusive reference to the verb if the verb is followed by a complement can only be expressed by an added sentence such as /ǹya nɔ́ ɓe/ 'that's it' ('it only it-is'). The usual uses of /nɔ́/ are illustrated by the following:

ńâŋ nɔ́ ɓé mɔlɔŋ yâ	'it's only my father who bought rice'
mɔlɔŋ nɔ́ ɓé ńâŋ è ǹyà	'it's only rice my father bought'
ńâŋ è mɔlɔŋ nɔ́ yà	'my father bought only rice'
è pà nɔ́ à mɔlɔŋ	'he brought only rice'
è pà nɔ́ wéɛ	'he came yesterday only'
è pà nɔ́, é 'tí káa	'he had no more than come when he saw them' ('he came only and he saw them')

An adverb /kpɔ́/, with a kind of intensive meaning best reflected by an English exclamation, often with words characteristic of exclamations, is used immediately after a verb or predicative adjectival. It refers to the predicate if nothing follows or otherwise to what follows. E.g.,

ŋuŋ a sôlii kpɔ́	'My head is splitting!'
(cf.: ŋuŋ a sôlii	'my head hurts')
ǹélɛɛì kpɔ́	'That's swell!'
(cf.: ǹélɛɛì	'it's fine, it's alright')
è 'kɛ̀ kpɔ́ à ǹélɛɛ	'He really did it well!'

An adverb /kpaâ/ 'almost' is used in the same pre-verbal position as temporal adverbs. E.g.,

| ŋaâ kpaâ 'kpɛɛ | 'I've almost finished it' |

Expressions for 'almost' in a number of other languages are verbal; typical of such is the Igbo /ọ́ fọ̀dừrừ ńtàkịrị́/ 'it remains a little' followed by a consecutive. E.g.,

ọ́ fọ̀dụ̀rụ̀ ńtàkị́rị́ ńrí   'the food is almost gone'
'ágwụ́cá

A Kpelle adverb /sôla/ 'about, approximately' is used after expressions including a reference to number or quantity. E.g.,

kóraŋ lɔ́ɔlu sôla   'about five years'

Again, expressions for the same idea in other languages are not necessarily adverbs. In Igbo, the noun /íhé/ 'thing (general)' is used, modified by the relative /'dị̀ kà/ 'which is like'; compare the English 'something like' in the meaning 'approximately'. E.g.,

íhé 'dị̀ kà áfọ̀ ìsé   'about five years'

The Kpelle word /kpéni/ was described in 14.2 as a noun with a meaning something like 'something done for nothing or in vain'. It also has an adverbial use, at the end of a sentence, but a reduplicated form of it, /kpénikpɛni/, is more common in this usage, with the same meaning. E.g.,

è 'kɛ̀ kpénikpɛni   'he did it free, he did it in vain'

There is thus a good deal of variation among languages in the specific ideas expressed by words in a class which may be called adverbs. It seems typical of Niger-Congo, however, that such a class is restricted, and that a number of ideas we might expect to be expressed by simple adverbs are expressed in quite different ways.

Among the non-Bantu languages, there seems to be no pattern for forming adverbs from words in other classes, comparable to the English suffix used with adjectives to form adverbs like 'quickly'. In at least some Bantu languages, however, one or two of the noun class prefixes may have such a function. In Swahili, the Class 8 prefix, which normally forms noun plurals corresponding to singulars in class 7, is used with adjective stems to form adverbs of manner like /vi-zuri/ 'well, in good way'; of course, such forms are also used adjectivally modifying class 8 nouns. The class 7 prefix is used with some noun stems, particularly those referring to tribes, peoples, and places, to form nouns which may also be used adverbially, referring to the manner or custom associated with the noun stem. Unless the context excludes such an interpretation, such forms refer to the language or dialect of a tribe, people, or place. Thus in the broadest sense /ki-Swahili/ is '(in) the Swahili manner', but it generally refers specifically to 'the Swahili language'.

Other Bantu languages have similar adverbial formations with noun-class prefixes, but not all of them with the same class references. Classes 14 and 11 are among those used to form adverbials in some other languages.

15.2. Along with adverbs in the narrow sense, adverbial phrases must be considered. In English, a very common type of adverbial complement is a preposition followed by a noun phrase. In Niger-Congo languages, there are very few words which can properly be called prepositions; in some languages there may be none at all, and it is difficult to find more than two in any one language. Even the few forms that one might decide to call prepositions may have a grammatically marginal status. In 11.3-4, for example, a case was made for the hypothesis that the Igbo /ná ∼ nà ∼ n'/ and the Yoruba /ní ∼ n'' ∼ l''/, both referring to location in a general way, are verbal in the underlying structure, ultimately derivable from verbs meaning 'be located at'. Yet in the present structure of these languages, at least for practical purposes and without introducing any unnecessary confusion, these forms may well be called prepositions.

To a large extent, ideas expressed by prepositions referring to motion in English are expressed in Niger-Congo languages by verbs, and ideas expressed by prepositions referring to location in English by nouns. It really ought to be trivial, but may be important in the light of the traditionalism still prevalent in African language studies, to note that many things have frequently been labelled "prepositions" which clearly are not. This is especially true in the case of languages which have serial verb constructions; verbs with meanings like 'take, use', 'start from', 'arrive at', 'give, do for', frequently used in serial constructions, are commonly translatable by, and thus frequently but wrongly analyzed as, prepositions meaning 'with', 'from', 'to', and 'for' respectively. Similarly, relational nouns with locative meaning in the Mande languages are commonly thought to be merely or primarily preposition-like, though they may be called "postpositions" because they occur after the possessing noun (cf. 8.5). In other languages, the verbal or nominal character of constructions translatable as adverbial complements introduced by prepositions is perhaps more conspicuous, but it is equally demonstrable in the case of serial verbs and relational nouns.

In Igbo, 'from' is commonly expressed by the stative of the verb /í'sí/ 'be from, start from'. With the more specific meaning 'beginning at', the consecutive of the same verb root with the base formative /-tá ∼ -té/, /í'síté/, is used. The sequence 'from . . . to . . .' is expressed by the consecutives /síté . . . rúé . . ./; the second consecutive is from the verb /í'rú/ 'arrive at'. The noun phrases used after these consecutives may be either locative or temporal. The forms in question are often used just as other consecutive verb forms are, but an unusual use which is grammatically more preposition-like is also permissible: /síté/ may be used at the beginning of a sentence, with or without /rúé/ introducing the destination, without a subject, like a nominal referring to place or time. Typical uses are:

ó sì Àbá byá	'he came from Aba'
ọ́ kwùsìrì n'òbòdò ní'ílé	'he stopped in every town
síté 'Ábá rúé Ụ̀mụ̀áhyà	from Aba to Umuahia'
ọ́ mụ̀rụ̀ ákwụ́kwọ́ síté élékéré	'he studied from three
'átọ́ rúé élékéré 'ísé	o'clock to five o'clock'
síté élékéré 'átọ́ rúé élékéré	'from three o'clock to five
'ísé, á gà m̀ ánọ̀ n'ụ́lọ̀	o'clock, I'll be at home'

·The consecutive form /bànyéré/ from the verb /íbànyè/ 'go into' is used in the meaning 'about, concerning'. The forms /bàtárá/ from /íbàtà/ 'come into' and /gbásárá/ from /í'gbásá/ 'pertain to' are sometimes used in the same way. E.g.,

ọ́ gwàrà m̀ bànyéré 'yá	'he told me about it'
ọ́ kwùrù ókwú bànyéré ńnà yá	'he talked about his father'

Often substitutable for /bànyéré/ etc., but with a somewhat different shade of meaning in other contexts, is a form /màkà/. This word implies an interest or involvement in what follows; it often means 'for the purpose of' or 'for the sake of'. Grammatically, there seems to be no alternative to calling this a preposition. A common use of it, illustrated and discussed in 14.3, is in the phrase /màkà gí'nị́/ 'for what?, why?'.

The only other preposition in Igbo is the one mentioned previously, with the alternant forms /nà/ before a consonant (which is rare) or before a syllabic nasal with low tone, /ná/ before a syllabic nasal with high tone, and /n'/ before a vowel. This has a general locative meaning 'at', though translations such as 'on' and 'in' are sometimes required by the context. It is used before any noun or noun phrase referring to place or time, but is not required if such a phrase appears in sentence-initial position followed by a pause. The following noun may be a word like 'house' or 'town', a place name, a noun like 'inside', 'top', 'back', 'underneath' followed by another noun in an associative construction, or an expression of time. E.g.,

ọ́ nà àrụ́ ọ́'rụ́ n'ụ́lọ̀	'he works at home'
ọ́ nà àrụ́ ọ́'rụ́ n'Àbá	'he works in Aba'
ọ́ nà àrụ́ ọ́'rụ́ n'ímé ụ́lọ̀	'he works indoors' ('at the inside of the house')
ọ́ nà arụ́ ọ́'rụ́ n'ébé áhụ̀	'he works there' ('at that place')
ọ́ byàrà n'á'fọ́ 'gárá ágá	'he came last year'
ọ́ byàrà nà ǹgbè áhụ̀	'he came then' ('at that time')

Such adverbial complements include phrases which fill gaps in the restricted repertoire of simple adverbs in Igbo—expressions for 'here', 'there', 'then', and perhaps others.

Rather unexpectedly, such locative complements are used after a few verbs which seem clearly to refer to motion, particularly /í'lá/ 'return to' and /íbà/ 'enter'. Other verbs of motion are followed by noun phrases without a preposition; as in Niger-Congo languages generally, it must be emphasized that such verbs have meanings like 'go to', 'be from', 'arrive at', and the like, and nothing like a preposition is used with them. E.g.,

ọ́ làrà n'ụ́lọ̀	'he returned home'
ọ́ bàrà n'ụ́lọ̀	'he entered the house'
ọ́ gàrà Àbá	'he went to Aba'
ọ́ byàrà ébé à	'he came here'

Complements referring to duration in time are also noun phrases without a preposition. There are also a few noun phrases referring to manner which are similarly used. Such phrases are adverbial simply by virtue of their position in the sentence. E.g.,

ọ́ nọ̀ n'ébé áhụ̀ àbàlì àtọ́	'he stayed there three days' (lit. 'three nights')
á nà m̀ àsụ́ Ìgbò ŋwáńtị́ńtị́	'I speak Igbo a little'
ó mèrè yà ŋ̀kè ọ́má	'he did it well' (lit. 'a good one')
ọ́ dì m̀'má ŋ̀kè úkwú	'it's very good' (lit. 'a big one')

For Igbo as well as several other languages, adverbial complements corresponding to English subordinate clauses referring to time, place, manner, reason, etc. were discussed at considerable length in chapter 14. These are typically nouns modified by relative clauses. Along with what has been said in this and the preceding section, the types of adverbials in Igbo have been pretty well covered.

A number of other languages have closely similar patterns for adverbial complements. Yoruba also has a preposition with a general locative reference, /ní ∼ n'' ∼ l''/, and phrases with and without this preposition have usages closely parallel to those discussed above for Igbo. Efik also has a similar preposition, /ké ∼ k'/ with similar uses and restrictions. Jukun has a comparably preposition /kí/.

Swahili also has a comparable form which may justifiably be called a preposition, /katika/. This appears to be derived from a noun /kati/ whose basic meaning is 'middle', and which is used in an associative construction with another noun for '(in) the middle of'; the derivation, however, does not follow any productive pattern in Swahili. The basic meaning of the preposition is 'in', but a specific reference to an area inside is frequently secondary to a reference determined by a verb or something else in the context. With literal locative reference, /katika/ plus a noun is an alternative for another locative formation; locative adverbials may also be formed by a suffix /-ni/ with a noun, and such adverbials are used more frequently than phrases with /katika/. Some of the relevant uses are:

alikiweka sandukuni	'he put it in the box'
∼ alikiweka katika sanduku	
alitoka katika shamba	'he came from the farm'
iandika katika karatasi hii	'write it on this paper'
alikuwa katika kuifanya	'he was in the act of doing it' (with infinitive)

In Swahili, unlike Igbo, other locative references and temporal references are not introduced by a preposition. They are simply noun phrases. Locative phrases consist of a locative noun in an associative construction with another noun; the locative noun in the first of the following is /juu/ 'top'. E.g.,

alikiweka juu ya meza	'he put it on the table'
alikifanya mwaka jana	'he did it last year'

The phrase /mwaka jana/ in the second of the above is peculiar. The word /mwaka/ means 'year', but /jana/ by itself means 'yesterday'. There is a similar phrase with /juzi/, which by itself means 'a few days ago, day before yesterday'; /mwaka juzi/ is 'year before last'. In these phrases, the two words appear to be in apposition. An alternative formation is an associative construction: /mwaka wa jana/, /mwaka wa juzi/.

In Kpelle, there is no preposition at all with adverbial complements of place and time. The phrases in question are adverbial simply by virtue of their position in the sentence. Locative complements are noun phrases, which in other positions may be verbal subjects or objects. A place name may be a complement by itself. Otherwise, a locative complement consists of a locative relational noun with a possessor. Such phrases in Kpelle and other Mande languages are discussed more fully in 8.5; the following are illustrative:

è lì Dukɔ̀ɔ	'he went to Monrovia'
ŋá 'kàa Dukɔ̀ɔ	'I saw him in Monrovia'
è lì 'taai sû	'he went into town' ('he went-to the-town's inside')
ŋá 'kàa 'taai sû	'I saw him in town'
ŋá 'kàa 'taai pôlu	'I saw him on the other side of town' (/pôlu/ 'back')

A detail worth nothing in this connection is that the phrase /'pérɛi sù/, which one would expect to mean 'the inside of the house', refers only to the area above the rafters; the area where people and furniture normally are is /'pérɛi mù/, with /mù/ which otherwise means 'the underneath part'.

Temporal complements in Kpelle may be noun phrases of the same type, or they may be marked complements—noun phrases without a locative relational noun, but introduced by a morpheme /à/ which will be more fully discussed in the following section, but which is not analyzed as a preposition. It is of interest that expressions like 'that week' may refer to either 'last week' or 'next week'; compare the Igbo /écí/ 'yesterday, tomorrow' noted in the preceding section. Examples of the alternative formations are as follows:

è pà 'kóraŋ tí sù	'he came last year'
～ è pà à 'kóraŋ tí	
a pâi pâi 'kóraŋ tí sù	'he will come next year'
～ a pâi pâi à 'kóraŋ tí	
è pà 'kóraŋ ŋí sù	'he came this year'
～ è pà à 'kóraŋ ŋí	
a kɔ́lɛì tɑ̂iī ŋí sù	'he's sick at present'
～ a kɔ́lɛì à tɑ̂iī ŋí	
è kɛ̀ à 'kɔ́lɛɛ tɑ̂iī tí sù	'he was sick at that time'
～ è kɛ̀ à 'kɔ́lɛɛ à tɑ̂iī tí	

Two other temporal adverbial phrases require special treatment. The phrase /ɣele 'ta/, literally 'some day' or 'some days', is used only in sentence-initial position. With reference to customary action, it means 'sometimes'; with other references, it means 'perhaps'. The phrase /ɣele támaa/ is used primarily if not exclusively in a marked complement; it literally means 'many days', but is the usual expression for 'often'. E.g.,

ɣele 'ta a tíi kɛ̀ ɓɛ́	'sometimes he works here'
ɣele 'ta a pâi pâi	'perhaps he will come'
è 'kɛ̀ à ɣele támaa	'he did it often'

Apart from locative and temporal complements, there is one word in Kpelle which may be analyzed as a preposition, though it may be used before a predicative clause as well as before a noun. It is /yɛ̂ɛ/ 'like', illustrated in the following:

'káa nɔ́ yɛ̂ɛ niŋa	'it's just like a cow'
'kɛ́ yɛ̂ɛ 'perei ŋa 'kɛ̀ là	'do it like (the way) I do it (with it)'
'káa yɛ̂ɛ 'fé pâi pâi	'it looks as if he isn't going to come'

In English, we speak of going to a place or going to a person, using the same construction. I know of no Niger-Congo language in which this is possible. One goes only to a person's place or location, or where a person is. In Kpelle, the relational noun /pɔ́/ is used for this purpose, followed by the adverb /nãa/ 'there'. The same noun without /nãa/ is used after a few other verbs; all that can be said is that it appears to refer to one's location or direction. E.g.,

è lì 'kâloŋ pɔ́ nãa	'he went to the chief'
è 'tɛ̀ɛ 'kâloŋ pɔ́	'he sent (∼ gave) it to the chief'
è lòno 'kâloŋ pɔ́	'he spoke to the chief'

Again, the constructions discussed in Chapter 14, primarily nouns modified by relatives, must be included with adverbial complements of the types outlined in this section. With natural variations in different languages, the overall theme is that of a restricted number of simple adverbs, an even more restricted repertoire of adverbials introduced by anything comparable to English prepositions, and a large number of noun phrases whose adverbial function is marked only by syntax.

15.3. Associative constructions constituting noun modifiers have been discussed in several contexts for several languages; familiarity with the situation in Bantu, as outlined in 10.1, is assumed for this section. A special usage of the associative /a/ is commonly found in the Bantu languages with no antecedent noun. The usual Bantu prefix for infinitives, class 15, is /ku-/, and infinitives share a number of usages with nouns. With reference to an action, which is specified by a verb in any construction, the associative /a/ with the concord for the infinitive, with a following noun or noun phrase, constitutes an adverbial complement. Several kinds of reference are involved, including means, material, manner, cause, and time. The following examples from Swahili are fairly typical of Bantu in general:

alikuja kwa miguu	'he came on foot'
alikifanya kwa kisu	'he made it with a knife'
alikifanya kwa mti	'he made it out of wood'
alikifanya kwa haraka	'he made it hastily'
alikufa kwa njaa	'he died of hunger'
mvua ilikunya kwa siku nyingi	'it rained for several days'

Another adverbial of this type was noted in 14.7 in connection with a discussion of question words in Swahili:

aliifanya kwa nini	'why did he do it?'

Adverbials of exactly the same form, but with nouns or concords referring to persons only, refer to the place where a person is; compare the note on going to a person in the preceding section. Such adverbials are probably best interpreted as involving the locative class 17 rather than the infinitive class 15; the concords for the two classes are identical in any case, and the two classes may ultimately be derived from one, though they are distinguished in the light of certain uses in some Bantu languages today. Thus:

alikwenda kwa Bwana Hamisi	'he went to Hamisi('s)'
alitoka kwa Bwana Hamisi	'he came from Hamisi('s)'
yuko kwa Bwana Hamisi	'he is at Bwana Hamisi's'
yuko kwangu	'he is at my place'

I have no evidence for adverbials of a similar type, based on an associative construction, in other noun class languages, though such adverials may well exist outside of Bantu. In some of the Mande languages, however, which show no trace of a functional noun class and concord system, there is a remarkable parallel to the class 15 associative adverbials of Bantu. Among the Southwestern Mande languages, Kpelle and Mende have a morpheme /à/ which is used after a verb to associate the action with a following nominal or adjectival expression; the combination constitutes an adverbial. Even prior to any knowledge of a Bantu language or of associative constructions involving class concord, I felt that the morpheme /à/ in Kpelle was in a special category, and I avoided calling it a preposition. A major reason was that /à/ is used not only before a noun, but also before an adjectival with prefixed low tone (cf. 9.2); perhaps such forms can be included under nominals in a sophisticated analysis, but they are not conspicuously nominal. Further, the morpheme marks several kinds of relationship between what precedes and what follows. On the basis of such facts, I chose to label constructions with /à/ "marked complements", and the morpheme /à/ itself a "complement marker". It later became clear that, both in form and in this usage, the parallelism with Bantu associatives is too close to be dismissed as coincidence.[1] Some of the following Kpelle examples are precise equivalents of some of the Swahili examples above:

---

[1] This has previously been discussed in Welmers 1963a.

è 'kpὲtε à 6óa	'he made it with a knife'
è 'kpὲtε à wúru	'he made it out of wood'
è 'kpὲtε à ɲέlεε	'he made it well'
tina è pù à ɣele-kû támaa	'it rained for several days'
è pà à 6óa	'he brought (came with) a knife'
è 'kpὲtε à konâ	'he made it into a mortar'
'káa à 6óa	'it is a knife'
è kὲ à ɲέlεε	'it was good'

As noted in the preceding section, this is one of two alternative constructions for adverbials referring to time; the other, which is used also for adverbials of place, is an "unmarked complement" with a possessed locative relational noun.

In Loma, the corresponding morpheme, used in very much the same way, is /gà/. Since the divergence of Kpelle, Mende, and Loma is relatively recent, and particularly since there is some evidence that Mende and Loma are slightly more closely related to each other than either is to Kpelle, one would hardly expect that /à/ in two of these languages and /gà/ in the other would have different origins. Loma /g/, however, ordinarily corresponds to Mende /ŋg/ and Kpelle /ɣ/. If both forms are from a proto-Southwestern-Mande */à/, the initial consonant in Loma can only be explained as an innovation; arguments can be adduced both for and against such a hypothesis. It is also possible, however, that the Loma /gà/ comes from an older form /*kà/; if so, proto-Southwestern-Mande had two alternative morphemes which were used as complement markers. An associative /ka/ is also attested in Bantu (cf. 10.1); if both existed in the rather recent proto-Southwestern-Mande, the parallelism with Bantu is even more striking than the Kpelle evidence by itself suggests. As noted in 10.3, an associative /ká/ is attested also in Northwestern Mande, though not in this usage.

All of this leads up to the observation that adverbials of the types illustrated above are formed with a morpheme /ká/ in the Southern and Eastern Mande languages. The construction differs, however, in that /ká/ appears in final position in the complement, rather than in initial position as the Kpelle and Mende /à/ and the Loma /gà/. The following illustrations from Dan (Gio) are equivalents of four of the illustrations from Kpelle above:

è à kə̀ làa ká	'he made it with a knife'
è à kə̀ wɔ́ ká	'he made it out of wood'
è à kə̀ sə̀ ká	'he made it well'
è nu làa ká	'he brought a knife'

15.4. In virtually every Niger-Congo language, as well as typically in Nilo-Saharan languages and at least in languages of the Chadic branch of Afro-Asiatic, but apparently not in the Khoisan languages, there is a fairly large group of words now generally known as "ideophones." Many of these have some kind of adverbial use, and so should be considered here. Unfortunately, when it comes to talking about ideophones, for almost every student of African languages—including con-

spicuously the present author—the "Peter Principle" begins to apply: we are
rapidly reaching the level of our own incompetence. Everyone seems to recognize
that some words are ideophones, but no one finds it easy to define an ideophone
with any precision.

For one not familiar with ideophones in an African language, some observations about some peculiar words in English may serve to set the stage. First,
we have a group of words representative of certain sounds. These include 'bang'
or 'bang-bang', 'bow-wow' or 'arf-arf', 'meow', and 'moo'. At least some of
these have perfectly normal grammatical uses; we speak of 'the bang of a gun',
and we say 'the cat meowed' and 'I heard a cow mooing'. They are also used,
however, in a unique way in sentences like 'the gun went bang-bang', 'the dog
went bow-wow', etc. In such sentences, the forms in question may be preceded
by a pause, and may be pronounced with unusual stress or accompanied by special
paralinguistic vocal effects. Thus 'meow' may be pronounced with a high-pitched
melody intended to represent the actual sound a cat makes; 'moo' may be prolonged far more than any normal English syllable, and pronounced with a low
falling pitch and either a "hushed" or a glottally interrupted voice. In this use
they rather resemble interjections, and of course such forms may also be used in
isolation as actual interjections. In quite a different category, but also rather
anomalous in English, is a group of partially reduplicated forms. In one type,
the reduplicated part of the form begins with a consonant or consonant cluster different from the initial consonant; examples are 'willy-nilly', 'teeny-
weeny', 'hurdy-gurdy', 'nitty-gritty', 'hum-drum'. In another type, the vowel
[ɪ] in the first part is echoed by [æ] in the second; I can think of ten of these, plus
an eleventh which was perhaps originally pronounced with [æ] instead of the
present [ɔ]:

fiddle-faddle	knick-nack	flim-flam
riff-raff	mish-mash	pitter-patter
zig-zag	wig-wag	wishy-washy
dilly-dally	shilly-shally	

An inspection of these reduplicated forms reveals that some of them are verbs,
some nouns, and some adjectives. A few of them have an interjection-like use,
as in 'pitter-patter went the rain', but most of them are not syntactically unusual. We may feel that some of them are onomatopoeic, and all of them seem to
have a rather picturesque connotation. It would not be difficult to imagine adverbial uses for comparable forms in other languages. For English, perhaps
phrases like 'tit for tat' and 'spick and span' should be included in this category.
Another set of words that might be mentioned is a surprisingly large number of
pseudo-agentives of the type of 'swash-buckler', 'four-flusher', and 'two-timer';
it is only for a special humorous effect that we speak of 'the most swaggering pirate
who ever buckled a swash'—and a fun game can be played by making up questions
like 'Do you have any fours you'd like flushed?' Such forms are phonologically

and syntactically normal, but peculiar in that their apparent derivation is not valid; they also seem to have a picturesque connotation.

It is forms with characteristics somewhat like these that are known as "ideophones" in African languages. In earlier works (prior to 1935) they have also been given labels such as "interjections", "descriptive adverbs", "picture words", "onomatopoeic adverbials". Many—probably most—African languages have hundreds of them; William J. Samarin (personal communication) has a file of over three thousand in Gbeya. At the same time, the repertoire and significance of ideophones in specific languages has, until recently, been appreciated by a relatively few linguists, primarily those who have had the opportunity to achieve a very high level of competence in a language, and whose rapport with native speakers of the language in virtually all aspects of their culture is unusually good. Even though one may be sure that the lexicon of a particular language includes a great many ideophones, they are extremely difficult to elicit, and they are often avoided by native speakers when speaking to someone whose competence in their language is clearly at a low level. It is hardly possible to predict the kinds of ideas that may be expressed by ideophones, and in many cases the bare denotative content of what one wishes to say can be conveyed without the connotative characteristics typical of ideophones. In the case of Igbo, I described the use of English forms like 'meow' to one informant, and after some consideration he cited sentences descriptive of noises, largely from the animal kingdom, using something like thirty ideophones. A female missionary of my acquaintance transcribed twenty or more ideophones in another language, which she had overheard spoken by men who were apparently talking about her and who did not realize that she understood quite a bit of their language; checking them later with her informants, she discovered that they all referred to her physical characteristics—many of them highly amusing because the local standards of what constitutes female desirability are in somewhat less than total agreement with those most talked about in our culture, and the entirely admirable and good-natured woman in question admitted to being visibly distinguishable from the latest Hollywood sex symbol. Short of acquiring a high level of competence in a language and laboriously collecting ideophones from conversation, narrative, and vivid description, about all that can be done is to help an informant to become conscious of such forms as a special type or set of types, and have him study his own usage for as many examples as he can think of—which is, of course, exactly what I did for English as a basis for the preceding paragraph.

The term "ideophone" seems to have been first suggested by C. M. Doke; he defined, or at least described, an ideophone as "a vivid representation of an idea in sound. A word, often onomatopoeic, which describes a predicate, qualificative or adverb in respect to manner, colour, smell, action, state or intensity" (Doke 1935, p. 118.). This seems to suggest that ideophones are a grammatical class of words, a type of adverbial, but no formal criterion is given for distinguishing them from other adverbs. In the Bantu languages with which Doke was concerned, the invariable or indeclinable nature of ideophones has often been noted, in contrast with adverbials like those formed with the locative class (16, 17, 18) prefixes; but the languages in question have at least a few other invariable words, such as a term for 'today', which are also adverbial but which one would hardly want to call ideophones. Calling some ideophones onomatopoeic is quite understandable and in some cases perhaps valid, but subjective judgment is often heavily involved; /tùwà tùwà/ may—and is said to—"sound like" the crack of a whip to a speaker of Igbo, but it doesn't to me, though I will readily accept /ùwúù ùwúù/ as genuinely imitative of the cry of an owl. In a category somewhat similar to onomatopoeia, phonaesthemics appears to play a rather minor role in ideophones in African languages, though it is attested. (A phonaestheme is a sound or sequence of sounds recurring in a number of words associated in some way with the same idea; English /sn-/ is a phonaestheme associated with the nose in words like 'sniff, sniffle, snuff, snore, snicker' and perhaps also 'snide, snit', but of course not 'snow, snake'.)

It has also been noted for some languages that ideophones are frequently phonologically anomalous. They may contain phonemes not found in other types of words, or unique sequences of phonemes, and they may be aberrant in respect to the rules of tone that apply to them. Paul Newman (1968, p. 107n) has aptly pointed out, however, that "It should be emphasized that the phonological distinctiveness of ideophones is a property of the set as a whole and not necessarily of each member of that set." That is, some words that one would like to call ideophones may be phonologically normal, and a particular word cannot be identified as an ideophone on purely phonologic grounds in all cases. Yet Newman would like to define ideophones in African languages generally on the basis of phonological and semantic criteria. For Hausa, he defines ideophones purely phonologically, but he is less successful for Tera. Karen Courtenay (1969, pp. 138-54) applies a phonological definition also to Yoruba, in which several different phonotactic patterns are peculiar to different sets of ideophones. If such a phonological definition is possible for a particular language, it should be all means be used; it may well be that phonological anomalies may be diagnostic for many or most languages, though of course the particular anomalies will vary from language to language. Semantic criteria would seem to be extremely difficult if not impossible to apply in any satisfactorily rigid fashion, although we may well have an intuitive impression that ideophones share some vaguely defined semantic characteristics.

William J. Samarin (1965), on the other hand, maintains that ideophones must be defined on a language-specific basis, in terms of grammatical function. He clearly implies that ideophones constitute a morphological class, which may be true for some of the languages with which he has worked; this does not seem to be the case, however, for all languages. Courtenay (1969, p. 138) explicitly says that "Yoruba ideophones can be adverbs, adjectives, or nouns." George Fortune (1962), whose phonosemantic definition of ideophones in Shona does not seem as rigid as one would like, describes them as a subcategory of verbs in that language.

Judging from the literature on ideophones and from my own experience—which is not intensive for any one language but includes a sketchy sampling in a good many—I would suggest that, for African languages as a whole, both phonological and grammatical criteria may be found necessary for defining ideophones. A phonological definition should come first. Then the functions of the ideophones so defined should be studied. If at least some ideophones have a special grammatical function—such as adverbial in unique collocations with particular verbs—it may then be possible to add to the class other forms which share the same grammatical function but which could not be included on phonologic grounds. Other phonologically defined ideophones may be, for example, normal nouns from a grammatical point of view; it would not be possible to add to such a class by applying grammatical criteria, since any form sharing the same function is simply a phonologically normal noun.

Before going farther into the specifics of ideophones in particular languages, it should be added that a spoken ideophone, particularly of the interjectional type, may regularly be accompanied by some activity, such as a gesture, which is not part of the linguistic system as such. In Igbo, the ideophone /kpáṁ-kpàṁ/ is always accompanied by two claps of the hands in time with the pronunciation; the palms of the hands are held vertically, with the right hand higher than the left, and the claps are produced in the process of opposing vertical movements of the hands, like cymbals in a march rhythm. Let these claps be represented by asterisks in the following:

ọ́ 'gwúlá *kpáṁ-*kpàṁ	'it's all-l-l gone; there's not a smidgin left'
à cọ́'ghị́ ṁ íhé 'ọ̀búlà *kpáṁ-*kpàṁ	'I don't want a cotton-pickin' thing'

As might be expected, such paralinguistic phenomena are not very consistently reported, though they are probably far more common than the available sources would suggest. It is reported that Shona has an interjection used as an extremely rude insult, consisting of the syllable [ŋɔ́] accompanied by an unguidental snap—the right thumbnail is simultaneously snapped from behind the upper right cuspid. Entirely paralinguistically, but of very great practical importance for the field worker, it may be added that, almost universally in Africa, noises produced in the labial or dental area are considered highly insulting—noises such as that produced by sucking air between the pursed lips or between the upper teeth, or by a dental click. Don't try to suck out those stringy mango fibers from between your teeth, or you may end up in court; use dental tape instead—or, even better, cut the mango cross-grain and there won't be any fibers.

It has frequently been said that ideophones are at least to some extent idiosyncratic—that is, that individual speakers may make up new ideophones as they feel like it, with the effect of intensifying what has been said, and without any specific relationship between sound and meaning. Such reports seem to be wild exaggerations, based on insufficient or insufficiently scientific observation—

though they may seem plausible if one listens to an expert story teller dramatically punctuate his narrative with seemingly *ad hoc* phonologically anomalous forms. With possible occasional exceptions, ideophones in any language are, like other forms, part of the community-accepted lexicon of arbitrary associations between sound and meaning.

15.5. In many Bantu languages, one type of form commonly included in the category of ideophones is derived from verb roots. There appears to be almost total freedom for such formations—virtually any verb may be the source of such an ideophone. Such forms generally accompany the verbs from which they are derived, and have an adverbial function. They are frequently reduplicated or triplicated. Samarin cites examples from several languages; the following from Mwera, with an intensive or continuative meaning, is typical:[2]

> kujenda jende jende   'to walk far, to keep on walking'

The justifiability of classifying such forms as ideophones may be called into question. I find no evidence that they are phonologically anomalous, as other types of ideophones commonly are. They are, to be sure, distinctive in other ways. Morphologically, unlike almost all other words, they are invariable or indeclinable. Syntactically, their reduplicated or triplicated usage is unique. Semantically, they seem to share some kind of intensive reference. Is all of this sufficient reason to put them in the special category of ideophones, rather than simply calling them adverbs derived from verbs? If they are to be called ideophones, they would at least appear to be a definable subtype.

A somewhat similar phenomenon is found in Igbo, but there is no reason at all to call the forms in question ideophones; they are simply nouns derived from verbs. Such a noun is used as the object of the verb from which it is derived, and may be called a "cognate object." Not all nouns derived from verbs belong in this category. The noun /ńrí/ 'food' is derived from the verb whose infinitive is /íˈrí/ 'eat'; it is frequently used as the object of the verb from which it is derived, as in /íˈrí ńrí/ 'to eat' (without specifying the particular food eaten), but it is used freely in many other combinations as well. The noun /ùtọ́/, having to do with good taste or desirability, is derived from the verb /íˈtọ́/, which is not attested except with the derived noun as object, as in /ọ́ tọ̀rọ̀ ùtọ́/ 'it is delicious'; the noun, however, may also be used after the verb /íˈdị́/ 'be described as' with the same meaning. The derived cognate objects in question are restricted to nouns with the prefix /à- ~ è-/. Their functions have not been fully analyzed, but there is clearly something special about them. The following examples seem to represent three different uses:

> òròmá áhụ̀ cáá ˈácá   'if those oranges are ripe'
> ọ́ kọ̀càrà àkọ́cá   'he cursed'
> háˈcébìrì m̀mírí ˈányị́ ˈécébì 'they limited our water supply'

---

[2] Cited in "Survey of Bantu Ideophones," *African Language Studies. In press.*

The verb in the first of these, /í'cá/, may also be used by itself, as in /òròmá áhù àcáálá/ 'those oranges are ripe (have ripened)'. The use of the cognate object appears to imply a contrast. The statement /òròmá áhù àcáálá/ is neutral; it merely observes that the oranges are ripe, when one might as easily have commented that they are large or expensive. The condition cited above, on the other hand, implies a concern as to whether the oranges are ripe as opposed to unripe. In the case of the second example above, the verb /í'kọ́cá/ can be used with a personal object, in the meaning 'speak abusively to or about', as in /ọ́ kọ̀càrà hà/ 'he cursed them'. If the target of the cursing is not specified, the cognate object is required. In the case of the third example, the verb /í'cébì/ is not attested without the cognate object. Another noun phrase, /m̀mírí 'ányị́/ 'our water', appears between the verb and the cognate object, and the cognate object may perhaps be said to have an adverbial use. It is definitely a noun, however; other obvious nouns are found in the same type of construction, as in the following:

ó tìrì yà ósísí   'he hit him with a stick'

Apart from the deverbal forms usually classified as ideophones in Bantu, as noted above, the same languages appear generally to have a number of other forms which can be treated together in terms of their unique phonological characteristics, and which also have the kinds of semantic peculiarities—however ill-defined they may be—which suggested the term ideophone in the first place. The treatments of ideophones that seem to be on the firmest ground are those which begin with such a phonological definition. Although Courtenay considers her discussion of Yoruba ideophones inconclusive, she gives an explicit justification for her approach—a justification which has very possibly been subconsciously used by students of other languages as a basis for distinguishing a set of forms called ideophones, but which is not otherwise overtly stated. Courtenay (1969, pp. 140-41) mentions that there are several phonological structures unique to what she calls ideophones, and then observes, "If one were to include these unique formatives in the regular morphological classes (i.e., in the class of nouns, verbs, etc.) it would be impossible to reveal the generalities concerning the regular structure of these classes, and thereby weaken the description of general phonological processes in the language." As an example, she cites the fact that normal Yoruba nouns have, or can be derived from, the structure VCV(CV). Nouns such as /šẹ̀kẹ̀rẹ̀/ 'rattling musical instrument' and /kẹ̀lẹ̀bẹ̀/ 'throat-phlegm' do not conform to this structure, and in addition have structural peculiarities of their own: all the vowels are identical, and have the same tone. Such forms are ideophones—in this case, specifically ideophonic nouns. Among the phonological characteristics unique to ideophones, she also cites longer sequences of segments than are found in regular formatives, immediate sequences of vowels in other than initial position, identical or regularly patterned tone sequences, and various types of reduplication and triplication. Twelve structural types of ideophones are listed, showing one or more of these characteristics in various combinations. As has been noted for ideophones in other languages, some Yoruba ideophones appear only in unique collocations, and in general they seem to be semantically pictures-que. For some types, reduplication is optional, and has an intensive force. One type, represented by fourteen cited examples, has the specific semantic property of suggesting some kind of irregularity, often but not exclusively pejorative. These are all segmentally full reduplications of two-syllable sequences, in all cases but one with the same vowel in each syllable, and with the unique tone sequence high-mid-low-mid. Some of these are:

kpálakpàla	'nonsense'	šákašàka	'shaggy'
wókowòko	'zigzag'	játijàti	'worthless'

Forms like the above, and many other Yoruba ideophones as well, would probably be immediately suspected of being ideophones by a student of other African languages exposed to them for the first time. Such reduplication and such a tone sequence, which seems to be a kind of echo, seem to be exceedingly widespread in ideophones, at least in West African Niger-Congo languages. Other Yoruba ideophones, however, are defined as such because they are phonologically anomalous in Yoruba, though comparable forms might be perfectly normal in other languages. Examples of such are /fúú/ 'suddenly', or /kíún/ 'a tiny bit', or /tòò/, used only after the verb /ké/ 'shout', the combination meaning 'shout at the top of the lungs'.

The phonological definitions for the various types and subtypes of Yoruba ideophones are for the most part highly specific. Each of one group of six, for example, has four syllables with identical vowels and all low tones; the first and third consonants are labial or velar (including doubly articulated stops), the second is /r/, and the fourth is /t/ or /d/. E.g.,

gbàràgàdà	'wide open'	kòròbòtò	'fat'
fèrègèdè	'broad'	bìrìkìtì ~ kìrìbìtì	'round'

Another type has the structure CVVCV, with identical vowels and tones, and with only /r/ as the second consonant; specifically this type reduplicates by suffixing only the first CV. E.g.,

gbiiri	'continuously'	:	gbiirigbi

Other CVVCV ideophones have identical tones, but not necessarily identical vowels, and a variety of second consonants; these reduplicate by complete repetition. E.g.,

tùùlù	'puffy'	:	tùùlù tùùlù
(sòrò) jééjé	'(speak) softly'	:	(sòrò) jééjé jééjé
(še) kpéékí	'(fit) accurately'	:	(še) kpéékí kpéékí

A variety of types of reduplication may be seen in the following, some of which reduplicate further by complete repetition as indicated; each of these is only one of a larger set:

kpéńkpé	'small'	:	kpéńkpé kpéńkpé
gbè̀ngbè̀	'large'	:	gbè̀ngbè̀ gbe̅ngbe̩
kòkòrò	'insect'		
šókíšòkìšókí	'in little drops'	:	šókíšòkìšókí šókíšòkìšókí
kpò̩tò̩kpó̩tò̩	'mud'		
fákáfìkì	'chug-chug' (of train)	:	fákáfìkì fákáfìkì
jàgídíjàga̅	'violent, violence'		

Courtenay does not specify whether repeated ideophones are or may be separated by pause, as suggested by word division written in some of the above. It would seem likely that they may. Some of the glosses given above are also undoubtedly less than perfect. In addition to ideophones with meanings such as 'small' and 'large', there are phonologically normal forms with similar meanings; the ideophones in all probability give a colorful impression to the native-speaking hearer, an impression which is difficult to isolate and even more difficult to represent in translation.

In Yoruba ideophones, unlike those of many other languages, there seems to be no use of sounds not found in the rest of the language. Apart from the number and types of syllables as noted above, the only phonotactic peculiarity found in ideophones is the permissibility of non-final nasalized vowels. Ideophones are primarily distinguished by their morpheme and word structure.

To her list of ideophones of various types, Courtenay appends a set of "restricted adverbs." These are regular in their phonological structure, but resemble a number of ideophones in usage, appearing only in unique collocations. These forms are reduplications of a single syllable, as in the phrase /sọ šášá/ 'speak clearly'. The existence of such a set of forms, which appear to share the rather vague but intuitively perceptible semantic qualities of ideophones, suggests that in other languages also the borderline between the normal lexicon and ideophones may not be sharply defined in all respects. Yet no one can quarrel with giving special treatment to the types of forms described above. And the label "ideophone," though not as yet formally defined for African languages in general, seems entirely appropriate.

15.6. Ideophones are not confined to the Niger-Congo languages. Newman (1968, pp. 107-17) defines and describes ideophones in two Chadic languages, Hausa and Tera. In each case, he starts with a phonological definition. For Hausa, this appears to be airtight: ideophones are forms which have final consonants. For Tera, the definition does not appear to be as satisfactory. Some initial consonants found elsewhere in the language do not appear in ideophones, but those which do appear are normal. Some types of ideophones show reduplication or special phonotactics, but other types appear not to violate normal phonotactics. There is "a high incidence of consonants in word final position"—in fact, all of the examples cited have final consonants—but at least some final consonants appear in the normal lexicon as well. Newman also speaks of "expressive intonation," or "expressive tone and stress," but does not say whether this invariably accompanies all ideophones. It would appear that some types of ideophones can be unambiguously defined in phonological terms, but Newman may have included some other forms on the basis of their similarity in grammatical function or perhaps their semantic characteristics.

There are some interesting differences between Hausa and Tera in the grammar of ideophones. In Hausa, ideophones appear in unique collocations; in Tera, they are used more freely, limited only by the bounds of semantic compatability. Some Hausa ideophones are used only after an adjective, and serve to intensify the meaning of the adjectives. Others are used only after verbs; these are of two semantic types, verbal intensifiers and descriptive adverbs, which are also formally distinguished by the range of syntactic constructions in which they may occur. In Tera, ideophones are either adjectives or adverbs; the adverbs are of two syntactic types, distinguished by the range of constructions in which they may occur. In addition, ideophonic adjectives and adverbs in Tera are distinguished by their canonical forms. Adjectives are either reduplicated forms of the type CVC-CVC, or trisyllabic forms with a restricted selection of final consonants and with identical vowels in at least the first and third syllables; adverbs have the structure CVCVC, some with and some without reduplication, or the structure CVC. A number of the Tera ideophonic adverbs are descriptive of sound or motion.

Newman appends to his discussion an observation and suggestion that certainly deserve further study in connection with ideophones in other languages: "An important syntactic feature of ideophonic descriptive-adverbs shared by Hausa and Tera is the tendency to limit these words to affirmative declarative sentences. I would suggest that the restriction of a subset of ideophones to certain basic sentence types is probably a common syntactic feature of ideophones in all African languages." This is another example, and an excellent one, of the kind of detail that may well underlie, subconsciously, the feeling that almost all students of African languages have had concerning the distinctive character of ideophones.

15.7. My own work on Kpelle has never included a systematic analysis of ideophones, in spite of the fact that my study of the language has been fairly thorough in other respects, and my competence at one time extended to complete ease in most conversational situations and in public speaking, and to being mistaken for a native speaker on a cloudy, moonless night. I have heard a number of apparent ideophones that I had no opportunity to record at the time, but have recorded relatively few. At the time of my first major work on the language, I was only vaguely aware of the existence of such forms that might be investigated as a set, and it did not occur to me to try to devise a technique for discovering them apart from accidentally running into them. A few forms I would now like to call ideophones were elicited as equivalents of English adjectives in limited situations; one turned up first in a proverb. The very limitation of the available data, however, makes it interesting to consider the direction in which it appears to be leading.

Kpelle roots are typically of the structures CV(ŋ), CVV(ŋ), and CVCV(ŋ). The structures CVVCV(ŋ) and CVCVV(ŋ), although uncommon, must apparently also be considered part of the normal phonotactics for roots. Roots with three or more syllable-initial consonants, and forms showing full reduplication except for a final /ŋ/, may tentatively be considered aberrant. Further study reveals, however, that virtually all roots with more than two syllable-initial consonants are free nouns, and these show none of the semantic peculiarities typical of ideophones in other languages. Many of these are adopted words, as /ˈⁱɔŋkɔ́rɔŋ/ 'papaya' and /ˈkaménɛ/ 'orange' from Gola, or /sɔ́ɓeli/ 'shovel' from English. Others are probably also adopted words, and some are very possibly originally compounds which can no longer be analyzed as such. Quite possibly none of them is an original Kpelle root. In the present state of the language, however, it is quite possible to include these forms as having a normal phonotactic structure for free nouns only.

Apart from these free nouns, only one recorded form with three syllable-initial consonants remains to be considered. It is recorded in only two expressions, in both cases followed by a noun with the low tone replacive characteristic of compounds; in one of these two expressions, it appears with full reduplication. The expressions are:

> kámelaŋ-kpɛ̀lɛe-wòo   'learnèd Kpelle' (Kpelle characterized by many allusions to tradition and legend, metaphors, etc., difficult for young people to understand, only rarely spoken by myself)
>
> kamelaŋ-kámelaŋ-kpùnəɓeli   'misshapen cocoyams' (if you plant them, you dig them, the proverb says)

In the first of the above, /kámelaŋ/ could readily be analyzed as a noun, except for the fact that it is not attested in any independent use. In the second expression, the reduplication is abnormal. I did not, and do not remember if I tried to, record it in a predicative usage. Semantically, it is a typical ideophone. Perhaps there may be other forms similar to this to constitute one type of ideophone.

The remaining aberrant forms, somewhat over thirty of which are recorded, are full reduplications as far as their segmental structure is concerned. The two parts of each form are tonally independent—and in a few cases may be incorrectly transcribed. The tonal combinations appear to be lexically determined. A few of these reduplicated forms are reduplications of roots otherwise attested in the same or a similar meaning. It might be possible to exclude these from the category of ideophones on this morphological ground. Most of these are recorded after nouns, and appear to function as attributive adjectivals. The last two of the following are used adverbially. These are:

pɛlɛ-pɛlɛ	'small'	tɛi-tɛi	'one or a few at a time'
pɔlɔ-pɔlɔ	'old, ancient'	kpéni-kpéni	'in vain, for nothing, in fun'
tuɛ-túɛ	'the first'		
fólɔ-fólɔ	'the very first'	wɔ́lɔ-wɔ́lɔ	'forever'
tɔnɔ-tɔ́nɔ	'one by one'		

The remaining reduplicated forms are not derived from stems used independently. These can be called ideophones without hesitation. Several of these are free nouns, including a number referring to physical disorders and insects—a phenomenon noted for ideophonic nouns in Yoruba and other languages also:

ɓola-ɓólaŋ	'hernia'
kérɛ-kérɛ	'a mild form of ringworm'
mɛɛ-mɛ̂ɛ	'rainy season foot itch' (apparently of fungus origin)
kpai-kɛ̂ɛ-kɛ̀ɛ	'ringworm of the scalp'
kpíli-kpíli	'bedbugs'
ŋwɛi-ŋwɛi	'yellow-jacket (bee)'
'fɔ̃-'fɔ̃	'bee (sp.)'
kwéi-kwéiŋ	'bee (sp.)'
ŋîna-ŋîna	'mosquito'
ɓóŋ-ɓòŋ	'elf' (or similar mischievous being)
mèlɛ-mèlɛ	'sheet glass, mirror'
wála-wála	'power, authority, strength'
kpɔ̀lɔ-kpɔ̀lɔ	'female tribal initiate'

A few similar forms are relational nouns:

-péɣɛ-péɣɛ	'lowest rib' (or that area)
-wólo-wòloŋ	'scab'
-fɔ̃lɔ-fɔ̃lɔ	'lungs'
-ɓele-ɓéleŋ	'corner of edge'

A third type of reduplicated form is represented by only eight recorded examples, but I would be very much surprised if there are not a great many more in the language. These are all characterized by having low tone throughout, which is not a normal tone for stems in Kpelle. The first of the examples below is recorded attributively after a noun; it is not known whether any or all of the others can be so used, but it seems rather likely. All are recorded in a construction indicating predication, but unlike predicates involving nouns or adjectivals. They are used exactly like locative adverbials in expressions simply stating the location of something. That is, a predication like /'káa lèɣɛ-lèɣɛ/ 'it is soft' is like /'káa nãa/ 'it is there', not like /'káa à ɓóa/ 'it is a knife'. In the following examples, a gloss like 'soft (of food)' is not to be taken as meaning that the form cannot be used for any other substance, but merely that I recorded it only in that context. These ideophones are:

kpèya-kpèya	'large, important'
lèɣɛ-lèɣɛ	'soft (of food)'
pùtɛ-pùtɛ	'soft (of ground)'
nèŋɛ-nèŋɛ	'smooth (of wood surface)'
kpɔ̀lɔwɔ-kpɔ̀lɔwɔ	'smooth (of wood surface)'
kàla-kàla	'rough (of wood surface)'
kpèrɛ-kpèrɛ	'soft (from being cooked')'
pùtu-pùtu	'scattered around haphazardly'

I have not recorded, but have certainly heard, ideophones of the interjective type, particularly some which are imitative of or represent specific sounds. If the sound described is continuing or repeated (unlike the single "bang" of a gun), the ideophone is generally repeated at least three times, with a pause after each occurrence. I cannot be sure, but seem to recall, that such ideophones sometimes contain segmental sounds not typical of the regular phonemic system. They are frequently accompanied by unusual vocal effects, such as a hushed voice, abnormally high pitch, or falsetto voice. There are several points in folk stories which I have recorded where I would rather expect such an ideophone. An adequate reason for it not to be included is that the stories were dictated sentence by laborious sentence, not in the context or style that lends itself to the addition of optional dramatic sound effects.

15.8. I have not as yet defined ideophones in Igbo to my own satisfaction. Verb root morphemes have the structure CV. Noun root morphemes are commonly the same structure; a typical full noun has the structure VCV or NCV, with a prefix. There are, however, many nouns with a prefix followed by two to four syllables. There seems to be no strong motivation for including all of these in a category of ideophones. As in Kpelle, the phonotactics of noun root structure may be considered more varied than that of verb root structure. There is some reason to believe that some such nouns are the result of derivational processes which probably cannot be adequately defined unless relevant evidence turns up in related languages. Some others of these nouns are clearly adopted words. Some types of reduplication or echoing are found, but forms like the following cannot be neatly classified or characterized, and it is dubious whether they should be called ideophones:

ànyìnyà	'horse'	ŋgbírígbá	'bell'
árírí	'millipede'	ìmìrìkítí	'the majority'
ḿmùmùwárì	'firefly'	ọ́kpọ́gọ́rọ́	'lock'

Some bird names belong in this category, and are certainly interesting sounding, and even onomatopoeic. Still, they cannot be concisely differentiated from all other nouns, though reduplication must be noted; a considerable majority of the bird names recorded are normal. The nouns in question are:

ikwìghìkwíghí	'owl'	òkóòkó	'parrot'
(~ òkwúkwú'ú)		kpálákúkú	'pigeon'

Some nouns of a type described in 9.6, referring to qualities and here glossed as if they were adjectives, show a peculiar type of reduplication. A VCV sequence (which in only one case appears apart from these forms) is fully reduplicated with a consonant, /d/, /l/, or /n/, between the two parts. In one case, an NCV sequence is similarly reduplicated, with /dá/ between the two parts; in other cases, NCV sequences are simply fully reduplicated. The tones are all high. This type of descriptive noun, however, includes other members which show no particular phonological peculiarity, though they happen to have two-syllable roots. Yet there is some reason to consider the reduplicated forms a type of ideophone, particularly in light of the three similar alternative forms of the first listed below; some speakers use two or all three of these freely, though the variation may originally have been dialectal. Forms of this type are:

óbódóbó	'wide'	ńtí-ńtí	'a little'
(~ íbédíbé, ábádíbá)		ŋ́kpó-ŋ́kpó	'short of stature'
ógólógó	'long, tall'	ŋ́kéré-ŋ́kéré	'thin, fine (not
(~ ákánáká)			coarse)'
ḿbádáḿbá	'wide, flat'		

A few expressions for colors may be considered ideophonic. These show full reduplication and are derived by special tonal rules. They are:

úhyé-'úhyé	'brownish-red'
ḿmé-'ḿmé	'bright red'
(~ òbàrá-òbàrà, in northern dialects)	
èdó-èdò	'yellow'

I can think of only one form that might be called an ideophonic adverb; it is /gbùrùgbúrù/ 'in a circle, around and around'.

The most serious problem in handling the types of data mentioned so far is to work out an adequate definition of ideophonic nouns of other than the descriptive type. The candidates for such a category include a number of nouns which are in no way semantically unusual. For Igbo, it may be preferable to state the recognizable or apparent types of noun derivation, and leave everything else to the phonotactics of noun roots. This suggests the possibility that the concept of ideophones may have been overworked in some other language studies.

Apart from the above, Igbo has a number of ideophones of the interjective type. Almost all of the recorded examples are imitative or representative of specific sounds. This does not mean that there may not be many more with other semantic references; it may only reflect the fact that these were supplied by an informant after I had asked about expressions comparable to the English 'the gun went bang'. Of the thirty or so forms recorded, one—and the only one recorded prior to the deliberate attempt to find such ideophones—is used attributively after a noun. It has got to be my favorite ideophone in any African language. The noun /úgbó/ refers broadly to any vehicle in which (not on which) one can ride—car, cart, train, canoe, steamer, plane, or undoubtedly space capsule. A vehicle used on the water may be specified by the phrase /úgbó ḿ'mírí/. Some years ago, slow and elderly side-wheel (or were they stern-wheel?) steamers used to ply the Niger river, and they had to labor pretty hard to move upstream. Such a steamer was /úgbó ḿ'mírí 'túḿ-túḿ-túḿ/.

Other interjective ideophones are used after a predicate. They are often preceded by a slight pause, which may be considered a phonological peculiarity distinguishing these as a class from all other words in the language; the phenomenon may be indicated in writing by a colon. Those which represent continuing or repeated sounds are repeated two to four times, with intervening pauses. Several of them have a final syllabic /m/, which is also found, though much less commonly, in other words which one would not want to classify as ideophones. Many of these ideophones have peculiar phonotactics, but the structures do not lend themselves to a simple classification. There are no phonemes other than those of the regular phonemic system, and the only violation of normal rules for immediate phonemic sequences is abnormal duration. When I recorded one form, representative of the sound of a cannon, I transcribed it as /kìm̀m̀/; the informant, who was watching me from across the table, instructed me, "Put one more to it." Some of these may be accompanied by unusual vocal effects, particularly hushed or tense voice. The following are the ideophones of this type recorded, in the sentences as given to me, with no indication of possible freedom in the preceding predicates; "X" is used as a gloss where necessary:

úgòló ọ̀mà nà ètí : ŋwọ̀ọ́, ŋwọ̀ọ́. ŋwọ̀ọ́.
　　'A crow (of a small variety) calls "caw, caw, caw".'
áwọ̀ nà ètí : wọ̀ọ́, wọ̀ọ́, wọ̀ọ́.
　　'A frog (?) calls "X, X, X".'
àkị̀rị́ nà ètí : tụ̀rụ́ tàá, tụ̀rụ́ tàá.
　　'A frog calls "X, X".'
ìkwìghìkwíghí nà ètí : ùwúù, ùwúù.
　　'An owl calls "who-o-o, who-o-o".'
ŋ́kị́'tá tìrì ŋ́kpụ́ : húyị̀, húyị̀.
　　'A dog called "X, X".' (May refer to barking, but most dogs in Igbo-
　　land bark very little.)
ŋwá 'óló'gbó tìrì ŋ́kpụ́ : mìá'ŋwụ́.
　　'A kitten called "meow".'
ŋwá é'wú tìrì ŋ́kpụ́ : m̀má'á, m̀má'á.
　　'A young goat called "ba-a-a, ba-a-a".' (Also of a sheep.)
ị̀gbè ọ̀kụ́kọ̀ tìrì : kwọ́ kwọ́ kwọ́ kwọ́, úmụ̀ yá 'kpákọ̀rọ̀.
　　'When the hen clucked "kpɔ kpɔ kpɔ kpɔ", her chicks gathered.'
ọ̀kụ́kọ̀ tìrì ŋ́kpụ́ : kọ̀ kọ̀ kọ̀ kọ̀ tụ̀á, ị̀gbè égbé byàrà í'bú ŋwá 'yá.
　　'The hen cackled "X X X X" when the kite came to carry away her
　　chick.' (Also after laying an egg.)
òbù nà ékù : ọ̀rúkú tùú, tùú, tùú.
　　'A coucal cries (lit. 'blows') "X X X X".'
ọ̀kụ́kọ̀ bèrè ákwá : ọ̀kụ̀ kóró òkòóò.
　　'The rooster crowed (lit. 'cried') "cockadoodle doo".'
èkpètè nà ádà : kpèghèm̀bụ́, kpèghèm̀bụ́.
　　'A (variety of single-headed) drum goes (lit. 'falls') "X X".'
égbè áhụ̀ dàrà : cáká fòm.
　　'The gun (a musket in this case) went "bang".'
égbè áhụ̀ dàrà : kìm̀m̀.
　　'The gun (a cannon in this case) went "boom".'

ṁmí'rí nà ádà : pèṁ pèṁ pèṁ.
'The water is dripping, "drip, drip, drip".'

ọ́ nà àgá íjè : kọ̀yì, kọ̀yì, kọ̀yì.
'He's walking "clomp, clomp, clomp".' (In leather shoes or boots, as a soldier.)

ŋ̀gbè ọ́ pyàrà yà ụ̀tàrì, ọ́ nà ádà : tụ̀wà, tụ̀wà.
'When he whipped him, it went "crack, crack".'

ŋ́kwụ́ dàrà n'àlà : dìṁ.
'A bunch of palm nuts fell on the ground, "X".'

òròmá dàrà n'àlà : kpìṁ.
'An orange fell on the ground, "X".'

ọ̀kụ́kọ̀ nà àbọ́ ábụ́bọ́ : ékpékéré kpàcí.
'The chicken is scratching, "X X".'

òké gbàghàrìrì n'ọ́hyá : yághá yághá.
'The rat ran around in the bush : "X X".' (In dry leaves.)

ùdèlè békwàsìrì n'élú ụ́lọ̀ : jàghàṁ.
'The vulture landed on the roof, "X".'

ńnụ̀nụ̀ nà àgbá ọ́'sọ́ n'ụ́zọ̀ : wéréwéré.
'A bird is running down the road, "X".' (As when a bicycle comes along.)

ágwọ́ 'gáfèrè n'ụ́zọ̀ : wéréréré.
'The snake slithered across the road, "X".

ọ́ gbàrà ọ́sọ́ n'ímé ḿ'mírí: tákpá tákpá.
'He ran through the water (a puddle), "splash splash".'

égbè í'gwé zèrè : gbúùm.
'The thunder rumbled, "X".'

There is one instance of a normal short sentence being used as an interjective ideophone; the situation is after bush has been burned for a farm:

égbé nà ètí : nyé 'ḿ ń'né ṁ.
'The kite calls, "Give me my mother".'

There are two instances of interjective ideophones referring to appearance; they are recorded as different in tone, which I hope was not a case of neglecting to finish the marking. There is also one instance referring to a situation. These are:

ḿ'má à cáfụ̀rụ̀ : bárìṁ.
'This knife is bright shining new.'

àmụ̀mà gbùrù : bárịḿ.
'The lightning flashed, "X".'

nọ̀ọ́ : ńsé ńsé ńsé.
'Don't be meddlesome.', 'Don't get involved.' (/nọ̀ọ́/ is an imperative, 'stay'.)

Perhaps this discussion can be concluded with my own definition of ideophones: ideophones are those words that are such fun to use.

15.9. A discussion of semantic ranges, the definition of lexical entries, cannot in the nature of the case be systematic, and it may seem trivial to one with some sophistication about language. A few examples of unexpected semantic ranges may, however, be instructive to two types of people—those who are attempting to learn an African language after a minimum of technical training and who are too easily satisfied with a superficial explanation, and the new breed of advanced student who is immersed in the complexities of contemporary theoretical linguistics but learns little about the realities of languages in their daily use.

At least a few decades ago, but hopefully not any more, American missionaries in Liberia could be heard making a remark like "These Kpelle people are so grateful that we are here. Whenever we go through a village or past a farm, they tell us 'Thank you'." And indeed, tribespeople who speak a little English use exactly those words under such circumstances. Warm and hospitable as the Kpelle people may be, however, gratitude has nothing to do with the message intended. The English expression 'Thank you' has uncritically been used as a translation of a Kpelle expression /í sɛγê/ (to one person; to more than one it is /ká sɛγê/) in all of its varied usages. The Kpelle expression is used, among other things, after receiving assistance, a service, or a gift—circumstances under which we would commonly say 'Thank you'. It is also used, however, as an expression of congratulation for work well done, to parents when a baby is born, or on the occasion of any pleasant event. And it is used as a greeting to someone at work, or as a word of welcome. Thinking of 'Thank you' as an appropriate translation under all of these circumstances is a distortion of Kpelle culture. The range of ideas conveyed by /í sɛγê/ in the many situations in which it is used can far better be represented by 'Hey, this is great!'

Expressions with a comparable versatility are common throughout West Africa. It should be expected that greetings and daily amenities in almost any language must be understood in terms of the situations in which they are used, rather than in terms of translation. (The same is ultimately true, of course, of any word in any language, but in many cases translation gives a reasonably accurate picture.) Greeting formalities range from simple exchanges comparable to our "How are you?" "Fine." to ceremonies taking up to fifteen minutes and involving special postures including kneeling and even lying prostrate. It is unfortunately impossible to represent in writing the interminable exchanges, in Bariba, of monosyllables like /fɔ/ and /mm/, with substantive words of greeting and questions about each other's well-being substituted from time to time, all in an inexorable metronomic rhythm; a five-word question has to be compressed into the same time as a single /fɔ/. When will well-meaning individuals, greeting card companies, and Hollywood entrepreneurs ever stop calling me and my colleagues to ask how to say 'Hello' or 'Merry Christmas' or 'Dear Sir' in eighteen African languages? (Assuming, of course, that they realize that there are languages other than Swahili in Africa. One Hollywood character, looking for a title for a planned film, asked me how to say "Sex!" in Swahili, obviously thinking of all the connotations of the English word; deadpan, I read to him from my

English-Swahili dictionary: "Sex: *hali ya kuwa kiume au kike*"— which being interpreted is 'the quality of being male or female'.)

What is done with the English expression 'Thank you' as described above might be called "under-translation". Another example of it, very widespread in West Africa, is found in the common reports that, in this or that language, you 'hear' an odor. You do not, of course. In many languages, however, there is a single verb for perceiving a sound or an odor—and in some languages such a verb includes also perceiving a flavor or a tactile sensation, 'perceive by other than sight'. Similarly, Africans do not talk about 'drinking' a cigarette, but many languages have a single verb covering the range of 'drink' and 'suck on'.

On the other hand, words may have more specific uses than we are accustomed to. In Igbo, the verb /í'rí/ corresponds to 'eat' if the object is /ńrí/ 'food' or almost any soft food. If the object is anything chewy or crisp—including meat, fowl, and fish, though good fish properly cooked in palm oil "melts in the mouth" —the verb used is /í'tá/. If licking or sucking is prominently involved, as in sucking on an orange or eating icecream, the verb used is /í'rá/. This sort of situation presents a more serious problem for the learner; he has to learn to incorporate more in his vocabulary than he expected to. Even finer distinctions are often made, as one might expect, in technical vocabulary which the non-African learner may have much less occasion to use; in the Southern Bantu languages, for example, there are scores of specific lexical units—ideophones, if I am not mistaken—for various cattle colorings and markings; a single word may mean something like 'brown with a white spot on the left flank'.

It is sometimes said that African languages do not have general terms for large categories, but only specific terms for members of such categories. Such observations are usually gross exaggerations, and unfortunately seem to be intended to suggest that there is something "primitive" about African languages. I know of no language that does not have general terms such as 'animal', 'bird', 'fish', 'snake', and even 'monkey'. In Kpelle, however, I have learned and almost totally forgotten about twenty words for various species of ants, but there is no general term for 'ant', though there is a more general term for all creeping insects. Furthermore, termites are never confused with ants, nor chimpanzees with monkeys, as is common among speakers of English. It is totally unfair to say that generalization is not typical of African languages; is is entirely true, and significant for the learner, that the generalizations may not be the same as ours.

Greater generalization—such as covering the spectrum of colors with fewer labels than we use—must not be construed as implying that speakers of such a language cannot perceive finer distinctions than they generally talk about. Any of us can perceive a wide variety of colors and sizes in the remarkable range of flowers lumped together under the name "crysanthemum"; in fact, I have long marveled that only one term is used, by the same flower-lovers who pettily distinguish jonquils from daffodils—as far as I am concerned, the wide variety of perceptibly different flowers that continually beautify the surroundings of my house, putting Solomon's glory to shame, are more conveniently referred to as roses and other non-tulips. In Kpelle, a single word /kpolo/—which may, to be sure, be modified to specify members of the category—may by itself refer to salt, soap (a product of lye and oil), lye, or baking soda; the word clearly means 'sodium', though with no implication that it originated with laboratory analysis. It should go without saying that this does not mean that a Kpelle tribesman would be satisfied to sprinkle lye on his rice. Whoever first said it, it should be constantly remembered that "words do not equal words."

It is entirely fitting that this work should conclude with a striking example supported by data provided by the great master of them all, J. G. Christaller. In his monumental *Dictionary of the Asante and Fante Language* (1881, second edition 1933), six full double-column pages are devoted to the entry *dì*, which just about any speaker of Akan will tell you means 'eat'. Christaller divides its uses into twenty-six major categories, with a total of one hundred ten subcategories. By way of introduction, he gives an underlying meaning '*to take (in the hands)* and *to handle*, or *to use, make use of, employ*', to which he hastily adds that it is used also, and in fact more commonly, with abstract nouns to express an abstract activity. I have attempted to sum up its uses under the geneal definition 'partake of or participate in'. It is indeed the general word for 'eat', but with other objects it refers among other things to using up or wasting money, taking a day off, having sexual relations with someone, accepting a bribe, inheriting goods, winning a victory, defeating an opponent, playing a game, holding an office, enduring suffering, making a bargain, living in some specified way, and so on at considerable length. A language has not been well studied until the nature of such semantic ranges, if not an exhaustive list of all recordable collocations, has been noted.

References

Abraham, R. C. 1940a. *A dictionary of the Tiv language*. London: Crown Agents for the Colonies.

———. 1940b. *The principles of Tiv*. London: Crown Agents for the Colonies.

———. 1941. *A modern grammar of spoken Hausa*. London: Crown Agents for the Colonies.

———. 1967. *The principles of Ibo*. University of Ibadan, Institute of African Studies, Occasional Publication No. 4.

Andrzejewski, B. W. 1964. *The declensions of Somali nouns*. London: University of London School of Oriental and African Studies.

Ansre, Gilbert. 1966. "The verbid—a caveat to 'serial verbs'." *Journal of West African Languages* 3: 29-32.

Armstrong, Lilias E. 1934. "The phonetic structure of Somali." *Mitteilungen des Seminars für orientalische Sprachen* 37: 116-61.

Armstrong, Robert G. 1968. "Yala (Ikom): a terraced-level language with three tones." *Journal of West African Languages* 5: 49-58.

Arnott, D. W. 1960. "Some features of the nominal class system of Fula in Nigeria, Dahomey, and Niger." *Afrika und Übersee* 43: 241-78.

———. 1964. "Downstep in the Tiv verbal system." *African Language Studies* 5: 34-51.

Ashton, E. O. 1944. *Swahili grammar*. London: Longmans.

Bamgboṣe, Ayọ. 1965. "Assimilation and contraction in Yoruba." *Journal of West African Languages* 2: 21-27.

Bargery, G. P. 1934. *A Hausa-English dictionary and English-Hausa vocabulary*. London: Oxford University Press.

Berry, Jack, and Nii Amon Kotei. 1969. *An introductory course in Ga*. Washington: Department of Health, Education, and Welfare (Office of Education).

Bird, Charles S. 1971. "Observations on initial consonant change in Southwestern Mande." In *Papers in African Linguistics*, edited by Chin-Wu Kim and Herbert Stahlke, pp. 153-74. Edmonton and Champaign: Linguistic Research, Inc.

Bleek, D. F. 1927. "The distribution of the Bushman languages in South Africa." In *Festschrift Meinhof*, pp. 55-64. Hamburg: Friederichsen.

———. 1929. *Comparative vocabularies of Bushman languages*. Publication of the School of African Life and Language (University of Cape Town). Cambridge.

Bleek, W. H. I. 1858. *The library of . . . Sir George Grey, K. C. B.: Philology*, *vol. 1, pt. 2*. London: Trübner.

Bloomfield, Leonard. 1942. *Outline guide for the practical study of foreign languages*. Baltimore: Waverly Press for the Linguistic Society of America.

Bryan, Margaret A. 1959. "The T/K languages: a new substratum." Africa 29: 1-21.

Carrell, Patricia L. 1970. *A transformational grammar of Igbo*. West African Language Monographs, No. 8. Cambridge: The University Press, 1964.

Christaller, J. G. 1875. *A grammar of the Asante and Fante language called Tshi*. Basel. Reprinted by the Gregg Press.

——. 1881. *Dictionary of the Asante and Fante language called Tshi*. Second edition, 1933. Basel: Basel Evangelical Missionary Society.

Cole, Desmond T. 1955. *Introduction to Tswana grammar*. London and Capetown: Longmans, Green.

——. 1967. *Some features of Ganda linguistic structure*. Johannesburg: Witwatersrand University Press.

——. 1971. "The History of African linguistics to 1945", in *Current trends in linguistics*, Vol. 7, edited by Thomas A Sebeok, pp. 1-29. The Hague, Paris: Mouton.

Cook, Thomas L. 1969. "The Efik Consonant System". Manuscript of paper presented at the Linguistics Seminar, University of Ibadan.

Courtenay, Karen Ruth. 1969. *A generative phonology of Yoruba*. Doctoral dissertation (1968), University of California, Los Angeles. Ann Arbor: University Microfilms.

Crabb, David W. 1965. *Ekoid Bantu languages of Ogoja*. West African Language Monographs, No. 4. Cambridge: The University Press.

Dalby, David. 1965. "The Mel languages." *African Language Studies* 6: 1-17.

——. 1966. "Levels of relationship in the comparative study of African languages." *African Language Studies* 7: 71-79.

——. 1970. "Reflections on the classification of African languages." *African Language Studies* 11: 147-71.

Doke, Clement. 1935. *Bantu linguistic terminology*. London: Longmans, Green.

Dunn, Ernest F. 1968. *An introduction to Bini*. African Language Monograph No. 9. East Lansing: Michigan State University (African Studies Center).

Fivaz, Derek. 1969. *Shona morphophonemics and morphosyntax*. Doctoral thesis, University of the Witwatersrand.

Fortune, G. 1955. *An analytical grammar of Shona*. London and Capetown: Longmans, Green.

——. 1962. *Ideophones in Shona*. London: Oxford University Press.

Gleason, H. A. 1961. *An introduction to descriptive linguistics*. Revised edition. New York: Holt, Rinehart, and Winston.

Green, M. M. 1949. "The classification of West African tone languages: Igbo and Efik." *Africa* 19: 213-19.

Green, M. M., and G. E. Igwe. 1963. *A descriptive grammar of Igbo*. London: Oxford University Press; Berlin: Akademie-Verlag.

Greenberg, Joseph H. 1955. *Studies in African linguistic classification*. New Haven: Compass Publishing Co.

———. 1963. *The languages of Africa*. Indiana University Research Center in Anthropology, Folklore, and Linguistics, Publication No. 25. *International Journal of American Linguistics* 29.1, part 2.

Gregerson, Edgar A. 1970. "Kongo-Saharan." Manuscript.

Guthrie, Malcolm. 1948. *The classification of the Bantu languages*. London: Oxford University Press for the International African Institute.

———. 1962. "Bantu origins: A tentative new hypothesis." *Journal of African Languages* 1: 9-21.

Hancock, Ian F. 1971. "West Africa and the Atlantic creoles." In *The English language in West Africa*, edited by John Spencer. London: Longmans. Pp. 113-22.

Harding, Deborah Ann. 1966. *The phonology and morphology of Chinyanja*. Doctoral dissertation, University of California, Los Angeles.

Hilders, J. H., and J. C. D. Lawrence. 1956. *An introduction to the Ateso language*. Kampala: Eagle Press.

Hodge, Carleton T. 1947. *An outline of Hausa grammar*. Language Dissertation 41. *Language* 23.4, supplement.

Hodge, Carleton T., and Helen E. Hause. 1944. "Hausa tone." *Journal of the American Oriental Society* 64: 51-52.

Hulstaert, G. 1938. *Praktische grammatica van het Lonkundo (Lomongo)*. Antwerp: De Sikkel.

Hyman, Larry M. 1970. "How concrete is phonology?" *Language* 46: 58-76.

Hyman, Larry M., and Erhard F. K. Voeltz. 1971. "The linguistic status of Bamileke." In *Papers in African Linguistics*, edited by Chin-Wu Kim and Herbert Stahlke. Champaign and Edmonton: Linguistic Research, Inc. Pp. 55-70.

Innes, Gordon. 1962. *A Mende grammar*. London: Macmillan.

International Phonetic Association. 1949. *The Principles of the International Phonetic Association*. London: International Phonetic Association.

Jacquot, A., and I. Richardson. 1956. "Report of the Western Team." In *Linguistic survey of the northern Bantu borderland*, vol. 1. London: Oxford University Press for the International African Institute.

Johnston, H. H. 1919. *A comparative study of the Bantu and semi-Bantu languages*. Volume 1. Oxford: Clarendon Press.

Ladefoged, Peter. 1964. *A phonetic study of West African languages*. West African Language Monographs, No. 1. Cambridge: the University Press.

Laman, Karl Edward. 1936. *Dictionnaire kikongo-française avec une étude phonétique décrivant les dialectes les plus importants de la langue dite kikongo*. Institute Royal colonial belge, section des Sciences Morales et Politiques, Mémoires. Brussels: Librairie Falk.

Lanham, L. W. 1963. "The tonemes of Xhosa: A restatement." *Studies in Linguistics* 17: 35-68.

Leslau, Wolf. 1941. *Documents tigrigna, grammaire et textes*. Paris: Klincksieck.

————. 1958. "Moča, a tone language of the Kafa group in southwestern Ethiopia." *Africa* 28: 135-47.

McCawley, James D. 1970. "A note on tone in Tiv conjunction." *Studies in African Linguistics* 1: 123-29.

Manessy, G. 1964. "Determination et predication en kpelle." *Bulletin de la Societé de Linguistique de Paris* 59: 119-29.

Mbiti, John S. 1969. "Eschatology." Chapter 8 in *Biblical revelation and African beliefs*, edited by Kwesi Dickson and Paul Ellingworth, Maryknoll, N. Y.: Orbis Books. Pp. 159-84.

Meeussen, A. E. 1964. *Eléments de grammaire lega*. Tervuren: Koninklijk Museum voor Centraal Afrika.

Meeussen, A. E., and D. Ndembe. 1964. "Principes de tonologie yombe (Kongo occidental)." *Journal of African Languages* 3: 135-61.

Meinhof, Carl. 1899. *Grundriss einer Lautlehre der Bantusprachen*. Leipzig: Brockhaus. Second edition, 1910. Berlin: D. Reimer.

————. 1911. "Sudansprachen und Hamitensprachen." *Zeitschrift für Kolonialsprachen* 1: 164.

——. 1932. *Introduction to the phonology of the Bantu languages*. Translated and revised (from Meinhof 1910) by N. J. van Warmelo. Berlin: D. Reimer/ E. Vohsen.

Melzian, Hans. 1937. *A concise dictionary of the Bini language of Southern Nigeria*. London: Kegan Paul, Trench, Trubner.

Methodist Book Depot. 1947. *Mfantse nkasafua nkyerewee nye ho mbra (Fante word list with principles and rules of spelling)*. Fourth edition. Cape Coast: Methodist Book Depot.

Montgomery, C. A. 1966. *The morphology of Sebei*. Doctoral dissertation, University of California, Los Angeles.

Newman, Paul. 1968. "Ideophones from a syntactic point of view." *Journal of West African Languages* 5: 107-18.

————. 1970. *A grammar of Tera: Transformational syntax and texts*. University of California Publications in Linguistics, No. 57. Berkeley and Los Angeles: University of California Press.

Ogbalu, F. Chidozie. 1959. *Igbo-English dictionary*. Port Harcourt and Lagos: C.M.S. Press (African Literature Bureau).

Pia, Joseph J. 1963. *An outline of the structure of Somali*. Los Angeles.

Pike, Kenneth L. 1948. *Tone languages*. Ann Arbor: University of Michigan Press.

————. 1966. *Tagmemic and matrix linguistics applied to selected African languages*. Washington: Department of Health, Education, and Welfare (Office of Education, Bureau of Research).

Sadler, Wesley. 1951. *Untangled Loma*. (New York): United Lutheran Church (Board of Foreign Missions), for the Evangelical Lutheran Church in Liberia.

Samarin, William J. 1965. "Perspective on African Ideophones." *African Studies* 24: 117-21.

————. In press. "Survey of Bantu ideophones." *African Language Studies.*

Schachter, Paul. 1961. "Phonetic similarity in tonemic analysis, with notes on the system of Akwapim Twi." *Language* 37: 231-38.

Schachter, Paul, and Victoria Fromkin. 1968. *A phonology of Akan: Akuapem, Asante, and Fante.* Working Papers in Phonetics, No. 9. Los Angeles: University of California.

Siertsema, B. 1963. "Intonation phenomena in tone languages." *Actes du second colloque international de linguistique négro-africaine.* Dakar: Université de Dakar; West African Languages Survey.

Stahlke, Herbert F. 1971. *Topics in Ewe phonology.* Doctoral dissertation, University of California, Los Angeles.

Stevick, Earl W., and Kingston Machiwana. 1960. *Manyika step by step.* Cleveland, Transvaal; Central Mission Press.

Stewart, J. M. 1965. "The typology of the Twi tone system, with comments by Paul Schachter and Wm. E. Welmers." Preprint of *Bulletin of the Institute of African Studies.* Legon: University of Ghana.

Swift, L. B., A. Ahaghotu, and E. Ugorji. 1962. *Igbo Basic Course.* Washington: Foreign Service Institute.

Tucker, A. N., and M. A. Bryan. 1957. *Linguistic survey of the northern Bantu borderland, vol. 4.* London: Oxford University Press for the International African Institute.

————. 1964. "Noun classification in Kalenjin: Nandi-Kipsigis." *African Language Studies* 5: 192-247.

————. 1966. *Linguistic analyses: the non-Bantu languages of northeastern Africa.* Handbook of African Languages, Part 5. London: Oxford University Press for the International African Institute.

Tucker, A. N., and J. Tompo Ole Mpaayei. 1955. *A Maasai grammar, with vocabulary.* London: Longmans, Green.

Ward, Ida C. 1933. *The phonetic and tonal structure of Efik.* Cambridge: Heffer.

————. 1936. *An introduction to the Ibo language.* Cambridge: Heffer.

Welmers, Beatrice F., and William E. Welmers. 1968a. *Igbo, a learner's dictionary.* Los Angeles: African Studies Center, University of California.

————. 1968b. *Igbo, a learner's manual.* Los Angeles: Wm. E. Welmers.

Welmers, William E. 1946. *A descriptive grammar of Fanti.* Language Dissertation 39. *Language* 22.3, supplement.

————. 1950a. "Notes on two languages in the Senufo group: I. Senadi." *Language* 26: 126-46.

————. 1950b. "Notes on two languages in the Senufo group: II. Sup'ide." *Language* 26: 494-531.

————. 1952a. "Notes on the structure of Bariba." *Language* 28: 82-103.

————. 1952b. "Notes on the structure of Saho." *Word* 8: 145-63, 236-51.

————. 1956. *Notes on two dialects known as Jukun; Notes on the structure of Kutep.* Hartford: H. A. Gleason Microcards.

———. 1958. "The Mande languages." Georgetown University Monograph Series in Languages and Linguistics 11. Washington: Georgetown University Press. Pp. 9-24.

———. 1959. "Tonemics, morphotonemics, and tonal morphemes." *General Linguistics* 4: 1-9.

———. 1961. "Internal evidence of borrowing in Kpelle." *General Linguistics* 5: 47-57.

———. 1962. "The phonology of Kpelle." *Journal of African Languages* 1: 69-93.

———. 1963a. "Associative *a* and *ka* in Niger-Congo." *Language* 39: 432-47.

———. 1963b. Review of *The languages of Africa* by Joseph H. Greenberg. *Word* 19: 407-17.

———. 1963c. Review of *Sierra Leone Language Review, No. 1. Bulletin of the School of Oriental and African Studies* 26: 677-78.

———. 1964. "The syntax of emphasis in Kpelle." *Journal of West African Languages* 1: 13-26.

———. 1968a. *Efik.* University of Ibadan, Institute of African Studies, Occasional Publication No. 11. (Originally available in mimeographed form, 1966.)

———. 1968b. *Jukun of Wukari and Jukun of Takum.* University of Ibadan, Institute of African Studies, Occasional Publication No. 16.

———. 1969a. "Structural notes on Urhobo." *Journal of West African Languages* 6: 85-107.

———. 1969b. "The morphology of Kpelle nominals." *Journal of African Languages* 8: 73-101.

———. 1970a. "The derivation of Igbo verb bases." *Studies in African Linguistics* 1: 49-59.

———. 1970b. "Igbo Tonology." *Studies in African Linguistics* 1: 255-78.

———. 1970c. "Language change and language relationships in Africa." *Language Sciences* (Indiana University, Research Center for the Language Sciences) 12: 1-8.

———. 1971a. "The typology of the proto-Niger-Kordofanian noun class system." In *Papers in African linguistics*, edited by Chin-Wu Kim and Herbert Stahlke, pp. 1-16. Champaign and Edmonton: Linguistic Research, Inc.

———. 1971b. "Niger-Congo, Mande." In *Current trends in linguistics*, vol. 7, edited by Thomas A. Sebeok. The Hague, Paris: Mouton. Pp. 113-40.

Welmers, William E., and Beatrice F. Welmers. 1969. "Noun modifiers in Igbo." *International Journal of American Linguistics* 35: 315-22.

Westermann, D. 1952. "African linguistic classification." *Africa* 22: 250-56.

Westermann, D., and M. A. Bryan. 1952. *The languages of West Africa.* Handbook of African Languages, Part 2. London: Oxford University Press for the International African Institute.

Westermann, D., and H. J. Melzian. 1930. *The Kpelle language in Liberia.* Berlin: D. Reimer.

Westphal, E. O. J. 1957. "On linguistic relationship." Zaïre 11: 513-24.

————. 1971. "The click languages of southern and eastern Africa." In *Current trends in linguistics*, vol. 7, edited by Thomas A. Sebeok. The Hague, Paris: Mouton. Pp. 367-420.

Whinnom, Keith. 1971. "Linguistic hybridization and the 'special case' of pidgins and creoles." In *Pidginization and creolization of languages* (Proceedings of a conference held at the University of the West Indies, Mona, Jamaica, April 1968), edited by Dell Hymes. London: Cambridge University Press.

Williamson, Kay. 1965. *A grammar of the Kolokuma dialect of Ịjọ*. West African Languages Monographs, No. 2. Cambridge: the University Press.

Wilson, W. A. A. 1962. "Temne, Landuma, and the Baga languages." *Sierra Leone Language Review* 1: 27-38.

Winston, F. D. D. 1960. "The 'mid tone' in Efik." *African Language Studies* 1: 185-92.

Zwernemann, Jurgen. 1967. "Versuch einer Analyse der Nominalen Klassifizierung in einigen Gur-Sprachen." In *La classification nominale dans les langues négro-africaines*. Paris: Centre National de la recherche scientifique. Pp. 75-98.

Index of Language Names

This index includes all names of African languages, language groups, and language families referred to in this volume. Although there are occasional references in the text to linguistic entities from other parts of the world, they are not included in the index. Bantu language names with class prefixes are alphabetized under the first letter of the stem, which appears with internal capitalization. The classification of each language is given, usually only up to the major branch of the language family to which it belongs. The location of each language is given in terms of the political unit or units in which it is spoken, or sometimes more specifically.